[英 汉 对 照]

西方学术经典文库

心理学原理

THE PRINCIPLES OF PSYCHOLOGY

[美] 威廉·詹姆斯 著

郭 宾 译

九州出版社 JIUZHOUPRESS | 全国百佳图书出版单位

图书在版编目(CIP)数据

心理学原理/（美）詹姆斯著；郭宾译.
—北京:九州出版社,2007.1（2010.2重印）
ISBN 978-7-80195-569-2

Ⅰ.心… Ⅱ.①詹…②郭… Ⅲ.心理学—英、汉
Ⅳ.B84

中国版本图书馆CIP数据核字（2006）第157822号

心理学原理

作　　者（美）威廉·詹姆斯 著　郭　宾 译
出版发行 九州出版社
出 版 人 徐尚定
地　　址 北京市西城区阜外大街甲35号（100037）
发行电话 （010）68992190/2/3/5/6
网　　址 www.jiuzhoupress.com
电子信箱 jiuzhou@jiuzhoupress.com
印　　刷 九洲财鑫印刷有限公司
开　　本 630毫米×970毫米　16开
印　　张 43.5
字　　数 464千字
版　　次 2007年1月第1版
印　　次 2010年2月第2次印刷
书　　号 ISBN 978-7-80195-569-2
定　　价 86.00元

出版说明

在西方学术思想的发展流变中，出现过很多影响深远的经典著作，这些著作穿越时空，为人们长久研读，有的甚至影响了整个人类文明的发展进程。这套《西方学术经典文库》（英汉对照本），精选了其中最有代表性的一些名著，计划达到一百部，将陆续分批出版直至全部完成。

《西方学术经典文库》由多位专家学者指导分类选目，内容涵盖哲学、文学、宗教学、政治学、经济学、社会学、人类学、心理学、法学、历史学等类，注重权威性、学术性和影响性，收录了不同国家、不同时代、不同流派的诸多名著。

《西方学术经典文库》中译本译自英文原著或其他文种的英文译本，以英汉对照的形式出版，读者可以参照原文对作品有更加客观的理解，更好地把握西方学术思想的精髓。

为加以区别，原文中的英文注释，注释号用①、②……形式表示；中文译者注释则以〔1〕、〔2〕……形式表示。至于英译本中出现的原文页码和特殊索引等问题，中文译者在“译者后记”中将予以解释、说明。另外，在英文原著中，有一些表示着重意义的斜体或大写等字体，考虑到读者可以在对照英文阅读中看到，因此在中译文中，没有照样标出，还望读者理解。

九州出版社

The Principles Of Psychology
By *William James*

本书根据 Macmillan And Co. ,Ltd. 1907 年版本译出

CONTENTS
目录

威廉 · 詹姆斯（1842—1910）

PREFACE

The treatise which follows has in the main grown up in connection with the author's class-room instruction in Psychology, although it is true that some of the chapters are more 'metaphysical,' and others fuller of detail, than is suitable for students who are going over the subject for the first time. The consequence of this is that, in spite of the exclusion of the important subjects of pleasure and pain, and moral and æsthetic feelings and judgments, the work has grown to a length which no one can regret more, than the writer himself. The man must indeed be sanguine who, in this crowded age, can hope to have many readers for fourteen hundred continuous pages from his pen. But *wer Vieles bringt wird Manchem etwas bringen*; and, by judiciously skipping according to their several needs, I am sure that many sorts of readers, even those who are just beginning the study of the subject, will find my book of use. Since the beginners are most in need of guidance, I suggest for their behoof that they omit altogether on a first reading chapters 6, 7, 8, 10 (from page 330 to page 371), 12, 13, 15, 17, 20, 21, and 28. The better to awaken the neophyte's interest, it is possible that the wise order would be to pass directly from chapter 4 to chapters 23, 24, 25, and 26, and thence to return to the first volume again. Chapter 20, on Space-perception, is a terrible thing, which, unless written with all that detail, could not be fairly treated at all. An abridgment of it, called 'The Spatial Quale,' which appeared in the Journal of Speculative Philosophy, vol. XIII. p. 64, may be found by some persons a useful substitute for the entire chapter.

I have kept close to the point of view of natural science throughout the book. Every natural science assumes certain data uncritically,

序　言

虽然由于本书的一些章节太“形而上”，而其他一些章节又太细致，因而对于首次接触这一学科的学生来说，不太适合，但以下论述的形成却主要和作者的心理学课堂教学有关。其结果是，尽管除去了愉快与痛苦、道德的和审美的情感与判断这些重要的题目，但这本书篇幅的冗长之憾还是令作者本人比任何人都感觉更甚。在这急速前进的时代，期望笔下那连续 1400 页的书拥有很多读者的人必定是乐观派。但是，谁做的事情多，谁就会对某些事情有帮助；而且我确信，通过按照各自的一些需要进行明智的跳读，多种类型的读者，甚至那些刚刚开始学习这一学科的人，都将会发现我这本书的用处。由于初学者最需要指导，为他们着想，我建议他们在首次阅读时完全省略掉第六、七、八、十（从 330 至 371 页）、十二、十三、十五、十七、二十、二十一和二十八章。为了更好地唤起初学者的兴趣，可能明智的顺序是读完第四章就直接进入第二十三、二十四、二十五和二十六章，并从那儿再返回第一卷。关于空间知觉的第二十章棘手一些，如果不那样细致地叙述，则根本不能清楚地对它加以处理。它的一个删节本，题为《空间感觉质》，刊登在《思辨哲学杂志》第十三卷 64 页上，一些人可能会发现它是整个二十章的一个有用的替代本。

我整本书都紧跟自然科学的观点。每门自然科学都不加批

and declines to challenge the elements between which its own 'laws' obtain, and from which its own deductions are carried on. Psychology, the science of finite individual minds, assumes as its data (1) *thoughts and feelings*, and (2) *a physical world* in time and space with which they coexist and which (3) *they know*. Of course these data themselves are discussable; but the discussion of them (as of other elements) is called metaphysics and falls outside the province of this book. This book, assuming that thoughts and feelings exist and are vehicles of knowledge, thereupon contends that psychology when she has ascertained the empirical correlation of the various sorts of thought or feeling with definite conditions of the brain, can go no farther—can go no farther, that is, as a natural science. If she goes farther she becomes metaphysical. All attempts to *explain* our phenomenally given thoughts as products of deeper-lying entities (whether the latter be named 'Soul,' 'Transcendental Ego,' 'Ideas,' or 'Elementary Units of Consciousness') are metaphysical. This book consequently rejects both the associationist and the spiritualist theories; and in this strictly positivistic point of view consists the only feature of it for which I feel tempted to claim originality. Of course this point of view is anything but ultimate. Men must keep thinking; and the data assumed by psychology, just like those assumed by physics and the other natural sciences, must some time be overhauled. The effort to overhaul them clearly and thoroughly is metaphysics; but metaphysics can only perform her task well when distinctly conscious of its great extent. Metaphysics fragmentary, irresponsible, and half-awake, and unconscious that she is metaphysical, spoils two good things when she injects herself into a natural science. And it seems to me that the theories both of a spiritual agent and of associated 'ideas' are, as they figure in the psychology-books, just such metaphysics as this. Even if their results be true, it would be as well" to keep them, *as thus presented*, out of psychology as it is to keep the results of idealism out of physics.

判地假定某种论据,然后再挑战它自己的“规律”所由以获得的、它自己的推论所由以展开的要素。心理学这门有限个体心灵的科学,假设它的论据如下,(1)思想和感受,(2)与它们共同存在的时空中的物质世界,(3)它们所知的物质世界。当然,这些论据本身尚可探讨,但是对这些论据(以及其他要素)的探讨被称作形而上学,而且也超出了本书的范围。由于假设思维和感受是存在的,而且是知识的媒介物,因此本书主张,一旦心理学确定了各种思想和感受同大脑的明确条件的经验关系,她就不能走得更远了——就是说,作为一门自然科学不能走得更远了。如果她再走得远些的话就变成形而上学的了。所有将现象界赋予的思想解说成深层本体(不管后者被称作“灵魂”、“先验自我”、“理念”或是“意识的基本单元”)的产物的尝试,均是形而上学的。因而本书拒绝联想主义者和唯灵论者的理论,并且本书的唯一特征就在于其严格的实证观点,而这也是我乐于称道的原创性之所在。当然,这绝不是终极的观点。人必须不断地思索,而且心理学所假设的论据,如同物理学和其他自然科学所假设的论据一样,必须在某个时期予以检验。对它们进行明晰的和彻底的检验之努力是形而上学,但是只有当形而上学清楚地意识到它极大的范围时,才能够完成好她的任务。当不完整的、不可靠的、半清醒的和没有意识到自己是形而上学的形而上学将自己注入一门自然科学中时,她就会把两种好的事物都破坏掉。并且,精神执行者的理论和联想“观念”的理论,就其在心理学书籍中出现的情况而言,在我看来它们就是这样的形而上学。即使它们的结果是真实的,也还是让它们和如此呈现的一样,同心理学分离为好,如同让唯心主义的结果和物理学分离一样。

I have therefore treated our passing thoughts as integers, and regarded the mere laws of their coexistence with brain – states as the ultimate laws for our science. The reader will in vain seek for any closed system in the book. It is mainly a mass of descriptive details, running out into queries which only a metaphysics alive to the weight of her task can hope successfully to deal with. That will perhaps be centuries hence; and meanwhile the best mark of health that a science can show is this unfinished – seeming front.

The completion of the book has been so slow that several chapters have been published successively in Mind, the Journal of Speculative Philosophy, the Popular Science Monthly, and Scribner's Magazine. Acknowledgment is made in the proper places.

The bibliography, I regret to say, is quite unsystematic. I have habitually given my authority for special experimental facts; but beyond that I have aimed mainly to cite books that would probably be actually used by the ordinary American college – student in his collateral reading. The bibliography in W. Volkmann von Volkmar's Lehrbuch der Psychologie(1875) is so complete, up to its date, that there is no need of an inferior duplicate. And for more recent references, Sully's Outlines, Dewey's Psychology, and Baldwin's Handbook of Psychology may be advantageously used.

Finally, where one owes to so many, it seems absurd to single out particular creditors; yet I cannot resist the temptation at the end of my first literary venture to record my gratitude for the inspiration I have got from the writings of J. S. Mill, Lotze, Renouvier, Hodgson, and Wundt, and from the intellectual companionship (to name only five names) of Chauncey Wright and Charles Peirce in old times, and more recently of Stanley Hall James Putnam, and Josiah Royce.

HABVARD UNIVERSITY,

AUGUST 1890.

因此，我将我们逝去的思想当作整体来加以对待，并且把关于它们和大脑状态共同存在的纯粹规律当作我们科学的最终规律。读者在本书中寻求任何封闭的体系都将是徒然的。本书有大量描述性的细节，而它们所引起的质疑，只有可以承担她重任的形而上学才能有希望成功地解决。那可能是此后几百年的事情了，同时，一门科学能展示出的最好的健康标志就是这种表面上未完成的样子。

由于本书的完成过于缓慢，一些章节已经相继在《心灵》、《思辨哲学杂志》、《大众科学月刊》和《斯克里布纳杂志》上发表过了。我在适当的地方承认了这一事实。

我很遗憾地指出，参考文献很不系统。我习惯性地授权自己采纳了一些特殊的实验事实，但除此之外，我的目标主要是引用一些普通的美国大学生在他们进行辅助阅读时可能会实际用到的书籍。W. 沃尔克曼·冯沃尔克玛的《心理学教科书》里的参考文献迄今为止都是相当全面的，我们不需要对其加以劣等的复制。而就较为近期的参考书目来看，我们可以方便地使用萨利的《提纲》、杜威的《心理学》和鲍德温的《心理学手册》。

最后，如果一个人对太多的人有所亏欠，那么从中挑选出几个特殊的债权人似乎是荒唐的，然而，在结束我第一次写作冒险之际，我还是忍不住要说，感谢 J. S. 密尔、洛采、雷诺维尔、霍奇森和冯特，我从他们的著作中获得了启发；感谢（仅列出五个人的名字）昌西·赖特、查尔斯·皮尔士、斯坦利·霍尔、詹姆斯·普特南和赛亚·罗伊斯，我在同前两位旧时进行的以及和后三位近期进行的智慧的交往中获得了启发。

哈佛大学

1890 年 8 月

CHAPTER I.

The Scope Of Psychology.

Psychology is the Science of Mental Life, both of its phenomena and of their conditions. The phenomena are such things as we call feelings, desires, cognitions, reasonings, decisions, and the like; and, superficially considered, their variety and complexity is such as to leave a chaotic impression on the observer. The most natural and consequently the earliest way of unifying the material was, first, to classify it as well as might be, and, secondly, to affiliate the diverse mental modes thus found, upon a simple entity, the personal Soul, of which they are taken to be so many facultative manifestations. Now, for instance, the Soul manifests its faculty of Memory, now of Reasoning, now of Volition, or again its Imagination or its Appetite. This is the orthodox 'spiritualistic' theory of scholasticism and of common-sense. Another and a less obvious way of unifying the chaos is to seek common elements *in* the divers mental facts rather than a common agent behind them, and to explain them constructively by the various forms of arrangement of these elements, as one explains houses by stones and bricks. The 'associationist' schools of Herbart in Germany, and of Hume the Mills and Bain in Britain have thus constructed a *psychology without a soul* by taking discrete 'ideas,' faint or vivid, and showing how, by their cohesions, repulsions, and forms of succession, such things as reminiscences, perceptions, emotions, volitions, passions, theories, and all the other furnishings of an individual's mind may be engendered.

第一章 心理学的范围

心理学是关于心理生活的现象及其条件的科学。这些现象指的是诸如所谓的情感、欲望、认知、推理、决定等等的东西；若是肤浅地考虑它们，这些现象的多样性和复杂性便会使观察者留下一种混乱的印象。最寻常、因而也是最早被用来统一这些材料的方法是，首先，尽量将其分类；其次，将由此找到的不同种类的心理模型从属于一个单纯本体——个人灵魂，这些心理模型被看作是个人灵魂的大量随机显现。例如，灵魂时而展露出记忆的能力，时而展现出推理的能力，时而又表现出意志力，又或者是想像力与自然欲望。这便是经院哲学与常识理论所说的“唯灵论”。此外，还有一种不太显著的用来统一这些混乱材料的方法，那便是在诸种心理事实中寻求共同的元素，而不是寻求这些事实背后共同的执行者，如同用石头和砖块来解释房屋一样，通过对构成心理事实的不同元素之间排列的不同形式的研究，对这些心理事实做出建设性的阐释。包括德国的赫尔巴特和英国的休谟、密尔父子以及贝恩在内的“联想主义”学派，已经以此种方式创建了一门无灵魂的心理学，他们采用分离的“构想”（是模糊的或者清晰的），通过展示心理事实之间的联结、排斥及序列形式，来说明诸如记忆、知觉、情绪、意志、激情、理论以及所有其他的

The very Self or *ego* of the individual comes in this way to be viewed no longer as the pre-existing source of the representations, but rather as their last and most complicated fruit.

Now, if we strive rigorously to simplify the phenomena in either of these ways, we soon become aware of inadequacies in our method. Any particular cognition, for example, or recollection, is accounted for on the soul-theory by being referred to the spiritual faculties of Cognition or of Memory. These faculties themselves are thought of as absolute properties of the soul; that is, to take the case of memory, no reason is given why we should remember a fact as it happened, except that so to remember it constitutes the essence of our Recollective Power. We may, as spiritualists, try to explain our memory's failures and blunders by secondary causes. But its *successes* can invoke no factors save the existence of certain objective things to be remembered on the one hand, and of our faculty of memory on the other. When, for instance, I recall my graduation-day, and drag all its incidents and emotions up from death's dateless night, no mechanical cause can explain this process, nor can any analysis reduce it to lower terms or make its nature seem other than an ultimate *datum*, which, whether we rebel or not at its mysteriousness, must simply be taken for granted if we are to psychologize at all. However the associationist may represent the present ideas as thronging and arranging themselves, still, the spiritualist insists, he has in the end to admit that *something*, be it brain, be it 'ideas,' be it 'association,' *knows* past time as past, and fills it out with this or that event. And when tile spiritualist calls memory an 'irreducible faculty,' he says no more than this admission of the associationist already grants.

And yet the admission is far from being a satisfactory simplification of the concrete facts. For why should this absolute god-given Faculty retain so much better the events of yesterday than those of last year, and, best of all, those of an hour ago? Why,

个体心灵备件是如何可能产生。通过表象这种方式，个体的那个自己或是自我就不再被认作是表象的先在根源，而是表象的最终和最复杂的结果。

现在，假如我们严格用上述两种方法中的一种来简化心理生活的现象，我们很快就会意识到我们的方法是不完备的。例如，任何一种独特的认知或回忆，都是在“唯灵论”的框架内诉诸认知和记忆的精神能力而加以阐释的。这些能力被认为是灵魂的特有性质；以记忆为例，那便是说，此理论除了指出记住某个已经发生的事实是我们的记忆能力的本质以外，并未给出为什么一个事实发生时我们应该记住这个事实的理由。按唯灵论者的观点，我们可以试图用次级原因来解释我们记忆的错误与误差。但是这种理论的成功，除了一方面肯定了被记忆的特定客观事物的存在，以及另一方面肯定人的记忆能力的存在，此处它并未涉及任何其他因素。例如，当我回忆毕业典礼，以及从死寂般的漫漫长夜里搜寻出当时的情景和情绪时，不仅机械的原因对此过程无从说明，而且也没有任何分析可将之还原为较低级的元素，或者说不能使其性质显得是一种终极论据，即如果我们要进行心理学的研究，不论对其神秘性反对与否，都必须认为这是理所当然。无论联想主义者如何将当前的观念表象为它们自身的群集和排列，唯灵论者仍坚持认为联想主义者最终必须承认，某种东西，不论它是大脑、“观念”或“联想”，知道过去的时间便是过去，并用这样或那样的事情将它填满。还有就是当唯灵论者称记忆是“不可还原的能力”时，他们只是说出了联想主义者业已认可的东西。

然而，这种认可远非是一种对具体事实的圆满简化。这一绝对的、神授的能力为何会对昨天发生的事情比去年发生的事情记得更清楚，而对一小时以前的事情记得最清楚呢？却又为何在年

again, in old age should its grasp of childhood's events seem firmest? Why should illness and exhaustion enfeeble it? Why should repeating an experience strengthen our recollection of it? Why should drugs, fevers, asphyxia, and excitement resuscitate things long since forgotten? If we content ourselves with merely affirming that the faculty of memory is so peculiarly constituted by nature as to exhibit just these oddities, we seem little the better for having invoked it, for our explanation becomes as complicated as that of the crude facts with which we started. Moreover there is something grotesque and irrational in the supposition that the soul is equipped with elementary powers of such an ingeniously intricate sort. Why *should* our memory cling more easily to the near than the remote? Why should it lose its grasp of proper sooner than of abstract names? Such peculiarities seem quite fantastic; and might, for aught we can see *a priori*, be the precise opposites of what they are. Evidently, then, *the faculty does not exist absolutely, but works under conditions*, and *the quest of the conditions* becomes the psychologist's most interesting task.

However firmly he may hold to the soul and her remembering faculty, he must acknowledge that she never exerts the latter without a *cue*, and that something must always precede and *remind* us of whatever we are to recollect. "An *idea*!" says the associationist, "an idea associated with the remembered thing; and this explains also why things repeatedly met with are more easily recollected, for their associates on the various occasions furnish so many distinct avenues of recall." But this does not explain the effects of fever, exhaustion, hypnotism, old age, and the like. And in general, the pure associationist's account of our mental life is almost as bewildering as that of the pure spiritualist. This multitude of ideas, existing absolutely, yet clinging together, and weaving an endless carpet of themselves, like dominoes in ceaseless change, or the bits of glass in a kaleidoscope,—whence do they get their fantastic laws of clinging,

长以后对儿时的事情的记忆似乎是最牢固的呢？为什么疾病与疲惫会使其衰弱？为什么一个经验的不断重复会加固对它的记忆？药物、发热、窒息和激动又是如何使久被遗忘的事物被记起的呢？假如我们仅仅以下述断言就感到满意的话，即大自然是如此独特地构造了记忆能力而使其展示奇异之处，那么我们似乎并未因援用它而优越多少，因为我们的解释会变得同我们所由以开始的对那些未经加工事实的解释一样复杂。而且，就灵魂具有如此复杂的天才般基本能力的假设来说，其中含有奇怪且非理性的东西。为什么我们的记忆应该更容易把握近期的事物而不是远期的事物？为什么它对专有名称应该比抽象名称忘得更快？这些特性似乎相当奇异，而且如果我们先天地去理解，这些特性可能同它们自身刚好相反。那么显然，这能力并非绝对的存在着，而是有条件地工作着，而对这些条件的探求就成为心理学家最感兴趣的任务。

不论某人如何坚定地认同灵魂及其记忆的能力，他必须承认灵魂从未没有某种提示就可应用其记忆的能力，并且这些事物必须总是在先并且使我们想起所要回忆的一切。“一个观念！”联想主义者谈到，“一个同被记起的事件形成联想关系的观念，并且它还解释了为何重复遇到的事物更容易回忆，因为它们在各种情形之下的联想关系促生了很多独特的回忆途径。”但这并没有说明由发热、疲惫、催眠术、年老等对记忆能力所造成的影响。大体来说，纯联想主义者对心理生活的解释和纯唯灵论的解释同样令人困惑。这众多观念绝对存在，且依附在一起，编织出一块由观念自身组成的无止境的地毯，像不停变化的多米诺骨牌，又或是万花筒中的玻璃碎片。它们是从哪里获得了那相互依附的神奇法则，

and why do they cling in just the shapes they do ?

For this the associationist must introduce the order of experience in the outer world. The dance of the ideas is a copy, somewhat mutilated and altered, of the order of phenomena. But the slightest reflection shows that phenomena have absolutely no power to influence our ideas until they have first impressed our senses and our brain. The bare existence of a past fact is no ground for our remembering it. Unless we have seen it, or somehow *undergone* it, we shall never know of its having been. The experiences of the body are thus one of the conditions of the faculty of memory being what it is. And a very small amount of reflection on facts shows that one part of the body, namely, the brain, is the part whose experiences are directly concerned. If the nervous communication be cut off between the brain and other parts, the experiences of those other parts are non-existent for the mind. The eye is blind, the ear deaf, the hand insensible and motionless. And conversely, if the brain be injured, consciousness is abolished or altered, even although every other organ in the body be ready to play its normal part. A blow on the head, a sudden subtraction of blood, the pressure of an apoplectic hemorrhage, may have the first effect; whilst a very few ounces of alcohol or grains of opium or hasheesh, or a whiff of chloroform or nitrous oxide gas, are sure to have the second. The delirium of fever, the altered self of insanity, are all due to foreign matters circulating through the brain, or to pathological changes in that organ's substance. The fact that the brain is the one immediate bodily condition of the mental operations is indeed so universally admitted nowadays that I need spend no more time in illustrating it, but will simply postulate it and pass on. The whole remainder of the book will be more or less of a proof that the postulate was correct.

Bodily experiences, therefore, and more particularly brain-experiences, must take a place amongst those conditions of the mentallife of which Psychology need take account. *The spiritualist and the associationist must both be 'cerebralists,'* to the extent at least of admitting that certain peculiarities in the way of working of their own favorite principles are explicable only by the fact

又为何恰恰以相互依附的那些形式而结合在一起呢？

为此，联想主义者不得不引进外部世界中的经验秩序。观念之舞是现象秩序的有些许残缺和变化的模本。然而通过最细微的反思可以看到，除非现象首先给我们的感官和大脑留下印象，否则它们绝对没有影响观念的能力。光是已往事实的存在不足以说明我们记得它的理由。除非我们看见过它，或以某种方式经历过它，否则我们将永远也不知道它存在过。因此亲身的体验便是如其所是的记忆能力的条件之一。通过对事实的稍许反思便可知晓，人体中被称作大脑的那一部分所得到的经验与此直接相关。如果中断大脑和其他人体部分的神经传输，那么其他人体部分所得到的经验对于心灵来说就不存在。因而眼睛便是瞎的，耳朵就是聋的，手是不能感觉也不能动的。相反，如果大脑受伤，意识便会被毁灭或者发生改变，尽管身体中的所有其他器官已经准备好行使其平常的功能。头部遭到重击、血液突然减少、因中风出血而造成的压迫可能导致第一种后果；而喝一点酒、吸食一些鸦片或大麻、摄取少量氯仿或一氧化二氮则一定会造成第二种后果。发热时的精神错乱、疯癫时改变了的自我，这些都是由于外来物质在脑内循环、或者是那一器官组织的病变所致。大脑是心灵运作的一个直接的身体条件，这一事实如今已得到了普遍的认可，因此本书无需花更多的时间对此加以阐明，而仅是将其作为一个基本假定，而后由此展开。并且本书的其余部分将或多或少地证明这一假设是正确的。

因此，身体获得经验，特别是大脑获得经验，必须在心理学需要加以考虑的那些心理生活条件中占有一席之地。唯灵论者和联想主义者得承认，只有依据大脑法则是结果的共同决定因素这一事实，他们自己所偏爱的原理在起作用的方式中的某些特殊情

that the brain laws are a codeterminant of the result.

Our first conclusion, then, is that a certain amount of brain-physiology must be presupposed or included in Psychology. ①

In still another way the pyschologist is forced to be something of a nerve-physiologist. Mental phenomena are not only conditioned *a parte ante* by bodily processes; but they lead to them *a parte post*. That they lead to *acts* is of course the most familiar of truths, but I do not merely mean acts in the sense of voluntary and deliberate muscular performances. Mental states occasion also changes in the calibre of blood-vessels, or alteration in the heart-beats, or processes more subtle still, in glands and viscera. If these are taken into account, as well as acts which follow at some *remote period* because the mental state was once there, it will be safe to lay down the general law *that no mental modification ever occurs which is not accompanied or followed by a bodily change*. The ideas and feelings, e. g., which these present printed characters excite in the reader's mind not only occasion movements of his eyes and nascent movements of articulation in him, but will some day make him speak, or take sides in a discussion, or give advice, or choose a book to read, differently from what would have been the case had they never impressed his retina. Our psychology must therefore take account not only of the conditions antecedent to mental states, but of their resultant consequences as well.

But actions originally prompted by conscious intelligence may grow so automatic by dint of habit as to be apparently unconsciously performed. Standing, walking, buttoning and unbuttoning, piano-playing, talking, even saying one's prayers, may be done when the mind is absorbed in other things. The performances of animal *instinct* seem semi-

---

① Cf. Geo. T. Ladd: Elements of Physiological Psychology (1887), pt III, chap. III, §§9,12.

况,才能得到解释说明。至少在这种程度上讲,他们都必须是“大脑主义者”。

那么,我们的第一个结论便是,特定数量的脑生理学必须作为心理学研究的前提,或说它就包含在心理学的研究之中。①

在另一方面,心理学家不得不在一定程度上像一个神经生理学家。心理现象不仅在前面以身体运动为前提条件,而且在后面又引起了身体运动。心理现象引起人的动作行为,这当然是人们最为熟悉的真相,但这里的行为并不仅仅意味着主动或有意的肌肉运动。心理状态的改变也会使血管的粗细发生变化,使心跳发生变化,还会使腺体和内脏发生极为精细的变化。如果把这些都考虑在内,并且还考虑到由某一较早时期曾出现的心理状态导致的行为,我们就可以放心得出这样一条基本法则:如果没有身体变化相伴随发生或随后发生,心理变化便不会发生。例如,由当前的印刷文字所激发的在读者心中的观念和情感,不仅引起他的眼睛和体内初始发声的动作,而且还在某天让他开口讲话,或者在某次讨论中支持一方的观点,或者提供建议,又或者选择一本书来读;如果这些文字从来没有在视网膜上留下印象,情形将会大不相同。因此,我们的心理学必须不仅考虑到形成心理状态的前提条件,还必须考虑到这些心理状态所造成的结果。

然而,最初由有意识的理智所促成的动作,可以凭借习惯的力量变得自动化,以至于能在明显的无意识状态下进行。起立、行走、系扣子、解扣子、弹钢琴、说话、甚至祷告,都可以在心灵专注于其他事物时完成。动物的本能活动似乎是半自动的,自我保

---

① 参见 G. T. 莱德:《生理心理学基础》(1887),第 3 部分,第 3 章,第 9、12 节。

automatic, and the *reflex acts* of self-preservation certainly are so. Yet they resemble intelligent acts in bringing about the *same ends* at which the animals' consciousness, on other occasions, deliberately aims. Shall the study of such machine-like yet purposive acts as these be included in Psychology?

The boundary-line of the mental is certainly vague. It is better not to be pedantic, but to let the science be as vague as its subject, and include such phenomena as these if by so doing we can throw any light on the main business in hand. It will ere long be seen, I trust, that we can; and that we gain much more by a broad than by a narrow conception of our subject. At a certain stage in the development of every science a degree of vagueness is what best consists with fertility. On the whole, few recent formulas have done more real service of a rough sort in psychology than the Spencerian one that the essence of mental life and of bodily life are one, namely, 'the adjustment of inner to outer relations.' Such a formula is vagueness incarnate; but because it takes into account the fact that minds inhabit environments which act on them and on which they in turn react; because, in short, it takes mind in the midst of all its concrete relations, it is immensely more fertile than the old-fashioned 'rational psychology,' which treated the soul as a detached existent, sufficient unto itself, and assumed to consider only its nature and properties. I shall therefore feel free to make any sallies into zoology or into pure nerve-physiology which may seem instructive for our purposes, but otherwise shall leave those sciences to the physiologists.

Can we state more distinctly still the manner in which the mental life seems to intervene between impressions made from without upon the body, and reactions of the body upon the outer world again? Let us look at a few facts.

If some iron filings be sprinkled on a table and a magnet brought near them, they will fly through the air for a certain distance and stick to its surface. A savage seeing the phenomenon

护的反射行为自然也是如此。然而,这些行为与智能行为的相似之处在于,这些行为的结果同其他情况中动物有意识、有目的的行为所造成的结果是相同的。那么,心理学应该包括对这些机械般的、然而却又是有目的的行为的研究吗?

心灵的界限必然是模糊的,最好不要过于书生气,就让这门科学同它的主题一样模糊吧,可以将这类现象囊括进来,如果这样做有助于我们手头的主要任务的话。我相信,人们不久就会看到我们已能够这样做,而且还会看到通过对研究主题广义而非狭义的理解,我们收获得更多。在每一门科学发展的某一特定阶段,某种程度的模糊性都蕴涵着多产性。总体而言,目前的学术讨论对心理学中这种模糊性的实际贡献尚未超过斯宾塞,他的理论主张:心理生活和肉体生活的本质是同一的,即"内部关系对外部关系的适应"。这种阐述是模糊性的典型,但是由于他考虑到了这样的事实,即心灵栖息于周围的环境之中,这个环境作用于心灵,心灵又反过来作用于环境;简单地说,又由于它将心灵置于所有具体的关系之中来加以考虑,因此它就比过时的"理性心理学"更富有成就。"理性心理学"将灵魂看作是独立自足的存在,并试图只考虑它的本质和属性。如果到动物学和纯神经生理学中去畅游一番会对我们要实现的目标有所帮助,那么我就将这样做,否则,我会将这些科学留给生理学家们。

关于心理生活介入由外部施加于人体的印象和身体对外部世界的反应之间的方式,我们能表达得更清楚一些吗?让我们看几个事例。

如果把一些铁屑撒在桌上,并用一块磁铁靠近它们,铁屑便会在空中飞上一段距离而后被吸附在磁铁表面。看到这一现象

explains it as the result of an attraction or love between the magnet and the filings. But let a card cover the poles of the magnet, and the filings will press forever against its surface without its ever occurring to them to pass around its sides and thus come into more direct contact with the object of their love. Blow bubbles through a tube into the bottom of a pail of water, they will rise to the surface and mingle with the air. Their action may again be poetically interpreted as due to a longing to recombine with the mother-atmosphere above the surface. But if you invert a jar full of water over the pail, they will rise and remain lodged beneath its bottom, shut in from the outer air, although a slight deflection from their course at the outset, or a re-descent towards the rim of the jar when they found their upward course impeded, would easily have set them free.

If now we pass from such actions as these to those of living things, we notice a striking difference. Romeo wants Juliet as the filings want the magnet; and if no obstacles intervene he moves towards her by as straight a line as they. But Romeo and Juliet, if a wall be built between them, do not remain idiotically pressing their faces against its opposite sides like the magnet and the filings with the card. Romeo soon finds a circuitous way, by scaling the wall or otherwise, of touching Juliet's lips directly. With the filings the path is fixed; whether it reaches the end depends on accidents. With the lover it is the end which is fixed, the path may be modified indefinitely.

Supposes a living frog in the position in which we placed our bubbles of air, namely, at the bottom of a jar of water. The want of breath will soon make him also long to rejoin the mother-atmosphere, and he will take the shortest path to his end by swimming straight upwards. But if a jar full of water be inverted over him, he will not, like the bubbles, perpetually press his nose against its unyielding roof, but will restlessly explore the neighborhood until by re-descending again he has discovered a path round its brim to the goal of his desires.

的原始人将它解释为这是磁铁和铁屑间的吸引或爱的结果。但是,如果用纸片盖住磁铁的两极,那么铁屑就只会永远被吸附在它的表面上,并且铁屑永远也不会从纸片的两边绕过去,从而可以更直接地同它所爱的对象相接触。将一根管子插到水桶底部,并用它来吹泡泡,气泡会浮出水面并同空气混合。气泡的运动也可以被诗意地解释为它渴望再度回到水面上空气妈妈的怀抱。可是,如果将一个盛满水的罐子倒扣在水桶里,气泡会上升到罐子底部,被关在里面,同外面的空气相隔绝,尽管它们如果在一开始就在上升的路线上做少许倾斜,或者当发现上升的道路被阻断后就再次朝着罐口下降,那么它们便会轻松地获得自由。

现在,如果我们把像这样的一些行为变化成有生命的事物的行为,我们就会发现有惊人的区别。罗密欧需要朱丽叶如同铁屑需要磁铁一般,并且如果没有障碍干涉的话,他就会和铁屑一样沿直线朝她走去。但是,如果有一堵墙在他们之间的话,罗密欧和朱丽叶就不会像磁铁和铁屑遭遇卡片一样,白痴般地将他们的脸一直贴在墙的正反两边。罗密欧很快就会发现一种迂回的方式,通过翻墙或者通过其他方式,从而和朱丽叶接吻的。对于铁屑来说,道路是固定的,它是否可以达到目标取决于偶然性。对于恋人来说,目标是固定的,而道路可以不确定地加以修正。

假设一只活青蛙处于我们放置空气泡的位置,即在一罐水的底部。由于需要呼吸,很快它也将渴望回到空气妈妈的怀抱,并且它将以最短的路径直线向上游到它的目的地。但是如果一个装满水的罐子倒扣在它上面,它将不会像气泡那样,将它的鼻子永久的顶在罐子坚硬的顶部,而是一直不安地探索邻近的地方,通过再次潜入水里,直到在罐口周围发现了一条可以达到它欲求

Again the fixed end, the varying means!

Such contrasts between living and inanimate performances end by leading men to deny that in the physical world final purposes exist at all. Loves and desires are to-day no longer imputed to particles of iron or of air. No one supposes now that the end of any activity which they may display is an ideal purpose presiding over the activity from its outset and soliciting or drawing it into being by a sort of *vis a fronte*. The end, on the contrary, is deemed a mere passive result, pushed into being *a tergo*, having had, so to speak, no voice in its own production. Alter the pre-existing conditions, and with inorganic materials you bring forth each time a different apparent end. But with intelligent agents, altering the conditions changes the activity displayed, but not the end reached; for here the idea of the yet unrealized end co-operates with the conditions to determine what the activities shall be.

The pursuance of future ends and the choice of means for their attainment are thus the mark and criterion of the presence of mentality in a phenomenon. We all use this test to discriminate between an intelligent and a mechanical performance. We impute no mentality to sticks and stones, because they never seem to move for *the sake of* anything, but always when pushed, and then indifferently and with no sign of choice. So we unhesitatingly call them senseless.

Just so we form our decision upon the deepest of all philosophic problems: Is the Kosmos an expression of intelligence rational in its inward nature, or a brute external fact pure and simple ? If we find ourselves, in contemplating it, unable to banish the impression that it is a realm of final purposes, that it exists for the sake of something, we place intelligence at the heart of it and have a religion. If, on the contrary, in surveying its irremediable flux, we can think of the present only as so much mere mechanical sprouting from the past, occurring with no reference to the future, we are atheists and materialists.

目标的路径。这又是固定的目标，变化的方法！

这种有生命和无生命的活动的对比最终造成了人们根本否认物质世界的终极目标的存在。爱和欲望在今天不再被归之于铁或空气粒子了。现在没有人假设任何可能展现出来的行为的目标是一种理想的目的，这目的从一开始就统辖这活动，并且通过一种前面的力量恳请或吸引它实现。相反，目标被认为仅仅是一种被动的结果，是随后形成的，对其自身的产生可以说没有任何发言权。改变预先存在的条件，就无机质料来说，你每次会实现显然不同的目标。但就智能执行者来说，改变条件能改变展现出来的行为，但改变不了达到的目标，因为在这里，那尚未实现的目标的观念同条件相互合作来决定行为将会是什么样的。

对未来目标的追求和达到它们方法的选择因此就是某种现象中心理活动呈现的标志和规范。我们全部使用这种检验来区分智能活动与机械活动。我们不将心理活动归之于棍子和石头，因为它们从来不因为任何事物而移动，而总是在被推了以后才冷淡地、没有任何选择迹象地移动。因此我们毫不犹豫地称它们为无感觉的。

正是如此我们形成了对所有最深奥的哲学问题的判断：宇宙是它内在本性中理智的理性表达，还是纯粹而简单的无理性的外部事实的表达？在沉思之时，如果我们发现自己不能消除这样的印象，即它是终极目的的领域，它因为某种东西的缘故而存在，我们将理智置于其中心，于是就有了宗教。相反，如果我们对它那不可挽回的流变加以审视，我们可以认为现在仅仅是从过去机械地萌发而来，它的出现对未来没有指涉，那我们就是无神论者和唯物主义者。

In the lengthy discussions which psychologists have carried on about the amount of intelligence displayed by lower mammals, or the amount of consciousness involved in the functions of the nerve-centres of reptiles, the same test has always been applied: Is the character of the actions such that we must believe them to be performed *for the sake* of their result? The result in question, as we shall hereafter abundantly see, is as a rule a useful one,—the animal is, on the whole, safer under the circumstances for bringing it forth. So far the action has a teleological character; but such mere outward teleology as this might still be the blind result of *vis a tergo*. The growth and movements of plants, the processes of development, digestion, secretion, eto., in animals, supply innumerable instances of performances useful to the individual which may nevertheless be, and by most of us are supposed to be, produced by automatic mechanism. The physiologist does not confidently assert conscious intelligence in the frog's spinal cord until he has shown that the useful result which the nervous machinery brings forth under a given irritation *remains the same when the machinery is altered*. If, to take the stock instance, the right knee of a headless frog be irritated with acid, the right foot will wipe it off. When, however, this foot is amputated, the animal will often raise the *left* foot to the spot and wipe the offending material away.

Pflüger and Lewes reason from such facts in the following way: If the first reaction were the result of mere machinery, they say; if that irritated portion of the skin discharged the right leg as a trigger discharges its own barrel of a shotgun ; then amputating the right foot would indeed frustrate the wiping, but would not make the *left* leg move. It would simply result in the right stump moving through the empty air (which is in fact the phenomenon sometimes observed). The right trigger makes no effort to discharge the left barrel if the right one be unloaded; nor does an electrical machine ever get restless because it can only emit sparks, and not hem pillow-cases like a sewing-machine.

If, on the contrary, the right leg originally moved for the *purpose* of wiping the acid, then nothing is more natural than that, when the easiest means of effecting that purpose prove fruitless, other means should be tried. Every failure must keep the animal in a state of disappointment

在心理学家关于低等哺乳动物所展示出的智能程度或爬虫动物的神经中枢的功能所涉及的意识程度的长期讨论中，同样的检验一直在应用着：这样的行为的特征是否在于我们必须相信它们的实施是为了寻求其结果的缘故？被讨论的这种结果，正如我们此后会完全明白的，是一条规则，一条有用的规则——总体来说，动物在产生结果的境况下更安全。由此，行为具有了一种目的论的特征，但是像这样仅仅是外表上的目的论，可能依然是它背后的力量的盲目结果。植物的生长与活动，动物的发展、消化、分泌等过程对个体提供了无数有用的活动实例，而它们可能依然被认为，并且我们大多数人也这么假设，它们是由自动机构产生的。生理学家不能自信地断言在青蛙的脊髓中有意识的智能，除非他能表明在给定刺激下神经机构所产生的有用结果在神经机构发生变化后仍保持不变。举个常用的例子，如果无头青蛙的右膝盖受到了酸的刺激，它的右脚会把酸擦掉。然而，当右脚被切除以后，它常常会将它的左脚抬到那里，擦拭掉那讨厌的材料。

弗吕格和路易斯从这些事实中用下述的方法进行了推论：他们说如果第一次反应仅仅是那种机制的结果；如果那受了刺激的一部分皮肤让右腿活动就像扳机让它自己的枪管开火一样，那么切除右脚确实会阻碍擦拭活动，却不会让左脚移动。它只会造成右边的残肢在空洞的空气中移动（这事实上是有时候观察到的现象）。如果右边的枪管被卸掉了，右边的扳机是不会尽力地让左边的枪管开火的；一台电机也从来不会因为它只能发出火花却不能像缝纫机一样缝制枕套而不停运动。

相反，如果原先右脚的移动是以擦掉酸为目的，那么这就是最自然不过的事了，即当用来达到目的的最简单的方式证明无效时，其他的方式就会被尝试。每一次失败一定让这动物处于一种

which will lead to all sorts of new trials and devices; and tranquillity will not ensue till one of these, by a happy stroke, achieves the wished-for end.

In a similar way Goltz ascribes intelligence to the frog's optic lobes and cerebellum. We alluded above to the manner in which a sound frog imprisoned in water will discover an outlet to the atmosphere. Goltz found that frogs deprived of their cerebral hemispheres would often exhibit a like ingenuity. Such a frog, after rising from the bottom and finding his farther upward progress checked by the glass bell which has been inverted over him, will not persist in butting his nose against the obstacle until dead of suffocation, but will often re-descend and emerge from under its rim as if, not a definite mechanical propulsion upwards, but rather a conscious desire to reach the air by hook or crook were the main-spring of his activity. Goltz concluded from this that the hemispheres are not the sole seat of intellect in frogs. He made the same inference from observing that a brainless frog will turn over from his back to his belly when one of his legs is sewed up, although the movements required are then very different from those excited under normal circumstances by the same annoying position. They seem determined, consequently, not merely by the antecedent irritant, but by the final end,—though the irritant of course is what makes the end desired.

Another brilliant German author, Liebmann,① argues against the brain's mechanism accounting for mental action, by very similar considerations. A machine as such, he says, will bring forth right results when it is in good order, and wrong results if out of repair. But both kinds of result flow with equally fatal necessity from their conditions. We cannot suppose

① Zur Analysis der Wirklichkeit, p. 489.

失望的状态中，而这又会导致各种新的实验和设计，直到通过一次快乐的努力，其中的一次尝试实现了所希望的目标，平静才随之到来。

戈尔茨以相似的方式将智能归因于青蛙的视叶和小脑。上文我们间接提到了一个健全的青蛙被困在水里时会发现一个通往空气的出口的方式。戈尔茨发现，失去大脑半球的青蛙通常会表现出相似的灵活性。这样的一只青蛙，从底部游上来并发现它进一步向上前进的道路被一个倒扣在它身上的玻璃罐所阻碍之后，将不会一直把它的鼻子贴在障碍物上直到窒息而死，而通常会在罐的边缘里游上游下，好像不是一种明确向上的机械推进力，而是通过各种不寻常的方式来到达空气中的有意识的欲望构成了它活动的主要原动力。戈尔茨由此得出结论，脑半球不是青蛙智力存在的唯一场所。从下述观察中他得出了相同的推论：一个无脑的青蛙当它的一条腿被缝起来时，它便会从背到肚皮翻转过来，尽管这一所需运动和在正常的情况下被同样令它厌烦的姿势所激起的运动十分不同。因此，它们似乎不仅仅是由先行刺激所决定，而是由最终的目标所决定，——尽管是经历的刺激造就了期望实现的目标。

另一个有才气的德国作家李普曼，[①]通过非常相似的考虑来反对心理活动取决于大脑的机制。他说，像这样一架机器当处于正常状态下会产生正确的结果，假如破损失修的话会产生错误的结果。但是这两种结果都随着从它们的条件而来的同样不可避免的必然性而产生。我们不能假设由于自身的结构而不可避免

① 《论现实的分析》，第 489 页。

the clock-work whose structure fatally determines it to a certain rate of speed, noticing that this speed is too slow or too fast and vainly trying to correct it. Its conscience, if it have any, should be as good as that of the best chronometer, for both alike obey equally well the same eternal mechanical laws—laws from behind. But if the *brain* be out of order and the man says " Twice four are two," instead of " Twice four are eight," or else " I must go to the coal to buy the wharf," instead of " I must go to the wharf to buy the coal," instantly there arises a consciousness of error. The wrong performance, though it obey the same mechanical law as the right, is nevertheless condemned,—condemned as contradicting the inner law—the law from in front, the purpose or ideal for which the brain *should* act, whether it do so or not.

We need not discuss here whether these writers in drawing their conclusion have done justice to all the premises involved in the cases they treat of. We quote their arguments only to show how they appeal to the principle that *no actions but such as are done for an end, and show a choice of means, can be called indubitable expressions of Mind.*

I shall then adopt this as the criterion by which to circumscribe the subject-matter of this work so far as action enters into it. Many nervous performances will therefore be unmentioned, as being purely physiological. Nor will the anatomy of the nervous system and organs of sense be described anew. The reader will find in H. N. Martin's 'Human Body,' in G. T. Ladd's 'Physiological Psychology,' and in all the other standard Anatomies and Physiologies, a mass of information which we must regard as preliminary and take for granted in the present work. ① Of the functions of the cerebral hemispheres, however, since they directly subserve consciousness, it will be well to give some little account.

---

① Nothing is easier than to familiarize one's self with the mammalian brain. Get a sheep's head, a small saw, chisel, scalpel and forceps (all three can best be had from a surgical-instrument maker) and unravel its parts either by the aid of a human dissecting book, such as Holden's 'Manual of Anatomy.' or by the specific directions *ad hoc* given in such books as Foster and Langley's 'Practical Physiology' (Macmillan) or Morrell's 'Comparative Anatomy and Dissection of Mammalia' (Longmans).

地决定了自身某一特定的运动速度的时钟机构，注意到了这速度太快或太慢，并且徒劳地尽力去把它纠正过来。它的良心，如果它有的话，应该和最好的记时器一样好，因为二者都以同样的方式、同样好地遵守这同样的永恒机械规律——来自背后的规律。但是，如果大脑失控，如果一个人说“二四得二”，而不是“二四得八”，或者另外说“我必须去煤那儿买码头”，而不是“我必须到码头去买煤”，则错误的意识马上就出现了。错误的行为活动，虽然和正确的一样遵守同样的机械规律，但它仍然受到责难——因为它同内部的规律——来自前面的规律相矛盾，即为了目的或最终目标，大脑应该行动，不管它是否这样做了。

我们在这里不需要讨论，这些作者在得出他们的结论的时候，是否对他们论及的事例中所包含的前提都公正地处理过。我们引用他们的辩论就是要展示出他们是如何诉诸于这一原理的，即只有那些为了目标而发生，并且展示出对方式的某种选择的行为活动，能够被称作是心灵不容置疑的表现。

那么在本书涉及行为的地方，我将以此作为标准来限定本书的主旨。因此，很多神经活动由于是纯生理学的，就不会被提及。神经系统和感觉器官的解剖学也不会被重新加以描述。读者将会在H. N. 马丁的《人的身体》、G. T. 莱德的《生理心理学》和所有其他标准的解剖学和生理学的书籍中发现在本书中我们肯定地看作是初级的和理所当然的大量知识。① 然而，关于脑半球的功能，由于它们直接促进意识，所以做一点儿说明是恰当的。

---

① 用哺乳动物的大脑来熟悉自己的大脑是再容易不过的事了。取一个羊头、一个小锯子、凿子、解剖刀和镊子（这三样最好能从外科手术器械制造者那里获得），然后在人体解剖书（如霍尔登的《解剖学指南》）的帮助下，或者根据在诸如福斯特和兰利的《实用生理学》（麦克米兰）以及莫雷尔的《比较解剖学和哺乳动物解剖》（朗文）这些书中所特别给出的具体指导，将羊头的各个部分拆开。

CHAPTER II.

The Functions Of The Brain.

If I begin chopping the foot of a tree, its branches are unmoved by my act, and its leaves murmur as peacefully as ever in the wind. If, on the contrary, I do violence to the foot of a fellow-man, the rest of his body instantly responds to the aggression by movements of alarm or defence. The reason of this difference is that the man has a nervous system whilst the tree has none; and the function of the nervous system is to bring each part into harmonious co-operation with every other. The afferent nerves, when excited by some physical irritant, be this as gross in its mode of operation as a chopping axe or as subtle as the waves of light, conveys the excitement to the nervous centres. The commotion set up in the centres does not stop there, but discharges itself, if at all strong, through the efferent nerves into muscles and glands, exciting movements of the limbs and viscera, or acts of secretion, which vary with the animal, and with the irritant applied. These acts of response have usually the common character of being of service. They ward off the noxious stimulus and support the beneficial one; whilst if, in itself indifferent, the stimulus be a sign of some distant circumstance of practical importance, the animal's acts are addressed to this circumstance so as to avoid its perils or secure its benefits, as the case may be. To take a common example, if I hear the conductor calling 'All aboard!' as I enter the depot, my heart first stops, then palpitates, and my legs respond to the air-waves falling on my tympanum by quickening their movements. If I stumble as I run,

第二章　大脑的功能

如果我开始砍一棵树的根部，它的枝干不会由于我的行动而移动，而且它的叶子也会和往常在风中一样平静地低语。相反，如果我向一个同胞的脚施加暴力，他身体的其余部分会立刻通过警告或防卫的动作回应这进攻。这种区别的原因在于，人有神经系统而树没有，而神经系统的功能就是让每个部分同其他部分和谐地相互合作。当传入神经受到某物理刺激物的刺激时，不管这刺激在操作方式上像砍树的斧子一样粗重还是像光线一样细微，它都会将这刺激传入神经中枢。在神经中枢产生的骚动不会在那儿停下，如果确实很强的话，它就会通过传出神经进入肌肉和腺体来释放自己，激起四肢和内脏的运动或者是分泌活动，而这因动物不同而变化，因所用刺激物的不同而变化。这些反应的行动通常具有共同的服务性特征。它们躲开有害的刺激而扶持有益的刺激。同时，如果本身无关紧要的刺激是有重要的实用意义的某种远处情境的征兆，动物的活动就会致力于这情境以便避免危险和确保其利益，而这随情况而定。举一个普通的例子，如果当我进入火车站时听到列车长喊“全部上车!”，我的心脏先停了一下，而后接着跳动起来，并且我的双腿通过加速它们的运动来对落在我鼓膜上的声波做出反应。如果当我跑的时候绊倒了，摔倒的感

the sensation of falling provokes a movement of the hands towards the direction of the fall, the effect of which is to shield the body from too sudden a shock. If a cinder enter my eye, its lids close forcibly and a copious flow of tears tends to wash it out.

These three responses to a sensational stimulus differ, however, in many respects. The closure of the eye and the lachrymation are quite involuntary, and so is the disturbance of the heart. Such involuntary responses we know as 'reflex' acts. The motion of the arms to break the shock of falling may also be called reflex, since it occurs too quickly to be deliberately intended. Whether it be instinctive or whether it result from the pedestrian education of childhood may be doubtful; it is, at any rate, less automatic than the previous acts, for a man might by conscious effort learn to perform it more skilfully, or even to suppress it altogether. Actions of this kind, into which instinct and volition enter upon equal terms, have been called 'semi-reflex.' The act of running towards the train, on the other hand, has no instinctive element about it. It is purely the result of education, and is preceded by a consciousness of the purpose to be attained and a distinct mandate of the will. It is a 'voluntary act.' Thus the animal's reflex and voluntary performances shade into each other gradually, being connected by acts which may often occur automatically, but may also be modified by conscious intelligence.

An outside observer, unable to perceive the accompanying consciousness, might be wholly at a loss to discriminate between the automatic acts and those which volition escorted. But if the criterion of mind's existence be the choice of the proper means for the attainment of a supposed end, all the acts seem to be inspired by intelligence, for *appropriateness* characterizes them all alike. This fact, now, has led to two quite opposite theories about the relation to consciousness of the nervous functions. Some authors, finding that the higher voluntary ones seem to require the guidance of feeling, conclude that over the lowest reflexes some such feeling also presides, though it may be a feeling of which *we* remain unconscious. Others, finding that

觉引起了双手向倒下的方向运动,这样做的结果就是为了避免身体受到太过突然的冲击。如果煤渣进入我的眼里,眼皮就会用力关闭,大量的眼泪流出来试图把它冲洗出去。

然而,对感觉刺激的这三种反应在很多方面都不相同。闭眼和流泪是相当自然而然的,而心脏跳动的干扰也是如此。这种自然而然的反应我们称之为"反射"行为。用来削弱摔倒时的冲击的胳膊的运动也可以称为是反射,因为它发生得太快而不能有意地加以谋划。它是否是本能的,或者它是否是儿童时代步行教育的结果,这或许值得怀疑,但不管怎么说它不如前面的动作那么自动,因为人可以通过有意识的努力,学会更有技巧地执行这一动作,或者甚至学会完全抑制住它。像这样由本能和意识以同等条件涉入的行为,已经被称作是"半反射"的。而另一方面,跑向火车的行动没有本能的成分与之相关。它纯粹是教育的结果,并且是要达到这目的的意识与意志的明确命令先于这一行动。它是"主动的行动"。因此动物的反射和主动的活动逐渐地交织在了一起,由那些常常可以自动发生,但也可以被有意识的理智所修改的行动所联系起来了。

一个外部观察者,由于不能察觉相伴随的意识,可能会在区别自动行动和意识相伴的行动时完全不知所措。但是如果心灵存在的标准就是对实现设定目标的恰当方法的选择,似乎所有的行动都是由理智引发的,因为它们都同样以适当性为特征。这一事实现在已经引发了两种截然不同的就神经功能的意识关系的理论。一些作者发现较高级的主动行动似乎需要感受的指引,于是得出结论,虽然我们可能对这种感受一直是无意识的,但某种这样的感受也统摄着最低级的反射行动。其他人发现反射与半

reflex and semi-automatic acts may, notwithstanding their appropriateness, take place with an unconsciousness apparently complete, fly to the opposite extreme and maintain that the appropriateness even of voluntary actions owes nothing to the fact that consciousness attends them. They are, according to these writers, results of physiological mechanism pure and simple. In a near chapter we shall return to this controversy again. Let us now look a little more closely at the brain and at the ways in which its states may be supposed to condition those of the mind.

The Frog's Nerve-Centres.

Both the minute anatomy and the detailed physiology of the brain are achievements of the present generation, or rather we may say (beginning with Meynert) of the past twenty years. Many points are still obscure and subject to controversy; but a general way of conceiving the organ has been reached on all hands which in its main feature seems not unlikely to stand, and which even gives a most plausible scheme of the way in which cerebral and mental operations go hand in hand.

The best way to enter the subject will be to take a lower creature, like a frog, and study by the vivisectional method the functions of his different nerve-centres. The frog's nerve-centres are figured in the accompanying diagram, which needs no further explanation. I will first proceed to state what happens when various amounts of the anterior parts are removed, in different frogs, in the way in which an ordinary student removes them; that is, with no extreme precautions as to the purity of the operation. We shall in this way reach a very simple conception of the functions of the various centres, involving the strongest possible contrast between the cerebral hemispheres and the lower lobes. This sharp conception will have didactic advantages, for it is often very instructive to start with too simple a formula and correct it later on.

自动的行动，尽管有其适当性，却可以显然完全无意识地发生，于是他们飞向另一个极端，主张即便是主动动作的适当性也不能证实意识参与了行动。按照这些作者的意思，它们是纯粹而简单的生理学意义上的机械装置的结果。在临近的章节中我们将会再次返回到这一辩论中来。现在让我们更进一步地考察一下大脑以及它的方式，在其方式中，大脑的状态可被看作是心灵状态的条件。

青蛙的神经中枢

关于大脑的仔细而准确的解剖学和详细的生理学都是当代人的成就，或者我们毋宁说（从梅纳特开始）是过去20年的成就。很多观点依然是模糊的并且受到争论，但是大家已经对思考这一器官的一般方法达成共识，在它的主要特征方面它似乎不可能站不住脚，而且它甚至给出了大脑和心理运作携手进行之方法的似乎最合理的图解。

进入这一主题的最佳方式就是取来像青蛙这种较低级的生物，通过活体解剖的方法研究它不同神经中枢的功能。青蛙的神经中枢由附随的图示来表示（见图1），图示无需更多的解释。我首先进行陈述的将是当不同量的前面部分在不同的青蛙那里被取掉时，会发生什么情况，取掉它们的方式和普通学生取掉它们的方式一样；也就是说，对手术的纯净度没有过高的要求。用这种方法我们将获得一个非常简单的各种中枢功能的概念，这涉及大脑半球和较低级脑叶之间可能有的最强烈的对比。这一鲜明的概念有说教的优势，因为从一个相当简单的公式开始然后再去修正它，

Our first formula, as we shall later see, will have to be softened down somewhat by the results of more careful experimentation both on frogs and birds, and by those of the most recent observations on dogs, monkeys, and man. But it will put us, from the outset, in clear possession of some fundamental notions and distinctions which we could otherwise not gain so well, and none of which the later more completed view will overturn.

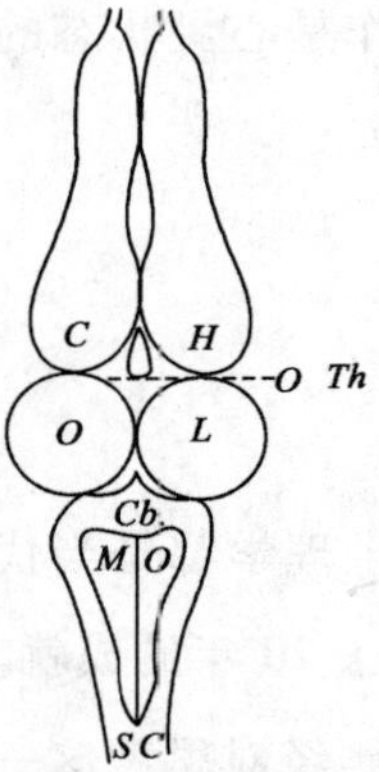

FIG. 1.—*C H*, Cerebral Hemispheres; *O Th*, Optic Thalami; *O L*, Optic Lobes; *Cb*, Cerebellum; *M O*, Medulla Oblongata; *S C*, Spinal Cord.

If, then, we reduce the frog’s nervous system to the spinal cord alone, by making a section behind the base of the skull, between the spinal cord and the medulla oblon-gata, thereby cutting off the brain from all connection with the rest of the body, the frog will still continue to live, but with a very peculiarly modified activity. It ceases to breathe or swallow; it lies flat on its belly, and does not, like a normal frog, sit up on its fore paws, though its hind legs ate kept, as usual, folded against its body and immediately resume this position if drawn out. If thrown on its back, it lies there quietly, without turning over like a normal frog. Locomotion and voice seem entirely abolished. If we suspend it by the nose, and irritate different portions of its skin by acid, it performs a set of remarkable ‘defensive’ movements calculated to wipe away the irritant. Thus, if the breast be touched, both fore paws will rub it vigorously; if we touch the outer side of the elbow, the hind foot of the same side will rise directly to the spot and wipe it. The back of the foot will rub the knee if that be attacked, whilst if the foot be cut away, the stump will make ineffectual movements, and then, in many frogs, a pause will come, as if for deliberation, succeeded by a rapid passage of the opposite unmutilated foot to the acidulated spot.

这通常是很有教育意义的。如我们后面将看到的那样，我们的第一个公式，将不得不由于对青蛙和鸟类所做的更仔细的实验结果，以及对狗、猴子和人所做的最近期的观察结果而被削弱了。但是，它使我们从一开始就对一些基本的概念和区分有了明确的把握，用其他方式我们是不能这么好地获得它们的，而且任何随后更加完善的观点都不能推翻它们。

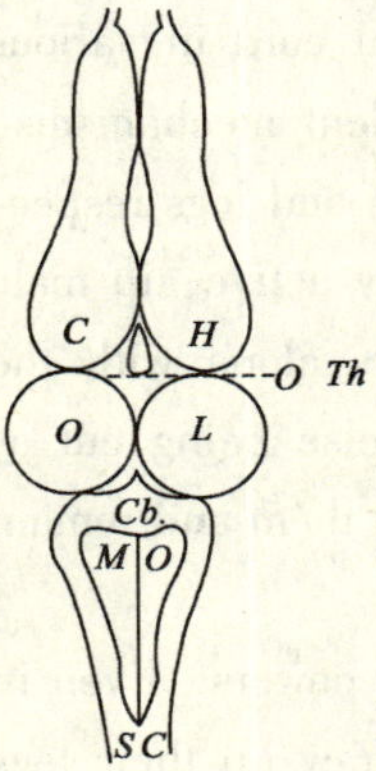

图 1　*C H*，大脑半球；*O Th*，视丘；*O L*，视叶；*Cb*，小脑；*M O*，延髓；*S C*，脊髓

那么，如果我们在青蛙颅骨底部的后面，在脊髓和延髓之间做一次切断，从而切断了大脑和其他身体部分的所有联系，这样我们就将青蛙的神经系统缩减到只剩下脊髓了，青蛙将继续活着，但行为却发生了很特别的变化。它停止了呼吸和吞咽，肚皮着地趴着，而不是和正常的青蛙一样用前爪支撑着坐在那里，尽管它的后腿和平常一样对着身体折叠着，而且当后腿被拽出来后又立刻恢复到这姿势。如果让它背部朝下，它静静地躺在那里，没有像正常青蛙一样翻转过来。运动和声音似乎完全消失了。如果我们拴住它的鼻子将它悬挂起来，用酸刺激它皮肤的不同部分，它将实施一系列显著的、有计划的消除刺激的“防御”活动。因此，如果胸部被触碰，两个前爪就会精神旺盛地摩擦那里；如果我们触碰它肘部的外侧，同侧的后脚会直接伸到那个地方并擦掉它。如果膝盖受到攻击，后脚就会摩擦膝盖，如果同时那脚被切除了，残肢就会做无效的运动，而且在大多数青蛙那里，接下来会出现停顿，就好像是为了思考，而后另一只没有受伤的脚向涂有酸的地方迅速移动过去。

The most striking character of all these movements, after their teleological appropriateness, is their precision. They vary, in sensitive frogs and with a proper amount of irritation, so little as almost to resemble in their machine-like regularity the performances of a jumping-jack, whose legs must twitch whenever you pull the string. The spinal cord of the frog thus contains arrangements of cells and fibres fitted to convert skin irritations into movements of defence. We may call it the *centre for defensive movements* in this animal. We may indeed go farther than this, and by cutting the spinal cord in various places find that its separate segments are independent mechanisms, for appropriate activities of the head and of the arms and legs respectively. The segment governing the arms is especially active, in male frogs, in the breeding season; and these members alone with the breast and back appertaining to them, everything else being cut away, will then actively grasp a finger placed between them and remain hanging to it for a considerable time.

The spinal cord in other animals has analogous powers. Even in man it makes movements of defence. Paraplegics draw up their legs when tickled; and Robin, on tickling the breast of a criminal an hour after decapitation, saw the arm and hand move towards the spot. Of the lower functions of the mammalian cord, studied so ably by Goltz and others, this is not the place to speak.

If, in a second animal, the cat be made just behind the optic lobes so that the cerebellum and medulla oblongata remain attached to the cord, then swallowing, breathing, crawling, and a rather enfeebled jumping and swimming are added to the movements previously observed.① There are other reflexes too. The animal, thrown on his back, immediately turns over to his belly. Placed in a shallow bowl, which is floated on water and made to rotate,

---

① It should be said that this particular cut commonly proves fatal. The text refers to the rare cases which survive.

所有这些运动的最显著的特征,除了它们在目的论意义上的适当性以外,就是它们的精确性。在有感觉的青蛙身上使用适量的刺激,这些动作几乎没有变化,在其机械般的规律性方面很像“跳娃娃”[1]表演,你随时拉动“跳娃娃”身上的线,它的腿都会抽动一下。因此,青蛙的脊髓含有细胞和纤维的排列组织,它们可以将皮肤刺激转变成防御动作。我们可将之称为这个动物中的防御动作中枢。我们确实可以走得比这更远,通过在不同的位置切掉脊髓,我们发现它分开的部分是独立的机构,分别控制头、手臂和腿的适当行动。在繁殖的季节,在雄性青蛙中控制手臂的部分尤其活跃;让这些青蛙只留下胸部和与它们相连的背部,其他的全部切除,那它们也会很活跃地抓住放在它们手臂之间地手指,并且悬上相当长的一段时间。

其他动物身上的脊髓有类似的能力。甚至在人这里它也产生防御动作。当给截瘫患者挠痒时他们会提起腿来;当罗宾胳肢一个已经被斩首一小时的罪犯的胸部时,他看到胳膊和手朝着被触摸的地方移动。关于哺乳动物脊髓较低级的功能,戈尔茨和其他人对它们的研究非常巧妙,但这儿不是讨论的地方。

在另一只动物身上,如果切割就在视叶的后面进行,结果是小脑与延髓依然同脊髓相连,那么在先前观察到的行动之上会加上吞咽、呼吸、爬行以及一种相当微弱的跳跃和游泳的动作。① 也有一些其他的反射动作。让动物背部朝下,它会立刻翻转到肚皮朝下的姿势。把它放在一个漂浮在水面上并且旋转着的浅碗里,

---

① 应该指出的是这一特殊的切割通常证明是致命的。本文指的是那些生还的罕见例子。

〔1〕 一种玩具。

he responds to the rotation by first turning his head and then waltzing around with his entire body, in the opposite direction to the whirling of the bowl. If his support be tilted so that his head points downwards, he points it up; he points it down if it be pointed upwards, to the right if it be pointed to the left, etc. But his reactions do not go farther than these movements of the head. He will not, like frogs whose thalami are preserved, climb up a board if the latter be tilted, but will slide off it to the ground.

If the cut be made on another frog between the thalami and the optic lobes, the locomotion both on land and water becomes quite normal, and, in addition to the reflexes already shown by the lower centres, he croaks regularly whenever he is pinched under the arms. He compensates rotations, etc., by movements of the head, and turns over from his back; but still drops off his tilted board. As his optic nerves are destroyed by the usual operation, it is impossible to say whether he will avoid obstacles placed in his path.

When, finally, a frog's cerebral hemispheres alone are cut off by a section between them and the thalami which preserves the latter, an unpractised observer would not at first suspect anything abnormal about the animal. Not only is he capable, on proper instigation, of all the acts already described, but he guides himself by sight, so that if an obstacle be set up between him and the light, and he be forced to move forward, he either jumps over it or swerves to one side. He manifests sexual passion at the proper season, and, unlike an altogether brainless frog, which embraces anything placed between his arms, postpones this reflex act until a female of his own species is provided. Thus far, as aforesaid, a person unfamiliar with frogs might not suspect a mutilation; but even such a person would soon remark the almost entire absence of spontaneous motion—that is, motion unprovoked by any *present* in-citation of sense. The continued movements of swimming, performed by the creature in the water,

它对旋转的反应最初是转动它的头，然后开始朝着浅碗转动的相反方向旋转整个身子。如果让它的支撑物倾斜，使它的头朝下了，它会让头朝上；如果头朝上，它就让头朝下；如果头朝左，它就让头朝右，等等。但它的反应不会超出头部的这些动作。它不会像丘脑被保留下来的青蛙那样，如果被倾斜会沿着板子向上爬，而是会顺着板子滑到地面上。

如果在另一只青蛙那里切割在丘脑和视叶之间进行，它在陆地和水上的动作就变得很正常了，而且，除了已经由较低级的中枢显示出来的反射动作以外，每当它的臂下被刺痛，它都有规律地呱呱叫。它通过头部的运动和从它的背部翻转过来的方式来抵消旋转，等等；但它仍然会从倾斜的板子上掉下来。由于它的视觉神经被通常的手术破坏了，要说出它能否避开放在道路上的障碍物是不可能的。

最后，在青蛙的两个大脑半球和丘脑之间进行切割，只将大脑半球切割掉而留下丘脑，一个经验不足的观测者起初不能怀疑这动物有任何不正常的情况。在适当的刺激下，它不仅能够做出上面已经描述的所有动作，而且它还能通过视觉来指引它自己，以致如果在它与发光体之间设置一个障碍物，并迫使它向前移动，它会或者跳过障碍物或者突然转向另一边。在适当的季节它会表现出性激情，并且不像一个完全没有大脑的青蛙那样会抱住任何放在它胳膊之间的东西，而是会推迟它的反射行动直到获得了它的一个同类雌性。由此，如前所述，一个不熟悉青蛙的人可能不会怀疑切割的发生；但即使是这样的人也会很快就注意到自发动作几乎完全丧失了——也就是说，不是由当前的任何感官刺激所引起的动作丧失了。这动物在水中执行的不断游泳的动作似乎是它

seem to be the fatal result of the contact of that fluid with its skin. They cease when a stick, for example, touches his hands. This is a sensible irritant towards which the feet are automatically drawn by reflex action, and on which the animal remains sitting. He manifests no hunger, and will suffer a fly to crawl over his nose unsnapped at. Fear, too, seems to have deserted him. In a word, he is an extremely complex machine whose actions, so far as they go, tend to self-preservation; but still a *machine*, in this sense—that it seems to contain no incalculable element. By applying the right sensory stimulus to him we are almost as certain of getting a fixed response as an organist is of hearing a certain tone when he pulls out a certain stop.

But now if to the lower centres we add the cerebral hemispheres, or if, in other words, we make an intact animal the subject of our observations, all this is changed. In addition to the previous responses to present incitements of sense, our frog now goes through long and complex acts of locomotion *spontaneously*, or as if moved by what in ourselves we should call an idea. His reactions to outward stimuli vary their form, too. Instead of making simple defensive movements with his hind legs like a headless frog if touched, or of giving one or two leaps and then sitting still like a hemisphereless one, he makes persistent and varied efforts at escape, as if, not the mere contact of the physiologist's hand, but the notion of danger suggested by it were now his spur. Led by the feeling of hunger, too, he goes in search of insects, fish, or smaller frogs, and varies his procedure with each species of victim. The physiologist cannot by manipulating him elicit croaking, crawling up a board, swimming or stopping, at will. His conduct has become incalculable. We can no longer foretell it exactly. Effort to escape is his dominant reaction, but he *may* do anything else, even swell up and become perfectly passive in our hands.

Such are the phenomena commonly observed, and such the impressions which one naturally receives. Certain general conclusions follow irresistibly. First of all the following:

的皮肤和液体相接触而造成的不可避免的结果。比如，当用棍子碰它的手时动作就停止了。这棍子是可感觉刺激物，通过反射动作脚朝着它自动地伸过来，并且这动物坐在了它上面。它没有饥饿的表现，而且会容忍一只苍蝇爬过它的鼻子并放过它。恐惧似乎也离开了它。总之，就目前它的行为来看，它是一架异常复杂的机器，虽倾向于自我保存；但是，它似乎不包含任何无法预料的因素，从这个意义上来说，它依然是一架机器。对它施加适当的感官刺激，我们对所要获得的固定反应极为确定，就如同管风琴家拉出某根音栓时对将要听到的某一音高那样确定。

但是，如果我们在低级中枢之上加上脑半球，或者换句话说，我们将一只完整无缺的动物当作我们的观测对象，所有这一切全部变化了。除了对目前感官刺激的前述反应之外，我们的青蛙现在能够自然地做出长时间的和复杂的运动动作，或者好像是被在我们这里称其为观念的东西所激励。对外部刺激反应的形式也很多样。如果被触碰，它不会像无头青蛙那样用后腿做简单的防御动作，也不会像没有脑半球的青蛙那样跳上一两下之后接着仍旧坐在那里，而是对逃跑做持久而多变的努力，仿佛此时对它的驱策并不仅仅是由于和生理学家的手发生了接触，而是由此所暗示出的危险的观念所造成。也由于饥饿感的驱使，它会搜寻昆虫、鱼、或者更小的青蛙，其程序随着猎物种类的不同而变化。心理学家不能凭意愿操纵它，让它发出叫声、爬上木板、游泳或者停下来。它的行为已经变得不能预测了。我们不能再对它做出准确预言。逃跑的努力是它的主要反应，但是它还可能做任何其他事情，甚至鼓胀起来，在我们手中变得完全被动起来。

这些便是一般被观测到的现象，也是人们自然获得的印象。某些一般性的结论不可避免地随之而来。首先如下：

The acts of all the centres involve the use of the same muscles. When a headless frog's hind leg wipes the acid, he calls into play all the leg-muscles which a frog with his full medulla oblongata and cerebellum uses when he turns from his back to his belly, Their contractions are, however, *combined* differently in the two cases, so that the results vary widely. We must consequently conclude that specific arrangements of cells and fibres exist in the cord for wiping, in the medulla for turning over, etc. Similarly they exist in the thalami for jumping over seen obstacles and for balancing the moved body; in the optic lobes for creeping backwards, or what not. But in the hemispheres, since the presence of these organs *brings no new elementary form of movement* with it, *but only determines differently the occasions* on which the movements shall occur, making the usual stimuli less fatal and machine-like; we need suppose no such machinery *directly* co-ordinative of muscular contractions to exist We may rather assume, when the mandate for a wiping-movement is sent forth by the hemispheres, that a current goes straight to the wiping-arrangement in the spinal cord, exciting this arrangement as a whole. Similarly, if an intact frog wishes to jump over a stone which he sees, all he need do is to excite from the hemispheres the jumping-centre in the thalami or wherever it may be, and the latter will provide for the details of the execution. It is like a general ordering a colonel to make a certain movement, but not telling him how it shall be done. ①

The same muscle, then, is repeatedly represented at different heights; and at each it enters into a different combination with other muscles to co-operate in some special form of concerted movement. *At each height the movement is discharged by some particular form of*

---

① I confine myself to the frog for simplicity's sake. In higher animals, especially the ape and man, it would seem as if not only determinate combinations of muscles, but limited groups or even single muscle could be innervated from the hemispheres.

所有中枢的行动涉及相同肌肉的使用。当无头青蛙的后腿擦掉酸液的时候，它调用了所有的腿部肌肉，这也是完全拥有延髓和小脑的青蛙在从其背部着地的姿势翻转到肚皮朝下的姿势时所用的肌肉。然而，在这两个例子里肌肉的收缩是被不同组合了的，以致结果有很大的变化。从而我们必须得出结论，许多具体的细胞和纤维排列分别存在于脊髓中控制擦拭动作，存在于延髓中控制翻转动作，等等。同样地，它们也存在于丘脑控制跳过所见障碍物的动作和控制平衡移动了的身体的动作，存在于视叶中控制向后爬的动作，等等。但是，在两个脑半球那里，由于这些器官的出现没有随之带来新的基本运动形式，而仅仅是不同地决定动作应当发生的时机，使通常的刺激行动显得不是那么不可避免，不那么像机器了。我们不需要假设直接协调肌肉收缩的机器存在，我们宁可假设，当脑半球下达了擦拭动作的命令之时，一股电流直接进入脊髓中控制擦拭的排列组织，将这排列组织作为一个整体加以刺激。同样地，如果一个健全的青蛙想要越过一个它看到的石头，它所需做的就是由脑半球刺激存在于丘脑或无论什么地方的跳跃中枢，后者将提供实施的细节。它就像将军命令上校完成某项活动，却不告诉他应该怎样完成它。①

那么，同样的肌肉会在不同的高度被重复表现，而且在每一个高度，它都和其他肌肉有一种不同的组合，从而在某种特殊谐和动作形式中互相协作。在每一个高度，动作在某种特殊的感觉

① 为了简单起见，我将自己局限于对青蛙的讨论。在更高等的动物尤其是猩猩和人那里，大脑半球似乎不仅可以促使确定的肌肉组合活动，而且可以使有限的肌肉群甚至单块儿肌肉活动。

sensorial stimulus. Thus in the cord, the skin alone occasions movements; in the upper part of the optic lobes, the eyes are added; in the thalami, the semi-circular canals would seem to play a part; whilst the stimuli which discharge the hemispheres would seem not so much to be elementary sorts of sensation, as groups of sensations forming determinate *objects* or *things*. *Prey* is not pursued nor are *enemies* shunned by ordinary hemisphereless frogs. Those reactions upon complex circumstances which we call instinctive rather than reflex, are already in this animal dependent on the brain's highest lobes, and still more is this the case with animals higher in the zoological scale.

The results are just the same if, instead of a frog, we take a pigeon, and cut out his hemispheres as they are ordinarily cut out for a lecture-room demonstration. There is not a movement natural to him which this brainless bird cannot perform if expressly excited thereto; only the inner promptings seem deficient, and when left to himself he spends most of his time crouched on the ground with his head sunk between his shoulders as if asleep.

General Notion Of Hemispheres.

All these facts lead us, when we think about them, to some such explanatory conception as this: *The lower centres act from present sensational stimuli alone; the hemispheres act from perceptions and considerations*, the sensations which they may receive serving only as suggesters of these. But what are perceptions but sensations grouped together? And what are considerations but expectations, in the fancy, of sensations which will be felt one way or another according as action takes this course or that? If I step aside on seeing a rattlesnake, from considering how dangerous an animal he is, the mental materials which constitute my prudential reflection are

刺激形式下释放出来。因此,在脊髓那里,皮肤单独引起运动;在视叶的上半部分,眼睛加了进来;在丘脑那里,半规管似乎在独立作用;同时释放脑半球的刺激行动似乎不完全是基本类型的感觉,而是形成对象和事物的感觉群。没有脑半球的青蛙不会追逐猎物也不会躲避敌人。那些就复杂情境所做出的反应我们称之为本能的而不是反射的,这些反应在这动物身上已经依赖于大脑最高级的视叶,在动物学等级中较高级的动物那里情形就更是如此。

如果我们用一只鸽子来替代青蛙,就像在教室中展示时所进行的普通切割那样,将它的脑半球切割掉,其结果也是一样。如果清楚地往鸽子那里施加刺激,对这只无头的鸟而言,只要是自然的动作它是没有不能完成的;只有内部的动力似乎是缺乏的,当让它自已待着时,它大部分时间都蜷伏在地上,将头埋在肩膀中间,仿佛睡着了一般。

关于脑半球的一般观点

当我们对所有这些事实进行思考时,它们将我们引入了某种诸如此类的解释概念:低级的中枢由于当前的感觉刺激而单独行动;大脑半球是由于知觉和思考而行动,它们收到的感觉只是作为这些知觉和思考的提示物。但是除了组合在一起的感觉,知觉又是什么呢?而且,除了以由这样或那样发生的动作而形成的这样或那样的方式在想像中对感受到的感觉的期待以外,思考又是什么呢?如果我看到一条响尾蛇,考虑到这只动物是多么的危险,于是避到一边,构成我的谨慎反射的心理材料是多少有些生

images more or less vivid of the movement of his head, of a sudden pain in my leg, of a state of terror, a swelling of the limb, a chill, delirium, unconsciousness, etc., and the ruin of my hopes. But all these images are constructed out of my past experiences. They are *reproductions* of what I have felt or witnessed. They are, in short, *remote* sensations; and the *difference between the hemi-sphereless animal and the whole one* may be concisely expressed by saying that the *one obeys absent, the other only present, objects.*

The hemispheres would then seem to be *the seat of memory.* Vestiges of past experience must in some way be stored up in them, and must, when aroused by present stimuli, first appear as representations of distant goods and evils; and then must discharge into the appropriate motor channels for warding off the evil and securing the benefits of the good. If we liken the nervous currents to electric currents, we can compare the nervous system, C, below the hemispheres to a direct circuit from sense-organ to muscle along the line S... C... M of Fig. 2 (p. 21). The hemisphere, H, adds the long circuit or loop-line through which the current may pass when for any reason the direct line is not used.

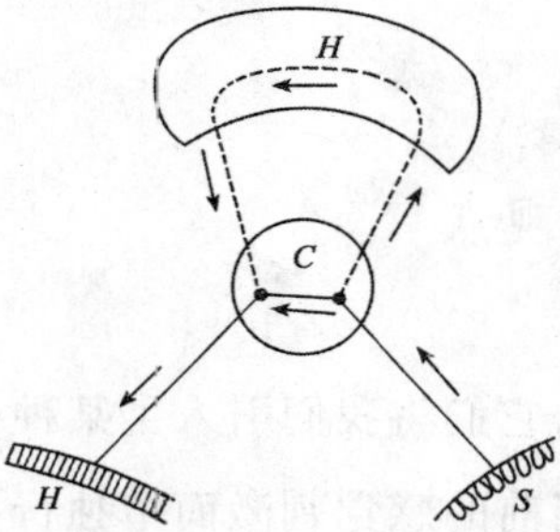

FIG. 2.

Thus, a tired wayfarer on a hot day throws himself on the damp earth beneath a maple-tree. The sensations of delicious rest and coolness pouring themselves through the direct line would naturally discharge into the muscles of complete extension: he would abandon himself to the dangerous repose. But the loop-line being open, part of the current is drafted along it, and awakens rheumatic or catarrhal reminiscences, which prevail over the instigations of sense, and make the man arise and pursue his way to where he may enjoy his rest more safely. Presently we shall examine the manner in which the hemispheric loop-line may be supposed to serve as a reservoir for such reminiscences as these. Mean-while I will ask the reader to notice some corollaries of its being such a reservoir.

动的意象，诸如蛇头的运动、腿部突然疼痛、恐怖的状态、肢体的肿胀、一阵寒战、暂时精神错乱、意识不清，等等，以及我的希望的破灭。但所有这些意象都是由我过去的经验构成的，它们是我曾经感受到或目击过的东西的再现。简而言之，它们是遥远的感觉，而且无脑半球的动物和健全的动物之间的区别可以被精确地表述为：一个服从不在场的对象，另一个服从在场的对象。

于是大脑就被看成是记忆的场所。过去经验的痕迹一定以某种方式储存于其中，而且当它被现在的刺激所引起时，它一定首先是作为遥远的善与恶的表象而显现的；并且接下来它一定流入了用来避开坏事、确保好事所带来的利益的运动通道。如果我们把神经流比喻成电流，我们可以将脑半球下的神经系统 C 比作图 2（第 21 页）[1] 中沿着线 C…S…M 从感觉器官到肌肉的一条直接电路。脑半球 H 加入了这条长电路或说回路线中来，当不论什么原因而导致直接电路线未被使用时，电流便可以通过 H。

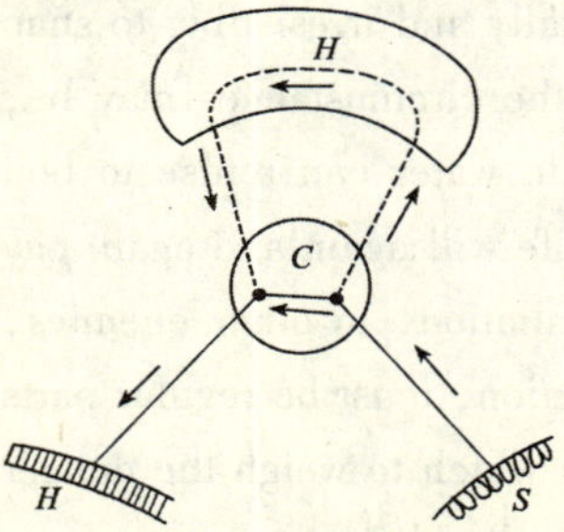

图 2

因此，在一个炎热日子里，疲惫的徒步旅行者会一头倒在枫树下潮湿的土地上。令人愉快的休息和凉爽的感觉通过直接电路线奔流着，它们将自然地流入完全舒展开的肌肉里：他将自己遗弃在这危险的睡眠里。但是回路线是打开的，一部分神经流沿着它流动，并且唤醒了风湿病和黏膜炎的记忆，它们胜于感官的鼓动，并使得他站了起来，去寻找能让他更安全地享受休息的地方。不久，我们将会检查这样一种方式，在这种方式下，回路线可被认为是充当了诸如此类记忆的储藏所。与此同时，我将请读者注意到它作为这样一个储藏所而招致的一些必然结果。

---

〔1〕 英文圆括号中页码，为原版书页码。本书此类情形不再另作说明。

First, no animal without it can deliberate, pause, postpone, nicely weigh one motive against another, or compare. Prudence, in a word, is for such a creature an impossible virtue. Accordingly we see that nature removes those functions in the exercise of which prudence is a virtue from the lower centres and hands them over to the cerebrum. Wherever a creature has to deal with complex features of the environment, prudence is a virtue. The higher animals have so to deal; and the more complex the features, the higher we call the animals. The fewer of his acts, then, can *such* an animal perform without the help of the organs in question. In the frog many acts devolve wholly on the lower centres; in the bird fewer; in the rodent fewer still; in the dog very few indeed; and in apes and men hardly any at all.

The advantages of this are obvious. Take the prehension of food as an example and suppose it to be a reflex performance of the lower centres. The animal will be condemned fatally and irresistibly to snap at it whenever presented, no matter what the circumstances may be; he can no more disobey this prompting than water can refuse to boil when a fire is kindled under the pot. His life will again and again pay the forfeit of his gluttony. Exposure to retaliation, to other enemies, to traps, to poisons, to the dangers of repletion, must be regular parts of his existence. His lack of all thought by which to weigh the danger against the attractiveness of the bait, and of all volition to remain hungry a little while longer, is the direct measure of his lowness in the mental scale. And those fishes which, like our cunners and sculpins, are no sooner thrown back from the hook into the water, than they automatically seize the hook again, would soon expiate the degradation of their intelligence by the extinction of their type, did not their exaggerated fecundity atone for their imprudence. Appetite and the acts it prompts have consequently become in all higher vertebrates functions of the cerebrum. They disappear when the physiologist's knife has left the subordinate centres alone in place. The brainless pigeon will starve though left on a corn-heap.

首先,如果没有它,没有任何动物可以思考、踌躇、延迟、精细地在动机之间加以权衡,或者比较。一言以蔽之,对这样一种动物来说审慎是一种不可能的优点。从而我们看到自然从较低等的中枢那里移走了这些功能,而就这些功能的实施来说审慎是一种优点,并且把它们交给了大脑。无论动物在何种情况下应对复杂的环境特点,审慎都是一种优点。较高级的动物必须应对环境,而且这些环境特点越复杂,我们说这种动物越高级。那么,没有被讨论的器官的帮助,这种动物所能完成的动作就较少。在青蛙那里,很多动作完全移交给了中枢;在鸟那里,这样的动作较少;在啮齿动物那里,这样的动作还要少些;在狗那里,这样的动作更是少有;而在猩猩和人那里,这样的动作几乎完全没有了。

这样的好处是显而易见的。以抓取食物为例,并假设它是较低级中枢的反射活动,不管情形怎样,只要食物出现,这动物就命中注定地、无法抗拒惩罚地咬住它;就和用壶烧水时壶里的水不能拒绝沸腾一样,它不能违背这刺激。它的生命将一次次地因为贪食而丧失。暴露于报复、其他敌人、陷阱、毒药和贪食的危险之中,一定是其生存时经常发生的事情。它缺乏权衡危险与诱饵诱惑的思维,缺乏再多忍耐一会饥饿的意志,而这就是对它在心理等级中处于较低位置的直接度量。而像青鲈和杜父鱼那样的鱼,刚从钩子上摘下来被扔到水里,它们又会自动地再次咬钩。如果不是它们夸张的生育能力弥补了它们的轻率行为,它们将很快通过其族类的灭绝来为其智能低下付出代价。食欲和它激起的行动从而在所有较高级的脊椎动物那里变成了大脑的功能。当生理学家的刀下只保留次级中枢的话,它们就消失了。即使将无脑的鸽子扔在玉米堆上,它也会饿死。

Take again the sexual function. In birds this devolves exclusively upon the hemispheres. When these are shorn away the pigeon pays no attention to the billings and coo-ings of its mate. And Goltz found that a bitch in heat would excite no emotion in male dogs who had suffered large loss of cerebral tissue. Those who have read Darwin's 'Descent of Man' know what immense importance in the amelioration of the breed in birds this author ascribes to the mere fact of sexual selection. The sexual act is not performed until every condition of circumstance and sentiment is fulfilled, until time, place, and partner all are fit. But in frogs and toads this passion devolves on the lower centers. They show consequently a machine-like obedience to the present incitement of sense, and an almost total exclusion of the power of choice. Copulation occurs *per fas aut nefas*, occasionally between males, often with dead females, in puddles exposed on the highway, and the male may be cut in two without letting go his hold. Every spring an immense sacrifice of batrachian life takes place from these causes alone.

No one need be told how dependent all human social elevation is upon the prevalence of chastity. Hardly any factor measures more than this the difference between civilization and barbarism. Physiologically interpreted, chastity means nothing more than the fact that present solicitations of sense are overpowered by suggestions of æsthetic and moral fitness which the circumstances awaken in the cerebrum; and that upon the inhibitory or permissive influence of these alone action directly depends.

Within the psychic life due to the cerebrum itself the same general distinction obtains, between considerations of the more immediate and considerations of the more remote. In all ages the man whose determinations are swayed by reference to the most distant ends has been held to possess the highest intelligence. The tramp who lives from hour to hour; the bohemian whose engagements are from day to day; the bachelor who builds but for a single life; the father who acts for another generation; the patriot who thinks of a whole community and many generations; and finally, the philosopher and saint whose cares are for humanity and for eternity,—these range themselves in an unbroken hierarchy, wherein each successive grade results from an increased manifestation of the special form of action by which the cerebral

再来看性功能。在鸟类那里它专属于脑半球掌管。当它们被切掉时,鸽子对配偶求爱的叫声无动于衷。而且,戈尔茨发现,一条发情的母狗不能激起脑组织大量丧失的公狗的任何情绪。阅读过达尔文《人类的由来》的人都知道,在鸟类繁殖的改善方面,作者将多么大的重要性归因于性选择这一单纯事实。只有到情境和情感的每一个条件都得以实现,并且时间、地点、配偶都合适,性行为才能执行。但是在青蛙和蟾蜍那里,这激情移交给了低级中枢。它们从而对目前的感官刺激展示了一种机械般的顺从,而且几乎完全消除了选择的能力。在公路上的泥水坑里,偶尔在雄性之间,或者通常是雄性和已死的雌性之间,性交竟然发生了,而且雄性还没有做完就可能被压成两半了。每年春天单单由于这些原因大量蛙类丧失了生命。

众所周知,人类社会的一切提升是何等地依赖于贞洁的盛行。几乎没有任何因素比这更能度量出文明与野蛮的区别了。从生理学来解释,贞洁只能意味这样的事实,即当前的感官诱惑被在大脑中由情境唤起的审美的和道德的适切性的暗示所压制了,并且贞洁直接取决于这些单独行动的抑制性的或许可性的影响。

在由大脑自身引起的精神生活中,在对较近事物的考虑和对较远事物的考虑之间有同样的一般性区别。在所有时代,通过参照最远的目标而转变其决定的人被认为拥有最高的智慧。以小时过活的乞丐,按天被雇佣的吉普赛人,只为此生而奋斗的单身汉,为下一代而劳作的父亲,为整个社会和许多代人着想的爱国者,最后还有关心人性和不朽的哲学家和圣人——这些人将自己排列到了一个完整等级层次中,在这里每一连续的等级成因于增强了的特殊行为方式的表现,而通过这行为方式大脑中枢同

centres are distinguished from all below them.

In the 'loop-line' along which the memories and ideas of the distant are supposed to lie, the action, so far as it is a physical process, must be interpreted after the type of the action in the lower centres. If regarded here as a reflex process, it must be reflex there as well. The current in both places runs out into the muscles only after it has first run in; but whilst the path by which it runs out is determined in the lower centres by reflections few and fixed amongst the cell-arrangements, in the hemispheres the reflections are many and instable. This, it will be seen, is only a difference of degree and not of kind, and does not change the reflex type. The conception of *all* action as conforming to this type is the fundamental conception of modern nerve-physiology. So much for our general preliminary conception of the nerve-centres! Let us define it more distinctly before we see how well physiological observation will bear it out in detail.

The Education Of The Hemispheres.

Nerve-currents run in through sense-organs, and whilst provoking reflex acts in the lower centres, they arouse ideas in the hemispheres, which either permit the reflexes in question, check them, or substitute others for them. All ideas being in the last resort reminiscences, the question to answer is: *How can processes become organized in the hemispheres which correspond to reminiscences in the mind?*①

---

① I hope that the reader will take no umbrage at my so mixing the physical and mental, and talking of reflex acts and hemispheres and reminiscences in the same breath, as if they were homogeneous quantities and factors of one causal chain. I have done so deliberately; for although I admit that from the radically physical point of view it is easy to conceive of the chain of events amongst the cells and fibres as complete in itself, and that whilst so conceiving it one need make no mention of 'ideas,' I yet suspect that point of view of being an unreal abstraction. Reflexes in centres may take place even where accompanying feelings or ideas guide them. In another chapter I shall try to show reasons for not abandoning this common-sense position; meanwhile language lends itself so much more easily to the mixed way of describing, that I will continue to employ the latter. The more radical-minded reader can always read 'ideational process' for 'idea.'

所有低于它们的东西区分开来。

对于遥远事物的记忆和观念被认为位于“回路线”之中,行为,只要它是一个物理过程,就必须按照低级中枢的行为类型来加以解释。如果在这里它被看作是一种反射过程,那么在那里它也必须是反射的。两个地方的神经流只有当它先流入之后才能流出并进入肌肉里;但同时在较低级的中枢那里,它流出的路径是由在细胞排列中少且固定的反射所决定的,在脑半球那里反射很多且不稳定。这将被看作只是程度上的不同,而不是种类上的不同,而且这并没有改变反射类型。关于所有行为都和此种类型相一致的概念是现代神经生理学的基础概念。我们关于神经中枢的一般的初步概念就谈到这里!在我们详细地看到生理学观测是如何彻底地证实它之前,让我们对它做更清楚的说明。

脑半球的教育

神经流通过感觉器官流入,并且在低级中枢那里引起反射动作的同时,它们在脑半球引出观念,观念或者容许可疑反射的发生,或者阻止它们,或者用其他反射替代它们。所有的观念最终都诉诸记忆,要回答的问题是:与心中的记忆相应合的过程是如何能够在脑半球中组织起来的?①

① 我希望读者不要因为我这样做而不快,即我如此将物理的和心理的东西混合起来,并且同时谈论反射动作、脑半球和记忆,好像它们是一个因果链条上同类的量和因素一般。我是故意这样做的,因为尽管我承认从激进的物理观点出发,人们很容易设想细胞和纤维中的事件系列自身是完善的,而且在如此设想它时,人们不需要提及“观念”,但是我怀疑那种观点是一种不真实的抽象。在中枢里的反射可以发生在甚至是相伴随的感受和观念指引它们的地方。在另一章,我将试图展示我不放弃这一常识立场的原因;同时,语言对这种混合的描述方式更加容易适应,以至我继续使用了后者。内心比较激进的读者总是能将“观念形成的过程”读作“观念”。

Nothing is easier than to conceive a *possible* way in which this might be done, provided four assumptions be granted. These assumptions (which after all are inevitable in any event) are:

1) The same cerebral process which, when aroused from without by a sense-organ, gives the perception of an object, will give an *idea* of the same object when aroused by other cerebral processes from within.

2) If processes 1, 2, 3, 4 have once been aroused together or in immediate succession, any subsequent arousal of any one of them (whether from without or within) will tend to arouse the others in the original order. (This is the so-called law of association.)

3) Every sensorial excitement propagated to a lower centre tends to spread upwards and arouse an idea.

4) Every idea tends ultimately either to produce a movement or to check one which otherwise would be produced.

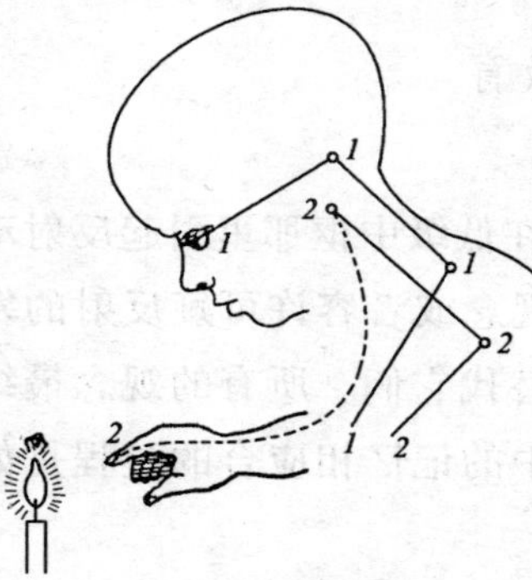

FIG. 3.

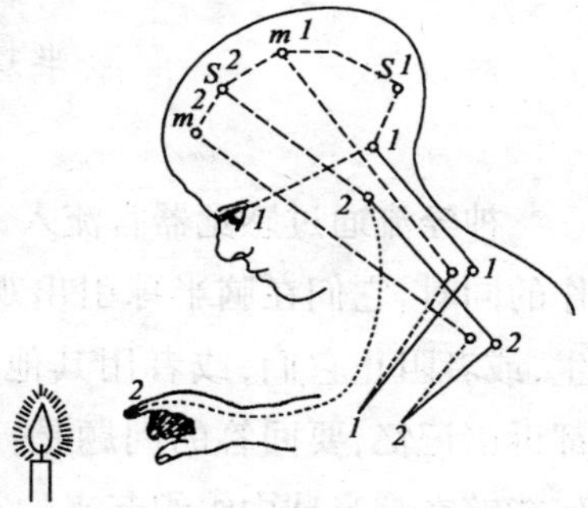

FIG. 4.—The dotted lines stand for afferent paths, the broken lines for paths between the centres; the entire lines for efferent paths.

Suppose now (these assumptions being granted) that we have a baby before us who sees a candle-flame for the first time, and, by virtue of a reflex tendency common in babies of a certain age, extends his hand to grasp it, so that his fingers get burned. So far we have two reflex currents in play: first, from the eye to the extension movement,

如果承认以下述提供的四个假设的话，设想这一过程得以完成的方式就会变得再简单不过了。这些假设(它们在任何情况下都毕竟是不可避免的)是：

(1)同一个大脑过程，当从外部通过某种感觉器官被引起时，它产生对某一对象的知觉，当它被其他的大脑过程从内部被激发时，它会引起对同一对象的观念。

(2)如果过程1、2、3、4曾共同或紧跟着相继被激发，随后它们中任意一个过程的激发(不管是来自外部还是来自内部)，将趋向于以最初的顺序引起其他过程。(这就是所谓的联想律。)

(3)每一个传播到较低级中枢的感觉刺激趋向于向上传播并引起一个观念。

(4)每一个观念最终或者引起一个动作，或者阻止一个将要产生的动作。

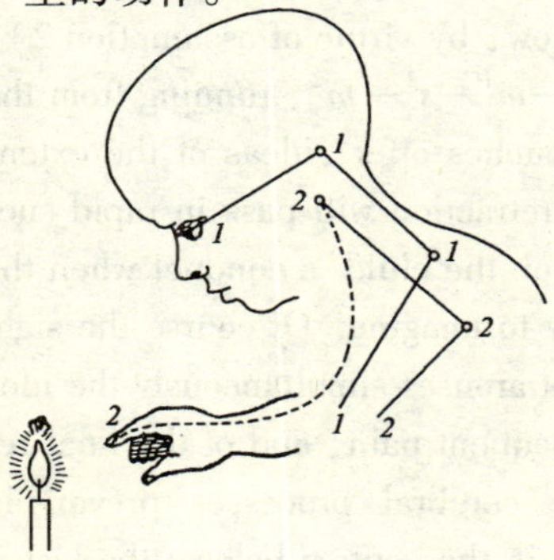

图3

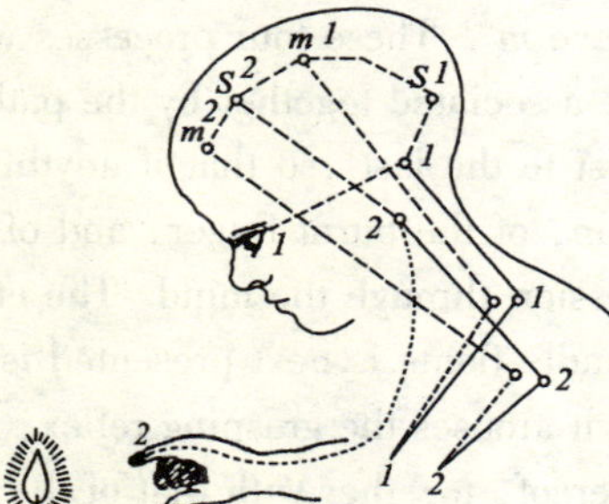

图4

由点组成的虚线表示传入的路径；断开的线表示中枢之间的路径；实线表示传出的路径。

现在设想(在承认这些假设的情况下)，在我们面前有个婴儿，他第一次看见烛光，而且由于在某一特定年龄婴儿中共同的反射倾向的品格，他伸手去抓火焰，结果手被烧伤了。到目前为止我们有两条反射流在行动(见图3)：第一条，从眼睛到伸展动

along the line 1—1—1—1 of Fig. 3; and second, from the finger to the movement of drawing back the hand, along the line 2—2—2—2. If this were the baby's whole nervous system, and if the reflexes were once for all organic, we should have no alteration in his behavior, no matter how often the experience recurred. The retinal image of the flame would always make the arm shoot forward, the burning of the finger would always send it back. But we know that 'the burnt child dreads the fire,' and that one experience usually protects the fingers forever. The point is to see how the hemispheres may bring this result to pass.

We must complicate our diagram (see Fig. 4). Let the current 1—1, from the eye, discharge upward as well as downward when it reaches the lower centre for vision, and arouse the perceptional process s^1 in the hemispheres; let the feeling of the arm's extension also send up a current which leaves a trace of itself, m^1; let the burnt finger leave an analogous trace, s^2; and let the movement of retraction leave m^2. These four processes will now, by virtue of assumption 2), be associated together by the path s^1—m^1—s^2—m^2, running from the first to the last, so that if anything touches off s^1, ideas of the extension, of the burnt finger, and of the retraction will pass in rapid succession through the mind. The effect on the child's conduct when the candle-flame is next presented is easy to imagine. Of course the sight of it arouses the grasping reflex; but it arouses simultaneously the idea thereof, together with that of the consequent pain, and of the final retraction of the hand; and if these cerebral processes prevail in strength over the immediate sensation in the centres below, the last idea will be the cue by which the final action is discharged. The grasping will be arrested in mid-career, the hand drawn back, and the child's fingers saved.

In all this we assume that the hemispheres do not natively couple any particular sense-impression with any special motor discharge. They only register, and preserve traces of, such couplings as are already organized in the reflex centres below. But this brings it inevitably about that, when a chain of experiences has been already registered and the first link is impressed once again from without, the last

作，沿着图3中的线1～1～1～1；第二条，从手指到抽回手的动作，沿着线2～2～2～2。如果这便是婴儿的全部神经系统，而且如果反射曾完全是因为器官的，那么不论经验如何频繁地重复，我们都不应该在他的行为中看到变化。火焰在视网膜上的图像将总会让胳膊向前伸出，而手指被烧伤总是让它缩回来。但是我们知道"烧伤的孩子害怕火"，并且一次经历通常会使手指永远得到保护。问题在于要看到脑半球是如何让这结果通过的。

我们必须把我们的图示变得复杂起来（见图4）。从眼睛开始的神经流1～1，当它到达控制视觉的低级中枢时，让它向上流也向下流，并且引起脑半球中的知觉过程 s^1；让手臂伸出的触觉也送出一条神经流，留下一个它自己的痕迹 m^1；让烧伤的手指留下相似的痕迹 s^2；让缩回的动作留下痕迹 m^2。根据假设2），这四个过程通过路径 $s^1 \sim m^1 \sim s^2 \sim m^2$ 从第一个到最后一个被共同联系起来了，结果是如果任何事物触动了 s^1，伸展的观念、烧伤手指的观念和缩回的观念就会在心中快速相继闪过。当蜡烛的火焰下一次出现时，关于孩子行为的结果就很容易想像得出了。当然，对火焰的视觉引起了抓握反射，但它同时也引起了由此作为结果而发生的疼痛的观念和最终缩回手的观念；而且如果这些大脑过程在强度上胜过了低级中枢的直接感觉，最终的观念将是最终行动由以执行的提示。抓握动作将在中途被阻止，手缩了回来，孩子的手指得救了。

在这里我们假设大脑半球并非生来就将任何独特的感官印象同任何特殊的行为动作相连接起来。它们只是记录和保存诸如已经在下面的反射中枢中组织起来的那些联结的痕迹。而这就不可避免地让它产生这样的情况，当一条经验链条已经被记录下来，而且当它的第一个链环再次从外部被引起时，那最后一个

link will often be awakened in *idea* long before it can exist in *fact*. And if this last link were previously coupled with a motion, that motion may now come from the mere ideal suggestion without waiting for the actual impression to arise. Thus an animal with hemispheres acts in *anticipation* of future things; or, to use our previous formula, he acts from considerations of distant good and ill. If we give the name of *partners* to the original couplings of impressions with motions in a reflex way, then we may say that the function of the hemispheres is simply to bring about *exchanges among the partners*. Movement m^n, which natively is sensation s^n's partner, becomes through the hemispheres the partner of sensation s^1, s^2 or s^3. It is like the great commutating switch-board at a central telephone station. No new elementary process is involved; no impression nor any motion peculiar to the hemispheres; but any number of combinations impossible to the lower machinery taken alone, and an endless consequent increase in the possibilities of behavior on the creature's part.

All this, as a mere scheme,① is so clear and so concordant with the general look of the facts as almost to impose itself on our belief; but it is anything but clear in detail. The brain-physiology of late years has with great effort sought to work out the paths by which these couplings of sensations with movements take place, both in the hemispheres and in the centres below.

So we must next test our scheme by the facts discovered in this direction. We shall conclude, I think, after taking them all into account,

---

① I shall call it hereafter for shortness 'the Meynert scheme;' for the child-and-flame example, as well as the whole general notion that the hemispheres are a supernumerary surface for the projection and association of sensations and movements natively coupled in the centres below, is due to Th. Meynert, the Austrian anatomist. For a popular account of his views, see his pamphlet 'Zur Mechanik des Gehirobaues,' Vienna, 1874. His most recent development of them is embodied in his 'Psychiatry,' a clinical treatise on diseases of the forebrain, translated by B. Sachs, New York, 1885.

链环通常在它变成事实之前已经在观念中被唤醒了。而且如果这最后一个链环先前同一个动作相联结,这动作现在就可以由于纯粹观念的暗示而发生,不用等待真实印象的出现。因此,一个具有脑半球的动物是在对未来事物的预期中行动;或者用先前的话说,它通过对远处的好与坏的考虑而行动。如果我们将最初以反射方式相连接的印象和动作叫做搭档的话,那我们就可以说脑半球的功能只不过就是促成这些搭档之间的转换。运动 m^n 生来就是感觉 s^n 的搭档,它通过脑半球变成了感觉 s^1、s^2 或者 s^3 的搭档。它就像一个在电话中心局的巨大整流接线总机。没有新的基本过程涉及进来,没有对脑半球来说是特有的印象和动作,有的只是低级机构不可能单独完成的大量的联合,以及随之而来的动物行为可能性的永无止境的增加。

作为一种最起码的方案,①所有这些是如此的清晰,它同事实的普通外表是如此的协调一致,以至于我们几乎要相信它了;但是它在细节上还很不清晰。近些年来的脑生理学付出了巨大的努力,试图找出在脑半球和低级中枢中造成感觉与动作相联合的途径。

因此,接下来我们必须用在这一方向上所发现的事实来检验我们的方案。在把它们全部考虑在内之后,我想我们可以得出结

① 为简短起见,此后我将称之为"梅纳特方案",因为婴儿与火焰的例子以及这整个一般观念,即脑半球是一个额外的表面,适用于在下面的中枢里先天相连接的感觉和行动的投射和联合,都应归功于奥地利解剖学家 Th. 梅纳特。就其观点的通俗说明,见他的小册子《论大脑结构的构造》,维也纳,1874 年。他对它们的最新发展在他的《精神病学》中得以体现,这是一篇关于前脑疾病的临床学论文,由 B. 萨克斯翻译,纽约,1885 年。

that the scheme probably makes the lower centres too machine-like and the hemispheres not quite machine-like enough, and must consequently be softened down a little. So much I may say in advance. Meanwhile, before plunging into the details which await us, it will somewhat clear our ideas if we contrast the modern way of looking at the matter with the *phrenological* conception which but lately preceded it.

The Phrenological Conception.

In a certain sense Gall was the first to seek to explain in detail how the brain could subserve our mental operations. His way of proceeding was only too simple. He took the faculty-psychology as his ultimatum on the mental side, and he made no farther psychological analysis. Wherever he found an individual with some strongly-marked trait of character he examined his head; and if he found the latter prominent in a certain region, he said without more ado that that region was the 'organ' of the trait or faculty in question. The traits were of very diverse constitution, some being simple sensibilities like 'weight' or 'color;' some being instinctive tendencies like 'alimentiveness' or 'amativeness;' and others, again, being complex resultants like 'conscientiousness,' 'individuality.' Phrenology fell promptly into disrepute among scientific men because observation seemed to show that large faculties and large 'bumps' might fail to coexist; because the scheme of Gall was so vast as hardly to admit of accurate determination at all—who of us can say even of his own brothers whether their perceptions of *weight* and of *time* are well developed or not?—because the followers of Gall and Spurzheim were unable to reform these errors in any appreciable degree; and, finally, because the whole analysis of faculties was vague and erroneous from a psychologic point of view. Popular professors of the lore have nevertheless continued to command the admiration of popular audiences; and there seems no doubt that Phrenology,

论，这一方案可能使得低级中枢太像机器了，而脑半球又不那么像机器，因此它必须被弱化一些。我事先要说的就这么多了。同时，在我们跳入等待我们的细节之前，如果我们将现代看待这问题的方法和仅是最近才领先于它的颅相学的概念相比较，这会略微地让我们的观念清晰一些。

颅相学的概念

从某种意义上说，高尔是第一个试图详细解释大脑是如何促进我们心理活动的人。可他的进行方式却太简单。他将官能心理学当作他精神方面的最后一张底牌，而没有做进一步的心理学分析。无论在什么情况下他发现一个个体具有某种非常显著的性格特征，他就去检查他的头颅；如果他发现头颅在某一区域隆起，他就小题大做地说那个区域就是相关特征或官能的器官。特征具有极为多变的构造，一些是如“重量”或“颜色”般简单的感受性，一些是如“食物供给”或“求爱”般的本能倾向，还有其他一些如“良知”，“个性”的复杂合成物。颅相学迅速地在科学人员中声名狼藉了，因为观察似乎显示出大的官能和大的“肿块”可能并不共存；又因为高尔的方案是如此的庞大而几乎根本不能容许有精确的测定——我们中有谁敢说他自己兄弟的重量和时间的知觉是否发展完善呢？——还因为高尔和施普茨海姆的追随者们不能在任何可觉察的程度上革新这些错误；最后，因为从心理学的观点来看，关于官能的整个分析都是模糊和错误的。然而，迎合大众口味的这门学问的教授们还是继续博得了大众的赞赏；并且似乎可以确定的是，无论颅相学多么不能满足我们

however little it satisfy our scientific curiosity about the functions of different portions of the brain, may still be, in the hands of intelligent practitioners, a useful help in the art of reading character. A hooked nose and a firm jaw are usually signs of practical energy; soft, delicate hands are signs of refined sensibility. Even so may a prominent eye be a sign of power over language, and a bull-neck a sign of sensuality. But the brain behind the eye and neck need no more be the *organ* of the signified faculty than the jaw is the organ of the will or the hand the organ of refinement. These correlations between mind and body are, however, so frequent that the 'characters' given by phrenologists are often remarkable for knowingness and insight.

Phrenology hardly does more than restate the problem. To answer the question, "Why do I like children?" by saying, "Because you have a large organ of philoprogenitiveness," but renames the phenomenon to be explained. What *is* my philoprogenitiveness? Of what mental elements does it consist? And how *can* a part of the brain be its organ? A science of the mind must reduce such complex manifestations as 'philoprogenitiveness' to their *elements*. A science of the brain must point out the functions of *its* elements. A science of the relations of mind and brain must show how the elementary ingredients of the former correspond to the elementary functions of the latter. But phrenology, except by occasional coincidence, takes no account of elements at all. Its 'faculties,' as a rule, are fully equipped persons in a particular mental attitude. Take, for example, the 'faculty' of language. It involves in reality a host of distinct powers. We must first have images of concrete things and ideas of abstract qualities and relations; we must next have the memory of words and then the capacity so to associate each idea or image with a particular word that, when the word is heard, the idea shall forthwith enter our mind. We must conversely, as soon as the idea arises in our mind, associate with it a mental image of the word, and by means of this image we must innervate our articulatory apparatus

对大脑不同部位功能的科学好奇，在那些伶俐的实践者手中，它依然可以是解读性格的技术上有用的辅助手段。带钩的鼻子和坚固的下巴通常是有实践活力的象征；温柔、纤细的手是有精确感受性的象征。凸出的眼睛甚至是有驾驭语言能力的象征，而粗脖子是好色的象征。但是，同下巴不是意志的器官，手不是品味高雅的器官一样，眼睛和脖子后面的大脑也无需是所指官能的器官了。然而，心灵和身体的相互关系是如此频繁，以至于由颅相学家给出的"性格"时常因为其获有的理解力和洞察力而变得显著起来。

颅相学除了重新陈述问题以外几乎没有做什么。"我为什么喜欢孩子?"对这一问题的回答是："你有一个具有爱子女能力的大器官。"这只是对有待解释的现象的重新命名而已。什么是我爱子女的能力？它由什么心理元素所构成？而且一部分大脑是如何能够成为它的器官的呢？心灵的科学必须将作为"爱子女的能力"如此复杂的表现还原成它们的元素。关于大脑的科学必须指出它的元素的功能。关于心灵和大脑关系的科学，必须指出前者的基本因素是如何与后者的基本功能相一致的。但是颅相学，除了偶然的巧合以外，根本没有对这些元素加以考虑。通常它的"官能"完全是被赋予了一种独特的心理态度的人。以语言"官能"为例，在现实中它涉及许多截然不同的能力。首先我们必须具有具体事物的意象和抽象的性质与关系的观念；其次我们必须具有词语的记忆力，然后是用一个特殊词汇同每一个观点和意象相联系的能力，即当词语被听到时，观念将直接进入我们的心里。相反，只要观念在我们的心里出现，我们必须将它同词语的心理意象相联系。并且通过这一意象的方式，我们必须促使我们的发

so as to reproduce the word as physical sound. To read or to write a language other elements still must be introduced. But it is plain that the faculty of spoken language alone is so complicated as to call into play almost all the elementary powers which the mind possesses, memory, imagination, association, judgment, and volition. A portion of the brain competent to be the adequate seat of such a faculty would needs be an entire brain in miniature,—just as the faculty itself is really a specification of the entire man, a sort of homunculus.

Yet just such homunculi are for the most part the phrenological organs. As Lange says:

"We have a parliament of little men together, each one of whom, as happens also in a real parliament, possesses but a single idea which he ceaselessly strives to make prevail"—benevolence, firmness, hope, and the rest. "Instead of one soul, phrenology gives us forty, each alone as enigmatic as the full aggregate psychic life can be. Instead of dividing the latter into effective elements, she divides it into personal beings of peculiar character. . . . 'Herr Pastor, sure there be a horse inside,' called out the peasants to X after their spiritual shepherd had spent hours in explaining to them the construction of the locomotive. With a horse inside truly everything becomes clear, even though it be a queer enough sort of horse—the horse itself calls for no explanation! Phrenology takes a start to get beyond the point of view of the ghost-like soul entity, but she ends by populating the whole skull with ghosts of the same order." ①

Modern Science conceives of the matter in a very different way. *Brain and mind alike consist of simple elements, sensory and motor.* "All nervous centres," says Dr. Hughlings Jackson, ② "from the lowest to the very highest (the substrata of consciousness),

① Geschichte des Materialismus, 2d ed., II. p. 345.
② West Riding Asylum Reports, 1876, p. 267.

音设备活动，以便让词语作为物理声音再现出来。如果要读或者写一种语言还必须要引入其他元素。而且很清楚的是，单独口头语言的官能就已如此的复杂，以至于几乎动用了所有心灵拥有的基本能力，即记忆、想像、联想、判断和意志。胜任于作为这种官能的适当处所的那部分大脑就应该是一个缩小了的完整大脑——就像官能自身实际是对整个人的一种具体化，像一种侏儒。

然而，恰恰是这样的矮子在很大程度上就是颅相学的器官。如兰格所说：

“我们有一个由小矮人在一起组成的议会，他们中的每一个人，就如在真的议会里发生的那样，仅仅拥有一个使他不停地努力使之胜出的观念”——仁慈、坚定、希望及其他。“颅相学给予我们的不是一个灵魂，而是四十个，单独每一个都能够如同完全聚合的精神生活一样那么高深莫测。不是将后者划分成有效的元素，她将它划分成具有独特性格的个人存在。……‘牧师先生，那里面确实有一匹马’，在农夫们精神上的看护人已经花了很长时间给他们解释运动的构造之后，农夫们向 X 叫嚷起来。有一匹马在里面的话一切就真地变得清晰起来，尽管它是一匹十足奇怪的马——这马本身不需要任何解释！颅相学起始于超越幽灵般灵魂本体的观点，却终结于让同样状态的幽灵居住进整个头骨。”①

现代科学以一种非常不同的方式考虑这一问题。大脑和灵魂同样由简单的元素构成，感觉的和运动的。“所有的神经中枢，”休林斯·杰克逊博士说②，“从最低级的到最高级的（意识的

① 《唯物史论》，第二版，2，第 345 页。
② 《西区精神病院报告》，1876 年，第 267 页。

are made up of nothing else than nervous arrangements, representing impressions and movements… I do not see of what other materials the brain *can* be made." Meynert represents the matter similarly when he calls the cortex of the hemispheres the surface of projection for every muscle and every sensitive point of the body. The muscles and the sensitive points are *represented* each by a cortical point, and the brain is nothing but the sum of all these cortical points, to which, on the mental side, as many *ideas* correspond. *Ideas of sensation*, *ideas of motion* are, on the other hand, *the elementary factors out of which the mind is built up by the associationists in psychology*. There is a complete parallelism between the two analyses, the same diagram of little dots, circles, or triangles joined by lines symbolizes equally well the cerebral and mental processes: the dots stand for cells or ideas, the lines for fibers or associations. We shall have later to criticise this analysis so far as it relates to the mind; but there is no doubt that it is a most convenient, and has been a most useful, hypothesis, formulating the facts in an extremely natural way.

If, then, we grant that motor and sensory ideas variously associated are the materials of the mind, all we need do to get a complete diagram of the mind's and the brain's relations should be to ascertain which sensory idea corresponds to which sensational surface of projection, and which motor idea to which muscular surface of projection. The associations would then correspond to the fibrous connections between the various surfaces. This distinct *cerebral localization* of the various elementary sorts of idea has been treated as a 'postulate' by many physiologists (e. g. Munk); and the most stirring controversy in nerve-physiology which the present generation has seen has been the *localization-question.*

The Localization Of Functions In The Hemispheres.

Up to 1870, the opinion which prevailed was that which the experiments of Flourens on pigeons' brains had made plausible, namely, that the different functions of the hemispheres were not locally separated, but carried on each by the aid of the whole organ. Hitzig in 1870 showed, however, that in a dog's brain highly specialized movements could

基础),都是由神经的排列构成,再现印象和运动……我看不出大脑还能用什么材料构成。"当梅纳特将脑半球的皮层称作对于身体的所有肌肉和所有有感觉的点的投射平面时,他表达了相同的观点。肌肉和有感觉的点通过脑皮层点被再现了,大脑就是所有这些脑皮层点的和,在精神方面,它和许多观念相对应。在另一方面,感觉观念、运动观念是心理学中联想主义者用来建构心灵的基本因素。这两种分析完全类似,小圆点、圆圈、或者三角形,再加上一些线条的相同图表,同样充分地象征出了大脑和心理的过程:圆点代表细胞或观念,线条代表纤维或关联。至于它同心灵相关,我们将在后面对这种分析提出批评;但毫无疑问的是,它是最方便的并且已是最有用的假说,它以一种极为自然的方式公式化地阐述了事实。

那么,如果我们承认不同地连接起来的运动和感觉的观念是心灵的材料,要得到一个关于心灵的和大脑关系的完整图表,我们所需要做的,应该是确定哪一个感觉观念和哪一个感觉的投射平面相对应,哪一个运动观念和哪一个肌肉的投射平面相对应。那么联想就应该和不同平面之间的纤维连接相对应。这一独特的关于各种基本种类的观点的大脑定位已经被很多生理学家(例如芒克)当作一种"基本条件"来加以对待;而且当代人所看到的在神经生理学中最激动人心的论战就是定位问题。

大脑半球中的功能定位

直到1870年,盛行的观点是弗路朗斯通过对鸽子大脑的实验而得到的似乎正确的观点,即脑半球的不同功能不是被局部地分离开的,每一种功能都是在整个器官的帮助下而得以实施的。然而,希齐格在1870年指出,在狗的大脑中非常专门的动作能

be produced by electric irritation of determinate regions of the cortex; and Ferrier and Munk, half a dozen years later, seemed to prove, either by irritations or excisions or both, that there were equally determinate regions connected with the senses of sight, touch, hearing, and smell. Munk's special sensorial localizations, however, disagreed with Ferrier's; and Goltz, from his extirpation-experiments, came to a conclusion adverse to strict localization of any kind. The controversy is not yet over. I will not pretend to say anything more of it historically, but give a brief account of the condition in which matters at present stand.

The one thing which is *perfectly* well established is this, that the 'central' convolutions, on either side of the fissure of Rolando, and (at least in the monkey) the calloso-marginal convolution (which is continuous with them on the mesial surface where one hemisphere is applied against the other), form the region by which all the motor incitations which leave the cortex pass out, on their way to those executive centres in the region of the pons, medulla, and spinal cord from which the muscular contractions are discharged in the last resort. The existence of this so-called 'motor zone' is established by the lines of evidence successively given below:

(1) *Cortical Irritations.* Electrical currents of small intensity applied to the surface of the said convolutions in dogs, monkeys, and other animals, produce well-defined movements in face, fore-limb, hind-limb, tail, or trunk, according as one point or another of the surface is irritated. These movements affect almost invariably the side opposite to the brain irritations: If the left hemisphere be excited, the movement is of the right leg, side of face, etc. All the objections at first raised against the validity of these experiments have been overcome. The movements are certainly not due to irritations of the base of the brain by the downward spread of the current, for: *a*) mechanical irritations will produce them, though less easily than electrical; *b*) shifting the electrodes to a point close by on the surface changes the movement in ways quite inexplicable by changed physical conduction of the current; *c*) if the cortical 'centre' for a certain movement be cut under with a sharp knife but left *in situ*, although the electric conductivity is physically unaltered by the operation,

通过脑皮层确定区域的电流刺激而产生；而且在六年之后，费里尔和芒克似乎证明了，或者通过刺激，或者通过切除，或者两者都使用，这里存在着和视觉、触觉、听觉和味觉相联系的同样确定的区域。然而芒克特殊的感觉定位和费里尔的不同；而且戈尔茨从他的根除实验中得出的结论同任何一种严格的定位都相反。论战还没有结束。我不打算从历史的角度对这再多说什么，我只是从目前的立场就相关的情况做一个简短的说明。

有一件事情是完全可以确定的，那就是在罗朗多沟两边的“中央”回，以及（至少在猴子那里）胼胝体额上回（它在一个脑半球和另一个脑半球互相紧贴的中央表面上和它们相连接），构成了这样的区域，所有离开脑皮层的运动刺激凭藉它穿出，踏上通往在脑桥、髓质和脊髓（由于它们肌肉收缩才在最后的常去之地得以释放）区域内的那些执行中枢的道路。下面相继给出的一系列证据确证了这一所谓运动区的存在。

（1）皮层刺激。小强度的电流作用于狗、猴子和其他动物中的上述脑回表面，依照表面的这个或另一个点所接受的刺激，它会造成在面部、前肢、后肢、尾巴或躯干的确定运动。这些运动几乎不变地作用于与大脑刺激相反的那一边：如果左脑被刺激了，运动来自右腿、右脸等等。最初提出的对这些实验有效性的所有异议都被战胜了。运动当然不是取决于通过向下传播的电流对大脑基部的刺激，因为：a）虽然不如电的刺激那么容易，但机械的刺激也能产生它们。b）在表面一个点的附近通过改变电极而改变了的运动，在方法上通过改变了的电流传导完全无法说明它。c）如果把负责某一动作的皮层“中枢”用一把锋利的刀切下，但留其在原来的位置，尽管电流的传导性通过手术未被物理地改变，生

the physiological conductivity is gone and currents of the same strength no longer produce the movements which they did; *d*) the time-interval between the application of the electric stimulus to the cortex and the resultant movement is what it would be if the cortex acted physiologically and not merely physically in transmitting the irritation. It is namely a well-known fact that when a nerve-current has to pass through the spinal cord to excite a muscle by reflex action, the time is longer than if it passes directly down the motor nerve: the cells of the cord take a certain time to discharge. Similarly, when a stimulus is applied directly to the cortex the muscle contracts two or three hundredths of a second later than it does when the place on the cortex is cut away and the electrodes are applied to the white fibres below. ①

(2) *Cortical Ablations*. When the cortical spot which is found to produce a movement of the fore-leg, in a dog, is excised (see spot 5 in Fig. 5), the leg in question becomes peculiarly affected. At first it seems paralyzed. Soon, however, it is used with the other legs, but badly. The animal does not bear his weight on it, allows it to rest on its dorsal surface, stands with it crossing the other leg, does not remove it if it hangs over the edge of a table, can no longer 'give the paw' at word of command if able to do so before the operation, does not use it for scratching the ground, or holding a bone as formerly, lets it slip out when running on a smooth surface or when shaking himself, etc., etc. Sensibility of all kinds seems diminished as well as motility, but of this I shall speak later on. Moreover the dog tends in voluntary movements to

---

① For a thorough discussion of the various objections, see Ferrier's 'Functions of the Brain,' 2d ed., pp. 227-384. and Francois-Franck's 'Lecons sur les Fonctions Motrices du Cerveau' (1887). Lecon 31. The most minutely accurate experiments on irritation of cortical points are those of Paneth, in Pfiüger's Archiv, vol 37. p. 528. —Recently the skull has been fearlessly opened by surgeons, and operations upon the human brain performed, sometimes with the happiest results. In some of these operations the cortex has been electrically excited for the purpose of more exactly localizing the spot, and the movements first observed in dogs and monkeys have then been verified in men.

理的传导性已经消失了，而且同样强度的电流不再产生它们曾产生的运动。d）电流刺激对大脑皮层的施用到作为结果而发生的运动的时间间隔是脑皮层生理地而不仅仅是物理地传递刺激并行动的时间间隔。即这是一个众所周知的事实，当神经流必须穿过脊髓通过反射行为刺激一块肌肉时，这一时间要比它直接向下传到运动神经的时间长：脊髓细胞要花一定的时间去释放。同样地，当一个刺激直接被施用于皮层时，肌肉收缩与当皮层上的这位置被切除了并且电极被施用于下面的白纤维相比，它将晚百分之二或三秒。①

（2）皮层切除。当被发现的造成狗前腿运动的皮层点被切除时，相关的腿就奇怪地受到了影响（见图5中点5）。起初它似乎瘫痪了。然而，很快它就与另外几条腿一起得到了使用，但很困难。这动物不让这条腿承受身体的重量，容许它靠在它的背上休息，让它和另一条腿交叉着站立，如果它挂在桌脚上，它也不移开它；如果在手术前它听到命令后能够“伸出爪子”，那么手术后它不能再这样做了；它不能像以前那样用它来挠地，或者按住骨头；当在平滑的表面上奔跑或者抖动身体时，它都让它呆在一边，诸如此类，不一而足。各种类型的感受性以及运动性似乎消失了，而就这一问题我将随后再谈。而且，狗在主动的运动中倾向于突然转向受损大脑那一边，

① 就各种异议的全面讨论，见费里尔《大脑的功能》，第二版，第227～384页。以及弗朗西斯－弗兰克的《大脑功能作用教程》（1887）第31讲。关于皮层点刺激的最详细、最精确的实验是帕内斯的，见《弗吕格文库》，第37卷，第528页。最近，外科医生勇敢地打开了头盖骨，而且对人脑实施手术，有时有最令人满意的结果。在一些这样的手术里，出于更加准确地定位点这一目的，大脑皮层被实施电刺激，而且起先在狗和猴子那里观察到的动作在人这里得到了核实。

swerve towards the side of the brain-lesion instead of going straight forward. All these symptoms gradually decrease, so that even with a very severe brain-lesion the dog may be outwardly indistinguishable from a well dog after eight or ten weeks. Still, a slight chloroformization will reproduce the disturbances, even then. There is a certain appearance of ataxic in-coordination in the movements —the dog lifts his fore-feet high and brings them down with more strength than usual, and yet the trouble is not ordinary lack of co-ordination. Neither

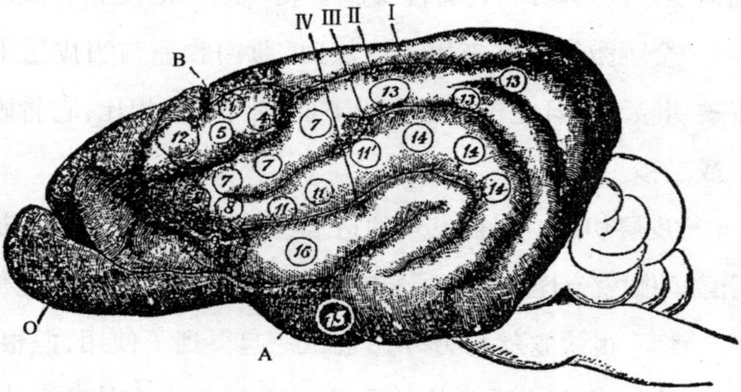

FIG. 5.—Left Hemisphere of Dog's Brain, after Ferrier.

A. the fissure of Sylvius. B, the crucial sulcus. O, the olfactory bulb. *I*, *II*, *III*, *IV*, indicate the first, second, third, and fourth external convolutions respectively. (1), (4), and (5) are on the sigmoid gyrus.

is there paralysis. The strength of whatever movements are made is as great as ever—dogs with extensive destruction of the motor zone can jump as high and bite as hard as ever they did, but they seem *less easily moved* to do *anything* with the affected parts. Dr. Loeb, who has studied the motor disturbances of dogs more carefully than any one, conceives of them *en masse* as effects of an increased inertia in all the processes of innervation towards the side opposed to the lesion. All such movements require an unwonted effort for their execution; and when only the normally usual effort is made they fall behind in effectiveness. ①

① J. Loeb: ' Beiträge zur Physiologie des Grosshirns; Pflüger's Archiv, XXXIX. 293. I simplify the author's statement.

而不是直着向前走。所有这些症状会逐渐减轻，以致在八或十周之后，一个大脑损伤严重的狗可能同一条健康的狗在表面上无法区分。尽管如此，甚至在那时，轻微的氯仿麻醉将使障碍再次产生。在运动中存在某种供给失调方面的不协调现象——这只狗抬高或放下它的前爪要用比通常更大的力气，而且麻烦不在于协调性的一般缺乏。也不存在瘫痪。无论做出何种动作的力量都

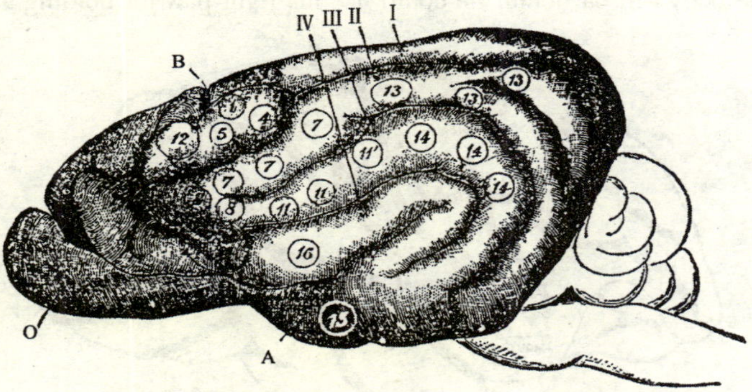

图5　狗脑的左半球，依照费里尔制作

A. 西耳维厄斯沟。B. 十字沟。O. 嗅球。Ⅰ. Ⅱ. Ⅲ. Ⅳ分别表示第一、第二、第三、第四外回。(1)、(4) 和 (5)在乙状回上。

和从前一样强大——运动区域被严重破坏了的狗能跳得和从前一样高，咬得和从前一样狠，但是，当它们移动受到影响的那部分来做任何动作时，这似乎不是很容易的。洛布博士对狗的运动障碍的研究比任何人都细致，他将它们看作是受了朝向损伤相反一边的所有神经支配过程中增加了的惯性的影响。所有这些运动都需要异常的努力来完成，而且当仅仅是付出了正常的普通努力时，它们在有效性上就差远了。①

---

① J. 洛布：《大脑生理学论文集》；《弗吕格文库》，39，第293页。我简化了作者的论述。

Even when the entire motor zone of a dog is removed, there is no permanent paralysis of any part, but only this curious sort of relative inertia when the two sides of the body are compared; and this itself becomes hardly noticeable after a number of weeks have elapsed. Prof. Goltz has described a dog whose entire left hemisphere was destroyed, and who retained only a slight motor inertia on the right half of the body. In particular he could use his right paw for holding a bone

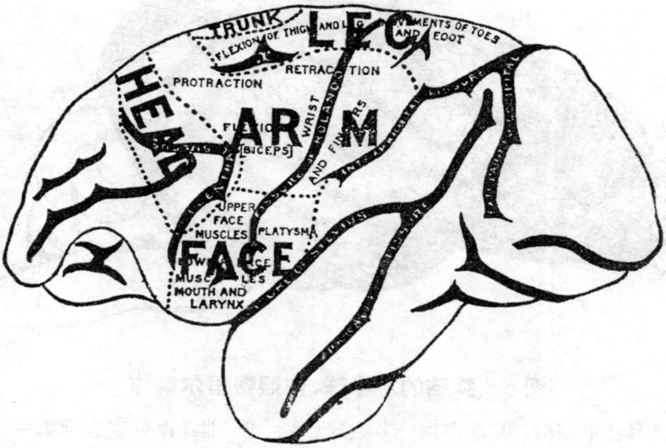

FIG. 6.—Left Hemisphere of Monkey's Brain. Outer Surface.

whilst gnawing it, or for reaching after a piece of meat. Had he been taught to give his paw before the operations, it would have been curious to see whether that faculty also came back. His tactile sensibility was permanently diminished on the right side.①In *monkeys* a genuine paralysis follows upon ablations of the cortex in the motor region. This paralysis affects parts of the body which vary with the brain-parts removed. The monkey's opposite arm or leg hangs flaccid, or at most takes

① Goltz: Pflüger's Arehiv, XLII. 419.

甚至当一条狗的整个运动区域都被取掉时,也不存在任何部位的永久瘫痪,只是当对身体的两边加以比较时,存在奇怪的某种相关惯性;并且这种情况在数周之后自身会变得几乎难以辨认。戈尔茨描述过一只狗,它的整个脑左半球被破坏掉了,在它右边的身体上只保留了一点点运动惯性。特别的是,它在啃骨头时能用右爪按

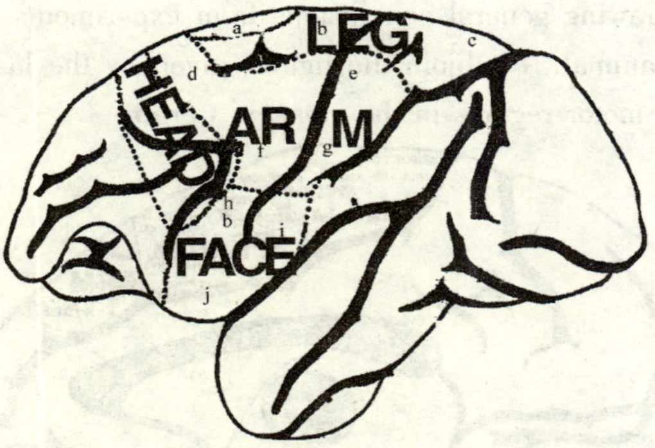

图6　猴脑左半球　外表面[1]

LEG. 腿。 ARM. 臂。 HEAD. 头。 FACE. 脸。 a. 躯干。 b. 股和腿的弯曲。 c. 脚趾和脚的运动。 d. 伸展 。e. 收缩。 f. 屈肌(二头肌)。 g. 腕和手指。 h. 脸上部肌肉。 i. 颈阔肌。 j. 脸下部肌肉嘴和喉。

住骨头,或者用右爪抓一块肉。若不是在手术前它未被训练过"伸出前爪",要不就可以很好奇地去看是否那项功能也回来了。它右边的触觉感受性被永久地减损了。① 在猴子那里,在运动区域中的皮层切除会导致真正的瘫痪。鉴于大脑切除部位的不同,这瘫痪会影响身体的不同部位。猴子相反一侧的胳膊或腿无力地挂在那里,或者

① 戈尔茨:《弗吕格文集》,42,第419页。

〔1〕 原书图中较小字号所标出的注文,译者以 a、b、c、d……字母在图中替代,然后在图下译出。后面有一些图也照此处理,不另注明。

a small part in associated movements. When the entire region is removed there is a genuine and permanent hemiplegia in which the arm is more affected than the leg; and this is followed months later by contracture of the muscles, as in man after inveterate hemiplegia. ① According to Schaefer and Horsley, the trunk-muscles also become paralyzed after destruction of the *marginal* convolution on *both* sides (see Fig. 7). These differences between dogs and monkeys show the danger of drawing general conclusions from experiments done on any one sort of animal. I subjoin the figures given by the last-named authors of the motor regions in the *monkey's brain.* ②

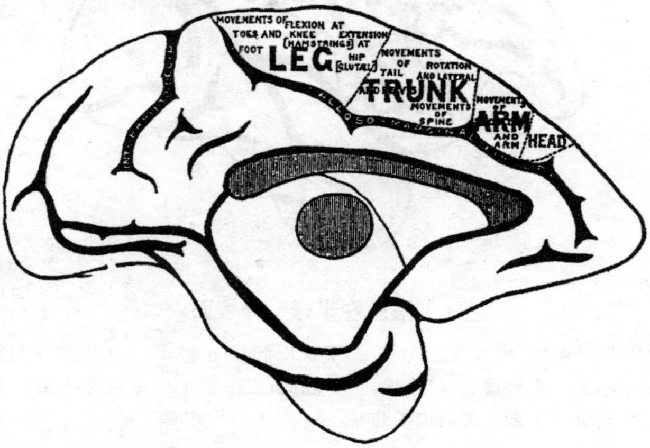

FIG. 7.—Left Hemisphere of Monkey's Brain. Mesial Surface.

In man we are necessarily reduced to the observation *post-mortem* of cortical ablations produced by accident or disease (tumor, hemorrhage, softening, etc.). What results during life

---

① 'Hemiplegia' means one-sided palsy.

② Philosophical Transactions, vol. 179, pp. 6.10(1888). In a later paper(*ilid.* p. 205) Messrs. Beevor and Horsley go into the localization still more minutely, showing spots from which single muscles or single digits can be made to contract.

至多在相关联的动作中起很小的作用。当整个区域被去除时，会出现真正的和永久的偏瘫，其中胳膊受到的影响要比腿受的影响更大，而且几个月之后随之而来的是肌肉挛缩，和人在长期的偏瘫后一样。① 依照谢弗和霍斯利，两边的缘回(见图 7)都受损之后，躯干肌肉也会变得瘫痪。狗和猴子之间的区别表明了，要从对任何一种动物所做的实验中得出普遍结论是危险的。我附加了由我最后提到的讨论猴脑中运动区域的作者给出的图示。②

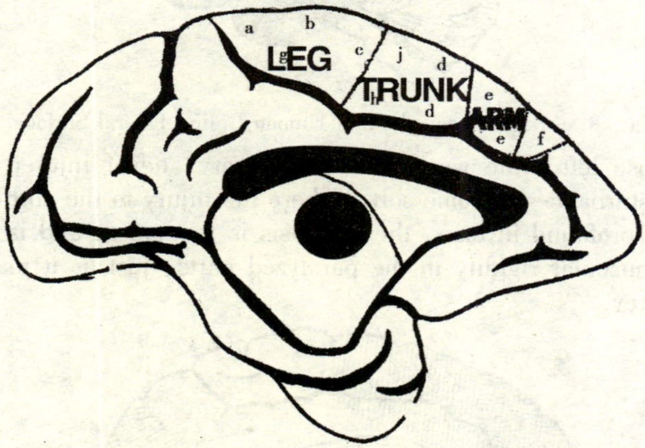

图 7　猴脑左半球中央表面

LEG. 腿。 TRUNK. 躯干。 ARM. 臂。 a. 脚趾和腿的运动。 b. 膝的弯曲(腿筋)。 c. 髋部伸展(臀肌)。 d. 脊柱的旋转和侧向运动。 e. 肩和臂的运动。 f. 头。 g. 腿。 h. 躯干。 i. 臂。 j. 尾部的运动。

在人这里，我们有必要将观察缩小到由事故和疾病(肿瘤、出血、软化等)造成的皮层切除的尸体检查上来。由这些情况在一生

① “偏瘫”指一边的瘫痪。

② 《哲学学报》，第 179 卷，第 6、10 页(1888 年)。在后来的一篇论文中(同前，第 205 页)比弗尔和霍斯利先生更加精确地进入定位，揭示出了一些点，通过它们，单块肌肉和单个手指、脚趾会引起收缩。

from such conditions is either localized spasm, or palsy of certain muscles of the opposite side. The cortical regions which invariably produce these results are homologous with those which we have just been studying in the dog, cat, ape, etc. Figs. 8 and 9 show the result of 169 cases carefully studied by Exner. The parts shaded are regions where lesions produced *no* motor disturbance.

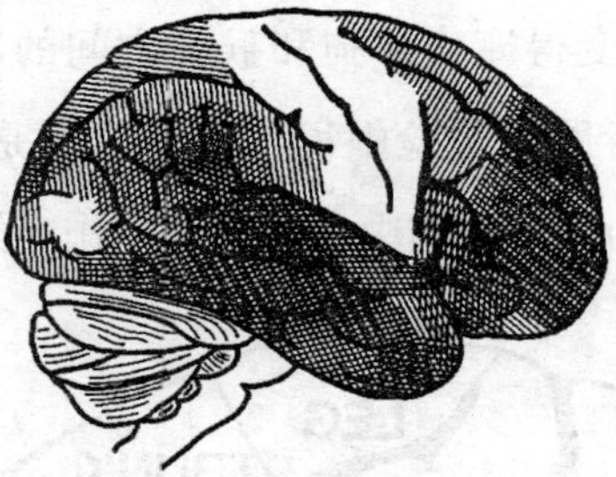

FIG. 8.—Right Hemisphere of Human Brain. Lateral Surface.

Those left white were, on the contrary, never injured without motor disturbances of some sort. Where the injury to the cortical substance is profound in man, the paralysis is permanent and is succeeded by muscular rigidity in the paralyzed parts, just as it may be in the monkey.

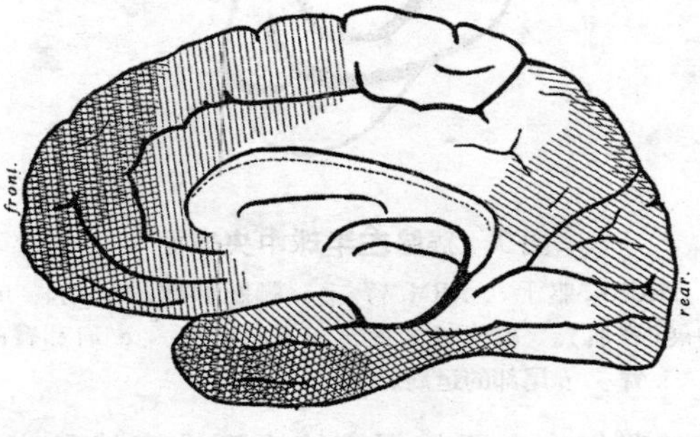

FIG. 9.—Right Hemisphere of Human Brain. Mesial Surface.

(3) *Descending degenerations* show the intimate connection of the rolandic regions of the cortex with the motor tracts of the cord. When, either in man or in the lower animals, these regions are destroyed, a peculiar degenerative change known as secondary sclerosis is found to extend downwards through the white fibrous substance of the brain in a perfectly definite manner, affecting certain distinct strands which pass through the inner capsule, crura, and pons, into the anterior pyramids of the medulla oblongata,

中造成的结果要么是局部痉挛，要么是相反一侧某些肌肉的瘫痪。造成这些结果的皮层区域和我们一直在狗、猫、猩猩那里研究的区域一致。图 8 和图 9 展示了由埃克斯纳仔细研究的 169 个病例的结果。阴影部分是损伤不造成运动障碍的区域。

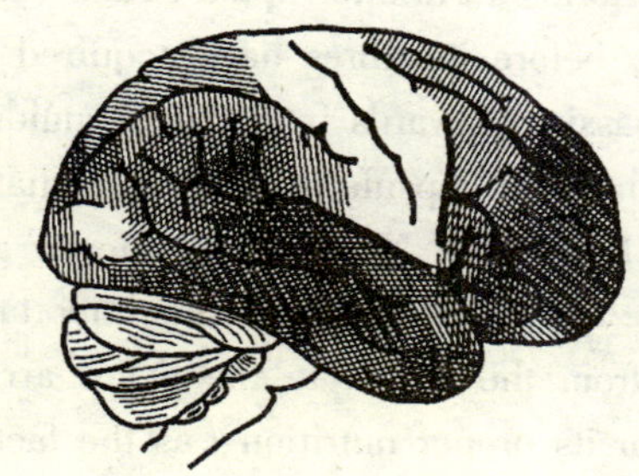

图 8　人脑右半球　侧面

相反，白色的部分只要受伤就会引起某种运动障碍。在人那里，如果对皮层物质的损伤很深，瘫痪就是永久的，而且继之而来的是瘫痪部位的肌肉硬化，就和在猴子那里发生的一样。

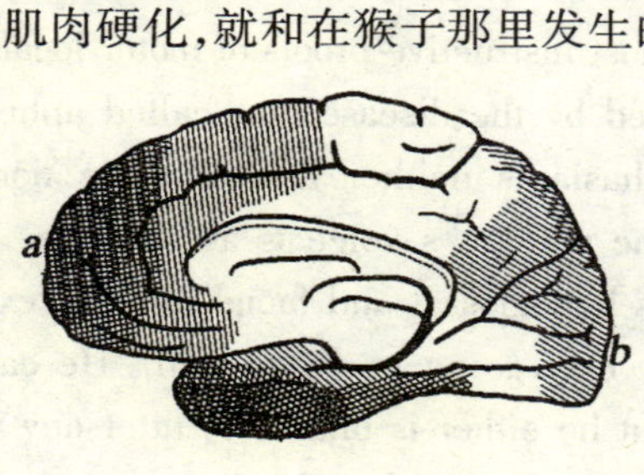

图 9　人脑右半球　中央表层

a. 前面　b. 后面

(3)下行的退化表明了脑皮层的罗朗多区域和脊椎运动束的密切联系。无论在人还是在低级动物这里，当这些区域被破坏了，一种独特的被称作是次级硬化的退化性质的变化就会被发现，它以一种完全确定的方式经由大脑纤维白质向下延伸，影响到某些独特的束，它们是穿过内囊、脑脚和脑桥而后进入延髓前

and from thence (partly crossing to the other side) downwards into the anterior (direct) and lateral (crossed) columns of the spinal cord.

(4) *Anatomical proof* of the continuity of the rolandic regions with these motor columns of the cord is also clearly given. Flechsig's 'Pyramidenbahn' forms an uninterrupted strand (distinctly traceable in human embryos, before its fibres have acquired their white 'medullary sheath') passing upwards from the pyramids of the medulla, and traversing the internal capsule and corona radiata to the convolutions in question (Fig. 10). None of the inferior gray matter of the brain seems to have any connection with this important fibrous strand. It passes directly from the cortex to the motor arrangements in the cord, depending for its proper nutrition (as the facts of degeneration show) on the influence of the cortical cells, just as motor nerves depend for their nutrition on that of the cells of the spinal cord. Electrical stimulation of this motor strand in any accessible part of its course has been shown in dogs to produce movements analogous to those which excitement of the cortical surface calls forth.

One of the most instructive proofs of motor localization in the cortex is that furnished by the disease now called aphemia, or *motor Aphasia*. Motor aphasia is neither loss of voice nor paralysis of the tongue or lips. The patient's voice is as strong as ever, and all the innervations of his hypoglossal and facial nerves, except those necessary for speaking, may go on perfectly well. He can laugh and cry, and even sing; but he either is unable to utter any words at all; or a few meaningless stock phrases form his only speech; or else he speaks incoherently and confusedly, *mispronouncing*, misplacing, and misusing his words in various degrees. Sometimes his speech is a mere broth of unintelligible syllables. In cases of pure motor aphasia the patient recognizes his mistakes and suffers acutely from them. Now whenever a patient dies in such a condition as this, and an examination of his brain is permitted, it is found that the lowest frontal gyrus (see Fig. 11) is the seat of injury. Broca first noticed this fact in 1861, and since then the gyrus has gone by the name of Broca's

椎体的束，并由此（部分地交叉到另一边）向下进入脊髓前柱（直接的）和侧柱（交叉的）。

（4）解剖学上的证明也清楚地表明了罗朗多区域同这些脊椎运动柱的连续性。弗莱西格的“椎体束”形成了一条不间断的索（可以清楚地追溯到人类胚胎，那时它的纤维还没有获得它们的白色“髓鞘”），它从髓质椎体向上走，并且越过内囊和辐射冠到达相关的脑回（图10）。所有大脑的次灰质似乎与这条重要的纤维束没有任何连接。它直接从脑皮层来到脊髓中的运动排列组织，它的适宜的营养（如退化的事实所显示）依赖于皮层细胞的影响，就和运动神经的营养依赖于脊髓细胞的影响一样。对这条运动束在其路线中任何容易接近的部分实施电刺激，在狗身上已经表明会产生类似于前面所说的由皮层表面的刺激而引起的动作。

关于脑皮层中运动定位的一个最有益的证据是由现在被称为失语症或运动失语症的疾病所提供的。运动失语症不是失声，也不是舌或唇的瘫痪。患者的声音和以前一样响亮，并且他的舌下神经和脸部神经的所有神经支配，除了那些为说话所必需的神经支配之外，都进行得很好。他能笑，能哭，甚至能唱歌；但是，他要么是根本不能说出任何词语，要么只能说出一些无意义的普通短语来构成他的讲话；又或者是他无条理地和混乱地说话，在不同程度上错误发音、错置词语、错用词语。有时，他的讲话就像是用无法了解的音节混成的一锅汤。在纯粹的运动失语症的病例中，患者知道他的错误，并且为此而极端痛苦。现在，只要患者在这样的情况下死去，并且对他大脑的检查获得容许时，就会发现损伤所在地位于最下面的额回（见图11）。布罗卡最先在1861年发现这一事实，并且从那时起，这一脑回被命名为布罗卡回。在

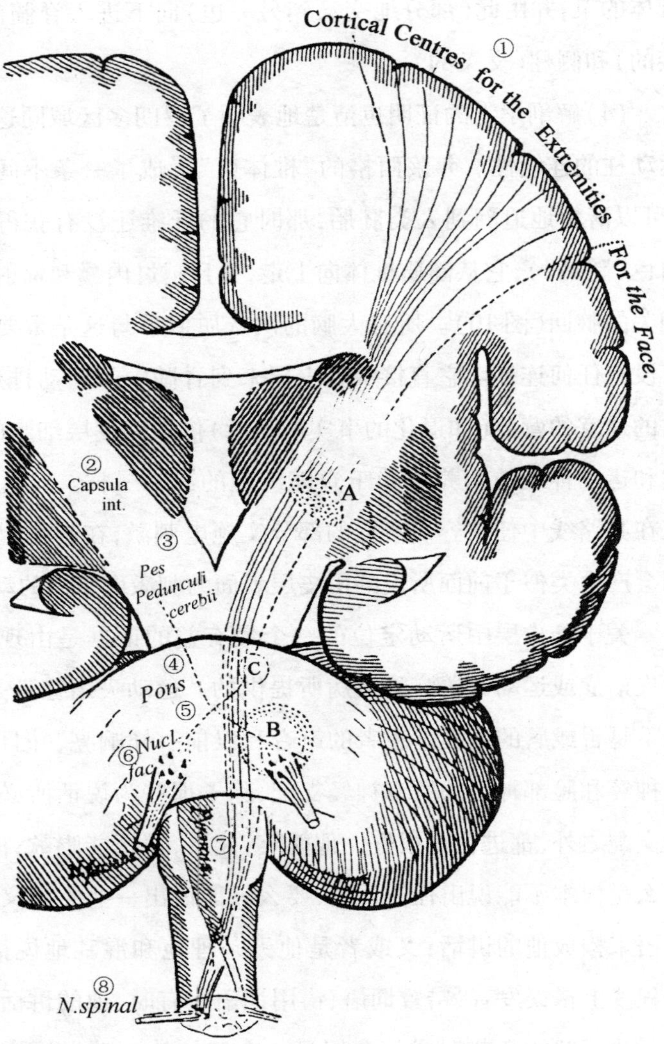

FIG. 10.—Schematic Transverse Section of Brain showing Motor Strand.—After Edinger.

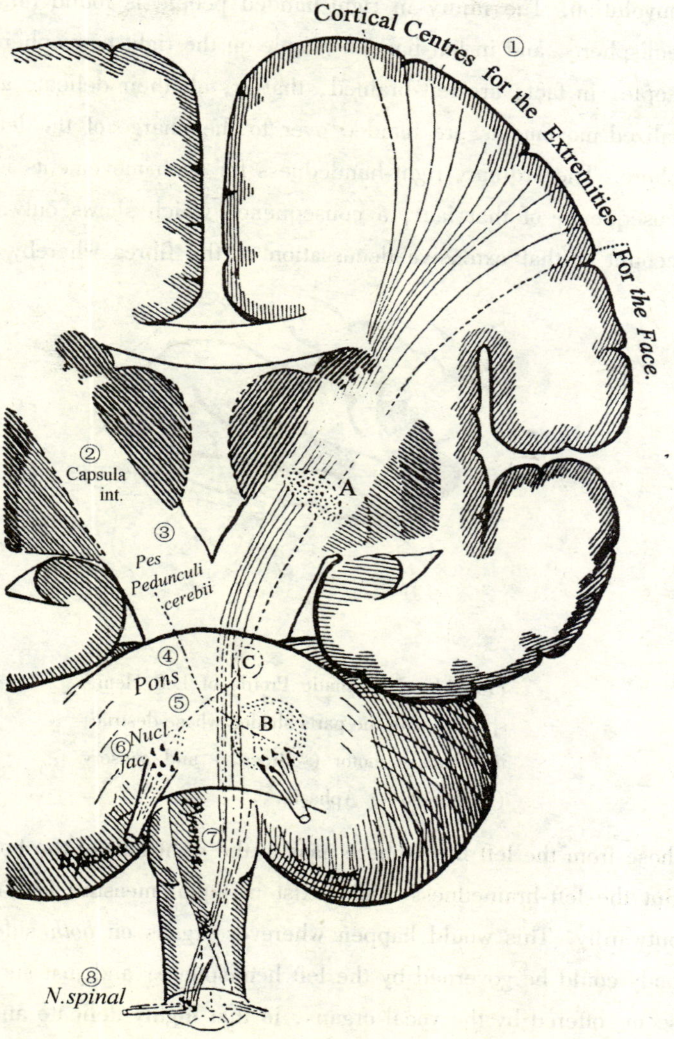

图 10　示意性的表示运动索的大脑横截面，依照埃丁格制作

①负责面部神经末端的皮层中枢　②内囊　③小脑下脚　④脑桥　⑤面神经核　⑥面神经　⑦椎体　⑧脊神经。

convolution. The injury in right-handed people is found on the left hemisphere, and in left-handed people on the right hemisphere. Most people, in fact, are left-brained, that is, all their delicate and specialized movements are handed over to the charge of the left hemisphere. The ordinary right-handedness for such movements is only a consequence of that fact, a consequence which shows outwardly on account of that extensive decussation of the fibres whereby most of

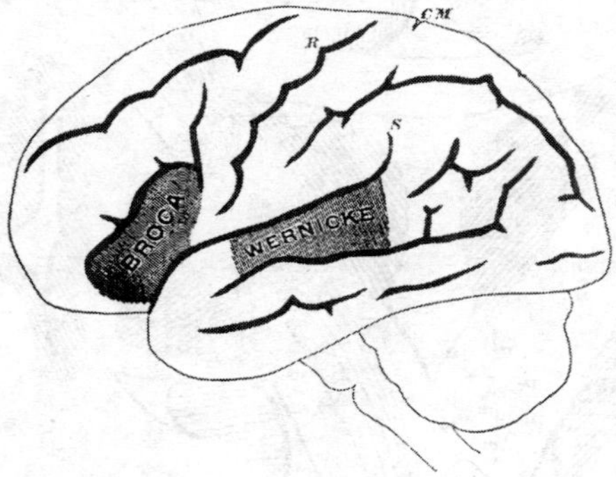

FIG. 11 —Schematic Profile of Left Hemisphere, with the parts shaded whose destruction causes motor ('Broca') and sensory ('wernicke') Aphasia.

those from the left hemisphere pass to the right half of the body only. But the left-brainedness might exist in equal measure and not show outwardly. This would happen wherever organs on *both* sides of the body could be governed by the left hemisphere; and just such a case seems offered by the vocal organs, in that highly delicate and special motor service which we call speech. Either hemisphere *can* innervate them bilaterally, just as either seems able to innervate bilaterally the muscles of the trunk, ribs, and diaphragm. Of the special movements of speech, however, it would appear (from the facts of aphasia) that the left hemisphere in most persons habitually takes exclusive charge.

惯用右手的人中，发现这种损伤在大脑的左半球，而在惯用左手的人中，发现这种损伤在大脑的右半球上。事实上，大多数人都是左脑发达的，也就是说，他们所有精巧的和专门化的动作都交由左半球负责。人们通常用右手来完成这些动作只是这一事实的结果而已，这一结果在外观上表明了这样一种情况，即借助那些纤维的广泛交叉，从左脑出来的大多数纤维只通向身体的右半部分。而且，左脑发达可以在相同操作上存在，并且不在外

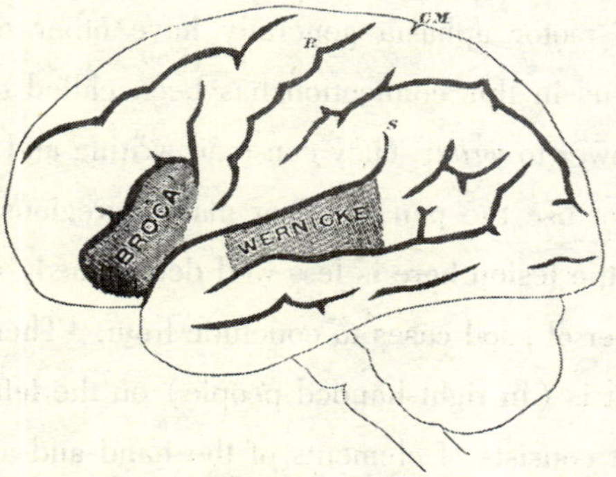

图 11　左半球侧面，阴影部分的损坏会引起运动（"Broca"）和感觉（"Wernicke"）失语症

观上显示出来。这会在两边的器官都能被左半球控制的情况下发生，而且在那种我们称之为说话的高度精巧和专门化的动作中，声音器官似乎提供了这一实例。两个半球都能够对它们进行双向神经支配，就如同它们似乎能够对躯干、肋、横膈膜的肌肉进行双向神经支配一样。然而，就说话这种专门的运动来说，会显示出（从失语症的事实看出）在大多数人那里左半球习惯性地实施全部控制。如果那个半球失灵了，说话就不能完成；尽

With that hemisphere thrown out of gear, speech is undone; even though the opposite hemisphere still be there for the performance of less specialized acts, such as the various movements required in eating.

It will be noticed that Broca's region is homologous with the parts ascertained to produce movements of the lips, tongue, and larynx when excited by electric currents in apes (cf. Fig. 6, p. 34). The evidence is therefore as complete as it well can be that the motor incitations to these organs leave the brain by the lower frontal region.

Victims of motor aphasia generally have other disorders. One which interests us in this connection has been called *agraphia*: they have lost the power to *write*. They can read writing and understand it; but either cannot use the pen at all or make egregious mistakes with it. The seat of the lesion here is less well determined, owing to an insufficient number of good cases to conclude from. ① There is no doubt, however, that it is (in right-handed people) on the left side, and little doubt that it consists of elements of the hand-and-arm region specialized for that service. The symptom may exist when there is little or no disability in the hand for other uses. If it does not get well, the patient usually educates his right hemisphere, i. e. learns to write with his left hand. In other cases of which we shall say more a few pages later on, the patient can write both spontaneously and at dictation, but cannot *read* even what he has himself written! All these phenomena are now quite clearly explained by separate brain-centres for the various feelings and movements and tracts for associating these together. But their minute discussion belongs to medicine rather than

① Nothnagel und Naunyn: Die Localization in den Gehirnkrankheiten (Wiesbaden, 1887), p. 34.

管另一个半球依然在那里负责执行不太专门化的行动，例如在进食中所需要的各种动作。

可以注意到的是，布罗卡区域和在猩猩身上当通过电击刺激时产生唇、舌以及喉运动的确定部位是一致的(见图6，第71页)。因此证明对这些器官的运动刺激，通过比较靠下的额部区域离开大脑的证据，已经如它能够达到的那样完善了。

运动失语症的患者一般还有其他紊乱。与此有关联并使我们感兴趣的一个叫做失写症：他们失去了写字的能力。他们可以阅读著述并理解它；但是他们要么根本不能使用笔，要么一用笔就犯异乎寻常的错误。由于用来得出结论的好的病例数量不够，损伤的所在地不能很好地加以确定。[①] 然而，毫无疑问的是它在(在惯用右手的人中)左边，并且可以确定是由专门负责那种职能的手臂区域的要素构成。这种病症可以存在于手被用于其他用途时很少存在或不存在无能的情况中。如果它没有好起来的话，患者通常就训练他的脑右半球，也就是学习用左手写字。在其他病例中，这些病例我们将在后面的几页纸上做更多的讨论，患者不仅可以自发地写字，还可以进行听写，但是他就是不能读出甚至是他自己写出来的东西。大脑中枢负责分离各种感受和运动，而神经束负责将它们联系起来，所有这些现象现在已经非常清楚地得到了解释。但是，这些仔细而准确的讨论属于医学而不是普通心

① 诺斯内格尔和农因：《大脑疾病定位》(威斯巴登，1887)第34页。

to general psychology, and I can only use them here to illustrate the principles of motor localization. ①Under the heads of sight and hearing I shall have a little more to say.

The different lines of proof which I have taken up establish conclusively the proposition *that all the motor impulses which leave the cortex pass out, in healthy animals, from the convolutions about the fissure of Rolando.*

When, however, it comes to defining precisely what is involved in a motor impulse leaving the cortex, things grow more obscure. Does the impulse start independently from the convolutions in question, or does it start elsewhere and merely flow through? And to what particular phase of psychic activity does the activity of these centres correspond? Opinions and authorities here divide; but it will be better, before entering into these deeper aspects of the problem, to cast a glance at the facts which have been made out concerning the relations of the cortex to sight, hearing, and smell.

Sight.

Ferrier was the first in the field here. He found, when the *angular* convolution (that lying between the 'intra parietal' and 'external occipital' fissures, and bending round the top of the fissure of Sylvius, in Fig. 6) was excited in the monkey, that movements of the eyes and head as if for vision occurred; and that when it was extirpated, what he supposed to be total and permanent blindness of the opposite eye followed. Munk almost immediately declared total and permanent blindness to follow from destruction of the *occipital lobe* in monkeys as well as dogs, and said that the angular gyrus had nothing to do with sight, but was only the centre for tactile sensibility of the eyeball. Munk's absolute tone about his observations and his theoretic arrogance have led to his ruin as an authority. But he did two things of permanent value.

① An accessible account of the history of our knowledge of motor aphasia is in W. A. Hammond's 'Treatise on the Diseases of the Nervous System,' chapter VII.

理学，而且我只能在这里使用它们来阐明运动定位原理。① 在视觉和听觉的标题之下，我还有更多的一些讨论。

我所采纳的不同的证明方式最终确立了这样一种主张，即在健康的动物那里，所有离开皮层的运动刺激都是从罗朗多沟周围的脑回中出来的。

然而，当要精确地确定出在运动刺激离开皮层中有什么东西涉及进来时，事情就变得更加模糊了。刺激是独立地从相关脑回中开始，还是从别处开始并且仅仅是从此流过吗？而且这些中枢的活动和哪一个精神活动的特殊阶段相对应呢？意见分化了，权威人士对此有分歧；然而，当进入这些问题的纵深方面时，最好看一下关于皮层与视觉、听觉和嗅觉关系的已知事实。

视 觉

费里尔是这领域中的第一人。当猴子身上的角回（位于"内顶骨"和"外枕骨"沟之间，并且沿着西耳维厄斯沟的顶部弯曲，见图6）被刺激时，好像是因视觉而产生了眼和头的运动；并且当它被切除时，随之而来的是他所认为的相反一侧眼睛完全和永久地失明。芒克也差不多马上宣布了猴子和狗的枕叶的损坏会招致完全和永久的失明，并且指出角回与视觉无关，它仅仅是负责眼球触觉感受性的中枢。芒克关于他的观察的绝对论调和他理论上的傲慢态度让他威信扫地。但是他做了两件具有永久价

① 关于运动失语症认知史的易得到的论述见 W. A. 哈蒙德的《论神经系统疾病》，第7章。

He was the first to distinguish in these vivisections between sensorial and *psychic* blindness, and to describe the phenomenon of *restitution* of the visual function after its first impairment by an operation; and the first to notice the *hemiopic* character of the visual disturbances which result when only one hemisphere is injured. Sensorial blindness is absolute insensibility to light; psychic blindness is inability to recognize the *meaning* of the optical impressions, as when we see a page of Chinese print but it suggests nothing to us. A hemiopic disturbance of vision is one in which neither retina is affected in its totality, but in which, for example, the left portion of *each* retina is blind, so that the animal sees nothing situated in space towards its right. Later observations have corroborated this hemiopic character of all the disturbances of sight from injury to a single hemisphere in the higher animals; and the question whether an animal's apparent blindness is sensorial or only psychic has, since Munk's first publications, been the most urgent one to answer, in all observations relative to the function of sight.

Goltz almost simultaneously with Ferrier and Munk reported experiments which led him to deny that the visual function was essentially bound up with any one localized portion of the hemispheres. Other divergent results soon came in from many quarters, so that, without going into the history of the matter any more, I may report the existing state of the case as follows: ①

In *fishes*, *frogs*, and *lizards* vision persists when the hemispheres are entirely removed. This is admitted for frogs and fishes even by Munk, who denies it for birds.

All of Munk's *birds* seemed totally blind (blind sensorially) after removal of the hemispheres by his operation. The following of a candle by the head and winking at a threatened blow, which are ordinarily

① The history up to 1885 may be found in A. Christiani: Zur Physiologie dear Gehirnes (Berlin, 1885).

值的事情。他是第一个在这些活体解剖中区分感觉失明和心理失明的人,并且描述了通过手术而造成的初次损伤之后视觉功能复原的现象;而且他是第一个注意到偏盲特性的人,这种偏盲是仅有一个脑半球受到损伤时而导致的视觉障碍。感觉失明是指对光完全没有感受性;心理失明是指没有能力认出视觉印象的意义,就如同当我们看到一张中文印刷物时,它对我们没有任何提示。视觉偏盲是指这样的情况,两个视网膜都没有全部受到影响,但是在其中,比如每个视网膜的左边一部分是盲的,那么这动物就看不见位于空间中朝向右边的东西。后来的观察已经确证了在高等动物那里由于单个脑半球的损伤而造成的所有视觉障碍的偏盲特性;而且在所有视觉功能的相关观察中,动物明显的失明是感觉的或者仅是心理的这一问题,自从芒克首次公布他的观点以来,就已经成为最急需回答的问题。

戈尔茨几乎同时与费里尔和芒克报告了这样的实验,这些实验使他否认了视觉功能在本质上和脑半球上任何一个定位部分有密切的关系。其他有分歧的结果很快从许多地方涌来,因此,无需再进入这一问题的历史记录,我就可以对这一情况的现状作如下报告了:①

在鱼、青蛙和蜥蜴那里,当脑半球被完全去除时,视觉会持续存在。芒克也承认在青蛙和鱼类那里情况是这样的,但他否认在鸟类那里情况也是如此。

芒克所有的鸟在通过手术切除脑半球之后似乎都完全失明(感觉失明)了。用头追逐蜡烛和朝着威胁性的攻击眨眼睛,这通

---

① 直至1885年的历史记录可以在A.克里斯蒂安尼的《大脑生理学》(柏林,1865年)中找到。

held to prove the retention of crude optical sensations by the lower centres in supposed hemisphereless pigeons, are by Munk ascribed to vestiges of the visual sphere of the cortex left behind by the imperfection of the operation. But Schrader, who operated after Munk and with every apparent guarantee of completeness, found that all his pigeons saw after two or three weeks had elapsed, and the inhibitions resulting from the wound had passed away. They invariably avoided even the slightest obstacles, flew very regularly towards certain perches, etc., differing *toto cœlo* in these respects with certain simply *blinded* pigeons who were kept with them for comparison. They did not pick up food strewn on the ground, however. Schrader found that they would do this if even a small part of the frontal region of the hemispheres was left, and ascribes their non-self-feeding when deprived of their occipital cerebrum not to a visual, but to a motor, defect, a sort of alimentary aphasia. ①

In presence of such discord as that between Munk and his opponents one must carefully note how differently significant is *loss*, from *preservation*, of a function after an operation on the brain. The *loss* of the function does not necessarily show that it *is* dependent on the part cut out; but its *preservation* does show that it is *not* dependent: and this is true though the loss should be observed ninety-nine times and the preservation only once in a hundred similar excisions. That birds and mammals *can* be blinded by cortical ablation is undoubted; the only question is, *must* they be so? Only then can the cortex be certainly called the ' seat of sight'. The blindness may always be due to one of those remote effects of the wound on distant parts, inhibitions, extensions of inflammation,—interferences, in a word,— upon which Brown-Séquard and Goltz have rightly insisted, and the

---

① Pflüger's Archiv, vol. 44, p. 176. Munk (Berlin Academy Sitzungsberichte, 1889, XXXI) returns to the charge, denying the extirpations of Schrader to be complete: "Microscopic portions of the Sehsphäre must remain."

常被用来证明无脑半球鸽子用低级中枢保留了天然的视觉，但芒克把这归因于不完善的手术而留下的皮层视觉区域的残余。可是，施拉德继芒克之后也做了这样的手术，并且手术的完善性得到了明显的保证，他发现他所有的鸽子在两、三周之后都看见了，并且因损伤所造成的障碍都消失了。它们总是能躲开甚至是最小的障碍物，非常有规律地飞向某些栖枝，等等，在这些方面它们和一些同它们关在一处用来做比较的完全失明的鸽子有极大的不同。然而，它们不去捡撒在地上的食物。施拉德发现，假如脑半球的额部区域有很小一部分被保留下来，它们就会去捡了，并且他没有将当枕部大脑切除时出现的非自我给食行为归因于视觉缺陷，而是将其归因于运动缺陷，一种进食失语症。①

面对芒克和他对手之间这样的不合意见，我们必须认真注意在大脑的手术之后，一种功能的丧失和保存有多么不同的重要意义。功能的丧失并不一定表明它依赖于切除的部分；但是它的保存也不能表明它不依赖它：在一百次的相似切除中，尽管丧失被观察到九十九次，保存只被观察到一次，这也是真实的。通过切除皮层，鸟和哺乳动物能够失明，这毫无疑问；唯一的问题是，它们必须这样吗？只有这样皮层才能确定地被称作“视觉的处所”。失明总是可以归因于任何那些遥远影响中的一个，这些影响由远处部位的损伤、阻碍、炎症的扩展，——总之是干涉，——而造成，布朗—西夸和戈尔茨很正确地坚持了这一点，而且它的重要性

① 《弗吕格文库》，第 44 卷，第 176 页。芒克(《柏林科学院会刊》，1889，31)进行了反驳，否认施拉德的切除是完全的：“视觉区域用显微镜可见的部分一定留了下来。”

importance of which becomes more manifest every day. Such effects are transient; whereas the *symptoms of deprivation* (*Ausfallserscheinungen*, as Goltz calls them) which come from the actual loss of the cut-out region must from the nature of the case be permanent Blindness in the pigeons, *so far as it passes away*, cannot possibly be charged to their seat of vision being lost, but only to some influence which temporarily depresses the activity of that seat. The same is true *mutatis mutandis* of all the other effects of operations, and as we pass to mammals we shall see still more the importance of the remark.

In rabbits loss of the entire cortex seems compatible with the preservation of enough sight to guide the poor animals' movements, and enable them to avoid obstacles. Christiani's observations and discussions seem conclusively to have established this, although Munk found that all *his* animals were made totally blind. ①

In dogs also Munk found absolute stone-blindness after ablation of the occipital lobes. He went farther and mapped out determinate portions of the cortex thereupon, which he considered correlated with definite segments of the two retinæ, so that destruction of given portions of the cortex produces blindness of the retinal centre, top, bottom, or right or left side, of the same or opposite eye. There seems little doubt that this definite correlation is mythological. Other observers, Hitzig, Goltz, Luciani, Loeb, Exner, etc., find, whatever part of the cortex may be ablated on one side, that there usually results a *hemiopic* disturbance of *both* eyes, slight and transient when the anterior lobes are the parts attacked, grave when an occipital lobe is the seat of injury, and lasting in proportion to the latter's extent. According to Loeb, the defect is a dimness of vision ('hemiamblyopia') in

---

① A. Christiani: Zur Physiol, d. Gehirnes (Berlin, 1885), chaps, II, III, IV. H. Munk: Berlin Akad. Stzgsb. 1884, XXIV.

也一天天地变得愈加明显了。这样的影响是短暂的;而由切除区域的真正丧失而出现的剥夺症状(戈尔茨称之为机能缺失现象),从这种情况的本质而言,则一定是永久的。到目前为止,鸽子的失明,因为它能消失,所以不能肯定地将其归因于它们的视觉处所的丧失,而只能够认为它是由于某种影响暂时抑制了那个处所的活动所致。手术的所有其他效果在细节上不同也同样是真实的,而且当我们对哺乳动物进行讨论时,我们将认识到这一情况的更进一步的重要性。

在兔子那里,整个皮层的丧失似乎和指引这可怜的动物的运动、并让它们避开障碍物的足够视觉的保存互不排斥。克里斯蒂安尼的观察和讨论似乎结论性地确立了这一点,尽管芒克发现他所有的动物都因此被弄得完全失明了。①

在狗那里,芒克也发现了枕叶切除之后出现了绝对的全盲。于是他更进一步画出了皮层的确定部位,他认为这部位和两个视网膜确定的部位相关联,这样一来,给定皮层部位的损伤就会产生同侧和相反一侧眼睛视网膜中心、顶部、下部、或者右边、或者左边的失明。似乎毫无疑问的是,这确定的相互关系是虚构的。希齐格、戈尔茨、卢西亚尼、洛布、埃克斯纳等其他观察者发现,无论脑皮层的哪一个部分在一边被切除,通常会导致双眼的偏盲,当前叶是损伤的部位时,偏盲是轻微和暂时的;当枕叶是受损的部位时,偏盲是严重的,并且其持续的时间和后者被切除的程度成正比。依照洛布,缺陷是视觉模糊("偏侧弱视"),在这里(不

① A. 克里斯蒂安尼:《大脑生理学》(柏林,1885 年),第 2、3、4 章。H. 芒克:《柏林科学院会刊》,1884 年,24。

which (however severe) the centres remain the best seeing portions of the retina, just as they are in normal dogs. The lateral or temporal part of each retina seems to be in exclusive connection with the cortex of its own side. The centre and nasal part of each seems, on the contrary, to be connected with the cortex of the opposite hemispheres. Loeb, who takes broader views than any one, conceives the hemiamblyopia as he conceives the motor disturbances, namely, as the expression of an increased inertia in the whole optical machinery, of which the result is to make the animal respond with greater effort to impressions coming from the half of space opposed to the side of the lesion. If a dog has right hemiamblyopia, say, and two pieces of meat are hung before him at once, he invariably turns first to the one on his left. But if the lesion be a slight one, *shaking* slightly the piece of meat on his right (this makes of it a stronger stimulus) makes him seize upon it first. If only one piece of meat be offered, he takes it, on whichever side it be.

When both occipital lobes are extensively destroyed total blindness may result. Munk maps out his ' Sehsphäre' definitely, and says that blindness *must* result when the entire shaded part, marked *A*, *A*, in Figs. 12 and 13, is involved in the lesion. Discrepant reports of other observations he explains as due to incomplete.

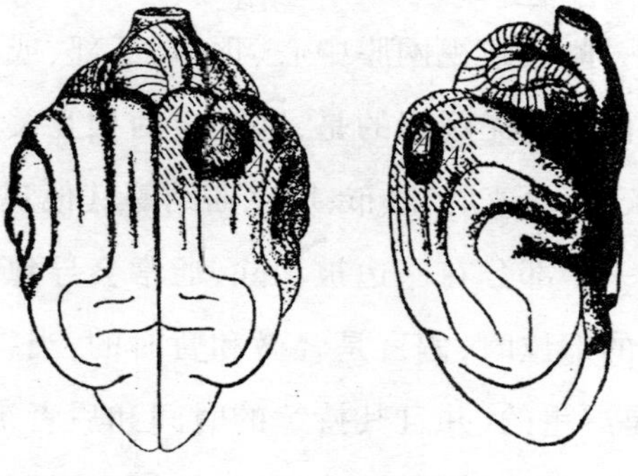

FIG. 12. FIG. 13.

The Dog's visual centre according to Munk, the entire striated region, *A*, *A*, being the exclusive seat of vision, and the dark central circle, *A'*, being correlated with the retinal centre of the opposite eye.

Luciani, Goltz, and Lannegrace, however, contend that they have

论如何严重),中心依然是视网膜最好的视觉部分,就如同它们在正常的狗身上的情况一样。每个视网膜的侧面和颞侧的部分似乎和它自己同侧皮层有专属的联系。相反,每个视网膜中心部分与鼻部似乎和相反一侧脑半球的皮层有联系。洛布比别人持有更宽泛的观点,他像自己构想运动障碍一样来构想偏侧弱视,即认为它是在整个视觉机构中增加了的惯性的表现,其结果就是让这动物以更大的努力来对来自损伤相反一侧的那半个空间里的印象做出反映。比如说,如果一条狗有右侧偏侧弱视,并且同时有两块肉挂在它面前,它总是不变地先转向在它左边的那一块。但如果损伤是很轻微的话,轻微地晃动它右边的那块肉(这造成了一个很强的刺激),就会让它先去咬右边的一块。如果只提供一块肉的话,不论它在哪一边,这狗都会去抓它。

当两边的枕叶都大面积受到损伤,就会导致全盲。芒克确定地绘制出了他的“视觉区域”,并且指出当损伤涉及整个阴影部分(在图 12、13 中标出的 *A*,*A*)时,就会导致失明。其他有差异的观

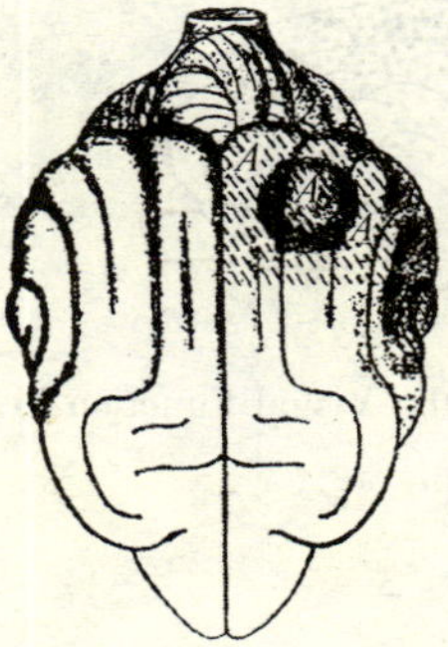

图 12

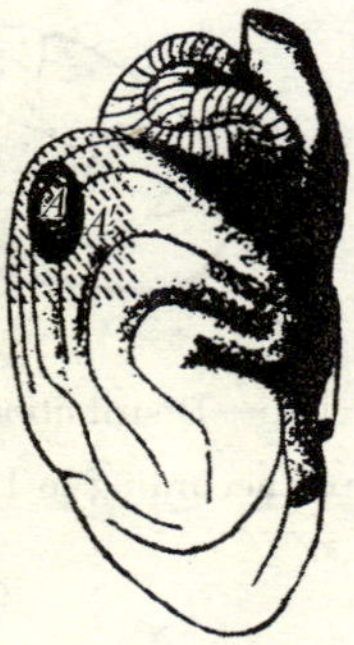

图 13

依照芒克的狗视觉中枢,整个有条纹的区域 *A*、*A*,是唯一的视觉处所,而且暗色的中心圆 *A′* 与相反一侧眼睛的视网膜中枢相关联。

察报告他解释说是由于切除不完全造成的。然而,卢西亚

made complete bilateral extirpations of Munk's Sehsphäre more than once, and found a sort of crude indiscriminating ablation. sight of objects to return in a few weeks. ① The question whether a dog is blind or not is harder to solve than would at first appear; for simply blinded dogs, in places to which they are accustomed, show little of their loss and avoid all obstacles; whilst dogs whose occipital lobes are gone may run against things frequently and yet see notwithstanding. The best proof that they may see is that which Goltz's dogs furnished: they carefully avoided, as it seemed, strips of sunshine or paper on the floor, as if they were solid obstacles. This no really blind dog would do. Luciani tested his dogs when hungry (a condition which sharpens their attention) by strewing pieces of meat and pieces of cork before them. If they went straight at them, they *saw*; and if they chose the meat and left the cork, they *saw discriminatingly*. The quarrel is very acrimonious; indeed the subject of localization of functions in the brain seems to have a peculiar effect on the temper of those who cultivate it experimentally. The amount of preserved vision which Goltz and Luciani report seems hardly to be worth considering, on the one hand; and on the other, Munk admits in his penultimate paper that out of 85 dogs he only 'succeeded' 4 times in his operation of producing complete

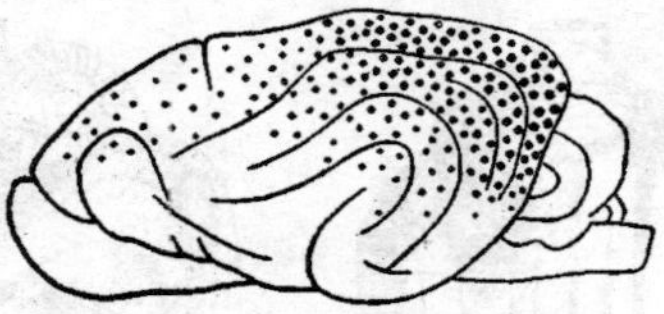

FIG. 14. —Distribution of the Visual Function in the Cortex, according to Luciani.

---

① Luciani und Seppili: Die Functions – Localization auf der Grosshirn – rinde (Deutsch von Fraenkel), Leipzig, 1886, Dogs M, N, and S. Goltz in Pflüger's Archiv, vol. 34, pp. 490 – 6; vol. 42, p. 454. Cf. also Munk: Berlin Akad. Stzgsb. 1886, VII, VIII, pp. 113 – 121, and Loeb: Pflüger's Archiv, vol. 39, p. 337.

尼、戈尔茨和兰格雷斯声称他们已经不止一次地对芒克的视觉区域做过完整的双面切除，并且发现一种对对象原始的、无辨别力的视觉在几周之后又回来了。① 狗是否失明这一问题比它起先出现时更难解决；因为完全失明的狗在它们熟悉的地方很少表现出它们丧失了视力，而且能够避开所有障碍；而失去了枕叶的狗会经常撞上东西，尽管它们还可以看得见。它们能够看到的最好的证据是戈尔茨的狗所提供的：它们似乎小心地避开光线和地面上的纸，好像它们是坚固的障碍物一样。真正失明的狗是不能这样做的。卢西亚尼对他的狗进行了实验，当它们饥饿时（集中它们注意力的一个条件），他在狗的面前撒下几块肉和几块软木。如果狗径直走向它们，则它们能看见；而且如果它们选择肉留下软木，则它们能有辨别力地看见。争论是非常尖刻的；确实，关于大脑中功能定位这一课题似乎对用实验方法研究它的人的脾气有一种特殊的影响。一方面，由戈尔茨和卢西亚尼所报告的被保存的视力，似乎不值得考虑；在另一方面，芒克在他倒数第二篇论文中承认，他对85条狗做了"视觉区域"的完

图14　大脑皮层中视觉功能的分布，依照卢西亚尼制作

---

① 卢西亚尼和塞皮里：《大脑皮层功能定位》（弗伦克尔德文版），莱比锡，1886年，狗M，N，S。《弗吕格文集》中的戈尔茨，第34卷，第490～496页，第42卷，第454页。也可参见芒克：《柏林科学院会刊》，1886年，7，8，第113～121页，以及洛布：《弗吕格文集》，第39卷，第337页。

blindness by complete extirpation of his ' Sehsphäre. ' [1] The safe conclusion for *us* is that Luciani's diagram, Fig. 14, represents something like the truth. The occipital lobes are far more important for vision than any other part of the cortex, so that their complete destruction makes the animal almost blind. As for the crude sensibility to light which *may* then remain, nothing exact is known either about its nature or its seat.

In the monkey, doctors also disagree. The truth seems, however, to be that the *occipital lobes* in this animal also are the part connected most intimately with the visual function. The function would seem to go on when very small portions of them are left, for Ferrier found no 'appreciable impairment' of it after almost complete destruction of them on both sides. On the other hand, he found complete and permanent blindness to ensue when they and the *angular gyri* in addition were destroyed on both sides. Munk, as well as Brown and Schaefer, found no disturbance of sight from destroying the *angular gyri* alone, although Ferrier found blindness to ensue. This blindness was probably due to inhibitions exerted *in distans*, or to cutting of the white optical fibres passing under the angular gyri on their way to the occipital lobes. Brown and Schaefer got complete and permanent blindness in one monkey from total destruction of both occipital lobes. Luciani and Seppili, performing this operation on two monkeys, found that the animals were only mentally, not sensorially, blind. After some weeks they saw their food, but could not distinguish by sight between figs and pieces of cork. Luciani and Seppili seem, however, not to have extirpated the entire lobes. When one lobe only is injured the affection of sight is hemiopic in monkeys: in this all observers agree. On the whole, then, Munk's original location of vision

---

① Berlin Akad. Sitzungsberichte, 1886, VII, VIII, p. 124.

全切除手术,其中只有四次成功地产生了全盲。① 对我们来说稳妥的结论是卢西亚尼的图示(见图 14)再现了某种类似真相的东西。枕叶对视觉来说比皮层的任何其他部分都更重要,以至于它们的完全损伤会使动物几乎失明。就对光的自然感受性此后可以保存下来而言,关于它的性质和所在地都不能确切地得到了解。

在对猴子的实验中,博士们意见也不一致。然而,真相似乎是这动物的枕叶也是和视觉功能联系最密切的部分。当枕叶的极小部分被保留下来时,视觉功能似乎能继续存在,因为在两边的枕叶都被完全损坏之后,费里尔没有发现这种功能的"可察觉的损伤"。在另一方面,他发现当两边的枕叶再加上角回都被损坏时,完全且永久的失明会跟着发生。芒克以及布朗和谢弗发现,单独的角回损坏不会导致视觉障碍,尽管费里尔发现了随之而来的失明。这种失明可能是由于远处施加的抑制所致,或者是因为切掉了在角回下面通往枕叶的白色视觉纤维所致。布朗和谢弗在一只猴子那里获得了由于两个枕叶的损伤而造成的完全且永久的失明。卢西亚尼和塞皮里对两只猴子做了这种手术,发现它们只是心理失明,而不是感觉失明。数周之后它们能看见它们的食物,但不能用视觉区分出无花果和软木块。然而,卢西亚尼和塞皮里似乎没有摘除整个枕叶。当只有一个枕叶受到损伤时,对猴子的视觉所造成影响就是偏盲:在这一点上所有观察者都意见一致。那么总体来说,芒克最初将视觉定位在枕叶中

① 《柏林科学院会刊》,1886 年,7,8,第 124 页。

in the occipital lobes is confirmed by the later evidence. ①

In man we have more exact results, since we are not driven to interpret the vision from the outward conduct. On the other hand, however, we cannot vivisect, but must wait for pathological lesions to turn up. The pathologists who have discussed these (the literature is tedious *ad libi-tum*) conclude that the occipital lobes are the indispensable part for vision in man. Hemiopic disturbance in both eyes comes from lesion of either one of them, and total blindness, sensorial as well as psychic, from destruction of both.

Hemiopia may also result from lesion in other parts, especially the neighboring angular and supra-marginal gyri, and it may accompany extensive injury in the motor region of the cortex. In these cases it seems probable that it is due to an *actio in distans*, probably to the interruption of fibres proceeding from the occipital lobe. There seem to be a few cases on record where there was injury to the occipital lobes without visual defect. Ferrier has collected as many as possible to prove his localization in the angular gyrus. ② A strict application of logical principles would make one of these cases outweigh one hundred contrary ones. And yet, remembering how imperfect observations may be, and how individual brains may vary, it would certainly be rash for their sake to throw away the enormous amount of positive evidence for the occipital lobes. Individual variability is always a *possible* explanation of an anomalous case. There is no more prominent

---

① H. Munk: Functionen der Grosshirnrinde (Berlin, 1881), pp. 36 – 40. Ferrier : Functions, etc., 2d ed, chap. IX, pt. I. Brown and Schaefer: Philos. Transactions, vol. 179, p. 321. Luciani u. Seppili, op. cit. pp. 131 – 138. Lannegrace found traces of sight with both occipital lobes destroyed, and in one monkey even when angular gyri and occipital lobes were destroyed altogether. His paper is in the Archives de Médecine Expérimental for January and March, 1889. I only know it from the abstract in the Neurologisches Centralblatt, 1889, pp. 108 – 420. The reporter doubts the evidence of vision in the monkey. It appears to have consisted in avoiding obstacles and in emotional disturbance in the presence of men.

② Localization of Cerebral Disease (1878). pp. 117 – 8.

被后来的证据所证实了。①

在人这里，我们有更准确的结果，因为我们不是被迫从外在行为来解释视觉。然而在另一方面，我们不能进行活体解剖，而必须等待病理损伤的出现。对这些问题已经讨论过的病理学学者（文献非常单调乏味）得出结论，认为对人的视觉来说枕叶是不可缺少的部分。两眼的偏盲障碍来自它们两者中其中一个的损伤，而感觉的和心理的全盲，是由于两者的损伤。

偏盲也可以由其他部位的损伤所致，尤其是临近的角回和缘上回，而且偏盲可以伴随着皮层运动区域的大面积损伤而出现。在这些病例中，它似乎可能是因为超距作用所致，也可能是因为从枕叶出来的纤维中断所致。这里似乎有一些病例记录了当枕叶受损时并未出现视觉障碍。费里尔收集了尽可能多的例子来证明他在角回的定位。② 逻辑法则的一次精确应用将会让一个病例从一百个相反的病例中脱颖而出。然而，考虑到观察可能是多么的不完善，个体的大脑可能是多么的不同，为了它们的缘故而抛弃掉大量支持枕叶定位的积极证据无疑是草率的。个体的可变性始终是对反常病例的一种可能的解释。这里没有任何解剖学

① H. 芒克：《大脑皮层功能》（柏林，1881 年），第 36～40 页。费里尔：《功能》，第二版，第 9 章，第 1 部分。布朗和谢弗：《哲学学报》，第 179 卷，第 321 页。卢西亚尼和塞皮里，在前面引用书中，第 181～188 页。兰格雷斯发现在两个枕叶一起被损坏之后有视觉迹象，而且在一只猴子那里甚至当角回和枕叶一起被损坏时也有视觉迹象。他的论文在 1889 年 1 月和 3 月的《实验医学文库》中。我只是从 1889 年的《精神病学中心报》第 108～420 页的摘要中了解到它的。报告者怀疑关于那猴子视觉的证据。它似乎是在躲避障碍，并且当人出现时表现出情绪上的不安。

② 《大脑疾病定位》（1878 年），第 117～118 页。

anatomical fact than that of the 'decussation of the pyramids,' nor any more usual pathological fact than its consequence, that left-handed hemorrhages into the motor region produce right-handed paralyses. And yet the decussation is variable in amount, and seems sometimes to be absent altogether①. If, in such a case as this last, the left brain were to become the seat of apoplexy, the left and not the right half of the body would be the one to suffer paralysis.

The *schema* on the opposite page, copied from Dr. Seguin, expresses, on the whole, the probable truth about the regions concerned in vision. Not the entire occipital lobes, but the so-called cunei, and the first convolutions, are the cortical parts most intimately concerned. Nothnagel agrees with Seguin in this limitation of the essential tracts.②

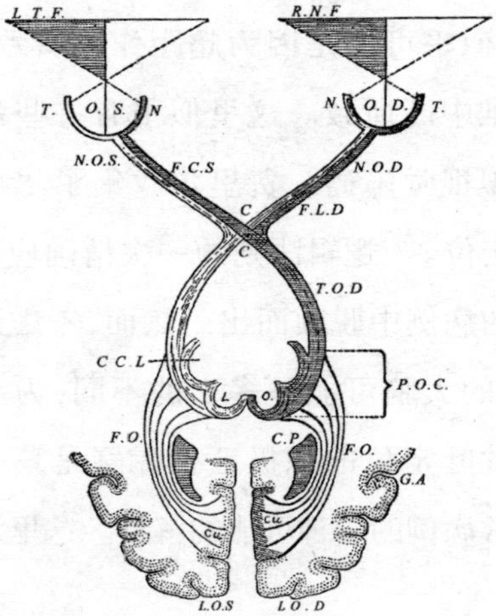

FIG. 15.—Scheme of the mechanism of vision, after Seguin.

---

① For cases see Flechsig: Die Leitungsbahnen in Gehirn u. Rückenmark (Leipzig, 1876), pp. 112,272; Exner's Untersuchungen, etc., p. 83; Ferrier s Localization, etc., p. 11; Francois-Franck's Cerveau Moteur, p. 63, note.

② E. C. Seguin: Hemianopsia of Cerebral Origin, in Journal of Nervous and Mental Disease, vol. VIII. p. 30. Nothnagel und Naunyn: Ueber die Localization der Gehirnkrankheiten (Wiesbaden, 1887), p. 10.

事实比“椎体的 X 形交”叉更显著的了，也没有任何病理事实比它的结果更平常的了，其结果是，左边的血管出血流入了运动区域，造成了右边的瘫痪。然而，这种 X 形交叉在程度上是可变的，有时似乎完全不存在。① 在最后指出的这类情况的病例中，如果中风的地方是左脑，瘫痪的就不是身体的右半部分，而是身体的左半部分。

从塞甘博士那里拷贝来的图示总体上表达了涉及视觉区域的可能真实的情况。不是整个枕叶，而是所谓的楔叶和第一脑回是皮层中最为密切相关的部分。诺斯内格尔在对基本神经束的限制方面同意塞甘的意见。②

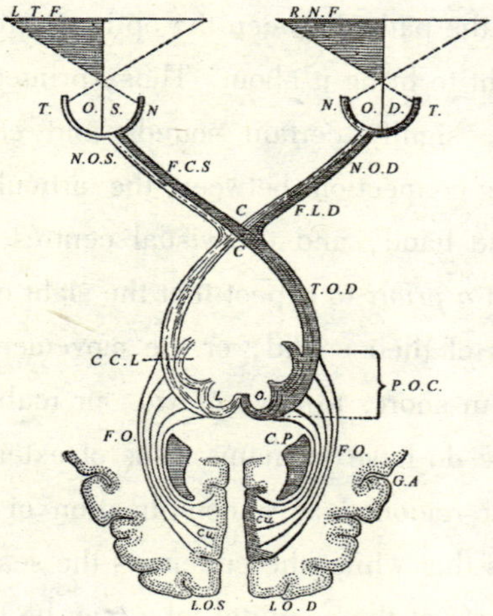

图 15　视觉机制图示，依照塞甘制作

---

① 病例见弗莱西格：《大脑和脊髓中的传导通道》（莱比锡，1874 年），第 112、272 页。埃克斯纳的《研究》，第 83 页；以及费里尔的《定位》，第 11 页；以及弗朗西丝－弗兰克的《大脑动力》，第 63 页，注释。

② E. C. 塞甘：《由大脑起因的偏盲》，见《神经和精神疾病杂志》，第 8 卷，第 30 页。诺斯内格尔和农因《关于大脑疾病的定位》（威斯巴登，1887 年），第 10 页。

The *cuneus* convolution (*Cu*) of the right occipital lobe is supposed to be injured, and all the parts which lead to it are darkly shaded to show that they fail to exert their function. *F. O.* are the intra-hemispheric optical fibres. *P. O. C.* is the region of the lower optic centres (corpora geniculata and quadrigemina). *T. O. D.* is the right optic tract; C, the chiasma; . *F. L. D.* are the fibres going to the lateral or temporal half T of the right retina; and *F. C. S* are those going to the central or nasal half of the left retina. *O. D.* is the right, and *O. S.* the left eyeball. The rightward half of each is therefore blind: in other words, the right nasal field, *R. N. F.*, and the left temporal field, *L. T. F.*, have become invisible to the subject with the lesion at *Cu*.

A most interesting effect of cortical disorder is *mental blindness*. This consists not so much in insensibility to optical impressions, as in *inability* to *understand them*. Psychologically it is interpretable as *loss of associations* between optical sensations and what they signify; and any interruption of the paths between the optic centres and the centres for other ideas ought to bring it about. Thus, printed letters of the alphabet, or words, signify certain sounds and certain articulatory movements. If the connection between the articulating or auditory centres, on the one hand, and the visual centres on the other, be ruptured, we ought *a priori* to expect that the sight of words would fail to awaken the idea of their sound, or the movement for pronouncing them. We ought, in short, to have *alexia*, or inability to read: and this is just what we do have in many cases of extensive injury about the fronto-temporal regions, as a complication of *aphasic* disease. Nothnagel suggests that whilst the cuneus is the seat of optical *sensations*, the other parts of the occipital lobe may be the field of optical *memories and ideas*, from the loss of which mental blindness should ensue. In fact, all the medical authors speak of mental blindness as if it must consist in the loss of visual images from the memory. It seems to me, however, that this is a psychological misapprehension. A man whose power of visual imagination has decayed (no unusual phenomenon in its lighter grades) is not mentally blind in the least, for he recognizes perfectly all that he sees. On the other hand, he *may* be mentally blind, with his optical imagination well preserved;

假设右枕叶的楔状回(*Cu*)受损了,所有通向它的部分都涂成暗色以显示它们不能执行其功能。*F. O.* 是大脑半球内部的视觉纤维。*P. O. C.* 是低级视觉中枢区域(膝状体和四叠体)。*O. T. D.* 是左视束;*C.* 是交叉;*F. L. D.* 是通向右视网膜的侧面或者颞部T的纤维;*F. C. S.* 是通向左视网膜中心或者鼻部的纤维。*O. D.* 是右眼球,*O. S.* 是左眼球。因此每一个的右半部分是盲的;换言之,右眼的鼻域 *R. N. F.* 和左眼的颞域 *L. T. F.* 对于在 *Cu* 处受损的被试者来说是不可见的。

皮层紊乱的一个最有趣的结果是心理失明。这种情况不是在于对视觉印象没有感受性,而是在于没有能力理解它们。按照心理学来说,它可被解说成视觉与视觉所指之间联想的丧失;视觉中枢和负责其他观念的中枢之间的任何路径的中断会导致其产生。因此,字母表中的印刷字母或者词语都意味着特定的声音和特定的发声动作。一方面是发声和听觉中枢而另一方面是视觉中枢,如果它们之间的联系被切断,我们先天就应预料到,对词语的视觉将不能唤起它们声音的观念,或者不能唤起发出它们的动作。简言之,我们会有失语症,或者无能力阅读:这确实是我们在额颞区域附近的大面积损伤(作为失语症的并发症)的许多病例中所遇到的情况。诺斯内格尔提出,当楔叶是视觉的所在地的同时,枕叶的其他部分可能是视觉记忆和观念的领域,心理失明将由于它们的丧失而跟着发生。事实上,所有的医学作者在谈到心理失明时,就好像它必定是记忆中视觉意象的丧失所致似的。然而,对我来说,这是一种心理学上的误解。一个视觉想像力已经衰退的人(在其程度较轻时不会有不正常的现象)至少不是心理失明,因为他完全认出了他所看到的一切。在另一方面,他可能心理失明了,而他的视觉想像力却保存完好;如同威尔布

as in the interesting case published by Wilbrand in 1887.[1] In the still more interesting case of mental blindness recently published by Lissauer,[2] though the patient made the most ludicrous mistakes, calling for instance a clothes-brush a pair of spectacles, an umbrella a plant with flowers, an apple a portrait of a lady, etc. etc., he seemed, according to the reporter, to have his mental images fairly well preserved. It is in fact the momentary loss of our *non*-optical images which makes us mentally blind, just as it is that of our *non*-auditory images which makes us mentally deal. I am mentally deaf if, *hearing* a bell, I can't recall how it *looks*; and mentally blind if, *seeing* it, I can't recall its *sound* or *its name*. As a matter of fact, I should have to be not merely mentally blind, but stone-blind, if all my visual images were lost. For although I am blind to the right half of the field of view if my left occipital region is injured, and to the left half if my right region is injured, such hemianopsia does not deprive me of visual *images*, experience seeming to show that the unaffected hemisphere is always sufficient for production of these. To abolish them entirely I should have to be deprived of both occipital lobes, and that would deprive me not only of ray inward images of sight, but of my sight altogether.[3] Recent pathological annals seem to offer a few such cases.[4] Meanwhile there are

---

① Dic Seelenblindheit, etc., p. 51 ff. The mental blindness was in this woman's case moderate in degree.

② Archiv f. Psychiatrie, vol. 21, p. 222.

③ Nothnagel (*loc. cit.* p. 22) says: "*Dies trifft aber nicht zu.*" He gives, however, no case in support of his opinion that double – sided cortical lesion may make one stone – blind and yet not destroy one's visual images; so that I do not know whether it is an observation of fact or an *a priori* assumption.

④ In a case published by C. S. Freund: Archivf. Psychiatric, vol. XX, the occipital lobes were injured, but their cortex was not destroyed, on both sides. There was still vision. Cf. pp. 291 – 5.

兰德在 1887 年发表的有趣的病例中的情况一样。[①] 在最近才由利索尔发表的心理失明的那个更有趣的病例中,[②]尽管病人犯了最可笑的错误,例如,他将一把衣刷称作眼镜,将一把雨伞称作一株开了花的植物,将一个苹果称作一位小姐的肖像画,等等,等等,然而依照报告者,他似乎将他的心理意象很好地保存了下来。事实上这种情况是由于致使我们心理失明的非视觉意象的瞬间丧失所致,就如同非听觉意象的丧失使我们心理失聪一样。如果我听到铃声,我不能回忆起铃儿看上去是什么样子的,我就是心理失聪了;如果我看到它,我不能回忆起它的声音或者是它的名字,我就是心理失明了。事实上,如果我的所有视觉意象都丧失了,则我将不仅仅是心理失明了,而是全盲了。因为即使我的左枕区域受损,对于我视野的右半部分来说我是失明的,我的右枕区受损,对于我视野的左半部分来说我是失明的,但是这样的偏盲并没有剥夺我的视觉意象,经验似乎表明未受影响的脑半球总是足以产生它们。如果要完全废止视觉意象,我将必须丧失两个枕叶,而且这不仅会让我的内部视觉意象丧失,还会让我的全部视觉丧失。[③] 最近的病理年报似乎提供了这样一些病例。[④] 与此同时,也存在

---

① 《心理失明》等,第 51 页以后。在这个女人的病例中心理失明是中等程度的

② 《精神病学文集》,第 21 卷,第 222 页。

③ 诺斯内格尔(在上述引文中的第 22 页)说:“但这却不符合实际情况。”然而,他没有给出任何实例支持他的观点,即两侧皮层的损伤可以让人全盲,并且还不会破坏人的视觉意象;因此我不知道是否它来自于对事实的观察,还是一种先天的假设。

④ 在由 C.S. 弗罗因德发表的一个病例中(《精神病学文库》,第 20 卷),两侧的枕叶都损伤了,但他们的皮层没有损伤。视觉依然存在。参见第 291 ~ 295 页。

a number of cases of mental blindness, especially for written language, coupled with hemianopsia, usually of the rightward field of view. These are all explicable by the breaking down, through disease, of the *connecting tracts* between the occipital lobes and other parts of the brain, especially those which go to the centres for speech in the frontal and temporal regions of the left hemisphere. They are to be classed among disturbances of *conduction* or of *association*; and nowhere can I find any fact which should force us to believe that optical images need① be lost in mental blindness, or that the cerebral centres for such images are locally distinct from those for direct sensations from the eyes. ②

Where an object fails to be recognized by sight, it often happens that the patient will recognize and name it as soon as he touches it with his hand. This shows in an interesting way how numerous the associative paths are which all end by running out of the brain through the channel of speech. The hand-path is open, though the eye-path be closed. When mental blindness is most complete, neither sight, touch, nor sound avails to steer the patient, and a sort of dementia which has been called *asymbolia* or *apraxia* is the result.

---

① I say ' need,' for do not of course deny the *possible* coexistence of the two symptoms. Many a brain – lesion might block optical associations and at the same time impair optical imagination, without entirely stopping vision. Such a case seems to have been the remarkable one from Charcot which I shall give rather fully in the chapter on Imagination.

② Freund (in the article cited above ' Ueber optische Aphasie und Seelenblindheit') and Bruns(' Ein Fall von Alexie. ' etc, in the Neuro – logisches Centralblatt for 1888, pp. 581, 509) explain their cases by broken – down conduction. Wilbrand, whose, painstaking monograph on mental blindness was referred to a moment ago, gives none but *a priori* reasons for his belief that the optical' Erinnerungsfeld' must be locally distinct from the Wahrnehmungsfeld (cf. pp. 84, 93). The *a priori* reasons are really the other way. Mauthner(' Gehim u. Auge' (1881), p. 487 ff.) tries to show that the ' mental blindness' of Munk's dogs and apes after occipital mutilation was not such, but real dimness of sight. The best case of mental blindness yet reported is that by Lissauer, as above. The reader will also do well to read Bernard: De l' Aphasie (1885) chap, v; Ballet: Le Langage Intérieur (1886), chap, VIII; and Jas. Ross's little book on Aphasia (1887), p. 74.

着一些心理失明的病例，特别是对阅读语言的心理失明，它们同偏盲相伴随发生，而且通常是同视觉右侧领域的偏盲相伴随发生。由于疾病而导致的枕叶和大脑其他部分之间的联系束的断裂，尤其是那些通向大脑左半球额颞区域的语言中枢的束的断裂，可以完全作为这些情况的解释。它们可被归入传导和联想障碍一类；而且我在那里也找不到任何事实可以迫使我们承认在心理失明中视觉意象需要丧失，[①]或者承认负责这种意象的大脑中枢在位置上与负责来自眼睛的直接感觉的中枢是截然不同的。[②]

当眼睛不能认出一个对象时，通常会发生的情况是患者一用他的手触摸它，就会认出它并叫出它的名字。这就以一种非常有趣的方式表明，以通过言语的路线从大脑中出来为全部终点的联想路径是怎样的众多。虽然眼睛的联想路径关闭了，但手的联想路径还开着。当心理失明最彻底时，视觉、触觉和听觉都不利于引导患者，而且结果是出现一种被称之为失示意能或说精神性失用

---

① 我说“需要”是因为我当然不否认这两种症状可能共存。很多大脑的损伤可以阻碍视觉联想，并与此同时削弱视觉想像力，而且还没有完全失去视觉。这样的情况出现在来自夏尔科的一个显著病例中，我将在关于想像力的那一章里更充分地对它加以说明。

② 弗罗因德（在前面引用的文章“视觉失语症与心理失明”中）和布伦斯（“一个失读症病例”等，在1888年的《神经病学中心报》，第581～509中）通过传导故障来解释它们的病例。威尔布兰德（他关于心理失明的艰辛专论刚刚被提到过）关于他的视觉“记忆区”和感觉区在位置上必须是不同的这一信仰仅仅给出了先天的理由（参见第84、93页）。这些先天的理由实际上不对路。模特纳（《大脑与眼睛》，1881年，第487页以后）试图表明，芒克的狗和猩猩在枕叶切除之后而出现的“心理失明”不是如此，而是视觉的真正模糊。已经报告的视觉失明的最好病例是由利索尔提供的，如上述。读者还可以阅读伯纳德：《失语症》（1885），第5章；巴利特：《内部语言》，（1886），第8章；以及詹姆斯·罗斯关于失语症的小书（1887），第74页。

The commonest articles are not understood. The patient will put his breeches on one shoulder and his hat upon the other, will bite into the soap and lay his shoes on the table, or take his food into his hand and throw it down again, not knowing what to do with it, etc. Such disorder can only come from extensive brain-injury. ①

The *method of degeneration* corroborates the other evidence localizing the tracts of vision. In young animals one gets secondary degeneration of the occipital regions from destroying an eyeball, and, *vice versa*, degeneration of the optic nerves from destroying the occipital regions. The corpora geniculata, thalami, and subcortical fibres leading to the occipital lobes are also found atrophied, in these cases. The phenomena are not uniform, but are indisputable②; so that, taking all lines of evidence together, the special connection of vision with the occipital lobes is perfectly made out. It should be added that the occipital lobes have frequently been found shrunken in cases of inveterate blindness in man.

Hearing.

Hearing is hardly as definitely localized as sight. *In the dog*, Luciani's diagram will show the regions which directly or indirectly affect it for the worse when injured. As with sight, one-sided lesions produce symptoms on both sides. The mixture of black dots and gray dots in the diagram is meant to represent this mixture of 'crossed' and 'uncrossed' connections, though of course no topographical exactitude is aimed at. Of all the region, the temporal lobe is the most important part; yet permanent absolute deafness did not result in a dog of Luciani's,

---

① For a case see Wernicke's Lehrb. d. Gehirnkrankheiten, vol. II. p. 554(1881).

② The latest account of them is the paper 'über die optischen Centren u. Bahnen' by von Monakow in the Archiv für Psychiatrie, vol. XX. p. 714.

症的痴呆。他连最简单的文章也不能理解。病人会将他的马裤搭在一个肩上,将他的帽子搭在另一个肩上,他会去咬肥皂并且把他的鞋放在桌子上,或者把他的食物放在手里并且再次把它扔下,不知道拿它来做什么,等等。这样的失控只能来自于大脑的大面积损伤。①

退化方法巩固了定位视觉束的其他证据。在年幼的动物那里,它们会由于一个眼球的损伤而产生枕部区域的次级退化,而且,反之亦然,由于损坏了枕部区域会造成视神经的退化。在这些病例中,发现通向枕叶的膝状体、丘脑和皮层下纤维也萎缩了。现象虽不统一,但无争论之余地;②那么,将各类证据都集中在一起,枕叶和视觉的特殊联系就完全被了解了。还要补充的是,在人的长期失明的病例中,通常发现枕叶也萎缩了。

听　觉

对听觉的定位不如视觉那样明确。在狗那里,卢西亚尼的图示展示了当其受损时会直接地或者间接地引起听觉的恶化的区域。和视觉一样,一侧的损伤会产生两侧的症状。在图中灰点和黑点的混合是有意要再现出"交叉的"和"非交叉的"连接的混合,尽管这样做的目的当然不是为了局部解剖图的精确性起见。在所有的区域中,颞叶是最重要的部分;然而,在卢西亚尼的一只狗

① 病例见威尔尼克的《大脑疾病教程》(1881 年),第 2 卷,第 554 页。

② 有关它们的最新讨论见冯莫纳科的论文"论视觉中枢与通道",《精神病学文集》,第 20 卷,第 714 页。

even from bilateral destruction of both temporal lobes in their entirety ①.

In the monkey, Ferrier and Yeo once found permanent deafness to follow destruction of the upper temporal convolution (the one just below the fissure of Sylvius in Fig. 6) on both sides.

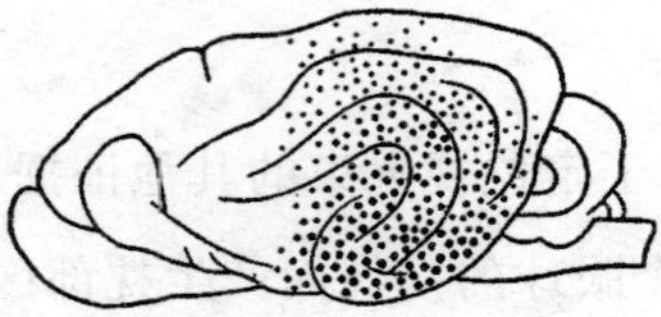

FIG. 16. —Luciani's Hearing Region.

Brown and Schaefer found, on the contrary, that in several monkeys this operation failed to noticeably affect the hearing. In one animal, indeed, both entire temporal lobes were destroyed. After a week or two of depression of the mental faculties this beast recovered and became one of the brightest monkeys possible, domineering over all his mates, and admitted by all who saw him to have all his senses, including hearing, 'perfectly acute.'② Terrible recriminations have, as usual, ensued between the investigators, Ferrier denying that Brown and Schaefer's ablations were complete,③ Schaefer that Ferrier's monkey was really deaf.④ In this unsatisfactory condition the subject must be left, although there seems no reason to doubt that Brown and Schaefer's observation is the more important of the two.

In man the temporal lobe is unquestionably the seat of the hearing function, and the superior convolution adjacent to the sylvian fissure is its most important part. The phenomena of aphasia show this. We studied motor aphasia a few pages back; we must now consider *sensory aphasia*.

---

① Die Functions - Localization, etc. Dog X; see also p. 161.

② Philos. Trans., vol. 179, p. 312.

③ Brain, vol. XI. p. 10.

④ *Ibid.* p. 147.

那里,甚至是两边颞叶的完全损伤,也没有导致绝对的永久性失聪。①

在猴子那里,费里尔和约一度发现,永久性失聪会随着两侧颞上回(刚好位于图6中西耳维厄斯沟的下部)的损伤而出现。

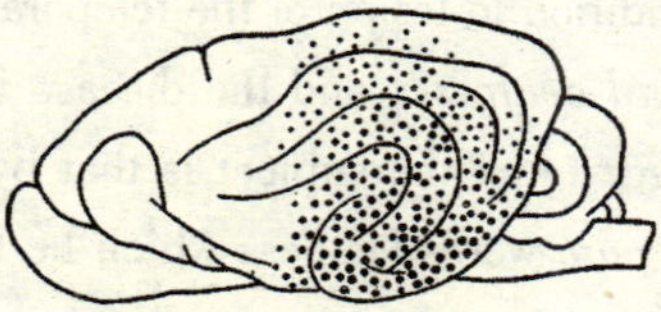

图16　卢西亚尼的听觉区域

相反,布朗和谢弗发现,对几只猴子做的这种手术不能显著地影响听力。确实,在一只猴子身上,它的两个完整的颞叶都被破坏掉了。在一到两周的心理能力衰退之后,这只动物恢复了,并且变成了可能是最聪明的猴子,它对它的所有配偶横行霸道,而且所有看到它的人都承认它的所有感官都"很敏锐",包括听力。② 和通常一样,糟糕的反责在调查者之间随即出现。费里尔否认布朗和谢弗的切除是完全的,③谢弗否认费里尔的猴子是真的聋了。④ 在这种令人不满意的情况下,问题只有被搁置起来,尽管这里似乎没有理由怀疑布朗和谢弗的观察在两者中更重要。

在人这里,颞叶毫无疑问是听觉功能的处所,而且邻近希尔维安沟的上回是其最重要的部分。失语症现象表明了这一点。我们在前边几页研究了运动失语症;我们现在必须考虑感觉失语

---

① 《功能定位》等,狗10;也可参见第161页。

② 《哲学学报》,第179卷,第321页。

③ 《大脑》,第11卷,第10页。

④ 同上,第147页。

Our knowledge of this disease has had three stages: we may talk of the period of Broca, the period of Wernicke, and the period of Charcot What Broca's discovery was we have seen. Wernicke was the first to discriminate those cases in which the patient can *not even understand* speech from those in which he can understand, only not talk; and to ascribe the former condition to lesion of the temporal lobe. ① The condition in question is *word-deafness*, and the disease is *auditory aphasia.* The latest statistical survey of the subject is that by Dr. Allen Starr, ② In the seven cases of *pure* word-deafness which he has collected, cases in which the patient could read, talk, and write, but not understand what was said to him, the lesion was limited to the first and second temporal convolutions in their posterior two thirds. The lesion (in right-handed, i. e. left-brained, persons) is always on the left side, like the lesion in motor aphasia. Crude hearing would not be abolished, even were the left centre for it utterly destroyed; the right centre would still provide for that. But the *linguistic use* of hearing appears bound up with the integrity of the left centre more or less exclusively. Here it must be that words heard enter into association with the things which they represent, on the one hand, and with the movements necessary for pronouncing them, on the other. In a large majority of Dr. Starr's fifty cases, the power either to name objects or to talk coherently was impaired. This shows that in most of us (as Wernicke said) speech must go on from auditory cues; that is, it must be that our ideas do not innervate our motor centres directly, but only after first arousing the mental sound of the words. This is the immediate stimulus to articulation; and where the possibility of this is abolished by the destruction of its usual channel in the left temporal lobe, the articulation must suffer. In the few cases in which the channel is abolished

① Der aphasische Symptomencomplex (1874). See in Fig. 11 the convolution marked Wernicke.

② 'The Pathology of Sensory Aphasia,' 'Brain,' July, 1889.

症。我们关于这一疾病的知识经历了三个阶段：我们将讨论布罗卡阶段、韦尔尼克阶段和夏尔科阶段。我们已经了解了布罗卡的发现是什么。韦尔尼克第一个区分出患者甚至不能听懂说话的病例和患者能听懂说话但只是不能说话的病例；他把前一种情况归因于颞叶的损伤。① 前一种情况是词聋，这种疾病是听觉失语症。关于这个问题的最近的统计调查是由艾伦·斯塔尔博士提供的。② 在他收集的七个纯粹的词聋病例中，病人可以读、说和写，但是不能听懂对他所说的话，损伤局限在第一和第二颞回后面的三分之二处。损伤（在习惯用右手的人那里，即左脑发达的人那里）总是在左边，像运动失语症的损伤一样。天生的听觉不会丧失，即使是左边控制它的中枢被完全损坏了；右侧中枢依然提供这种功能。但是听觉在语言的使用上或多或少专有地和左侧中枢的完整性紧密地联系在一起。这里的情况一定是这样，听到的语言一方面和它们所象征的事物联系在一起，另一方面，和为了发出它们的必要的动作联系在一起。在斯塔尔博士的 50 个病例的大部分病例中，叫出对象的名字和连贯谈话的能力都被削弱了。这种情况表明在我们大多数人中（如韦尔尼克所说），说话必须通过听觉的刺激才能进行；也就是说，情况一定是我们的观念不直接对我们的运动中枢进行神经支配，而是在先引起语言的心理声音之后才对运动中枢进行神经支配。这是对发音的直接刺激；若左颞叶中往常的通道被破坏，这种可能就没有了，发音必然受损。在一些病例中，通道被取消了，但对说话没有造成不良

① 《失语症综合症》（1874 年）。见图 11 标示为韦尔尼克的脑回。

② “感觉失语症病理学”，《大脑》，1889 年 7 月。

with no bad effect on speech we must suppose an idiosyncrasy. The patient must innervate his speech-organs either from the corresponding portion of the other hemisphere or directly from the centres of ideation, those, namely, of vision, touch, etc., without leaning on the auditory region. It is the minuter analysis of the facts in the light of such individual differences as these which constitutes Charcot's contribution, towards clearing up the subject.

Every namable thing, act, or relation has numerous properties, qualities, or aspects. In our minds the properties of each thing, together with its name, form an associated group. If different parts of the brain are severally concerned with the several properties, and a farther part with the hearing, and still another with the uttering, of the name, there must inevitably be brought about (through the law of association which we shall later study) such a dynamic connection amongst all these brain-parts that the activity of any one of them will be likely to awaken the activity of all the rest. When we are talking as we think, the *ultimate* process is that of utterance. If the brain-part for *that* be injured, speech is impossible or disorderly, even though all the other brain-parts be intact: and this is just the condition of things which, on page 37, we found to be brought about by limited lesion of the left inferior frontal convolution. But back of that last act various orders of succession are possible in the associations of a talking man's ideas. The more usual order seems to be from the tactile, visual, or other properties of the things thought-about to the sound of their names, and then to the latter's utterance. But if in a certain individual the thought of the *look* of an object or of the *look* of its printed name be the process which habitually precedes articulation, then the loss of the *hearing* centre will *pro tanto* not affect that individual's speech. He will be mentally deaf, i. e. his *understanding* of speech will suffer, but he will not be aphasic. In this way it is possible to explain the seven cases of *pure* word-deafness which figure in. Dr. Starr's table.

影响,我们必须假定它们是一种特异性。患者肯定要么是从另一个大脑半球的相应部分,要么直接从观念中枢,即视觉中枢、触觉中枢等,对他的语言器官进行神经支配,而没有依靠听觉区域。正是基于这样一些个体差异而对事实所做的详细分析,构成了夏尔科为澄清这一问题所做的贡献。

所有可指明的事物、动作或关系都有众多的属性、性质或方面。在我们心中,每一个事物的属性同它的名称一起构成了一个联想群。如果大脑的不同部分分别和几个属性有关,另外一部分和听觉有关,还有一部分和名称的发声有关,那么在所有这些大脑的不同部分中就一定会不可避免地(通过我们将在后面研究的联想律)产生这样一种动态联系,以至于它们中任何一部分的活动都有可能唤起所有其余部分的活动。当我们一边思考一边谈话时,最终的步骤就是发声这一步骤。如果负责这一步骤的大脑部分受损了,讲话是不可能的或混乱的,尽管大脑的其他部分是完整的:这就是我们发现由于左额下回的有限损伤而造成的事态(见 37 页)的情况。但是,在最后那个动作之前,各种相继次序在谈话人的观念联想中都是可能出现的。比较正常的次序似乎是从所想事物的视觉的、触觉的、或其他方面的属性到它们名称的声音,然后再到最后的发声。但是,如果在某一个体那里对一个对象外表的思考或者它的印刷出来的名称的思考是习惯性地先于发声的步骤,那么听觉中枢的丧失在此范围之内就不会影响个体的讲话。它将是心理失聪的,也即他理解讲话会有困难,但他不会患失语症。通过这样的方法就有可能解释在斯塔尔博士的表格中所描述的七个纯粹的词聋病例了。

If this order of association be ingrained and habitual in that individual, injury to his visual centres will make him not only word-blind, bat aphasic as well. His speech will become confused in consequence of an occipital lesion. Naunyn, consequently, plotting out on a diagram of the hemisphere the 71 irreproachably reported cases of aphasia which he was able to collect, finds that the lesions concentrate themselves in three places: first, on Broca's centre; second, on Wernicke's; third, on the supra-marginal and angular gyri under which those fibres pass which connect the visual centres with the rest of the brain[1] (see Fig. 17). With this result Dr. Starr's analysis of purely sensory cases agrees.

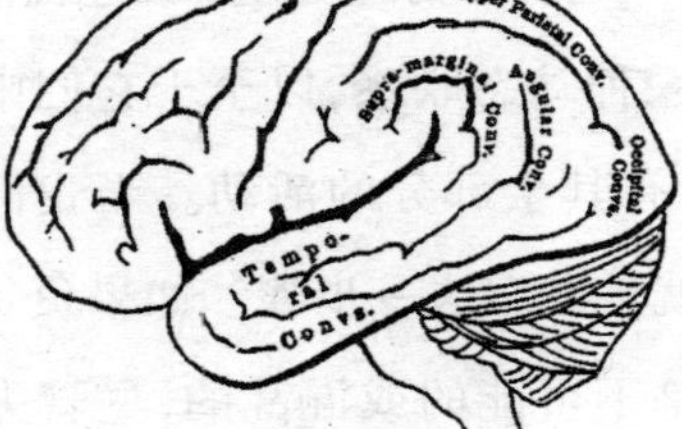

FIG. 17.

In a later chapter we shall again return to these differences in the effectiveness of the sensory spheres in different individuals. Meanwhile few things show more beautifully than the history of our knowledge of aphasia how the sagacity and patience of many banded workers are in time certain to analyze the darkest confusion into an orderly display.[2] There is no 'centre of Speech' in the brain any more than there is a faculty of Speech in the mind. The entire

① Nothnagel and Naunyn; *op. cit*, plates.

② Ballet's and Bernard's works cited on p. 51 are the most accessible documents of Charcot's school. Bastian's book on the Brain as an Organ of Mind (last three chapters) is also good.

如果这种联想次序在那个个体中是根深蒂固的，而且是习惯性的，对他视觉中枢的损伤将不仅使他成为词盲，而且也会使他患有失语症。枕部损伤的结果是他的语言变得混乱了。因此，农因在一个大脑半球的图示上标出了他能够收集到的71个失语症病例的无过失报告，发现损伤集中在三个部位：首先，在布罗卡中枢；其次，在韦尔尼克中枢；第三，在缘上回和角回，那些将视觉中枢和大脑其余部分连接起来的纤维从这下面通过（见图17）。[①]斯塔尔博士对纯粹的感觉病例的分析与这一结果相一致。

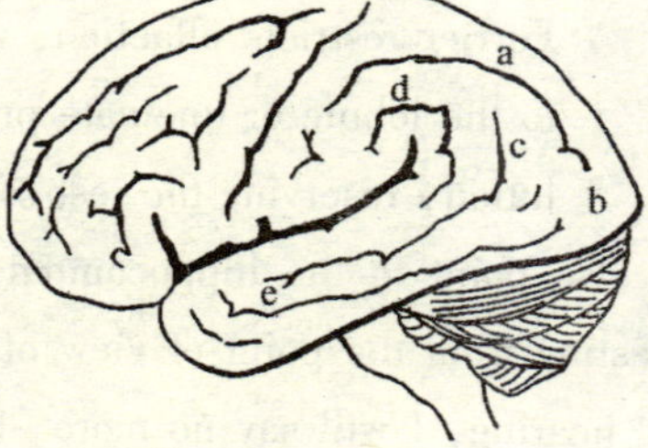

图17

a. 顶上回。b. 枕回。c. 角回。d. 缘上回。e. 颞回。

在后面的章节中，我们将再次回到那些在不同个体中的感觉半球的效力差异上来。同时，几乎没有什么能够比失语症的认知史更美好地表明，众多被蒙着双眼的工作者的睿智与耐心是如何及时地保证了将最隐讳的混乱分析成了有序的程式。[②] 正如同大脑中不存在讲话官能一样，大脑中不存在“讲话中枢”。在一个使

① 诺斯内格尔和农因；见前面所引用的书中的插图。

② 前面在51页引用的巴利特和伯纳德的著作是最容易获得的关于夏尔科学派的文献。巴斯琴的《作为心灵器官的大脑》这本书（最后三章）也不错。

brain, more or less, is at work in a man who uses language. The subjoined diagram, from Ross, shows the four parts most critically concerned, and, in the light of our text, needs no farther explanation (see Fig. 18).

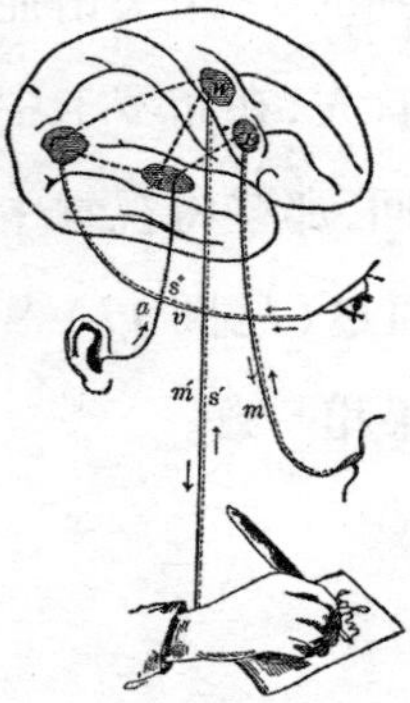

FIG. 18.

Smell.

Everything conspires to point to the median descending part of the temporal lobes as being the organs of smell. Even Ferrier and Munk agree on the hippocampal gyrus, though Ferrier restricts olfaction, as Munk does not, to the lobule or uncinate process of the convolution, reserving the rest of it for touch, Anatomy and pathology also point to the hippocampal gyrus; but as the matter is less interesting from the point of view of human psychology than were sight and hearing, I will say no more, but simply add Luciani and Seppili's diagram of the dog's smell-centre. ①

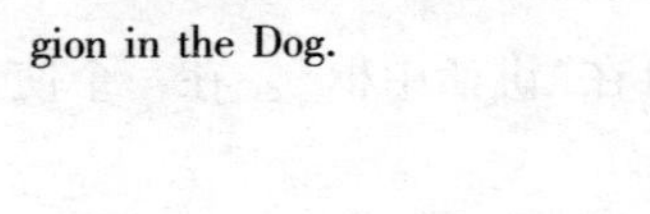

FIG 19.—Luciani's Olfactory Region in the Dog.

Taste.

Of we know little that is definite. What little there is points to the lower temporal regions again. Consult Ferrier as below.

① For details, see Ferrier's 'Functions, chap, IX pt. lll, and Chas. K. Mills: Transactions of Congress of American Physicians and Surgeons, 1888, vol. I. p. 278.

用语言的人身上，整个大脑或多或少地在工作着。来自罗斯的附图表明了最为关键的四个相关部分，而且，鉴于本文的考虑，不需要对它做进一步地解释了。（见图18）。

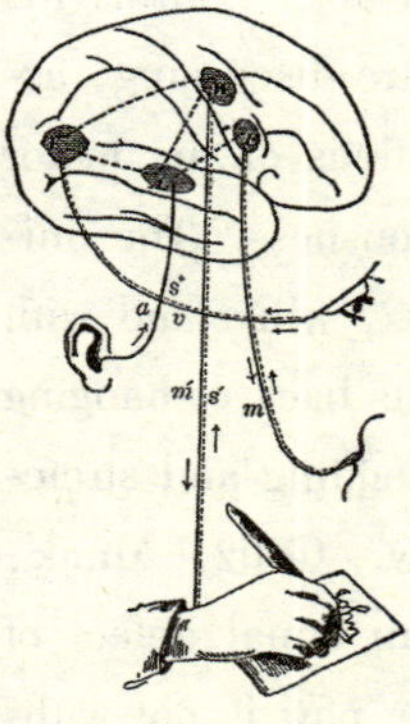

图 18

嗅 觉

所有的观察都凑合起来指向颞叶中间向下的部分，将之作为嗅觉的器官。甚至费里尔和芒克都对海马回持有一致意见，尽管和芒克有所不同，费里尔将嗅觉局限在海马回的小叶或者钩的突起上，将其余部分保留给了触觉。解剖学和病理学也指向了海马回；但是由于从人类心理学的观点来看这一问题没有视觉和听觉那么有趣，我就不再多言了，只是附加上卢西亚尼和塞皮里关于狗的味觉中枢的图示（见图19）。[①]

图 19　卢西亚尼的狗的嗅觉区域

味 觉

关于味觉我们所知道的确定的东西很少。所知道的那一点点东西也再次指向了靠下的颞部区域。可参考下述费里尔的内容。

① 详细内容可参见费里尔的《功能》，第9章，第3部分，以及C. K. 米尔斯：《美国内科医生和外科医生协会学报》，1888年，第1卷，第278页。

Touch.

Interesting problems arise with regard to the seat of tactile and muscular sensibility. Hitzig, whose experiments on *dogs' brains* fifteen years ago opened the entire subject which we are discussing, ascribed the disorders of motility observed after ablations of the motor region to a loss of what he called muscular consciousness. The animals do not notice eccentric positions of their limbs, will stand with their legs crossed, with the affected paw resting on its back or hanging over a table's edge, etc.; and do not resist our bending and stretching of it as they resist with the unaffected paw. Goltz, Munk, Schiff, Herzen, and others promptly ascertained an equal defect of cutaneous sensibility to pain, touch, and cold. The paw is not withdrawn when pinched, remains standing in cold water, etc. Ferrier meanwhile denied that there was any true anæsthesia produced by ablations in the motor zone, and explains the appearance of it as an effect of the sluggish motor responses of the affected side.① Munk② and Schiff③, on the contrary, conceive of the 'motor zone' as essentially sensory, and in different ways explain the motor disorders as secondary results of the anæsthesia which is always there. Munk calls the motor zone the Fühlsphäre of the animal's limbs, etc., and makes it coördinate with the Sehsphäre, the Hörsphäre, etc., the entire cortex being, according to him, nothing but a projection-surface for sensations, with no exclusively or essentially motor part. Such a view would be important if true, through its bearings on the psychology of volition.

---

① Functions of the Brain, chap. X. § 14.

② Ueber die Functionen d. Grosshirnrinde (1881), p. 50

③ Lezioni di Fisiologia sperimentale sul sistema nervoso encefalico (1873), p. 527ff. Also 'Brain,' vol. IX. p. 298.

触 觉

当我们思考触觉和肌肉感受性的处所时,有趣的问题就出现了。我们现在所讨论的整个题目都肇始于希齐格在15年前对狗的大脑所做的实验,他将运动区域切除后而观察到的运动混乱归因于他所称作的肌肉意识的丧失。那些动物不能注意到它们四肢的古怪位置,将它们的腿交叉起来站立着,让受到影响的爪子靠在它的背上休息,或者将它搭在桌子的边上,等等;并且我们弯曲和拉直那只爪子它们也不反抗,只是我们对未受影响的爪子这样做时,它们才会反抗。戈尔茨、芒克、希夫等人很快探知,对疼痛、触碰和寒冷的皮肤感受性也出现了相同的缺失。受到影响的爪子当被夹住时不会缩回来,一直站在冷水里,等等。同时,费里尔否认了在运动区域进行的切除会产生任何真正的感觉缺失,并且将这种现象解释为受影响一侧的迟缓的运动反应的结果。[①] 相反,芒克[②]和希夫[③]认为运动区域本质上是感觉的,并且用不同的方式将运动失序解释为一直存在的感觉缺失的次级结果。芒克将运动区域称为动物四肢等等的触觉区域,并且让它和视觉区域与听觉区域等等相并列,按照他的观点,整个皮层都是感觉的一块投射表面,没有专门的和本质上的运动部分。这样的观点如果是真的,它会很重要,因为它关涉到意志心理学。什么是真的

① 《大脑的功能》,第10章,第14节。

② 《论大脑皮层的功能》(1881年),第50页。

③ 《大脑神经系统实验生理学教程》(1873年),第527页以后。还有《大脑》,第9卷,第298页。

What is the truth? As regards the fact of cutaneous anæsthesia from motor-zone ablations, all other observers are against Ferrier, so that he is probably wrong in denying it. On the other hand, Munk and Schiff are wrong in making the motor symptoms *depend* on the anæsthesia, for in certain rare cases they have been observed to exist not only without insensibility, but with actual hyperæsthesia of the parts.① The motor and sensory symptoms seem, therefore, to be independent variables.

In monkeys the latest experiments are those of Horsley and Schaefer,② whose results Ferrier accepts. They find that excision of the hippocampal convolution produces transient insensibility of the opposite side of the body, and that permanent insensibility is produced by destruction of its continuation upwards above the corpus callosum, the so-called *gyrus fornicatus* (the part just below the 'calloso-marginal fissure' in Fig. 7). The insensibility is at its maximum when the entire tract comprising both convolutions is destroyed. Ferrier says that the sensibility of monkeys is 'entirely unaffected' by ablations of the motor zone,③ and Horsley and Schaefer consider it by no means necessarily abolished.④ Luciani found it diminished in his three experiments on apes.⑤

---

① Bechterew (Pflüger's Archiv., vol, 35, p. 137) found *no* anæsthesia in a cat with motor symptoms from ablation of sigmoid gyrus. Luciani got hyperæsthesia coexistent with cortical motor defect in a dog, by simultaneously hemisecting the spinal cord (Lucianiu. Seppili, *op. cit.* p. 234). Goltz frequently found hyperæsthesia of the whole body to accompany motor defect after ablation of both frontal lobes, and he once found it after ablating the motor zone (Pflüger's Archiv, vol. 34, p. 471).

② Philos. Transactions, vol. 179, p. 20 ff.

③ Functions, p. 375.

④ Pp. 15–17.

⑤ Luciani u. Seppili, *op. cit.* pp. 275–288.

呢？就运动区域的切除而导致的皮肤感觉缺失的事实而言，所有其他的观察者都反对费里尔，以致他对这一事实的否认可能是错误的。另一方面，芒克和希夫将那些运动症状依赖于感觉缺失也是错误的，因为在某些罕见的例子中，它们被观察到不仅没有和感受性缺失共存，而是和一些部位的感觉过敏共存。① 因此，运动和感觉的症状似乎是独立的变量。

在猴子那里，最近的实验是霍斯利和谢弗所做的实验，②费里尔认可他们的实验结果。他们发现，对海马回的切除产生了相反一侧身体的短暂的感受性缺失，而破坏其向上至胼胝体以上的延续部分，即所谓的穹隆状回（在图 7 中恰好在“胼胝体额上沟”之下的那一部分），则会产生永久的感受性缺失。当包含两个脑回的整个区域都被损坏时，感受性缺失就达到了最大的限度。费里尔说运动区域的切除“完全不影响”猴子的感受性，③而霍斯利和谢弗认为这种情况的出现绝不是必要的切除所致。④ 卢西亚尼在他对三个猩猩做的实验中发现这种情况被削弱了。⑤

---

① 贝克特莱尔（《弗吕格文集》，第 35 卷，第 137 页）在一只由于乙状回的切除而出现运动症状的猫身上发现没有感觉缺乏出现。卢西亚尼在一只狗身上观察到，通过同时将脊髓对半切开而导致的皮层运动缺陷与感觉过敏共存（卢西亚尼和塞皮里，在前面引用的书中，第 234 页）。戈尔茨经常发现双额叶切除之后运动缺陷伴随有整个身体的感觉过敏，而且他有一次发现这种情况出现在运动区域切除之后（《弗吕格文集》，第 34 卷，第 471 页）。

② 《哲学学报》，第 179 卷，第 20 页及其后。

③ 《功能》，第 875 页。

④ 第 15 ~ 17 页。

⑤ 卢西亚尼和塞皮里，在前面引用的书中，第 275 ~ 288 页。

In man we have the fact that one-sided paralysis from disease of the opposite motor zone may or may not be accompanied with anæsthesia of the parts.

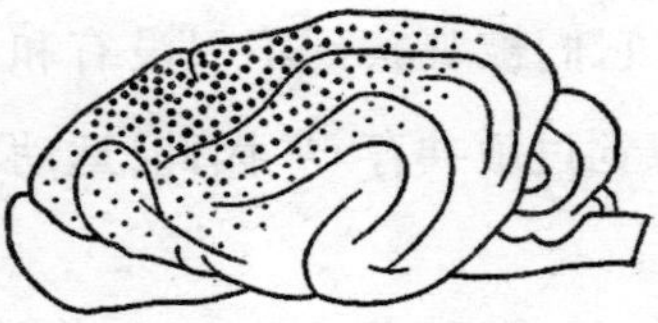

FIG. 20.—Luciani's Tactile Region in the Dog.

Luciani, who believes that the motor zone is also sensory, tries to minimize the value of this evidence by pointing to the insufficiency with which patients are examined He himself believes that in dogs the tactile sphere extends backwards and forwards of the directly excitable region, into the frontal and parietal lobes (see Fig. 20). Nothnagel considers that pathological evidence points in the same direction; ① and Dr. Mills, carefully reviewing the evidence, adds the gyri fornicatus and hippocampi to the cutaneo-muscular region in man. ② If one compare Luciani's diagrams together (Figs. 14, 16, 19, 20) one will see that the entire parietal region of the dog's skull is common to the four senses of sight, hearing, smell, and touch, including muscular feeling. The corresponding region in the human brain (upper parietal and supra-marginal gyri—see Fig. 17, p. 56) seems to be a somewhat similar place of conflux. Optical aphasias and motor and tactile disturbances all result from its injury, especially when that is on the left side. ③The lower we go in the animal scale the less differentiated the functions of the several brain-parts seem to be. ④ It may be that the region in question still represents in ourselves something like this primitive condition, and that the surrounding parts, in adapting themselves more and more to specialized and narrow functions,

① *Op. cit.* p. 18.

② Trans, of Congress, etc, p. 272.

③ See Exner's Unters. üb. Localization, plate XXV.

④ Cf. Ferrier's Functions, etc., chap. IV and chap. X, §§ 6 to 9.

在人这里我们获有这样的事实，即由于相反一侧运动区域的疾病而造成的身体一侧的瘫痪，可能会伴有，也可能不会伴有瘫痪一侧的感觉缺失。

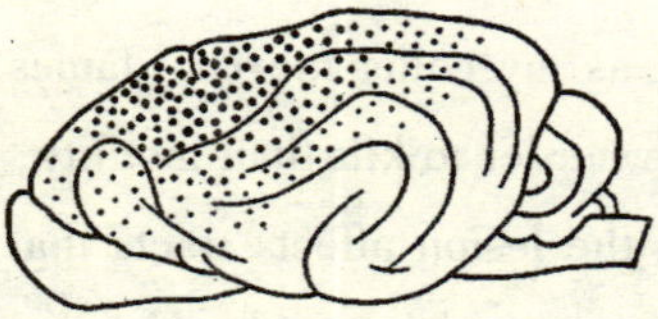

图 20　卢西亚尼的狗的嗅觉区域

卢西亚尼认为运动区域也是感觉的，他试图以指出病人的检查不充分为由将这一证据的价值减到最低。他自己认为狗的触觉区域从直接能被刺激的区域向后和向前伸展直至额叶和顶叶（见图 20）。诺斯内格尔认为病理证据指向了同一方向；[1]米尔斯博士仔细地回顾了这一证据，在人的皮肤－肌肉区域上又补充进了穹隆状回和海马回。[2] 如果我们将卢西亚尼的图示搁在一起做比较（图 14、16、19、20），我们将会看到，狗脑的整个顶部区域为视觉、听觉、嗅觉和触觉以及肌肉感觉等所共有。在人脑中的相应区域（顶上回和缘上回——见图 17，56 页）似乎是有些相似的汇流之地。视觉失语症以及运动和触觉障碍都是由于它的损伤所致，尤其当损伤发生在左侧时情况更是这样。[3] 在动物的等级序列中我们越是往下走，不同大脑部位的功能似乎就分化得越少。[4] 情况似乎是，所讨论的区域在我们自己这里依然代表了像这种原始条件一样的东西，而周围的部分，在使它们自身越来越适应于专门化的和有限的功能中，已经使这

① 前面引用的书中，第 18 页。

② 《协会学报》，第 272 页。

③ 见埃克斯纳的《定位研究》，插图 25。

④ 参见费里尔的《功能》，第 4 章和第 10 章的第 6~9 节。

have left it as a sort of *carrefour* through which they send currents and converse. That it should be connected with musculo-cutaneous feeling is, however, no reason why the motor zone proper should not be so connected too. And the cases of paralysis from the motor zone with no accompanying anæsthesia may be explicable without denying all sensory function to that region. For, as my colleague Dr. James Putnam informs me, sensibility is always harder to kill than motility, even where we know for a certainty that the lesion affects tracts that are both sensory and motor. Persons whose hand is paralyzed in its movements from compression of arm-nerves during sleep, still feel with their fingers; and they may still feel in their feet when their legs are paralyzed by bruising of the spinal cord. In a similar way, the motor cortex might be sensitive as well as motor, and yet by this greater subtlety (or whatever the peculiarity may be) in the sensory currents, the sensibility might survive an amount of injury there by which the motility was destroyed. Nothnagel considers that there are grounds for supposing the *muscular* sense to be exclusively connected with the parietal lobe and not with the motor zone. "Disease of this lobe gives pure ataxy without palsy, and of the motor zone pure palsy without loss of muscular sense."[①] He fails, however, to convince more competent critics than the present writer,[②] so I conclude with them that as yet we have no decisive grounds for locating muscular and cutaneous feeling apart. Much still remains to be learned about the relations between musculo-cutaneous sensibility and the cortex, but one thing is certain: that neither the

---

① *Op. cit.* p. 17.

② E. g. Starr, *loc, cit.* p 272; Leyden, Beiträge zur Lehre v. d. Localization im Gehirn (1888), p. 72.

一区域作为一种交叉路口而存留下来，通过它，它们发送和接受神经流。然而，就它应该同肌肉－皮肤感觉相联系而言，这一点并不成为适当的运动区域不应该也如此相连的原因。因运动区域所致且不伴有感觉缺失的瘫痪病例，可以在不否认对那个区域的所有感觉功能的情况下而得到解释。因为，如我的同事詹姆斯·普特南博士告知我的那样，甚至我们明确地知道损伤影响的区域既是感觉的又是运动的，感受性总是比运动性更加难以破坏。由于在睡觉过程中压迫了臂神经而造成了手臂在运动方面瘫痪的人，依然对他们的手指是有感觉的；当他们的腿部由于脊髓的挫伤而瘫痪时，他们可能依然对他们的脚是有感觉的。同样的道理，运动皮层可能和运动神经一样是有感受性的，而且正是由于在感觉流中的这种更加微妙的精确性（或者无论这种独特性会是什么），感受性才可能在足以破坏运动性的损伤之后，依然存留下来。诺斯内格尔认为这里有假设肌肉感觉只是和顶叶相联系，而没有和运动区域相联系的根据。“这个叶的疾病会引起单纯的供给失调，而没有伴有瘫痪；而且运动区域的疾病会引起单纯的瘫痪，而没有伴有肌肉感觉的丧失。”[①]然而，除了当前的笔者之外，它没有说服更多有力的批评者，[②]因此我和他们一道得出结论，到现在为止我们还没有将肌肉感觉和皮肤感觉分开定位的决定性依据。关于肌肉－皮肤感受性和皮层的关系还有许多地方需要研究，但有一点是确定的：在人身上既不是枕叶与额前叶也不是

---

① 前面引用过的书，第 17 页。

② 例如，斯塔尔，在上述引文中，第 272 页；莱登，《大脑定位原理论文集》（1888 年），第 72 页。

occipital, the forward frontal, nor the temporal lobes seem to have anything essential to do with it in man. It is knit up with the performances of the *motor zone and of the convolutions backwards and midwards of them.* The reader must remember this conclusion when we come to the chapter on the Will.

I must add a word about the connection of aphasia with the tactile sense. On p. 40 I spoke of those cases in which the patient can write but not read his own writing. He cannot read by his eyes; but he can read by the feeling in his fingers, if he retrace the letters in the air. It is convenient for such a patient to have a pen in hand whilst reading in this way, in order to make the usual feeling of writing more complete.[①] In such a case we must suppose that the path between the optical and the graphic centres remains open, whilst that between the optical and the auditory and articulatory centres is closed. Only thus can we understand how the look of the writing should fail to suggest the sound of the words to the patient's mind, whilst it still suggests the proper movements of graphic imitation. These movements in their turn must of course be felt, and the feeling of them must be associated with the centres for hearing and pronouncing the words. The injury in cases like this where very special combinations fail, whilst others go on as usual, must always be supposed to be of the nature of increased resistance to the passage of certain currents of association. If any of the *elements* of mental function were destroyed the incapacity would necessarily be much more formidable. A patient who can both read and write with his fingers most likely uses an identical 'graphic' centre, at once sensory and motor, for both operations.

I have now given, as far as the nature of this book will allow, a complete account of the present state of the localization-question. In its main outlines it stands firm, though much has still to be discovered. The anterior frontal lobes, for example, so far as is yet known, have no definite functions. Goltz finds that dogs bereft of them both are incessantly in motion, and excitable by

① Bernard, *op. cit.* p. 84.

颞叶和它有任何本质的联系。它是同运动区域的活动以及后部与中部脑回的活动紧密联系在一起的。当我们进入意志这一章时,读者一定要记得这一结论。

我必须就失语症和触觉之间的联系再说两句。在40页我谈到的那些病例中,患者只能写出但是不能读出他自己写下的东西。他不能用眼睛阅读;但如果他在空中再描画那些字的话,他能够通过手指的感觉阅读。对患者来说在用这种方法阅读的同时,为了使书写的正常感觉更加完备而在手里拿一支笔的话就会很方便。① 在这样的情况下,我们必须假定,视觉中枢和图描中枢之间的路径是敞开的,同时视觉中枢和听觉中枢与发声中枢之间的路径是关闭的。只有这样我们才能理解笔迹的外表是如何未能对患者的心灵提示出文字的声音,同时又是如何提示出"图描"模仿的恰当动作的。这些动作在其进行中当然一定被感受到了,而且对它们的感受一定和负责听出与说出这些文字的中枢相联系。在这样的病例中,非常专门的连接中断了,而其他的连接正常如故,其损伤必须总是被假定为具有对某些联想流的路径增加阻力的本质。如果心理功能的任何元素被破坏了,无能必定将变得更加厉害。一个能用手指阅读和书写的患者很可能使用着同一个"图描"中枢,对于这两种操作来说,它既是感觉的也是运动的。

就本书的性质所承认的情况来说,现在我要对定位问题的现状做出全面的说明。它在其主要观点的论述方面是稳固的,虽然还有许多内容尚待发现。例如,就目前所知额前叶还没有确定的功能。戈尔茨发现,丧失掉两个额前叶的狗会不停的运动,并且

① 伯纳德,前面引用过的书,第84页。

every small stimulus. They are irascible and amative in an extraordinary degree, and their sides grow bare with perpetual reflex scratching; but they show no *local* troubles of either motion or sensibility. In monkeys not even this lack of inhibitory ability is shown, and neither stimulation nor excision of the prefrontal lobes produces any sympuoms whatever. One monkey of Horsley and Schaefer's was as tame, and did certain tricks as well, after as before the operation. ① It is probable that we have about reached the limits of what can be learned about brain-functions from vivisecting inferior animals, and that we must hereafter look more exclusively to human pathology for light. The existence of separate speech and writing centres in the left hemisphere in man; the fact that palsy from cortical injury is so much more complete and enduring in man and the monkey than in dogs; and the farther fact that it seems more difficult to get complete sensorial blindness from cortical ablations in the lower animals than in man, all show that functions get more specially localized as evolution goes on. In birds localization seems hardly to exist, and in rodents it is much less conspicuous than in carnivora. Even for man, however, Munk's way of mapping out the cortex into absolute areas within which only one movement or sensation is represented is surely false. The truth seems to be rather that, although there is a correspondence of certain regions of the brain to certain regions of the body, yet the several *parts* within each bodily region are represented throughout the *whole* of the corresponding brain-region like pepper and salt sprinkled from the same caster. This, however, does not prevent each 'part' from having its *focus* at one spot within the brain-region. The various brain-regions merge into each other in the same mixed way. As Mr. Horsley says: "There are border centres, and the area of representation of the face merges into that for the representation of the upper limb.

---

① Philos. Trans., vol. 179. p. 3.

易于为非常小的刺激所激发。它们易怒且好色到了不同寻常的程度,而且它们的两侧伴随着永久的反射性挠抓而变得光秃了;但是它们没有显示出运动性或感受性的局部障碍。在猴子身上甚至没有显示出这种抑制能力的缺乏,而且对额前叶的刺激或切除不会产生任何不论是何种的症状。霍斯利和谢弗的一只猴子在手术后和手术前一样驯服,一些小把戏也和以前一样做得不错。① 可能我们通过活体解剖低等动物这种方式已经达到了我们所能获得的关于大脑功能知识的极限,于是今后我们必须更加专注地研究人类的病理学来得到知识了。在人的左半球大脑中单独的说话中枢和书写中枢的存在;由于皮层的损伤而造成的瘫痪在人与猴子身上比在狗身上要更加彻底与持久这一事实,以及由于皮层的切除而导致的彻底的感觉失明在低等动物那里比在人那里更难出现这一事实,都表明随着进化的进行,功能被更加专门地加以定位了。在鸟类中,定位好像几乎不存在,而在啮齿类动物那里,定位不如在食肉动物那里那么显著。然而,即使对人来说,芒克那种将皮层划分成绝对的区域,并且在每一个区域只有一种运动或感觉得以表现的方法当然也是错的。真相似乎是,尽管存在大脑的某些区域与身体的某些区域的对应关系,但是在每个身体区域中的一些部分都是通过整个相应的大脑区域而得以表现的,就像同一个调味瓶中撒出的胡椒和盐一样。然而,这并没有妨碍让每一"部分"在大脑区域中聚焦于一点。各种大脑区域以相同的混合方法各自融合在一起。如霍斯利先生所说:"有边缘中枢存在,并且表现面部的区域和表现上肢

① 《哲学学报》,第179卷,第3页。

If there was a focal lesion at that point, you would have the movements of these two parts starting together."[1] The accompanying figure from Paneth shows just how the matter stands in the dog.[2]

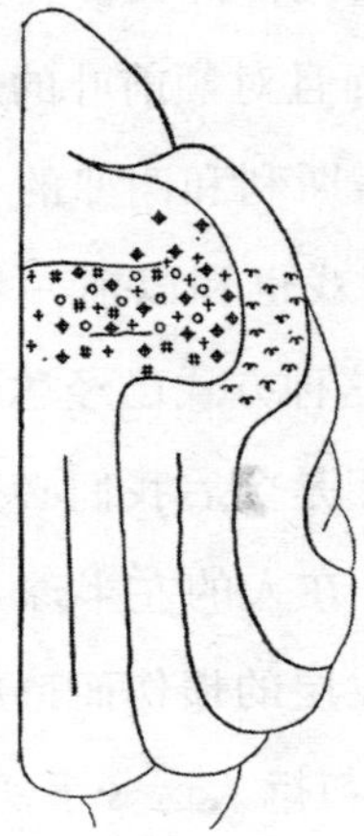

FIG. 21.—Dog's motor centres, right hemisphere, according to Paneth. —The points of the motor region are correlated as follows with muscles: the loops with the *orbicularis palpebrarum*; the *plain crosses* with the *flexor*, the *crosses inscribed in circles* with the *extensor*, *digitorum communis* of the fore-paw; the *plain circles* with the *abductor pollicis longus*; the *double crosses* with the *extensor communis* of the hind-limb.

I am speaking now of localizations breadthwise over the brain-surface. It is conceivable that there might be also localizations depthwise through the cortex. The more superficial cells are smaller, the deepest layer of them is large; and it has been suggested that the superficial cells are sensorial, the deeper ones motor;[3] or that the superficial ones in the motor region are correlated with the extremities of the organs to be moved (fingers, etc.), the deeper ones with the more central segments (wrist, elbow, etc).[4] It need hardly be said that all such theories are as yet but guesses.

We thus see that the postulate of Meynert and Jackson which we started with cn p. 30

① Trans. of Congress of Am. Phys. and Surg. 1888, vol. 1. p. 343. Beevor and Horsley's paper on electric stimulation of the monkey's brain is the most beautiful work yet done for precision. See Phil. Trans., voL 179, p. 205, especially the plates.

② Pflüger's Archiv, Vol. 37, p. 523 (1885).

③ By Luys In his generally preposterous book "The Brain'; also by Horsley.

④ C. Mercier: The Nervous System and the Mind, p. 124.

的区域是融合在一起的。如果在那一点上出现了集中的损伤,你就会让这两个部分的运动一起开始。"[①]来自帕内斯的附图表明了这种情况是如何在狗身上也成立的。[②]

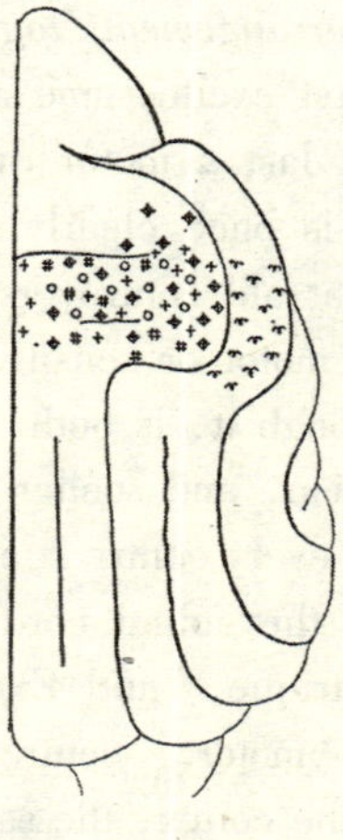

图 21　狗的运动中枢,大脑右半球,依照帕内斯制作

运动区域上的点以下述方式和肌肉相关联:搭环与环状眼睑肌肉相关联;普通的十字形和屈肌相关联;标在圆圈中的十字形和前爪指伸肌相关联;普通的圆圈和拇指展肌相关联;双十字和后肢伸肌相关联。

我现在谈论的是大脑表层的横向定位。可以想像,也可能存在大脑皮层的纵向定位。越是接近表层的细胞就越小,越是深层的细胞就越大;有人指出表层细胞是感觉的,深层细胞是运动的;[③]或者运动区域中的表层细胞和运动器官的末端相关联(手指等),而深层的细胞和较中间的部位相关联(手腕、肘部等)。[④]几乎无需说的是,这些理论到目前为止还都是猜测。

因此,我们看到我们从30页开始讨论的梅纳特和杰克逊的设想,

---

① 《美国内科医师和外科医生学报》,1888 年,第 1 卷,第 343 页。比弗和霍斯利关于对猴子的大脑进行电刺激的论文是迄今为止在精确性方面做得最好的文章。见《哲学学报》,第 179 卷,第 205 页,特别是插图。

② 《弗吕格文集》,第 37 卷,第 523 页(1885 年)

③ 这种观点由卢伊斯在其总体上来说是荒谬的书《大脑》中提出,霍斯利也这么认为。

④ C. 默西埃:《神经系统与心灵》,第 124 页。

is on the whole most satisfactorily corroborated by subsequent objective research. *The highest centres do probably contain nothing but arrangements for representing impressions and movements, and other arrangements for coupling the activity of these arrangements together.* ① Currents pouring in from the sense-organs first excite some arrangements, which in turn excite others, until at last a motor discharge downwards of some sort occurs. When this is once clearly grasped there remains little ground for keeping up that old controversy about the motor zone, as to whether it is in reality motor or sensitive. The whole cortex, in as much as currents run through it, is both. All the currents probably have feelings going with them, and sooner or later bring movements about. In one aspect, then, every centre is afferent, in another efferent, even the motor cells of the spinal cord having these two aspects inseparably conjoined. Marique,② and Exner and Paneth③ have shown that by cutting *round* a 'motor.' centre and so separating it from the influence of the rest of the cortex, the same disorders are produced as by cutting it out, so that really it is only the mouth of the funnel, as it were, through which the stream of innervation, starting from elsewhere, pours; ④ consciousness accompanying the stream, and being mainly of things seen if the stream is strongest occipitally, of things heard if it is strongest temporally, of things felt, etc., if the stream occupies most intensely the 'motor zone.'

---

① The frontal lobes as yet remain a puzzle. Wundt tries to explain them as an organ of 'apperception' (Grundzüge d. Physiologischen Psychologie, 3d ed. vol. l. p. 233 ff), but I confess myself unable to apprehend clearly the Wundtian philosophy so far as this word enters into it, so must be contented with this bare reference. – Until quite recently it was common to talk of an 'ideational centre' as of something distinct from the aggregate of other centres, Fortunately this custom is already on the wane.

② Rech. Exp. sur le Fonctionnement des Centres Psycho – moteurs (Brussels, 1885).

③ Pflüger's Archiv, vol. 44, p. 544.

④ I ought to add, however, that Francois – Franck (Fonctions Motrices, p. 370) got, in two dogs and a cat, a different result from this sort of 'circumvallation.'

在总体上令人满意地被后来的客观研究所确证。最高级的中枢可能只是包含这样一些再现印象和运动的排列，以及用来将这些排列的活动联结起来的其他一些排列。[①] 由感觉器官涌入的神经流最先刺激一些排列，然后这些排列刺激其他排列，直到最后某种向下的运动释放发生。当这一点一旦被清楚地掌握之后，再继续关于运动区域实际是运动的还是有感觉的这一古老的争论，便没有多少根据了。整个皮层，由于所有的神经流从此通过，因而它既是感觉的，也是运动的。所有的神经流可能都伴有感受，并且迟早会引起动作。那么，一方面每一个中枢都是传入的，另一方面它们又都是传出的，甚至脊髓的运动细胞也有不可分离地结合在一起的这两个方面。马克[②]、埃克斯纳和帕内斯[③]已经表明，通过在“运动”中枢周围进行切割，以便让它不受剩余皮层的影响，这样做所引起的紊乱和将它切除所引起的紊乱是一样的，因此可以说，它实际上只是个漏斗口，如其所示，开始于别处的神经支配流从此流过；[④]意识伴随着这流，如果这流在枕部最强，意识就主要是关于所见之物的，如果这流在颞部最强，意识就主要是关于所听之物的，如果这流在“运动区”最强，意识就是关

---

① 额叶现在还是个谜。冯特试图将它们作为“统觉”器官来解释(《生理心理学的基本特征》，第3版，第1卷，第233页以后)，一旦这一术语进入了冯特的哲学，我承认我就不能清楚地领会这种哲学，因此我只能满足于这种泛泛的提及。——直到现在将“观念中枢”作为一种和其他中枢集合不同的东西来谈论都是很普通的，好在这一习惯已经逐渐消逝了。

② 《关于心理动力中枢功能的实验研究》(布鲁塞尔，1885年)。

③ 《弗吕格文集》，第44卷，第544页。

④ 然而，我应该补充一句，弗朗西斯－弗兰克(《驱动功能》，第370页)在两只狗和一只猫身上，通过这种“壁垒化”的方式而得到了不同的结果。

It seems to me that some broad and vague formulation like this is as much as we can safely venture on in the present state of science; and in subsequent chapters I expect to give confirmatory reasons for my view.

Man's Consciousness Limited To The Hemispheres.

But is the consciousness which accompanies the activity of the cortex the only consciousness that man has? Or are his lower centres conscious as well?

This is a difficult question to decide, how difficult one only learns when one discovers that the cortex-consciousness itself of certain objects can be seemingly annihilated in any good hypnotic subject by a bare wave of his operator's hand, and yet be proved by circumstantial evidence to exist all the while in a split-off condition, quite as 'ejective'[①] to the rest of the subject's mind as that mind is to the mind of the bystanders,[②] The lower centres themselves may conceivably all the while have a split-off consciousness of their own, similarly ejective to the cortex-consciousness; but whether they have it or not can never be known from merely introspective evidence. Meanwhile the fact that occipital destruction in man may cause a blindness which is apparently absolute (no feeling remaining either of light or dark over one half of the field of view), would lead us to suppose that if our lower optical centres, the corpora quadrigemina, and thalami,

---

① For this word, see T. K. Clifford's Lectures and Essays (1879), vol. II. p. 72.

② See below, Chapter VIII.

于所触知之物等等这类事物的。似乎对我来说,像这样一些宽泛的且模糊的简洁陈述是我们在目前的科学发展阶段只能如此稳妥尝试的内容;而在后面的章节中,我想就我的观点给出确定的理由。

局限于大脑半球的人的意识

但是,和大脑皮层的活动相伴随的意识是人所具有的唯一意识吗?或者说,他的低级中枢也具有意识吗?

这是一个难以决断的问题,当我们获悉下面所说的情况时,我们就知道这一问题有多么难回答了。我们发现,在任何一个较易被催眠的受试者那里,只要他的医生干练地挥挥手,某一对象的皮层意识自身表面上就被消除掉了,但是皮层意识还被相关证据所证明一直以一种分裂出去的状态存在着,对受试者的心灵的其余部分来说它是“放逐的”,就像受试者的心灵对旁观者来说是“放逐的”[①]一样。[②] 低级中枢自身也可以被想像成一直拥有它们自己的分裂出去的意识,同样,对于皮层意识来说它们是“放逐的”;但是,由于仅仅是通过反省的证据,所以它们是否拥有意识将永远不能被知晓。同时,人的枕部的损伤会引起明显的完全失明(在视野的一半区域之外对光和黑暗仍然没有任何感觉)这一事实,将会导致我们假设,如果我们的低级视觉中枢、四叠

① 关于这个词,参见 T. K. 克利福德的《讲演与论文集》,(1879 年),第 2 卷,第 72 页。

② 参见下面的第 8 章。

do have any consciousness, it is at all events a consciousness which does not mix with that which accompanies the cortical activities, and which has nothing to do with our personal Self. In lower animals this may not be so much the case. The traces of sight found (supra, p. 46) in dogs and monkeys whose occipital lobes were entirely destroyed, may possibly have been due to the fact that the lower centres of these animals saw, and that what they saw was not ejective but objective to the remaining cortex, i. e. it formed part of one and the same inner world with the things which that cortex perceived. It may be, however, that the phenomena were due to the fact that in these animals the cortical 'centres' for vision reach outside of the occipital zone, and that destruction of the latter fails to remove them as completely as in man. This, as we know, is the opinion of the experimenters themselves. For practical purposes, nevertheless, and limiting the meaning of the word consciousness to the personal self of the individual, we can pretty confidently answer the question prefixed to this paragraph by saying that *the cortex is the sole organ of consciousness in man.* ①If there be any consciousness pertaining to the lower centres, it is a consciousness of which the self knows nothing.

The Restitution Of Function.

Another problem, not so metaphysical, remains. The most general and striking fact connected with cortical injury is that of the *restoration of function.* Functions lost at first are after a few days or weeks restored.

---

① Cf. Ferrier's Functions, pp. 120, 147, 414. See also Vulpian: Leçons sur la Physiol. du Syst. Nerveux, p. 548; Lucianiu. Seppili, *op. cit.* pp. 404 – 5; H. Maudsley: Physiology of Mind (1876), pp. 138 ff., 197 ff., and 241 ff. In G. H. Lewes's Physical Basis of Mind, Problem IV: 'The Reflex Theory,' a very full history of the question is given.

体、丘脑的确有一些意识，它必定是和伴随皮层活动的意识不相混合的意识，必定是同我们的个人自我没有关系的意识。在低等动物那里，情况可能不尽如此。在枕叶完全受损的狗和猴子身上发现的视觉迹象（前面第46页）很可能基于这样的事实，即这些动物的低级中枢能看见，并且它们所看到的对于剩下来的皮层来说不是“放逐的”，而是真实的，也就是说，它们所看到的东西和那个皮层所感知的东西一起形成了一个、并且是同一个内部世界的一部分。然而，情况可能是这现象基于这样的事实，即在这些动物身上负责视觉的皮层中枢延伸到了枕部以外，而且对枕部的破坏未有像在人身上一样能将它们完全地去除掉。据我们所知，这是试验者们自己的观点。不过，出于实用的目的，并且为了将意识这一术语的意义局限于个体的个人自我之上，我们能够相当自信地回答在这一段之前的那个问题了：我们认为对人而言皮层是意识的唯一器官。① 如果有任何为低级中枢所固有的意识存在的话，它也是自我对其一无所知的意识。

功能的复原

还存在一个不那么形而上的问题。与大脑皮层的损伤相关联的最普遍的和最令人吃惊的事实是功能复原这一事实。起先丧失的功能在几天或几周之后又恢复了。我们应该如何理解这

① 参见费里尔的《功能》，第120、147、414页。也可参见武尔皮安：《神经系统生理学教程》，第548页；卢西亚尼和塞皮里，前面引用过的书，第404－405页；H. 莫兹利：《心之生理学》（1876年），第138页以后，第197页以后，第241页以后。G. H. 路易斯的《心的物理基础》，问题4："反射理论"，对这一问题的历史做了非常全面的论述。

How are we to understand this restitution ?

Two theories are in the field:

1) Restitution is due to the vicarious action either of the rest of the cortex or of centres lower down, acquiring functions which until then they had not performed;

2) It is due to the remaining centres (whether cortical or 'lower') resuming functions which they had always had, but of which the wound had temporarily inhibited the exercise. This is the view of which Goltz and Brown-Séquard are the most distinguished defenders.

Inhibition is a *vera causa*, of that there can be no doubt. The pneumogastric nerve inhibits the heart, the splanch-nic inhibits the intestinal movements, and the superior laryngeal those of inspiration. The nerve-irritations which may inhibit the contraction of arterioles are innumerable, and reflex actions are often repressed by the simultaneous excitement of other sensory nerves. For all such facts the reader must consult the treatises on physiology. What concerns us here is the inhibition exerted by different parts of tne nerve-centres, when irritated, on the activity of distant parts. The flaccidity of a frog from 'shock,' for a minute or so after his medulla oblongata is cut, is an inhibition from the seat of injury which quickly passes away.

What is known as 'surgical shock' (unconsciousness, pallor, dilatation of splanchnic blood-vessels, and general syncope and collapse) in the human subject is an inhibition which lasts a longer time. Goltz, Freusberg, and others, cutting the spinal cord in dogs, proved that there were functions inhibited still longer by the wound, but which reestablished themselves ultimately if the animal was kept alive. The lumbar region of the cord was thus found to contain independent vaso-motor centres, centres for erection, for control of the sphincters, etc., which could be excited to activity by tactile stimuli and as readily reinhibited by others simultaneously applied. ①

---

① Goltz: Pflüger's Archiv, vol. 8, p. 460; Freusberg: *ibid.* vol. 10, p. 174.

种复原呢?

在这一领域有两种理论:

(1)复原归因于剩余皮层的各种活动或较低级中枢的各种活动,它们获得了直到当时都没有行使过的功能。

(2)复原归因于剩余中枢(不论是皮层的还是"低级的")恢复了它们一直具有的功能,而损伤只是暂时抑制了功能的行使。戈尔茨和布朗-西夸是这一观点的最著名的辩护者。

抑制是真正的原因,对此不可能存在任何疑问。迷走神经抑制心脏,内脏神经抑制肠的运动,而喉上神经抑制呼吸运动。可以抑制细动脉收缩的神经是无数的,而反射活动通常会被其他感觉神经所同时产生的刺激所抑制。对于这些事实,读者必须参考生理学的论著。在这里与我们相关的内容是,当神经中枢的不同部分被刺激时,它就会对远端部位的活动施加抑制。当青蛙的延髓被切除后,由于"休克"而引起的一分钟左右的软弱无力,是一种由损伤之处造成的、很快就会过去的抑制。

当受试者是人时,所谓的"手术休克"(无意识、脸色苍白、内脏血管扩张、以及一般的昏厥和虚脱)是持续较长时间的抑制。戈尔茨、弗罗斯伯格和其他一些人,通过切除狗的脊髓,证明了存在一些功能,它们由于损伤而被抑制的时间更长,但是如果这动物能存活下来的话,这些功能自身最终会复原。脊髓的腰部区域因此被发现包含独立的血管收缩中枢、负责勃起的中枢和负责控制括约肌的中枢等等,这些中枢能够因触觉刺激而兴奋起来进行活动,如同其他同时施加的刺激再次轻易地抑制它们一样。[1]

---

① 戈尔茨:《弗吕格文集》,第 8 卷,第 460 页;弗罗斯伯格:同前,第 10 卷,第 174 页。

We may therefore plausibly suppose that the rapid reappearance of motility, vision, etc., after their first disappearance in consequence of a cortical mutilation, is due to the passing off of inhibitions exerted by the irritated surface of the wound. The only question is whether *all* restorations of function must be explained in this one simple way, or whether some part of them may not be owing to the formation of entirely new paths in the remaining centres, by which they become 'educated' to duties which they did not originally possess. In favor of an indefinite extension of the inhibition theory facts may be cited such as the following: In dogs whose disturbances due to cortical lesion have disappeared, they may in consequence of some inner or outer accident reappear in all their intensify for 24 hours or so and then disappear again. ① In a dog made half blind by an operation, and then shut up in the dark, vision comes back just as quickly as in other similar dogs whose sight is exercised systematically every day. ② A dog which has learned to beg before the operation recommences this practice quite *spontaneously* a week after a double-sided ablation of the motor zone. ③ Occasionally, in a pigeon (or even, it is said, in a dog) we see the disturbances less marked immediately after the operation than they are half an hour later. ④ This would be impossible were they due to the subtraction of the organs which normally carried them on. Moreover the entire drift of recent physiological and pathological speculation is towards enthroning inhibition as an ever-present and indispensable condition of orderly activity. We shall see how great is its importance, in the chapter on the Will. Mr. Charles Mercier considers that no muscular contraction,

---

① Goltz: Verrichtungen des Grosshirns, p. 78

② Loeb: Pflüger's Archiv, VOl. 39, p. 276.

③ Ibid. p. 289.

④ Schrader: *ibid.* vol. 44, p. 218.

因此我们可以似真的假定，运动性、视觉等等在它们最初由于皮层切除而消失后，能够很快地恢复，是因为由受刺激的创伤表面而招致的抑制消除了。唯一的问题是，是否所有的功能恢复必须以这种简单的方式加以解释，或者它们中的一部分是否可以不被归因于在剩余中枢中全新路径的形成，通过这些路径，它们“被训练”得可以承担它们当初并不承担的责任。为了便于抑制理论无明确限制的扩展，一些事实引用如下：在由于皮层损伤而产生的障碍已经消失的狗那里，这些障碍可以因为某些内部或外部的意外事件而以最大的强度再次出现，并持续 24 小时左右，然后再次消失。[①] 一条通过手术而变得半盲、而后被关在黑暗中的狗，它的视觉恢复得与它处境类似、但视觉每天都受系统训练的狗一样快。[②] 一条在手术前已经学会乞求动作的狗，在运动区域双侧切除一周之后，又非常自然地重新开始做这种动作。[③] 偶尔，在鸽子那里（或者，据说甚至在狗那里）我们看到，刚刚做完手术后出现的障碍不如手术后半小时出现的障碍那么明显。[④] 如果这些障碍的产生是因为在正常情况下执行这些功能的器官被去除掉了，这种情况将是不可能出现的。而且，最近生理学和病理学论断的整个走势，是趋向于将抑制作为有序活动的一种始终存在的和不可缺少的条件来加以推崇的。在关于意志的那一章里，我们将会看到它的重要性是何等之大。查尔斯·默西埃先生认为，如果没有它

---

① 戈尔茨：《大脑的日常工作》，第 78 页。

② 洛布：《弗吕格文集》，第 39 卷，第 276 页。

③ 同前，第 289 页。

④ 施拉德：同前，第 44 卷，第 218 页。

once begun, would ever stop without it, short of exhaustion of the system;[①] and Brown-Séquard has for years been accumulating examples to show how far its influence extends.[②] Under these circumstances it seems as if error might more probably lie in curtailing its sphere too much than in stretching it too far as an explanation of the phenomena following cortical lesion.[③]

On the other hand, if we admit *no* re-education of centres, we not only fly in the face of an a *priori* probability, but we find ourselves compelled by facts to suppose an almost incredible number of functions natively lodged in the centres below the *thalami* or even in those below the *corpora quadrigemina.* I will consider the *a priori* objection after first taking a look at the facts which I have in mind. They confront us the moment we ask ourselves just *which are the parts which perform the functions abolished by an operation after sufficient time has elapsed for restoration to occur*?

The first observers thought that they must be the *corresponding parts of the opposite or intact hemisphere.* But as long ago as 1875 Carville and Duret tested this by cutting out the fore-leg-centre on one side, in a dog, and then, after waiting till restitution had occurred, cutting it out on the opposite side as well. Goltz and others have done the same thing.[④] If the opposite side were really the seat of the restored function, the original palsy should

---

① The Nervous System and the Mind (1888), chaps, llI, VI; also in Brain, vol. XI p. 361.

② Brown – Séquard has given a résumé of his opinions in the Archives de Physiologie for Oct. 1889, 5me. Série, vol. I. p. 751.

③ Goltz first applied the inhibition theory to the brain in his ' Verrich – tungen des Grosshirns, ' p. 39 ff. On the general philosophy of Inhibition the reader may consult Brunton ' s ' Pharmakology and Therapeutics, ' p. 154 ff., and also ' Nature, ' vol. 27, p. 419 ff.

④ E. g. Herzen, Herman u. Schwalbe ' s Jahres – bericht for 1886, Abth. p. 38. (Experiments on new – born puppies.)

的话，肌肉收缩一旦开始将不会停下，除非系统耗尽枯竭了；[①]而布朗－西夸用了多年时间一直在收集可以表明它的影响能有何等深远的例子。[②] 在这种情况下，就对皮层损伤而产生的现象的解释而言，似乎错误更可能出在过分缩小了它的范围，而不是在于将它拓展得太远。[③]

在另一方面，如果我们不承认中枢的再训练，我们就不仅要公然对抗一种先天的可能性，而且我们会发现自己由于事实所迫而必须假设有多得令人难以置信的功能先天寄宿于丘脑下面的中枢中，或者甚至是寄宿于四叠体下面的中枢中。我将在先看看我心中所获有的事实之后再考虑那一先天的异议。当我们自问，在使复原能够发生的足够的时间过去之后，是哪一个部分执行了由于手术而废止的功能时，这些事实就会出现在我们面前。

第一个观察者认为，它们一定是相反一侧或完整无缺的大脑半球的相应部分。但是，早在 1875 年卡维尔和杜莱特就对这一推测进行了检验，方法是先切除狗一侧的前腿中枢，然后当复原发生之后，再切掉相反一侧的前腿中枢。戈尔茨和其他人也做了同样的事情。[④] 如果相反一边真的是恢复了的功能的处所，起初

---

① 《神经系统与心灵》(1888 年)，第 3、4 章，以及《大脑》，第 11 卷，第 361 页。

② 布朗－西夸已经在 1889 年 10 月的《生理学文库》中给出了其观点的摘要，第 5 集，第 1 卷，第 751 页。

③ 戈尔茨最先在他的《大脑的日常工作》中将抑制理论应用于大脑，第 39 页以后。关于一般的抑制哲学，读者可以参考布伦顿的《药物学与治疗学》，第 154 页以后，以及《自然》，第 27 卷，第 419 页以后。

④ 如赫茨恩、赫尔曼和施瓦柏的《生理学年刊》，1886 年，第 38 页。(对新生小狗的实验。)

have appeared again and been permanent. But it did not appear at all; there appeared only a palsy of the hitherto unaffected side. The next supposition is that *the parts surrounding the cut-out region* learn vicariously to perform its duties. But here, again, experiment seems to upset the hypothesis, so far as the motor zone goes at least; for we may wait till motility has returned in the affected limb, and then both irritate the cortex surrounding the wound without exciting the limb to movement, and ablate it, without bringing back the vanished palsy. ① It would accordingly seem that *the cerebral centres below the cortex* must be the seat of the regained activities. But Goltz destroyed a dog's entire left hemisphere, together with the *corpus striatum* and the *thalamus* on that side, and kept him alive until a surprisingly small amount of motor and tactile disturbance remained. ② These centres cannot here have accounted for the restitution. He has even, as it would appear,③ ablated both the hemispheres of a dog, and kept him alive 51 days, able to walk and stand. The corpora striata and thalami in this dog were also practically gone. In view of such results we seem driven, with M. Francois-Franck,④ to fall back on the *ganglia lower still*, or even on the *spinal cord* as the 'vicarious' organ of which we are in quest. If the abeyance of function between the operation and the restoration was due *exclusively* to inhibition, then we must suppose these lowest centres to be in reality extremely accomplished organs. They must always have done what we now find them doing after function is restored, even

---

① Francois – Franck: op. cit. p. 382. Results are somewhat contradictory.

② Pflüger's Archiv, vol. 42, p. 419.

③ Neurologisches Centralblatt, 1889, p. 372.

④ Op. cit. p. 387. See pp. 378 to 388 for a discussion of the whole question. Compare also Wundt's Physiol. Psych., 3d ed., I. 225 ff., and Luciani u. Seppili, pp. 243, 293.

的瘫痪应该再次出现并且应该是永久性的。但是这种情况根本没有出现;仅仅出现了迄今为止一直未受影响的那一边的瘫痪。下一个推测是沿着被切除区域周围的部分替代性地学会了履行这一职责。但是在这里,至少就运动区域的运行状况而言,实验似乎又一次推翻了这一假设,因为我们可以一直等到运动性再次回到那一受影响的肢体,然后刺激伤口周围的皮层,却不能激起那一肢体运动,或者切除这部分皮层,却不能让已经消失的瘫痪再度产生。[①] 因此,情况似乎应该是皮层下面的大脑中枢一定是重新获得活动的处所。可是,戈尔茨破坏了一只狗的整个大脑左半球以及左侧的纹状体和丘脑,并且让它存活下来直到其只剩下了令人惊讶的少许运动和触觉障碍为止。[②] 这里的这些中枢不可能引起复原。如这种情况将会出现的那样,[③]他甚至切除了一条狗的两个脑半球,并让它存活了 51 天,其间它能够行走和站立。实际上这只狗的纹状体和丘脑也都不存在了。考虑到这样的结果,我们似乎和弗朗西丝 - 弗兰克先生一道,[④]被迫落回到更低级的神经节,或者甚至落回到脊髓,将其作为我们所寻找的“替代性”器官。如果手术和功能恢复之间的功能中止仅仅是由于抑制,那么我们必须假定这些低级中枢实际上是相当完善的器官。它们一定总是在做着我们现在发现在功能恢复之后它们所做的事情,甚

---

① 弗朗西丝 - 弗兰克:前面引用过的书,第 382 页。结果有些矛盾。

② 《弗吕格文集》,第 42 卷,第 419 页。

③ 《神经病学中心报》,1889 年,第 372 页。

④ 上面引用的书,第 387 页。关于整个问题的讨论,见第 378 ~ 388 页。同时比较冯特的《生理心理学》,第 3 版,第一部分,第 225 页以后,以及卢西亚尼和塞皮里,第 243、293 页。

when the hemispheres were intact. Of course this is conceivably the case; yet it does not seem very plausible. And the *a priori* considerations which a moment since I said I should urge, make it less plausible still.

For, in the first place, the brain is essentially a place of currents, which run in organized paths. Loss of function can only mean one of two things, either that a current can no longer run in, or that if it runs in, it can no longer run out, by its old path. Either of these inabilities may come from a local ablation; and 'restitution' can then only mean that, in spite of a temporary block, an inrunning current has at last become enabled to flow out by its old path again—e. g., the sound of 'give your paw' discharges after some weeks into the same canine muscles into which it used to discharge before the operation. As far as the cortex itself goes, since one of the purposes for which it actually exists is the production of new paths,① the only question before us is: Is the formation of *these particular 'vicarious' paths* too much to expect of its plastic powers? It would certainly be too much to expect that a hemisphere should receive currents from optic fibres whose *arriving*-place within it is destroyed, or that it should discharge into fibres of the pyramidal strand if their *place of exit* is broken down. Such lesions as these must be irreparable *within that hemisphere*. Yet even then, through the other hemisphere, the *corpus callosum*, and the bilateral connections in the spinal cord, one can imagine some road by which the old muscles might eventually be innervated by the same incoming currents which innervated them before the block. And for all minor interruptions, not involving the arriving-place of the 'cortico-petal' or the place of exit of the 'cortico-fugal' fibres, roundabout paths of some sort through the affected hemisphere itself must exist,

---

① The Chapters on Habit, Association, Memory, and Perception will change our present preliminary conjecture that that is one of its essential uses, into an unshakable conviction.

至当脑半球完整无缺时它们也是这样。当然,这是可以想像到的情况,但这似乎却不大可能。而且我在前不久提到的我要强调的那种先天意见,使它变得更不可能了。

因为,首先大脑在本质上是在组织起来的路径中流动的神经流的处所。功能的丧失只能意味着两件事情中的任何一件,即或者神经流不能再流入了,或者如果它流进来,它不能通过它的老路再流出去了。这两种抑制中的任何一种都可以由于局部切除而出现;而且复原只能意味着尽管有暂时性的阻塞,流入的神经流最终还是变得能从它的老路再次流出去——例如"伸出前爪"的声音在几周之后又释放到了手术前它通常释放进去的相同犬肌中去。就皮层自身运行的情况来说,由于它存在的目的之一是产生新的路径,①那么我们面前的唯一问题就是:就这些"替代性"路径的形成而言,我们是否对皮层的可塑性能力期望过高了? 如果我们认为脑半球应该接受来自视觉纤维、并且其内部的目的地已被损坏的神经流的话,或者认为当神经流的所在地被破坏后,脑半球应该将其释放入椎体索的纤维中去的话,我们对它的期望就过高了。像这样的损伤在那个大脑半球之内肯定是无法补救的。但即使是这样,通过另一个半球、胼胝体以及脊髓中的双侧连接,我们可以想像一些路径,通过这些路径,原来的肌肉可以最终被阻塞前对它们进行神经支配的相同的流入神经流所支配。而就所有不涉及"向皮层"纤维的目的地、也不涉及"离皮层"的所在地的小的中断来说,一定存在有穿过受影响半球自身的某种迂

① 关于习惯、联想、记忆和知觉的章节将把我们认为这是它本质的用途之一这一当前的初步推测变成一种不可动摇的信念。

for every point of it is, remotely at least, in potential communication with every other point. The normal paths are only paths of least resistance. If they get blocked or cut, paths formerly more resistant become the least resistant paths under the changed conditions. It must never be forgotten that a current that runs in has got to run out *somewhere*; and if it only once succeeds by accident in striking into its old place of exit again, the thrill of satisfaction which the consciousness connected with the whole residual brain then receives will reinforce and fix the paths of that moment and make them more likely to be struck into again. The resultant feeling that the old habitual act is at last successfully back again, becomes itself a new stimulus which stamps all the existing currents in. It is matter of experience that such feelings of successful achievement do tend to fix in our memory whatever processes have led to them; and we shall have a good deal more to say upon the subject when we come to the Chapter on the Will.

My conclusion then is this: that some of the restitution of function (especially where the cortical lesion is not too great) is probably due to genuinely vicarious function on the part of the centres that remain; whilst some of it is due to the passing off of inhibitions. In other words, both the vicarious theory and the inhibition theory are true in their measure. But as for determining that measure, or saying which centres are vicarious, and to what extent they can learn new tricks, that is impossible at present.

Final Correction Of The Meynert Scheme.

And now, after learning all these facts, what are we to think of the child and the candle-flame, and of that scheme which provisionally imposed itself on our acceptance after surveying the actions of the frog? (*Cf.* pp. 25-6, *supra.*) It will be remembered that we

回路径,因为它的每一个点,至少是遥远地和其他每一个点具有潜在的交流。平常的路径仅是阻力最小的路径。如果它们被堵住了或者是被切除了,在这种变化了的情况下,以前阻力较大的路径变成了阻力最小的路径。一定永远不要忘记的是流入的神经流必须要在某个地方流出去;而且如果仅仅有一次它成功地再次闯入了它原来的所在地,那么由与全部残留大脑相联系的意识所接受到的满足的震颤,将会加强和固定那一时刻的路径,使神经流更有可能再次闯入它们。作为结果而发生的感受,即以前的习惯性动作最终又成功地回来了的这样一种感受,它自身又变成了一个新的刺激,它让所有现存的神经流艰难地挤了进来。无论何种过程所引起的这类成就感确实趋向于在我们的记忆中固定下来,这是一个经验事实;并且当我们进入关于意志这一章时,我们将就这一问题做更多的讨论。

那么我的结论就是:一些功能复原(尤其是在皮层损伤不是很重的地方)可能是由于存留下来的那部分中枢的真正的替代性功能所致;同时另一些功能复原是因为抑制的逐渐消失而造成的。换言之,替代理论和抑制理论在它们各自的范围里都是正确的。但是,就确定出范围,或者说出哪个中枢是替代性的,并且在何种程度上它们可以习得新的技能来说,目前这都是不可能的。

对梅纳特方案的最后修正

现在,在了解了所有这些事实之后,就婴儿和烛焰、以及那个在考察了青蛙的活动之后而暂时让我们接受的方案,我们该想些什么呢(参见前面第25~26页)?应当记得的是,我们

then considered the lower centres en *masse* as machines for responding to present sense-impressions exclusively, and the hemispheres as equally exclusive organs of action from inward considerations or ideas; and that, following Meynert, we supposed the hemi-spheres to have no native tendencies to determinate activity, but to be merely superadded organs for breaking up the various reflexes performed by the lower centres, and combining their motor and sensory elements in novel ways. It will also be remembered that I prophesied that we should be obliged to soften down the sharpness of this distinction after we had completed our survey of the farther facts. The time has now come for that correction to be made.

Wider and completer observations show us both that the lower centres are more spontaneous, and that the hemispheres are more automatic, than the Meynert scheme allows. Schrader's observations in Goltz's Laboratory on hemisphereless frogs① and pigeonst ②give an idea quite different from the picture of these creatures which is classically current. Steiner's ③ observations on frogs already went a good way in the same direction, showing, for example, that locomotion is a well-developed function of the medulla oblongata. But Schrader, by great care in the operation, and by keeping the frogs a long time alive, found that at least in some of them the spinal cord would produce movements of locomotion when the frog was smartly roused by a poke, and that swimming and croaking could sometimes be performed when nothing above the medulla oblongata remained. ④ Schrader's hemisphereless frogs moved spontaneously, ate flies, buried themselves in the ground, and in short did many things which before his observations were supposed to be impossible unless the hemispheres remained.

---

① Pflüger's Archiv, vol. 41, p. 75 (1887).

② *lbid.*, vol. 44, p. 175 (1889).

③ Untersuchungen über die Physiologie des Froschhirns, 1885.

④ *Loc. cit.* pp. 80, 82 – 3. Schrader also found a *biting* – reflex developed When the medulla oblongata is cut through just behind the cerebellum.

将整个低级中枢看作是专门对当前的感官印象做出反应的机器，而大脑半球也同样被看作是由于内部的考虑和观念而引起的行动的专门器官；而且，继梅纳特之后，我们设想大脑半球不具有与生俱来的对确定行为的倾向，而仅仅是附加器官，它负责打破由低级中枢所执行的各种反射，并且以新颖的方式将其运动和感觉因素连接起来。还应该记得的是，我曾预言，在完成对进一步事实的考察之后，我们将不得不弱化这一明显的区分。现在是进行这种修正的时候了。

更宽泛且更完善的观测向我们表明，与梅纳特方案所承认的内容相比，低级中枢在活动时要更自发一些，而大脑半球在活动时则要更机械一些。施拉德在戈尔茨实验室对无脑的青蛙①与鸽子②的观测提供了一种与当前对这些动物的经典论述所截然不同的观点。斯坦纳③在这同一研究方向上已经有了很好的进展，例如，他表明移动是延髓的一个良好地发展了的功能。但是，施拉德通过更细心地做手术，并且让青蛙活得时间更长一些才发现，当青蛙由于被刺了一下而被激起时，至少在一些青蛙身上的脊髓可以产生移动的动作，而且当延髓以上的部分都没有了的时候，游泳和蛙鸣有时能够进行。④ 施拉德的无大脑半球的青蛙可以自发地移动、吃苍蝇、把自己隐藏在地下，简言之，它们做了很多在他的手术之前被认为是除非脑半球存在否则根本不可能完成的

① 《弗吕格文集》，第41卷，第75页(1887年)

② 同上，第44卷，第175页(1889年)。

③ 《蛙脑生理学研究》，1885年。

④ 在上述引文中，第80、82、83页。施拉德还发现当延髓正好是在小脑后面被切穿时，仍然有刺痛反射显示出来。

Steiner[1] and Vulpian have remarked an even greater vivacity in fishes deprived of their hemispheres. Vulpian says of his brainless carps[2] that three days after the operation one of them darted at food and at a knot tied on the end of a string, holding the latter so tight between his jaws that his head was drawn out of water. Later, "they see morsels of white of egg; the moment these sink through the water in front of them, they follow and seize them, sometimes after they are on the bottom, sometimes before they have reached it. In capturing and swallowing this food they execute just the same movements as the intact carps which are in the same aquarium. The only difference is that they seem to see them at less distance, seek them with less impetuosity and less perseverance in all the points of the bottom of the aquarium, but they struggle (so to speak) sometimes with the sound carps to grasp the morsels. It is certain that they do not confound these bits of white of egg with other white bodies, small pebbles for example, which are at the bottom of the water. The same carp which, three days after operation, seized the knot on a piece of string, no longer snaps at it now, but if one brings it near her, she draws away from it by swimming backwards before it comes into contact with her mouth." [3] Already on pp. 9-10, as the reader may remember, we instanced those adaptations of conduct to new conditions, on the part of the frog's spinal cord and thalami, which led Pflüger and Lewes on the one. hand and Goltz on the other to locate in these organs an intelligence akin to that of which the hemispheres are the seat.

When it comes to birds deprived of their hemispheres, the evidence that some of their acts have conscious purpose behind them is quite as persuasive. In pigeons Schrader found that the state

---

① Berlin Akad. Sitzungsberichte for 1886.

② Comptes Rendus, vol. 102, p. 90.

③ Comptes Rendus de l'Acad. d. Sciences, vol. 102, p. 1530.

事情。斯坦纳[1]和武尔皮安在被夺去了脑半球的鱼身上注意到了一种甚至是更大的活力。武尔皮安谈到他的那些手术后三天的无脑鲤鱼[2]时说,其中的一条鱼朝着食物和在绳子的一端系着的结飞奔过去,把后者紧紧地咬在两颌之间,以至于头都被拉出了水面。后来,"它们看到了少量蛋白;当这些蛋白在它们面前沉入水中时,它们追上去并咬住它们,有时是在这些蛋白沉到底部之后,有时是在它们沉到底部之前。在捕获和吞咽这些食物的过程中,它们执行的动作和在同一养鱼池中完好的鲤鱼所做的动作是相同的。唯一的区别是,它们似乎在较近的距离才看见食物,在养鱼池底部的所有地方寻找食物的时候也没有那么性急和坚定,但是它们有时和健全的鲤鱼进行争斗(可以这么说)来逮住蛋白。可以肯定的是它们没有将这些蛋白碎块和其他沉在水底的例如像小鹅卵石这样的白色物体相混淆。那条在手术三天后咬住绳结的鲤鱼,现在不再去咬绳结了,而且如果有人将那个绳结靠近它,它会在绳结和它的嘴接触之前向后面游去,从而躲开它。"[3]如读者可以记起的那样,在第 9 ~ 10 页我们列举了那些与青蛙的脊髓和丘脑相关的对新条件的行为适应的情况,这使得弗吕格和路易斯在一方面、戈尔茨在另一方面将某种与以大脑半球为处所的智能相类似的智能定位在了这些器官之中。

当提到丧失了大脑半球的鸟时,表明在它们一些行为的背后有有意识的目的的证据是相当令人信服的。在鸽子那里,施拉德

---

① 《柏林科学院会刊》,1886 年。

② 《报告》,第 102 卷,第 90 页。

③ 《科学院报告》,第 102 卷,第 1530 页。

of somnolence lasted only three or four days, after which time the birds began indefatigably to walk about the room. They climbed out of boxes in which they were put, jumped over or flew up upon obstacles, and their sight was so perfect that neither in walking nor flying did they ever strike any object in the room. They had also definite ends or purposes, flying straight for more convenient perching places when made uncomfortable by movements imparted to those on which they stood; and of several possible perches they always chose the most convenient "If we give the dove the choice of a horizontal bar (*Reck*) or an equally distant table to fly to, she always gives decided preference to the table. Indeed she chooses the table even if it is several meters farther off than the bar or the chair." Placed on the back of a chair, she flies first to the seat and then to the floor, and in general "will forsake a high position, although it give her sufficiently firm support, and in order to reach the ground will make use of the environing objects as intermediate goals of flight, showing a perfectly correct judgment of their distance. Although able to fly directly to the ground, she prefers to make the journey in successive stages. ... Once on the ground, she hardly ever rises spontaneously into the air."①

Young rabbits deprived of their hemispheres will stand, run, start at noises, avoid obstacles in their path, and give responsive cries of suffering when hurt. Rats will do the same, and throw themselves moreover into an attitude of defence. Dogs never survive such an operation if performed at once. But Goltz's latest dog, mentioned on p. 70, which is said to have been kept alive for fifty-one days after both hemispheres had been removed by a series of ablations and the corpora striata and thalami had softened away, shows how much the mid-brain centres and the cord can do even in the canine species. Taken together,

---

① *Loc. cit.* P. 216.

发现嗜睡状态只持续三到四天,此后,这些鸟开始在房间里不知疲倦地走来走去。它们从用来放它们的盒子里爬出来,跳过或飞过障碍物,而且它们的视觉是如此的好,以至于不论是在行走中还是在飞行中,它们都不会撞上房间中的任何东西。它们也有确定的目标或目的,当它们所站的地方由于受到运动的影响而变得不舒适时,它们会直接飞到更合适的栖息地;而且在几个可供选择的栖息地当中它们总是选择最合适的那一个。“如果我们提供给鸽子可供飞往的一块水平横木和距离同样远的一张桌子让其选择,它总是确定地优先选择桌子。甚至当桌子比横木或椅子还要远上几米时,它也会选择桌子。”把它放在一把椅子的靠背上,它先是飞到座位上,然后再飞到地面上,而且一般而言“它将会放弃高的位置,尽管这位置给它以十分牢固的支撑,而且为了到达地面,它会使用周围的物体作为它飞行的中间目标,对这些目标的距离它显示出一种非常正确的判断。尽管能够直接飞到地面,它还是乐于将它的旅程分成几个相继的阶段……一旦到了地面,它几乎不会再自发地飞到空中了。”①

丧失了脑半球的仔兔会站立、跑、因噪音而运动、躲开它们道路中的障碍,并且当受到伤害时会发出痛苦的叫声以给予回应。老鼠会做同样的事情,此外还会让自己进入一种防御的状态。如果立刻对狗进行这种手术的话,它们从来没有存活下来过。但是在70页提到的戈尔茨的最近的那只狗,据说在其两个半球通过一系列的切除而被去除,并且它的纹状体和丘脑都被软化了之后,还存活了51天,这表明即使在犬类中,中脑中枢和脊髓能起

---

① 在上述引文中,第216页。

the number of reactions shown to exist in the lower centres by these observations make out a pretty good case for the Mey-nert scheme, as applied to these lower animals. That scheme demands hemispheres which shall be mere supplements or organs of repetition, and in the light of these observations they obviously are so to a great extent. But the Meynert scheme also demands that the reactions of the lower centres shall all be *native*, and we are not absolutely sure that some of those which we have been considering may not have been acquired after the injury; and it furthermore demands that they should be machine-like, whereas the expression of some of them makes us doubt whether they may not be guided by an intelligence of low degree.

Even in the lower animals, then, there is reason to soften down that opposition between the hemispheres and the lower centres which the scheme demands. The hemispheres may, it is true, only supplement the lower centres, but the latter resemble the former in nature and have some small amount at least of 'spontaneity' and choice.

But when we come to monkeys and man the scheme well-nigh breaks downaltogether; for we find that the hemispheres do not simply repeat voluntarily actions which the lower centres perform as machines. There are many functions which the lower centres cannot by themselves perform at all. When the motor cortex is injured in a man or a monkey genuine paralysis ensues, which in man is incurable, and almost or quite equally so in the ape. Dr. Seguin knew a man with hemi-blindness, from cortical injury, which had persisted unaltered for twenty-three years. 'Traumatic inhibition' cannot possibly account for this. The blindness must have been an 'Ausfallser-scheinung,' due to the loss of vision's essential organ. It would seem, then, that in these higher creatures the lower centres must be less adequate than they are farther down in the zoological scale; and that even for certain elementary combinations of movement and impression the co-operation of the hemispheres is necessary from the start. Even in birds and dogs

到的作用是何等之大。总之,通过这些观察所显示出的存在于低级中枢的反应活动的数量,很好地支持了梅纳特方案,这是就其应用于低等动物而言的。这一方案要求脑半球仅仅作为补充物或重复器官,而且鉴于这些观察,它们在很大程度上确实如此。但是,梅纳特方案还要求低级中枢的反应活动应该全部都是与生俱来的,然而我们也不是绝对确信,我们所一直考虑的其中一些反应活动不是在受伤后才获得的;此外这一方案还要求这些反应活动应该是机械般的,然而它们中的一些表现使我们怀疑,它们可否不用较低级的智能来引导。

那么,甚至在低级动物这里,也存在着弱化这个方案所要求的脑半球和低级中枢之间的对立的原因。的确,脑半球可能仅是低级中枢的补充物,但是后者在本质上类似于前者,并且至少具有少量的"自发性"和选择性。

可是,当我们提及猴子和人的时候,这个方案就几乎完全被打破了;因为我们发现大脑半球并不仅仅是自愿地重复低级中枢作为机器而执行的动作。这里有许多功能低级中枢仅凭借自身是根本无法行使的。当人或者猴子的运动皮层受损时,真正的瘫痪就会跟着发生,人的这种瘫痪是无法治愈的,猩猩的这种瘫痪也几乎同样如此。塞甘博士认识一个由于皮层损伤而导致偏盲的人,他的偏盲一直未改变地持续了 23 年。用"创伤抑制"不可能说明这种情况。这种失明一定是一种基于视觉的基本器官丧失的"机能缺失现象"。那么,情况似乎是这样,高等动物的低级中枢一定不如处于动物学等级中更靠下的动物的低级中枢那么令人满意;而且甚至对于运动和印象的某种基本结合来说,脑半球的合作从一开始就是必要的。甚至在鸟和狗那里,当额叶被切

the power of *eating properly* is lost when the frontal lobes are cut off. ①

The plain truth is that neither in man nor beast are the hemispheres the virgin organs which our scheme called them. So far from being unorganized at birth, they must have native tendencies to reaction of a determinate sort. ② These are the tendencies which we know as *emotions* and *instincts*, and which we must study with some detail in later chapters of this book. Both instincts and emotions are reactions upon special sorts of objects of *perception*; they depend on the hemispheres; and they are in the first instance reflex, that is, they take place the first time the exciting object is met, are accompanied by no forethought or deliberation, and are irresistible. But they are modifiable to a certain extent by experience, and on later occasions of meeting the exciting object, the instincts especially have less of the blind impulsive character which they had at first. All this will be explained at some length in Chapter XXIV. Meanwhile we can say that the multiplicity of emotional and instinctive reactions in man, together with his extensive associative power, permit of extensive recouplings of the original sensory and motor partners. The *consequences* of one instinctive reaction often prove to be the inciters of an opposite reaction, and being *suggested* on later occasions by the original object, may then suppress the first reaction altogether, just as in the case of the child and the flame. For this education the hemispheres do not need to be *tabulæ rasæ* at first, as the Meynert scheme would have them;

① Goltz: Pflüger's Archiv, vol. 42, p. 447; Schrader: *ibid.* vol. 44, p. 219 ff. It is possible that this symptom may be an effect of traumatic inhibition, however.

② A few years ago one of the strongest arguments for the theory that the hemispheres are purely supernumerary was Soltmann's often-quoted observation that in new-born puppies the motor zone of the cortex is not excitable by electricity and only becomes so in the course of a fortnight, presumably after the experiences of the lower centres have educated it to motor duties. Paneth's later observations, however, seem to show that Soltmann may have been misled through overnarcotizing his victims (Pflüger's Archiv, vol. 37, p. 202). In the Neurologisches Centralblatt for 1889, p. 513, Bechterew returns to the subject on Soltmann's side with out, however, noticing Paneth's work.

除时,正常进食的能力都会丧失。①

显见的真相是,在人和兽类的身上,大脑并非如我们方案所说是尚未开发的器官。它们从生下来就远非是无组织的,它们一定具有与生俱来的确定种类的反应倾向。② 这些倾向我们称之为情绪和本能,对它们我们必须在本书的后面一些章节予以详细的研究。本能和情绪都是对特殊种类的知觉对象的反应;它们依赖大脑半球;它们处于最初阶段的反射中,也就是说,它们发生在初次遇到刺激对象之时,不伴随有预谋与深思,并且是不可抗拒的。但是通过经验它们在某种程度上是可以更改的,而且在今后遇到刺激对象的情况下,尤其是本能将较少具有它们起先具有的盲目冲动的特性。在 24 章中,所有这些情况将在某种程度上给予解释。同时我们能够说明的是,人的情绪和本能反应的多样性,与他那广阔的联想能力一起,准许了最初感觉和运动搭档之间的再连接。一种本能反应的结果常常被证明是相反反应的刺激物,而且在今后的情况下它可以被最初的对象所提示,从而可以一起抑制最初的反应,就像婴儿和烛焰那一事例中的情况一样。大脑半球无需像梅纳特所要求它们的那样,最初作为一块白板来接受这

---

① 戈尔茨:《弗吕格文库》,第 42 卷,第 447 页;施拉德:同上,第 44 卷,第 219 页以后。然而,有可能这种症状是创伤抑制的结果。

② 在几年前,关于脑半球是纯粹多余的理论的最强论据之一是索特曼那经常被人引用的观察,即新降生的小狗皮层的运动区域不能够因电击而被激发,而只有在两周之后才变得可以如此,据说这是在低级中枢的经验训练了皮层而使之承担起运动职责之后才出现的。然而,帕内斯后来的观察似乎表明,索特曼由于过度麻醉了它的实验对象而可能被误导了(《弗吕格文集》,第 37 卷,第 202 页)。在 1889 年《神经病学中心报》的第 513 页,贝克特莱尔站在索特曼一边又返回到了这一问题中,然而他却没有注意到帕内斯的工作。

and so far from their being educated by the lower centres exclusively, they educate themselves.①

We have already noticed the absence of reactions from fear and hunger in the ordinary brainless frog. Schrader gives a striking account of the instinctless condition of his brainless pigeons, active as they were in the way of locomotion and voice. " The hemisphereless animal moves in a world of bodies which…are all of equal value for him…He is, to use Goltz's apt expression, *impersonal*…Every object is for him only a space-occupying mass, he turns out of his path for an ordinary pigeon no otherwise than for a stone. He may try to climb over both. All authors agree that they never found any difference, whether it was an inanimate body, a cat, a dog, or a bird of prey which came in their pigeon's way. The creature knows neither friends nor enemies, in the thickest company it lives like a hermit. The languishing cooing of the male awakens no more impression than the rattling of the peas, or the call-whistle which in the days before the injury used to make the birds hasten to be fed. Quite as little as the earlier observers have I seen hemisphereless she-birds answer the courting of the male. A hemisphereless male will coo all day long and show distinct signs of sexual excitement, but his activity is without any object, it is entirely indifferent to him whether the she-bird be there or not.

① Münsterberg (Die Willenshandlung, 1888, p. 134) challenges Meynert's scheme *in toto*, saying that whilst we have in our personal experience plenty of examples of acts which were at first voluntary becoming secondarily automatic and reflex, we have no conscious record of a single originally reflex act growing voluntary. – As far as conscious record is concerned, we could not possibly have it even if the Meynert scheme were wholly true, for the education of the hemispheres which that scheme postulates must in the nature of things antedate recollection. But it seems to me that Münsterberg's rejection of the scheme may possibly be correct as regards reflexes from the *lower centres*. Everywhere in this department of psychogenesis we are made to feel how ignorant we really are.

一训练；而且它们不是专门通过低级中枢而获得训练，它们自己训练自己。[①]

我们已经注意到，普通无脑的青蛙缺乏由于恐惧和饥饿而引起的反应。施拉德对无脑鸽子（这些鸽子在移动和发音方面还和以前一样活跃）的无本能状况做出了惊人的论述。“无大脑半球的动物在一个所有的物体……对它来说都具有相等的价值的世界中活动……。用戈尔茨对其猩猩的措辞来说，它是不具有人格的……。对它来说每一个对象只是一种占据空间的东西，它朝一只普通的鸽子走去和向一块石头走去没有什么不同。它会试图爬到它们上面去。所有的作者都同意，不论是一个无生命的物体、一只猫、一条狗或是一只猛禽出现在他们的这只鸽子跟前，他们从未发现有什么特别之处。这家伙不知道朋友也不知道敌人，在密集的鸽群中它活得像个隐士。雄性鸽子那渴望的咕咕的叫声、豌豆的咔咔声以及在鸽子受伤前的日子里用来催促鸽子前来进食的口哨声都不能再唤起印象了。同早期的观察者一样，我很少看见雌性鸽子回应雄性鸽子的求爱。无脑半球的雄性鸽子会一整天地咕咕叫个不停，而且显示出了明显的性兴奋迹象，但是它的行动没有任何对象，不论雌性在与不在，对它来说都无关紧要。如果将

① 芒斯特伯格（《意志行为》，1888 年，第 134 页）在总体上挑战了梅纳特方案，他说我们关于行为最初由主动的变成次级自动的和反射的例子在我们的个人经验中有很多，同时，我们没有任何关于最初是反射的行动变成主动的行动的意识记录。——就有意识的记录而言，即使是假设梅纳特方案完全正确，我们也不可能获得它，因为方案所假设的脑半球的训练在本质上一定是先于记忆而发生的事情。但是，似乎对我来说，如果考虑到反射来自于低级中枢这一观点，芒斯特伯格对这方案的反对似乎是正确的。在心理发生学这一领域中，我们处处都感觉到自己真的是多么地无知。

If one is placed near him, he leaves her unnoticed···As the male pays no attention to the female, so she pays none to her young. The brood may follow the mother ceaselessly calling for food, but they might as well ask it from a stone··· The hemisphereless pigeon is in the highest degree tame, and fears man as little as cat or bird of prey." ①

Putting together now all the facts and reflections which we have been through, it seems to me that *we can no longer hold strictly to the Meynert scheme.* If anywhere, it will apply to the lowest animals; but in them especially the lower centres seem to have a degree of spontaneity and choice. On the whole, I think that we are driven to substitute for it some such general conception as the following, which allows for zoological differences as we know them, and is vague and elastic enough to receive any number of future discoveries of detail.

Conclusion.

All the centres, in all animals, whilst they are in one aspect mechanisms, probably are, or at least once were, organs of consciousness in another, although the consciousness is doubtless much more developed in the hemispheres than it is anywhere else. The consciousness must everywhere *prefer* some of the sensations which it gets to others; and if it can remember these in their absence, however dimly, they must be its *ends* of desire. If, moreover, it can identify in memory any motor discharges which may have led to such ends, and associate the latter with them, then these motor discharges themselves may in turn become desired as *means.* This is the development of *will*; and its realization must of course

① Pflüge's Archiv, vol. 44. p. 230-1.

一只雌性放在它跟前,它对它也不在意……。雄鸟不关注雌鸟,雌鸟也不关注它的孩子。幼鸟可以跟着母亲不停地要吃的,也可以向一块石头要吃的……。无脑半球鸽子的驯服程度最高,它们像不怕猫和猛禽一样不怕人。"①

现在将我们所谈论过的事实和思考全部放在一起,似乎对我来说,我们已经不能再严格地坚持梅纳特方案了。如果它有适用地方的话,它将适用于最低级的动物;但是在它们那里,低级中枢似乎尤其具有某种程度的自发性和选择性。总之,我想我们不得不用下述这种一般概念来取代它,这种概念能够容纳如我们所了解到的那些动物学差异,而且它足够模糊且有弹性,可以接受无数未来的详细发现。

结　论

一切动物的所有中枢,它们一方面是机械装置,同时,在另一方面它们也可能是,或者至少曾经是意识的器官,尽管意识无疑在脑半球中比在其他任何地方都要发达得多。意识在任何地方都一定倾向于选择它获得的一些感觉,而不是其他感觉;而且如果它能在这些感觉缺失的情况下记起它们(无论是多么模糊),它们就一定是欲望的目标。而且,如果它在记忆中能够识别出可能曾经实现这类目标的任何运动释放,并且将这些运动释放和这些目标联系起来,那么这些运动释放就可能反过来作为手段而成为被欲求的对象。这就是意志的发展;而且其实现当然

① 《弗吕格文集》,第 44 卷,第 230 ~ 231 页。

be proportional to the possible complication of the consciousness. Even the spinal cord may possibly have some little power of will in this sense, and of effort towards modified behavior in consequence of new experiences of sensibility. ①

All nervous centres have then in the first instance one essential function, that of 'intelligent' action. They feel, prefer one thing to another, and have ' ends. ' Like all other organs, however, they *evolve* from ancestor to descendant, and their evolution takes two directions, the lower centres passing downwards into more unhesitating automatism, and the higher ones upwards into larger intellectuality. ② Thus it may happen that those functions which can safely grow uniform and fatal become least accompanied by mind, and that their organ, the spinal cord, becomes a more and more soulless machine; whilst on the contrary those functions which it benefits the animal to have adapted to delicate environing variations pass more and more to the hemispheres, whose anatomical structure and attendant consciousness grow more and more elaborate as zoological evolution proceeds.

---

① Naturally, as Schiff long ago pointed out (Lehrb. d. Muskel – u. Ner – venphysiologie, 1859, p. 213 ff.), the ' Rückenmarksseele,' if it now exist, can have no higher sense – cocsciousness, for its incoming currents are solely from the skin. But it may, in its dim way, both feel, prefer, and desire. See, for the view favorable to the text: G. H. Lewes, The Physiology of Common Life (1860), chap. Ix. Goltz (Nervencentren des Frosehes 1869, pp. 102 – 130) thinks that the frog's cord has no adaptative power. This may be the case in such experiments as his, because the beheaded frog's short span of life does not give it time to learn the new tricks asked for. But Rosenthal (Biologisches Centralblatt. vol. iv. p. 247) and Mendelssohn (Berlin Akad. Sitzungsberichte, 1885, p. 107) in their investigations ou the simple reflexes of the frog's cord, show that there is some adaptation to new conditions, inasmuch as when usual paths of conduction are interrupted by a cut, new paths are taken. According to Rosenthal, these grow more pervious (i. e. require a smaller stimulus) in proportion as they are more often traversed.

② Whether this evolution takes place through the inheritance of habits acquired, or through the preservation of lucky variations, is an alternative which we need not discuss here. We shall consider it in the last chapter in the book. For our present purpose the *modus operandi* of the evolution makes no difference, provided it be admitted to occur.

必须是和意识的可能复杂性成比例的。从这个意义上说,即使脊髓也可能有一些意志力,拥有鉴于新的感性经历而努力修正自己行为的能力。①

因而,所有的神经中枢首先都具有一种基本的功能,即"理智的"行动的功能。它们有感受,倾向于选择一个东西而不是另外一个,并且还有"目的"。然而,和其他所有器官一样,它们由祖先向后代进化,并且它们的进化有两个方向,低级中枢向上进入更加敏捷的自动化阶段,而高级中枢向上进入智能水平更高的阶段。② 因此,可能发生的情况就是有些功能确实变得始终如一且不可避免,而且这些功能至少有心灵相伴随,而它们的器官,脊髓,变成了一架越来越没有灵魂的机器;同时,与此相反,那些使动物受益于适应细微的环境变化的功能,则逐渐地传到了脑半球,随着动物学中所说的进化的进行,脑半球的解剖学结构和相

---

① 自然,如希夫在很久以前所指出的那样(《肌肉神经生理学教科书》,1859 年,第 213 页以后),"脊髓精神",如果它现在存在的话,不可能有高级的感觉意识,因为流入的神经流都是来自皮肤的。但是它可以通过它那模糊的方式去感受、去喜好、去欲求。就支持本文的观点可参见:G. H. 路易斯,《普通生命生理学》(1860),第 9 章。戈尔茨(《青蛙的神经中枢》,1869 年,第 102 ~ 130 页)认为青蛙的脊髓没有适应能力。在他的这类实验中情况可能是这样的,无头青蛙的短暂生命使得它没有时间来学习所需要的新技能。但是罗森塔尔(《生物学中心报》,第 4 卷,第 247 页)和门德尔松(《柏林科学院会刊》,1885 年,第 107 页)在他们对青蛙脊髓简单反射的研究中表明,存在一些对新条件的适应,因为当通常的传导路径由于切除而被阻断之时,新的路径被采用了。根据罗森塔尔的观点,由于这些路径经常被穿过,它们变得更加通畅了(即所需的刺激更小了)。

② 这种进化是否是由于所获得习惯的遗传而发生,或者是由于幸运变异的保存而发生,是另一个问题,在这里我们无需讨论。我们将在本书的最后一章探讨这个问题。就我们现在的目的而言,进化的进行方式是无关紧要的,提出它是为了承认它发生了。

In this way it might come about that in man and the monkeys the basal ganglia should do fewer things by themselves than they can do in dogs, fewer in dogs than in rabbits, fewer in rabbits than in hawks,[1] fewer in hawks than in pigeons, fewer in pigeons than in frogs, fewer in frogs than in fishes, and that the hemispheres should correspondingly do more. This passage of functions forward to the ever-enlarging hemispheres would be itself one of the evolutive changes, to be explained like the development of the hemispheres themselves, either by fortunate variation or by inherited effects of use. The reflexes, on this view, upon which the education of our human hemispheres depends, would not be due to the basal ganglia alone. They would be tendencies in the hemispheres themselves, modifiable by education, unlike the reflexes of the medulla oblongata, pons, optic lobes and spinal cord. Such cerebral reflexes, if they exist, form a basis quite as good as that which the Meynert scheme offers, for the acquisition of memories and associations which may later result in all sorts of 'changes of partners' in the psychic world. The diagram of the baby and the candle (see page25) can be re-edited, if need be, as an entirely cortical transaction. The original tendency to touch will be a cortical instinct; the burn will leave an image in another part of the cortex, which, being recalled by association, will inhibit the touching tendency the next time the candle is perceived, and excite the tendency to withdraw—so that the retinal picture will, upon that next time, be coupled with the original motor partner of the pain. We thus get whatever psychological truth the Meynert scheme possesses without entangling ourselves on a dubious anatomy and physiology.

Some such shadowy view of the revolution of the centres, of the relation of consciousness to them, and of the hemispheres to the other lobes, is, it seems to me, that in which it is safest to indulge.

---

① See Schroder's Observations, *loc. cit.*

伴随的意识变得越来越精致了。通过这种方法,情况可以被认为是,人和猴子的基底神经结自身比狗的基底神经结所能够做的事情应该少一些,而狗的比兔子的又少一些,而兔子的比老鹰的更少一些,而老鹰的比鸽子的又再少一些,[①]而鸽子的比青蛙的又更少一些,而青蛙的比鱼的再更少一些,并且脑半球应当相应地做得更多。功能向不断扩大的脑半球的迁移,其自身就是一种进化上的变化,它可以像大脑半球本身的发展一样,通过幸运的变异或者使用的遗传结果而得到解释。据此观点,我们人类脑半球的训练所依赖的反射活动就不应该仅仅归因于基底神经结。它们是大脑半球自身中的倾向,可以通过训练而更改,和延髓、脑桥、视叶和脊髓的反射活动不同。这些大脑反射活动,如果它们存在的话,构成了一种用来获得以后可以导致在心灵世界中各种"搭档变化"的记忆和联想的基础,这基础与梅纳特方案所提供的一样好。如果需要的话,婴儿和蜡烛的图示(见 25 页)可以作为一种完全是大脑皮层的事物而被重新修订。最初的触摸倾向是一种皮层本能;灼伤在皮层的另一部位留下意象,这意象通过联想被回忆起来,在下一次感知蜡烛时将会抑制触摸的倾向并激发出缩回手的倾向——结果视网膜的图片在下一次将会和最初的疼痛的运动搭档联系起来。因此,我们就获得了梅纳特方案所拥有的所有心理学的真相,而没有使我们卷入令人怀疑的解剖学和生理学之中。

关于中枢进化、意识与中枢的关系、以及大脑半球与其他脑叶的关系的这些模糊观点,似乎对我来说,是可以最安全地沉湎

---

① 参见施拉德的《观察》,在上述引文中。

If it has no other advantage, it at any rate makes us realize how enormous are the gaps in our knowledge, the moment we try to cover the facts by any one formula of a general kind.

于其中的。如果它没有其他的优势的话,它至少可以使我们认识到,在我们试图以任何一种普遍的公式来囊括那些事实之时,在我们知识中的缝隙是何等之大。

CHAPTER III.

On Some General Conditions Of Brain-activity.

The elementary properties of nerve-tissue on which the brain-functions depend are far from being satisfactorily made out. The scheme that suggests itself in the first instance to the mind, because it is so obvious, is certainly false: I mean the notion that each cell stands for an idea or part of an idea and that the ideas are associated or 'bound into bundles' (to use a phrase of Locke's) by the fibres. If we make a symbolic diagram on a blackboard, of the laws of association between ideas, we are inevitably led to draw circles, or closed figures of some kind, and to connect them by lines. "When we hear that the nerve-centres contain cells which send off fibres, we say that Nature has realized our diagram for us, and that the mechanical substratum of thought is plain. In *some* way, it is true, our diagram must be realized in the brain; but surely in no such visible and palpable way as we at first suppose. ① An enormous number of the cellular bodies in the hemispheres are fibreless. Where fibres are sent off they soon divide into untraceable ramifications; and nowhere do we see a simple coarse anatomical connection, like a line on the blackboard, between two cells. Too much anatomy has been found to order for theoretic purposes, even

① I shall myself in later places indulge in much of this schematization. The reader will understand once for all that it is symbolic; and that the use of it is hardly more than to show what a deep congruity there is between mental processes and mechanical processes of *some* kind, not necessarily of the exact kind portrayed.

第三章 大脑活动的一些一般条件

人们还远远没有满意地了解大脑功能所依赖的神经组织的基本性质。由于其非常明显而最先出现在我们心中的方案一定是错误的:我是指这样的观点,即每一个细胞代表一个观念或观念的一部分,而且观念间发生联系或(用洛克的话来说)被“绑成一捆”是通过纤维来实现的。如果我们就观念间的联想律在黑板上画一个象征性的图示,我们不可避免地会画出一些圆圈或者是某种闭合的图形,并且用线将它们连起来。当我们听说神经中枢包含有送出纤维的细胞时,我们就说大自然为我们实现了这一图示,并且思维的机械基础是简单的。确实,我们的图示一定以某种方式在大脑中被实现了;但肯定不是以我们起先假设的那种明显的方法。[①] 脑半球中有大量的细胞体是无纤维的。一旦纤维被送出,它们就很快分解为无法追踪的分支;并且我们在哪里也看不到在两个细胞之间有任何如黑板上的线条一样简单的、粗糙的解剖学连接。人们发现很多解剖学是为了维护理论的目的,甚至

---

① 我将在后面的地方对这个图解给予更多的关注。读者将一劳永逸地理解它是象征性的;并且对它的使用只能表明在心理过程和非常复杂的机械过程之间存在着多么复杂的一致性,而不必是所确切描述的这种一致性。

by the anatomists ; and the popular-science notions of cells and fibres are almost wholly wide of the truth. Let us therefore relegate the subject of the *intimate* workings of the brain to the physiology of the future, save in respect to a few points of which a word must now be said. And first of in the same nerve-tract. This is a property extremely important for the understanding of a great many phenomena of the neural, and consequently of the mental life; and it behooves us to gain a clear conception of what it means before we proceed any farther.

The Summation Of Stimuli.

The law is this, that *a stimulus which would be inadequate by itself to excite a nerve-centre to effective discharge may, by acting with one or more other stimuli (equally ineffectual by themselves alone) bring the discharge about.* The natural way to consider this is as a summation of tensions which at last overcome a resistance. The first of them produce a ' latent excitement ' or a ' heightened irritability '—the phrase is immaterial so far as practical consequences go; the last is the straw which breaks the camel' s back. Where the neural process is one that has consciousness for its accompaniment, the final, explosion would in all cases seem to involve a vivid state of feeling of a more or less substantive kind. But there is no ground for supposing that the tensions whilst yet submaximal or outwardly ineffective, may not also have a share in determining the total consciousness present in the individual at the time. In later chapters we shall see abundant reason to suppose that they do have such a share, and that without their contribution the fringe of relations which is at every moment a vital ingredient of the mind' s object, would not come to consciousness at all.

解剖学家也是如此;并且大众科学关于细胞和纤维的观点几乎完全偏离了真理。因此,让我们将关于大脑内部工作的课题移交给未来的生理学吧,而只留下现在必须要讨论的几点。首先要讨论的是在同一神经束中的刺激聚合。这一性质对于理解神经系统的众多生命现象以及由此而造成的精神生活的众多现象是极为重要的;而且在我们进一步探讨它之前,我们有必要就其意义获得一个清晰的概念。

刺激的聚合

这个规律是,一个自身不足以激起神经中枢进行有效释放的刺激,通过和另一个或更多刺激(这些刺激在单独情况下也是无效的)的共同作用,就会使释放发生。用自然的方法来考虑这一规律就是将其看作是最终克服了阻力的张力的积累。它们中的第一个刺激产生了一种“潜在的兴奋”或说一种“提升了的兴奋强盛”——就实际的结果来说,这种表达是非实质性的;最后的刺激就是那能压跨驼峰的稻草(俗语)。如果神经系统的过程有意识相伴随的话,那么在所有情形中最后的爆发似乎将涉及或多或少真实存在的一种生动的感受状态。但是这里却没有理由作出假设说,由于这些紧张还不是最大程度的,并且表面上看来是无效的,所以它们也不会在决定当前出现在个体中的全部意识方面起作用。在后面的章节,我们将会看到有充足的理由可以假设它们确实在这方面起作用,并且如果没有它们的贡献的话,作为始终都是心理对象的重要因素的边际关系将根本不会出现于意识之中。

The subject belongs too much to physiology for the evidence to be cited in detail in these pages. I will throw into a note a few references for such readers as may be interested in following it out,① and simply say that the direct electrical irritation of the cortical centres sufficiently proves the point. For it was found by the earliest experimenters here that whereas it takes an exceedingly strong current to produce any movement when a single induction-shock is used, a rapid succession of induction-shocks (' faradization ') will produce movements when the current is comparatively weak. A single quotation from an excellent investigation will exhibit this law under further aspects:

"If we continue to stimulate the cortex at short intervals with the strength of current which produces the minimal muscular contraction [of the dog's digital extensor muscle], the amount of contraction gradually increases till it reaches the maximum. Each earlier stimulation leaves thus an effect behind it, which increases the efficacy of the following one. In this summation of the stimuli.... the following points may be noted:

1) Single stimuli entirely inefficacious when alone may become efficacious by sufficiently rapid reiteration. If the current used is very

---

① Valentin: Archiv f, d. gesammt. Physiol., 1873, p. 458. Stirling: Leipzig Acad. Berichte, 1875, p. 372 (Journal of Physiol., 1875). J. Ward: Archiv f. (Anat. u.) Physiol., 1880, p, 72. H. Sewall: Johns Hopkins Studies, 1880, p. 30. Kronecker u. Nicolaides: Archiv f. (Anat. u.) Physiol., 1880, p. 437. Exner: Archiv f, die ges. Physiol., Bd. 28, p. 487 (1882). Eckhard: in Hermann's Hdbch. d. Physiol., Bd. I. Thl. II. p. 31. Francois-Franck: Lecons sur les Fonctions motrices du Cerveau, p. 51 ff., 339. -For the process of summation in *nerves* and *muscles*, cf. Hermann: *ibid*. Thl. Ⅰ. p. 109, and vol. Ⅰ. p. 40. Also Wundt: Physiol. Psych., Ⅰ. 243 ff.; Richet: Travaux du Laboratoire de Marey, 1877, p. 97; L'Homme et l'Intelligence, pp. 24 ff., 468; Revue Philosophique, t. XXI. p. 564. Kronecker u. Hall: Archiv f. (Anat. u.) Physiol., 1879; Schönleín: *ibid*. 1882, p. 357. Sertoli (Hofmann and Schwalbe's Jahres-bericht, 1882. p. 25. De Watteville: Neurologisches Centralblatt, 1883, No. 7. Grünhagen: Arch. f. d. ges. Physiol., Bd. 34, p. 301 (1884).

就这几页将要详细引用的论据而言，这一主题更属于生理学的范畴。对于那些可能对此会感兴趣且会将它研究到底的读者，我将会在注释中提供一些参考书目，[①]简单地说，对皮层中枢的直接电刺激可以充分地证明这一观点。因为，最早期的实验人员发现，尽管在使用单一诱导电击时，要产生任何运动都需要极强的电流，而快速的连续诱导电击（"感应电流疗法"）会在电流相对较弱时产生运功。一段来自一项出色研究中的引文将在更多的方面展示这一规律：

"如果我们用造成（狗指伸肌）肌肉最小收缩的电流强度以较短的时间间隔持续刺激皮层，肌肉收缩量会逐渐增加直到达到最大值。因此前一个刺激会作用于后一个刺激，这种作用会增加随后刺激的功效。在这种刺激聚合中……，应该注意以下几点：

（1）当单独存在时完全没有效力的单一刺激，可以通过充分的快速重复而变得有效力。如果所使用的电流比首次引起收缩

---

① 瓦伦丁：《全部生理学文库》，1873 年，第 458 页。斯特林：《莱比锡科学院报告》，1875 年，第 372 页（《生理学杂志》，1875 年）。J. 沃德：《（解剖学和）生理学文库》，1880 年，第 72 页。H. 休厄尔：《约翰·霍普金斯研究》，1880 年，第 30 页。克罗耐克和尼古莱德斯：《（解剖学和）生理学文库》，1880 年，第 437 页。埃克斯纳：《生理学文库》，第 28 卷，第 487 页，1882 年。埃克哈德：在赫尔曼的《生理学手册》，第 1 卷，第 2 册，第 31 页。弗朗西丝－弗兰克：《大脑驱动功能作用教程》，第 51 页以后，第 339 页。—就神经和肌肉的聚合过程，参见赫尔曼：同上，第 1 册，第 109 页，和第 1 卷，第 40 页。以及冯特：《生理心理学》，1，第 243 页以后；里奇特：《莫雷实验室的业绩》，1877 年，第 97 页；《人与智能》，第 24 页以后，第 468 页；《哲学评论》，第 21 册，第 564 页。克罗耐克和霍尔：《（解剖学和）生理学文库》，第 1879 年；舍恩雷：同上，1882 年，第 357 页。瑟托利：《霍夫曼和施瓦尔伯年刊》，1882 年，第 25 页。德沃特威尔：《神经病学中心报》，1883 年，No. 7。格伦哈根：《生理学文库》，第 34 卷，第 301 页，1884 年。

much less than that which provokes the first beginning of contraction, a very large number of successive shocks may be needed before the movement appears—20, 50, once 106 shocks were needed. 2) The summation takes place easily in proportion to the shortness of the interval between the stimuli. A current too weak to give effective summation when its shocks are 3 seconds apart will be capable of so doing when the interval is shortened to 1 second. 3) Not only electrical irritation leaves a modification which goes to swell the following stimulus, but every sort of irritant which can produce a contraction does so. If in any way a reflex contraction of the muscle experimented on has been produced, or if it is contracted spontaneously by the animal (as not unfrequently happens 'by sympathy,' during a deep inspiration), it is found that an electrical stimulus, until then inoperative, operates energetically if immediately applied." ①

Furthermore:

"In a certain stage of the morphia-narcosis an ineffectively weak shock will become powerfully effective, if, immediately before its application to the motor centre, the skin of certain parts of the body is exposed to gentle tactile stimulation…If, having ascertained the subminimal strength of current and convinced one's self repeatedly of its inefficacy, we draw our hand a single time lightly over the skin of the paw whose cortical centre is the object of stimulation, we find the current at once strongly effective. The increase of irritability lasts some seconds before it disappears. Sometimes the effect of a single light stroking of the paw is only sufficient to make the previously ineffectual current produce a very weak contraction. Repeating the tactile stimulation will then, as a rule,

① Bubnoff und Heidenhain: Ueber Erregungs – und Hemmungsvorgünge innerhalb der motorischen Hirncentren. Archive f. d. ges. Physiol., Bd. 26, p. 156 (1881).

的电流要弱很多，在运动出现之前就需要进行大量的连续电击——需要20次、50次电击，甚至有一次需要106次电击。(2)聚合发生的难易程度和刺激时间间隔的缩短成正比。当电击时间间隔为三秒时，电流由于太弱而不能产生有效聚合，而当时间间隔被缩短到一秒时，这一电流就能产生有效聚合了。(3)不仅电刺激可以造成这种增大随后刺激的变化，而且每种可以引起肌肉收缩的刺激都能如此。如果不论通过任何方式使受试肌肉发生了反射收缩，或者如果动物自发地收缩了那块肌肉(如并非不经常发生的在深呼吸中'由于共感'而引起的收缩)，人们会发现，一直不起作用的电刺激，如果立即被施用的话，就会强有力地起作用。"①

还有：

"在由于吗啡麻醉而导致昏迷的特定阶段，无效的弱电击，如果就在它施用于运动中枢之前，身体特定部位的皮肤受到温和的触觉刺激，这种无效的弱电击会变得非常有效……。在已经确定电流为亚极小强度、并且已经反复使自己确信它的无效性之后，如果我们用手在它的爪子上轻轻地划上一下来对它的皮层进行刺激，我们发现电流立刻就强有力地产生效用了。兴奋性的增强在它消失之前会持续几秒钟。有时，轻抚爪子而产生的影响仅足以使以前无效的电流产生一种非常微弱的收缩。通常，重复施用

---

① 巴诺夫和海登汉："论大脑运动中枢的兴奋和抑制过程"，《生理学文库》，第26卷，第156页(1881年)。

increase the contraction's extent." ①

We constantly use the summation of stimuli in our practical appeals. If a car-horse balks, the final way of starting him is by applying a number of customary incitements at once. If the driver uses reins and voice, if one bystander pulls at his head, another lashes his hind quarters, and the conductor rings the bell, and the dismounted passengers shove the car, all at the same moment, his obstinacy generally yields, and he goes on his way rejoicing. If we are striving to remember a lost name or fact, we think of as many 'cues' as possible, so that by their joint action they may recall what no one of them can recall alone. The sight of a dead prey will often not stimulate a beast to pursuit, but if the sight of movement be added to that of form, pursuit occurs. "Brücke noted that his brainless hen, which made no attempt to peck at the grain under her very eyes, began pecking if the grain were thrown on the ground with force, so as to produce a rattling sound." ② "Dr. Allen Thomson hatched out some chickens on a carpet, where he kept them for several days. They showed no inclination to scrape, …but when Dr. Thomson sprinkled a little gravel on the carpet, …the chickens immediately began their scraping movements." ③ A strange person, and darkness, are both of them stimuli to fear and mistrust in dogs (and for the matter of that, in men). Neither circumstance alone may awaken outward manifestations, but together, i. e.

---

① Archiv f. d. ges. Physiol., Bd. 26, p. 176 (1881). Exuer thinks (*ibid.* Bd. 28, p. 497 (1882)) that the summation here occurs in the spinal cord. It makes no difference where this particular summation occurs, so far as the general philosophy of summation goes.

② G. H. Lewes: Physical Basis of Mind, p. 479, where many similar examples are given, 487 -9.

③ Romanes: Mental Evolution in Animals, p. 163.

触觉刺激会增大收缩程度。”①

在生活实践中我们经常使用刺激聚合。如果一匹马不肯前进,让它开始走路的最后方法就是同时施用几种它所习惯的刺激。如果车夫使用鞭子并吆喝着,一个旁观者拽它的头,另一个旁观者鞭打它身体的后部,指挥者摇着铃,下车的乘客猛推车厢,所有这一切同时发生,那么它的固执一般会有所收敛,从而高兴地上路了。如果我们正在努力地回忆已被遗忘的一个名字或一个事实,我们会尽可能多得去寻找“线索”,以便通过它们的共同作用,可以召回它们中的任何一个都无法单独召回的东西。一只野兽看到死了的猎物,这样的刺激通常不会促使它去追击,但如果在那一外观上再加入运动的视觉刺激,追逐就产生了。“布吕克注意到,他的无脑母鸡不会试图啄食它眼皮底下的谷粒,如果为了产生卡嗒卡嗒的声音而将谷粒用力的撒到地上,它就开始啄食了。”②“艾伦·汤姆森博士让一些小鸡在一块地毯上孵了出来,并让它们在地毯上待了几天。它们没有刮擦地毯的倾向,……但是当汤姆森博士往地毯上撒了一些沙砾时,……小鸡就立刻开始了它们的刮擦运动。”③对狗来说,陌生人与黑暗这二者都是引起恐惧和猜疑的刺激物(其实对人来说也一样)。这两种情况单独出现都不会唤起外在的表现,但是它们在一起时,就是说,

---

① 《生理学文库》,第26卷,第176页(1881年)。埃克修尔认为(同上,第28卷,第497页,1882年),这里的聚合发生在脊髓。就对于聚合的一般哲学思考而言,这一特殊的聚合发生在哪里都是无关紧要的。

② G. H. 路易斯:《心灵的物理基础》,第479页,这里给出了很多相似的例子,第487~489页。

③ 罗马尼斯:《动物心理进化》,第163页。

when the strange man is met in the dark, the dog will he excited to violent defiance. ① Street-hawkers well know the efficacy of summation, for they arrange themselves in a line upon the sidewalk, and the passer often buys from the last one of them, through the effect of the reiterated solicitation, what he refused to buy from the first in the row. Aphasia shows many examples of summation. A patient who cannot name an object simply shown him, will name it if he touches as well as sees it, etc.

Instances of summation might be multiplied indefinitely, but it is hardly worth while to forestall subsequent chapters. Those on Instinct, the Stream of Thought, Attention, Discrimination, Association, Memory, Æsthetics, and Will, will contain numerous exemplifications of the reach of the principle in the purely psychological field.

Reaction-Time.

One of the lines of experimental investigation most diligently followed of late years is that of the ascertainment of the *time occupied by nervous events*. Helmholtz led off by discovering the rapidity of the current in the sciatic nerve of the frog. But the methods he used were soon applied to the sensory nerves and the centres, and the results caused much popular scientific admiration when described as measurements of the ' velocity of thought'

① See a similar instance in Mach : Beiträge zur Analyse der Empfin – dungen, p. 36, a sparrow being the animal. My young children are afraid of their own pug – dog, if he enters their room after they are in bed and the lights are out. Compare this statement also: " The first question to a peasant seldom proves more than a flapper to rouse the torpid adjustments of his ears. The invariable answer of a Scottish peasant is, ' What' s your wull?' – that of the English, a vacant stare. A second and even a third question may be required to elicit an answer. " (R. Fowler: Some Observations on the Mental State of the Blind, and Deaf, and Dumb (Salisbury, 1843), p. 14.)

当狗在黑暗中遇见陌生人时，就会激起它的强烈反抗。[①] 沿街叫卖的小贩非常了解聚合的效力，因为他们沿着人行道排成一行，由于反复诱惑的作用，路过的人常常从他们中的最后一人那里买上了他们在队伍的头一个人那里所拒绝购买的东西。失语症展示了很多聚合的例子。一个不能叫出展示给他的东西的名称的病人，如果他在看见它的同时又触摸它的话，他就会叫出它的名称，等等。

聚合的例子可以毫无限制地增加，但是若要抢在后来的章节之前来考虑它们，这样做是不值得的。那些关于本能、思想之流、注意、辨别力、联想、记忆、审美和意志的章节，将包含这一原理在纯心理学领域中所涉及的大量范例。

反应时间

近些年来，为实验研究所最为不懈追随的路线之一是对神经事件所占据时间的探察。赫姆霍尔兹通过发现青蛙坐骨神经流的速度而开始了这方面的研究。但是他所使用的方法很快被应用于感觉神经和中枢，并且当研究的结果被描述为对"思想速率"

---

① 参见马奇的《感觉分析论文集》第 36 页中的一个相似的例子。我的年幼的孩子们会害怕他们的哈巴狗，如果它在他们上了床并且熄了灯之后进入他们的房间的话。也可以和这一段话相比较："对农民的第一个提问通常被证明仅仅如同一声拍击，以使他开始迟钝地调整他的耳朵。一个苏格兰农民对此的不变回答是：'你呜什么？'——这样一句英语之后，他茫然地注视着你。如果要引出一个回答就需要提第二个甚至第三个问题。"（R. 福勒：《对盲、聋、哑人心理状态的一些观察》，索尔兹伯里，1843 年，第 14 页。）

The phrase ' quick as thought' had from time immemorial signified all that was wonderful and elusive of determination in the line of speed; and the way in which Science laid her doomful hand upon this mystery reminded people of the day when Franklin first ' *eripuit cœlo fulmen*, ' foreshadowing the reign of a newer and colder race of gods. We shall take up the various operations measured, each in the chapter to which it more naturally pertains. I may say, however, immediately, that the phrase ' velocity of *thought*' is misleading, for it is by no means clear in any of the cases what particular act of thought occurs during the time which is measured. ' Velocity of nerve-action' is liable to the same criticism, for in most cases we do not know what particular nerve-processes occur. What the times in question really represent is the total duration of certain *reactions upon stimuli*. Certain of the conditions of the reaction are prepared beforehand; they consist in the assumption of those motor and sensory tensions which we name the expectant state. Just what happens during the actual time occupied by the reaction (in other words, just what is added to the pre-existent tensions to produce the actual discharge) is not made out at present, either from the neural or from the mental point of view.

The method is essentially the same in all these investigations. A signal of some sort is communicated to the subject, and at the same instant records itself on a time-registering apparatus. The subject then makes a muscular movement of some sort, which is the ' reaction, ' and which also records itself automatically. The time found to have elapsed between the two records is the total time of that observation. The time-registering instruments are of various types.

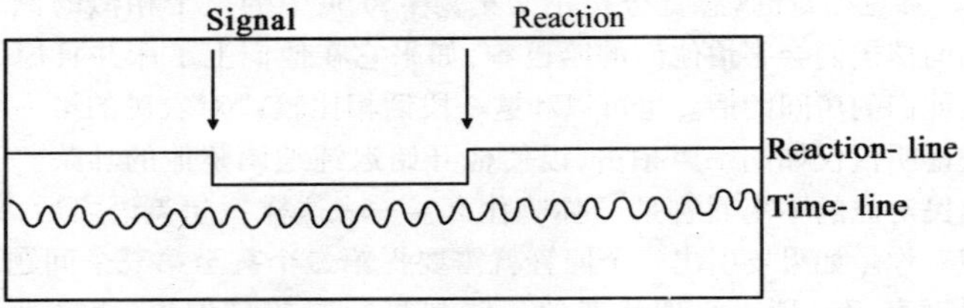

FIG. 21

的测量时，它赢得了极为广泛的科学赞赏。短语“像思维一样快”，从远古时期就意味着在速度的确定方面有奇妙和难以琢磨的东西；科学将它充满厄运的手伸向这一神秘事物的方式，使人们回想起由富兰克林所最先预示的被更新、更冷酷的神所统治的日子的到来。我们将在更适宜的章节继续逐一讨论得到测量的各种运作活动。然而，我即刻可以说的是，短语“思维速率”会令人误解，因为，在任何情况下，人们一点也不清楚在所测量的时间中有什么样的特殊的思维活动发生了。“神经活动的速率”也易于受到同样的批评，因为在大多数情况下我们不知道发生了什么样的特殊的神经过程。所探讨的时间真正代表的是某种刺激反应所持续的全部时间。反应的特定条件已经预先准备好了；它们存在于我们对被称为预期状态的运动和感觉张力的假设之中。无论是从神经的还是从心理的角度来看，在反应所占据的时间中究竟发生了什么（换言之，究竟是什么被添加到了先在的张力之上从而产生了实际的释放），这在目前还未弄明白。

在所有这些研究中，方法在本质上是相同的。传达某种信号给被试，并且在同一时刻将它记录在计时装置上。然后，被试做出某种肌肉运动，这便是反应，并且它也自动地将自己记录下来。所发现的在两个记录之间流逝的时间就是观察的全部时间。计时装置有各种不同的类型。

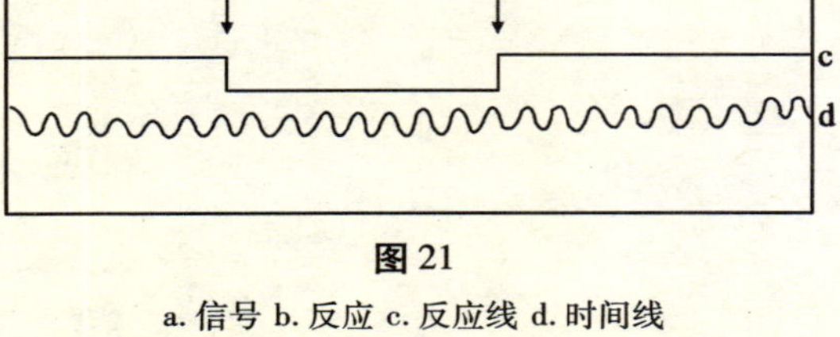

图 21

a. 信号 b. 反应 c. 反应线 d. 时间线

One type is that of the revolving drum covered with smoked paper, on which one electric pen traces a line which the signal breaks and the 'reaction' draws again; whilst another electric pen (connected with a pendulum or a rod of metal vibrating at a known rate) traces alongside of the former line a 'time-line' of which each undulation or link stands for a certain fraction of a second, and against which the break in the reaction-line can be measured. Compare Fig. 21, where the line is broken by the signal at the first arrow, and continued again by the reaction at the second. Ludwig's Kymograph, Marey's Chronograph are good examples of this type of instrument.

Another type of instrument is represented by the stop-watch, of which the most perfect form is Hipp's Chrono-scope. The hand on the dial measures intervals as short as $\frac{1}{1000}$ of a second. The signal (by an appropriate electric Connection) starts it; the reaction stops it; and by reading off its initial and terminal positions we have immediately and with no farther trouble the time we seek. A still simpler instrument, though one not very satisfactory in its working, is the 'psychodometer' of Exner & Obersteiner, of which I picture a modification devised by my colleague Professor H. P. Bowditch, which works very well.

有一种计时工具是这样的，在一个旋转着的鼓形圆筒上覆盖有熏纸，一只电子笔在上面画着一条线，信号将它中断，而“反应”又使它继续画线；同时，另一只电子笔（和已知摆动速度的钟摆和金属棒相连接）在前面那条线旁边画着一条“时间线”，每一个波动和链环代表每秒中的特定片断，通过这条线，在“反应线”上的中断就可以得到测量。试比较图 21，“反应线”在第一个箭头处被信号所中断，在第二个箭头处又因反应而继续。路德维希的转筒记录器和马瑞的计时器是这种类型装置的很好的范例。

另一种类型装置的代表是秒表，希普的极微时间测定器是其最完善的形式。表盘上的指针可以测量千分之一秒的时间间隔。信号（通过一种适当的电连接）让它开始工作；反应让它停下来；通过读出指针的起始位置，我们立刻就可以知道我们所寻求的时间，不必再做其他麻烦的事情。还有一种更简单的装置是埃克斯纳和奥博斯坦纳的“心理反应测时器”，可是它的运作不是很令人满意。我画出的是由我的同事鲍迪奇教授所设计的对其更改后的图示，它运作得非常好。

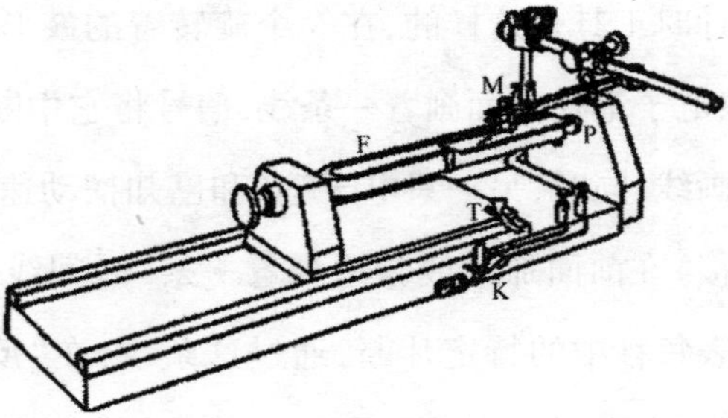

FIG. 22. —Bowditch's Reaction-timer. F, tuning-fork carrying a little plate which holds the paper on which the electric pen *M* makes the tracing, and sliding in grooves on the base-board. *P*, a plug which spreads the prongs of the fork apart when it is pushed forward to its extreme limit, and releases them when it is drawn back to a certain point. The fork then vibrates, and, its backward movement continuing, an undulating line is drawn on the smoked paper by the pen. At *T* is a tongue fixed to the carriage of the fork, and at *K* an electric key which the tongue opens and with which the electric pen is connected. At the instant of opening, the pen changes its place and the undulating line is drawn at a different level on the paper. The opening can be made to serve as a signal to the reacter in a variety of ways, and his reaction can be made to close the pen again, when the line returns to its first level. The reaction time = the number of undulations traced at the second level.

The manner in which the signal and reaction are connected with the chronographic apparatus varies indefinitely in different experiments. Every new problem requires some new electric or mechanical disposition of apparatus. ①

The least complicated time-measurement is that known as *simple reaction-time*, in which there is but one possible signal and one possible movement, and both are known in advance. The movement is generally the closing of an electric key with the hand. The foot, the jaw, the lips,

① The reader will find a great deal about chronographic apparatus in J. Mary: La Méthode Graphique, pt. II. chap. II. One can make pretty fair measurements with no other instrument than a watch, by making a large number of reactions, each serving as a signal for the following one, and dividing the total time they take by their number. Dr. O. W. Holmes first suggested this method, which has been ingeniously elaborated and applied by Professor Jastrow. See Science' for September 10, 1886.

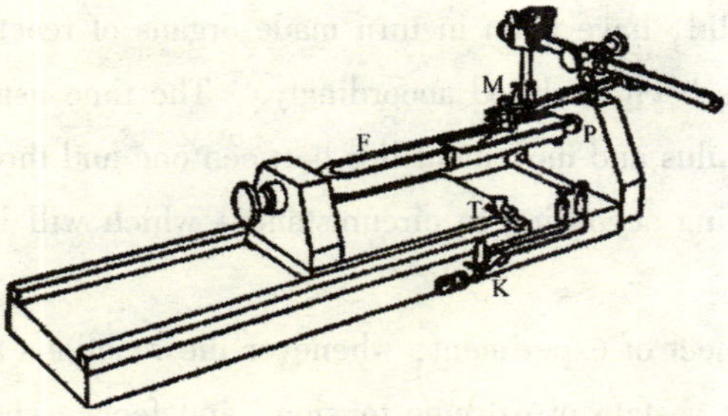

图 22　鲍迪奇的反应测时器

F,带着金属板的转叉,金属板上有纸,电子笔 M 在上面做着图录,并且滑入到底板凹槽中。P,是一个栓子,当它向前被推至极限时,它将转叉的叉头伸展,当它被拉回到某一位置时,它就放开了叉头。这样转叉就会震动,它向后的运动一直持续着,笔就在熏纸上画下了一条波形线。在 T 处有一个固定在转叉架上的舌状物,在 K 处有一个舌状物可以开启的电子键,电子笔和它相连。开启时,笔会改变它自己的位置,从而在纸上画下一条高度不同的波形曲线。开启可以以各种方式作为一种对反应者的信号,而他的反应让笔停下,此时线回到了原来的高度。反应时间 = 在第二高度图录下的波形数量。

在不同的实验中,信号和反应与计时装置相联系的方式是不确定地变化着的。每一个新的问题都要求对装置进行新的电子的或机械的部署。①

最不复杂的时间测量就是人们所知道的对简单反射时间的测量,在其中只有一种可能信号和一种可能动作,而且二者都是事先已知的。动作一般是用手合上一个电键。脚、下巴、嘴唇、甚

① 读者可以在 J. 马瑞的《图解法》第 2 部分第 2 章中找到大量关于测时装置的资料。人们可以仅仅使用一只手表而无需其他的装置来进行很好的测量,方法是进行大量的反应活动,把每一个反应都当作是下一个反应的信号,并且用所占用的整个时间除以反应的数量。W. 霍尔姆斯博士最先提出这一方法,贾斯特罗教授独创性地详尽阐述并应用了这一方法。见《科学》,1886 年 9 月 10 日。

even the eyelid, have been in turn made organs of reaction, and the apparatus has been modified accordingly.① The time usually elapsing between stimulus and movement lies between one and three tenths of a second, varying according to circumstances which will be mentioned anon.

The subject of experiment, whenever the reactions are short and regular, is in a state of extreme tension, and feels, when the signal comes, as if *it* started the reaction, by a sort of fatality, and as if no psychic process of perception or volition had a chance to intervene. The whole succession is so rapid that perception seems to be retrospective, and the time-order of events to be read off in memory rather than known at the moment. This at least is my own personal experience in the matter, and with it I find others to agree. The question is, What happens inside of us, either in brain or mind? and to answer that we must analyze just what processes the reaction involves. It is evident that some time is lost in each of the following stages:

1. The stimulus excites the peripheral sense-organ adequately for a current to pass into the sensory nerve;

2. The sensory nerve is traversed;

3. The transformation (or reflection) of the sensory into a motor current occurs in the centres;

4. The spinal cord and motor nerve are traversed;

5. The motor current excites the muscle to the contracting point.

Time is also lost, of course, outside the muscle, in the joints, skin, etc., and between the parts of the apparatus; and when the stimulus which serves as signal is applied to the skin of the trunk or limbs, time is lost in the sensorial conduction through the spinal cord.

---

① See, for a few modifications, Catell, Mind, XI. 220 ff.

至眼睑都轮流成为了反应的器官，而且计时装置也相应的进行了改变。[①] 刺激和运动之间所流逝的时间在 1/10 和 3/10 秒之间，它依情形的不同而发生变化，不久我们就会谈到这一点。

只要反应是短暂和规则的，被实验的主体一定处于一种极端紧张的状态，而且当信号到来的时候，他感受到讯号似乎是以某种不可避免的方式产生了反应活动，而且知觉和意志的心理过程似乎都没有机会介入这一反应。整个相继的过程是如此之快，以至于知觉好像成了反省式的，而且事件的时间顺序好像是在记忆中被完成的，而不是在那一刻被知觉了的。这至少是我自己在这一事件中的个人经历，并且我发现其他人也认同它。问题是，在我们内部，不论是在大脑中还是在心灵中，究竟发生了什么事情？而要回答这一问题我们必须分析出反应到底涉及什么样的过程。显然，在下列的每一个阶段中都有一些时间被耗费掉了：

1. 刺激物对外围感觉器官予以充分地刺激，致使神经流进入感觉神经；

2. 感觉神经被穿过；

3. 在中枢中发生了感觉流向运动流的转化（或反射）；

4. 脊髓和运动神经被穿过；

5. 运动流激起肌肉运动至收缩点。

当然，在肌肉之外，在关节、皮肤等等这些地方中，在装置的不同部分之间，也有时间被耗费掉了；而且当刺激作为信号施加于躯干或者四肢的皮肤上时，在脊髓中的感觉传导也耗费了一些时间。

---

① 关于对它们一些修改，见凯特尔，《心灵》，11，第 220 页以后。

The stage marked 3 is the only one that interests us here. The other stages answer to purely physiological processes, but stage 3 is psycho-physical; that is, it is a higher-central process, and has probably some sort of consciousness accompanying it. What sort?

Wundt has little difficulty in deciding that it is consciousness of a quite elaborate kind. He distinguishes between two stages in the conscious reception of an impression, calling one *perception*, and the other *apperception*, and likening the one to the mere entrance of an object into the periphery of the field of vision, and the other to its coming to occupy the focus or point of view. *Inattentive awareness* of an object, and *attention* to it, are, it seems to me, equivalents for perception and apperception, as Wundt uses the words. To these two forms of awareness of the impression Wundt adds the conscious volition to react, gives to the trio the name of 'psycho-physical' processes, and assumes that they actually follow upon each other in the succession in which they have been named. ① So at least I understand him. The simplest way to determine the time taken up by this psycho-physical stage No. 3 would be to determine separately the duration of the several purely physical processes, 1, 2, 4, and 5, and to subtract them from the total reaction-time. Such attempts have been made. ② But the data for calculation are too inaccurate for use, and, as Wundt himself admits, ③ the precise duration of stage 3

---

① Physiol. Psych., II. 221 – 2. Cf. also the first edition, 728 – 9. I must confess to finding all Wundt's utterances about 'apperception' both vacillating and obscure. I see no use whatever for the word, as he employs it, in Psychology. Attention, perception, conception, volition, are its ample equivalents. Why we should need a single word to denote all these things by turns, Wundt fails to make clear. Consult, however, his pupil Staude's article, 'Ueber den Beg riff der Apperception,' etc., in Wundt's periodical Philosophische Student, I. 149, which may be supposed official. For a minute criticism of Wundt's 'apperception,' see Marty. Vierteljahrschrift f. wiss. Philos., X. 346.

② By Exner, for example, Pflüger's Archiv, VII. 628 ff.

③ P. 222. Cf. also Richet, Rev. Philos., VI. 395 – 6.

标记为3的阶段是引起我们兴趣的唯一阶段。其他阶段都是对纯生理过程做出的反应,但阶段3是心理-物理的;即它是一个高级中枢的过程,并且可能有某种意识相伴。是什么类型的意识呢?

冯特几乎没有任何困难就断定出它是一种相当精细的意识。他将印象的有意识接受区分成了两个阶段,叫它们中的一个为知觉,叫另一个为统觉,并且把其中的一个比作对象刚刚进入视野的外围,把另一个比作对象的到来占据了视野的焦点。一个是对对象的疏忽性知晓,另一个是对对象的关注,似乎对我来说,当冯特使用这些术语时,知觉和统觉是一样的。在这两种印象的知晓形式之上,冯特又加入了进行反应的有意识意志,将这三重唱命名为"心理-物理"过程,并且设想它们是按照其被命名的顺序而相继发生的。① 所以我至少理解了他。要确定心理-物理阶段3所耗费的时间,最简单的办法就是分别确定出其他几个纯物理过程1、2、4和5的持续时间,然后从整个反应时间中减去它们。已经有人进行了这样的尝试。② 但是,对我们来说用来计算的数据太不准确了,而且,如冯特自己所承认的那样,阶段3③ 的准确持

① 《生理心理学》,2,第221~222页。也可参见第一版,第728~729页。我必须承认,我发现冯特关于"统觉"的所有说法既模糊又犹豫。我认为就他对这个术语的使用来看,无论怎样使用,它在心理学中都没有用处。注意、知觉、概念、意志都是其充分的等价物。为什么我们需要这一单个的术语来轮流表示所有这些东西,冯特并没有表述清楚。然而,可以参考他的学生斯托德的文章,"统觉的概念"等,其发表于冯特的期刊《心理学研究》第1卷,第149页,这些文章可被看作是具有权威性的。关于对冯特"统觉"的详细批评,参见马蒂:《科学哲学季刊》,10,第346页。

② 例如,埃克斯纳对此做了尝试,《弗吕格文集》,7,第628页以后。

③ 第222页,也可参见里奇特,《哲学评论》,6,第395~396页。

must at present be left enveloped with that of the other processes, in the total reaction-time.

My own belief is that no such succession of conscious feelings as Wundt describes takes place during stage 3. It is a process of central excitement and discharge, with which doubtless some feeling coexists, but *what* feeling we cannot tell, because it is so fugitive and so immediately eclipsed by the more substantive and enduring memory of the impression as it came in, and of the executed movement of response. Feeling of the impression, attention to it, thought of the reaction, volition to react, *would*, undoubtedly, all be links of the process *under other conditions*① and would lead to the same reaction—after an indefinitely longer time. But these other conditions are not those of the experiments we are discussing; and it is mythological psychology (of which we shall see many later examples) to conclude that because two mental processes lead to the same result they must be similar in their inward subjective constitution. The feeling of stage 3 is certainly no articulate perception. It can be nothing but the mere sense of a reflex discharge. *The reaction whose time is measured is*, in short, *a reflex action pure and simple, and not a psychic act.* A foregoing psychic condition is, it is true, a prerequisite for this reflex action. The preparation of the attention and volition; the expectation of the signal and the readiness of the hand to move, the instant it shall come; the nervous tension in which the subject waits, are all conditions of the formation in him for the time being of a new path or arc of reflex discharge. The tract from the sense-organ which receives the stimulus, into the motor centre which discharges the reaction, is already tingling with premonitory innervation, is raised to such a pitch of heightened irritability by the expectant attention, that the signal is instantaneously sufficient to cause the

① For instance, if, on the previous day, one had resolved to act on a signal when it should come, and it now came whilst we were engaged in other things, and reminded us of the resolve.

续时间目前还必须和其他过程的持续时间一起封装在整个反应时间之中。

我坚信，阶段3中如冯特所描述的那种相继的有意识的感受并没有发生。这是一个中枢的兴奋和释放过程，毫无疑问有某种感受存在，但是我们却不能说出它是什么样的感受，因为它是如此的难以捕捉，并且当印象进来之时，对印象和对执行了的反应动作更具实体性、更持久的记忆立刻就覆盖了它。对印象的感受、对它的注意、对反应的思考、做出反应的意志力，在其他情况下无疑都是这过程的环节，①并且会导致同样的反应——在一段不确定的较长的时间之后。但是这些其他的情况不是我们所讨论的实验中的情况；而且神话心理学（后面我们将会看到很多关于它的例子）得出结论，因为两种心理过程导致了同样的结果，所以它们在其内部主观构造上一定是相似的。阶段3中的感受一定不是清晰的知觉。它只能是对反射释放的纯粹感觉。简而言之，其时间得到测量的反应是一个纯粹的和简单的反射动作，而不是心理行为。确实，前述的心理状况是这一反射动作的先决条件。注意力和意志力的准备，对信号的期待与使手运动的准备，被试主体等待中的神经紧张，都是当时在他那里形成新的反射释放路径或弧的条件。从接受刺激的感觉器官到释放反应的运动中枢的神经束，已经随着有预兆的神经支配而兴奋起来了，通过预期注意，它的兴奋性提高到了一个足够的高度，以至于信号足以即刻引起

① 例如，如果在前一天我们决定要在一个信号到来时对它做出反应，而现在它来了，可与此同时我们正忙于其他的事情，它让我们回想起了我们的决定。

overflow.[①]No other tract of the nervous system is, at the moment, in this hair-trigger condition. The consequence is that one sometimes responds to a *wrong* signal especially if it be an impression of the same *kind* with the signal we expect[②] But if by chance we are tired, or the signal is unexpectedly weak, and we do not react instantly, but only after an express perception that the signal has come, and an express volition, the time becomes quite disproportionately long (a second or more, according to Exner [③]), and we feel that the process is in nature altogether different.

In fact, the reaction-time experiments are a case to which we can immediately apply what we have just learned about the summation of stimuli. 'Expectant attention' is but the subjective name for what objectively is a partial stimulation of a certain pathway, the pathway from the 'centre' for the signal to that for the discharge. In Chapter XI we shall see that all attention involves excitement from within of the tract concerned in feeling the objects to which attention is given. The tract here is the excito-motor arc about to be traversed. The signal is but the spark from without which touches off a train already laid. The performance, under these conditions, exactly resembles any reflex action. The only difference is that whilst, in the ordinarily so-called reflex acts, the reflex arc is a permanent result of organic growth, it is here a

---

① "I need hardly mention that success in these experiments depends in a high degree on our concentration of attention. If inattentive, one gets very discrepant figures…This concentration of the attention is in the highest degree exhausting. After some experiments in which I was concerned to get results as uniform as possible, I was covered with perspiration and excessively fatigued although I had sat quietly in my chair all the while." (Exner, *loc. cit.* VII. 618.).

② Wundt, Physiol. Psych., II. 286.

③ Pflüger's Archiv, VII. 616.

流溢。[1] 此时,神经系统中没有其他神经束处于这种一触即发的情形之中。结果是有的时候人们对错误的信号做出反应,尤其当这信号和我们所预期的信号具有同样类型的印象之时。[2] 但是如果偶尔我们累了,或者信号出人意料地微弱,那么我们就不会立刻做出反应,而只是在快速知觉信号已经到来之后、在一种迅速的意志活动之后,我们才会做出反应,时间会不成比例地变得很长(按照埃克斯纳的研究,[3]会是一秒钟或更长),并且我们感到过程在本质上也完全不同。

事实上,反应时间的实验是我们可以立即将我们所知晓的刺激聚合应用于其上的实例。"预期注意"只是一个主观称谓,用来指出某种从"信号"中枢到释放中枢的路径的局部刺激在客观上是什么样的。在第 11 章我们将会看到,所有的注意都涉及神经束内部的兴奋,这神经束与对所注意对象的感受相关联。这里的神经束是将要被打通的兴奋－运动弧。信号好似来自外面的火花,它将已经铺好的导火线点燃。在这些条件下的活动类似于任何一种反射活动。唯一的区别在于,在所谓普通的反射动作中,反射弧是由于器官生长而造成的永久结果,而这里的反射弧是由于

---

① "我几乎无需提及的是,实验的成功在很大程度上取决于我们注意力的集中。如果注意力不集中的话,我们就会得到差异极大的数据……这种注意力的集中是最令人疲惫不堪的。在一些我想要得到尽可能一致的结果的实验之后,我浑身是汗,极度疲劳,虽然其间我一直安静地坐在我的椅子上。"(埃克斯纳,在上述引文中,7,第 618 页。)

② 冯特,《生理心理学》,2,第 286 页。

③ 《弗吕格文集》,7,第 616 页。

transient result of previous cerebral conditions. ①

I am happy to say that since the preceding paragraphs (and the notes thereto appertaining) were written, Wundt has himself become converted to the view which I defend. He now admits that

---

① In short, what M. Delbœuf calls an '*organe adventice*.' The reaction – time, moreover, is quite compatible with the reaction itself being of a reflex order. Some reflexes (sneezing, e. g.) are very slow. The only time – measurement of a reflex act in the human subject with which I am acquainted is Exner's measurement of winking (in Pflüger's Archiv f. d. gesammt. Physiol., Bd. VIII. p. 526, 1874). He found that when the stimulus was a flash of light it took the wink 0.2168 sec. to occur. A strong electric shock to the cornea shortened the time to 0.0578 sec. The ordinary 'reaction – time' is midway between these values. Exner 'reduces' his times by eliminating the physiological process of conduction. His 'reduced minimum winking – time' is then 0.0471 (*ibid.* 531), whilst his reduced reaction – time is 0.0828 (*ibid.* VII. 637). These figures have really no scientific value beyond that of showing, according to Exner's own belief (VII. 531), that reaction – time and reflex – time measure processes of essentially the same order. His description, moreover, of the process is an excellent description of a reflex act. "Every one," says he, "who makes reaction – time experiments for the first time is surprised to find how little he is master of his own movements, so soon as it becomes a question of executing them with a maximum of speed. Not only does their energy lie, as it were, outside the field of choice, but even the time in which the movement occurs depends only partly upon ourselves. We jerk our arm, and we can afterwards tell with astonishing precision whether we have jerked it quicker or slower than another time, although we have no power to jerk it exactly at the wished – for moment." – Wundt himself admits that when we await a strong signal with tense preparation there is no consciousness of any duality of 'apperception' and motor response; the two are continuous (Physiol. Psych., II. 226). – Mr. Cattell's view is identical with the one I defend. "I think," he says, "that if the processes of perception and willing are present at all they are very rudimentary.... The subject, by a voluntary effort [before the signal comes], puts the lines of communication between the centre for" the stimulus "and the centre for the co – ordination of motions... in a state of unstable equilibrium. When, therefore, a nervous impulse reaches the" former centre, "it causes brain – changes in two directions; an impulse moves along to the cortex and calls forth there a perception corresponding to the stimulus, while at the same time an impulse follows a line of small resistance to the centre for the co – ordination of motions, and the proper nervous impulse, already prepared and waiting for the signal, is sent from the centre to the muscle of the hand. When the reaction has often been made the entire cerebral process becomes automatic, the impulse of itself takes the well – travelled way to the motor centre, and releases the motor impulse." (Mind, XI. 232 – 3.) – Finally, Prof. Lipps has, in his elaborate way (Grundtatsachen, 179 – 188), made mince – meat of the view that stage 3 involves either conscious perception or conscious will.

先前的大脑条件而造成的暂时结果。①

我很高兴的是，由于写下了前面的段落（以及另外属于那一段的注释），冯特本人已经转向了我所辩护的观点。现在他承认

---

① 简而言之，M. 德尔博夫称其为“外感官”。而且，反应时间与自身作为反射顺序的反应是十分符合的。一些反射是（如打喷嚏）很慢的。我唯一知晓的把人作为被试而进行反射动作的测量是埃克斯纳的眨眼测量（在《全部生理学弗吕格文集》，第 8 卷，第 526 页，1874 年）。他发现当刺激物是闪光时，眨眼产生所花费的时间是 0.2168 秒。对角膜进行强电击使时间缩短到了 0.0578 秒。普通的“反射时间”介于这些时值之间。埃克斯纳通过消除生理传导时间而“缩短”了他的时间。他的“缩短了的最小眨眼时间”为 0.0471 秒（同上，第 531 页），同时他的缩短了的反应时间是 0.0828 秒（同上，第 7 卷，第 637 页）。按照埃克斯纳的观点（第 7 卷，第 531 页）这些数据除了表明反应时间和反射时间的进行具有本质上相同的顺序以外，它们真的没有任何科学价值。而且，他对这过程的描述是对反射动作的一种极好描述。他说：“所有第一次做反应时间实验的人，会很惊奇地发现一旦他自己的动作要以最大的速度来执行时，他是多么难以驾驭这个动作。不仅他们的力气似乎位于可供他们选择的范围之外，而且甚至动作产生的时间也只是部分地取决于他们自己。我们猛拉胳膊，而且之后我们能够以令人惊异的精确性说出，和上次相比我们是动得快了还是慢了，尽管我们没有能力在我们想猛拉胳膊的时刻拉动它。”——冯特自己承认，当我们紧张地准备好等待一个强信号时，这里不存在任何对“统觉”和运动反应的二元性意识；二者是连续的（《生理心理学》，2，第 226 页）。——凯特尔先生的观点和我所辩护的观点是一致的。他说：“我认为，如果有知觉和意愿过程的出现，它们也是非常初步的……被试通过主动的努力（在信号到来之前），将‘刺激’中枢和运动协调中枢……之间的联系通道置于一种不稳定的平衡状态之中。因此，当一个神经刺激到达‘前一个中枢’时，它造成了两个方向的大脑变化；一个刺激来到皮层并且引起与刺激物相对应的知觉，与此同时一个刺激沿着带有少量阻力的路径来到运动协调中枢，而且已经准备好的并且正在等待信号的适当的神经刺激已经由中枢被送到了手的肌肉中了。如果经常做出这样的反应，整个大脑过程就变得自动化了，刺激本身通过经常穿越的道路来到运动中枢，并且释放运动刺激。”（《心灵》，11，第 232 ~ 233 页。）——最后，利普斯教授用详细阐述的方式（《基本事实》第 179 ~ 188 页）驳倒了阶段 3 涉及有意识的知觉或有意识的意志这种观点。

in the shortest reactions "there is neither apperception nor will, but that they are merely *brain-reflexes due to practice.*" ① The means of his conversion are certain experiments performed in his laboratory by Herr L. Lange, ② who was led to distinguish between two ways of setting the attention in reacting on a signal, and who found that they gave very different time-results. In the '*extreme sensorial*' way, as Lange calls it, of reacting, one keeps one's mind as intent as possible upon the expected signal, and 'purposely avoids' ③ thinking of the movement to be executed; in the '*extreme muscular*' way one 'does not think at all' ④ of the signal, but stands as ready as possible for the movement. The muscular reactions are much shorter than the sensorial ones, the average difference being in the neighborhood of a tenth of a second. Wundt accordingly calls them 'shortened reactions' and, with Lange, admits them to be mere reflexes; whilst the sensorial reactions he calls 'complete,' and holds to his original conception as far as they are concerned. The facts, however, do not seem to me to warrant even this amount of fidelity to the original Wundtian position. When we begin to react in the 'extreme sensorial' way, Lange says that we get times so very long that they must be rejected from the count as non-typical. "Only after the reacter has succeeded by repeated and conscientious practice in bringing about an extremely precise co-ordination of his voluntary impulse with his sense-impression do we get times which can be regarded as typical sensorial reaction-times." ⑤ Now it seems to me that these excessive and 'untypical' times are probably the real 'complete times,' the only ones in which distinct processes of actual perception and volition occur (see above, pp. 88-9).

---

① Physiol. Psych., 3d edition (1887), vol. II. p. 266.

② Philosophische Studien, vol. IV. p. 479 (1888).

③ *Loc. cit.* p. 488.

④ *Loc. cit.* p. 487.

⑤ *Loc. cit.* p. 489.

在最短的反射中"既不存在统觉也没有意志,而它们仅仅是由于练习而导致的大脑反射。"①促使他发生转变的是赫尔·兰格在他的实验室中所进行的某些实验,②这些实验导致兰格区分出了在对信号做出反应时两种调整注意力的方式,并且兰格发现它们形成了不同的时间结果。当人们以兰格所命名的"极端感觉的"方式进行反应时,人们让大脑对预期的信号尽可能的保持专注,并且"有目的地避免"③思考将要执行的动作;当人们以"极端肌肉的"方式进行反应时,人们"根本不思考"④信号,而是尽可能的准备好运动。肌肉反应比感觉反应要短得多,平均差异大约在十分之一秒。冯特因此称它们为"缩短了的反应",并且和兰格一起承认它们仅仅是反射;同时他认为感觉反应是"完全的",并且就它们而言,他坚持他原初的观点。然而事实在我看来似乎是,甚至这样的精确程度也没有确保冯特的最初立场是合理的。当我们以"极端感觉的"方式开始反应,兰格说我们所得到的时间是如此的长,以至于人们一定会认为它们是非典型的,从而拒绝考虑它们。"只有在反应者通过反复认真的练习,成功地获得其主动刺激和感官印象极度精确的协调之后,我们才能够获得被认为是典型的感觉反应时间。"⑤现在,似乎对我来说,这些过长的和"非典型"的时间可能就是真正的"完全时间",是唯一在其中有明显是真实的知觉和意志过程发生的时间(见

---

① 《生理心理学》,第3版(1887年),第2卷,第266页。

② 《哲学研究》,第4卷,第497页(1888年)。

③ 在上述引文中,第488页。

④ 在上述引文中,第487页。

⑤ 在上述引文中,第489页。

The typical sensorial time which is attained by practice is probably another sort of reflex, less perfect than the reflexes prepared by straining one's attention towards the movement.① The times are much more variable in the sensorial way than in the muscular. The several muscular reactions differ little from each other. Only in them does the phenomenon occur of reacting on a false signal, or of reacting before the signal. Times intermediate between these two types occur according as the attention fails to turn itself exclusively to one of the extremes. It is obvious that Herr Lange's distinction between the two types of reaction is a highly important one, and that the 'extreme muscular method,' giving both the shortest times and the most constant ones, ought to be aimed at in all comparative investigations. Herr Lange's own muscular time averaged 0″.123; his sensorial time, 0″.230.

These reaction-time experiments are then in no sense measurements of the swiftness of thought. Only when we complicate them is there a chance for anything like an intellectual operation to occur. They may be complicated in various ways. The reaction may be withheld until the signal has consciously awakened a distinct idea (Wundt's discrimination-time, association-time) and then performed. Or there may be a variety of possible signals, each with a different reaction assigned to it, and the reacter may be uncertain which one he is about to receive. The reaction would then hardly seem to occur without a preliminary recognition and choice. We shall see, however, in the appropriate chapters, that the discrimination and choice involved in such a reaction are widely different from the intellectual operations of which we are ordinarily conscions under those names. Meanwhile the simple reaction-time remains as the starting point of all these superinduced complications.

---

① Lange has an interesting hypothesis as to the brain-process concerned in the latter, for which I can only refer to his essay.

上述第88～89页)。通过练习而获得的典型感觉时间可能是另一种类型的反射,可能不如某人通过集中对动作的注意力而准备好的反射那么完善。[①] 时间在感觉的方式中比在肌肉的方式中有更多的可变性。几个肌肉反应彼此之间很少有区别。只有在它们当中,才会出现对错误信号做出反应和在信号之前就开始反应的现象。如果注意力没有专门地朝向其中的一个极端,就会产生这两种反应时间的中间的时间。显而易见,兰格对这两种类型的反应进行区分是非常重要的,而且,在所有的比较研究中,因为"极端肌肉法"可以给出最短和最恒定的时间,所以我们都应该致力于它。兰格自己的肌肉时间平均为0.123秒,他的感觉时间平均为0.230秒。

因此反应时间的实验绝不是对快速思维的测量。只有当我们把它们复杂化的时候,才可能有机会出现如智性活动的这类东西。它们可以通过各种方式被复杂化。反应可以一直被抑制住,直到信号有意识地唤醒了一个截然不同的观念之后(冯特的辨别时间和联想时间),它才被执行出来。或者也可能存在多种可能信号,每一个信号都配置有一个不同的反应,而且反应者并不确定他将接收到哪一个信号。因此,如果没有一个初步的识别和选择的话,反应似乎很难发生。然而,在适当的章节中我们将会看到,在这种反应中所涉及的辨别和选择与我们在这些名称之下通常所意识到的智性活动是非常不同的。与此同时,这种简单的反应依然是作为所有这些增加了的复杂性的起点而存在的。在所

① 关于涉及后者的大脑过程,兰格提出了一个有趣的假说,对此我只能参考他的论文。

It is the fundamental physiological constant in all time-measurements. As such, its own variations have an interest, and must be briefly passed in review. ①

The reaction-time varies with the *individual* and his *age.* An individual may have it particularly long in respect of signals of one sense (Buccola, p. 147), but not of others. Old and uncultivated people have it long (nearly a second, in an old pauper observed by Exner, Pflüger's Archiv, VII. 612-4). Children have it long (half a second, Herzen in Buccola, p. 152).

Practice shortens it to a quantity which is for each individual a minimum beyond which no farther reduction can be made. The aforesaid old pauper's time was, after much practice, reduced to 0.1866 sec. (*loc. cit.* p. 626).

Fatigue lengthens it.

Concentration of attention shortens it. Details will be given in the chapter on Attention.

The *nature of the signal* makes it vary. ② Wundt writes:

---

① The reader who wishes to know more about the matter will find a most faithful compilation of all that has been done, together with much original matter, in G. Buccola's 'Legge del Tempo,' etc. See also chapter XVI of Wundt's Physiol. Psychology; Exner in Hermann's Hdbch., Bd. 2, Thl. II. pp. 252-280; also Ribot's Contemp. Germ. Psych. chap. VIII.

② The nature of the movement also seems to make it vary. Mr. B. I. Gilman and I reacted to the same signal by simply raising our hand, and again by carrying our hand towards our back. The moment registered was always that at which the hand broke an electric contact in *starting* to move. But it started one or two hundredths of a second later when the more extensive movement was the one to be made. Orchansky, on the other hand, experimenting on contractions of the masseter muscle, found (Archiv f. (Anat. u.) Physiol., 1889, p. 187) that the greater the amplitude of contraction intended, the shorter grew the time of reaction. He explains this by the fact that a more ample contraction makes a greater *appeal to the attention*, and that this shortens the times.

有的时间测量中，它是基本的生理学常数。既然这样，它本身的变化就很有趣了，从而必须对其做一简单的回顾。①

反应时间随个体及其年龄的不同而变化。个体可能对一种感官信号的反应时间特别长（布科拉，第147页），但对其他信号却不是这样。年老的和未受教育的人反应时间长（埃克斯纳观察到一个年老的乞丐反应时间接近一秒，《弗吕格文集》，7，第612~614页）。儿童的反应时间长（半秒，布科拉书中之“赫茨恩”，第152页）。

练习可以使反应时间缩短到对每一个个体来说不可能再进一步缩短的最小值。上述年老乞丐在大量训练之后，其反应时间缩短到了0.1866秒。（在上述引文中，第626页。）

疲劳会延长反应时间。

注意力的集中会缩短反应时间。在注意力一章中会对其详细内容加以讨论。

信号的性质使它发生变化。② 冯特写道：

---

① G. 布科拉在其《时间法则》中对所有已经做过的工作做了最忠实的编辑，想对这一问题做更多的了解的读者可以在其中找到它们，其中还有一些更为新颖的问题。也可参见冯特的《生理心理学》，第16章；赫尔曼《手册》中的“埃克斯纳”，卷2，册2，第252~280页；以及里伯特的《当代德国心理学》，第8章。

② 运动的性质似乎也使运动时间发生变化。B. J. 吉尔曼和我通过简单地举起手，以及把手伸向后背分别对同一个信号做出反应。记录下的时刻总是手开始运动时断开电接触的时刻。可是，当人们做伸展幅度更大的动作时，反应开始的时间总是要晚百分之一或百分之二秒。另一方面，奥尔查斯克对嚼肌的收缩做了实验，发现（《（解剖学和）生理学文库》，1889年，第187页）意图收缩的幅度越大，反应的时间就越短。他是这样解释这种情况的：收缩幅度越大，对注意力的要求就越高，而这就会缩短反应时间。

"I found that the reaction-time for impressions on the skin with electric stimulus is less than for true touch-sensations, as the following averages show:

	Average.	Average Varilation.
Sound.	0.167 sec.	0.0221 sec.
Light	0.222 "	0.0219 "
Electric skin-sensation.	0.201 "	0.0115 "
Touch-sensations	0.213 "	0.0134 "

I here bring together the averages which have been obtained by some other observers:

	Hirsch.	Hankel.	Exner.
Sound	0.149	0.1505	0.1360
Light	0.200	0.2246	0.1506
Skin-sensation	0.182	0.1546	0.1337"①

Thermic reactions have been lately measured by A. Goldscheider and by Vintschgau (1887), who find them slower than reactions from touch. That from heat especially is very slow, more so than from cold, the differences (according to Goldscheider) depending on the nerve-terminations in the skin.

Gustatory reactions were measured by Vintschgau. They differed according to the substances used, running up to half a second as a maximum when identification took place. The mere perception of the presence of the substance on the tongue varied from 0″.159 to 0″.219 (Pflüger's Archiv, XIV. 529).

Olfactory reactions have been studied by Vintschgau, Buccola, and Beaunis. They are slow, averaging about half a second (cf. Beaunis, Recherches exp. sur l'Activité Cérébrale, 1884, p. 49 ff.).

① Physiol. Psych., II. 223.

“我发现对皮肤电刺激印象的反应时间比真正的触摸感觉的反应时间要短，如下面的平均值所表示的那样：

	平均值	平均变化值
声音	0.167 秒	0.0221 秒
光	0.222“	0.0219“
皮肤电感觉	0.201“	0.0115“
触摸感觉	0.213“	0.0134“

我在这里将其他观察者获得的平均值放在一起：

	赫希	汉克尔	埃克斯纳
声音	0.149	0.1505	0.1360
光	0.200	0.2246	0.1506
皮肤感觉	0.182	0.1546	0.1337”①

最近 A. 戈德施艾德和温特施高（1887 年）对温度反应进行了测量，他们发现温度反应比触觉反应慢。尤其是对热的反应非常慢，比对冷的反应还慢，差异（根据戈德施艾德的观点）取决于皮肤神经终端。

温特施高测量了味觉反应。反应时间随使用物质的变化而不同，当识别发生时，反应时间最长可达半秒。对物质出现在舌头上的单纯知觉时间在 0″.159 至 0″.219 秒之间变化（《弗吕格文集》，14，第 529 页）。

温特施高、布科拉和博尼斯研究了嗅觉反应。它们比较慢，平均时间约为半秒（参见博尼斯，《大脑活动实验研究》，1884 年，第 49 页以后）。

① 《生理心理学》，2，第 223 页。

It will be observed that *sound* is more promptly reacted on than either *sight* or *touch*. *Taste* and *smell* are slower than either. One individual, who reacted to touch upon the tip of the tongue in 0″. 125, took 0″. 993 to react upon the taste of quinine applied to the same spot. In another, upon the base of the tongue, the reaction to touch being 0″. 141, that to sugar was 0″. 552 (Vintschgau, quoted by Buccola, p. 103). Buccola found the reaction to odors to vary from 0″. 334 to 0″. 681, according to the perfume used and the individual.

The *intensity of the signal* makes a difference. The in-tenser the stimulus the shorter the time. Herzen (Grund-linien einer allgem. Psychophysiologie, p. 101) compared the reaction from a *corn* on the toe with that from the skin of the hand of the same subject. The two places were stimulated simultaneously, and the subject tried to react simultaneously with both hand and foot, but the foot always went quickest. When the sound skin of the foot was touched instead of the corn, it was the hand which always reacted first. Wundt tries to show that when the signal is made barely perceptible, the time is probably the same in all the senses, namely, about 0″. 332 (Physiol. Psych., 2d ed., Ⅱ. 224).

Where the signal is of touch, the place to which it is applied makes a difference in the resultant reaction-time. G. S. Hall and V. Kries found (Archiv f. Anat. u. Physiol., 1879) that when the finger-tip was the place the reaction was shorter than when the middle of the upper arm was used, in spite of the greater length of nerve-trunk to be traversed in the latter case. This discovery invalidates the measurements of the rapidity of transmission of the current in human nerves, for they are all based on the method of comparing reaction-times from places near the root and near the extremity of a limb. The same observers found that signals seen by the periphery of the retina gave longer times than the same signals seen by direct vision.

将会观察到的是，对声音的反应比视觉反应和触觉反应更迅速一些。味觉和嗅觉反应比视觉和触觉反应更慢。一个个体对触碰舌尖做出反应的时间是0.125秒，对施用于舌尖同一点上的奎宁的味道做出反应花了0.993秒。在另一个体那里，位置在舌的根部，触觉反应时间为0.141秒，对糖的反应时间为0.552秒（温特施高，由布科拉引用，第103页）。布科拉发现，根据所使用香水和个体的不同，对气味的反应时间介于0.334秒至0.681秒之间。

信号的强度也会产生差异。刺激的强度越大，时间越短。赫茨恩（《普通心理生理学概要》，第101页）比较了同一被试对象从脚趾上的鸡眼而来的反应和从手的皮肤而来的反应。两个地方同时受到刺激，并且被试对象尽量用手和脚同时做出反应，但是脚总是动得最快。当被触碰的是脚上的健康皮肤而不是鸡眼时，手的反应总是最先出现。冯特试图说明，当信号仅仅能被感知时，所有感官的反应时间可能都是一样的，即，大约0.332秒（《生理心理学》，第2版，2，第224页）。

当信号是触觉信号时，触碰所施用的位置会使作为结果而发生的反应时间发生变化。G. S. 霍尔和V. 克里斯发现（《解剖学和生理学文库》，1879年），当触碰位置在指尖时，反应时间比触碰位置在上臂中部时的反应时间要短一些，虽然在后一种情况下需要穿越的神经主干要长很多。这一发现使对人的神经流传送速度的测量变得无效了，因为这些测量的方法都是建立在比较四肢根部附近和四肢末端附近的反应时间的基础之上的。同样的观察者还发现通过视网膜边缘看到信号比通过直接视觉看到同一信号需要花费更长的时间。

The *season* makes a difference, the time being some hundredths of a second shorter on cold winter days (Vintschgau *apud* Exner, Hermann's Hdbh., p. 270).

Intoxicants alter the time. *Coffee* and *tea* appear to shorten it. Small doses of *wine* and *alcohol* first shorten and then lengthen it; but the shortening stage tends to disappear if a large dose be given immediately. This, at least, is the report of two German observers. Dr. J. W. Warren, whose observations are more thorough than any previous ones, could find no very decided effects from ordinary doses (Journal of Physiology, Ⅷ. 311). *Morphia* lengthens the time. *Amyl-nitrite* lengthens it, but after the inhalation it may fall to less than the normal. Ether and chloroform lengthen it (for authorities, etc., see Buccola, p. 189).

Certain *diseased states* naturally lengthen the time.

The *hypnotic trance* has no constant effect, sometimes shortening and sometimes lengthening it (Hall, Mind, Ⅷ. 170; James, Proc. Am. Soc. for Psych. Research, 246).

The time taken to *inhibit* a movement (e.g. to cease con-traction of jaw-muscles) seems to be about the same as to produce one (Gad, Archiv f. (Anat. u.) Physiol., 1887, 468; Orchansky, *ibid.*, 1889, 1885).

An immense amount of work has been done on reaction-time, of which I have cited but a small part. It is a sort of work which appeals particularly to patient and exact minds, and they have not failed to profit by the opportunity.

Cerebral Blood-Supply

The next point to occupy our attention is the *changes of circulation which accompany cerebral activity.*

季节也会造成差异，在寒冷的冬天，反应时间会缩短百分之几秒（温特施高，根据埃克斯纳的《赫尔曼手册》，第 270 页）。

能令人麻醉的东西使时间有所改变。咖啡和茶水显得缩短时间。少量的红酒和酒精先是缩短时间，然后会延长时间；但是如果立刻施加大的剂量，缩短时间的阶段就会趋向于消失。至少，这是两个德国观察人员的报告。J. W. 沃伦博士的观察比任何先前的观察都更加彻底，他发现普通的剂量不会导致十分确定的结果（《生理学杂志》，8，第 311 页）。吗啡延长时间。亚硝酸戊酯延长时间，但是在吸入以后，时间可能会降低至正常水平以下。乙醚和氯仿延长时间（关于权威论述等，参见布科拉，第 189 页）。

某些患病状态自然会延长时间。

由催眠导致的恍惚状态不会产生恒定的作用，有时缩短时间，有时延长时间（霍尔，《心灵》，8，第 170 页；詹姆士，《美国心理学研究协会会刊》，第 246 页）。

抑制一种动作的时间（例如，停止下巴肌肉的收缩）似乎和产生一种动作的时间相等（盖德，《（解剖学和）生理学文库》，1887 年，第 468 页；奥查斯基，同上，1889 年，1885 年）。

对于反应时间人们已经做了大量的工作，而我在这里只引用了其中一个小的部分。做这种工作需要有特别的耐心和严谨的态度，通过把握机会，观察人员一定会因此而受益的。

大脑供血

占据我们注意力的下一个问题是与大脑活动相伴随的血液循环的变化。

All parts of the cortex, when electrically excited, produce alterations both of respiration and circulation. The blood-pressure rises, as a rule, all over the body, no matter where the cortical irritation is applied, though the motor zone is the most sensitive region for the purpose. Elsewhere the current must be strong enough for an epileptic attack to be produced. ①Slowing and quickening of the heart are also observed, and are independent of the vaso-constrictive phenomenon. Mosso, using his ingenious ‘plethysmograph’ as an indicator, discovered that the blood-supply to the arms diminished during intellectual activity, and found furthermore that the arterial tension (as shown by the sphygmograph) was increased in these members (see Fig23).

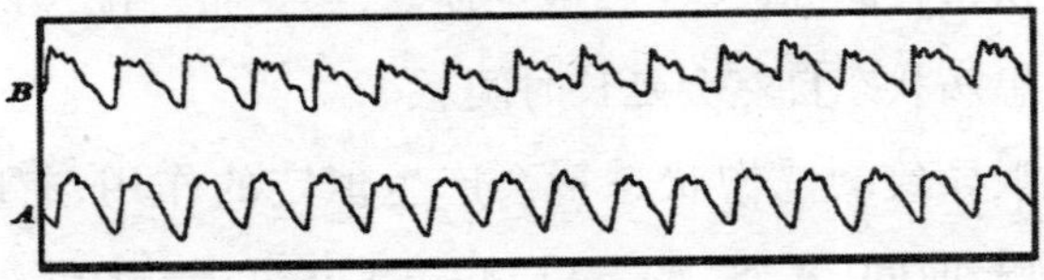

FIG. 23.—Sphymographic pulse-tracing.

A, during intellectual repose; *B*, during intellectual activity. (Moso)

So slight an emotion as that produced by the entrance of Professor Ludwig into the laboratory was instantly followed by a shrinkage of the arms. ② The brain itself is an excessively vascular organ, a sponge full of blood, in fact; and another of Mosso's inventions showed that when less Blood went to the arms, more went to the head. The subject to be observed lay on a delicately balanced table which could tip downward either at the head or at the foot if the weight of either end were increased.

---

① Francois – Franck, Fonctions Motrices, Lecon XXII.

② La Paura (1884), p. 117.

皮层的所有部位，当受到电刺激时，就会产生呼吸和血液循环的变化。不论将皮层刺激施加在什么部位，全身的血压通常都会升高，尽管运动区域是造成血压升高的最敏感区域。在其他地方，电流必须足够强，才能引起癫痫病的发作。① 心跳的减慢和加速也得到观察，而且它们是独立于血管收缩现象的。莫索将他那具有独创性的“体积描记器”作为指示器来使用时发现，在智性活动过程中，对胳膊的供血减少了，而且他还进一步发现，动脉压（如脉搏描记器所显示的那样）在这些肢体中升高了（见图 23）。

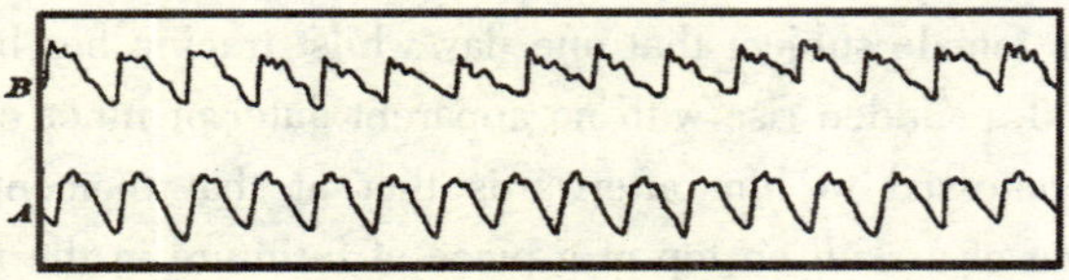

图 23 脉搏记录仪的脉搏图录

A，智性活动停止之时；*B*，智性活动进行之时。（莫索）

像因路德维希教授进入实验室而产生的那么细微的情绪，随后也会立刻造成胳膊供血的减少。② 大脑本身是一个血管太多的器官，事实上是一块充满血液的海绵体；而且莫索的另一项发明表明，当胳膊中的血液减少时，很多血液去了大脑。被观察的主体躺在一张非常平稳的桌子上，如果头部和脚部这两端的重量有

---

① 弗朗西斯－弗兰克，《驱动功能》，第 22 讲。

② 拉波拉（1884 年），第 117 页。

The moment emotional or intellectual activity began in the subject, down went the balance at the head-end, in consequence of the redistribution of blood in his system. But the best proof of the immediate afflux of blood to the brain during mental activity is due to Mosso's observations on three persons whose brain had been laid bare by lesion of the skull. By means of apparatus described in his book, ① this physiologist was enabled to let the brain-pulse record itself directly by a tracing. The intra-cranial blood-pressure rose immediately whenever the subject was spoken to, or when he began to think actively, as in solving a problem in mental arithmetic. Mosso gives in his work a large number of reproductions of tracings which show the instantaneity of the change of blood-supply, whenever the mental activity was quickened by any cause whatever, intellectual or emotional. He relates of his female subject that one day whilst tracing her brain-pulse he observed a sudden rise with no apparent outer or inner cause. She however confessed to him afterwards that at that moment she had caught sight of a *skull* on top of a piece of furniture in the room, and that this had given her a slight emotion.

The fluctuations of the blood-supply to the brain were independent of respiratory changes, ② and followed the quickening of mental activity almost immediately. We must suppose a very delicate adjustment whereby the circulation follows the needs of the cerebral activity. Blood very likely may rush to each region of the cortex according as it is most active, but of this we know nothing. I need hardly say that the activity of the nervous matter is the primary phenomenon, and the afflux of blood its secondary consequence. Many popular writers talk as if it were the other way about, and as if mental activity were due to the afflux of blood. But,

① Ueber den Kreislauf des Blutes im menschlichen Gehirn (1881) chap. II. The Introduction gives the history of our previous knowledge of the subject.

② In this conclusion M. Gley (Archives de Physiologie 1881, p. 742) agrees with Professor Mosso. Gley found his pulse rise 1-3 beats, his carotid dilate, and his radial artery contract during hard mental work.

所增加，这张桌子就会朝增重的那一端倾斜。当被试的情绪和智性活动开始时，由于他体内的血液重新分布的缘故，头部那一端就会向下倾斜。但是，对心理活动之时血液立即流入大脑这一事实的最好证明是莫索对三个由于头盖骨损伤而致使大脑暴露在外的病人的观察。借助于他书中所描述的仪器，①这位生理学家能够让脑脉冲直接通过图录被记录下来。只要有人和被试说话，或者当他开始积极思考的时候，如通过心算来解决一个问题时，颅内血压就会立即升高。莫索在其著作中复制了大量的图录，它们表明，无论什么原因，不管它是智性方面的还是情绪方面的，只要心理活动被加快，供血都会发生瞬时性变化。他在讲述他的女性被试时说，有一天当他对她的脑脉冲进行图录时，他观察到了一个没有明显内部或外部原因的突然升高。然而，她后来向他承认，当时她看到房间里有一个摆在家具顶部的头盖骨，而这使她产生了一些轻微的情绪变化。

大脑供血的波动独立于呼吸的变化，②并且几乎立刻随着心理活动的加快而变化。我们必须假定血液循环随着大脑活动的需要而产生了非常微妙的调节。血液很可能会依照每一皮层区域的活跃程度而流动，即当某一区域最活跃的时候，血液就会流向它，但是对此我们一无所知。我几乎无需提及，神经物质的活动是主要现象，而血液的流入是次级结果。很多有名的作者在谈论这一问题时似乎持有不同的观点，似乎认为心理活动是基于血

---

① 《论人脑中的血液循环》，1881 年，第 2 章，导论部分考察了我们以前对这一问题的认知史。

② 格雷先生在这一结论上与莫索教授的意见一致（《生理学文集》，1881 年，第 742 页）。格雷发现在艰苦的脑力工作中，他的脉搏加快了一到三下，他的颈动脉扩张了，他的桡骨动脉收缩了。

as Professor H. N. Martin has well said, "that belief has no physiological foundation whatever; it is even directly opposed to all that we know of cell life." ① A chronic pathological congestion may it is true, have secondary consequences, but the primary congestions which we have been considering *follow* the activity of the brain-cells by an adaptive reflex vaso-motor mechanism doubtless as elaborate as that which harmonizes blood-supply with cell-action in any muscle or gland.

Of the changes in the cerebral circulation during sleep, I will speak in the chapter which treats of that subject.

Cerebral Thermometry.

Brain-activity seems accompanied by a local disengagement of heat. The earliest careful work in this direction was by Dr. J. S. Lombard in 1867. Dr. Lombard's latest results include the records of over 60,000 observations. ② He noted the changes in delicate thermometers and electric piles placed against the scalp in human beings, and found that any intellectual effort, such as computing, composing, reciting poetry silently or aloud, and especially that emotional excitement such as an anger fit, caused a general rise of temperature, which rarely exceeded a degree Fahrenheit. The rise was in most cases more marked in the middle region of the head than elsewhere. Strange to say, it was greater in reciting poetry silently than in reciting it aloud. Dr. Lombard's explanation is that "in internal recitation an additional portion of energy, which in recitation aloud was converted into nervous and muscular force, now

---

① Address before Med. and Chirurg. Society of Maryland, 1879.

② See his book; "Experimental Researches on the Regional Tempera ture of the Head" (London, 1879).

液的流入。但是,正如H.N.马丁教授所说:“那种信念没有任何生理学基础,它甚至与我所知道的细胞生命的知识直接对立。”[①]确实,慢性病理充血会产生次级结果,但是我们一直在探讨的主要充血,通过适应性反射血管收缩机制的作用跟随脑细胞活动而发生,适应性反射血管收缩机制无疑与在任何肌肉和腺体中协调供血和细胞运动的机制一样精细。

关于在睡眠中大脑血液循环的变化,我将在论述那个问题的章节中谈到它。

大脑测温

大脑活动似乎伴随有局部的放热。在这一研究方向上最早的细致工作是由J.S.隆巴德做出的。隆巴德博士最近的观察结果囊括了60000多项观察记录。[②] 他注意到了挨着人的头皮被放置的精密温度计和电池组的变化,并且发现任何智性的努力,例如计算、写作、默背或朗读背诵诗歌,还有尤其是如愤怒之类的情绪激动,都会导致温度的普遍升高,温度升高很少会超过华氏1度。在大多数情况下,头部中间区域的温度升高得比其他区域更显著一些。奇怪的是,默背诗歌时,温度升高得比朗读背诵时要多一些。隆巴德博士对此的解释是,“在朗读背诵时,一部分额外的能量转化成了神经和肌肉的力,而在默背时,这部分能量作为

① 《对Med.和Chirurg.的演讲》,马里兰协会,1879年。

② 参见他的著作:《关于头部局部温度的实验研究》(伦敦,1879年)。

appears as heat." [1]I should suggest rather, if we must have a theory, that the surplus of heat in recitation to one's self is due to inhibitory processes which are absent when we recite aloud. In the chapter on the Will we shall see that the *simple* central process is to *speak* when we think; to think silently involves a check in addition. In 1870 the indefatigable Schiff took up the subject, experimenting on live dogs and chickens, plunging thermo-electric needles into the substance of their brain, to eliminate possible errors from vascular changes in the skin when the thermometers were placed upon the scalp. After habituation was established, he tested the animals with various sensations, tactile, optic, olfactory, and auditory. He found very regularly an immediate deflection of the galvanometer, indicating an abrupt alteration of the intra-cerebral temperature. When, for instance, he presented an empty roll of paper to the nose of his dog as it lay motionless, there was a small deflection, but when a piece of meat was in the paper the deflection was much greater. Schiff concluded from these and other experiments that sensorial activity heats the brain-tissue, but he did not try to localize the increment of heat beyond finding that it was in both hemispheres, whatever might be the sensation applied. [2] Dr. R. W. Amidon in 1880 made a farther step forward, in localizing the heat produced by voluntary muscular contractions. Applying a number of delicate surface-thermometers simultaneously against the scalp, he found that when different muscles of the body were made to contract vigorously for ten minutes or more, different regions of the scalp rose in temperature, that the regions were well focalized, and that the rise of temperature was often considerably over a Fahrenheit degree. As a result of his investigations he gives a diagram in which numbered regions

---

① *Loc. cit.* p. 195.

② The most convenient account of Schiff's experiments is by Prof. Herzen, in the Revue Philosophique, vol. III. p. 36.

热量而表现了出来”。[1] 如果我们必须要提出一种理论的话，我还要进一步指出，在自己默背时多出来的热量是由于抑制过程而导致的，并且这种抑制过程当我们朗读背诵时是不存在的。在关于意志的那一章中，我们将会看到，当我们思考时，简单的中枢过程是说出来；不出声地思考涉及额外的抑制。在1870年，不知疲倦的希夫就开始致力于这一问题，他用活着的狗和鸡做实验，将温差电针插入其大脑的物质当中，以消除当温度计放在头皮上时由于皮肤脉管的变化而可能造成的误差。当适应形成后，他对这些动物的各种感觉进行了测试，包括触觉、视觉、嗅觉和听觉。他有规律地发现了检流计上立刻出现的偏转，这表明脑内温度有突然的改变。例如，当他的狗一动不动地躺在那里时，他将一个空纸卷放到它的鼻子前，就会出现很小的偏转，而当纸里有一块肉的时候，偏转会大很多。希夫从这些实验和其他实验中得出结论，认为是感觉活动让脑组织发热的，但是他只是发现，不论所涉及的是哪一种感觉，发热都发生在两个脑半球中，却没有对发热的地方做出定位。[2] 1880年，R. W. 阿米登博士在对由主动的肌肉收缩而产生的发热进行定位方面向前迈进了一步。通过同时将一些精密的体表温度计紧贴头皮，他发现当使身体的不同肌肉有力地收缩十分钟或更长一段时间时，头皮不同区域的温度就会升高，这些区域很容易定位，并且温度的升高经常会大大超过华氏1度。他给出了一个图示作为他研究的结果，其中被编了号的区域

---

① 在上述引文中，第195页。

② 赫茨恩教授对希夫的实验做出了最适宜的说明，见《哲学评论》，第3卷，第36页。

represent the centres of highest temperature for the various special movements which were investigated. To a large extent they correspond to the centres for the same movements assigned by Ferrier and others on other grounds; only they cover more of the skull. ①

Phosphorus and Thought.

Chemical action must of course accompany brain-activity. But little definite is known of its exact nature. Cholesterin and creatin are both excrementitious products, and are both found in the brain. The subject belongs to chemistry rather than to psychology, and I only mention it here for the sake of saying a word about a wide-spread popular error about brain-activity and phosphorus. '*Ohne Phosphor, kein Gedanke*,' was a noted war-cry of the 'materialists' during the excitement on that subject which filled Germany in the '60s. The brain, like every other organ of the body, contains phosphorus, and a score of other chemicals besides. Why the phosphorus should be picked out as its essence, no one knows. It would be equally true to say 'Ohne Wasser kein Gedanke,' or 'Ohne Kochsalz kein Gedanke'; for thought would stop as quickly if the brain should dry up or lose its NaCl as if it lost its phosphorus. In America the phosphorus-delusion has twined itself round a saying quoted (rightly or wrongly) from Professor L. Agassiz, to the effect that fishermen are more intelligent than farmers because they eat so much fish, which contains so much phosphorus. All the facts may be doubted.

The only straight way to ascertain the importance of phosphorus to thought would be to find whether more is excreted by the brain during mental activity than during rest. Unfortunately we cannot do this directly, but can only gauge the amount of PO_5 in the urine,

---

① A New Study of Cerebral Cortical Localization (N. Y., Putnam. 1880), pp. 48-53.

代表所研究的因为各种特殊运动而产生的最高温度中心。它们在很大程度上和由费里与其他人在不同基础上指出的负责相同运动的中枢相符和;只是它们覆盖了头盖骨的更大的部分。①

磷与思维

化学作用一定和大脑活动相伴随。但是我们却很少有关于其确切本质的确定知识。胆固醇和肌氨酸都是排泄物,并且在大脑中都可以找到它们。这一课题属于化学而不是心理学,我在这里提到它只是为了对关于大脑活动和磷的一个广为传播的流行的错误观点提出一些看法。“没有磷,就没有思维”是对这一问题的兴趣弥漫在60年代的德国之时由“唯物主义者”提出的著名口号。和身体中所有其他器官一样,大脑中含有磷,此外还含有其他许多化学元素。为什么磷被挑选出来成为其本质要素,没有人知道。说“没有水就没有思维”或“没有盐就没有思维”也同样正确;因为如果大脑耗尽了水或者失去了氯化钠,思维也会同大脑失去磷一样而很快停止的。在美国,对磷的错觉与从L.阿加西斯教授那里引来(正确地或错误地)的一句谚语交织在一起,之所以渔夫比农民更聪明是因为他们吃了很多鱼,而鱼中含有很多磷。所有这些事实都值得怀疑。

探知磷对思维的重要性的唯一直接方式,就是去发现是否在心理活动过程中大脑分泌的磷比在其休息时要多。遗憾的是我们不能直接这样做,而只能测量尿液中五氧化磷的含量,用它来

① 《对大脑皮层定位的新研究》(N.T.普特曼,1880年),第48~53页。

which represents other organs as well as the brain, and this procedure, as Dr. Edes says, is like measuring the rise of water at the mouth of the Mississippi to tell where there has been a thunder-storm in Minnesota.① It has been adopted, however, by a variety of observers, some of whom found the phosphates in the urine diminished, whilst others found them increased, by intellectual work. On the whole, it is impossible to trace any constant relation. In maniacal excitement less phosphorus than usual seems to be excreted. More is excreted during sleep. There are differences between the alkaline and earthy phosphates into which I will not enter, as my only aim is to show that the popular way of looking at the matter has no exact foundation.② The fact that phosphorus-preparations may do good in nervous exhaustion proves nothing as to the part played by phosphorus in mental activity. Like iron, arsenic, and other remedies it is a stimulant or tonic, of whose intimate workings in the system we know absolutely nothing, and which moreover does good in an extremely small number of the cases in which it is prescribed.

The phosphorus-philosophers have often compared thought to a secretion. "The brain secretes thought, as the kidneys secrete urine, or as the liver secretes bile," are phrases which one sometimes hears. The lame analogy need hardly be pointed out. The materials which the brain *pours into the blood*(cholesterin, creatin, xanthin, or whatever they may be)are the analogues of the urine and the bile, being in fact real material excreta. As far as these matters go, the brain is a ductless gland. But we know of nothing connected with liver -and kidney-activity which can be in the remotest degree compared with the stream of thought

---

① Archives of Medicine, vol. X, No. 1(1883).

② Without multiplying references, I will simply cite Mendel (Archiv f. Psychiatrie vol. III, 1871), Mairet(Archives de Neurologie, vol. IX, 1885), and Beaunis (Rech. Expérimentales sur I' Activité Cérébrale, 1887). Riches gives a partial bibliography in the Revue Scientifique, vol. 38, p. 788(1886).

代表大脑和其他器官中的磷的含量，而这种测量程序，如伊兹博士所说，就好比通过在密西西比河口测量河水的上涨，来断定在明尼苏达是否有过一场雷暴一样。① 然而，很多观察人员采用了它，他们中的一些人发现由于脑力劳动而使得尿液中的磷酸盐减少了，而另外一些人发现它们增加了。总之，追踪任何不变的关系是不可能的。在狂乱的兴奋状态中，磷分泌得似乎比平常少。睡觉的时候磷分泌得多。碱性的磷酸盐和自然的磷酸盐之间有差异，对此我就不讨论了，因为我的唯一目的就是要表明，看待这一问题的那种流行方法没有切实的基础。② 磷制剂可能对精神衰竭有疗效这一事实不能证明磷在心理活动中所起的作用。像铁、砷以及其他药物一样，它是一个刺激物或滋补剂，它在身体系统内部的作用方式我们绝对一无所知，而且在开了磷制剂处方的病例中，它只有在极少数病例中有疗效。

那些思考磷的哲人们时常将思维比作分泌。“大脑分泌出思想，就如同肾脏分泌出尿液，或肝脏分泌出胆汁一样，”这就是人们有时能听到的一些措辞。这种类比没有说服力是显而易见的。大脑注入血液中的物质（胆固醇、肌氨酸、叶黄素或无论什么东西），作为在事实上是真正的排泄物，才是尿液和胆汁的相似之物。就这些物质被分泌出来而言，大脑是一种内分泌腺。但是，就肝脏和肾脏活动在最低程度上与大脑的物质分泌相伴的思想

① 《医学文库》，第 10 卷，第 1 期（1883 年）。

② 为了不增加参考书目，我只引用了门德尔（《精神病学文库》，第 3 卷，1871 年）、梅莱特（《神经病学文库》，第 9 卷，1885 年）以及博尼斯（《大脑活动实验研究》，1887 年）。里奇特在《科学评论》中给出了部分参考书目，第 38 卷，第 788 页（1886 年）。

that accompanies the brain's material secretions.

There remains another feature of general brain-physiology, and indeed for psychological purposes the most important feature of all. I refer to the aptitude of the brain for acquiring *habits*. But I will treat of that in a chapter by itself.

之流做比较来说,我们对此一无所知。

在普通大脑生理学中还有一个特征这里没有讨论,对心理学的目的而言,它确实是所有特征中最重要的一个。我是指大脑有获得习惯的天生能力。我将在独立的章节中讨论它。

CHAPTER IV. [①]

Habit.

When we look at living creatures from an outward point of view, one of the first things that strike us is that they are bundles of habits. In wild animals, the usual round of daily behavior seems a necessity implanted at birth; in animals domesticated, and especially in man, it seems, to a great extent, to be the result of education. The habits to which there is an innate tendency are called instincts; some of those due to education would by most persons be called acts of reason. It thus appears that habit covers a very large part of life, and that one engaged in studying the objective manifestations of mind is bound at the very out-set to define clearly just what its limits are.

The moment one tries to define what habit is, one is led to the fundamental properties of matter. The laws of Nature are nothing but the immutable habits which the different elementary sorts of matter follow in their actions and reactions upon each other. In the organic world, however, the habits are more variable than this. Even instincts vary from one individual to another of a kind; and are modified in the same individual, as we shall later see, to suit the exigencies of the case. The habits of an elementary particle of matter cannot change (on the principles of the atomistic philosophy), because the particle is itself an unchangeable thing; but those of a compound mass of matter can change, because they are in the last instance due to the structure of the compound,

---

① This chapter has already appeared in the Popular Science Monthly for February 1887.

第四章　习　惯①

当我们以外在的角度观察有生命的动物时，最先打动我们的事情之一，就是看到它们有许多习惯。野生动物的一系列日常行为似乎是在其出生时就被灌注到它们身上的一种必需之物；在被驯养的动物那里，尤其是在人那里，它似乎在很大程度上是教育的结果。具有先天倾向的习惯被称为本能；一些由于教育而形成的习惯，大多数人称其为理性行为。因此，似乎习惯涵盖了生活的很大一部分内容，而对致力于研究心灵的客观表现的人来说，他理应在一开始就清楚地对其界限做出规定。

当人们试图定义什么是习惯时，就马上被引到了物质的基本属性上来。自然规律仅仅是不同元素种类的物质在其相互之间的作用和反作用中所遵循的不变的习惯。然而，在有机界，习惯要比这易变得多。甚至本能在同一种类的不同个体中也有变化；而且，如我们后面将要看到的那样，为了适应紧急情况，在同一个体那里本能也会被改良。一粒单纯物质的习惯不会变化（据原子理论哲学的原理），因为粒子本身是不可变化的东西；但是复合的物质集团的习惯就会变化，因为在最后，习惯是由于复合物的结

---

① 本章在1887年2月的《通俗科学月刊》上发表过。

and either outward forces or inward tensions can, from one hour to another, turn that structure into something different from what it was. That is, they can do so if the body be plastic enough to maintain its integrity, and be not disrupted when its structure yields. The change of structure here spoken of need not involve the outward shape; it may be invisible and molecular, as when a bar of iron becomes magnetic or crystalline through the action of certain outward causes, or India-rubber becomes friable, or plaster 'sets.' All these changes are rather slow; the material in question opposes a certain resistance to the modifying cause, which it takes time to overcome, but the gradual yielding whereof often saves the material from being disintegrated altogether. When the structure has yielded, the same inertia becomes a condition of its comparative permanence in the new form, and of the new habits the body then manifests. *Plasticity*, then, in the wide sense of the word, means the possession of a structure weak enough to yield to an influence, but strong enough not to yield all at once. Each relatively stable phase of equilibrium in such a structure is marked by what we may call a new set of habits. Organic matter, especially nervous tissue, seems endowed with a very extraordinary degree of plasticity of this sort; so that we may without hesitation lay down as our first proposition the following, that *the phenomena of habit in living beings are due to the plasticity*[①] *of the organic materials of which their bodies are composed.*

But the philosophy of habit is thus, in the first instance, a chapter in physics rather than in physiology or psychology. That it is at bottom a physical principle is admitted by all good recent writers on the subject. They call attention to analogues of acquired habits exhibited by

① In the sense above explained, which applies to inner structure as well as to outer form.

构而形成的，而且外部的力量或内部的张力每时每刻都能够将结构变得和先前不一样。也就是说，如果身体有足够的可塑性来保持它的完整性，并且当它结构改变时也不会受到破坏，那么习惯就能够改变。这里所谈到的结构变化不需要涉及外部形状的变化；变化可以是看不见的，并且是分子的变化，就如同铁块由于某种外部因素的作用而变得有磁性或者变成了晶状体，或者如印度橡胶变成脆的或膏状的。所有这些变化都相当缓慢；相关的质料形成某种阻力与形成变化的因素相对抗，而阻力需要时间来克服，然而对变化因素的逐渐让步常常使质料得以免遭被完全分解的厄运。在结构已经改变了的时候，相同的惯性变成了在新形式中一个其保持相对持久性的条件，同时也变成了产生身体此时显现出来的新习惯的一个条件。因此，从广义上来说，可塑性意味着获有一种结构，其脆弱得足以屈从于影响，却又有不会一下子就屈服的力量。在这种结构中，每一个相对稳定的状态都被标记以我们称之为一组新的习惯的东西。有机物，尤其是神经组织，在极大程度上被赋予了这种可塑性；从而我们可以毫不犹豫地提出我们下述第一个命题，即在有生命的存在物中的习惯现象应归因于构成其身体的有机物的可塑性。①

因此，关于习惯的哲学在最初就是物理学中的一章，而不是生理学和心理学中的一章。它根本就是一条物理原理，并且这被最近所有研究这一问题的优秀作者所承认。他们引起了人们对无生命物质所展示出来的获得习惯的这种类似情况的注意。因

① 从上面所解释的意义上说，它既适用于内部结构，也适用于外部形式。

dead matter. Thus, M. Léon Dumont, whose essay on habit is perhaps the most philosophical account yet published, writes:

"Every one knows how a garment, after having been worn a certain time, clings to the shape of the body better than when it was new; there has been a change in the tissue, and this change is a new habit of cohesion. A lock works better after being used some time; at the outset more force was required to overcome certain roughnesses in the mechanism. The overcoming of their resistance is a phenomenon of habituation. It costs less trouble to fold a paper when it has been folded already. This saving of trouble is due to the essential nature of habit, which brings it about that, to reproduce the effect, a less amount of the outward cause is required. The sounds of a violin improve by use in the hands of an able artist, because the fibres of the wood at last contract habits of vibration conformed to harmonic relations. This is what gives such inestimable value to instruments that have belonged to great masters. Water, in flowing, hollows out for itself a channel, which grows broader and deeper; and, after having ceased to flow, it resumes, when it flows again, the path traced by itself before. Just so, the impressions of outer objects fashion for themselves in the nervous system more and more appropriate paths, and these vital phenomena recur under similar excitements from without, when they have been interrupted a certain time." ①

Not in the nervous system alone. A scar anywhere is a *locus minoris resistentice*, more liable to be abraded, inflamed, to suffer pain and cold, than are the neighboring parts. A sprained ankle, a dislocated arm, are in danger of being sprained or dislocated again; joints that have once been attacked by rheumatism or gout, mucous membranes that have been the seat of catarrh, are with each fresh recurrence more prone to a relapse, until often the morbid state chronically substitutes itself for the sound one. And if we ascend to

---

① Revue Philosophique, I, 324.

此，L. 杜蒙先生（他关于习惯的论文可能是迄今已经出版的最富哲理性的论述）写道：

"每个人都知道，一件衣服在穿了一段时间之后为何会比它崭新时更贴身；这是因为织体发生了变化，这种变化就是新的结合习惯。锁在用过一段时间后会变得更好开，它在开始时需要更大的力量来克服机械装置的粗糙所带来的阻力。对阻力的克服就是一种形成习惯的现象。折叠一张已经被折叠过的纸就不会那么麻烦。麻烦减少了是由于习惯的根本性质所造成的，正是由于它，当重新产生结果时，就需要较少量的外因了。通过有才能的艺术家的双手使用，一把小提琴的音质会有所提高，因为木头的纤维最终养成了与和声关系相一致的振动习惯。就是习惯赋予了大师们手中的乐器以如此不可估量的价值。流淌的水为自己冲出一条水道，这水道变得越来越宽、越来越深；而当它停止流动一段时间后再重新开始流动，它仍会继续以前流过的路线。就像这样，对外部对象的印象在神经系统中为它们自己塑造出了越来越适宜的路径，并且当它们被截断一段时间后，这些重要的现象会在相似的外部条件刺激下又再次重现。"①

这种情况不单单在神经系统中存在。任何地方的疤痕都是一个抵抗力轻微的部位，和它邻近的部分相比，更容易擦伤、发炎，以及遭受疼痛和寒冷之苦。扭伤的踝关节、脱臼的胳膊有再次扭伤和脱臼的危险；曾经换过风温病和痛风的关节、曾经得过粘膜炎的黏膜，随着每一次新的复发都会使它们更易于重演，直到慢性的病变状态替代了原来的健康状态。而且如果我们上升

① 《哲学评论》，第 1 卷，第 324 页。

the nervous system, we find how many socalled functional diseases seem to keep themselves going simply because they happen to have once begun; and how the forcible cutting short by medicine of a few attacks is often sufficient to enable the physiological forces to get possession of the field again, and to bring the organs back to functions of health. Epilepsies, neuralgias, convulsive affections of various sorts, insomnias, are so many cases in point. And, to take what are more obviously habits, the success with which a 'weaning' treatment can often be applied to the victims of unhealthy indulgence of passion, or of mere complaining or irascible disposition, shows us how much the morbid manifestations themselves were due to the mere inertia of the nervous organs, when once launched on a false career.

Can we now form a notion of what the inward physical changes may be like, in organs whose habits have thus struck into new paths? In other words, can we say just what mechanical facts the expression 'change of habit' covers when it is applied to a nervous system? Certainly we cannot in anything like a minute or definite way. But our usual scientific custom of interpreting hidden molecular events after the analogy of visible massive ones enables us to frame easily an abstract and general scheme of processes which the physical changes in question *may* be like. And when once the possibility of *some* kind of mechanical interpretation is established, Mechanical Science, in her present mood, will not hesitate to set her brand of ownership upon the matter, feeling sure that it is only a question of time when the exact mechanical explanation of the case shall be found out.

If habits are due to the plasticity of materials to out-ward agents, we can immediately see to what outward influences, if to any, the brain-matter is plastic. Not to mechanical pressures, not to thermal changes, not to any of the forces to which all the other organs of our body are exposed; for nature has carefully shut up our brain and spinal cord in bony boxes, where no influences of this sort can get at

到神经系统,我们就会发现,似乎许多功能性疾病只是因为其碰巧出现过一次就一直存在;通过药物强制性地阻止了几次疾病的发作,而这又足以使生理的力量重新占据那一领域,并且使器官重新获得健康的功能。癫痫症、神经痛、各种痉挛性疾病、失眠症都属于这种情况。再则,举个属于习惯的更加明显的例子,"断念"疗法常常可以成功地施用于不健康地放纵情欲的患者,以及沉湎于单纯抱怨中或有暴躁倾向的患者。这种成功向我们表明,一旦神经器官误入歧途,有多少病态的表现自身便会由于神经器官的纯粹惯性而造成。

现在我们能够形成一个定义用来说明在习惯如此挤入新路径的器官中,其内部的物理变化是什么样的吗?换言之,当"习惯的变化"这一表述被应用于神经系统,我们能够说出这一表述涵盖了什么样的机械事实吗?当然,我们不能以任何详细的和确定的方式来这样做。但是,我们通常的科学习惯,即通过对可见的宏观事件的类推来解释隐藏着的分子事实,使我们能够很容易地设计出一种抽象的和普通的方案,用它来表述相关的物理变化过程可能是什么样的。并且,一旦当某种机械解释的可能性被确立下来,机械科学,以其现在的状态,将会毫不犹豫地在这一问题上贴上其所有权的标签,并且很确定地认为,找出对这一问题的切实的机械解释只是个时间问题。

如果习惯归因于质料对于外部手段所表现出来的可塑性,我们立刻就可以看到大脑物质对什么样的外部影响(如果有的话)来说是可塑的。外部影响不是机械压力,不是温度变化,不是我们身体的所有其他器官所面临的任何力;因为自然已经小心翼翼地将我们的大脑和脊髓封闭在骨头匣子中了,这类影响不可能到

them. She has floated them in fluid so that only the severest shocks can give them a concussion, and blanketed and wrapped them about in an altogether exceptional way. The only impressions that can be made upon them are through the blood, on the one hand, and through the sensory nerve-roots, on the other; and it is to the infinitely attenuated currents that pour in through these latter channels that the hemispherical cortex shows itself to be so peculiarly susceptible. The currents, once in, must find a way out. In getting out they leave their traces in the paths which they take. The only thing they *can* do, in short, is to deepen old paths or to make new ones; and the whole plasticity of the brain sums itself up in two words when we call it an organ in which currents pouring in from the sense—organs make with extreme facility paths which do not easily disappear. For, of course, a simple habit, like every other nervous event—the habit of snuffling, for example, or of putting one's hands into one's pockets, or of biting one's nails—is, mechanically, nothing but a reflex discharge; and its anatomical substratum must be a path in the system. The most complex habits, as we shall presently see more fully, are, from the same point of view, nothing but *concatenated* discharges in the nerve centres, due to the presence there of systems of reflex paths, so organized as to wake each other up successively—the impression produced by one muscular contraction serving as a stimulus to provoke the next, until a final impression inhibits the process and closes the chain. The only difficult mechanical problem is to explain the formation *de novo* of a simple reflex or path in a pre-existing nervous system. Here, as in so many other cases, it is only the *premier pas qui coûte.* For the entire nervous system is nothing but a system of paths between a sensory *terminus a quo* and a muscular, glandular, or other *terminus ad quem.* A path once traversed by a nerve-current might be expected to follow the law of most of the paths we know, and to be scooped out and made more permeable

达那里。它让它们漂浮在液体中,以至于只有最激烈的振荡才能给它们以冲击,并且它用一种完全异常的方式将它们覆盖和包裹起来。被施加于其上的仅有印痕,一方面是通过血液来完成的,另一方面是通过感觉神经根来完成的。正是由于从这些神经通道中流入的无限减弱的神经流,脑半球皮层才表现出它自己是特别容易受影响的。神经流一旦流入的话,一定会找条路出来。当它们出来的时候,它们在其所走的道路上留下了自己的痕迹。简言之,它们仅仅能做的事情要么是深化原来的路径,要么就是找到新的路径;而且,如果我们称大脑是这样的一个器官:在其中从感觉器官中流入的神经流开辟出极为便捷且不易消失的路径,那么我们就把大脑的全部可塑性用一句话总结完了。因为,一个简单的习惯,和所有其他神经事实一样——例如,抽鼻子的习惯、把手放在口袋里的习惯、咬指甲的习惯——当然只是一种机械性的反射释放;其解剖学基础一定是系统中的一条路径。如我们不久将更加全面地了解到的那样,从同样的观点看,最复杂的习惯也只是神经中枢中的连锁释放,这些释放是由存在于那里的反射路径系统造成的,反射路径是以依次唤醒对方的方式组织起来的——由一次肌肉收缩而产生的印象是唤醒下一个印象的刺激,直到最后一个印象抑制了这一程序并且关闭了这一链条为止。唯一困难的机械问题是,如何解释在一个预先存在的神经系统中一个简单反射或说路径的形成。这里,像在很多其他情况中一样,只是第一步费力。因为整个神经系统只是从感官的由此终端到肌肉的、腺体的或其他的至此终端之间的路径系统。一条路径一旦被一条神经流穿过,可以预期它遵循我们所知道的大部分路径的规律,它被挖掘开来并且比以前更

than before;[1] and this ought to be repeated with each new passage of the current. Whatever obstructions may have kept it at first from being a path should then, little by little, and more and more, be swept out of the way, until at last it might become a natural drainage-channel. This is what happens where either solids or liquids pass over a path; there seems no reason why it should not happen where the thing that passes is a mere wave of rearrangement in matter that does not displace itself, but merely changes chemically or turns itself round in place, or vibrates across the line. The most plausible views of the nerve current make it out to be the passage of some such wave of rearrangement as this. If only a part of the matter of the path were to 'rearrange' itself, the neighboring parts remaining inert, it is easy to see how their inertness might oppose a friction which it would take many waves of rearrangement to break down and overcome. If we call the path itself the 'organ,' and the wave of rearrangement the 'function,' then it is obviously a case for repeating the celebrated French formula of '*La fonction fait l'organe.*'

So nothing is easier than to imagine how, when a current once has traversed a path, it should traverse it more readily still a second time. But what made it ever traverse it the first time? [2] In answering this question we can only fall back on our general conception of a nervous system as a mass of matter whose parts, constantly kept in states of different

---

① Some paths, to be sure, are banked up by bodies moving through them under too great pressure, and made impervious. These special cases we disregard.

② We cannot say *the will*, for, though many, perhaps most, human habits were once voluntary actions, no action, as we shall see in a later chapter, can be *primarily* such. While an habitual action may once have been voluntary, the voluntary action must before that, at least once, have been impulsive or reflex. It is this very first occurrence of all that we consider in the text.

容易通过;[①]而这种情况应该在神经流每次重新通过时得以重复。不管最初有什么障碍物使它不能成为一条路径,这些障碍物被一点点地、越来越多地清除了出去,直到最后它能成为一条自然的排出通道。这正是当固体或者液体通过一条路径时所发生的情况;当通过的东西仅仅是物质中重新排列的一种波,它没有替换掉自己,而仅仅是发生了化学变化,或者自己就地转向,或者穿越中线往复摆动,这里似乎没有理由说明这种情况为什么不能发生。关于神经流最可信的观点就是,由于某些诸如此类的、重新排列了的波的通过,神经流使得这种情况的发生得以完成。如果路径中只有一部分物质可以"重新排列"自己,并且其周围部分保持着惰性,那么就不难看到,它们的惰性可以引起一种阻力的对抗,并且这阻力必须通过许多重新排列的波才能被瓦解和克服掉。如果我们将路径自身称作一个器官,并且将重新排列的波称作功能,那么它显然就是一个例子,其重复了那句著名的法国陈词"功能造就器官"。

因此,很容易设想,当神经流第一次穿过一条路径时,它应当如何在第二次更容易地穿过它。但是,是什么让它第一次穿过了它呢?[②] 要回答这一问题,我们只能回到我们关于神经系统的一般观念上来,即作为一团物质的神经系统,它的各个部位不变地

---

① 确实,有一些路径在过大的压力之下被通过的物体堵塞了,而且变得不畅通了。对这些特殊情况我们不予考虑。

② 我们不能说是意志,因为尽管很多、甚至可能大多数人类的习惯都曾经是主动的行为,但是如我们在后来的章节中所看到的那样,没有任何行为起初是这样的。虽然一个习惯性行为可以曾经是主动的,但是在这之前,主动的行为一定至少曾有一次是冲动的或反射的。我们在文章中考虑的正是这所有习惯行为中最初发生的事情。

tension, are as constantly tending to equalize their states. The equalization between any two points occurs through whatever path may at the moment be most pervious. But, as a given point of the system may belong, actually or potentially, to many different paths, and, as the play of nutrition is subject to accidental changes, blocks may from time to time occur, and make currents shoot through unwonted lines. Such an unwonted line would be a new-created path, which if traversed repeatedly, would become the beginning of a new reflex arc. All this is vague to the last degree, and amounts to little more than saying that a new path may be formed by the sort of chances that in nervous material are likely to occur. But, vague as it is, it is really the last word of our wisdom in the matter. ①

It must be noticed that the growth of structural modification in living matter may be more rapid than in any lifeless mass, because the incessant nutritive renovation of which the living matter is the seat tends often to corroborate and fix the impressed modification, rather than to counter act it by renewing the original constitution of the tissue that has been impressed. Thus, we notice after exercising our muscles or our brain in a new way, that we can do so no longer at that time; but after a day or two of rest, when we resume the discipline, our increase in skill not seldom surprises us. I

---

① Those who desire a more definite formulation may consult J. Fiske's 'Cosmic Philosophy,' vol. Ⅱ. pp. 142-146 and Spencer's 'Principles of Biology,' sections 302 and303, and the part entitled 'Physical Synthesis' of his 'Principles of Psychology.' Mr. Spencer there tries, not only to show how new actions may arise in nervous systems and form new reflex arcs therein, but even how nervous tissue may actually be born by the passage of new waves of isometric transformation through an originally indifferent mass. I cannot help thinking that Mr. Spencer's data, under a great show of precision, conceal vagueness and improbability, and even self contradiction.

处于不同的紧张状态，它们同样趋向于不停地使自己的状态达到平衡。此刻不论什么路径，只要它最容易通过，那么由于它的性质使然，任何两点间的平衡就会出现。但是，由于系统中给定的点可能会实际地或潜在地属于很多不同的路径，并且由于营养的作用可以发生偶然的变化，因而，阻塞会不时地发生，迫使神经流流入非习惯性路径中。这种非习惯性路径将是一条新开辟的路径，如果它被重复穿过的话，它就是一个新的反射弧的开端。所有这一切都极端空泛，差不多就是说，由于在神经质料中很可能发生的某种偶然事件所致，一条新的路径可能形成。而且，虽然它很空泛，可这真的是用我们的智慧对这一问题所能说出的最后的话了。①

必须注意的是，在有生命的物质中，结构更改进程比在任何无生命物质中要快很多，因为在有生命物质中不停的营养革新常常趋向于将留有印象的更改加以强化并固定下来，而不是通过更新被留下印象的最初组织结构来对抗这种更改。因此我们注意到，在通过新的方式训练过我们的肌肉或大脑之后，我们在那时就不能再做这种训练了；但是，在一到两天的休息之后，当我们重新开始训练的时候，我们技能的增进不能不令我们感到惊讶。我

---

① 那些想要获得更明确的简洁陈述的人可以参考 J. 菲斯克的《宇宙哲学》，第 2 卷，第 142 ~ 146 页，以及斯宾塞的《生物学原理》，第 302 ~ 303 页，以及他的《心理学原理》中标题为“物理综合”的部分。在其中，斯宾塞先生不仅试图表明新的行为如何可以在神经系统中产生并且在那里形成新的反射弧，而且还试图说明神经组织如何可以通过新的等量转化波穿过一团最初无关的质料而最终被创生了出来。我禁不住认为，斯宾塞先生的数据，在其显示出极大精确性的背后，隐藏着空泛的和不大可能的事物，还有甚至是自相矛盾的东西。

have often noticed this in learning a tune; and it has led a German author to say that we learn to swim during the winter and to skate during the summer.

Dr. Carpenter writes: ①

"It is a matter of universal experience that every kind of training for special aptitudes is both far more effective, and leaves a more permanent impress, when exerted on the *growing* organism than when brought to bear on the adult. The effect of such training is shown in the tendency of the organ to ' grow to' the mode in which it is habitually exercised; as is evidenced by the increased size and power of particular sets of muscles, and the extraordinary flexibility of joints, which are acquired by such as have been early exercised in gymnastic performances. . . . There is no part of the organism of man in which the *reconstructive activity* is so great, during the whole period of life, as it is in the ganglionic substance of the brain. This is indicated by the enormous supply of blood which it receives. . . . It is, moreover, a fact of great significance that the nerve-substance is specially distinguished by its *reparative* power. For while injuries of other tissues (such as the muscular) which are distinguished by the *specialty* of their structure and endowments, are repaired by substauce of a lower or less specialized type, those of nerve-substance are repaired by a complete reproduction of the normal tissue; as is evidenced in the sensibility of the newly forming skin which is closing over an open wound, or in the recovery of the sensibility of a piece of 'transplanted' skin, which has for a time been rendered insensible by the complete interruption of the continuity of its nerves. The most remarkable example of this reproduction, however, is afforded by the results of M. Brown-Séquard's ② experiments upon the gradual restoration of the functional activity of the spinal cord after its complete division; which takes place in a way that

① 'Mental Physiology' (1874.) pp. 339-345.

② [See, later, Masius in Van Benedens' and Van Bambeke's 'Archives de Biologie,' vol. I (Liége, 1880). -W. J.]

在学习一个曲调时经常注意到这一点；而且这种情况还令一个德国作家写到：我们在冬天学游泳，在夏天学溜冰。

卡彭特博士写道：①

“这是一个普遍经验，即对特殊天资的各种训练施加于成长中的生物体时，比施加于成年生物体时要更有效，也会留下更为持久的印象。这种训练的效果表现为器官‘生长入’它习惯性练习的模式中的倾向；例如由于体操表演的早期训练，特殊肌肉群获得了体积和力量的增加，并且关节获得了非同寻常的灵活性，这些都证实了这种情况……人这种生命体中的任何部位，只有大脑神经节这种物质在其一生当中重建活动最为活跃。它获得大量的血液供应这一事实可以表明这一点……而且，神经物质具有特别显著的修复功能，这是一个具有重要意义的事实。因为，虽然其他以结构和能力的特殊性而著称的组织（例如肌肉），其损伤可以通过类型较低级或不那么专门化的物质而得以修复，但是神经物质是通过正常组织的完全再生而得以修复的；在一个敞开的伤口上，新长出来的皮肤覆盖了它，这皮肤的感受性可以证实这种情况；又如一块被‘移植’的皮肤，由于神经连续性的完全中断它有一段时间全无感觉，而其感受性的恢复也可以证实这种情况。然而，这种再生的最显著的例子是由布朗－西夸先生②的实验结果所提供的，这是一项关于脊髓被完全分裂之后其功能活动逐渐恢复的实验；实验结果以其产生的方式表明，是整个脊

① 《心理生理学》(1874 年)，第 339～345 页。

② 参见后面，范本尼登斯和范班伯克《生物学文集》(列日，1880 年)第 1 卷中的马修斯。—W. J.

indicates rather a *reproduction* of the whole, or the lower part of the cord and of the nerves proceeding from it, than a mere *reunion* of divided surfaces. This reproduction is but a special manifestation of the reconstructive change which is *always* taking place in the nervous system; it being not less obvious to the eye of reason that the 'waste' occasioned by its functional activity must be constantly repaired by the production of new tissue, than it is to the eye of sense that such reparation supplies an actual *loss* of substance by disease or injury."

"Now, in this constant and active reconstruction of the nervous system, we recognize a most marked conformity to the general plan manifested in the nutrition of the organism as a whole. For, in the first place, it is obvious that there is a tendency to the production of a *determinate type* of structure; which type is often not merely that of the species, but some special modification of it which characterized one or both of the progenitors. But this type is peculiarly liable to modification during the early period of life; in which the functional activity of the nervous system (and particularly of the brain) is extraordinarily great, and the reconstructive process proportionally active. And this modifiability expresses itself in the formation of the mechanism by which those *secondarily automatic* modes of movement come to be established, which, in man, take the place of those that are *congenital* in most of the animals beneath him; and those modes of sense-perception come to be *acquired*, which are elsewhere clearly *instinctive*. For there can be no reasonable doubt that, in both cases, a nervous mechanism is *developed* in the course of this self-education, corresponding with that which the lower animals inherit from their parents. The plan of that *rebuilding* process, which is necessary to maintain the integrity of the organism generally, and which goes on with peculiar activity in this portion of it, is thus being incessantly modified; and in this manner all that portion of it which ministers to the *external* life of sense and motion that is shared by man with the animal kingdom at large, becomes at adult age the expression of the habits which the individual has acquired during the period of growth and development. Of these habits,

髓或者脊髓的下半部分以及由它发出的神经的再生，而不仅仅是分裂了的表面的再结合。这种再生是在神经系统中一直发生着的重建性变化的特殊表现；对‘理性之眼’来说，由其功能性活动而引起的‘损耗’必须不断地通过新组织的产生而得以修复，这是显而易见的，而对‘感性之眼’来说，这种修复实际上填补了由于疾病和损伤而造成的物质损耗，这同样是显而易见的。”

“现在，在这种持续的、活跃的神经系统的重建之中，我们识别出了一种最显著的一致性，即与在对生物体进行总体供养时表现出来的一般规划的一致性。因为，首先，显然存在着产生确定结构类型的倾向；这种结构类型通常不仅仅是物种的类型，而是物种类型的某种特殊更改，而这种更改表现了个体自身或者个体自身和其祖先的特征。而且这种类型尤其在早年之时易于更改，在早年，神经系统的功能性活动（尤其是大脑的功能性活动）异常活跃，并且重建过程也相应地活跃。而且这种可更改性是在机制的形成之中来表达自身的，通过形成机制，那些次级自动化的运动模式确立了下来。在人这里，这种运动模式取代了存在于人之下的大部分动物中的天生的运动模式；并且感官知觉模式逐渐地被获得了，而在其他地方它们显然是本能。因为没有理由怀疑，在两种情形中，神经机制都是在自我教育的过程中发展的，与低等动物从其父母那里继承的神经机制的发展相应。因而重建过程的计划不断地被改变，重建过程的计划对于一般性地保持生物体的完整性来说是必要的，并且它与生物体这一部分的特殊活动一同进行；而且，以这种方式，生物体中负责人与动物王国所普遍共享的外部的感觉和运动生活的所有部位，在其成年阶段就变成了个体在成长和发展阶段获得的习惯的表达物。就这些习惯来

some are common to the race generally, while others are peculiar to the individual; those of the former kind (such as Walking erect) being universally acquired, save where physical inability prevents; while for the latter a special training is needed, which is usually the more effective the earlier it is begun—as is remarkably seen in the case of such feats of dexterity as require a conjoint education of the perceptive and of the motor powers. And when thus developed during the period of growth, so as to have become a part of the constitution of the adult, the acquired mechanism is thenceforth maintained in the ordinary course of the nutritive operations, so as to be ready for use when called upon, even after long inaction."

"What is so clearly true of the nervous apparatus of animal life can scarcely be otherwise than true of that which ministers to the automatic activity of the mind. For, as already shown, the study of psychology has evolved no more certain result than that there are uniformities of mental action which are so entirely conformable to those of bodily action as to indicate their intimate relation to a 'mechanism of thought and feeling,' acting under the like conditions with that of sense and motion. The psychical principles of *association*, indeed, and the physiological principles of *nutrition*, simply express—the former in terms of mind, the latter in terms of brain—the universally admitted fact that any sequence of mental action which has been frequently repeated tends to perpetuate itself; so that we find ourselves automatically prompted to *think*, *feel*, or *do* what we have been before accustomed to think, feel, or do, under like circumstances, without any consciously formed *purpose*, or anticipation of results. For there is no reason to regard the cerebrum as an exception to the general principle that. while each part of the organism tends to *form itself* in accordance with the mode in which it is habitually exercised, this tendency will be especially strong in the nervous apparatus, in virtue of that *incessant regeneration* which is the very condition of its functional activity. It scarcely, indeed, admits of doubt that every state of ideational consciousness which is either *very strong* or

说，有一些通常是种族所共有的，而其他一些是个体所特有的；前一种习惯（例如直立行走）可以普遍获得，除非身体的缺陷阻碍了它们的获得；而后一种习惯的获得需要专门的训练，通常开始得越早，就越有效——正如人们在灵巧技艺的获得需要对知觉和运动能力进行综合训练这一实例中明显看到的那样。而且，当这个机制在成长期间如此发展了起来，以至于成为了成年人体质的一部分时，所获得的机制此后在营养作用的日常过程中被保持下来，以至于甚至在很长一段时间没有活动之后，当需要的时候，就可以拿来使用。”

“对动物生命的神经机制来说是如此明显真实的东西，对与负责心灵的自动化行动的东西来说几乎不可能不真实。因为，如已经表明的那样，心理学的研究还没有推算出比下面更确定的结果，即存在着一些心理活动的一致性，它们和身体活动的一致性是如此的一致，以至于暗示出了它们与‘思维和感受机制’的亲密相关性，这个机制与感觉和运动机制在相同条件下活动。确实，心理的联想原理和营养的生物原理仅仅表达了——前者在心灵方面，后者在大脑方面——普遍承认的事实，即被经常重复的心理活动序列，都倾向于使自己永久化；以致我们发现我们自动地促使自己去思考、感受或者做我们以前在类似情况下已经习惯于思考、感受和做的事情，而不带有任何有意识形成的目的或者对结果的预期。因为这里没有任何理由将大脑看成是下述一般原理的例外情况，即当生物体的每一个部位都趋向于依照其习惯性训练的模式来形成自身时，这种倾向在神经机制中尤其强烈，这是由于作为其功能活动的绝对条件的那种不断重建所致。确实，几乎无可怀疑的是，观念意识的所有状态，不论它非常强还是

is *habitually repeated* leaves an organic impression on the cerebrum ; in virtue of which that same state may be reproduced at any future time, in respondence to a suggestion fitted to excite it.... The 'strength of early association' is a fact so universally recognized that the expression of it has become proverbial; and this precisely accords with the physiological principle that, during the period of growth and development, the formative activity of the brain will be most amenable to directing influences. It is in this way that what is early 'learned by heart' becomes branded in (as it were) upon the cerebrum; so that its 'traces' are never lost, even though the conscious memory of it may have completely faded out. For, when the organic modification has been once *fixed* in the growing brain, it becomes a part of the normal fabric, and is regularly *maintained* by nutritive substitution; so that it may endure to the end of life, like the scar of a wound."

Dr. Carpenter's phrase that *our nervous system grows to the modes in which it has been exercised* expresses the philosophy of habit in a nutshell. We may now trace some of the practical applications of the principle to human life.

The first result of it is that *habit simplifies the movements required to achieve a given result, makes them more accurate and diminishes fatigue.*

"The beginner at the piano not only moves his finger up and down in order to depress the key, he moves the whole hand, the forearm and even the entire body, especially moving its least rigid part, the head, as if he would press down the key with that organ too. Often a contraction of the abdominal muscles occurs as well. Principally, however, the impulse is determined to the motion of the hand and of the single finger. This is, in the first place, because the movement of the finger is the movement *thought of*, and, in the second place, because its movement and that of the key are the movements we try to *perceive*, along with the results of the latter on the ear. The more often the process is repeated, the more easily the movement follows, on account of the increase in permeability of the nerves engaged."

"But the more easily the movement occurs, the slighter is the

习惯性地重复着，都在大脑中留下了有机印象；这是由于在对一个适合于激起同样状态的暗示做出反应时，同样的状态可以在未来的任何时间被重现出来……‘早期联想强度’是这样一个被普遍公认的事实，以至于这种表达变得众所周知了；并且它正好和这种生理学原理相一致，即在成长和发展期间，形成中的大脑活动最顺从于引导性影响。正是通过这种方式早期‘用心学会’的东西（就好像）被刻在了脑子里，以致即使是对它的有意识的记忆已经完全消失了，可它的‘痕迹’却从来不会失去。因为，一旦有机更改已经固定在了成长着的大脑中，它就成为了正常组织的一部分，并且通过营养置换而被有规律地保持着，以致它可以持续到生命的结束为止，就像一块伤疤。”

卡彭特博士一语“我们的神经系统生长入它习惯性练习的模式中”，简约地表达出了习惯哲学。我们现在可以追溯一下这一原理对人类生活的实际应用。

它的第一个结果是习惯使实现一个特定结果的动作简单化了，它使得动作更加精确并且减少了疲劳。

“初学钢琴的人为了按下琴键不仅会上下动他的手指，他还会动整个手、前臂、甚至整个身体，尤其还会动他最僵硬的部分——头部，好像他要用那个器官按下琴键似的。通常，腹部肌肉的收缩也会出现。然而，神经脉冲主要是为了让手和单个手指运动。首先，这是因为手指的运动是被思考到了的运动，第二，因为手指的运动和琴键的运动都是我们尽力知觉的运动，还有琴键的运动对耳朵产生的影响也是我们所尽力知觉的。由于所使用神经的渗透性的增加，越频繁地重复这一过程，动作就越容易发生。”

“但是动作发生得越容易，开始这动作所需的刺激就越轻微；

stimulus required to set it up; and the slighter the stimulus is, the more its effect is confined to the fingers alone."

"Thus, an impulse which originally spread its effects over the whole body, or at least over many of its movable parts, is gradually determined to a single definite organ, in which it effects the contraction of a few limited muscles. In this change the thoughts and perceptions which start the impulse acquire more and more intimate causal relations with a particular group of motor nerves."

"To recur to a simile, at least partially apt, imagine the nervous system to represent a drainage system, inclining, on the whole, toward certain muscles, but with the escape thither somewhat clogged. Then streams of water will, on the whole, tend most to fill the drains that go towards these muscles and to wash out the escape. In case of a sudden 'flushing,' however, the whole system of channels will fill itself, and the water overflow everywhere before it escapes. But a moderate quantity of water invading the system will flow through the proper escape alone."

"Just so with the piano-player. As soon as his impulse, which has gradually learned to confine itself to single muscles, grows extreme, it overflows into larger muscular regions. He usually plays with his fingers, his body being at rest. But no sooner does he get excited than his whole body becomes 'animated,' and he moves his head and trunk, in particular, as if these also were organs with which he meant to belabor the keys."①

Man is born with a tendency to do more things than he has ready-made arrangements for in his nerve-centres. Most of the performances of other animals are automatic. But in him the number of them is so enormous, that most of them must be the fruit of painful study. If practice did not make perfect, nor habit economize the expense of nervous

---

① G. H. Schneider: 'Der menschliche Wille' (1882). pp. 417-419 (freely translated). For the drain simile, see also Spencer's 'Psychology,' part V, chap. Ⅷ.

而刺激越轻微，其作用就越是单独局限在手指上。”

“因此，最初将自己的效用遍及全身、或者至少遍布很多可移动部位的神经脉冲，逐渐致力于一个确定的单一器官，在其中它造成了有限的几个肌肉的收缩。在这种变化中，引起神经脉冲的思维和知觉获得了一种与一组特殊运动神经越来越亲密的因果关系。”

“借助于一个至少是部分切题的明喻，将神经系统想像成一个排水系统，在整体上向某些肌肉倾斜，但是到那边的出口有些堵塞了。那么水流在整体上最倾向于充满朝向这些肌肉的水沟，并且冲开那个出口。然而，在突然间‘奔流’的情况中，整个通道系统将充满水，并且水会在流出之前到处泛滥。但如果流入系统中的水是适量的，那么它就会单独从适当的出口流出去。”

“钢琴演奏人员的情况和这一样。他已经逐渐学会将神经脉冲局限在个别肌肉中，一旦他的这种神经脉冲达到极限，它就会蔓延到更大的肌肉区域中。他通常用他的手指弹奏，而他的身体在休息，但是，一旦他变得激动起来，他的整个身体就立刻变得‘充满活力’了，并且他尤其要将他的头和躯干运动起来，就好像它们也是他想要用来狠击琴键的器官一样。”①

人生下来就有一种倾向，要做比他在神经中枢里已经安排好了的更多的事情。其他动物的大多数行为都是自动的。但是在人这里，行为的数量非常之大，而且大多数行为都是艰苦学习的结果。如果练习没有达到完美，习惯没有节省神经和肌肉能量的

① G. H. 施奈德：《人的意志》（1882 年），第 417 ~419 页（意译的）。就排水沟这一明喻，也可参见斯宾塞的《心理学》，第 5 部分，第 8 章。

and muscular energy, he would therefore be in a sorry plight. As Dr. Maudsley says: ①

"If an act became no easier after being done several times, if the careful direction of consciousness were necessary to its accomplishment on each occasion, it is evident that the whole activity of a lifetime might be confined to one or two deeds—that no progress could take place in development. A man might be occupied all day in dressing and undressing himself; the attitude of his body would absorb all his attention and energy; the washing of his hands or the fastening of a button would be as difficult to him on each occasion as to the child on its first trial; and he would, furthermore, be completely exhausted by his exertions. Think of the pains necessary to teach a child to stand, of the many efforts which it must make, and of the ease with which it at last stands unconscious of any effort. For while secondarily automatic acts are accomplished with comparatively little weariness—in this regard approaching the organic movements, or the original reflex movements—the conscious effort of the will soon produces exhaustion. A spinal cord without... memory would simply be an idiotic spinal cord.... It is impossible for an individual to realize how much he owes to its automatic agency until disease has impaired its functions."

The next result is that *habit diminishes the conscious attention with which our acts are performed.*

One may state this abstractly thus: If an act require for its execution a chain, *A*, *B*, *C*, *D*, *E*, *F*, *G*, etc., of successive nervous events, then in the first performances of the action the conscious will must choose each of these events from a number of wrong alternatives that tend to present themselves; but habit soon brings it about that each event calls up its own appropriate successor without any alternative

---

① Physiology of Mind, p. 155.

损失，他会因此而处于令人遗憾的困境之中。正如莫兹利博士所说：①

“如果一个动作在做了几次之后还没有变得容易起来，如果每一次完成它时都必须得有意识的悉心指导，那么显然一生的全部活动将局限在一种或两种行为中——在发展中就不可能有进步发生。人可能会整天忙碌于穿衣服和脱衣服；身体的姿势可能会完全吸引他的注意力并吸尽他的能量；每一次洗手和扣纽扣对他来说都会像小孩第一次尝试这些事情时那么困难；此外，由于自己的努力他会变得完全地精疲力竭。想想教会一个孩子站起来所必须经历的痛苦吧，想想孩子必须做出的多种努力吧，再想想他最后站立起来并且意识不到任何努力时的从容吧。因为次级自动动作的完成伴随有相对较少的疲劳——考虑到它接近器官运动，或者最初的反射运动——而意志的有意识努力很快就会产生疲劳。没有……记忆的脊髓简直就是白痴般的脊髓……对个体来说，除非疾病削弱了他的自动机构的功能，否则他不可能认识到他有多么依赖自动机构。”

下一个结果是，习惯减少了我们执行动作所需要的有意识的注意力。

人们可以抽象地如此陈述：如果一个动作的执行需要相继的神经事件链条 A、B、C、D、E、F、G，等等，那么在第一次执行动作时，有意识的意志必须从很多错误地倾向于呈现自身的可选事件中——选择出这些事件；但是习惯很快就会使这样的情况发生，即每一个事件唤起适合它自己的后继事件，其间没有任何可供选

① 《心灵生理学》，第 155 页。

offering itself, and without any reference to the conscious will, until at last the whole chain, *A*, *B*, *C*, *D*, *E*, *F*, *G*, rattles itself off as soon as *A* occurs, just as if *A* and the rest of the chain were fused into a continuous stream. When we are learning to walk, to ride, to swim, skate, fence, write, play, or sing, we interrupt ourselves at every step by unnecessary movements and false notes. When we are proficients, on the contrary, the results not only follow with the very minimum of muscular action requisite to bring them forth, they also follow from a single instantaneous 'cue.' The marksman sees the bird, and, before he knows it, he has aimed and shot. A gleam in his adversary's eye, a momentary pressure from his rapier, and the fencer finds that he has instantly made the right parry and return. A glance at the musical hieroglyphics, and the pianist's fingers have rippled through a cataract of notes. And not only is it the right thing at the right time that we thus involuntarily do, but the wrong thing also, if it be an habitual thing. Who is there that has never wound up his watch on taking off his waistcoat in the daytime, or taken his latchkey out on arriving at the door-step of a friend? Very absent-minded persons in going to their bedroom to dress for dinner have been known to take off one garment after another and finally to get into bed, merely because that was the habitual issue of the first few movements when performed at a later hour. The writer well remembers how, on revisiting Paris after ten years' absence, and, finding himself in the street in which for one winter he had attended school, he lost himself in a brown study, from which he was awakened by finding himself upon the stairs which led to the apartment in a. house many streets away in which he had lived during that earlier time, and to which his steps from the school had then habitually led. We all of us have a definite routine manner of performing certain daily offices connected with the toilet, with the opening and shutting of familiar cupboards, and the like. Our lower centres know the order of these movements, and show their knowledge by their 'surprise' if the objects are altered so as to oblige the movement to be made in a different way.

择的事件提供它们自己，而且也没有涉及任何有意识的意志，直到最后，只要 A 一发生，B、C、D、E、F、G 就轻快地展开了，就好像 A 和链条的剩余部分变化融会成了一条连续的川流一般。当我们正在学习走路、骑马、游泳、滑冰、写字、游戏和歌唱时，我们的每一步骤都被不必要的动作和错误的音符所打断。相反，当我们精通之时，不仅以最少所需肌肉动作就会产生那些结果，而且单一的瞬间提示就会产生它们。神射手看到了鸟，而且在他认出它以前，他已经瞄准了它，并把它射了下来。对手眼睛里一丝光芒的闪烁，来自他剑上的瞬间压力，击剑者就发现他已经即刻做出了正确的躲避和回击。只要瞟上一眼乐谱，钢琴家的手指就已经波浪般地弹奏出了奔流的音符。而且我们不仅仅是这样不知不觉地在恰当的时间做着正确的事情，我们也做着错误的事情，好像它也是习惯中做的事情。有谁从来不会在白天脱掉马夹时拧紧手表的发条，又有谁从来不会在到达朋友门前时拿出自己的家门钥匙？人们知道一些很是心不在焉的人，他们走进卧室为晚餐换衣服，却脱去一件又一件衣服，最后还睡到了床上，因为这仅仅是一个习惯问题，前几个动作是在晚些时候要执行的习惯性动作。作者还清楚地记得自己在离开巴黎十年之后重返那里时的情形：自己走在一条街上，这条街曾经是他在某个冬天里去上学的必经之路，他在恍惚的遐想中迷失了，当他回过神来时，他发现自己已经在几条街之外的一间房子中了，他站在进入公寓的楼梯上，这里曾是他早年一直居住的地方，是从学校回来的脚步习惯性地把他引到这里来的。我们所有人都以一种确定的常规方式来处理某些日常事物，例如洗漱、开关熟悉的碗橱，以及与此类似的事情。我们的低级中枢知道这些动作的顺序，如果对象的变化导致其被迫以不同

But our higher thought-centres know hardly anything about the matter. Few men can tell off-hand which sock, shoe, or trousers leg they put on first. They must first mentally rehearse the act; and even that is often insufficient—the act must be *performed*. So of the questions, Which valve of my double door opens first? Which way does my door swing? etc. I cannot *tell* the answer; yet my *hand* never makes a mistake. No one can *describe* the order in which he brushes his hair or teeth; yet it is likely that the order is a pretty fixed one in all of us.

These results may be expressed as follows:

In action grown habitual, what instigates each new muscular contraction to take place in its appointed order is not a thought or a perception, but the *sensation occasioned by the muscular contraction just finished*. A strictly voluntary act has to be guided by idea, perception, and volition, throughout its whole course. In an habitual action, mere sensation is a sufficient guide, and the upper regions of brain and mind are set comparatively free, A. diagram will make the matter clear:

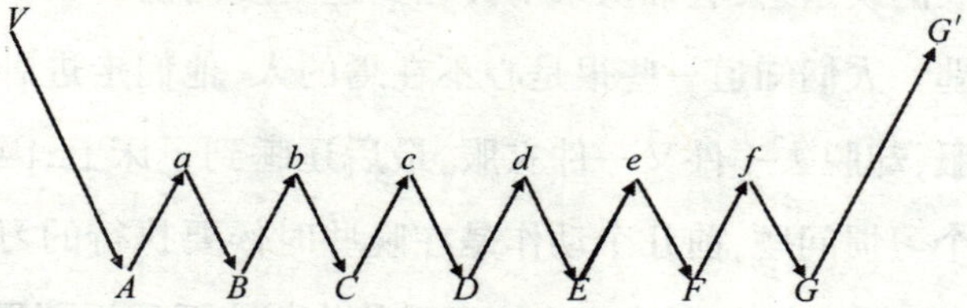

FIG. 24

Let A, B, C, D, E, F, G represent an habitual chain of muscular contractions, and let a, b, c, d, e, f stand for the respective sensations which these contractions excite in us when they are successively performed. Such sensations will usually be of the muscles, skin, or joints of the parts moved, but they may also be effects of the movement upon the eye or the ear. Through them, and through them alone, we are made aware whether the contraction has or has not occurred. When the

的方式做出动作，它们就通过“惊讶”向我们表明它们的知识。很少有人能够当即说出他们是先穿哪只袜子、哪只鞋和那条裤腿。他们必须在心里预演那个动作；而且甚至这样也不够——动作必须执行出来。我先开双扇门的哪一扇？我的门先朝哪边转动？等等。这些问题也是无法回答的。我不能说出答案，但是我的手从来不会犯错。没有人能够描述出他梳头和刷牙的顺序，然而很可能的是，顺序在我们所有人中是相当固定的。

对这些结果可以做如下表述：

在已经成为习惯的行为中，每一次激起新的肌肉收缩并以其指定的顺序发生的东西，不是一次思维，也不是一次知觉，而是由刚刚完成的肌肉收缩引起的感觉。严格的主动动作必须在其整个过程中由观念、知觉和意志所指引。在习惯性的行为中，仅仅感觉就足以成为向导，而大脑和心灵的高级区域则相对比较自由。下面的图示可以使这一问题清楚起来：

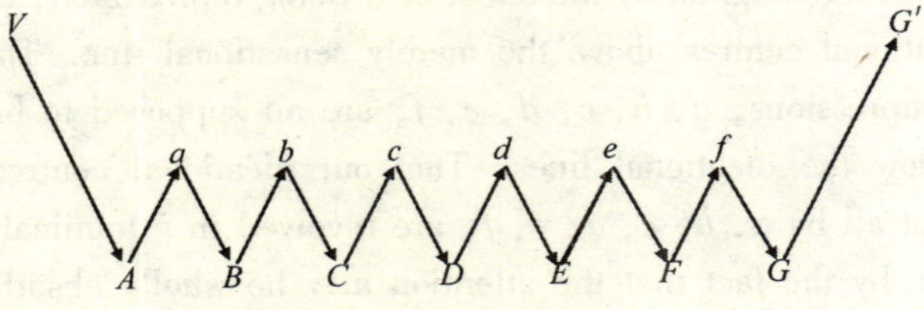

图 24

让 A、B、C、D、E、F、G 代表肌肉收缩的习惯性链条，让 a、b、c、d、e、f 代表当肌肉收缩相继发生时在我们身上分别被激起的感觉。这些感觉通常是肌肉的、皮肤的、或者是运动部位关节的感觉，但是它们也可能是运动对眼睛或耳朵产生的效果。通过它们，而且是单独通过它们，我们意识到了收缩是否发生。当 A、

series, *A*, *B*, *C*, *D*, *E*, *F*, *G*, is being learned, each of these sensations becomes the object of a separate perception by the mind. By it we test each movement, to see if it be right before advancing to the next we hesitate, compare, choose, revoke, reject, etc., by intellectual means; and the order by which the next movement is discharged is an express order from the ideational centres after this deliberation has been gone through.

In habitual action, on the contrary, the only impulse which the centres of idea or perception need send down is the initial impulse, the command to *skart*. This is represented in the diagram by *V*; it may be a thought of the first movement or of the last result, or a mere perception of some of the habitual conditions of the chain, the presence, e. g., of the keyboard near the hand. In the present case, no sooner has the conscious thought or volition instigated movement *A*, than *A*, through the sensation a of its own occurrence, awakens *B* reflexly; *B* then excites *C* through *b*, and so on till the chain is ended, when the intellect generally takes cognizance of the final result. The process, in fact, resembles the passage of a wave of ' peristaltic' motion down the bowels. The intellectual perception at the end is indicated in the diagram by the effect of *G* being represented, at *G'*, in the ideational centres above the merely sensational line. The sensational impressions, *a*, *b*, *c*, *d*, *e*, *f*, are all supposed to have their seat below the ideational lines. That our ideational centres, if involved at all by *a*, *b*, *c*, *d*, *e*, *f*, are involved in a minimal degree, is shown by the fact that the attention may be wholly absorbed elsewhere. We may say our prayers, or repeat the alphabet, with our attention far away.

A musical performer will play a piece which has become familiar by repetition while carrying on an animated conversation, or while continuously engrossed by some train of deeply interesting thought; the accustomed sequence of movements being directly prompted by the *sight* of the notes, or by the remembered succession of the *sounds*(if the piece is played from memory), aided in both cases by the guiding sensations derived from the muscles themselves.

B、C、D、E、F、G 这一序列正在被学习时，这每一个感觉成为了心灵单个知觉的对象。通过它，我们按照理智的方式，犹豫、比较、选择、撤销、拒绝，等等，来检验每一个动作，看它在进入下一个动作之前是否正确；而在这种深思熟虑已经完成之后，释放下一个动作的命令就是直接来自观念中枢的命令。

相反，在习惯性动作中，观念中枢或知觉唯一需要发出的神经脉冲就是最初的神经脉冲，即开始的命令。在图示中这由 V 来表示；它可以是对最初动作或最后结果的一次思维，或者仅仅是对那个链条的一些习惯性条件的一次知觉，例如知觉到了手边的键盘。在目前这种情况下，一旦有意识的思维和意志激起了动作 A，那么 A 通过由于其自身的发生而产生的感觉 a，反射性地唤起了 B，B 然后又通过 b 激起了 C，就这样一直到链条结束为止，此时智性通常认识到了最后的结果。事实上，这种过程很像肠子里的“蠕动”波的通过。最后，智性的知觉在图示中是通过 G 的结果由在单纯“感觉线”上方的观念中枢中的 G’所代表并表示出来的。感觉印象 a、b、c、d、e、f 的位置被认为应该在观念线的下方。如果我们的观念中枢最终被 a、b、c、d、e、f 牵涉进来的话，其所关联的程度也是非常小的，这一点可以由注意力可以完全被吸引到其他地方这一事实而得以证明。我们可以在我们的注意力远离的情况下做祷告，或者重述字母表。

音乐演奏家可以在愉快地进行谈话的同时，或者在持续地全神贯注于一系列非常有趣的思想时，演奏一首因重复已经变得熟悉的乐曲，习惯了的运动顺序通过对音符的视觉而被直接提示出来，或者通过记忆中的连续的声音而被提示出来（如果乐曲是通过记忆来演奏的话），而且在这两种情况下，来自肌肉自身的指

But, further, a higher degree of the same 'training' (acting on an organism specially fitted to profit by it) enables an accomplished pianist to play a difficult piece of music at sight; the movements of the hands and fingers following so immediately upon the sight of the notes that it seems impossible to believe that any but the very shortest and most direct track can be the channel of the nervous communication through which they are called forth. The following curious example of the same class of *acquired aptitudes*, which differ from instincts only in being prompted to action by the will, is furnished by Robert Houdin:

"With a view of cultivating the rapidity of visual and tactile perception, and the precision of respondent movements, which are necessary for success in every kind of prestidigitation, Houdin early practised the art of juggling with balls in the air; and having, after a month's practice, become thorough master of the art of keeping up four balls at once, he placed a book before him, and, while the balls were in the air, accustomed himself to read without hesitation. 'This,' he says, 'will probably seem to my readers very extraordinary; but I shall surprise them still more when I say that I have just amused myself with repeating this curious experiment. Though thirty years have elapsed since the time I was writing, and though I have scarcely once touched the balls during that period, I can still manage to read with ease while keeping *three* balls up,'" (Autobiography, p. 26.) ①

We have called *a*, *b*, *c*, *d*, *e*, *f*, the antecedents of the successive muscular attractions, by the name of sensations. Some authors seem to deny that they are even this. If not even this, they can only be centripetal nerve-currents, not sufficient to arouse feeling, but sufficient to arouse motor response. ②It may be at once admitted that they

---

① Carpenter's 'Mental Physiology' (1874), pp. 217, 218.

② Von Hartmann devotes a. chapter of his 'Philosophy of the Unconscious (English translation, vol. I. p. 72) to proving that they must be both *ideas* and *unconscious*.

导性感觉也提供了帮助。此外,程度较高的相同“训练”(作用于特别适合于由此而受益的生物体),能使有造诣的钢琴家试奏难度很大的乐曲;手和手指的运动是如此快速地紧随着所看到的音符,以至于人们似乎不可能相信除了最短和最直接的神经束以外还有什么能够成为它们被由以唤起的神经交流的通道。罗伯特·霍丁提供了下面这个关于同样类型的习得能力的奇特例子,这种习得能力和本能的区别仅仅在于活动由意志所促使:

“为了培养视觉的和触觉的知觉速度,以及反应动作的精确性(这对任何一种杂技的成功来说都是必需的),霍丁早期练习过空中耍球的技艺,在一个月的练习之后,他已经完全精通了同时让四个球保持在空中的技艺,他在他前面放了一本书,并且当球在空中时,他让自己习惯于毫不犹豫地阅读。他说,‘这对我的观众来说可能似乎很不寻常;但是当我说我在重复这项奇特的实验时很开心,我会更令他们感到惊讶。尽管从我开始写作算起,三十年已经过去了,而在此期间我几乎一次也没有碰过那些球,可是我依然能够设法让三个球保持在空中的同时,轻松地进行阅读。’”(《自传》,第26页。)①

我们将吸引肌肉活动的先前事物a、b、c、d、e、f,冠以感觉之名。一些作者似乎都否认它们是感觉。如果它们连这都不是的话,它们只能是传入的神经流,不足以引起感受,但足以引起运动反应。而且立刻就可以承认的是,它们不是明显的意志。② 即使

① 卡彭特的《心理生理学》(1874年),第217、218页。

② 冯哈特曼在其《无意识哲学》(英译本,第1卷,第72页)中,用了一章的内容来努力证明它们不仅必须是观念,而且还必须是无意识的。

are not distinct *volitions*. The will, if any will be present, limits itself to a *permission* that they exert their motor effects. Dr. Carpenter writes:

"There may still be metaphysicians who maintain that actions which were originally prompted by the will with a distinct intention, and which are still entirely under its control, can never cease to be volitional; and that either an infinitesimally small amount of will is required to sustain them when they have been once set going, or that the will is in a sort of pendulum—like oscillation between the two actions—the maintenance of the train of *thought*, and the maintenance of the train of *movement*. But if only an infinitesimally small amount of will is necessary to sustain them, is not this tantamount to saying that they go on by a force of their own? And does not the experience of the *perfect continuity* of our train of thought during the performance of movements that have become habitual, entirely negative the hypothesis of oscillation? Besides, if such an oscillation existed, there must be *intervals* in which each action goes on *of itself*; so that its essentially automatic character is virtually admitted. The physiological explanation, that the mechanism of locomotion, as of other habitual movements, *grows* to the mode in which it is early exercised, and that it then works automatically under the general control and direction of the will, can scarcely be put down by any assumption of an hypothetical necessity, which rests only on the basis of ignorance of one side of our composite nature." ①

But if not distinct acts of will, these immediate antecedents of each movement of the chain are at any rate accompanied by consciousness of some kind. They are *sensations* to which we are *usually inattentive*, but which immediately call our attention if they go *wrong*. Schneider's account of these sensations deserves to be quoted. In the act of walking, he says, even when our attention is entirely off, "We are continuously aware of certain muscular feelings; and we have,

---

① 'Mental Physiology,' p. 20.

有任何意志出现,这意志也只会将自己局限于容许它们产生其运动结果之中。卡彭特博士写到:

“这里可能还会有形而上学者坚持认为,最初被具有明显意图的意志所促使,并且依然在其完全控制之下的行为,将永远也不会成为不是凭借意志的行为;并且这些行为一旦开始进行,持续这些行为的意志要么就变得无穷小,要么就好像钟摆一样在两种行为——思维序列的保持和运动序列的保持——之间摆动。但是,如果对持续行为来说仅有无限小的意志是必要的,那这不是就等于说,它们是通过自己的力量来继续下去的吗?而且在已经成为习惯性的动作的执行期间,我们关于思维序列的完美连续性的经历不是正好完全否定了摆动假说吗?此外,如果这样一种摆动确实存在,就必须存在每一个动作凭借自身进行运动的时间间隔;因此其自动化的本质特征实际上就得到了承认。和其他习惯性动作一样的运动机制,‘生长入’它早期训练的模式之中,然后它在意志的全面控制和指引下自动地行动,这种生理学的解释,很难被任何具有假定的必然性的假设所推翻,这些假设的基础仅仅建立在对我们复合性本性的某一方面的无知之上。”①

但是,如果不是明显的意志行为的话,链条中每一个动作所紧接着的前面的事件,无论如何也有某种意识相伴随。它们是我们通常忽略的感觉,如果动作出错的话,它们会立刻引起我们的注意。施奈德关于这些感觉的说明值得引用,他说,甚至当我们的注意力完全离开的时候,“我们不断地意识到某种来自肌肉的感受;而且我们还感受到某种使我们保持平衡,并且要求我们先

① 《心理生理学》,第20页。

moreover, a feeling of certain impulses to keep our equilibrium and to set down one leg after another. It is doubtful whether we could preserve equilibrium if no sensation of our body's attitude were there, and doubtful whether we should advance our leg if we had no sensation of its movement as executed, and not even a minimal feeling of impulse to set it down. Knitting appears altogether mechanical, and the knitter keeps up her knitting even while she reads or is engaged in lively talk. But if we ask her how this be possible, she will hardly reply that the knitting goes on of itself. She will rather say that she has a feeling of it, that she feels in her hands that she knits and how she must knit, and that therefore the movements of knitting are called forth and regulated by the sensations associated therewithal, even when the attention is called away."

"So of every one who practises, apparently automatically, a long familiar handicraft. The smith turning his tongs as he smites the iron, the carpenter wielding his plane, the lace-maker with her bobbin, the weaver at his loom, all will answer the same question in the same way by saying that they have a feeling of the proper management of the implement in their hands."

"In these cases, the feelings which are conditions of the appropriate acts are very faint. But none the less are they necessary. Imagine your hands not feeling; your movements could then only be provoked by ideas, and if your ideas were then diverted away, the movements ought to come to a standstill, which is a consequence that seldom occurs."①

Again:

"An idea makes you take, for example, a violin into your left hand. But it is not necessary that your idea remain fixed on the contraction of the muscles of the left hand and fingers in order that the violin may continue to be held fast and not let fall. The sensations themselves which the holding of the instrument awakens in the hand, since they are associated with the motor impulse of grasping,

① 'Der menschliche Wille,' pp. 447, 448.

后放下左右脚的神经脉冲。如果不存在对我们身体姿势的感觉，我们是否能够保持平衡是值得怀疑的，而且如果我们对执行了的动作没有感觉，并且对执行它的神经脉冲也没有一丝感受，我们是否能够迈出腿也是值得怀疑的。编织似乎是机械的，而且编织者在进行编织活动的同时，她甚至可以阅读或者进行生动的谈话。但是如果我们问她这是如何成为可能的，她几乎不会回答编织活动独自进行着，而宁愿说她对此有感受，她用她的手感受到她在编织并且她必须如何编织，因此编织的动作被那些与之相联系感觉所唤起，并被控制着，甚至当注意力离开之时也是如此。”

“这对长期以来显然是自动地从事一项熟悉的手工艺的人来说也是如此。打铁时旋转着钳子的铁匠，挥动着刨子的木匠，拿着卷线筒的花边工匠，织机旁的织布工，他们都会以同样的方式回答同样的问题，他们会说，他们对他们手中工具的恰当操作有一种感受。”

“在这些情况中，作为适当行为的条件的感受是非常微弱的。但它们依然是必需的。想像一下你的手不能够去感受了；那么你的动作因此只能受观念的驱使，而如果在那时你的观念也转向了一边，动作就应当停止下来，而这种结果很少发生。”①

还有：

“例如，一个观念使你将小提琴拿到了左手。但是，你的观念没有必要一直固定在左手和左手指的肌肉收缩上，以便小提琴可以继续被紧握在手中而没有掉下来。抓紧乐器的动作唤起了手中的感觉，由于它们和‘抓’这个动作的神经脉冲相联系，因此这些

① 《人的意志》，第447、448页。

are sufficient to cause this impulse, which then lasts as long as the feeling itself lasts, or until the impulse is inhibited by the idea of some antagonistic motion."

And the same may be said of the manner in which the right hand holds the bow:

"It sometimes happens, in beginning these simultaneous combinations, that one movement or impulse will cease if the consciousness turn particularly toward another, because at the outset the guiding sensations must *all* be strongly *felt*. The bow will perhaps slip from the fingers, because some of the muscles have relaxed. But the slipping is a cause of new sensations starting up in the band, so that the attention is in a moment brought back to the grasping of the how.

The following experiment shows this well: When one begins to play on the violin, to keep him from raising his right elbow in playing a book is placed under his right armpit, which he is ordered to hold fast by keeping the upper arm tight against his body. The muscular feelings, and feelings of contact connected with the book, provoke an impulse to press it tight. But often it happens that the beginner, whose attention gets absorbed in the production of the notes, lets drop the book. Later, however, this never happens; the faintest sensations of contact suffice to awaken the impulse to keep it in its place, and the attention may be wholly absorbed by the notes and the fingering with the left hand. The *simultaneous combination of movements is thus in the first instance conditioned by the facility with which in us, along side of intellectual processes, processes of inattentive feeling may still go on.*"①

This brings us by a very natural transition to the *ethical implications of the law of habit*. They are numerous and momentous. Dr. Carpenter,

① 'Der meuschliche Wille,' p. 439. The last sentence is rather freely translated the sense is unaltered.

感觉自身就足以引起这种神经脉冲，而后这种感受自身就会和神经脉冲持续同样长的时间，或者直到神经脉冲被某种敌对的运动观念所抑制时，它才停止。”

而且就右手持弓的方式也可以同样这么说：

“在开始这些同时性结合时，如果意识特别注意其中的一个动作或者神经脉冲，那么某个动作或神经脉冲将会停下来，这种情况有时候是会发生的，这是因为在开始的时候，指导性的感觉都必须全部被强烈的感受到。因为一些肌肉的放松，弓子将可能从手指间滑落。然而，滑落的动作又是手中开始出现的新感觉的原因，于是注意力又即刻回到持弓上来。

下面的实验很好地展示了这一点：当某人开始拉小提琴时，为了不让他在拉的时候抬起右肘，于是在他右臂的腋窝下面放了一本书，并且让他用右臂的上半部分紧贴着身体来夹紧这本书。肌肉的感受，以及同那本被夹着的书相接触的感受，激起了仅仅夹着它的神经脉冲。但是，刚刚开始做这项练习的人，他的注意力集中到了演奏乐曲之上，他就会让书掉下来，这种情况常常发生。然而，后来这种情况就再不发生了；最微弱的接触感觉足以唤起使书被夹住的神经脉冲，而且注意力可以完全被乐谱和左手的手指运动所吸引。动作的同时性结合，首先是以熟练性为条件，在我们这里，这种熟练性和智性过程一起，使无注意的感受可以持续进行。”①

而这又通过一种很自然的转变把我们带到了习惯规律的道德含义上来。它们为数众多，意义重大。我们曾引用过其《心理

---

① 《人的意志》，第439页。最后一句话是意译的——意思没有改变。

from whose 'Mental Physiology' we have quoted, has so prominently enforced the principle that our organs grow to the way in which they have been exercised, and dwelt upon its consequences, that his book almost deserves to be called a work of edification, on this account alone. We need make no apology, then, for tracing a few of these consequences ourselves:

"Habit a second nature! Habit is ten times nature," the Duke of Wellington is said to have exclaimed; and the degree to which this is true no one can probably appreciate as well as one who is a veteran soldier himself. The daily drill and the years of discipline end by fashioning a man completely over again, as to most of the possibilities of his conduct.

"There is a story, which is credible enough, though it may not be true, of a practical joker, who, seeing a discharged veteran carrying home his dinner, suddenly called out, 'Attention!' where upon the man instantly brought his hands down, and lost his mutton and potatoes in the gutter. The drill had been thorough, and its effects had become embodied in the man's nervous structure." ①

Riderless cavalry-horses, at many a battle, have been seen to come together and go through their customary evolutions at the sound of the bugle-call. Most trained domestic animals, dogs and oxen, and omnibus-and carhorses, seem to be machines almost pure and simple, undoubtingly, unhesitatingly doing from minute to minute the duties they have been taught, and giving no sign that the possibility of an alternative ever suggests itself to their mind. Men grown old in prison have asked to be readmitted after being once set free. In a railroad accident to a travelling menagerie in the United States some time in 1884, a tiger, whose cage had broken open, is said to have emerged,

---

① Huxley's 'Elementary Lessons in Physiology,' lesson XII.

生理学》的卡彭特博士，非常突出地强调了这一原则，即我们的器官“生长入”了它们所受训练的模式之中，并且会驻足于这样的结果之上，仅仅根据这一理由，他的著作几乎完全可以称得上是一部道德启迪的作品。因此，我们无需辩解，就可以追溯一些我们自己的这样一些结果：

“习惯是第二自然！习惯是十倍的自然，”人们说威灵顿公爵这样呐喊过；就这句话在何种程度上真实的而言，可能没有人会比一个退伍的老兵自己对这有更好的理解了。每日的操练和年复一年的训练最终将一个人的可能的行为完全重新塑造了。

“有一个故事，虽然可能并不真实，但却十足可信，故事说的是一个有实际经验且爱开玩笑的人，他看到一个退伍的老兵正拿着晚饭的食物回家，他突然叫道，‘立正！’于是那个老兵立刻放下双手，而他的羊肉和马铃薯都掉进了水沟里。训练曾经是彻底的，它的作用已经具体化到了老兵的神经结构中。”①

在很多战斗中都可以见到，无人骑的战马当听见军号的召唤时，会聚集到一起，并且做出它们所习惯的一系列动作。大多数受过训练的驯养的动物，如狗、牛、拉公共马车和小马车的马，好似近乎纯粹的和单纯的机器，时时刻刻都毫无疑问地和毫不犹豫地履行着交给它们的职责，而且没有任何迹象表明存在这种可能性，即可供选择的事物曾经向它们的心灵进行过暗示。在监狱中变老的人，曾经在释放以后请求再回到监狱中。1844 年，美国一家旅行动物园曾经发生一起铁路事故，据说关着老虎的笼子被撞开了，老虎出来了，似乎它觉得出来之后任务太繁重，不知道该怎

① 赫胥黎的《生理学基础教程》，第 12 讲。

but presently crept back again, as if too much bewildered by his new responsibilities, so that he was without difficulty secured.

Habit is thus the enormous fly-wheel of society, its most precious conservative agent. It alone is what keeps us all within the bounds of ordinance, and saves the children of fortune from the envious uprisings of the poor. It alone prevents the hardest and most repulsive walks of life from being deserted by those brought up to tread therein. It keeps the fisherman and the deck-hand at sea through the winter; it holds the miner in his darkness, and nails the countryman to his log-cabin and his lonely farm through all the months of snow; it protects us from invasion by the natives of the desert and the frozen zone. It dooms us all to fight out the battle of life upon the lines of our nurture or our early choice, and to make the best of a pursuit that disagrees, because there is no other for which we are fitted, and it is too late to begin again. It keeps different social strata from mixing. Already at the age of twenty-five you see the professional mannerism settling down on the young commercial traveller, on the young doctor, on the young minister, on the young counsellor-at-law. You see the little lines of cleavage running through the character, the tricks of thought, the prejudices, the ways of the ' shop, ' in a word, from which the man can by-and-by no more escape than his coat-sleeve can suddenly fall into a new set of folds. On the whole, it is best he should not escape. It is well for the world that in most of us, by the age of thirty, the character has set like plaster, and will never soften again.

If the period between twenty and thirty is the critical one in the formation of intellectual and professional habits, the period below twenty is more important still for the fixing of *personal* habits, properly so called, such as vocalization and pronunciation, gesture, motion, and address. Hardly ever is a language learned after twenty spoken without a foreign accent; hardly ever can a youth transferred to the society of his betters unlearn the nasality and other vices of speech bred in him by the associations of his growing years.

么办才好，于是它很快又爬回去了，以致它很容易地就又被关了起来。

因此，习惯是巨大的社会调速轮，是社会最宝贵的守旧工具。唯独它将我们所有人保持在了传统风俗习惯的限度之内，它使富人的孩子们免遭嫉妒的穷人们的暴动之厄运。它独自阻止了在那里成长起来的人们放弃那些最艰苦和最受人排斥的工作。它使得渔夫和甲板水手整个冬天都呆在海上；它让矿工在黑暗中坚持着，它让村里人在几个月的漫长雪天中呆在他们的小木屋和寂寞的农场里；它保护了我们，使我们没有受到居住在沙漠和严寒地带的人的侵袭。它使我们注定要根据我们的教养或早期的选择在生活中闯荡，并尽力处理好那些和教养与选择不一致的追求，因为没有其他的东西更适合我们，而重新开始又太晚了。它没有让不同社会阶层混合起来。你会看到，在25岁时，年轻的旅行推销员、医生、牧师和律师顾问都已经染上了职业怪癖。你会看到细小的裂痕划过了性格、思维技巧、成见以及“购物”的方式，一句话，人们对此最终无法逃脱，就像外衣袖子不能突然就有新的折痕一样。总体来说，他最好不要逃开。我们中的大多数人，到了30岁，性格固定得像一块石膏，将永远不会变软了，这对世界来说是件好事。

如果20到30岁之间是形成智性习惯和专业习惯的关键时期，那么20岁以下这段时间对固定个人习惯（我们可以比较恰当地如此称呼它）来说就更重要，这些个人习惯包括发声和发音方法、姿势、动作、言谈等。20岁以后学会的语言说出来时很少没有不带国外口音的；一个进入其上层圈子的年轻人，几乎很难忘记在他成长的年代中由其所在的团体给他带来的讲话中的鼻

Hardly ever, indeed, no matter how much money there be in his pocket, can he even learn to *dress* like a gentleman-born. The merchants offer their wares as eagerly to him as to the veriest 'swell,' but he simply *cannot* buy the right things. An invisible law, as strong as gravitation, keeps him within his orbit, arrayed this year as he was the last; and how his better-bred acquaintances contrive to get the things they wear will be for him a mystery till his dying day.

The great thing, then, in all education, is to *make our nervous system our ally instead of our enemy.* It is to fund and capitalize our acquisitions, and live at ease upon the interest of the fund. *For this we must make automatic and habitual*, *as early as possible*, *as many useful actions as we can*, and guard against the growing into ways that are likely to be disadvantageous to us, as we should guard against the plague. The more of the details of our daily life we can hand over to the effortless custody of automatism, the more our higher powers of mind will be set free for their own proper work. There is no more miserable human being than one in whom nothing is habitual but indecision, and for whom the lighting of every cigar, the drinking of every cup, the time of rising and going to bed every day, and the beginning of every bit of work, are subjects of express volitional deliberation. Full half the time of such a man goes to the deciding, or regretting, of matters which ought to be so ingrained in him as practically not to exist for his consciousness at all. If there be such daily duties not yet ingrained in any one of my readers, let him begin this very hour to set the matter right.

In Professor Bain's chapter on 'The Moral Habits' there are some admirable practical remarks laid down. Two great maxims emerge

音和其他讲话恶习。而且确实,不管他的口袋里有多少钱,他也几乎不可能学会如何穿戴得像个绅士出身的人。商人们向对待真正的"头面人物"一样热情地向他推销商品,但是他就是买不到合适的东西。一条看不见的规律,和地心引力一样强大,让他停留在自己的轨道上,在这一年里把他装扮得好像是最差的;而他的那些受过更好教育的熟人是如何设法得到他们所穿戴的东西的,这对他来说至死都是个谜。

因此,在所有的教育中,重要的事情在于让我们的神经系统成为我们的盟友,而不是敌人。教育的重点在于向我们的获得物进行投资并且将我们的获得物变成资本,然后靠这项投资的利息轻松过活。为此,我们必须尽可能早地、并且尽可能多地将我们能够获得的有用的行为变成自动的和习惯的行为,并且对那些可能不利于我们的方式,我们要提防它们生长进来,就如同提防瘟疫一样。如果我们能够将更多的生活细节交付给不费力气的自动作用来照管的话,我们将会有更多心灵的高级能力被释放出来,从而它们可以做适合自己的工作。如果一个人没有任何习惯,只有优柔寡断,对他来说,每点一根烟、每喝一杯水、每天起床和睡觉的时间、开始每一项工作,他都要凭借其意志力而深思熟虑一番,这样的人比任何人都悲惨。这种人的一半时间都用来对一些问题做出决定,或者为一些问题而感到后悔,而这些问题在他那里本该是根深蒂固的习惯,是实际上对意识来说根本不存在的问题。如果这类日常事物在我的读者那里还没有变成根深蒂固的习惯的话,让他从现在开始就把这个问题解决了吧。

贝恩教授在"道德习惯"一章中,写下了一些令人钦佩的很实用的论述。有两个伟大的座右铭来自他的论述。第一个座右铭

from his treatment. The first Is that in the acquisition of a new habit, or the leaving off of an old one, we must take care to *launch ourselves with as strong and decided an initiative as possible.* Accumulate all the possible circumstances which shall reenforce the right motives; put yourself assiduously in conditions that encourage the new way; make engagements incompatible with the old; take a public pledge, if the case allows; in short, envelop your resolution with every aid you know. This will give your new beginning such a momentum that the temptation to break down will not occur as soon as it otherwise might; and every day during which a breakdown is postponed adds to the chances of its not occurring at all.

The second maxim is: *Never suffer an exception to occur till the new habit is securely rooted in your life.* Each lapse is like the letting fall of a ball of string which one is carefully winding up; a single slip undoes more than a great many turns will wind again. *Continuity* of training is the great means of making the nervous system act infallibly right. As Professor Bain says:

"The peculiarity of the moral habits, contradistinguishing them from the intellectual acquisitions, is the presence of two hostile powers, one to be gradually raised into the ascendant over the other. It is necessary, above all things, in such a situation, never to lose a battle. Every gain on the wrong side undoes the effect of many conquests on the right. The essential precaution, therefore, is so to regulate the two opposing powers that the one may have a series of uninterrupted successes, until repetition has fortified it to such a degree as to enable it to cope with the opposition, under any circumstances. This is the theoretically best career of mental progress."

The need of securing success at the *outset* is imperative. Failure at first is apt to dampen the energy of all future attempts, whereas past experience of success nerves one to future vigor. Goethe says to a man who consulted him about an enterprise but mistrusted his own powers; "Ach! you need only blow on your hands!"

是，在获得一个新的习惯和摈弃一个旧的习惯中，我们必须要注意的是在我们开始时要有一种尽可能强硬和明确的主动性。积累能够增强正确动机的所有可能的情境；勤勉地将你自己置身于能够激励新习惯的条件之中；做出与旧习惯不相容的诺言；如果情况容许的话，做出公开的保证；总之，将你的决心包封在你所知道的对它有所帮助的每一件事物中。这将给你的新的开始带来这样一种动力，以至于半途而废的诱惑不会在它将要出现的时候立刻出现；半途而废的发生每被推迟一天，都增大了它最终不会出现的机会。

第二个座右铭是：除非有新的习惯已经安全地根植于你的生活之中，否则绝不能容忍意外情况的发生。每一次错误就像丢掉一个正在仔细缠绕的线团；一次滑落所放松的线，比缠绕好几次才能缠绕上的线还要多。连续的训练是使神经系统准确无误地正确行动的主要手段。正如贝恩教授所说：

“同智性习得的东西相对照，道德习惯的特性在于两种敌对势力的存在，一个将逐渐提升到可以支配另一个的高度。首先，在这种情况下，永远也不吃一次败仗是必要的。错误一方的每次获胜都使得正确一方由多次征服而产生的效果消解掉了。因此，基本的防范就是管制两种敌对力量，致使一方可以获得一系列不被打断的成功，直到重复将它强化到了它能在任何情况下对付对手为止。从理论上讲，这是心理进步的最佳进程。”

在一开始就要确保成功，这种需要是强制性的。最初的失败易于抑制未来所有努力的力量，而过去成功的经验会鼓舞人，给人增添未来的活力。有一个人要从事一项事业，但不相信自己的能力，他向歌德请教，歌德对他说：“啊！你只需向你的手吹口气

And the remark illustrates the effect on Goethe's spirits of his own habitually successful career. Prof. Baumann, from whom I borrow the anecdote,①says that the collapse of barbarian nations when Europeans come among them is due to their despair of ever succeeding as the new-comers do in the larger tasks of life. Old ways are broken and new ones not formed.

The question of 'tapering-off,' in abandoning such habits as drink and opium-indulgence, comes in here, and is a question about which experts differ within certain limits, and in regard to what may be best for an individual case. In the main, however, all expert opinion would agree that abrupt acquisition of the new habit is the best way, *if there be a real possibility of carrying it out.* We must be careful not to give the will so stiff a task as to insure its defeat at the very outset; but, *provided one can stand it*, a sharp period of suffering, and then a free time, is the best thing to aim at, whether in giving up a habit like that of opium, or in simply changing one's hours of rising or of work. It is surprising how soon a desire will die of inanition if it be *never* fed.

"One must first learn, unmoved, looking neither to the right not left, to walk firmly on the straight and narrow path, before one can begin 'to make one's self over again.' He who every day makes a fresh resolve is like one who, arriving at the edge of the ditch he is to leap, forever stops and returns for a fresh run. Without *unbroken* advance there is no such thing as accumulation of the ethical, forces possible, and to make this possible, and to exercise us and habituate us in it, is the sovereign blessing of regular work." ②

---

① See the admirable passage about success at the outset, in his Handbuch der Moral (1878), pp. 38-43.

② J. Bahnsen: 'Beitrtge zu Charakterologie' (1867), vol I. p 209.

就行了!"这句话表明了歌德的习惯性的成功生涯对他自己的精神所造成的影响。鲍曼教授说(我从他借来这段轶事),[①]当欧洲人来到那些野蛮国家时,那些国家的崩溃是因为他们看到他们永远不能和新来的人一样,成功地完成更加伟大的生活任务,他们于是绝望了。旧的习惯被打破了,新的习惯还没有形成。

在戒除像酗酒、吸食鸦片这样一些习惯中,这里涉及到了"逐渐停止"的问题,关于这个问题,专家们在特定的范围之内,在考虑到对个人情况而言什么是最好的办法这一方面,存在着分歧。然而,大体上所有专家都同意,迅捷地获得新习惯是最好的方法,如果存在有执行它的可能性的话。我们必须小心,不要交给意志太过艰巨的任务,致使它在一开始就注定失败;但是,无论是戒除像吸食鸦片那样的习惯,还是只改变起床或工作的时间,只要人们能承受得住,在一段时期的艰难困苦之后就是自由的时光了,而这是期望得到的最好的事情了。如果一种愿望从未得到培养,它很快就会死于营养不良,其速度快得令人吃惊。

"在人能够开始'重新做人之前',他必须先学习,不动摇,不左顾右盼,在笔直和狭长的道路上坚定地走下去。每天都要下一个新的决心的人,就像每一次到达了想要跳过去的壕沟边上,却又返回去重新起跑的人。伦理力量的积累不能没有不间断的进步,而要使这成为可能,并且使我们在其中得到练习从而形成习惯,只能取决于有规律的工作。"[②]

---

① 参见他那值得赞美的关于成功的开始的段落,《道德手册》,第38~43页。

② J. 巴恩森:《性格学论文集》(1867年),第1卷,第209页。

A third maxim may be added to the preceding pair: *Seize the very first possible opportunity to act on every resolution you make, and on every emotional prompting you may experience in the direction of the habits you aspire to gain.* It is not in the moment of their forming, but in the moment of their producing *motor effects*, that resolves and aspirations communicate the new 'set' to the brain. As the author last quoted remarks:

"The actual presence of the practical opportunity alone furnishes the fulcram upon which the lever can rest, by means of which the moral will may multiply its strength, and raise itself aloft. He who has no solid ground to press against will never get beyond the stage of empty gesture-making."

No matter how full a reservoir of *maxims* one may possess, and no matter how good one's *sentiments* may be, if one have not taken advantage of every concrete opportunity to act, one's character may remain entirely unaffected for the better. With mere good intentions, hell is proverbially paved. And this is an obvious consequence of the principles we have laid down. A 'character,' as J. S. Mill says, 'is a completely fashioned will'; and a will, in the sense in which he means it, is an aggregate of tendencies to act in a firm and prompt and definite way upon all the principal emergencies of life. A tendency to act only becomes effectively ingrained in us in proportion to the uninterrupted frequency with which the actions actually occur, and the brain *grows* to their use. Every time a resolve or a fine glow of feeling evaporates without bearing practical fruit is worse than a chance lost; it works so as positively to hinder future resolutions and emotions from taking the normal path of discharge. There is no more contemptible type of human character than that of the nerveless sentimentalist and dreamer, who spends his life in a weltering sea of sensibility and emotion, but who never does a manly concrete deed. Rousseau, inflaming all the mothers of Prance, by his eloquence, to follow Nature and nurse their babies themselves, while he sends his own children to the foundling hospital, is the classical example of what I mean.

除上述两个格言之外，还可以加上第三个：抓住每一个最初可能的机会来为你所下的每一个决心做出行动，并且依从在你渴望获得习惯的道路上所体会到的每一次情绪激励而行动。不是在它们的形成时刻，而是在产生运动结果的时刻，决心和渴望才将新的“设置结果”传递给大脑。正如上面所引述过的作者所说：

“实践机会的真实出现自身，就提供了杠杆得以支撑的支点，通过这样的手段，道德意志可以增加其强度，将自己向高处提升。一个人如果没有可以依靠的坚实基础，他将永远不会超越做出空洞姿态的阶段。”

不管一个人拥有的座右铭有多少，不管一个人的情操有多好，如果他不能利用每一个具体机会去行动，他的性格就完全不会受到好的方面的影响。众所周知，仅有好的意图，走向地狱。这是我们已经提出的那些原则的一个明显结果。而且正如 J. S. 密尔所说，“一种品格是一种被完全塑造了的意志”；而且，从他所指的意义上来说，意志就是以坚定、迅捷和明确的方式对生活中一切首要的突发事件做出行动的倾向的集合。一种行为倾向有效地根植于我们身上，是与行为实际发生的不间断次数成正比的，而且大脑“生长入”其用途当中。每当一次决心和一种情感的美好闪现没有任何实际结果地消失掉了，这比失去一次机会还糟糕；它肯定会阻碍未来的决心和情绪采用正常的释放渠道。无力的伤感主义者（他们将一生都耗费在其感性和情绪的汹涌大海上了），还有那从来不曾有果断的行动的梦想家，在人类的品格中没有比他们更令人鄙视的了。卢梭用他那雄辩的口才鼓动法国的所有母亲遵循自然规则亲自哺乳自己的婴儿，但他却把自己的孩子送进了育婴院，这是我所说的意思的一个典型例子。但

But every one of us in his measure, whenever, after glowing for an abstractly formulated Good, he practically ignores some actual case, among the squalid 'other particulars' of which that same Good lurks disguised, treads straight on Roussean's path. All Goods are disguised by the vulgarity of their concomitants, in this work-a-day world; but woe to him who can only recognize them when he thinks them in their pure and abstract form! The habit of excessive novel-reading and theatre-going will produce true monsters in this line. The weeping of a Russian lady over the fictitious personages in the play, while her coachman is freezing to death on his seat outside, is the sort of thing that everywhere happens on a less glaring scale. Even the habit of excessive indulgence in music, for those who are neither performers themselves nor musically gifted enough to take it in a purely intellectual way, has probably a relaxing effect upon the character. One becomes filled with emotions which habitually pass without prompting to any deed, and so the inertly sentimental condition is kept up. The remedy would be, never to suffer one's self to have an emotion at a concert, without expressing it afterward in *some* active way. ①Let the expression be the least thing in the world—speaking genially to one's aunt, or giving up one's seat in a horse-car, if nothing more heroic offers—but let it not fail to take place.

These latter cases make us aware that it is not simply *particular lines* of discharge, but also *general forms* of discharge, that seem to be grooved out by habit in the brain. Just as, if we let our emotions evaporate, they get into a way of evaporating; so there is reason to suppose that if we often flinch from making an effort,

① See for remarks on this subject a readable article by Miss V. Scudder on 'Musical Devotees and Morals,' in the Andover Review for January 1887.

是无论何时，我们每个人在其尺度之内为一种抽象描述出来的善而激动之后，在实践上会忽略掉一些肮脏的“其他细节”中的实际情况，从而直接走上卢梭的道路，其实同样的善却恰恰伪装性地潜伏在那里。在这个平凡的世界中，所有的善都被其伴随物的粗俗所伪装了起来；而且对那些只能以纯粹的和抽象的形式对善进行思考时才能够识别出善的人来说，这是一种悲哀！过度地阅读小说和看戏剧的习惯，会在这个方面造就出真正的恶人。一位俄国女士为剧中虚构的人物而哭泣，而她的马车夫却冻死在了外面他所坐的地方，这种事情到处都会发生，只是不太显眼罢了。甚至过度沉迷于音乐中的习惯，对那些自己既不是演奏家，也没有足够的天赋以一种纯粹智性的方式来欣赏它的人来说，可能会对品格造成一种松懈的影响。这样的人内心充满了只是习惯性通过却不激起行动的情绪，因此毫无生气的感伤性的情境就会一直保持着。补救的方法就是，在音乐会上永远不要让自我遭受某种情绪之苦，而在这之后也不要以某种积极的方式表达它们。[①] 使表达变成世界上最细小的事情——如果没有更崇高的事情可做，那就亲切地同自己的姑姑讲话，或者在马车上让出自己的座位——但就是不要让它不发生。

后面的这些例子使我们明白，不仅特殊的释放路线，而且一般的释放形式似乎都是通过习惯被刻印在大脑中的。就好像如果我们让自己的情绪消失的话，它们就进入了一条消失的道路中了；因此这里有理由假设，如果我们经常在做出努力上退缩，做出

① 关于这一问题的评论可参见 V. 斯卡德小姐的一篇易读的文章，“音乐热爱者与道德”，《安多瓦评论》，1887 年 1 月。

before we know it the effort making capacity will be gone; and that, if we suffer the wandering of our attention, presently it will wander all the time. Attention and effort are, as we shall see later, but two names for the same psychic fact. To what brainprocesses they correspond we do not know. The strongest reason for believing that they do depend on brain-processes at all, and are not pure acts of the spirit, is just this fact, that they seem in some degree subject to the law of habit, which is a material law. As a final practical maxim, relative to these habits of the will, we may, then, offer something like this: *Keep the faculty of effort alive in you by a little gratuitous exercise every day.* That is, be systematically ascetic or heroic in little unnecessary points, do every day or two something for no other reason than that you would rather not do it, so that when the hour of dire need draws nigh, it may find you not unnerved and untrained to stand the test. Asceticism of this sort is like the insurance which a man pays on his house and goods. The tax does him no good at the time, and possibly may never bring him a return. But if the fire does come, his having paid it will be his salvation from rum. So with the man who has daily inured himself to habits of concentrated attention, energetic volition, and self-denial in unnecessary things. He will stand like a tower when everything rocks around him, and when his softer fellowmortals are winnowed like chaff in the blast.

The physiological study of mental conditions is thus the most powerful ally of hortatory ethics, The hell to be endured hereafter, of which theology tells, is no worse than the hell we make for ourselves in this world, by habitually fashioning our characters in the wrong way. Could the young but realize how soon they will become mere walking bundles of habits, they would give more heed to their conduct while in the plastic state. We are spinning our own fates, good or evil, and

努力的能力就会在我们知道它消失之前就消失了;并且,如果我们一直让我们的注意力涣散,不久它就会一直涣散下去了。如我们后来所看到的那样,注意力和努力只是同一个心理事实的两个名字罢了。它们和什么大脑过程相应,我们不知道。相信它们完全依赖于大脑过程,而不仅仅是纯粹的精神活动,支持这种信念的最强有力的理由恰恰就是这个事实,即它们似乎在某种程度上服从习惯规律,而习惯规律是一个物质规律。作为最后一个和意志的这些习惯相关的实践的座右铭,我们可以提出:通过每天做一些免费的练习,使做出努力的能力在你身上保持活力。这就是说,在一些细小的并非必要的方面有规则地节制欲望或者变得英勇起来,每一两天就做一些你没有其他理由不做的事情,这样,当可怕的需要来临的时刻,你将发现自己不会再没有勇气和像未受过训练似地承受它了。这种类型的禁欲主义就像一个人给他的房屋和财产买的保险。税金当时对他来说没有好处,而且可能也永远不会给他带来回报。但是,如果火灾确实发生了,他曾经支付过的保险就会使他免于破产。对一个每天使自己在不必要的事情上习惯于集中注意力、保持精力充沛的意志和进行自我克制的人来说,情况就是这样。当所有的事情都在周围动摇,当他那些软弱的凡人同类像风中的谷壳一样被吹走,他将如铁塔一般屹立不动。

因此,有关心理条件的生理学研究是规劝伦理学的最强有力的同盟,神学所讲的来世将要忍受的地狱,并不比我们在现世为自己所造就的地狱更糟糕,而这地狱是我们以错误的方式习惯性地塑造我们的性格而造就的。如果年轻人能够意识到他们很快就会成为一捆行走着的习惯的话,他们就会在可塑阶段更加留意自身的行为。我们自己的命运,好或是坏,都是自己缠上的,永远

never to be undone. Every smallest stroke of virtue or of vice leaves its never so little scar. The drunken Rip Van Winkle, in Jefferson's play, excuses himself for every fresh dereliction by saying, 'I won't count this time!' Well! he may not count it, and a kind Heaven may not count it; but it is being counted none the less. Down among his nerve-cells and fibres the molecules are counting it, registering and storing it up to be used against him when the next temptation comes. Nothing we ever do is, in strict scientific literalness, wiped out. Of course, this has its good side as well as its bad one. As we become permanent drunkards by so many separate drinks, so we become saints in the moral, and authorities and experts in the practical and scientific spheres, by so many separate acts and hours of work. Let no youth have any anxiety about the upshot of his education, whatever the line of it may be. If he keep faithfully busy each hour of the workingday, he may safely leave the final result to itself. He can with perfect certainty count on waking up some fine morning, to find himself one of the competent ones of his generation, in whatever pursuit he may have singled out. Silently, between all the details of his business, the *power of judging in* all that class of matter will have built itself up within him as a possession that will never pass away. Young people should know this truth in advance. The ignorance of it has probably engendered more discouragement and faint heartedness in youths embarking on arduous careers than all other causes put together.

也解不开。每一个最小的德行或恶行的冲撞都会给它留下细小的疤痕。杰弗逊剧中醉酒的范温克尔，在每一次新的放弃之后都为自己找借口说："这次不算！哈！"他可以这次不算，仁慈的上帝也可以这次不算；可它仍然还是要算数的。他的神经细胞和纤维中的分子会算上这一次，记录下这一次并将它储存起来，以便当下次诱惑到来时用它来对付他。从严格的科学意义上来讲，我们所做的任何事情都不会被擦掉。当然，这有其好的一面也有坏的一面。就像许多次的喝酒，使我们成为了永远的酒鬼一样，我们也能通过多次的行动、许多小时的工作成为道德上的圣人、实践和科学领域中的权威和专家。无论年轻人受到的是哪一方面的教育，都要让他们对所受教育的结果不感到焦虑。如果他在工作的日子里每小时都尽心地忙碌着，他可以安稳地不管最后的结果。他可以完全肯定地期待，在某个晴朗的早晨醒来时，他发现，在他所挑选出来的不论哪一种追求中，他是他那一代人里最有能力的一个。静静地，在他所有的工作细节之中，对那类事物的判断力将在他的内部建立起来，并且这是一份永远不会消失的财产。年轻人应该预先了解这一真理。对于正从事艰辛的事业的年轻人来说，对它的无知引起了他们更多的气馁和懦弱，这原因超过了其他所有原因的总和。

CHAPTER V.

The Automaton-Theory.

In describing the functions of the hemispheres a short way back, we used language derived from both the bodily and the mental life, saying now that the animal made indeterminate and unforeseeable reactions, and anon that he was swayed by considerations of future good and evil; treating his hemispheres sometimes as the seat of memory and ideas in the psychic sense, and sometimes talking of them as simply a complicated addition to his reflex machinery. This sort of vacillation in the point of view is a fatal incident of all ordinary talk about these questions; but I must now settle my scores with those readers to whom I already dropped a word in passing (see page 24, note) and who have probably been dissatisfied with my conduct ever since.

Suppose we restrict our view to facts of one and the same plane, and let that be the bodily plane: cannot all the outward phenomena of intelligence still be exhaustively described? Those mental images, those 'considerations,' whereof we spoke,—presumably they do not arise without neural processes arising simultaneously with them, and presumably each consideration corresponds to a process *sui generis*, and unlike all the rest In other words, however numerous and delicately differentiated the train of ideas may be, the train of brain-events that runs alongside of it must in both respects be exactly its match, and we must postulate a neural machinery that offers a living counterpart for every shading, however fine, of the history of its owner's mind.

第五章 自动机理论

在前面描述大脑半球的功能时，我们使用了源自身体和心理生活的语言，说目前这种动物做出了不确定的和无法预料的反应，而后又说他由于对未来善与恶的考虑而摇摆不定；有时从精神的意义上我们将他的大脑半球当作记忆和观念的处所来加以对待，而有时又仅仅将它们作为其反射机器的复杂附加物而加以考虑。在观点上的这种游移不定，对所有对这些问题的一般性探讨来说都是致命的事；在前面的论述中我为一些读者留下了伏笔（见第24页的注释），可能从那时起，他们就对我的行为感到不满意了，现在，我必须和他们清算一下。

假设我们将我们的观点限定在一个方面并且是同一发展水平的事实之内，即事实是身体方面的：对理智的所有外部现象的描述依然不能得以穷尽吗？我们所谈到的那些心理意象，那些"考虑"——推测起来，如果没有神经过程与之同时发生，它们就不会发生，而且每一次考虑都和一种独特的过程相对应，并且和所有其他过程都不同。换句话说，不管观念系列的区别可以多么地众多和精细，和它一起运作的大脑事件的序列必须在这两个方面和它完全相称，而且我们必须假设一种神经机器，它为其所有者的精神史的每一次变化（不论是多么细小）都提供了一个活的

Whatever degree of complication the latter may reach, the complication of the machinery must be quite as extreme, otherwise we should have to admit that there may be mental events to which no brain-events correspond. But such an admission as this the physiologist is reluctant to make. It would violate all his beliefs. 'No psychosis without neurosis,' is one form which the principle of continuity takes in his mind.

But this principle forces the physiologist to make still another step. If neural action is as complicated as mind; and if in the sympathetic system and lower spinal cord we see what, so far as we know, is unconscious neural action executing deeds that to all outward intent may be called intelligent; what is there to hinder us from supposing that even where we know consciousness to be there, the still more complicated neural action which we believe to be its inseparable companion is alone and of itself the real agent of whatever intelligent deeds may appear? 'As actions of a certain degree of complexity are brought about by mere mechanism, why may not actions of a still greater degree of complexity be the result of a more refined mechanism?' The conception of reflex action is surely one of the best conquests of physiological theory; why not be radical with it? Why not say that just as the spinal cord is a machine with few reflexes, so the hemispheres are a machine with many, and that that is all the difference? The principle of continuity would press us to accept this view.

But what on this view could be the function of the consciousness itself? *Mechanical* function it would have none. The sense-organs would awaken the brain-cells; these would awaken each other in. rational and orderly sequence, until the time for action came; and then the last brainvibration would discharge downward into the motor tracts. But this would be a quite autonomous chain of occurrences, and whatever mind went with it would be there only as an 'epiphenomenon,' an inert spectator, a sort of 'foam, aura, or melody' as Mr. Hodgson says, whose opposition or whose furtherance would

副本。无论后者可以达到什么样的复杂程度，机器的复杂性也必须达到同样的极致，否则的话我们将不得不承认存在有和大脑事件不相应的心理事件。但是，生理学家不愿意承认这种情况。它会违背其所有的信念。“没有神经，就没有精神”，是这种连续性原理在他心中的一种呈现形式。

但是，这一原理迫使生理学家还要走出另一步。如果神经活动和心理活动一样复杂；而且就我们目前所知，如果在交感神经系统和下部的脊髓中，我们看到了什么是执行行为的无意识的神经活动，它们对于外部的意向来说都可以被称作是理智的；那么，是什么在妨碍着我们假设：在我们知道有意识存在的地方，被我们认作是意识的不可分离的伴随物的更加复杂的神经活动，这种神经活动是无论何种理智行为可能出现的唯一真正施动者？“既然一定复杂程度的行为是由纯粹的机械装置产生的，为什么复杂程度更高的行为不能是更精致的机械装置的结果呢？”反射行为的概念当然是生理学理论的最佳战利品之一；为什么不能让它更激进一些呢？为什么不说正是由于脊髓是一些反射的机械装置，因此大脑半球是更多反射的机械装置，而且这就是其所有的区别呢？连续性原理会迫使我们接受这一观点。

但是，根据这种功能，意识自身的功能是什么呢？它一点机械的功能也没有。感觉器官唤醒大脑细胞；大脑细胞又会以合理的和有秩序的顺序彼此唤醒对方，直到行动到来之时；然后，最后的大脑振动会向下释放到运动束中。但是，这是一个非常具有自治性质的发生事件的链条，并且无论有什么样的精神与之相伴，它也只能是一种“附带现象”，一个无自动力的观众，如霍奇森所说，是某种“气泡、气味和音调”，它的反对和促进对事件自身的发

be alike powerless over the occurrences themselves, When talking, some time ago, we ought not, accordingly, *as physiologists*, to have said anything about ' considerations ' as guiding the animal. We ought to have said ' paths left in the hemispherical cortex by former currents, ' and nothing more.

Now so simple and attractive is this conception from the consistently physiological point of view, that it is quite wonderful to see how late it was stumbled on in philosophy, and how few people, even when it has been explained to them, fully and easily realize its import. Much of the polemic writing against it is by men who have as yet failed to take it into their imaginations. Since this has been the case, it seems worth while to devote a few more words to making it plausible, before criticising it ourselves.

To Descartes belongs the credit of having first been bold enough to conceive of a completely self-sufficing nervous mechanism which should be able to perform complicated and apparently intelligent acts. By a singularly arbitrary restriction, however, Descartes stopped short at man, and while contending that in beasts the nervous machinery was all, he held that the higher acts of man were the result of the agency of his rational soul. The opinion that beasts have no consciousness at all was of course too paradoxical to maintain itself long as anything more than a curious item in the history of philosophy. And with its abandonment the very notion that the nervous system *per se* might work the work of intelligence, which was an integral, though detachable part of the whole theory, seemed also to slip out of men's conception, until, in this century, the elaboration of the doctrine of reflex action made it possible and natural that it should again arise. But it was not till 1870, I believe, that Mr. Hodgson made the decisive step, by saying that feelings, no matter how intensely they may be present, can have no causal efficacy whatever, and comparing them to the colors laid on the surface of a mosaic,

生来说都同样是无力的。我们在以前谈论的时候,作为生理学者,相应地,我们不应该说任何诸如“思考”作为动物的指导之类的话。我们应该说“以前的神经流在脑半球皮层中留下的路径”,而且仅此而已。

现在,来自一致的生理学观点的这一概念,是如此的简单和富有吸引力,虽然看到它这么晚才在哲学上被无意中发现,而且甚至当人们已经了解了关于这概念的解释之时,也只有极少数的人能够充分地和不费力地了解到它的重要性,但这也是非常令人高兴的。大部分反对它的那些争论性的文章都是由那些直到现在都不敢想像它的人写的。鉴于这种情况,在我们对它进行批判之时,似乎很有必要再花一些笔墨把那些似乎合理的地方表述出来。

笛卡儿首次大胆地设想出了能够执行复杂的和显然是理智行为的一种完全自足的神经机械装置。然而,出于一种令人无法理解地武断的限制,笛卡儿在人这里就停止不前了,而且,虽然他主张在兽类那里神经机械装置就是一切,但是他坚持认为人类的高级行为是理性灵魂作用的结果。兽类完全没有意识的观点当然十分荒谬,在哲学史中它除了作为一种奇怪的说法使自己保存下来以外,它什么也不是。而且随着对它的遗弃,神经系统本身可能会承担起理智工作的观点,作为整个理论所必需的,尽管也是可分的一个部分,似乎也滑出了人的概念之外,直到这个世纪,对反射动作学说的苦心经营,才使得这一观点的重新出现成为一个可能的和自然的事情。而且我认为,直到1870年,霍奇森先生才迈出了决定性的一步,他认为,不管感受的出现有多么强烈,它们不可能具有任何因果关系的功效,而且他把马赛克表面涂上的

of which the events in the nervous system are represented by the stones. ①Obviously the stones are held in place by each other and not by the several colors which they support.

About the same time Mr. Spalding, and a little later Messrs. Huxley and Clifford, gave great publicity to an identical doctrine, though in their case it was backed by less refined metaphysical considerations. ②

A few sentences from Huxley and Clifford may he subjoined to make the matter entirely clear. Professor Huxley says:

"The consciousness of brutes would appear to be related to the mechanism of their body simply as a collateral product of its working, and to be as completely without any power of modifying that working as the steam-whistle which accompanies the work of a locomotive engine is without influence on its machinery. Their volition, if they have any, is an emotion *indicative* of physical changes, not a cause of such changes.... The soul stands related to the body as the bell of a clock to the works, and consciousness answers to the sound which the bell gives out when it is struck.... Thus far I have strictly confined myself to the automatism of brutes.... It is quite true that, to the best of my judgment, the argumentation which applies to brutes holds equally good of men; and, therefore, that all states of consciousness in us, as in them, are immediately caused by molecular changes of the brain-substance.

① The Theory of Practice, vol. I, p, 416 ff.

② The present writer recalls, bow, in 1869, when still a medical student, he began to write an essay showing few almost every one who speculated about brain-processes illicitly interpolated into his account of them links derived from the entirely heterogeneous universe of Feeling. Spencer, Hodgson (in his Time and Space), Maudsley, Lockhart Clarke, Bain, Dr. Carpenter, and other authors were cited as having been guilty of the confusion. The writing was soon stopped because he perceived that the view which he, was upholding against these authors was a pure conception, with no proofs to be adduced of its reality. Later it seemed to him that whatever *proofs* existed really told in favor of their view.

颜色比作感受，而石块则代表神经系统中的事件。[1] 很明显，石头呆在其位置上是由于它们之间的相互作用，而不是由于它们所提供的那几种颜色。

大约在同一时间，斯波尔丁先生，以及稍晚一些的赫胥黎先生和克利福德先生，都广泛地公开了同一学说，尽管就当时的情况来说，支持他们学说的形而上思考的精细程度要差一些。[2]

为了把这一问题完全弄清楚，可以补充一些来自赫胥黎和克利福德的讨论。赫胥黎教授说：

“兽类的意识似乎是作为其身体机械装置工作的一种间接产品而与机械装置相联系的，而且它完全没有改变其工作的能力，就如同伴随着机车发动机工作的汽笛对其机械装置没有影响一样。它们的意志，如果它们有的话，是一种预示物理变化的情绪，而不是这些变化的原因，……灵魂和身体的关系就如同钟表的铃和机件的关系一样，而意识与敲击铃时发出的声音相符合。……至此，我一直严格地将自己限制在兽类的自动作用中。……就我可以做出的最佳判断而言，适用于兽类的争论也同样很好地适用于人类，这是相当真实的；因此，在我们这里，所有的意识状态，和在它们那里一样，都是立刻由大脑物质的分子变化所引起的。似

① 《实践理论》，第 1 卷，第 416 页以后。

② 当前的作者回忆，在 1869 年，当时他还是个医学院的学生，他开始写一篇论文，表明几乎所有思考大脑过程的人，都在自己对它们的解释中不正当地插入了源自整个异质感受世界的联系。他印证说斯宾赛、霍奇森（在其《时间与空间》中）、莫兹利、洛克哈特·克拉克、贝恩、卡彭特博士都曾犯过这种混淆的错误。写作很快就停止了，因为他觉察到，他所持有的用来反对这些作者的观点是一个纯粹的概念，关于它的真实性没有证据可以被列举出来。后来，似乎对他来说，所有现存的证据实际上都支持他们的观点。

It seems to me that in men, as in brutes, there is no proof that any state of consciousness is the cause of change in the motion of the matter of the organism. If these positions are well based, it follows that our mental conditions are simply the symbols in consciousness of the changes which take place automatically in the organism; and that, to take an extreme illustration, the feeling we call volition is not the cause of a voluntary act, but the symbol of that state of the brain which is the immediate cause of that act. We are conscious automata."

Professor Clifford writes:

"All the evidence that we have goes to show that the physical world gets along entirely by itself, according to practically universal rules. . . . The train of physical facts between the stimulus sent into the eye, or to any one of our senses, and the exertion which follows it, and the train of physical facts Which goes on in the brain, even when there is no stimulus and no exertion,—these are perfectly complete physical trains, and every step is fully accounted for by mechanical conditions. . . . . The two things are on utterly different platforms—the physical facts go along by themselves, and the mental facts go along by themselves. There is a parallelism between them, but there is no . interference of one with the other. Again, if anybody says that the will influences matter, the statement is not untrue, but it is nonsense. Such an assertion belongs to the crude materialism of the savage. The only thing which influences matter is the position of surrounding matter or the motion of surrounding matter. . . . The assertion that another man's volition, a feeling in his consciousness that I cannot perceive, is part of the train of physical facts which I may perceive,—this is neither true nor untrue, but nonsense; it is a combination of words whose corresponding ideas will not go together. . . . Sometimes one series is known better, and sometimes the other; so that in telling a story we speak sometimes of mental and sometimes of material facts. A feeling of chill made a man ran; strictly speaking, the nervous disturbance which coexisted with that feeling of chill

乎对我来说,在人这里和在兽类那里一样,没有证据表明任何状态的意识是引起生物体物质运动变化的原因。如果这些立场都有很好的基础,由它可以推知,我们的心理条件仅仅是在生物体中自动发生着变化的意识中的符号;而且,采取一种极端的说法,我们称之为意志的感受不是主动行为的原因,而是作为那种行为的直接原因的大脑状态的符号。我们是有意识的自动机。”

克利福德教授写到:

“我们所具有的所有证据表明,物理世界完全是依照实际的普遍规律通过自身来运行的。……在送入我们眼睛、或者其他任何感官中的刺激,和随后发生的动作之间的物理事实序列,以及甚至在没有刺激和动作之时在大脑中运行的物理事实序列,——这些是极为完全的物理序列,而且每一步都完全可以由机械条件加以说明。……这两类事物处于完全不同的平台上——物理事实通过它们自身而运行,而且心理事实也通过它们自身而运行。它们之间存在一种平行关系,但是它们之间不存在相互的干涉。再则,如果有人说意志影响物质,这种论述不是不真实,而是胡说。这样的假设属于野蛮人粗糙的唯物主义。唯一影响物质的东西是周围物质的位置,或者周围物质的运动。……另一个人的意志,以及我所不能知觉的他意识中的一种感受,是我可以知觉的物理事实序列的一部分,——这种主张既非真实,亦非不真实,而是胡说;这种主张是一些词语的结合,而其相应的观念是不能合在一处的。……人们有时对一个序列了解得较好,有时对另一个了解得较好;因此我们在讲述的时候,有时候谈到心理事实,有时候谈到物质事实。寒冷的感受使一个人跑起来;严格地讲,如果我们想谈论物理事实的话,就说是和寒冷的感受共存的神经的

made him run, if we want to talk about material facts; or the feeling of chill produced the form of sub-consciousness which coexists with the motion of legs, if we want to talk about mental facts. . . . When, therefore, we ask: ' What is the physical link between the ingoing message from chilled skin and the outgoing message which moves the leg?' and the answer is, 'A man's will,' we have as much right to be amused as if we had asked our friend with the picture what pigment was used in painting the cannon in the foreground, and received the answer, ' Wrought iron. ' It will be found excellent practice in the mental operations required by this doctrine to imagine a train, the fore part of which is an engine and three carriages linked with iron couplings, and the hind part three other carriages linked with iron couplings; the bond between the two parts being made up out of the sentiments of amity subsisting between the stoker and the guard."

To comprehend completely the consequences of the dogma so confidently enunciated, one should unflinchingly apply it to the most complicated examples. The movements of our tongues and pens, the flashings of our eyes in conversation, are of course events of a material order, and as. such their causal antecedents must be exclusively material. If we knew thoroughly the nervous system of Shakespeare, and as thoroughly all his environing conditions, we should be able to show why at a certain period of his life his hand came to trace on certain sheets of paper those crabbed little black marks which we for shortness' sake call the manuscript of Hamlet We should under stand the rationale of every erasure and alteration therein, and we should understand all this without in the slightest degree acknowledging the existence of the thoughts in Shakespeare's mind. The words and sentences would be taken, not as signs of anything beyond themselves, but as little outward facts, pure and simple. In like manner we might exhaustively write the biography of those two hundred pounds, more or less, of warmish albuminoid matter called Martin Luther, without ever implying that it felt.

But, on the other hand, nothing in all this could prevent us from

局部运动使他跑起来；或者如果我们要想谈论心理事实，就说寒冷的感受产生了和腿的运动共存的下意识形式。……因此，当我们问：'来自受到冷刺激的皮肤的进入的信息和移动双腿的出来的信息之间的联系是什么呢？'回答就是：'人的意志，'我们这时有足够的权利发笑，就好像我们拿着一张画问我们的朋友在前景中的大炮使用了什么颜料，而得到的回答是'熟铁'时一样。可以发现，由这一学说所要求的在心理活动中的最好的练习就是去想像一辆火车，它的前半部分是一个车头和由铁制连接器连在一起的三节车厢，它的后半部分也是由铁制连接器连在一起的三节车厢；而这两部分之间的结合出自司炉和列车员之间的友好情感。"

为了完全领会人们如此自信地阐明的信条所带来的结果，人们应该不畏缩地将它应用于最复杂的例子中。我们的舌头和笔的运动，在谈话中眼睛的闪烁，当然都是物质序列的事实，因而它们的先行原因也必须是物质的。如果我们完全了解莎士比亚的神经系统，并对他的所有环境条件也完全了解，我们就应该能够表明，为什么在他生活的某一阶段，他的手开始在一些纸上写下那些潦草的黑色小符号，而且为了简短起见，我们才称之为哈姆雷特手稿。我们也应该理解在那里所做的所有删除和添加的基本原因，而且我们应该在理解所有这一切的同时，一点也不承认莎士比亚心灵中思想的存在。那些词语和句子不应该被看作是任何超出它们自身的记号，而应该被看作是纯粹而简单的琐碎的外部事实。以同样的方式，我们可以毫无遗漏地写出那被叫做马丁·路德的大约二百磅重的微温蛋白物质的传记了，而根本不用指出他有感受。

在另一方面，所有这一切中，没有任何东西可以阻止我们对

giving an equally complete account of either Luther ' s or Shakespeare ' s spiritual history, an account in which every gleam of thought and emotion should find its place. The mind history would run alongside of the bodyhistory of each man, and each point in the one would correspond to, but not react upon, a point in the other. So the melody floats from the harp-string, but neither checks nor quickens its vibrations; so the shadow runs alongside the pedestrian, but in no way influences his steps.

Another inference, apparently more paradoxical still, needs to be made, though, as far as I am aware, Dr. Hodgson is the only writer who has explicitly drawn it. That inference is that feelings, not causing nerve-actions, cannot even cause each other. To ordinary common sense, felt pain is, as such, not only the cause of outward tears and cries, but also the cause of such inward events as sorrow, compunction, desire, or inventive thought. So the consciousness of good news is the direct producer of the feeling of joy, the awareness of premises that of the belief in conclusions. But according to the automaton-theory, each of the feelings mentioned is only the correlate of some nerve movement whose *cause* lay wholly in a previous nerve-movement. The first nerve-movement called up the second; whatever feeling was attached to the second consequently found itself following upon the feeling that was attached to the first. If, for example, good news was the consciousness correlated with the first movement, then joy turned out to be the correlate in consciousness of the second. But all the while the items of the nerve series were the only ones in causal continuity; the items of the conscious series, however inwardly rational their sequence, were simply juxtaposed.

Reasons For The Theory.

The ' conscious automaton-theory, ' as this conception is generally

路德和莎士比亚的精神的历史做出同样全面的说明，在这一说明中，思想和情绪的每一个闪光点都应该有自己的位置。每一个人的心灵的历史和身体的历史应该是并行的，两种历史中的每一点应该相互对应，但不会彼此做出反应。因此，竖琴的琴弦上飘散出了旋律，但这旋律既不阻止也不加快琴弦的振动；因此，影子伴随着行人一起走，但是却绝不会影响他的脚步。

这里还需要做另一个显然更加荒谬的推论，尽管据我所知，霍奇森博士是唯一明确做出这一推论的人。其推论就是，感受不能引起神经活动，甚至也不能彼此引起对方。从普通常识来看，感受到的痛苦本身，不仅是外部眼泪和哭声的原因，而且也是内部诸如悲哀、悔恨、愿望或者创造性思维之类的事件的原因。因此对好消息的意识是欢乐感受的直接产生者，关于前提的意识会产生对结论的信仰。但是按照自动理论，所提到的每一种感受仅仅是一些神经运动的相关物，而这些神经运动的起因完全存在于前一个神经运动中。第一个神经运动唤起了第二个；因此，不管第二个神经运动之上附加了什么感受，这感受都会发现自己跟随着附加在第一个神经运动之上的感受。例如，如果好消息是和第一个运动相联系的意识，那么欢乐就是意识中第二个运动的关联物。但是，神经序列中的东西始终是因果连续中唯一的东西；而意识序列中的东西，不论其序列如何具有内在的合理性，它们都只是被并置的。

支持这一理论的理由

“意识自动机理论”，如这一概念通常被称为的那样，因此是

called, is thus a radical and simple conception of the manner in which certain facts may possibly occur. But between conception and belief, proof ought to lie. And when we ask, 'What proves that all this is more than a mere conception of the possible?' it is not easy to get a sufficient reply. If we start from the frog's spinal cord and reason by continuity, saying, as that acts so intelligently, though unconscious, so the higher centres, *though conscious*, may have the intelligence they show quite as mechanically based; we are immediately met by the exact counter-argument from continuity, an argument actually urged by such writers as Pflüger and Lewes, which starts from the acts of the hemispheres, and says: "As *these* owe their intelligence to the consciousness which we know to be there, so the intelligence of the spinal cord's acts must really be due to the invisible presence of a consciousness lower in degree." All arguments from continuity work in two ways: you can either level up or level down by their means. And it is clear that such arguments as these can eat each other up to all eternity.

There remains a sort of philosophic faith, bred like most faiths from an aesthetic demand. Mental and physical events are, on all hands, admitted to present the strongest contrast in the entire field of being. The chasm which yawns between them is less easily bridged over by the mind than any interval we know. Why, then, not call it an absolute chasm, and say not only that the two worlds are different, but that they are independent? This gives us the comfort of all simple and absolute formulas, and it makes each chain homogeneous to our consideration. When talking of nervous tremors and bodily actions, we may feel secure against intrusion from an irrelevant mental world. When, on the other hand, we speak of feelings, we may with equal consistency use terms always of one denomination, and never be annoyed by what Aristotle calls 'slipping into another kind.'

关于某种事实可能发生的方式的一种激进而简单的概念。但是,在概念和信仰之间,应该存在证据。而且当我们问道:“是什么证明了所有这一切并非仅仅是一个可能的概念?”要得到一个充分的回答是不容易的。如果我们从青蛙的脊髓开始,并且通过连续性进行推论,由于其行为是如此的智能化,尽管是无意识的,所以高级中枢,尽管是有意识的,可以拥有智能,而且其表现出来的智能的基础是完全机械的;我们立刻就遇到了来自连续性的反论证,这一论点实际上是由诸如弗吕格和路易斯这样的作者所强烈主张的,他们从脑半球的动作开始,并且说:“由于这些动作将它们的智能归功于我们知道其存在的意识,因此,脊髓动作的智能必须真正被归因于程度较低的意识的不可见的存在。”所有来自连续性的争论以两种方式进行着:通过他们的方式你可以跟上面一致,也可以和下面一致。而且很清楚的是,像这样的辩论可以永远地互相争咬下去。

这里还存在一种哲学的信仰,它的产生像大多数来自审美需求的信仰一样。在所有方面,精神的和物理的事件都被认为可以在整个存在界呈现出最强烈的对比。通过心灵在它们之间的裂痕上架起一座桥梁,比通过我们所知道的任何其他的中间事物都更不容易。那么,为什么不将它称为是绝对的裂痕呢?并且不仅说这两个世界是不同的,而且还说它们是彼此独立的呢?这会给我们所有简单而且绝对的公式以安慰,并且它使得每一个链条都与我们的思考同质了。当谈论神经振动和身体动作时,我们将由于没有受到来自不相干的精神世界的侵扰而感到安全。在另一方面,当我们谈论感受的时候,我们可以同样一贯地使用总是同一种类的术语,而且永远也不会被亚里士多德称为“滑入另一种类”

The desire on the part of men educated in laboratories not to have their physical reasonings mixed up with such incommensurable factors as feelings is certainly very strong. I have heard a most intelligent biologist say: "It is high time for scientific men to protest against the recognition of any such thing as consciousness in a scientific investigation." In a word, feeling constitutes the 'unscientific' half of existence, and any one who enjoys calling himself a 'scientist' will be too happy to purchase an untrammelled homogeneity of terms in the studies of his predilection, at the slight cost of admitting a dualism which, in the same breath that it allows to mind an independent status of being, banishes it to a limbo of causal inertness, from whence no intrusion or interruption on its part need ever be feared.

Over and above this great postulate that matters must be kept simple, there is, it must be confessed, still another highly abstract reason for denying causal efficacity to our feelings. We can form no positive image of the *modus operandi* of a volition or other thought affecting the cerebral molecules.

"Let us try to imagine an idea, say of food, producing a movement, say of carrying food to the mouth. . . What is the method of its action? Does it assist the decomposition of the molecules of the gray matter, or does it retard the process, or does it alter the direction in which the shocks are distributed? Let us imagine the molecules of the gray matter combined in such a way that they will fall into simpler combinations on the impact of an incident force. Now suppose the incident force, in the shape of a shock from some other centre, to impinge upon these molecules. By hypothesis it will decompose them, and they will fall into the simpler combination. How is the idea of food to prevent this decomposition? Manifestly it can do so only by increasing the force which binds the molecules together. Good! Try to imagine the idea of a beefsteak binding two molecules together. It is impossible. Equally impossible is it to imagine a similar idea

的事物所烦扰。在实验室中被教育出来的人，有一部分人有种相当强烈的愿望，即他们不希望将他们的物理推论和诸如感受这类不能比较的因素混淆起来。我听到一位最聪明的生物学家说过："对科学人员来说，现在是起来抗议在科学研究中承认有任何诸如意识的东西的时候了。"一句话，感受构成了"非科学"的那半部分存在，而且任何乐于称自己为科学家的人，在他所爱好的研究中，都极不乐意以承认二元论为微小代价，来换取术语不受阻碍的同质性，这种二元论在承认心灵是独立的存在状态的同时，又将它驱逐进了无因果自动力的监狱之中，从此可以再也不需要惧怕来自心灵这方面的侵扰和打断。

在必须让问题保持简单这一伟大的基本原理之上，必须承认的是，这里还有另外一个高度抽象的理由用来否认我们感受的因果效力。我们对影响大脑分子的意志或其他思维的运作不能形成肯定的意象。

"让我们试着想像一个观念，比如说食物的观念，它造成了一个动作，比如说将食物送到嘴里的动作。……其行动的方式是什么？它帮助灰色物质的分子分解了吗，或者它延迟了这一过程吗，或者它改变了震荡分布的方向了吗？让我们想像灰色物质的分子是以这样的方式结合的，即在偶发力量的冲撞下他们会分解成更简单的化合物。现在假设，以来自其他中枢的震荡为形式的偶发力量撞击这些分子。根据假说，它将会分解它们，而且它们会分解成更简单的化合物。食物的观念是如何阻止这一分解的呢？显然，它只能通过增强将分子粘合在一起的力量来做到这一点。好！试着想像一个牛排的观念将两个分子粘合在一起。这是不可能的。同样也不可能想像的是一个相似的观点将两个分

loosening the attractive force between two molecules." ①

This passage from an exceedingly clever writer expresses admirably the difficulty to which I allude. Combined with a strong sense of the 'chasm' between the two worlds, and with a lively faith in reflex machinery, the sense of this difficulty can hardly fail to make one turn consciousness out of the door as a superfluity so far as one's explanations go. One may bow her out politely, allow her to remain as an 'epiphenomenon' (invaluable word!), but one insists that matter shall hold all the power.

"Having thoroughly recognized the fathomless abyss that separates mind from matter, and having so blended the very notion into his very nature that there is no chance of his ever forgetting it or failing to saturate with it all his meditations, the student of psychology has next to appreciate the association between these two orders of phenomena. . . . They are associated in a manner so intimate that some of the greatest thinkers consider them different aspects of the same process. . . When the rearrangement of molecules takes place in the higher regions of the brain, a change of consciousness simultaneously occurs. . . . The change of consciousness never takes place without the change in the brain; the change in the brain never . . . without the change in consciousness. But *why* the two occur together, or what the link is which connects them, we do not know, and most authorities believe that we never shall and never can know. Having firmly and tenaciously grasped these two notions, of the absolute separateness of mind and matter, and of the invariable concomitance of a mental change with a bodily change, the student will enter on the study of psychology with half his difficulties surmounted." ②

① Chas. Mercier: The Nervous System and the Mind (1888), p. 9.
② *Op. cit.* p. 11.

子间相互吸引的力减小了。”①

这个段落来自一位非常聪明的作者，它极好地表达出了我暗指的那个困难。对这一困难的见识，对两个世界之间的“裂缝”的强烈感觉，以及对反射机制的真实信仰，它们三者结合在一起，几乎不会不使人在做出其解释时将意识作为一种额外的东西而逐出门外。人们可以斯文地将她俯首送出，容许她作为一种“伴随物”（无价的用词！）而存在，可是人们却坚持物质应该拥有全部力量。

“如果已经完全认识到那将精神和物质分离开来的深不可测的深渊，并且已经将这种观点完全混合进了他的本性之中，以至于这里没有机会再让他忘记它，或者没有使它完全渗透到他的全部沉思中，心理学学者已经接近于赏识这两种现象秩序的联系了。……它们以如此亲密的方式联系在一起，以至于一些伟大的思想家将它们认为是同一过程的不同方面……当在大脑高级区域的分子重新排列发生时，意识的变化也同时发生。……如果没有大脑中的变化，意识的变化就永远不会发生；大脑中的变化从来不会……没有意识的变化相伴随。但是，为什么两者同时发生呢，或者将它们连接起来的连接物是什么呢，我们不知道，而且大部分权威人士认为我们将永远不会知道，也永远不能知道。如果已经坚定地并且顽强地把握住了这两种观点，即精神和物质是绝对分离的观点，以及心理变化和身体变化永远相互伴随的观点，学者在开始心理学研究时，就已经克服了一半的困难。”②

---

① C. 默西埃：《神经系统与心灵》（1888 年），第 9 页。

② 在前面所引用的书中，第 11 页。

Half his difficulties ignored, I should prefer to say. For this 'concomitance' in the midst of 'absolute separateness' is an utterly irrational notion. It is to my mind quite inconceivable that consciousness should have *nothing* to do with a business which it so faithfully attends. And the question, 'What has it to do?' is one which psychology has no right to 'surmount,' for it is her plain duty to consider it. The fact is that the whole question of interaction and influence between things is a metaphysical question, and cannot be discussed at all by those who are unwilling to go into matters thoroughly. It is truly enough hard to imagine the 'idea of a beefsteak binding two molecules together;' but since Hume's time it has been equally hard to imagine *anything* binding them together. The whole notion of 'binding' is a mystery, the first step towards the solution of which is to clear scholastic rubbish out of the way. Popular science talks of 'forces,' 'attractions' or 'affinities' as binding the molecules; but clear science, though she may use such words to abbreviate discourse, has no use for the conceptions, and is satisfied when she can express in simple 'laws' the bare space-relations of the molecules as functions of each other and of time. To the more curiously inquiring mind, however, this simplified expression of the bare facts is not enough; there must be a 'reason' for them, and something must 'determine' the laws. And when one seriously sits down to consider what sort of a thing one *means* when one asks for a 'reason,' one is led so far afield, so far away from popular science and its scholasticism, as to see that even such afact as the existence or non-existence in the universe of 'the idea of a beefsteak' may not be wholly indifferent to other facts in the same universe, and in particular may have something to do with determining the distance at which two molecules in that universe shall lie apart. If this is so, then common-sense, though the intimate nature of causality and of the connection of things in the universe lies beyond her pitifully bounded horizon,

我更愿意说，他有一半的困难被忽视了。因为在“绝对分离”之中的这种“伴随”是一个完全不合理的概念。对我来说似乎很难想像意识和它如此忠实参加的事业没有任何关系。而且“它不得不做什么”这一问题，是心理学无权“超越”的问题，因为考虑这一问题是其平常的职责所在。实际上，两种事物间的相互作用和影响，这整个问题，是一个形而上学的问题，而且那些不愿意完全深入到问题中的人是根本不能讨论它的。想像“一块将两个分子粘合在一起的牛排的观念”确实是足够困难的；可是自从休谟时代以来，想像将它们粘合在一起的任何事情也是同样困难。“粘合”的整个概念就是一个谜，解决这个谜的第一步就是要将经院哲学家的垃圾从道路上清扫出去。通俗科学谈论“力”、“吸引力”或“亲和力”，将它们作为粘合分子的东西；尽管清晰的科学可以使用这些词语来缩短论述，但它们对她来说是没有用的，当她能够以简单的“规律”将分子的单纯空间关系表示为相互间的作用以及时间的作用时，她就满足了。然而，对于更具好奇心并且爱寻根究底的心灵来说，这种对单纯事实的简单化表达是不够的；这里必须得有一个“理由”来支持它们，而且必须有一些东西可以“确定”那些规律。一个人坐下来认真思考：当人们索要一个理由的时候，他们所指的是什么一种东西，此时，他就被带到了一个遥远的领域，它远离通俗科学及其烦琐哲学，以至于他看到像“牛排的观念”在宇宙中的存在和不存在这样的事实，都不可能完全和同一宇宙中的其他事实无关，而且，就确定在那个宇宙中的分子将会由以分开的距离而言，它和这尤其相关。如果是这样的话，尽管因果关系的固有本质和宇宙中事物的联系的固有本质超越了常识的可怜的受限范围，当常识顽固地坚持感受和观念就是原因之

has the root and gist of the truth in her hands when she obstinately holds to it that feelings and ideas are causes. However inadequate our ideas of causal efficacy may be, we are less wide of the mark when we say that our ideas and feelings have it, than the Automatists are when they say they haven't it, As in the night all cats are gray, so in the darkness of metaphysical criticism all causes are obscure. But one has no right to pull the pall over the psychic half of the subject only, as the automatists do, and to say that *that* causation is unintelligible, whilst in the same breath one dogmatizes about *material causation* as if Hume, Kant, and Lotze had never been born, One cannot thus blow hot and cold. One must be impartially *naif* or impartially critical. If the latter, the reconstruction must be thorough-going or 'metaphysical' and will probably preserve the common-sense view that ideas are forces, in some translated form. But Psychology is a mere natural science, accepting certain terms uncritically as her data, and stopping short of metaphysical reconstruction. Like physics, she. must be *naive*; and if she finds that in her very peculiar field of study ideas *seem* to be causes, she had better continue to talk of them as such. She gains absolutely nothing by a breach with common-sense in this matter, and she loses, to say the least, all naturalness of speech. If feelings are causes, of course their effects must be furtherances and checkings of internal cerebral motions, of which in themselves we are entirely Without knowledge. It is probable that for years to come we shall have to infer what happens in the brain either from our feelings or from motor effects which we observe. The organ will be for us a sort of vat in which feelings and motions somehow go on stewing together, and in which innumerable things happen of which we catch but the statistical result. Why, under these circumstances, we should be asked to forswear the language of our childhood I cannot well imagine, especially as it is perfectly compatible with the language of physiology. The feelings can produce nothing absolutely new, they can only reinforce and inhibit reflex currents which already exist,

时,真理的根基和要旨就掌握在它的手中了。不论我们关于因果效力的观念有多么不充分,当我们说我们的观念和感受具有它时,我们比那些说它们没有因果效力的自动论者还要更接近目标一些,如在夜晚所有的猫都是灰色的一样,因此在形而上学批判的黑暗中所有的原因都是模糊的。但是人们没有权利只将帷幕盖住问题的精神那一半,如自动论者所做的一样,并且说那种因果作用是无法理解的,而与此同时又武断地提出物质的因果关系,就好像休谟、康德和洛采从来没有出生过一样,人不能因此而摇摆不定。人必须是没有偏见地天真,或者没有偏见地苛求。如果是后者,则重建必须是彻底的,或者是“形而上学”的,而且将可能保留常识的观点,即:观念在某种被转化了的形式中就是力。但是,心理学仅仅是一门自然科学,它不加批判地接受某些特定的术语以作为其资料,而且在形而上学的重建之前就停止了脚步。像物理学一样,它必须是天真的;而且如果它发现在其特殊的研究领域中观念似乎就是原因,它最好还是继续这样讨论它们。在这一问题上违背常识,它绝对不会得到任何好处,而且至少来说,它失去了讲话的全部自然性。如果感受就是原因,它们的作用当然就是促进和检验内在的大脑活动,关于大脑活动自身,我们一无所知。可能在很长的时间里,我们都将不得不从我们的感受中或者从我们所观察的运动结果中来推断在大脑中发生了什么。对我们来说,这器官就是一种大桶,在其中感受和运动不知何故就蒸煮在了一起,并且在其中有无数的事情发生了,而我们只能捕捉到关于它们的统计学结果。在这样的情况下,我不能很好地想像,为什么请求我们放弃儿时的语言,尤其当它和生理学的语言完全一致时。感受不能产生任何绝对新的东西,它们只能强化和

and the original organization of these by physiological forces must always be the ground-work of the psychological scheme.

My conclusion is that to urge the automaton-theory upon us, as it is now urged, on purely a *priori* and *quasi* metaphysical grounds, is an *unwarrantable impertinence in the present state of psychology*.

Reasons Against The Theory.

But there are much more positive reasons than this why we ought to continue to talk in psychology as if consciousness had causal efficacy. The *particulars of the distribution of consciousness*, so far as we know them, *point to its being efficacious*. Let us trace some of them.

It is very generally admitted, though the point would be hard to prove, that consciousness grows the more complex: and intense the higher we rise in the animal kingdom. That of a man must exceed that of an oyster. From this point of view it seems an organ, superadded to the other organs which maintain the animal in the straggle for existence; and the presumption of course is that it helps him in some way in the struggle, just as they do. But it cannot help him without being in some way efficacious and influencing the course of his bodily history. If now it could be shown in what way consciousness *might* help him, and if, moreover, the defects of his other organs (where consciousness is most developed) are such as to make them need just the kind of help that consciousness would bring provided it *were* efficacious; why, then the plausible inference would be that it came just *because* of its efficacy—in other words, its efficacy would be inductively proved.

Now the study of the phenomena of consciousness which we shall

抑制已经存在的反射流，而由生理力量完成的对这些反射流的最初的组织，必须永远是心理学方案的基础。

我的结论就是，在纯粹先天的和准形而上学的基础上，如现在所做的这样，向我们力劝自动机理论，在目前的心理学状态下，是一种不正当的鲁莽行为。

反对这一理论的理由

而且，这里还有比这多得多的肯定的理由来支持为什么我们应该在心理学的讨论中，要好像意识是有因果效力的。就我们所知，意识分布的细节表明了它的效力。让我们对此做一些探讨。

意识变得越复杂、越强烈，我们在动物王国中就升得越高，虽然这一点很难证明，但它得到了普遍的承认。人的意识必须超越牡蛎的意识。从这种观点来看，它似乎是一种器官，加上其他的器官，它们一起使动物在生存的斗争中得以保存；而且假定当然是它以某种方式在斗争中帮助了他，就和其他器官所做的一样。但是，如果它不能以某种方式发生效力并且影响他的身体的历史进程，它就不能帮助他。如果现在能够表明意识以什么方式可以帮助他，此外，如果他的其他器官（在那里意识最为发达）的缺陷是那样的一种缺陷，即它们需要意识提供帮助，而那种帮助只有假设意识有效用的时候，它才可以提供；那么，似乎合理的推论就是，它为什么出现，正是因为它的效用——换句话说，它的效用得到了归纳性的证明。

我们将在本书其余部分中论述的现今关于意识现象的研究

make throughout the rest of this book will show us that consciousness is at all times primarily a *selecting agency*. ① Whether we take it in the lowest sphere of sense, or in the highest of. intellection, we find it always doing one thing, choosing one out of several of the materials so presented to its notice, emphasizing and accentuating that and suppressing as far as possible all the rest. The item emphasized is always in close connection with some *interest* felt by consciousness to be paramount at the time.

But what are now the defects of the nervous system in those animals whose consciousness seems most highly developed? Chief among them must be *instability*. The cerebral hemispheres are the characteristically 'high' nerve-centres, and we saw how indeterminate and unforeseeable their performances were in comparison with those of the basal ganglia and the cord. But this very vagueness constitutes their advantage. They allow their possessor to adapt his conduct to the minutest alterations in the environing circumstances, any one of which may be for him a sign, suggesting distant motives more powerful than any present solicitations of sense. It seems as if certain mechanical conclusions should be drawn from this state of things. An organ swayed by slight impressions is an organ whose natural state is one of unstable equilibrium. We may imagine the various lines of discharge in the cerebrum to be almost on a par in point of permeability-what discharge a given small impression will produce may be called *accidental*, in the sense in which we say it is a matter of accident whether a raindrop falling on a mountain ridge descend the eastern or the western slope. It is in this sense that we may call it a matter of accident whether a child be a boy or a girl. The ovum is so unstable a body that certain causes too minute for our apprehension may at a certain moment tip it one way or the other. The natural law of an organ constituted after this fashion can be nothing but a law of caprice. I do not see how one

① See in particular the end of Chapter IX.

向我们表明,意识始终都主要是一个选择机制。[1] 不论我们将意识带入最低级的感觉领域来研究,还是将它带入最高级的智性活动来探讨,我们发现它总是做着一件事情,即它从呈现在它面前并引起它注意的几种材料中选择出一种,强调并注重这一材料,并且尽可能地抑制剩下的材料。得到强调的东西,总是与由意识所感觉到的在当时极为重要的某种利益有紧密的联系。

但是,在那些意识似乎得到了高度发展的动物中,当前神经系统的缺陷是什么呢?其中最主要的缺陷一定是不稳定性。脑半球的独特之处在于它是"高级"神经中枢,而且我们看到,同基底神经结和脊髓的运行相比,它们的运行是多么地不确定和不可预测。但恰恰是这种含混构成了它们的优势。它们使得其所有者的行为可以适应周围环境的最细微的变化,其中任何一个变化对他来说都可以是一个符号,它比任何当前的感觉诱惑都更有力地向他提示出了远端的目标。就好像从这些事物的状态中可以得出某种机械的结论。由于细小的印象而摇摆的器官,其自然状态是某种不稳定的平衡状态。我们可以想像大脑中的各种释放路线就渗透性这一点来说几乎处于同等地位——一个给定的小的印象将产生什么样的释放,这可以被认为是偶然的,这种意义上的偶然性就和我们说落在山坡上的雨点是从东边还是西边的山坡流下去是偶然的一样。就我们的理解而言,卵子是如此地不稳定,以至于某些非常细小的原因就可以使它在某一时刻滑向一条道路或者另一条道路之中。以这种方式构成器官的自然规律,只能是一种反复无常的规律。我没有见过一个人如何

① 尤其参见第9章的结束部分。

could reasonably expect from it any certain pursuance of useful lines of reaction, such as the few and fatally determined performances of the lower centres constitute within their narrow sphere. The dilemma in regard to the nervous system seems, in short, to be of the following kind. We may construct one which will react infallibly and certainly, but it will then be capable of reacting to very few changes in the environment-it will fail to be adapted to all the rest. We may, on the other hand, construct a nervous system potentially adapted to respond to an infinite variety of minute features in the situation; but its fallibility will then be as great as its elaboration. We can never be sure that its equilibrium will be upset in the appropriate direction. In short, a high brain may do many things, and may do each of them at a very slight hint. But its hair-trigger organization makes of it a happy-go-lucky, hit-or-miss affair. It is as likely to do the crazy as the sane thing at any given moment. A low brain does few things, and in doing them perfectly forfeits all other use. The performances of a high brain are like dice thrown forever on a table. Unless they be loaded, what chance is there that the highest number will turn up oftener than the lowest?

All this is said of the brain as a physical machino pure and simple. *Can consciousness increase its efficiency by loading its dice*? Such is the problem.

Loading its dice would mean bringing a more or less constant pressure to bear in favor of *those* its performances which make for the most permanent interests of the brain's owner; it would mean a constant inhibition of the tendencies to stray aside.

Well, just such pressure and such inhibition are what consciousness *seems* to be exerting all the while. And the interests in whose favor it seems to exert them are *its* interests and its alone,

能够理性地从它那里预期出一系列有用反应的任何确定的执行，就像预期出低级中枢在其狭窄的领域之内组成的那些为数不多且不可避免地确定了的行动一样。简而言之，神经系统的两难选择似乎是下面这一种。我们可以构造一个能够准确无误地和确定地做出反应的神经系统，但是它因此只能够对环境中的极少数变化做出反应——它不能适应所有其他的变化。在另一方面，我们可以构造一种神经系统，它潜在地适合于对环境中无限多的细微特征做出反应；但是它的易错性会因此和它的精致性一样巨大。我们永远也不能确定它的平衡将会在哪个适当的方向上被打破。简言之，一个高级的大脑可以做很多事情，而且可以根据非常微小的暗示来做每一件事情。但是，其一触即发的组织使它成为一个随遇而安的、遇到事情现打主意的东西。在任何给定的时刻，它都同样有可能做疯狂的事情和明智的事情。一个低级的大脑做很少的事情，并且在做这些事情时完全丧失了所有其他用途。一个高级大脑的行动就像是在桌子上一直扔骰子。除非它们被灌了铅，否则最大的数字比最小的数字经常出现的机率会是多少呢？

关于大脑作为一架纯粹的和简单的物理机器而言，所说的就这么多了。意识能够通过往骰子里灌铅来增加其效力吗？这是个问题。

给它的骰子灌铅的意思是，要带来一种多少可以持续忍受的压力，这种压力有利于给大脑的所有者带来最长久利益的那些行动；它意味着对偏离开来的倾向进行一种持续性的抑制。

好了，就是这种压力和这种抑制，是意识似乎一直施加着的东西。而且它看上去施加这些东西所为的那种利益，就是它所创造的它

interests which it *creates*, and which, but for it, would have no status in the realm of being what-ever. We talk, it is true, when we are darwinizing, as if the mere *body* that owns the brain had interests; we speak about the utilities of its various organs and how they help or hinder the body's survival; and we treat the survival as if it were an absolute end, existing as such in the physical world, a sort of actual *shouid-be*, presiding over the animal and judging his reactions, quite apart from the presence of any commenting intelligence outside. We forget that in the absence of some such superadded commenting intelligence (whether it be that of the animal itself, or only ours or Mr. Darwin's), the reactions cannot be properly talked of as 'useful' or 'hurtful' at all. Considered merely physically, all that can be said of them is that *if* they occur in a certain way survival will as a matter of fact prove to be their incidental consequence. The organs themselves, and all the rest of the physical world, will, however, all the time be quite indifferent to this consequence, and would quite as cheerfully, the circumstances changed, compass the animal's destruction. In a word, survival can enter into a purely physiological discussion only as an *hypothesis made by an onlooker*, about the future. But the moment you bring a consciousness into the midst, survival ceases to be a mere hypothesis. No longer is it, "*if* survival is to occur, then so and so must brain and other organs work." It has now become an imperative decree: "Survival *shall* occur, and therefore organs *must* so work!" *Real* ends appear for the first time now upon the world's stage. The conception of consciousness as a purely cognitive form of being, which is the pet way of regarding it in many idealistic schools, modern as well as ancient, is thoroughly anti-psychological, as the remainder of this book will show. Every actually existing consciousness seems to itself at any rate to be a *fighter for ends*, of which many, but for its presence, would not be ends at all. Its powers of cognition are mainly subservient to these ends,

的利益、它独自的利益，而且这利益若不是为了它，其在存在领域将没有任何地位。确实，当我们用达尔文的理论来思维时，我们的谈论就好像认为拥有大脑的身体才有利益；我们谈论其各种器官的效用，以及它们如何帮助或阻碍身体的生存；而且我们似乎将生存看作是一个绝对的目的，同样存在于物理世界之中，是某种实在的“将在”，它主管着动物并且评判其反应，并且远在外界的任何评论理智的存在之外。我们忘记了，若是没有这样一些被添加上的评论理智（不论它是那个动物自己的，或者仅是我们自己的或达尔文先生的），反应就根本不能被恰当地称作是“有用的”或者是“有害的”。如果仅仅从物理方面考虑，关于它们所能说的只是，如果它们以某种方式发生，生存事实上将证明是它们的附带结果。然而，器官自身以及所有物理世界的剩余部分将始终对这一结果毫不关心，假如环境变化了，它们将同样高高兴兴地实现动物的毁灭。一句话，生存只有作为一种由旁观者提出的关于未来的假说才能够进入纯粹生理学的讨论之中。但是，一旦你将意识带入其中，生存就不仅仅是一个假说了。它不再是“假如生存将要发生，那么大脑和其他器官就必须如此这般地工作。”它现在已经变成了一种强制性的命令：“生存将要发生，因此器官必须如此工作！”实在的目的首次出现在了世界的舞台上。将意识作为一种纯粹的对存在的认识形式，这种观念是许多近代以及古代的唯心主义学派的主张，正如本书其余部分将要表明的那样，它是彻底反心理学的。每一个实际存在的意识对它自身来说似乎无论如何都是为目的而战的战士，其中的许多目的，如若没有意识的存在，将根本不是目的。意识的认知能力主要是用来帮助这些目的的，辨别出哪种事实促进了这些目的，

discerning which facts further them and which do not.

Now let consciousness only be what it seems to itself, and it will help an instable brain to compass its proper ends. The movements of the brain *per se* yield the means of attaining these ends mechanically, but only out of a lot of other ends, if so they may be called, which are not the proper ones of the animal, but often quite opposed. The brain is an instrument of possibilities, but of no certainties. But the consciousness, with its own ends present to it, and knowing also well which possibilities lead thereto and which away, will, if endowed with causal efficacy, reinforce the favorable possibilities and repress the unfavorable or indifferent ones. The nerve-currents, coursing through the cells and fibres, must in this case be supposed strengthened by the fact of their awaking one consciousness and dampened by awaking another. *How* such reaction of the consciousness upon the currents may occur must remain at present unsolved: it is enough for my purpose to have shown that it may not uselessly exist, and that the matter is less simple than the brain-automatists hold.

All the facts of the natural history of consciousness lend color to this view. Consciousness, for example, is only intense when nerve-processes are hesitant. In rapid, automatic, habitual action it sinks to a minimum. Nothing could be more fitting than this, if consciousness have the teleological function we suppose; nothing more meaningless, if not. Habitual actions are certain, and being in no danger of going astray from their end, need no extraneous help. In hesitant action, there seem many alternative possibilities of final nervous discharge. The feeling awakened by the nascent excitement of each alternative nerve-tract seems by its attractive or repulsive quality, to determine whether the excitement shall abort or shall become complete. Where indecision is great, as before a dangerous leap,

哪些不能。

现在,就让意识仅仅成为对其自身来说似乎所是的东西吧,而且它将帮助不稳定的大脑实现其适宜的目的。大脑本身的运动机械地产生了实现这些目的的手段,而且还放弃了许多其他的目的,如果我们可以如此称呼它们的话,这些其他的目的不是动物的适宜目的,而通常是敌对的目的。大脑是可能性的工具,但却没有确定性。但是当意识自身的目的呈现在它面前,并且意识还知道哪些可能性会引导它到那里,哪些会偏离目的,那么意识如果被赋予因果效力,它就会强化有利的可能性,并且压制不利的或无关紧要的可能性。奔流过细胞和纤维的神经流,必须在这种情况下才能被认为由于它们唤醒了一个意识而得以强化,又由于它们唤醒了另一个意识而受到抑制。意识对神经流的这种反作用是如何可以发生的,目前来说,这必须保持未解决状态:就我的目的而言,表明它不是无用地存在着,并且问题并不像大脑自动机理论持有者所认为的那么简单,这就足够了。

关于意识的自然史中的所有事实都为这一观点增添了色彩。例如,当神经过程犹豫之时,意识恰恰是强烈的。在快速的、自动的和习惯性的动作中,它减弱到了最低的程度。如果意识具有我们所推测的目的论功能,那么没有什么比这更恰当的了;如果意识没有目的论的功能,那么没有什么比这更没有意义的了。习惯性动作是确定的,并且没有偏离目的陷入迷途的危险,它不需要外来的帮助。在犹豫不决的动作中,似乎存在很多可供选择的最后神经释放的可能性。由每个可供选择的神经束的最初兴奋而唤起的感受,似乎通过其吸引或者排斥的性质来决定是否这兴奋应该中断,还是应该完成。在极度优柔寡断之时,例如在一次危

consciousness is agonizingly intense. Feeling, from this point of view, may be likened to a cross-section of the chain of nervous discharge, ascertaining the links already laid down, and groping among the fresh ends presented to it for the one which seems best to fit the case.

The phenomena of 'vicarious function' which we studied in Chapter II seem to form another bit of circumstantial evidence. A machine in working order acts fatally in one way. Our consciousness calls this the right way. Take out a valve, throw a wheel out of gear or bend a pivot, and it becomes a different machine, acting just as fatally in another way which we call the wrong way. But the machine itself knows nothing of wrong or right: matter has no ideals to pursue. A locomotive will carry its train through an open drawbridge as cheerfully as to any other destination.

A brain with part of it scooped out is virtually a new machine, and during the first days after the operation functions in a thoroughly abnormal manner. As a matter of fact, however, its performances become from day to day more normal, until at last a practised eye may be needed to suspect anything wrong. Some of the restoration is undoubtedly due to 'inhibitions' passing away. But if the consciousness which goes with the rest of the brain, be there not only in order to take cognizance of each functional error, but also to exert an efficient pressure to check it if it be a sin of commission, and to lend a strengthening hand if it be a weakness or sin of omission,—nothing seems more natural than that the remaining parts, assisted in this way, should by virtue of the principle of habit grow back to the old teleological modes of exercise for which they were at first incapacitated. Nothing, on the contrary, seems at first sight more unnatural than that they should vicariously take up the duties of a part now lost without those *duties as such* exerting any persuasive or coercive force.

险的跳跃之前，意识令人苦恼地强烈。从这种观点来看，感受可以比作是神经释放链条的横截面，它确定链条已经断开，并且在出现在它面前的那些新的末端中探索，以便从中找到最适合当前情况的一个。

我们在第二章研究过的“替代功能”现象似乎构成了另外一些偶然的证据。一台工作中的机器以某种方式宿命式地制定活动。我们的意识将这称作是正确的方式。拆掉一个阀门，从传动装置中卸掉一个轮子或者弄弯一个枢轴，它就变成了一个不同的机器了，它以另一种方式同样宿命式地运行着，我们称其为错误的方式。但是，机器自身对正确和错误一无所知：物质没有用来追求的理想。一个火车头可以和驶向其他目的地一样，同样高高兴兴地拉着它的车厢驶向一个敞开着的吊桥。

其中的一部分被去除的大脑，实质上是一台新的机器，在手术后的最初几天，它以一种完全反常的方式运行着。然而事实上，它的运行一天天地变得正常起来，直到最后需要受过训练的眼睛才可以觉察出任何失常的事情。一些恢复无疑是由于“抑制”的消失所致。但是，如果伴随着大脑剩余部分的意识，其存在不仅仅是为了认识每一个功能的错误，而且也是为了施加一种有效的压力，如果是滥用之过，施加的压力就对其阻止，如果是虚弱或者疏忽之过，施加的压力就对其进行加固性的帮助，——那么，以这种方式得到帮助的大脑剩余部分，就应该通过习惯原则的效力变回到起初它们不能胜任的旧的目的论的运行模式中来，这是最自然不过的了。相反，它们应该替代性地肩负起现在已经丧失的那一部分的责任，却没有肩负起像这种施加说服的或者强制的力量的责任，初看上去，没有什么比这更不自然的了。在二十七

At the end of Chapter XXVII shall return to this again.

There is yet another set of facts which seem explicable on the supposition that consciousness has causal efficacy. It is a *well-known fact that pleasures are generally associated with beneficial*, *pains with detrimental*, *experiences.* All the fundamental vital processes, illustrate this law. Starvation, suffocation, privation of food, drink and sleep, work when exhausted, burns, wounds, inflammation, the effects of poison, are as disagreeable as filling the hungry stomach, enjoying rest and sleep after fatigue, exercise after rest, and a sound skin and unbroken bones at all times, are pleasant. Mr. Spencer and others have suggested that these coincidences are due, not to any pre-established harmony, but to the mere action of natural selection which would certainly kill off in the long-run any breed of creatures to whom the fundamentally noxious experience seemed enjoyable. An animal that should take pleasure in a feeling of suffocation would, if that pleasure were efficacious enough to make him immerse his head in water, enjoy a longevity of four or five minutes. But if pleasures and pains have no efficacy, one does not see (without some such *a priori* rational harmony as would be scouted by the ' scientific ' champions of the automaton-theory) why the most noxious acts, such as burning, might not give thrills of delight, and the most necessary ones, such as breathing, cause agony. The exceptions to the law are, it is true, numerous, but relate to experiences that are either not vital or not universal. Drunkenness, for instance, which though noxious, is to many persons delightful, is a very exceptional experience. But, as the excellent physiologist Pick remarks, if all rivers and springs ran alcohol instead of water, either all men would now be born to hate it or our nerves would have been selected so as to drink it with impunity. The only considerable attempt, in fact, that has been made to explain the *distribution* of our feelings is that of Mr. Grant Allen in his suggestive little work *Physiological Esthetics*; and his reasoning is based exclusively on that causal efficacy of pleasures and pains which the ' double-aspect' partisans so strenuously deny.

章的结尾，我将再次回到这一问题上来。

这里还有另外一组事实似乎可以说明意识具有因果效力这一假设。快乐一般和有益的经验相联系，痛苦一般和有害的经验相联系，这是一个众所周知的事实。所有基本的生命过程都阐明了这一规律。饥饿、窒息、缺乏食物、酗酒并且醉倒、疲惫时工作、烧伤、创伤、炎症、毒药的作用是不令人愉快的，填饱饥饿的肚子、疲惫时享受休息和睡眠、休息后锻炼、始终拥有健康的皮肤和完好的骨骼是令人愉快的。斯宾塞和其他人认为，这些巧合不是由于任何被预先设定的和谐所致，而是由于纯粹的自然选择的作用，任何对根本有害的经验感到愉快的物种，当然会被它毁灭掉。一个从窒息的感受中得到快乐的动物，如果那种快乐的效力足以使它将头浸在水中，它只能获有四或五分钟的寿命。但是，如果快乐和痛苦没有效力，人们将不会看到（如果没有自动机理论的“科学”拥护者所觅得的诸如此类的先天理性的和谐的话）为什么大多数有害的动作，例如烧灼，不可能造成愉快的震颤，而大多数必要的动作，例如呼吸，不会引起极大的痛苦。确实，这一规律的例外情况也有很多，但它们与不重要的或不普遍的经验相联系。例如，醉酒就是一个非常例外的体验，尽管它是有害的，但它对很多人来说是愉快的。但是，如杰出的生理学家菲克所述，如果所有的河流和泉水里流淌的都是酒，而不是水，那么或者现在所有人天生就讨厌它，或者我们的神经已经有了选择，可以饮酒而无患。事实上，用来解释我们的感受分布的唯一值得重视的尝试，是由格兰特·艾伦先生在其具有启发性的短篇著作《生理美学》中完成的；而且他的推理完全以快乐和痛苦的因果效力为基础，而这正是为“双重观点”的支持者们所极力反对的。

Thus, then, from every point of view the circumstantial evidence against that theory is strong. *A priori* analysis of both brain-action and conscious action shows us that if the latter were efficacious it would, by its selective emphasis, make amends for the indeterminateness of the former; whilst the study *a posteriori* of the *distribution* of consciousness shows it to be exactly such as we might expect in an organ added for the sake of steering a nervous system grown too complex to regulate itself. The conclusion that it is useful is, after all this, quite justifiable. But, if it is useful, it must be so through its causal efficaciousness, and the automaton-theory must succumb to the theory of common-sense. I, at any rate (pending metaphysical reconstructions not yet successfully achieved), shall have no hesitation in using the language of common-sense throughout this book.

因此，从各个方面来看，反对那一理论的间接证据是很有力的。对大脑活动和意识活动的先天分析向我们表明，如果后者是有效力的，通过其对选择的强调，它就会补偿前者的不确定性；而对意识分布的后天研究表明，它确实如我们在器官中所期待的那样，它是为了指导由于变得太复杂而不能管理好自身的神经系统而被添加上去的。鉴于这一切，意识是有用的这一结论就相当合理了。但是，如果意识是有用的，它就必须通过它的因果效力而有用，并且自动机理论就必须服从于常识理论。至少我(将还没有获得成功的形而上学的重建搁置起来)将在全书中毫不犹豫地使用常识的语言。

威廉·詹姆斯漫画像

CHAPTER VI.

The Mind-Stuff Theory.

The reader who found himself swamped with too much metaphysics in the last chapter will have a still worse time of it in this one, which is exclusively metaphysical. Metaphysics means nothing but an unusually obstinate effort to think clearly. The fundamental conceptions of psychology are practically very clear to us, but theoretically they are very confused, and one easily makes the obscurest assumptions in this science without realizing, until challenged, what internal difficulties they involve. When these assumptions have once established themselves (as they have a way of doing in our very descriptions of the phenomenal facts) it is almost impossible to get rid of them afterwards or to make any one see that they are not essential features of the subject. The only way to prevent this disaster is to scrutinize them beforehand and make them give an articulate account of themselves before letting them pass. One of the obscurest of the assumptions of which I speak is *the assumption, that our menial states are composite in structure, made up of smaller states conjoined.* This hypothesis has outward advantages which make it almost irresistibly attractive to the intellect, and yet it is inwardly quite unintelligible. Of its unintelligibility, however, half the writers on psychology seem unaware. As our own aim is *to understand* if possible,

第六章　精神素材理论

那些发现自己在上一章为太多的形而上学所淹没的读者，在这一章将会度过一段更加艰难的时光，这一章的内容完全是形而上学的。形而上学不是指别的什么，它就是意味着以一种异乎寻常地倔强的努力去清晰地思考。心理学的基本概念在实践上对我们来说是非常清楚的，但是在理论上它们是非常混乱的，并且人们很容易在这门科学中做出最模糊的假设，而且，除非这些假设受到了挑战，否则他们不会意识到它们涉及到了什么样的内在困难。当这些假设一旦自身确立了（由于它在我们对现象事实的特别描述中发挥了某种作用），此后要想摆脱它们，或者想要让任何人都了解它们不是问题的本质特征，都几乎是不可能的。防止这种灾难发生的唯一办法就是预先对它们进行详细的考察，并且在让它们通过之前，让它们就自身给出一个清晰明白的说明。我所谈到的假设中最模糊的一个假设是这样的：我们的心理状态在结构上是复合的，由结合在一起的更小的状态所组成。这一假说具有外在的优势，这使得它对我们的智性来说有着几乎不可抗拒的诱惑力，但是它在内涵上却很难被理解。然而，就其不可理解性而言，有一半的心理学作者都似乎没有觉察出来。由于我们自己的目的是在可能的情况下去理解，因此在开始从事我们工作

I make no apology for singling out this particular notion for very explicit treatment before taking up the descriptive part of our work. *The theory of 'mind-stuff' is the theory that our mental states are compounds*, expressed in its most radical form.

Evolutionary Psychology Demands A Mind-Dust.

In a general theory of evolution the inorganic comes first, then the lowest forms of animal and vegetable life, then forms of life that possess mentality, and finally those like ourselves that possess it in a high degree. As long as we keep to the consideration of purely outward facts, even the most complicated facts of biology, our task as evolutionists is comparatively easy. We are dealing all the time with matter and its aggregations and separations; and although our treatment must perforce be hypothetical, this does not prevent it from being *continuous*. The point which as evolutionists we are bound to hold fast to is that all the new forms of being that make their appearance are really nothing more than results of the redistribution of the original and unchanging materials. The self-same atoms which, chaotically dispersed, made the nebula, now, jammed and temporarily caught in peculiar positions, form our brains; and the 'evolution' of the brains, if understood, would be simply the account of how the atoms came to be so caught and jammed In this story no new *natures*, no factors not present at the beginning, are introduced at any later stage.

But with the dawn of consciousness an entirely new nature seems to slip in, something whereof the potency was not given in the mere outward atoms of the original chaos.

The enemies of evolution have been quick to pounce upon this undeniable discontinuity in the data of the world, and many of them, from the failure of evolutionary explanations at this point,

的描述性部分之前，选出这一观点并加以非常明晰的处理，我认为是合理的。“精神素材”理论是指，我们的心理状态是复合物，这种理论以其最激进的形式被表达了出来。

进化心理学需要精神微粒

在一般的进化论中，无机物首先出现，然后是最低级的动植物生命形式，而后是拥有精神的生命形式，最后是像我们自己这样在更高程度上拥有精神的生命形式。只要我们一直考虑纯粹的外部事实，甚至包括生物学中最复杂的事实，作为进化论者我们的任务相对而言就容易一些。我们所始终涉及的是物质及其聚合与分离；尽管我们的处理必须一定是假说性的，但这并不妨碍它是连续性的。作为进化论者我们一定要牢牢把握的要点是，所有使其显现的新的存在形式，实际上仅仅是原初的和不变的质料重新分布的结果。混乱散布着的、组成星云的自我同一的原子，现在被挤压在一起并且暂时被置于特殊的位置之中，形成了我们的大脑；大脑的“进化”如果可以理解的话，它将仅仅是对原子如何逐渐地被置于这样的位置并且这样挤在一处的说明。在这种论述中，没有新的性质，没有在开始不存在的要素在任何后来的阶段被引进来。

但是随着意识的首次出现，一种全新的本性似乎溜了进来，它是某种在最初混乱的单纯的外部原子那里没有获得其力量的东西。

进化论的敌人很快就对在世界的资料中这种不可否认的非连续性发起了突然的袭击，而且他们之中的很多人，由进化论在

have inferred their general incapacity all along the line. Every one admits the entire incommensurability of feeling as such with material motion as such. "A motion became a feeling!"—no phrase that our lips can frame is so devoid of apprehensible meaning. Accordingly, even the vaguest of evolutionary enthusiasts, when deliberately comparing material with mental facts, have been as forward as any one else to emphasize the 'chasm' between the inner and the outer worlds.

"Can the oscillations of a molecule," says Mr. Spencer, "be represented side by side with a nervous shock [he means a mental shock], and the two be recognized as one? No effort enables us to assimilate them. That a unit of feeling has nothing in common with a unit of motion becomes more than ever manifest when we bring the two into juxtaposition."①

And again:

"Suppose it to have become quite clear that a shock in conscious-ness and a molecular motion are the subjective and objective faces of the same thing; we continue utterly incapable of uniting the two, so as to conceive that reality of which they are the opposite faces."②

In other words, incapable of perceiving in them any common character. So Tyndall, in that lucky paragraph which has been quoted so often that every one knows it by heart:

"The passage from the physics of the brain to the corresponding facts of consciousness is unthinkable. Granted that a definite thought and definite molecular action in the brain occur simultaneously; we do

① Psychol. § 62.

② *Ibid.* § 272.

这一点上解释的失败,已经推导出了它们对沿着这条线索而来的所有问题的解释的普遍无能。每个人都承认同量的感受和同量的物质运动是完全不能比较的,“运动变成了感受!”——我们的嘴再不能构造出比这更缺乏可理解的含义的短句了。相应地,甚至最暧昧的进化论狂热者,当有意地将物质事实和精神事实相比较时,也和所有其他人一样激进地强调内部和外部世界之间的“裂口”。

斯宾塞先生说:“分子的振动和神经的震动(他是指心理的震颤)能够相互表象吗,并且它们能够被认作是一个东西吗?所有的努力都不能让我们将它们同化。当我们将感受单元和运动单元并置在一起时,它们之间没有任何共同之处这一事实就比以前变得更加明显了。”[①]

还有:

“假设意识中的震颤和分子的运动是同一事物的主观方面和客观方面这一事实已经变得非常清楚了;我们依然完全不能将二者统一起来,以便思考关于它们是相反的两个方面的那种事实。”[②]

换言之,我们无法在它们中间感知到任何共同的特征。廷德尔在那个经常被人引用、以至于每个人都将它铭记于心的幸运的段落中也如此说道:

“从脑物理学到相应的意识事实之间的通道是不可思议的。即使承认一种确定的思想和一种确定的分子运动在大脑中同时发生;我们还是没有拥有这种智性器官,或者显然是这器官的雏

① 《心理学》,第62节。

② 同前,第272节。

not possess the intellectual organ, nor apparently any rudiment of the organ, which would enable us to pass, by a process of reasoning, from one to the other." ①

Or in this other passage:

"We can trace the development of a nervous system and correlate with it the parallel phenomena of sensation and thought. We see with undoubting certainty that they go hand in hand. But we try to soar in a vacuum the moment we seek to comprehend the connection between them. . . . There is no fusion possible between the two classes of facts—no motor energy in the intellect of man to carry it without logical rupture from the one to the other."②

None the less easily, however, when the evolutionary afflatus is upon them, do the very same writers leap over the breach whose flagrancy they are the foremost to announce, and talk as if mind grew out of body in a continuous way. Mr. Spencer, looking back on his review of mental evolution, tells us how "in tracing up the increase we found ourselves passing *without break* from the phenomena of bodily life to the phenomena of mental life." ③And Mr. Tyndall, in the same Belfast Address from which we just quoted, delivers his other famous passage:

"Abandoning all disguise, the confession that I feel bound to

---

① Fragments of Science, 5th ed., p. 420.

② Belfast Address, 'Nature,' August 20, 1874. p. 318. I cannot help remarking that the disparity between motions and feelings on which these authors lay so much stress, is somewhat less absolute than at first sight it seems. There are categories common to the two worlds, Not only temporal succession (as Helmholtz admits, Physiol. Optik, p. 445), but such attributes as intensity, volume, simplicity or complication, smooth or impeded change, rest or agitation, are habitually predicated of both physical facts and mental facts. Where such analogies obtain, the things do have something in common.

③ Psychology, §131.

形，它可以使我们通过推理的过程从一方到达另一方。”①

在别的段落中他又说：

“我们可以追踪神经系统的发展，并且使它与平行的感觉和思维现象相关联。我们毫不怀疑地确知它们是携手共进的。但是，一旦我们试图理解它们之间的联系，我们就如同想要在真空中飞翔……这里不存在将这两种类别的事实融合在一起的可能性——在人的智性中没有这样一种动力可以在从一方到另一方时不出现逻辑的破裂情况下将它完成。”②

然而，当进化论的灵感降临到这些作者身上之时，尽管这裂痕的恶名是他们最先宣布的，但是这些相同的作者依旧很容易地越过了那条裂痕，而且说起话来就好像心灵是以一种连续的方式从身体中生长出来的。斯宾塞先生回顾了他对精神进化的评论，告诉我们如何“在追踪这种增长时，我们发现自己不断地从身体生活的现象到达了精神生活的现象。”③而且，廷德尔先生在我们刚刚引用过的同一个《贝尔法斯特演讲》中，写下了另外一个著名的段落：

“遗弃所有的掩饰，在你们面前我感到一定要承认的是，我将

① 《科学片断》，第5版，第420页。

② 《贝尔法斯特演讲》，《自然》，1874年8月20日，第318页。我不禁要指出的是，这些作者所如此强调的运动与感受之间的不一致，有点不如它似乎初看起来那么绝对。有一些范畴是两个世界所共有的，不仅时间的连续性（如赫姆霍尔茨所承认的那样，《视觉生理学》，第445页），还有诸如强度、体积、简单性或复杂性、平稳的变化或受到阻碍的变化、平静或兴奋这些属性，都被习惯性地断言为物理事实和精神事实的属性。在这种类比成立的地方，事物确实具有一些相同的地方。

③ 《心理学》，第131节。

make before you is that I prolong the vision backward across the boundary of the experimental evidence, and discern in that matter which we, in our ignorance and notwithstanding our professed reverence for its Creator, have hitherto covered with opprobrium the promise and potency of every form and quality of life."①

—mental life included, as a matter of course.

So strong a postulate is continuity! Now this book will tend to show that mental postulates are on the whole to be respected. The demand for continuity has, over large tracts of science, proved itself to possess true prophetic power. We ought therefore ourselves sincerely to try every possible mode of conceiving the dawn of consciousness so that it may *not* appear equivalent to the irruption into the universe of a new nature, non-existent until then.

Merely to call the consciousness 'nascent' will not serve our turn.②

---

① 'Nature,' as above, 317-8.

② 'Nascent' is Mr. Spencer's great word. In showing how at a certain point consciousness must appear upon the evolving scene this author fairly outdoes himself in vagueness.

"In its higher forms, Instinct is probably accompanied by a rudimentary consciousness. There cannot be co-ordination of many stimuli without some ganglion through which they are all brought into relation. In the process of bringing them into relation, this ganglion must be subject to the influence of each-must undergo many changes. And the quick succession of changes in a ganglion, implying as it does perpetual experiences of differences and likenesses, constitutes the *raw material* of consciousness. The implication is that as fast as Instinct is developed, some kind of consciousness becomes nascent." (Psychology, § 195.)

The words 'raw material' and 'implication' which I have italicized are the words which do the *evolving*. They are supposed to have all the rigor which the 'synthetic philosophy' requires. In the following passage, when 'impressions' pass through a common 'centre of communication' in succession (much as people might pass into a theatre through a turnstile) consciousness, non-existent until then, is supposed to result:

"Separate impressions are received by the senses-by different parts of the body. If they go no further than the places at which they are received, they are useless. Or if only some of them are brought into relation with one another, they are useless. That an effectual adjustment may be made, they must be

视野向后延伸从而越过了实验证据的边界，在由于我们的无知和我们所公开宣称的对其创造者的敬重而使得我们迄今对其加倍非难的那种物质中，我看到了每种生命形式及其性质的希望与力量。”①

——不用说，精神生活也包括在内。

对连续性的假定是如此的强烈！现在，本书将试图表明，对精神的假定在总体上来说是应该受到尊重的。在广泛的科学领域之内，对连续性的要求已经证明自身具有真正的预言能力。因此，我们自己应该真诚地尝试每一种构想意识开始出现的方式，以便使它的显现看上去不等同于直到那时都不存在的一种新的本性侵入了宇宙之中。

将意识仅仅称作是“初生的”并不符合我们的目的。②确实，

---

① 《自然》，同上，第317～318页。

② “初生的”是斯宾塞先生的重要措词。在表明意识如何在某一点必须出现在进化现场时，这位作者在模糊性方面完全超越了他自己。

“在其高级形式中，本能可能由一种初步的意识相伴随。如果没有某些使许多刺激全部联系起来的神经节，就不能够存在这些刺激间的协调。在将它们联系起来的过程中，这种神经节必须受每一个刺激的影响的支配——必须经历许多变化。而在神经节中的变化的快速演替，如它所暗示出了对差异性和相似性的永久持续的经验那样，构成了意识的原材料。这里的含义是，随着本能的快速发展，某种意识就成为了初生的。”（《心理学》，第195节。）

我将之变成斜体的“原材料”和“含义”这两个词就是解答进化的词。它们被期望具有“综合哲学”所要求的全部精确性。在下面的段落中，当“印象”相继穿过一个共同的“交流中心”时（很像人们穿过十字转门进入一个剧场），直到那时还不存在的意识就应该产生了。

“单独的印象接收通过的是感观——身体的不同部分。如果它们到达其接收所在地就不再前进了，它们就是无用的。或者，如果它们中间只有一些互相联系了起来，它们也是无用的。那么可以做一种有效的调整，它们必须

It is true that the word signifies not yet *quite* born, and so seems to form a sort of bridge between existence and nonentity. But that is a verbal quibble. The fact is that discontinuity comes in if a new nature comes in at all. The *quantity* of the latter is quite immaterial. The girl in 'Midshipman Easy' could not excuse the illegitimacy of her child by saying, 'it was a little small one.' And Consciousness, however little, is an illegitimate birth in any philosophy that starts without it, and yet professes to explain all facts by continuous evolution.

If evolution is to work smoothly, consciousness in some shape must have been present at the very origin, of things. Accordingly we find that the more clear-sighted evolutionary philosophers are beginning to posit it there. Each atom of the nebula, they suppose, must have had an aboriginal atom of consciousness linked with it; and, just as the material atoms have formed bodies and brains by massing them-selves together, so the mental atoms,

---

all brought into relation with one another. But this implies some centre of communication common to them all, through which they severally pass; and as they cannot pass through it simultaneously, they must pass through it in succession. So that as the external phenomena responded to become greater in number and more complicated in kind, the variety and rapidity of the changes to which this common centre of communication is subject must increase-there must result on unbroken series of these changes-*there must arise a consciousness.*

"Hence the progress of the correspondence between the organism and its environment necessitates a gradual reduction of the sensorial changes to a succession; and by so doing *evolves a distinct consciousness-a* consciousness that becomes higher as the succession becomes more rapid and the correspondence more complete." (*Ibid.* § 179.)

It is true that in the Fortnightly Review (vol. xiv. p. 716) Mr. Spencer denies that he means by this passage to tell us anything about the origin of consciousness at all. It resembles, however, too many other places in his Psychology (e.g. §§ 43, 110, 244) not to be taken as a serious attempt to explain how consciousness must at a certain point be 'evolved.' That, when a critic calls his attention to the inanity of his words, Mr. Spencer should say he never meant anything particular by them, is simply an example of the scandalous vagueness with which this sort of 'chromo-philosophy' is carried on.

这个词意指尚未完全出生，并且因此它在存在与虚无之间形成了某种桥梁。但那是一种言辞上的诡辩。事实是，如果有一种新的本性出现了，非连续性也就出现了。后者的量是没有物质实体的。在《军校学生小憩》里的女孩不能为其私生子辩解说："它是一个非常小的孩子。"无论意识有多么微小，它在任何开始时没有它、却声称通过连续的进化解释了所有事实的哲学中的出生都是不合法的。

如果进化要平稳地进行，某种形式的意识就必须在事物的最初起源时出现。相应地，我们发现，更加精明的进化论哲学家正开始将它定位在那里。他们推测，星云中的每一个原子一定获有一个与之相联系的原始的意识原子；而且，正如同质料原子通过将自己聚合在一起从而形成了身体和大脑一样，精神原子也通过

全部相互联系起来。但是，这就意味着某种交流中心对它们来说是共有的，它们各自从中穿过；而且由于它们不能同时由此穿过，它们必须相继穿过。结果，由于对其做出反应的外部现象在数量上变得越来越多，在性质上变得越来越复杂，支配这一共有的交流中心的变化的种类和数量也必须增加——这些变化的不间断的序列一定会产生——意识一定会出现。

"因此生物体和其环境间的一致性的发展要求感觉的变化逐渐变形为一种相继性；而且由此就进化出了一种截然不同的意识——这是一种随着相继性变得更迅速，一致性变得更完善，它就变得越高级的意识。"（同上，第 179 节。）

确实，在《双周评论》（第 14 卷，第 716 页）中，斯宾塞先生完全否认了通过这一段落他想要告诉我们关于意识起源的任何问题。然而，在他的《心理学》中（例如第 43 节、第 110 节、第 244 节），有太多的地方与这一段落相似，以至于我们不得不把它看作是对解释意识如何必须在某一点必须"进化"出来而做的一次认真的尝试。当一个批评者使他注意到其措词的空洞时，斯宾塞先生便会说他使用这些词从来没有任何特别的所指，这只不过是令人反感的含糊性的一个实例，而正是通过这种含糊性，这种"颜色哲学"才得以继续下去。

by an analogous process of aggregation, have fused into those larger consciousnesses which we know in ourselves and suppose to exist in our fellow-animals. Some such doctrine of *atomistic hylozoism* as this is an indispensable part of a thorough-going philosophy of evolution. According to it there must be an infinite number of degrees of consciousness, following the degrees of complication and aggregation of the primordial mind-dust. To prove the separate existence of these degrees of consciousness by indirect evidence, since direct intuition of them is not to be had, becomes therefore the first duty of psychological evolutionism.

Some Alleged Proofs That Mind-Dust Exists.

Some of this duty we find already performed by a number of philosophers who, though not interested at all in evolution, have nevertheless on independent grounds convinced themselves of the existence of a vast amount of sub-conscious mental life. The criticism of this general opinion and its grounds will have to be postponed for a while. At present let us merely deal with the arguments assumed to prove aggregation of bits of mind-stuff into distinctly sensible feelings. They are clear and admit of a clear reply.

The German physiologist A. Fick, in 1862, was, so far as I know, the first to use them. He made experiments on the discrimination of the feelings of warmth and of touch, when only a very small portion of the skin was excited through a hole in a card, the surrounding parts being protected by the card. He found that under these circumstances mistakes were frequently made by the patient,①

① His own words are: "Mistakes are made in the sense that he admits having been touched, when in reality it was radiant heat that affected his skin. In our own before-mentioned experiments there was never any deception on the entire palmar side of the hand or on the face. On the back of the hand in one case in a series of 60 stimulations 4 mistakes occurred, in another case 2 mistakes in 45 stimulations. On the extensor side of the upper arm 3 deceptions out of 48 stimulations were noticed,

一种相似的聚合过程而融合为那些更大的意识,我们知道这种意识就存在于我们自身当中,并且假设它们也存在于我们的动物同伴身上。一些像这样的原子物活论学说是彻底的进化论哲学所不可缺少的部分。根据这种学说,必须存在无限数量的意识等级,它与原始精神微粒的复杂程度和聚合程度相一致。由于将不会获有对这些意识等级的直接的直觉,因此,用间接的证据来证明它们的单独存在就成为了心理进化论的首要职责。

精神微粒存在的一些所谓证据

我们发现很多哲学家已经履行了一些这样的职责,尽管他们对进化完全不感兴趣,他们还是以独立的理由使自己深信有大量的下意识精神生活的存在。对这种一般观点及其理由的批评将不得不推迟一会再做讨论。现在,让我们仅仅涉及一下那些试图证明少许精神微粒可以聚合为被清楚感觉到的感受的论证。这些论证是清晰的,而且容许有清楚的回答。

据我所知,德国的生理学家 A. 菲克在 1862 年首先使用了这些论证。他就温暖和触碰感受的辨别做了实验,当穿过卡片上的一个小洞仅有非常小的一部分皮肤受到了刺激,而周围的部分得到了卡片的保护的时候,他发现在这种情况下,患者经常犯错误,①

① 用他自己的话说:"所犯的错误是这种意义上的,即当实际上是热辐射刺激了他的皮肤的时候,他却承认是被触碰了。在前面提到过的我们自己的实验中,整个手掌和面部从来没有受过任何欺骗。在一个案例中,在对手背实施的 60 次连续刺激中有 4 次出现了错误,在另一个案例中,在 45 次刺激中有 2 次出现了错误。在上臂的伸肌一侧,注意到在 48 次刺激中有 3

and concluded that this must be because the number of sensations from the elementary nerve-tips affected was too small to sum itself distinctly into either of the qualities of feeling in question. He tried to show how a different manner of the summation might give rise in one case to the heat and in another to the touch.

"A feeling of temperature," he says, "arises when the intensities of the units of feeling are evenly gradated, so that between two elements *a* and *b* no other unit can spatially intervene whose intensity is not also *between* that of *a* and *b*. A feeling of contact perhaps arises when this condition is not fulfilled. Both kinds of feeling, however, are composed of the same units."

But it is obviously far clearer to interpret such a gradation of intensities as a brain-fact than as a mind-fact. If in the brain a tract were first excited in one of the ways suggested by Prof. Fick, and then again in the other, it might very well happen, for aught we can say to the contrary, that the psychic accompaniment in the one case would be heat, and in the other pain. The pain and the heat would, however, not be composed of psychic units, but would each be the direct result of one total brain-process. So long as this latter interpretation remains open, Fick cannot be held to have proved psychic summation.

---

and in the case of another individual, 1 out of 31. In one case over the spine 3 deceptions in a aeries of 11 excitations were observed; in another, 4 out of 19. On the lumbar spine 6 deceptions came among 29 stimulations, and again 4 out of 7. There is certainly not yet enough material on which to rest a calculation of probabilities, but any one can easily convince himself that on the back there is no question of even a moderately accurate discrimination between warmth and a light pressure so far as but small portions of skin come into play. It has been as yet impossible to make corresponding experiments with regard to sensibility to cold." (Lehrb. d. Anat u, Physiol, d. Sinnesorgane (1862), p. 29.)

并且断定这一定是由于来自受影响的基本神经末梢的感觉数量太少了，它们显然不能令自己聚合出相关的具有任何一种性质的感受。他试图表明不同的聚合方式如何可以在一种情况下引发对热度的感受，而在另一种情况下引发对触碰的感受。

他说："当感受单元的强度被均匀的顺次排列，以至于在 a 和 b 两个元素之间，没有其他的单元（其强度也不在 a 和 b 的强度之间）能够在空间上介入时，温度感受就会出现。触碰的感受可能在这一条件没有得到满足时出现。然而，这两种感受都由同样的单元所组成。"

但是，将这一强度等级解释为大脑事实显然比解释为精神事实要清楚得多。如果在大脑中一个神经束最初以菲克教授提示的方法之一被激起，然后以另一种方式又被激起，由于我们说不出任何相反的东西，那么，很有可能发生的情况就是，在一种情况下精神伴随物是热，而在另一种情况下是痛。然而，痛和热就不是由精神单元所组成，它们各自都是一个完整的大脑过程的直接结果。只要这后一种解释仍然是开放的，就不能认为菲克已经证明了精神的聚合。

次受骗，而在另一个个体的案例中，在 31 次刺激中只有 1 次受骗。在一个案例中，在对脊骨的 11 次刺激中观察到有一次受骗；在另一个案例中，19 次有 4 次受骗。在对腰椎处的 29 次刺激当中有 6 次受骗，在另一个案例中，7 次有 4 次受骗。当然，这里还没有能够做出概率计算的足够资料，但是任何人都能很容易地让自己相信，如果只有很小一部分皮肤开始活动的话，在背部不可能存在对温暖与轻度压力的适度的精确辨别力。要做出相应的关于寒冷的感受性的实验至今都是不可能的。"（《感觉器官的解剖学和生理学教科书》（1862 年），第 29 页。）

Later, both Spencer and Taine, independently of each other, took up the same line of thought. Mr. Spencer's reasoning is worth quoting *in extenso*. He writes:

"Although the individual sensations and emotions, real or ideal, of which consciousness is built up, appear to be severally simple, homogeneous, unanalyzable, or of inscrutable natures, yet they are not so. There is at least one kind of feeling which, as ordinarily experienced, seems elementary, that is demonstrably not elementary. And after resolving it into its proximate components, we can scarcely help suspecting that other apparently-elementary feelings are also compound, and may have proximate components like those which we can in this one instance identify."

"Musical sound is the name we give to this seemingly simple feeling which is clearly resolvable into simpler feelings. Well-known experiments prove that when equal blows or taps are made one after another at a rate not exceeding some sixteen per second, the effect of each is perceived as a separate noise; but when the rapidity with which the blows follow one another exceeds this, the noises are no longer identified in separate states of consciousness, and there arises in place of them a continuous state of consciousness, called a tone. In further increasing the rapidity of the blows, the tone undergoes the change of quality distinguished as rise in pitch; and it continues to rise in pitch as the blows continue to increase in rapidity, until it reaches an acuteness beyond which it is no longer appreciable as a tone. So that out of units of feeling of the same kind, many feelings distinguishable from one another in quality result, according as the units are more or less integrated."

"This is not all. The inquiries of Professor Helmholtz have shown that when, along with one series of these rapidly-recurring noises, there is generated another series in which the noises are more rapid though not so loud, the effect is a change in that quality known as its *timbre*. As various musical instruments show us, tones which are alike in pitch

后来,斯宾塞和泰恩又各自独立地采纳了同一思路。斯宾塞先生的推论值得详尽地加以引证。他写到:

"尽管构成意识的单独的感觉和情绪(真实的或想像的)看上去各自是简单的、同一的、不可分析的,或者具有难以了解的本性,但它们却不是这样的。如通常所体验到的那样,至少有一种感受似乎是基本的,但它却被证明不是基本的。而且在将它分解成紧接的组成部分时,我们将不禁怀疑,其他显然是基本的感受也是复合的,而且也可能具有我们在这个例子中可以识别出来的紧接的组成部分。"

"乐音就是我们给这种表面上简单的感受所起得的名字,这种感受无疑可以被分解成更简单的感受。众所周知的实验证明,当同样的吹气和敲击以不超过大约每秒钟 16 次的速率依次做出时,每一次吹气和敲击的结果就会作为一种分离的噪音而被感知到;但是,当依次做出的吹气的速度超过了每秒钟 16 次时,这些噪音将不会再在分离的意识状态中被识别出来,并且代之而起的是一种被称作乐音的连续的意识状态。当进一步增加吹气的速度,乐音就会经历音调升高这种性质的变化;而且随着吹气速度的持续增加,乐音的音高也会持续增高,直到音高达到了一种极限,超过了这一极限,它就不能再作为乐音而被欣赏了。因此,根据同类感受单元或多或少地结合在了一起这一情况,从那些单元之中产生出很多相互之间在性质上可以区别开来的感受。"

"这还不是全部。赫姆霍尔茨教授的调查表明,当与这些快速反复发出的噪音序列一起,又产生出一个噪音发出速度更快但音量却不是很大的噪音序列的时候,结果就会出现被称之为音色的性质变化。正如不同的乐器向我们表明的那样,具有相同音高

and strength are distinguishable by their harshness or sweetness, their ringing or their liquid characters; and all their specific peculiarities are proved to arise from the combination of one, two, three, or more, supplementary series of recurrent noises with the chief series of recurrent noises. So that while the unlikenesses of feeling known as differences of pitch in tones are due to differences of integration among the recur-rent noises of one series, the unlikenesses of feeling known as differences of *timbre*, are due to the simultaneous integration with this series of other series having other degrees of integration. And thus an enormous number of qualitatively-contrasted kinds of consciousness that seem severally elementary prove to be composed of one simple kind of consciousness, combined and recombined with itself in multitudinous ways."

"Can we stop short here? If the different sensations known as sounds are built out of a common unit, is it not to be rationally inferred that so likewise are the different sensations known as tastes, and the different sensations known as odors, and the different sensations known as colors ? Nay, shall we not regard it as probable that there is a unit common to all these strongly-contrasted classes of sensations? If the unlikenesses among the sensations of each class may be due to unlike-nesses among the modes of aggregation of a unit of consciousness common to them all; so too may the much greater unlikenesses between the sensations of each class and those of other classes. There may be a single primordial element of consciousness, and the countless kinds of consciousness may be produced by the compounding of this element with itself and the recompounding of its compounds with one another in higher and higher degrees: so producing increased multiplicity, variety, and complexity."

"Have we any clue to this primordial element? I think we have. That simple mental impression whic proves to be the unit of composition of the sensation of musical tone, is allied to certain other simple mental impressions differently-originated. The subjective effect produced by a crack or noise that has no appreciable duration is little else

和强度的乐音，可以根据其粗糙或甜美、响亮或透明的特性而加以区别；而它们的所有具体特性都被证明来自一种、两种、三种或者更多种重复发出的噪音序列与重复发出的噪音主序列的结合。因此，被称之为乐音音高差异的这种感受的不相同，是由于在一个序列中重复出现的噪音结合的不同而造成的，同时，被称之为音色差异的这种感受的不相同，则是由于具有不同结合程度的其他序列与这一序列同时结合在一起而造成的。因此，大量单独看上去各自是基本的并且在性质上形成对比的各种意识，证明是由一种简单的意识构成的，这种意识以多种多样的方式将自己组合、再组合。”

“我们能够在这里突然停下来吗？如果被称之为声音的不同感觉是由一种共同的单元构成的，难道不能合理地推断出被称之为味道的不同感觉、被称之为气味的不同感觉、被称之为颜色的不同感觉都同样如此吗？不仅如此，难道我们不能认为可能存在一种为所有这些对比强烈的感觉种类所共有的单元吗？如果每种感觉中的差异可以归因于它们所共有的意识单元的结合方式的不同；那么，每类的感觉和其他种类的感觉之间的大得多的差异也可以归因于此。可能存在一种单一的原始意识要素，通过这一要素与自身的组合，以及它的复合物相互在越来越高的等级上的再组合，无数种类的意识都可以产生出来：如此就造成了增强了的多重性、多样性和复杂性。”

“我们对这一原始要素有任何线索吗？我认为我们有。那种被证明是乐音感觉的构成单元的简单的心理印象，与某些有着不同起源的其他简单的心理印象有关联。由劈啪声或噪音所造成并且无法感知其持续时间的主观印象，只不过是一次神经的震

than a nervous shock. Though we distinguish such a nervous shock as belonging to what we call sounds, yet it does not differ very much from nervous shocks of other kinds. An electric discharge sent through the body causes a feeling akin to that which a sudden loud report causes. A strong unexpected impression made through the eyes, as by a flash of lightning, similarly gives rise to a start of shock; and though the feeling so named seems, like the electric shock, to have the body at large for its seat, and may therefore be regarded as the correlative rather of the efferent than of the afferent disturbance, yet on remembering the mental change that results from the instantaneous transit of an object across the field of vision, I think it may be perceived that the feeling accompanying the efferent disturbance is itself reduced very nearly to the same form. The state of consciousness so generated is, in fact, comparable in quality to the initial state of consciousness caused by a blow (distinguishing it from the pain or other feeling that commences the instant after); which state of consciousness caused by a blow may be taken as the primitive and typical form of the nervous shock. The fact that sudden brief disturbances thus set up by different stimuli through different sets of nerves cause feelings scarcely distinguishable in quality will not appear strange when we recollect that distinguishableness of feeling implies appreciable duration; and that when the duration is greatly abridged, nothing more is known than that some mental change has occurred and ceased. To have a sensation of redness, to know a tone as acute or grave, to be conscious of a taste as sweet, implies in each ease a considerable continuity of state. If the state does not last long enough to admit of its being contemplated, it cannot be classed as of this or that kind; and becomes a momentary modification very similar to momentary modifications otherwise caused."

"It is possible, then-may we not even say probable—that something of the same order as that which we call a nervous shock is the ultimate

荡。尽管我们将这种神经震荡归入到我们称之为声音的东西中而加以区别,但是它和其他种类的神经震荡没有太多的区别。流经身体的电流的释放,会引起类似于响亮的突然爆炸声所引起的感受。通过眼睛而获得的强烈而意外的印象,如通过闪电所引起的印象,也会引起震荡的发生;尽管被如此命名的感觉,像电击一样,似乎将整个身体都作为它的处所,并且因此可能被认为与传出的骚乱相关,而和传入的骚乱不相关,但在回忆由对象在视野中瞬间经过而造成的心理变化的时候,我认为可以知觉到的是,与传出骚乱相伴随的感觉自身,已经还原到了非常接近于同一种形式的程度。事实上,如此产生的意识状态在性质上是可以与由一次吹气而引起的最初的意识状态(在将它与随后立即开始的疼痛或其他感受区别开来的同时)相比较的;由一次吹气而引起的意识状态可以被认作是神经震荡的原始的和典型的形式。当我们想起感受的可区分性意味着可感知的持续时间时,以下这个事实将不会显得那么奇怪了,即由穿过不同神经束而来的不同的刺激所导致的突然而短暂的骚乱,引起了在性质上几乎无法区分的感受;而且当持续时间被大大地缩短了的时候,所知道的仅仅是某种心理变化发生了并且停止了。要产生一种红色的感觉,要知道一个乐音是尖锐的还是低沉的,要意识到一种味道是甜的,这每一种情况都意味着一种相当大的状态的连续性。如果那种状态持续的时间不足以容许它受到关注,它就不能被归类到这个或者那个种类之中;并且它就变成了一种与由其他方式引起的瞬间改变非常相似的瞬间改变。”

“那么,有可能的是——我们甚至不能说有可能吗——与我们所说的神经震荡一样有相同顺序的某种东西是意识的最终单

unit of consciousness; and that all the unlikenesses among our feelings result from unlike modes of integration of this ultimate unit. I say of the same order, because there are discernible differences among nervous shocks that are differently caused; and the primitive nervous shock probably differs somewhat from each of them. And I say of the same order, for the further reason that while we may ascribe to them a general likeness in nature, we must suppose a great unlikeness in degree. The nervous shocks recognized as such are violent-must be violent before they can be perceived amid the procession of multitudinous vivid feelings suddenly interrupted by them. But the rapidly-recurring nervous shocks of which the different forms of feeling consist, we must assume to be of comparatively moderate, or even of very slight intensity. Were our various sensations and emotions composed of rapidly-recurring shocks as strong as those ordinarily called shocks, they would be unbearable; indeed life would cease at once. We must think of them rather as successive faint pulses of subjective change, each having the same quality as the strong pulse of subjective change distinguished as a nervous shock." ①

Insufficiency Of These Proofs.

Convincing as this argument of Mr. Spencer's may appear on a

① Principles of Psychology, § 60.

元;而且在我们感受中的所有差异都是由于这种最终单元的不同的结合方式所导致的。我说有相同的顺序,因为在由不同原因引起的神经震荡中存在着可以辨别的差异;而原始的神经震荡可能与它们中的每一个都多少有些区别。而且我说有相同的顺序,因为有更进一步的理由,即虽然我们可以将一种在本性上的一般相似性归于它们,但是我们必须假定它们在程度上有巨大的差异。被如此认识的神经震荡是激烈的——它们在由它们所突然中断的多种多样的生动感受队伍中能够被知觉到之前,它们必须是激烈的。但是,就由不同的感受形式所组成的快速重复出现的神经震荡来说,我们必须假设它们是比较温和的,或者甚至具有非常微弱的强度。假如我们的各种感觉和情绪所由以组成的快速反复发生的震荡和那些通常所说的震荡一样强烈的话,它们将会是令人无法忍受的;甚至生命都会立刻中止。我们必须将它们看作是相继发生的主体变化的微弱波动,每一个都和作为神经震荡而得以区别的主体变化的强烈波动具有相同的性质。”①

这些证据的不足之处

斯宾塞先生的这一论证初读起来似乎是令人信服的,但奇怪

---

① 《心理学原理》,第60节。

first reading, it is singular how weak it really is. [1] We do, it is true, when we study the connection between a musical note and its outward cause, find the note simple and continuous while the cause is multiple and discrete. Somewhere, then, there *is* a transformation, reduction, or fusion. The question is, Where? —in the nerve-world or in the mind-world ?

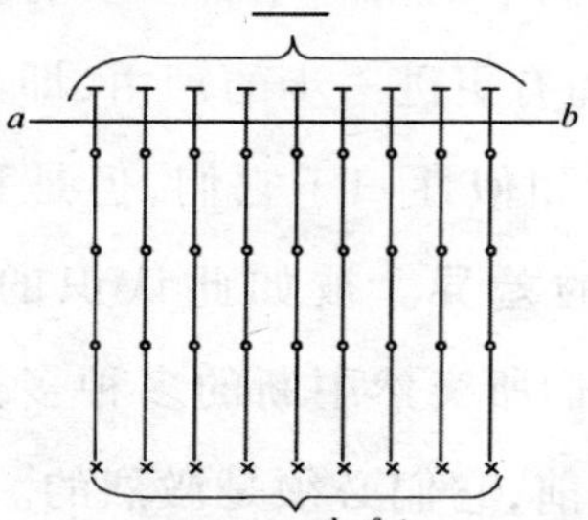

FIG. 25.

Really we have no experimental proof by which to decide; and if decide we must, analogy and a *priori* probability can alone guide us. Mr. Spencer assumes that the fusion must come to pass in the mental world, and that the physical processes get through air and ear, auditory nerve and medulla, lower brain and hemispheres, without their number being reduced. Figure 25, on the previous page, will make the point clear.

Let the line *a-b* represent the threshold of conscious-ness: then

---

① Oddly enough, Mr. Spencer seems quite unaware of the *general* function of the theory of elementary units of mind-stuff in the evolutionary philosophy. We have seen it to be absolutely indispensable, if that philosophy is to work, to postulate consciousness in the nebula,-the simplest way being, of course, to suppose every atom animated. Mr. Spencer, however, will have it (e. g. First Principles, § 71) that consciousness is only the occasional result of the' transformation ' of a certain amount of ' physical force' to which it is' equivalent' Presumably a brain must already be there before any such 'transformation' can take place; and so the argument quoted in the text stands as a mere local detail, without general bearings.

的是它实际上却是那么的脆弱。① 确实，当我们研究乐音和它的外部原因之间的联系时，我们的确发现了音符是简单而连续的，而原因却是多重的和不连续的。那么，在某个地方就存在着转化、缩减或者融合。问题是在哪里——是在神经世界还是在精神世界？

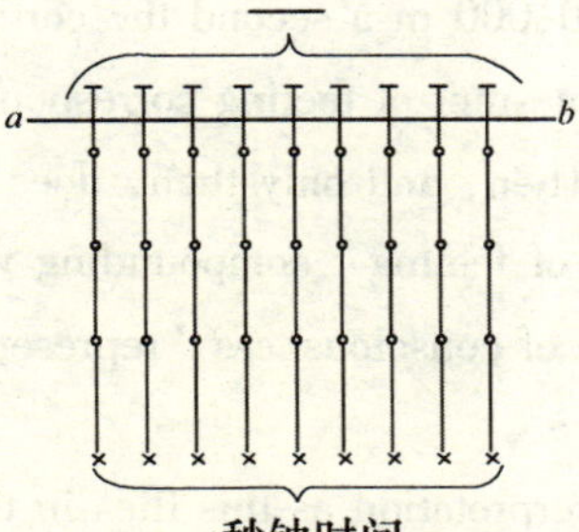

图 25

实际上我们还没有用来做出判断的实验证据；而如果我们必须做出判断的话，类比和先天的可能性是唯一能够指引我们的东西。斯宾赛先生假定融合一定发生在精神世界，而且物理过程经过空气和耳朵、听觉神经和髓质、大脑下部和大脑半球时，它们的数量并没有减少。在前一页上的图示 25 将清楚地表明这一点。

让线段 a－b 代表意识的阈限：那么画在这条线下面的所有

---

① 特别古怪的是，斯宾塞先生似乎完全没有意识到精神素材基本单元理论在进化论哲学中的一般功能。我们认为，如果那种哲学要起作用的话，绝对不可缺少的就是要假定星云中有意识，——当然，最简单的方法就是假设每一个原子都是活生生的。然而，斯宾塞先生（例如，《第一原理》，第 71 节）会认为意识仅仅是与之“相当的”一定量的“物理的力”的“转化”的偶然结果。在任何这种“转化”能够发生之前，推测起来大脑必须已经存在于那里了；因此文中所引用的论证只能作为局部的细节而存在，而不具有普遍的意义。

everything drawn below that line will symbolize a physical process, everything above it will mean a fact of mind. Let the crosses stand for the physical blows, the circles for the events in successively higher orders of nerve-cells, and the horizontal marks for the facts of feeling. Spencer's argument implies that each order of cells transmits just as many impulses as it receives to the cells above it; so that if the blows come at the rate of 20,000 in a second the cortical cells discharge at the same rate, and one unit of feeling corresponds to each one of the 20,000 discharges. Then, and only then, does 'integration' occur, by the 20,000 units of feeling 'compounding with themselves' into the 'continuous state of consciousness' represented by the short line at the top of the figure.

Now such an interpretation as this flies in the face of physical analogy, no less than of logical intelligibility. Consider physical analogy first.

A pendulum may be deflected by a single blow, and swing back. Will it swing back the more often the more we multiply the blows? No; for if they rain upon the pendulum too fast, it will not swing at all but remain deflected in a sensibly stationary state. In other words, increasing the cause numerically need not equally increase numerically the effect. Blow through a tube: you get a certain musical note; and increasing the blowing increases for a certain time the loudness of the note. Will this be true indefinitely? No; for when a certain force is reached, the note, instead of growing louder, suddenly disappears and is replaced by its higher octave. Turn on the gas slightly and light it: you get a tiny flame. Turn on more gas, and the breadth of the flame increases. Will this relation increase indefinitely? No, again; for at a certain moment up shoots the flame into a ragged streamer and begins to hiss. Bend slowly through the nerve of a frog's gastrocnemius muscle a succession of galvanic shocks:

东西将代表一个物理过程,线上面的所有东西将意味着一个心理事实。让小叉儿代表物理吹气,圆圈代表在依次升高的神经细胞等级中的事件,而水平的符号代表感受事实。斯宾塞的论证意味着每一个等级的细胞给它上面的细胞所传输的刺激和它所接受到的刺激是一样多的;因此,如果吹气以每秒20000次的速度吹来,皮层细胞会以同样的速度释放,而这20000次释放当中的每一次释放都和一个感受单元相对应。在那时,而且也只有在那时,“结合”才能发生,它是通过这20000个感受单元“与它们自身相复合”为“连续的意识状态”来完成的,图示顶部的短线代表“连续的意识状态”。

现在,像这样的一种解释公然违背了物理的类推,这不亚于违背了逻辑的可理解性。首先考虑一下物理的类推。

通过一次吹气,一只钟摆会偏离出去,然后再摆动回来。我们越多地增加吹气次数,它就会越频繁地摆动回来吗?不会的,因为如果对钟摆吹气吹得太快了,它将根本不会摆动回来,而是以一种可感觉地固定的状态一直偏离出去。换句话说,在数量上增加原因不必要同样地在数量上增加结果。向一根管子里吹气:你得到了某一个乐音;加大吹气的量会在一定的时间里增加音符的音量。可以无限地这样下去吗?不可以;因为当达到了某一强度的时候,这个音符的音量就不会变得更大了,这个音符反而会突然消失并且会被比它高八度的那个音符所替代。稍微打开一点煤气并且点燃它:你得到了一个微弱的火苗。将煤气开得再大一些,火苗的宽度增大了。这种关系会无限地递进吗?还是不会;因为在某一特定的时刻,火焰会向上喷射,变成粗糙的长条状,并且开始嘶嘶作响。缓慢地向一只青蛙的腓肠肌神经实施连

you get a succession of twitches. Increasing the number of shocks does not increase the twitching; on the contrary, it stops it, and we have the muscle in the apparently stationary state of contraction called tetanus. This last fact is the true analogue of what must happen between the nerve-cell and the sensory fibre. It is certain that cells are more inert than fibres, and that rapid vibrations in the latter can only arouse relatively simple processes or states in the former. The higher cells may have even a slower rate of explosion than the lower, and so the twenty thousand supposed blows of the outer air may be 'integrated' in the cortex into a very small number of cell-discharges in a second. This other diagram will serve to contrast this supposition with Spencer's. In Fig. 26 all 'integration' occurs below the threshold of consciousness. The frequency of cell-events becomes more and more reduced as we approach the cells to which feeling is most directly attached, until at last we come to a condition of things symbolized by the larger ellipse, which may be taken to stand for some rather massive and slow process of tension and discharge in the cortical centres, to which, *as a whole*, the feeling of musical tone symbolized by the line at the top of the diagram *simply and totally* corresponds. It is as if a long file of men were to start one after the other to reach a distant point. The Toad at first is good and they keep their original distance apart. Presently it is intersected by bogs each worse than the last, so that the front men get so retarded that the hinder ones catch up with them before the journey done,

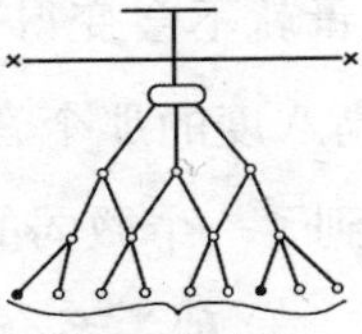

one second of time.

FIG. 26.

续的电击:你会得到连续的抽搐。增加电击的次数不会增加抽搐;相反,这会使抽搐停止,我们使得肌肉处于明显固定的收缩状态之中,这被称作肌肉痉挛。这最后一个事实真正类似于在神经细胞和感觉纤维之间所必定发生的情况。可以确定的是,细胞比纤维更具惰性,而且在后者中的快速振动只能在前者中引起相对简单的过程和状态。高级细胞可能比低级细胞的爆发速度更慢,因此在一秒中之内,那假定为20000次的外部空气的吹动可能会在皮层中"结合"为非常少量的细胞释放。这另一个图示是用来将这一推测与斯宾塞的推测相对照的。在图26中,所有的"结合"都发生在意识阈限之下。当我们接近与感受的关联最为直接的细胞时,细胞事件的发生次数就越来越少了,直到最后我们到达了由较大的椭圆所象征的事物的情形之中,这个椭圆可以被认为代表了在皮层中枢中规模相当大的、缓慢的紧张与释放过程,作为一个整体,由图示顶部的直线所象征的乐音感受简单并且完整地与它相对应。这就如同人们排成了一条长队,开始依次向远处的一点前行。开始的时候道路很好并且他们可以保持原来的距离。不久道路让一次比一次更糟的沼泽所切断,结果前面的人前进得是如此的缓慢,以至于后面的人在他们结束其旅程前

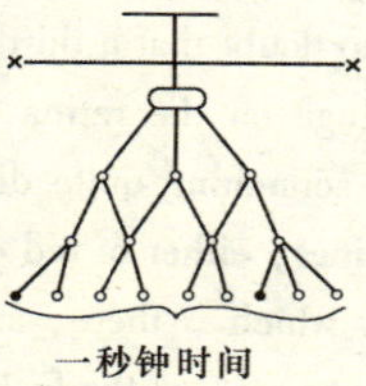

图26

and all arrive together at the goal. ①

On this supposition there *are* no unperceived units of mind-stuff preceding and composing the full consciousness. The latter is itself an immediate psychic fact and bears an immediate relation to the neural state which is its un-conditional accompaniment. Did each neural shock give rise to its own psychic shock, and the psychic shocks then combine, it would be impossible to understand why severing one part of the central nervous system from another should break up the integrity of the consciousness. The cut has nothing to do with the psychic world. The atoms of mind-stuff ought to float off from the nerve-matter on either side of it, and come together over it and fuse, just as well as if it had not been made. We know, however, that they do not; that severance of the paths of conduction between a man's left auditory centre or optical centre and the rest of his cortex will sever all communication between the words which he hears or sees written and the rest of his ideas.

Moreover, if feelings can mix into a *tertium quid*, why do we not take a feeling of greenness and a feeling of redness, and make a feeling of yellowness out of them? Why has optics neglected the open road to truth, and wasted centuries in disputing about theories of color-composition which two minutes of introspection would have settled forever? ②We cannot mix feelings as such,

---

① The compounding of colors may be dealt with in an identical way. Helmholtz has shown that if green light and red light fall simultaneously on the retina, we see the color yellow. The mind-stuff theory would interpret this as a case where the feeling green and the feeling red 'combine' into the *terlium quid* of feeling, yellow. What really occurs is no doubt that a third kind of nerve-process is set up when the combined lights impinge on the retina,-not simply the process of red plus the process of green, but something quite different from both or either. Of course, then, there *are* no feelings, either of red or of green, present to the mind at all; but the feeling of yellow which *is* there, answers as directly to the nerve-process which momentarily then exists, as the feelings of green and red would answer to their respective nerve-processes did the latter happen to be taking place.

② Cf. Mill's Logic, book VI. chap. IV. § 3.

就赶上了他们,并且所有人都一起到达了目的地。①

根据这一假定,不存在未被知觉到的精神素材单元先于整个意识并构成整个意识。后者自身是一个直接的精神事实,并且与作为其无条件伴随物的神经状态有直接的关系。如果每一次神经震荡都引起它自己的精神震荡,然后这些精神震荡就结合起来的话,就不可能理解为什么将中枢神经系统的一个部分与另一个部分切开会破坏意识的完整性。这一切断和精神世界没有任何关系。精神素材的原子应该从两边的神经物质中游离开来,然后越过它完好地聚集在一起并融合起来,就像切除从来没有做过一样。然而,我们知道它们不是这样的;切断人的左侧的听觉中枢或者视觉中枢与其剩余皮层的传导路径就会中断他听见或者看到所写下来的词语与他的其他观念之间的交流。

此外,如果感受能够混合为一种中间物,为什么我们不能拿来一个绿色的感受和一个红色的感受,并且从它们中做出一个黄色的感受呢?为什么光学忽视了通向真理的敞开大道,并且浪费了几个世纪的时间来争论用两分钟时间的内省就可以永远解决的颜色合成理论呢?② 虽然我们可以混合我们所感受到的对象,并且从它们的

① 颜色的混合可以用同样的方式来加以对待。赫姆霍尔茨已经表明,如果绿光和红光同时落在视网膜上,我们看见的颜色是黄色。精神素材理论将把这作为这样一种情况而加以解释,即绿色的感受和红色的感受"结合"为一种中间的感受,黄色的感受。实际上发生的情况无疑是,当组合的光撞击到视网膜上时,第三种神经过程开始了,——而不简单地是红色的过程加上绿色的过程,而是与两个一起或者每一个都完全不同的东西。当然,在那时,红色或者绿色的感受完全没有出现在心灵面前;而只有黄色的感受存在于那里,直接与于是即刻存在的神经过程相对应,就如同绿色和红色的感受如果恰巧正在产生的话,它们会直接和各自的神经过程相对应一样。

② 参见密尔的《逻辑学》,第6卷,第4章,第3节。

though we may mix the objects we feel, and from *their* mixture get new feelings. We cannot even (as we shall later see) have two feelings in our mind at once. At most we can compare together *objects previously presented* to us in distinct feelings; but then we find each object stubbornly maintaining its separate identity before consciousness, whatever the verdict of the comparison may be. ①

Self-Compounding Of Mental Facts Is Inadmissible.

But there is a still more fatal objection to the theory of mental units 'compounding with themselves' or 'integrating.' It is logically unintelligible; it leaves out the essential feature of all the 'combinations' we actually know.

All the 'combinations' which we actually know are EFFECTS, wrought by the units said to be 'combined,' UPON SOME ENTITY OTHER THAN THEMSELVES. Without this feature of a medium or vehicle, the notion of combination has no sense.

"A multitude of contractile units, by joint action, and by being all connected, for instance, with a single tendon, will pull at the same, and will bring about a dynamical effect which is undoubtedly the resultant of their combined individual energies. . . . On the whole, tendons are to muscular fibres, and bones are to tendons, combining recipients of mechanical energies. A medium of composition is indispensable to the summation of energies. To realize the complete dependence of

---

① I find in my students an almost invincible tendency to think that we can immediately perceive that feelings do combine. "What!" they say, "is not the taste of lemonade composed of that of lemon *plus* that of sugar?" This is taking the combining of objects for that of feelings. The physical lemonade contains both the lemon and the sugar, but its taste does not contain their tastes, for if there are any two things which are certainly *not* present in the taste of lemonade, those are the lemon-sour on the one hand and the sugar-sweet on the other. These tastes are absent utterly. The entirely new taste which is present *resembles*, it is true, both those tastes; but in Chapter XIII we shall see that resemblance can not always be held to involve partial identity.

混合中获得新的感受,但是我们却不能混合感受本身。我们甚至不能(如我们后来所看到的那样)在心灵中同时获有两种感受。我们最多只能在截然不同的感受中将先前展现给我们的对象合起来比较;但在当时我们会发现,无论这种比较的定论会是什么,每一个对象在意识面前都倔强地保持其个别的特性。①

精神事实的自我复合是不可接受的

而且,对精神单元"自我复合"或者"结合"的理论还有一个更加致命的反驳。它在逻辑上是无法理解的;它遗漏了我们所实际了解的所有"结合"的本质特征。

为我们所实际了解的所有"结合",都是在与自身不同的本体之上,由所谓被"结合"的单元而形成的。没有这种中介或媒介物的特征,结合的概念就毫无意义。

"例如,一群会收缩的单元,通过共同的行动,并且通过都和一个单一的腱相连接,将会同时拉动,并且会产生一种动力效果,这效果无疑是它们所结合起来的个别能量的矢量合……总之,腱对于肌肉纤维,骨骼对于腱,都是机械能量的联合接受者。合成媒介对于能量的聚合来说是不可缺少的。要了解机械的合成

① 我在我的学生中发现了一种几乎无法克服的倾向,认为我们能够立刻知觉到感受确实结合了。"什么!"他们说,"柠檬水的味道不是由柠檬的味道加上糖的味道组合起来的吗?"这是将对象的结合当作感受的结合了。物理的柠檬水包含有柠檬与糖,但是其味道不包含这两者的味道,因为假设有任意两样东西肯定没有出现在柠檬水的味道之中,那它们一个就是柠檬的酸味,另一个就是糖的甜味。这两种味道是完全不存在的。所出现的全新的味道确实像这两种味道;但是在第13章中,我们将会看到那种相似性不能总是被认为涉及到了部分的同一。

mechanical resultants on a combining substratum, one may fancy for a moment all the individually contracting muscular elements severed from their attachments. They might then still be capable of contracting with the same energy as before, yet no co-operative result would be accomplished. The medium of dynamical combination would be wanting. The multiple energies, singly exerted on no common recipient, would lose themselves on entirely isolated and disconnected efforts." ①

In other words, no possible number of entities (call them as you like, whether forces, material particles, or mental elements) can sum *themselves* together. Each remains, in the sum, what it always was; and the sum itself exists only *for a bystander* who happens to overlook the units and to apprehend the sum as such; or else it exists in the shape of some other *effect* on an entity external to the sum itself. Let it not be objected that H, and O combine of themselves into 'water,' and thenceforward exhibit new properties. They do not. The 'water' is just the old atoms in the new position, H-O-H; the 'new properties' are just their combined *effects*, when in this position, upon external media, such as our sense-organs and the various reagents on which water may exert its properties and be known.

"Aggregations are organized wholes only when they behave as such in the presence of other things. A statue is an aggregation of particles of marble; but as such it has no unity. For the spectator it is one; in itself it is an aggregate; just as, to the consciousness of an ant crawling over it, it may again appear a mere aggregate. No summing up of parts can make an unity of a mass of discrete constituents,

① E. Montgomery, in 'Mind,' V. 18-19. See also pp. 24-5.

对于结合基质的完全的依赖性,我们可以花一点时间来设想一下将所有单独收缩的肌肉要素都从它们的附着物上切下来。它们在那时依然能够用和以前一样的能量收缩,然而却不能形成协作的结果。所欠缺的是动力结合的媒介。单独施加的没有共同接受者的多重能量,将会在完全孤立和分离的努力中丧失掉它们自己。”①

换句话说,不管多少数量的本体(依照你的喜好,可以把它们称为力、质料粒子或者精神元素)都不可能将它们自己聚合在一起。在总体中,每一个本体都一直是它永远所是的东西;而总体自身只有对一个旁观者来说才是存在着的,这个旁观者碰巧忽视了单元,并且照此来理解总体;或者,它以对外在于总体自身的一种本体所表现出的某种其他作用的形式而存在。不要反驳 H_2 和 O 将它们自身结合成“水”,并且其后展现出了新的性质。它们没有这样。“水”只是在新位置中的旧原子,H-O-H;“新的性质”只是当其处于这一位置时对外部的媒介(例如我们的感觉器官和各种为人所知的可以让水表现出其性质的试剂)所表现出的联合效果。

“只有当聚合体在其他事物面前做如此的行为表现时,它们才是有组织的整体。一尊雕像是大理石微粒的聚合物;但是像这样的话它就不具有统一性。因为对于观看者来说它是一个东西;但它自身却是一个聚合物;正如同对于一只爬到它上面的蚂蚁的意识来说,它又可以显现为一种单纯的聚合物。部分间的聚合不能产生出许多离散成分的统一体,除非这个统一体对于某个其他

① E. 蒙哥马利,《心灵》,5,第18~19页。也可参见第24~25页。

unless this unity exist for some other subject, not for the mass itself."①

Just so, in the parallelogram of forces, the 'forces' themselves do not combine into the diagonal resultant.; a *body* is needed on which they may impinge, to exhibit their resultant effect. No more do musical sounds combine *per se* into concords or discords. Concord and discord are names for their combined effects on that external medium, the *ear*.

Where the elemental units are supposed to be feelings, the case is in no wise altered. Take a hundred of them, shuffle them and pack them as close together as you can (whatever that may mean); still each remains the same feeling it always was, shut in its own skin, windowless, ignorant of what the other feelings are and mean. There would be a hundred-and-first feeling there, if, when a group or series

---

① J. Royce, 'Mind,' VI. p. 376. Lotze has set. forth the truth of this law more clearly and copiously than any other writer. Unfortunately he is too lengthy to quote. See his Microcosmus, bk. II. ch. I. § 5; Metaphysik, §§ 242, 260; Outlines of Metaphysics, part Ⅱ. chap. I. §§ 3,4, 5. Compare also Reid's Intellectual Powers, essay V, chap. Ⅲ ad *fin.*; Bowne's Meta-physics, pp. 361-76; St. J. Mivurt: Nature and Thought, pp. 98-101; E. Gurney: 'Monism,' in 'Mind.' Ⅵ. 158; and the article by Prof. Royce, just quoted, on 'Mind-stuff and Reality.'

In defence of the mind-stuff view, see W. K. Clifford: 'Mind.' Ⅲ. 57 (reprinted in his 'Lectures and Essays,' Ⅱ. 71): G. T. Fechner, Psycho-pliysik, Bd. Ⅱ. cap. XIV: H. Taine: on Intelligence, bk. Ⅲ; E. Haeckel: 'Zellseelen u. Seelenzellen' in Gesammelte pop. Vorträge, Bd. I. p. 143; W. S. Duncan. Conscious Matter, *passim*, H. Zöllner: Natur d. Cometen, pp. 320 ff.; Alfred Barratt: 'Physical Ethic' and 'Physical Metempiric,' *passim*; J. Soury. 'Hylozoisimus,' in 'Kosmos,' V. Jahrg.. Heft X. p. 241; A. Main: 'Mind,' I. 292, 481, 566; Ⅱ 129, 402; *Id.* Revue Philos. Ⅱ. 86, 88, 419; Ⅲ. 51, 502; Ⅳ. 402; F. W. Frankland: 'Mind,' Ⅵ. 116; Whittaker: 'Mind.' Ⅵ. 498 (historical); Morton Prince: The Nature of Mind and Human Automatism (1885); A. Riehl: Der philosophische Kritlcismus. Bd. Ⅱ. Theil 2, 2ter Abschnitt, 2tes Cap. (1887). The clearest of all these statements is, as far as it goes, that of Prince.

主体来说，而不是对于那一大堆东西自身来说是存在着的。”①

正是如此，在力的平行四边形中，“力”自身并不结合成对角线的矢量合；为了展现它们的合力效果，需要有一个它们可以对其进行撞击的身体。乐音本身也不结合为和谐音与不和谐音。和谐音与不和谐音仅仅是它们对外部的媒介——耳朵所表现出的联合效果的名称而已。

在基本单元被设想成是感受的情况下，情形决不会变化。取来一百个感受，搅乱它们，并且尽你所能将它们紧紧地捆扎在一起(不论这意味着什么)；每一个感受依然是其一直所是的同一个感受，关闭在它自己的外壳里，没有窗户，也不知道其他感受是什么、意味着什么。如果当一组或一系列的这种感受被建立起来的

---

① J. 罗伊斯，《心灵》，6，第 376 页。洛采比其他任何作者都更加清楚和充分地阐明了这一规律的真相。可惜的是他的论述太长了，所以没能引用。参见他的《微观宇宙》，第 2 卷，第 1 章，第 5 节；《形而上学》，第 242、260 节；《形而上学纲要》，第 2 部分，第 1 章，第 3、4、5 节。也可以比较里德的《智能》，论文 5，第 3 章的最后；鲍恩的《形而上学》，第 361 ~ 367 页；圣 J. 米瓦特：《自然与思想》，第 98 ~ 101 页；E. 格尼："一元论"，《心灵》，6，第 158 页；还有刚刚引用过的罗伊斯教授的文章，“精神素材与实在”。

对精神素材观点的辩护，参见 W. K. 克利福德：《心灵》，3，57(在其《演讲与论文》中重印，2，71)；G. T. 费克纳，《精神物理学》，第 2 卷，第 14 章；H. 泰恩：《论理智》，第 3 卷；E. 黑科尔，“细胞精神与精神细胞”，《通俗演讲集》，第 1 卷，第 143 页；W. S. 邓肯，《意识物质》，各处；H. 佐尔纳：《彗星的性质》，第 320 页以后；阿尔弗雷德 · 巴勒特：“物理伦理”和“物理先验论”，各处；J. 索瑞：“物活论”，在《宇宙》中，第 5 年度，第 10 期，第 241 页；A. 梅因：《心灵》，1，292、481、566；2，129、402；《哲学评论》，2，86、88、419；3，51，502；4，402；F. W. 弗兰克兰：《心灵》，6，116；惠特克：《心灵》，6，498(历史的)；莫顿 · 普林斯：《心灵的本性和人的自动化》(1885 年)；A. 里尔：《哲学批评》，第 2 卷，第 2 部分，第 2 章，(1887 年)。就所有这些论述而言，其中论述最清晰的就是普林斯的论述。

of such feelings were set up, a consciousness *belonging to the group as such* should emerge. And this 101st feeling would be a totally new fact; the 100 original feelings might, by a curious physical law, be a signal for its *creation*, when they came together; but they would have no substantial identity with it, nor it with them, and one could never deduce the one from the others, or (in any intelligible sense) say that they *evolved* it.

Take a sentence, of a dozen words, and take twelve men and tell to each one word. Then stand the men in a row or jam them in a bunch, and let each think of his word as intently as he will; nowhere will there be a consciousness of the whole sentence. ①We talk of the 'spirit of the age,' and the 'sentiment of the people,' and in various ways we hypostatize 'public opinion.' But we know this to be symbolic speech, and never dream that the spirit, opinion, sentiment, etc., constitute a consciousness other than, and additional to, that of the several individuals whom the words 'age,' 'people,' or 'public' denote. The private minds do not agglomerate into a higher compound mind. This has always been the invincible contention of the spiritualists against the associationists in Psychology,—a contention which we shall take up at greater length in Chapter X. The associationists say the mind is constituted by a multiplicity of distinct 'ideas' *associated* into a unity. There is, they say, an idea of *a*, and also an idea of *b*. *Therefore*, they say, there is an idea of a + b,

① "Someone might say that although it is true that neither a blind man nor a deaf man by himself can compare sounds with colors, yet since one hears and the other sees they might do so both together. . . . But whether they are apart or close together makes no difference; not even if they permanently keep house together; no, not if they were Siamese twins, or more than Siamese twins, and were inseparably grown together, would it make the assumption any more possible. Only when sound and color are represented in the same reality is it thinkable that they should be compared." (Brentano: Psychologic, p. 209.)

时候，一个像这样属于那个系列的意识就应该出现了。那么，在那里就会有第一百零一个感受存在；当一百个原初的感受在一起的时候，通过一条奇怪的规律，它们就可能是其创生的一个信号；但是它们与它，或者它与它们都没有实质性的同一性，并且人们永远不能将一个感受从其他感受中演绎出来，或者（在任何可理解的意义上）说它们进化出了它。

拿来一个由12个词组成的句子，再找来12个人并且告诉每一个人一个词。然后让他们站成一行或者让他们排成一串，并且让每一个人尽可能专心地思考他的词；在哪里都不可能出现对整个句子的意识。[①] 我们谈论“时代精神”和“人民情操”，并且以各种方式具体化“公众意见”。但是我们知道这是一个象征性的说法，并且我们从来也不会梦想，精神、意见和情操等构成了这样一种意识，它不同于“时代”、“人民”或者“公众”这些词所表示的一些个体的意识，并且它是附加在这种意识之上的。这些个体的心灵不能聚合成一个更为高级的复合的心灵。这一直是心理学中唯灵论者用来反对联想主义者的战无不胜的论点——在第10章我们将进一步展开这一论点。联想主义者认为，心灵是由联结为一个统一体的许多截然不同的观点构成的。他们说，存在有观念a，并且也存在有观念b。因此，他们说就有一个a+b的观念，

①“有人可能会说，尽管一个盲人或者一个失聪的人确实都不能通过他自己将声音和颜色加以比较，但是，由于一个人听到了而另一个人看到了，因此他们可以两个人一起来这样做……但是，不论他们是分开的还是紧挨在一起的，这都一样不行；即使他们永远住在一起也不行；不行，即使他们是孪生双胞胎，或者比孪生双胞胎更甚，而且是不能分离地长在一起的，这都不会使这一假定有更多的可能性。只有当声音和颜色在相同的实在中得以表象时，才能够设想它们应该得到了比较。（布兰塔诺：《心理学》，第209页。）

or of *a* and *b* together; Which is like saying that the mathematical square of *a* plus that of *b* is equal to the square of *a* + *b*, a palpable untruth. Idea of *a* + idea of *b* is *not* identical with idea of (*a* + *b*). It is one, they are two; in it, what knows *a* also knows *b*; in them, what knows *a* is expressly posited as not knowing *b*; etc. In short, the two separate ideas can never by any logic be made to figure as one and the same thing as the 'associated' idea.

This is what the spiritualists keep saying; and since we do, as a matter of fact, have the 'compounded' idea, and do know *a* and *b* together, they adopt a farther hypothesis to explain that fact. The separate ideas exist, they say, but *affect* a third entity, the soul. *This* has the 'compounded' idea, if you please so to call it; and the compounded idea is an altogether new psychic fact to which the separate ideas stand in the relation, not of constituents, but of occasions of production.

This argument of the spiritualists against the associationists has never been answered by the latter. It holds good against any talk about self-compounding amongst feelings, against any 'blending,' or 'complication,' or 'mental chemistry,' or 'psychic synthesis,' which supposes a resultant consciousness to float off from the constituents *per se*, in the absence of a supernumerary principle of consciousness which they may affect. The mind-stuff theory, in short, is unintelligible. Atoms of feeling cannot compose higher feelings, any more than atoms of matter can compose physical things! The 'things,' for a clear-headed atomistic evolutionist, are not. Nothing is but the everlasting atoms. When grouped in a certain way, *we* name them this 'thing' or that;

或者一个 a 和 b 在一起的观念;这好像就是说,a 的数学平方加上 b 的平方等于 a+b 的平方,这是个明显的错误。观念 a+观念 b 不等于观念(a+b)。(a+b)是一个,a、b 是两个;在(a+b)那里,知道 a 者也知道 b;在 a、b 那里,知道 a 者是明确地被假定为不知道 b 的;等等。简而言之,这两个分离的观念是永远也不能够通过逻辑而变得可以和那个"联想的"观念一样来描述一个同样的事物的。

这就是唯灵论者一直在说的内容;而且既然事实上我们拥有"复合的"观念,并且确实一起知道了 a 和 b,他们就采用了一个更进一步的假说来解释那一事实。他们说,分离的观念是存在着的,但是他们影响着第三个本体——灵魂。这个东西拥有"复合的"观念,如果你愿意这样称呼它的话;并且复合的观念是一个全新的精神事实,分离的观念与它的关系不是构成的关系,而它们之间的关系是分离的观念是它得以产生的诱因。

唯灵论者反对联想主义者的这个论证,从来也没有得到后者的回应。它有效地反对了任何主张感受间的自我复合的言论,有效地反对了任何"混合"、"复杂化"、"心理化学"或"精神综合"的观点,这种观点设想一种合成的意识从其组成部分自身中漂浮开来,而此时缺少它们可以对其施加影响的额外法则。简而言之,精神素材理论是无法了解的。感受原子不能组成高级的感受,就如同物质原子不能组成物理事物一样。对一个头脑清醒的原子进化论者来说,"事物"是无。除了永恒的原子之外什么都不存在。当以某一特定的方式聚合在一起时,我们称它们为这个"事物"或那个"事物";但是,我们所

but the thing we name has no existence out of our mind. So of the states of mind which are supposed to be compound because they know many different things together. Since indubitably such states do exist, they must exist as single new facts, effects, possibly, as the spiritualists say, on the Soul (we will not decide that point here), but at any rate independent and integral, and not compounded of psychic atoms. ①

① The reader must observe that we are reasoning altogether about the *logic* of the mind-stuff theory, about whether it can *explain the constitution* of higher mental states by viewing them as *identical with lower ones* summed together. We say the two sorts of fact are not identical: a higher state *is* not a lot of lower states; it is itself. When, however, a lot of lower states have come together, or when certain brain-conditions occur together which, *if they occurred separately, would produce* a lot of lower states, we have not for a moment pretended that a higher state may not emerge. In fact it does emerge under those conditions; and our Chapter IX will be mainly devoted to the proof of this fact. But such emergence is that of a new psychic entity, and is *toto coelo* different from such an 'integration' of the lower states as the mind-stuff theory affirms.

It may seem strange to suppose that anyone should mistake criticism of a certain theory about a fact for doubt of the fact itself. And yet the confusion is made in high quarters enough to justify our remarks. Mr. J. Ward. in his article Psychology in the Encyclopedia Britannica, speaking of the hypothesis that "a series of feelings can be aware of itself as a series," says (p. 39): " Paradox is too mild a word for it, even contradiction will hardly suffice." Whereupon, Professor Bain takes him thus to task: "As to 'a series of states being aware of itself, I confess I see no insurmountable difficulty. It may be a fact, or not a fact; it may be a very clumsy expression for what it is applied to; but it is neither paradox nor contradiction. A series merely contradicts an individual, or it may be two or more individuals as coexisting; bat that is too general to exclude the possibility of self-knowledge. It certainly does not bring the property of self-knowledge into the foreground, which. however, is not the same as denying it. An algebraic series might know itself, without any contradiction : the only thing against it is the want of evidence of the fact.' ('Mind,' XI. 459). Prof. Bain thinks, then, that all the bother is about the difficulty of seeing how a series of feelings can have the knowledge of itself

命名的事物离开我们的心灵就不存在。那些因为同时知道很多不同的事物,所以被假设是复合的心理状态也是如此。既然这些状态不容置疑地存在着,它们必须作为单一的新事实而存在,或者可能如唯灵论者所说,作为施加于灵魂之上的效果而存在(在这里我们将不对这一观点做出决断),但无论如何它们都是独立的和完整的,并且不是由精神原子复合而成的。①

---

① 读者必须注意到,我们完全是在对精神素材理论的逻辑进行推论,通过将高级的精神状态看作是与聚合在一起的低级的精神状态一样的东西,我们在推论这种理论是否能够解释高级精神状态的构成。我们说这两种事实不是同一的:一个高级的状态不是许多低级状态;它就是它自身。然而,当很多低级的状态来到一起的时候,或者当某些大脑条件同时出现的时候,而且如果这些条件单独出现的话,它们会产生很多低级状态,我们片刻也没有冒险地自称高级的状态可以不出现。事实上,在那些条件下它确实出现了;而且我们的第9章将主要用来证明这一事实。但是,这种出现是全新的精神实体的出现,而且它与如精神素材理论所断言的那种低级状态的“结合”截然不同。

假设任何人都会将对关于一个事实的某种理论的批判错当成对那个事实自身有所怀疑的事实,这看起来好像很奇怪。然而,来自高层的混淆足以证明我们的评论是正当的。J. 沃德先生在他的文章“不列颠百科全书之心理学”中谈到“一个感受系列能够意识到自己是一个系列”这一假说时说(第39页),“用悖论这个词来称呼它太温和了,甚至矛盾这个词对它来说都几乎不够用。”于是,贝恩教授这样指责他说:“至于‘一个状态的序列意识到它自己’,我承认我看不出有任何不能克服的困难。它可以是一个事实,或者不是一个事实;它可以是对其适用事物的一种非常笨拙的表达;但是它既不是悖论也不是矛盾。一个序列仅仅和一个个体相矛盾,或者它可以和共存着的两个或者多个个体相矛盾;但是这太一般化了,因而不能排除自觉的可能性。它当然没有将自觉的性质带到最显著的位置上来,然而这与否认它还是有所不同的。一个代数序列可以知道它自己,同时没有任何矛盾:反对它的唯一东西就是它缺乏事实证据。”(《心灵》,11,第459页)。因而贝恩教授认为,所有的麻烦都在于了解一个感受序列如何能够将对它自己的知觉

Can States Of Mind Be Unconscious?

The passion for unity and smoothness is in some minds so insatiate that, in spite of the logical clearness of these reasonings and conclusions, many will fail to be influenced by them. They establish a sort of disjointedness in things which in certain quarters will appear intolerable. They sweep away all chance of 'passing without break' either from the material to the mental, or from the lower to the higher mental; and they thrust us back into a pluralism of consciousnesses-each arising discontinuously in the midst of two disconnected worlds, material and mental-which is even worse than the old notion of the separate creation of each particular soul. But the malcontents will hardly try to refute our reasonings by direct attack. It is more probable that, turning their back upon them altogether, they will devote themselves to sapping and mining the region roundabout until it is a bog of logical liquefaction, into the midst of which all definite conclusions of any sort may be trusted ere long to sink and disappear.

Our reasonings have assumed that the 'integration' of a thousand psychic units must be either just the units over again, simply rebaptized, or else something real, but then other than and additional to

added to it! ! ! As if anybody ever was troubled about that. That, notoriously enough, is a fact: our consciousness is a series of feelings to which every now and then is *added* a retrospective consciousness that they have come and gone. What Mr. Ward and I are troubled about is merely the silliness of the mind-stufflsts and associationists continuing to say that the 'series of states' is the 'awareness of itself ;' that if the states be posited severally, their collective consciousness is *eo ipso* given; and that we need no farther explanation, or 'evidence of the fact.'

心理状态可以是无意识的吗？

在一些人的心中，追求统一和顺畅的热情是如此地难以满足，以至于不论这些推理和结论在逻辑上有多么清晰，很多人还是没有受到它们的影响。他们使得一些事情变得杂乱无章，这在某些团体那里似乎是令人无法忍受的。他们扫除了所有从物质到精神，或者从较低级的精神到较高级的精神“不间断地过渡”的机会；而且他们强行使我们退回到了意识多元论中——每一个意识不连续地从物质和精神这两个分离的世界中产生出来——这甚至比每一个灵魂的单独创造这种古老观点更糟糕。而且这些不满的人几乎不会通过直接的攻击来尽力地反驳我们的推理。更有可能的是，在对这些推论完全置之不理的同时，他们却致力于迂回地侵蚀和破坏那个区域，直到它成为一片逻辑的泥沼，进入这片泥沼之中，任何种类的明确结论不久就必定会下沉和消失。

我们的推论已经假定，一千个精神单元的“聚合”，必须要么是仅被重新命名的那些单元的重复，要么是某些其他实在的东西，这样它就不同于那些单元，对那些单元来说它就是另外的；如

加到它之上的困难!!! 就好像所有人都一直为这所困扰似的。那是一个足够声名狼藉的事实：我们的意识是一个感受序列，来来去去的内省意识不时地加到它的上面去。精神素材论者和联想主义者不断地说，“状态序列”是“对它自己的意识”；如果状态被单独对待，它们的聚合意识就等于产生了；并且我们不需要做进一步的解释，也不需要“事实的证据”，沃德先生和我所感到的困扰仅仅是他们的愚蠢。

those units; that if a certain existing fact is that of a thousand feelings, it cannot at the same time be that of ONE feeling; for the essence of feeling is to be felt, and as a psychic existent *feels*, so it must *be*. If the one feeling feels like no one of the thousand, in what sense can it be said to *be* the thousand? These assumptions are what the monists will seek to undermine. The Hegelizers amongst them will take high ground at once, and say that the glory and beauty of the psychic life is that in it all contradictions find their reconciliation; and that it is just because the facts we are considering *are* facts of the self that they are both one and many at the same time. With this intellectual temper I confess that I cannot contend. As in striking at some unresisting gossamer with a club, one but overreaches one's self, and the thing one aims at gets no harm. So I leave this school to its devices.

The other monists are of less deliquescent frame, and try to break down distinctness among mental states by *making a distinction*. This sounds paradoxical, but it is only ingenious. The distinction is that *between the unconscious and the conscious being of the mental state*. It is the sovereign means for believing what one likes in psychology, and of turning what might become a science into a tumbling-ground for whimsies. It has numerous champions, and elaborate reasons to give for itself. We must there-fore accord it due consideration. In discussing the question:

Do Unconscious Mental States Exist?

it will be best to give the list of so-called proofs as briefly as possible,

果某一个存在的事实是关于那一千个感受的事实，那么它就不能同时又是关于一个感受的事实；因为感受的本质是被感受，而且是作为一个精神的存在着的感受，它就必须如此。如果一个感受在感受起来时不像那一千个感受中的任何一个感受，它在什么样的意义上能够被说成是一千个感受呢？这些假设是一元论者所想要破坏的。他们中黑格尔化了的人会立刻站在高处，并且说精神生活的荣耀和美丽在于其中所有的矛盾都得到了调和；而且正是因为我们所考虑的事实是关于自我的事实，它们同时既是一也是多。我承认，我无法同这样的智性趋向相争辩。这就像一个人用棍棒来敲击那不加抵抗的小蜘蛛网一样，除了弄巧成拙以外，他的目标毫无损伤。因此，我听任这一学派自行其是。

其他的一元论者就较少有这种容易消融的形质，它们试图通过做出一种区分来破坏心理状态之间的区别。这听起来是荒谬的，但也仅仅是机智的表现。区分是对心理状态的无意识存在和有意识存在之间的区分。这是让一个人相信他在心理学中所喜欢的东西的最高手段，也是将本来可以成为科学的东西变成怪念头的竞技场的最高手段。它有众多支持者，并且有详尽的理由来支持自己。因此我们必须对它做应有的思考。

无意识心理状态存在吗？

在对这个问题的讨论中，最好的方法就是尽可能简要地给出一个所谓的证明清单，并且在每一个的后面给出对它的反驳，就

and to follow each by its objection, as in scholastic books. ①

First Proof. The *minimum visibile*, *the minimum audibile*, are objects composed of parts. How can the whole affect the sense unless each part does? And yet each part does so without being separately sensible. Leibnitz calls the total consciousness an '*aperception*,' the supposed insensible consciousness by the name of '*petites perceptions*'.

"To judge of the latter," he says, "I am accustomed to use the example of the roaring of the sea with which one is assailed when near the shore. To hear this noise as one does, one must hear the parts which compose its totality, that is, the noise of each wave,... although this noise would not be noticed if its wave were alone. One must be affected a little by the movement of one wave, one must have some perception of each several noise, however small it be. Otherwise one would not hear that of 100,000 waves, for of 100,000 zeros one can never make a quantity." ②

Reply. This is an excellent example of the so-called 'fallacy of division,' or predicating what is true only of a collection, of each

---

① The writers about 'unconscious cerebration' seem sometimes to mean that and sometimes unconscious thought. The arguments which follow are culled from various quarters. The reader will find them most systematically urged by E. von Hartmann: Phffosophy of the Uncor scious, vol. I, and by E. Colsenet: La vie Inconaciente de l'Esprit (1880). Consult also T. Laycock: Mind and Brain, vol. I. chap, V (1860); W. B. Carpenter: Mental Physiology, chap. XIII; F P. Cobbe: Darwinism in Morals and other Essays, essay XI, Unconscious Cerebration (1872); F. Bowen: Modern Philosophy, pp. 428-480; R. H. Hutton: Contemporary Review, vol. XXIV. p. 201; J. S. Mill: Exam, of Hamilton, chap. XV; G. H. Lewess: Problems of Life and Mind, 3d series, Prob. II. chap. X. and also Prob. III chap. II; D. G. Thompson: A System of Psychology, chap. XXXIII, J. M. Baldwin, Hand-book of Psychology, chap, IV.

② Nouveaux Essais, Avant-propos.

好像在经院哲学家的书中所看到的那样。①

第一个证明：最小的可见物和最低的可听物是由部分所组成的对象。除非每一个部分影响了感官，否则整体如何能够影响感官呢？而且，在它们各自都是不可感觉的情况下，每一个部分都影响了感官。莱布尼兹将整个意识称作“统觉”，将假设是不可感觉的意识称作是“微知觉”。

“就对后者的断定而言，”他说，“我习惯于使用这样一个例子，即当一个人接近海岸的时候，他受到了大海咆哮的冲击。如果某人要听到这种噪音，他就必须听到组成其全体的部分，即每一个波浪的噪音，……但是如果只有一个波浪的话，这噪音就不会引起人的注意。人们必定受到了某一波动运动的些许影响，人们必定对每个个别的噪音有一些知觉，不论它有多么小。否则，他就不会听到那100000个波浪，因为从100000个零中永远也不能得出一个量来。”②

答复：这是所谓“分割谬误”的一个极好的例子，或者它是这种断言的极好例子，即仅仅对于集合物为真的东西，对于集合物

① 谈论“无意识用脑”的作者有时指的是这个，有时指的是无意识的思想。后面的论证是从各个层面精选出来的。读者会发现E.冯哈特曼与E.科尔塞尼在倡导它们时说得最为系统，E.冯哈特曼：《无意识哲学》，第1卷，E.科尔塞尼：《精神的无意识生活》（1880年）。也可参考T.莱科克，第1卷，第5章（1860年）；W.B.卡彭特：《心理生理学》，第13章；F.P.科博：《伦理道德中的达尔文主义和其他论文》，论文11，《无意识用脑》（1872年）；F.鲍恩《现代哲学》，第428～480页；R.H.赫顿：《当代评论》，第24卷，第201页；J.S.密尔：《汉密尔顿研究》，第15章；G.H.路易斯《生命与心灵的问题》，第3集，问题2，第10章，以及问题3，第2章；D.G.汤普森：《心理学体系》，第33章；J.M.鲍德温：《心灵学手册》，第4章。

② 《新评论》，序言。

member of the collection distributively. It no more follows that if a thousand things together cause sensation, one thing alone must cause it, than it follows that if one pound weight moves a balance, then one ounce weight must move it too, in less degree. One ounce weight does not move it *at all*; its movement *begins* with the pound. At most we can say that each ounce affects it in *some* way which helps the advent of that movement And so each infra-sensible stimulus to a nerve no doubt affects the nerve and helps the birth of sensation when the other stimuli come. But this affection is a nerve-affection, and there is not the slightest ground for supposing it to be a 'perception' unconscious of itself. "A certain *quantity* of the cause may be a necessary condition to the production of *any* of the effect,"[①] when the latter is a mental state.

Second Proof. In all acquired dexterities and habits, secondarily automatic performances as they are called, we do what originally required a chain of deliberately conscious perceptions and volitions. As the actions still keep their intelligent character, intelligence must still preside over their execution. But since our consciousness seems all the while elsewhere engaged, such intelligence must consist of unconscious perceptions, inferences, and volitions.

Reply. There is more than one alternative explanation in accordance with larger bodies of fact. One is that the perceptions and volitions in habitual actions may be performed consciously, only so quickly and inattentively that no *memory* of them remains. Another is that the conscious-ness of these actions exists, but is *split-off* from the rest of the consciousness of the hemispheres. We shall find in Chapter X numerous proofs of the reality of this split-off condition of portions of consciousness. Since in man the hemispheres

① J. S. Mill, Exam. of Hamilton, chap. XV.

中的每一个成员也分别为真。如果一磅的重量能够使天平移动，那么一盎司的重量必定也会在较小的程度上移动它，这一断言在此是不成立的，如果一千个东西一起引起感觉，那么一个东西也必定会单独地引起它，这一断言在此也同样是不成立的。一盎司的重量根本不会使天平移动；它的运动从磅开始。至多我们能够说，每一盎司以某种帮助那一运动出现的方式影响了它。因此，每一个对神经的亚可感刺激无疑影响了神经，并且当其他刺激到来的时候，帮助了感觉的产生。但是，这种影响是一种神经影响，这里没有理由可以用来假设它是没有意识到它自身的"知觉"。"特定量的原因可以是产生任何结果的一个必要条件，"[①]当后者是一种心理状态的时候。

第二个证明：在所有获得的机敏和习惯当中，在如他们所命名的次级自动操作中，我们所作的事情是最初需要有一系列有意的有意识的知觉和意志才能做到的事情。既然动作依然保持着它们的理智特征，理智就必须依旧掌管它们的执行。而且由于我们的意识似乎一直在别处忙碌着，这种理智就必须由无意识知觉、推理和意志所组成。

答复：这里有不止一种可选择的解释与这多得多的事实相符合。一个解释是，习惯性动作中的知觉和意志可以有意识地行动，只是行动地非常快而且没有引起注意，以至于对它们没有任何记忆保留下来。另一个解释是，对这些行为的意识是存在着的，但是它从脑半球的其他意识中分离了出去。我们将在第10章中发现大量关于部分意识处于分离状态的实在的证明。既然人的大脑半

① J.S.密尔，《汉密尔顿研究》，第15章。

indubitably co-operate in these secondarily automatic acts, it will not do to say either that they occur without consciousness or that their consciousness is that of the lower centres, which we know nothing about. But either lack of memory or split-off cortical consciousness will certainly account for all of the facts. ①

Third Proof. Thinking of A, we presently find our-selves thinking of C. Now B is the natural logical link between A and C, but we have no consciousness of having thought of B. It must have been in our mind '*unconsciously*,' and in that state affected the sequence of our ideas.

Reply. Here again we have a choice between more plausible explanations. Either B was consciously there, but the next instant forgotten, or its *brain-tract* alone was adequate to do the whole work of coupling A with C, without the idea B being aroused at all, whether consciously or 'unconsciously.'

Fourth Proof. Problems unsolved when we go to bed are found solved in the morning when we wake. Somnambulists do rational things. We awaken punctually at an hour predetermined overnight, etc. Unconscious thinking, volition, time-registration, etc., must have presided over these acts.

Reply. Consciousness forgotten, as in the hypnotic trance.

Fifth Proof. Some patients will often, in an attack of epileptiform unconsciousness, go through complicated processes, such as eating a dinner in a restaurant and paying for it, or making a violent homicidal attack. In trance, artificial or pathological, long and complex performances, involving the use of the reasoning powers, are executed, of which the patient is wholly unaware on coming to.

Reply. Rapid and complete oblivescence is certainly the explanation

---

① Cf. Dugald Stewart, Elements, chap. Ⅱ.

球无疑在次级自动动作中协作着,说它们的发生没有意识,或者说它们的意识是低级中枢的意识,但对此我们一无所知,这两种说法都是行不通的。但是,记忆的缺乏或者分离的皮层意识肯定能够解释所有的事实。①

第三个证明:当正在思考A的时候,我们马上就发现自己在思考C。现在,B是A和C之间自然的逻辑链环,但是我们对已经想到了B没有意识。它在我们心中肯定是无意识的,并且在那种状态下影响了我们观念的顺序。

答复:这里我们又可以在似乎更可靠的解释之间做出选择。要么是B有意识地存在于那里,但在下一个瞬间就被遗忘了,要么是它的大脑神经通道独自足以完成联结A和C的整个工作,而B的观念根本没有被唤醒,不管它是有意识的还是"无意识的"。

第四个证明:我们睡觉时还尚未解决的问题,当我们早晨醒来时发现它已经被解决了。梦游者做合理的事情。我们准时在头天晚上预定的时间里醒来,等等。无意识的思维、意志、时间感知等,肯定掌管着这些活动。

答复:忘记了的意识,就如同在催眠恍惚状态中一样。

第五个证明:一些患者经常会在癫痫样的无意识发作中经历一些复杂的过程,例如在饭店里吃顿饭并且付饭钱,或者进行暴力的杀人攻击。在人为的或者是病理的恍惚状态中,患者会完成长时间的复杂活动,这涉及了推理能力的使用,并且在这过程期间他对此完全没有察觉到。

答复:快速和完全的遗忘肯定是对此的解释。类似的情况还

① 参见杜格尔德·斯图尔德,《原理》,第2章。

here. The analogue again is hypnotism. Tell the subject of an hypnotic trance, during his trance, that he *will* remember, and he may remember everything perfectly when he awakes, though without your telling him no memory would have remained. The extremely rapid oblivescence of common *dreams* is a familiar fact.

Sixth Proof. In a musical concord the vibrations of the several notes are in relatively simple ratios. The mind must unconsciously count the vibrations, and be pleased by the simplicity which it finds.

Reply. The brain-process produced by the simple ratios may be as directly agreeable as the conscious process of comparing them would be. No counting, either conscious or 'unconscious,' is required.

Seventh Proof. Every hour we make theoretic judgments and emotional reactions, and exhibit practical tendencies, for which we can give no explicit logical justification, but which are good inferences from certain premises. We know more than we can say. Our conclusions run ahead of our power to analyze their grounds. A child, ignorant of the axiom that two things equal to the same are equal to each other, applies it nevertheless in his concrete judgments unerringly. A boor will use the *dictum de omni et nullo* who is unable to understand it in abstract terms.

"We seldom consciously think how our house is painted, what the shade of it is, what the pattern of our furniture is, or whether the door opens to the right or left, or out or in. But how quickly should we notice a change in any of these things! Think of the door you have most often opened, and tell, if you can, whether it opens to the right or left, out or in. Yet when you open the door you never put the hand on the wrong side to find the latch, nor try to push it when it opens with a pull. . . . What is the precise characteristic in your friend's step that enables you to recognize it when he is coming?

有催眠状态。当被催眠的被试者处于恍惚状态期间,告诉他说他将会记得,那么他在醒来的时候就会很好地记起所有的事情,但是你不那样告诉他的话,他就不会有任何记忆保留下来。将普通的梦境极为迅速地遗忘掉是一个常见的事实。

第六个证明:在一个音乐和弦中,几个音符以相对简单的比率振动。心灵必须无意识地将那些振动计算在内,并且由于它发现了这样的简单性而感到高兴。

答复:由简单的比率所产生的大脑过程,可能和将这些比率进行比较的意识过程一样,是直接使人愉快的。不需要有意识的或者是无意识的计算。

第七个证明:我们每时每刻都在做出理论判断和情绪反应,并且表现出实践的倾向,对此我们不能给出清楚的逻辑理由,但是这却是来自某些假设的好的推论。我们知道的比我们能够说的要多。我们的结论先于我们对其根据做出分析的能力。一个孩子虽然对与同一个事物相等的两个事物彼此也相等这一公理全然无知,却仍然能正确地将它应用于他的具体判断之中。一个无法以抽象的术语理解全部内容的农民,却可以使用它。

“我们很少有意识地思考我们的房子是如何粉刷的,它的色调是什么,我们的家具是什么样式的,或者门是朝右开还是朝左开,是朝里开还是朝外开。但是,我们是多么迅速地注意到了这所有东西中每一个东西的变化啊！想想你最经常打开的那扇门,如果可以的话说出它是朝右还是朝左开,朝里开还是朝外开。然而,在你开门的时候,你从来也不曾把手放在错误的一边去找插销,从来也不曾推开本来是应该拉开的门……你朋友的脚步有什么样的精确特征使得你在他正走来的时候能够认出它?你曾经

Did you ever consciously think the idea, 'if I run into a solid piece of matter I shall get hurt, or be hindered in my progress'? and do you avoid running into obstacles because you ever distinctly conceived, or consciously acquired and thought, that idea?"①

Most of our knowledge is at all times potential We act in accordance with the whole drift of what we have learned, but few items rise into consciousness at the time. Many of them, however, we may recall at will. All this co-operation of unrealized principles and facts, of potential knowledge, with our actual thought is quite inexplicable unless we suppose the perpetual existence of an immense mass of *ideas in an unconscious state*, all of them exerting a steady pressure and influence upon our conscious thinking, and many of them in such continuity with it as ever and anon to become conscious themselves.

Reply. No such mass of ideas is supposable. But there are all kinds of short-cuts in the brain; and processes not aroused strongly enough to give any 'idea' distinct enough to be a premise, may, nevertheless, help to determine just that resultant process of whose psychic accompaniment the said idea *would* be a premise, if the idea existed at all. A certain overtone may be a feature of my friend's voice and may conspire with the other tones thereof to arouse in my brain the process which suggests to my consciousness his name. And yet I may be ignorant of the overtone *perse*, and unable, even when he speaks, to tell whether it be there or no. It leads me to the *idea of the name*; but it produces in me no such cerebral process as that to which the *idea of* the overtone would correspond. And similarly of our learning. Each subject we learn leaves behind it a modification of the brain, which makes it impossible for the latter to react upon things just as it did before; and the result of the difference may be a tendency to act, though

---

① J. E. Maude: 'The Unconscious in Education,' in 'Education' voI L. p. 401 (1882).

有意识地思考过这个观念‘如果我撞上一块坚硬的物质，我就会受伤，或者我的前进就会受到阻碍’吗？而且你避免撞上障碍物是因为你曾经清楚地构思过那个观念，或者有意识地获得并思考过那个观念吗？”①

我们的大部分知识总是潜在的。我们按照我们所习得的东西的整体流动来行动，但是当时只有极少数的东西进入到了意识中。然而，我们可以随意回忆起其中很多东西。所有这些未被认识到的原理和事实、这些潜在的知识与我们的思想的合作，都是完全无法解释的，除非我们假定有大量的观念以一种无意识状态永久地存在着，所有观念都对我们的有意识的思维施加着稳定的压力和影响，而且其中很多观念和它处于这样一种连续性，即它们自己不久就会变成有意识的。

答复：难以想像有这么多观念。但是，在大脑中确实存在各种捷径；并且有些过程没有被那么强烈地激起，因而不足以产生任何清楚得足以成为一个前提的“观念”，不过这些过程可以帮助确定一种作为结果而发生的过程，而这些过程的精神伴随物，即所说的观念可以是一个前提，如果观念确实存在的话。某个泛音可能是我朋友的声音的一个特征，并且它可以与其中的其他音一起在我的大脑中引起向我的意识提示出我朋友的名字的过程。然而，我对那个泛音本身可以是无知的，并且甚至当他在说话的时候都不能分辨出它是否出现了。它将我引向那个名字的观念；但是它在我这里并没有引起与那个泛音观念相应的大脑过程。这和我们的学习相类似。我们所学的每一个问题都使得大脑此后发生了更改，这使得大脑以后不可能对事情做出和以前一样的反应；并且差异的结果可能就是行动的倾向，虽然没有观念

① J.E.莫德：《教育中的无意识》，《教育》，第1卷，第401页(1882年)。

with no idea, much as we should *if* we were consciously thinking about the subject. The becoming conscious of the latter at will is equally readily explained as a result of the brain-modification. This, as Wundt phrases it, is a 'predisposition' to bring forth the conscious idea of the original subject, a pre-disposition which other stimuli and brain-processes may convert into an actual result. But such a predisposition is no 'unconscious idea;' it is only a particular collocation of the molecules in certain tracts of the brain.

Eighth Proof. Instincts, as pursuits of ends by appropriate means, are manifestations of intelligence; but as the ends are not foreseen, the intelligence must be unconscious.

Reply. Chapter XXIV will show that all the phenomena of instinct are explicable as actions of the nervous system, mechanically discharged by stimuli to the senses.

Ninth Proof. In sense-perception we have results in abundance, which can only be explained as conclusions drawn by a process of unconscious inference from data given to sense. A small human image on the retina is referred, not to a pygmy, but to a distant man of normal size. A certain gray patch is inferred to be a white object seen in a dim light. Often the inference leads us astray: e. g., pale gray against pale green looks red, because we take a wrong premise to argue from. We think a green film is spread over everything; and knowing that under such a film a red thing would look gray, we wrongly infer from the gray appearance that a red thing must be there. Our study of space-perception in Chapter XVIII will give abundant additional examples both of the truthful and illusory percepts which have been explained to result from unconscious logic operations.

Reply. That chapter will also in many cases refute this explanation. Color- and light-contrast are certainly purely sensational affairs,

相伴随,但却和假如我们想到了那个问题,我们就应该去做是一样的。随意地变得对后者有意识了,这同样可以作为大脑变化的一个结果而容易地加以解释。如冯特所说,这是一种产生对原先问题的有意识观念的"倾向",一种其他刺激和大脑过程可以将其转变为真实结果的倾向。但是,这样一种倾向不是"无意识观念",它只是分子在大脑的某些神经束中的一种特殊排列。

第八个证明:本能,作为用适当的手段对目标的追求,是理智的表现;但是,由于目标不是预知的,所以理智一定是无意识的。

答复:第 24 章将会表明,所有的本能现象都可以作为神经系统的活动而加以解释,通过刺激,它们被机械地释放到了感官中。

第九个证据:在感官知觉中,我们有大量的结果,它们只能作为通过无意识的推理过程从赋予感官的资料中得出的结论而加以解释。视网膜上的小人图像不是被推断为一个小矮人,而是被推断为远处一个身材标准的人。某个灰色的斑纹被推断为在黯淡的光线下看到的一个白色的物体。这样的推断经常将我们引入歧途:例如,以淡绿色为背景的淡灰色看上去是红色的,因为我们使用了一个错误的前提来进行推论。我们认为一层绿色的薄膜覆盖了一切;并且知道在这样一层薄膜之下一个红色的东西看上去是灰色的,我们错误地从这种灰色的现象之下推断出一个红色的东西一定存在于那里。我们在 18 章关于空间知觉的研究中将给出大量其他例子,这些例子是关于曾被解释为由无意识逻辑活动所导致的真的和虚幻的知觉的例子。

答复:在很多情况下那一章节的内容也可以反驳这一解释。色对比和光对比无疑纯粹是感觉事件,推论不参与其中。赫林已

in which inference plays no part. This has been satisfactorily proved by Hering,[1]and shall be treated of again in Chapter XVII Our rapid judgments of size, shape, distance, and the like, are best explained as processes of simple cerebral association. Certain sense-impressions directly stimulate brain-tracts, of whose activity ready-made conscious percepts are the immediate psychic counterparts. They do this by a mech-anism either connate or acquired by habit. It is to be remarked that Wundt and Helmholtz, who in their earlier writings did more than any one to give vogue to the notion that unconscious inference is a vi-tal factor in sense-percep-tiou, have seen fit on later occasions to modify their views and to admit that results *like* those of reasoning may accrue without any actual reasoning process unconsciously taking place,[2]Maybe the excessive and riotous applications made by Hart-mann of their principle have led them to this change. It would be nat-ural to feel towards him as the sailor in the story felt towards the horse who got his foot into the stirrup, — " If you ' re going to get on, I must get off. "

Hartmann fairly boxes the compass of the universe with the prin-ciple of unconscious thought For him there is no namable thing that does not exemplify it But his logic is so lax and his failure to consider the most obvious alternatives so complete that it would, on the whole, be a waste of time to look at his arguments in detail. The same is true of Schopenhauer, in whom the mythology reaches its climax. The vis-ual perception, for example, of an object in space results, according to him, from the intellect performing the following operations, all un-conscious. First, it apprehends the inverted retinal image and turns it right side up, constructing *flat space* as & preliminary operation;

---

① Zur Lehre vom Lichtsinne (1878).

② Cf. Wundt: Ueber den Einfluss der Philosophic, etc. -Antritlsrede 1876), pp. 10 – 11;-Helmholtz: Die Thatsachen in der Wahrnehmung, 1879), p. 27.

经令人满意地证实了这一点,[①]这在十七章中再作讨论。我们对尺寸、形状、距离等等的快速判断最好应解释为简单的大脑联结过程。特定的感官印象直接刺激大脑神经束,现成的有意识的知觉是这些大脑神经束的活动的直接精神配对物。它们或者是通过先天的,或者是由习惯获得的机制来完成这种活动的。应当谈及的是,冯特和赫姆霍尔茨在他们的早期著作中为了使无意识推论在感官知觉中是一个至关重要的因素这一观念盛行起来,做的工作比任何人都多,他们后来看到,更改他们的观点,并且承认类似于推论结果的那些结果可以在没有任何真实的无意识推理过程发生的情况下产生是合适的。[②] 也许是哈特曼对他们的原理的过分的放纵应用使他们做出了这样的改变。很自然,他们对他的感受就像是故事中水手对马的感受一样,那个水手将他的脚放进马镫里,——"如果你准备继续前进,我就必须下来。"

哈特曼凭借着无意识思维原理相当彻底地变更了宇宙。在他看来,所有可命名的事物都可以作为这一原理的例子。但是他的逻辑是如此的松散,而且他对考虑最明显的不同观点疏忽得是如此的彻底,以至于总体来说,详细地考察他的论证是在浪费时间。这种说法同样适用于叔本华,在他那里,神话达到了它的极致。例如,根据他的观点,对于一个存在于空间中的视知觉是由于智性执行了下述完全无意识的操作而造成的。首先,它理解倒转的视网膜形象,并且把它正过来,这样一来,作为初步的操作便

① 《光感原理》(1878 年)。

② 参见冯特:《论哲学的影响及其他——就职演说》(1876 年),第 10 ~11 页;——赫姆霍尔茨:《感觉中的事实》(1879 年),第 27 页。

then it computes from the angle of convergence of the eye-balls that the two retinal images must be the projection of but a single *object*; thirdly, it constructs the third dimension and sees this object *solid*; fourthly, it assigns its *distance*; and fifthly, in each and all of these operations it gets the objective character of what it 'constructs' by unconsciously inferring it as the only possible *cause* of some sensation which it unconsciously feels. ①Comment on this seems hardly called for. It is, as I said, pure mythology.

None of these facts, then, appealed to so confidently in proof of the existence of ideas in an unconscious state, prove anything of the sort. They prove either that conscious ideas were present which the next instant were forgotten; or they prove that certain results, *similar* to results of reasoning, may be wrought out by rapid brain-processes to which no ideation seems attached. But there is one more argument to be alleged, less obviously insufficient than those which we have reviewed, and demanding a new sort of reply.

Tenth Proof. There is a great class of experiences in our mental life which may be described as discoveries that a subjective condition which we have been having is really something different from what we had supposed. We suddenly find ourselves bored by a thing which we thought we were enjoying well enough; or in love with a person whom we imagined we only liked. Or else we deliberately analyze our motives, and find that at bottom they contain jealousies and cupidities which we little suspected to be there. Our feelings towards people are perfect wells of motivation, unconscious of itself, which introspection brings to light. And our sensations likewise: we constantly

---

① Of. Satz vom Grunde, pp. 59-65. Compare also F. Zöllner's Natut der Kometen, pp. 342 ff., and 425

构建了一个平面空间；然后，它通过眼球聚焦的角度计算出两个视网膜上的意象一定只能是一个对象的投影；第三，它构建出了第三维度，并且将这一对象看作是立体的；第四，它将距离赋值给这一物体；第五，在所有的这些操作当中，通过无意识地推断出它是理智无意识地感受到的一些感觉的唯一可能的起因，理智获得了它所“构建”的东西的客观特征。① 对此似乎不需要做出任何评论。如我所说，它纯粹是神话。

那么，在无意识状态观念存在的证明中，人们非常自信地使用的那些事实，都不能证明任何这一类的问题。它们或者证明了有意识的观念出现了，而在下一个瞬间它又被遗忘了；或者证明了某些与推论结果相似的结果，可以通过似乎没有观念作用附着其上的快速的大脑过程而形成。接下来，这里还要提出一个论证，它不像我们已经评论过的那些证明那样显然是不充分的，对它需要给出一种新的回答。

第十个证明：在我们的精神生活中，存在着很大一类经验，它们可以被描述为这样一种发现，即我们所一直具有的主观条件实际上是某种与我们的假设有所不同的东西。我们突然发现自己对我们以为自己一直非常喜欢的事情感到厌烦；或者爱上了一个我们以为自己仅仅是喜欢的人。又或者我们有意分析我们的动机，发现实际上它们包含我们很少觉察到其存在的嫉妒和贪婪。我们对人们的情感是完美的动机之源，它本身是无意识的，是内省将它显现了出来。并且我们的感觉也同样如此：我们不断地在我

① 参见《基本原理》，第 59 ~ 65 页。也可以比较 F. 佐尔纳的《彗星的性质》，第 342 页以后，以及 425 页。

discover new elements in sensations which we have been in the habit of receiving all our days, elements, too, which have been there from the first, since otherwise we should have been unable to distinguish the sensations containing them from others nearly allied. The elements must exist, for we use them to discriminate by; but they must exist in an unconscious state, since we so completely fail to single them out. ① The books of the analytic school of psychology abound in examples of the kind. Who knows the countless associations that mingle with his each and every thought? Who can pick apart all the nameless feelings that stream in at every moment from his various internal organs, muscles, heart, glands, lungs, etc., and compose in their totality his sense of bodily life? Who is aware of the part played by feelings of innervation and suggestions of possible muscular exertion in all his judgments of distance, shape, and size? Consider, too, the difference between a sensation which we simply *have* and one which we *attend to*. Attention gives results that seem like fresh creations; and yet the feelings and elements of feeling which it reveals must have been already there-in an unconscious state. We all know *practically* the difference between the so-called sonant and the so-called surd consonants, between D, B, Z, G, V, and T, P, S, K, F, respectively. But comparatively few persons know the difference *theoretically*, until their attention has been called to what it is, when, they perceive it readily enough. The sonants are nothing but the surds plus a certain element, which is alike in all, superadded. That element is the laryngeal sound with which they are uttered, surds having no such accompaniment When we hear the sonant letter, both its component elements must really be in our mind; but we remain unconscious of what they really are, and mistake the letter for a simple quality of sound until an effort of attention teaches us its two components.

---

① Cf. the statements from Helmholtz to be found later in Chapter XIII.

们每天已经习惯获得的感觉中发现新的元素,这些元素也以应该从一开始就存在,因为否则的话我们将不能把包含它们的感觉与几乎同属一系的其他感觉区别开来。这些元素必须存在,因为我们使用它们来进行区分;但是它们必须在无意识状态下存在,因为我们完全不能将它们挑选出来。① 在心理分析学派的书中充满了这种例子。谁知道那些无数的与他的每个思想混合在一起的联系呢?谁能拆散每时每刻从他的内部器官、肌肉、心脏、腺、肺等流入的不可名状的感觉,并且从整体上构成他对肉体生命的感觉呢?在他对距离、形状和大小的判断中,谁能意识到对神经支配的感受与对可能肌肉运用的暗示所起的作用呢?也思考一下我们只是拥有的感觉与我们注意到的感觉之间的差别。由注意产生的结果似乎像是全新的创造;但是它揭示出的感受和感受元素肯定已经存在于那里了——以一种无意识状态。我们在实践上都知道 D、B、Z、G、V 与 T、P、S、K、F 之间分别存在着所谓浊辅音和清辅音之间的区别。但是,除非人们完全准备好了要感知它们,并且他们的注意力已经被引到了它是什么这一问题上了,否则相比较而言有很少的人在理论上知道这种区别。浊辅音不是别的,就是清音再加上某一特定的元素,这元素在所有的浊辅音中都是一样的,是外加上去的。那个元素是浊辅音发出时所使用的一种喉音,清音没有这样的伴随物。当我们听到浊辅音字母时,它的两个组成元素都必须真正存在于我们心中;但是,我们对它们真正是什么却一直是无意识的,并且将那个字母错当成一种简单的声音性质,直到通过尽力的注意,我们才了解它的两个组成部分。

---

① 参见来自赫姆霍尔茨的论述,可在后面的第 13 章中找到它。

There exist a host of sensations which most men pass through life and never attend to, and consequently have only in an unconscious way. The feelings of opening and closing the glottis, of making tense the tympanic membrane, of accommodating for near vision, of intercepting the passage from the nostrils to the throat, are instances of what I mean. Every one gets these feelings many times an hour; but few readers, probably, are conscious of exactly what sensations are meant by the names I have just used. All these facts, and an enormous number more, seem to prove conclusively that, in addition to the fully conscious way in which an idea may exist in the mind, there is also an unconscious way; that it is unquestionably the same identical idea which exists in these two ways; and that therefore any arguments against the mind-stuff theory, based on the notion that *esse* in our mental life is *sentiri*, and that an idea must consciously be felt as what it is, fall to the ground.

Objection. These reasonings are one tissue of confusion. Two states of mind which refer to the same external reality, or two states of mind the later one of which refers to the earlier, are described as the same state of mind, or 'idea,' published as it were in two editions; and then whatever qualities of the second edition are found openly lacking in the first are explained as having really been there, only in an 'unconscious' way. It would be difficult to believe that intelligent men could be guilty of so patent a fallacy, were not the history of psychology there to give the proof. The psychological stock-in-trade of some authors is the belief that two thoughts about one thing are virtually the same thought, and that this same thought may in subsequent reflections become more and more *conscious* of what it really was all along from the first But once make the distinction between simply *having an* idea at the moment of its presence and subsequently knowing all sorts of

存在着很多感觉，大部分人一生都在经历着它们，但却从来没有注意过，因此这些人只是以一种无意识的方式拥有着它们。打开和关闭声门的感受，拉紧鼓膜的感受，为适应近距离视觉而进行调节的感受，中断从鼻孔到咽喉的通道的感受，都是我所说的意思的例子。每个人在一小时之内多次获得这些感受；但是可能只有极少数的读者能够正确地意识到我刚刚使用过的那些名称所指的是一些什么样的感觉。所有这些事实，以及更加大量的事实似乎结论性地证明了，一个观念除了可以以完全有意识的方式在心中存在以外，这里还有一种无意识的方式支持其存在；同一个观念无疑以这两种方式存在着；由于任何反对精神素材理论的论证都建立在如下这种观点之上，即在我们精神生活中的存在就是感觉，并且一个观念必须有意识地被感觉为它所是的东西，因此它们便垮台了。

反对的理由：这些推论混乱连篇。指称同一个外部实在的两种心理状态，或者其中的后一种心理状态指称前一种心理状态的两种心理状态，被描述为同样的心理状态或"观念"，按照原来的样子以两个版本发表出来；于是，在第二个版本中可以发现在第一个版本中明显缺乏的任何性质，这些性质被解释为已经真实地存在于那里，只不过是以一种"无意识的"方式存在着。如果不是有心理学的历史作证，很难相信有才智的人会犯如此明显的错误。一些作者的心理学的惯用手段是这样一种信念，即关于同一个事物的两种思想事实上是同一个思想，并且这同一个思想可以在后来的反思中逐渐地意识到它从开始以来一直是什么。但是，一旦在观念出现之时简单地获有了一个观念与后来知道了关于这个观念的各种事情之间做出区分；而且在被认作是主观事实的

things *about it*; make moreover that between a state of mind itself, taken as a subjective fact, on the one hand, and the objective thing it knows, on the other, and one has no difficulty in escaping from the labyrinth.

Take the latter distinction first: Immediately all the arguments based on sensations and the new features in them which attention brings to light fall to the ground. The sensations of the B and the V when we attend to these sounds and analyze out the laryngeal contribution which makes them differ from P and F respectively, are *different sensations* from those of the B and the V taken in a simple way. They stand, it is true, or the *same letters*, and thus mean the *same outer realities*; but they are different mental affections, and certainly depend on widely different processes of cerebral activity. It is unbelievable that two mental states so different as the passive reception of a sound as a whole, and the analysis of that whole into distinct ingredients by voluntary attention, should be due to processes at all similar. And the subjective difference does not consist in that the first-named state *is* the second in an 'un-conscious' form. It is an absolute psychic difference, even greater than that between the states to which two different surds will give rise. The same is true of the other sensations chosen as examples. The man who learns for the first time how the closure of his glottis feels, experiences in this discovery an. absolutely new psychic modification, the like of which he never had before. He had another feeling before, a feeling incessantly renewed, and of which the same glottis was the organic starting point; but that was not the later feeling in an 'unconscious' state; it was a feeling *sui generis altogether*, although it took cognizance of the same bodily part, the glottis. We shall see, hereafter, that the same reality can be cognized by an endless number of psychic states, which may differ toto coelo among themselves, without ceasing on that account to refer to the reality in question. Each of them is a conscious fact; none of them has any mode of being whatever except a certain way of being felt at the moment of being present. It is simply unintelligible and fantastical to say, because they point to the same outer reality,

心理状态自身这一方面与它所知道的客观事实这另一方面之间做出区分,那么人们就可以毫无困难地逃离那个迷宫了。

首先来讨论第一个区分:所有以通过注意力而显现出来的感觉和这些感觉中的新的特征为基础的论证,立刻就垮台了。当我们注意B和V的声音,并且分析出是喉部的作用使得它们分别与P和F不同时,对B和V的感觉就和以简单的方式获得的B和V的感觉有所不同。确实,它们代表相同的字母,并且因此意指相同的外部事实;但是它们是不同的心理倾向,并且的确依赖于差别极大的不同的大脑活动过程。由于一个要将声音作为一个整体来被动地接受,并且另一个通过有意识的注意要将那个整体分析为截然不同的组成部分,因此将这两种如此不同的心理状态归因于完全相似的过程是令人难以置信的。并且这种主观的差别并不是在于那个起先被命名的状态就是以一种无意识状态存在的第二种状态。这是一种纯粹的精神差别,甚至比两个不同的清音所引起的差别还要大。其他被选中作为例子的感觉也同样如此。第一次习得关闭声门的感受是什么样的人,在这次发现中体验了一次全新的心理改变,像这样的事件他以前从来没有体验过。他以前有另一个感受,一个不断更新的感受,同样的声门是这个感受的器官起点;但那并不是处于"无意识"状态之下的后来的感受;它是一种完全独特的感觉,尽管它使我们认识到相同的身体部分——声门。此后我们将会看到,相同的实在可以通过数不清的精神状态被认识到,这些精神状态之间可以有天壤之别,却并不因此而停止指称那个相关的实在。它们每一个都是有意识的事实;除了在它们出现的那一时刻被感受到的这种方式以外,它们没有任何其他的存在方式。因为它们指向了同一个外部

that they must therefore be so many editions of the same 'idea,' now in a conscious and now in an 'unconscious' phase. There is only one 'phase' in which an idea can be, and that is a fully conscious condition. If it is not in that condition, then it is not at all Something else is, in its place. The something else may be a merely physical brain-process, or it may be another conscious idea. Either of these things may perform much the same *function* as the first idea, refer to the same object, and roughly stand in the same relations to the upshot of our thought. But that is no reason why we should throw away the logical principle of identity in psychology, and say that, however it may fare in the outer world, the mind at any rate is a place in which a thing can be all kinds of other things without ceasing to be itself as well.

Now take the other cases alleged, and the other distinction, that namely between *having* a mental state and knowing all *about* it The truth is here even simpler to unravel. When I decide that I have, without knowing it, been for several weeks in love, I am simply giving a name to a state which previously *I have not named*, but which was fully conscious; which had no residual mode of being except the manner in which it was conscious; and which, though it was a feeling towards the same person for whom I now have a much more inflamed feeling, and though it continuously led into the latter, and is similar enough to be called by the same name, is yet in no sense identical with the latter, and least of all in an 'unconscious' way. Again, the feelings from our viscera and other dimly-felt organs, the feelings of innervation (if such there be), and those of muscular exertion which, in our spatial judgments, are supposed unconsciously to determine what we shall perceive, are just exactly what we feel them, perfectly determinate conscious states, not vague editions of other conscious states.

实在,所以它们就一定是同一个“观念”的如此众多的版本,时而处于意识状态,时而处于“无意识”状态,这仅仅是一种令人难以理解和凭空想像的说法。这里只有一种“状态”观念能够存在其中,并且那是一种完全的有意识状态。如果它不是以那种状态存在,那么它就完全不存在。某种别的东西处于它的位置上。这种别的东西可以是一种单纯的物理的大脑过程,或者它可以是另外一个有意识的观念。这两种东西中的任何一种都可以行使和第一个观念差不多相同的功能,意指相同的客体,并且与我们的思维结果处于一种大致相同的关系中!但是,那并非是我们应该在心理学中将逻辑的同一性原理抛弃掉的原因,并且说不论它在外部世界中的进展如何,心灵无论如何都是这样一个地方,在其中一个东西可以是其他各种东西,同时它也一直是它自己。

现在讨论所提到的其他的例子,以及另外一个区别,即拥有一种心理状态和知道关于它的全部事情的区别。在这里拆解和澄清真理将更加简单。当我判定自己在不知道的情况下已经坠入爱河好几个星期的时候,我仅仅是赋予了我以前不曾命名、却完全有意识的状态一个名称;这种状态除了以有意识的方式存在之外,它没有任何其他的存在方式;尽管它是我现在对其怀有一种热烈得多的情感的人的感受,尽管它不断地向后者发展,并且与后者相似得足以用同一个名称来命名,然而它与后者绝不是同一的,更不是以一种“无意识”的方式与后者是同一的。此外,来自于我们的内脏和被隐约感受到的器官的感受,对神经支配的感受(如果存在这样的感受的话),以及在我们的空间判断中,被无意识地假定为决定我们将要知觉的东西的那种对肌肉运动的感受,的确就是我们对它们所感受到的内容 处于完全确定的意识状态,而不是处于其他意

They may be faint and weak; they may be very vague cognizers of the same realities which other conscious states cognize and name exactly; they may be unconscious of much in the reality which the other states are conscious of. But that does not make them *in themselves* a whit dim or vague or unconscious. They *are eternally* as they feel when they exist, and can, neither actually nor potentially, be identified with anything else than their own faint selves. A faint feeling may be looked back upon and classified and understood in its relations to what went before or after it in the stream of thought. But it, on the one hand, and the later state of mind which knows all these things about it, on the other, are surely not two conditions, one conscious and the other 'unconscious,' of the same identical psychic fact. It is the destiny of thought that, on the whole, our early ideas are superseded by later ones, giving fuller accounts of the same realities. But none the less do the earlier and the later ideas preserve their own several substantive identities as so many several successive states of mind. To believe the contrary would make any definite science of psychology impossible. The only identity to be found among our successive ideas is their similarity of cognitive or representative function as dealing with the same objects. Identity of *being*, there is none; and I believe that throughout the rest of this volume the reader will reap the advantages of the simpler way of formulating the facts which is here begun. ①

---

① The text was written before Professor Lipps's Grundtatsachen des Seelenlebens (1883) came into my hands. In Chapter III of that book the notion of unconscious thought is subjected to the clearest and most searching criticism which it has yet received, Some passages are so similar to what I have myself written that I must quote them in a note. After proving that dimness and clearness, incompleteness and completeness do not pertain to a state

识状态的模糊版本中。它们可能是模糊的和微弱的;它们可能是对其他意识状态能够确切地认识和命名的一些同样的实在的非常模糊的认识物;对于其他状态能够意识到的实在中的许多东西而言,它们可以是无意识的。但是这一点也没有使它们自身变得暗淡、模糊起来,或者变成无意识的。当它们存在时,它们永远和它们所感受的一样,而且,除了它们微弱的自身之外,不论是实际地还是潜在地,它们都不能和任何别的东西是同一的。根据在思想之流中的一个微弱的感受与在它之前或者之后的东西的关系,它可以被追忆、被归类并且被理解。但是,一方面是它,而另一方面是知道关于它的所有这些事情的后来的心理状态,这两者肯定不是关于同一个精神事实的两种状态,其中一种是有意识的,另一种是无意识的。大体上来说,思想的命运是,前面的观念被后面的观念所取代,同时给出对相同实在的更全面的解释。但是,先前的观念和后来的观念与许多单独的、相继的心理状态一样,依然保持着它们自己单独的实体性身份。如果要相信相反的观点的话,就不可能有任何确定的心理科学了。在我们相继的观念中所发现的唯一的统一性就是它们处理相同客体时其认知和表象功能的相似性。就存在的同一性而言,这里是无;我相信在本书的所有剩余部分中,读者将会受益于从这里开始的简洁地陈述这些事实的简单方式。①

---

① 原文写于我得到里普斯教授的《精神生活的基本事实》(1883 年)之前。在那本书的第三章,无意识思想的观点遭受到了它迄今所受到的最清晰和最透彻的批评,一些段落与我自己写出的东西是如此的相似,以至于我必须在注释中引用它们。在证明模糊与清晰、不完全与完全不是同样地属

So we seem not only to have ascertained the unintelligibility of the notion that a mental fact can be two things at once, and that what seems like one feeling, of blueness for example, or of hatred, may really and 'unconsciously' be ten thousand elementary feelings which do not resemble blueness or hatred at all, but we find that we can express all the observed facts in other ways. The mind-stuff theory, however, though scotched, is, we may be sure, not killed. If we ascribe consciousness to unicellular animalcules, then single cells can have it, and analogy should make us ascribe it to the several cells of the brain, each individually taken.

---

of mind *as such*-since every state of mind must be *exactly* what it is, and nothing else-but only pertain to the way in which states of mind stand for objects, which they more or less dimly, more or less clearly, *represent*; Lipps takes the case of those sensations which attention is said to make more clear. "I perceive an object," he says, " now in clear daylight, and again at night. Call the content of the day-perception *a*, and that of the evening-perception a^1. There will probably be a considerable difference between *a* and a^1. The colors of *a* will be varied and intense, and will be sharply bounded by each other; those of a^1 will be less luminous, and less strongly contrasted, and will approach a common gray or brown, and merge more into each other. Both percepts, however, as such, are completely determinate and distinct from all others. The colors of a^1 appear before my eye neither more nor less decidedly dark and blurred than the colors of *a* appear bright and sharply bounded. But now I know, or believe I know, that one and the same real Object A corresponds to both *a* and a^1. I am convinced, moreover, that *a* represents A better than does a^1. Instead, however, of giving to my conviction this, its only correct, expression, and keeping the content of my consciousness and the real object, the representation and what it means, distinct from each other, I substitute the real object for the content of the consciousness, and talk of the experience as if it consisted in one and the same object (namely, the surreptitiously introduced real one), constituting twice over the content of my consciousness, once in a clear and distinct, the other time in an obscure and vague fashion. I talk now of a distincter and of a less distinct *consciousness* of A, whereas I am only justified in talking of two consciousnesses, *a* and a^1, equally distinct *in se*, but to which the supposed external object A corresponds with different degrees of distinctness." (P. 38-9.)

因此,我们似乎不仅确定了下述观点是不可理解的,即一个心理事实能够同时是两个东西,而且似乎像是一种感受的东西,例如蓝色的感受或者憎恨的感受,可以真实地和"无意识地"是成千上万种与蓝色和憎恨一点也不相似的基本感受;但是我们发现我们能够以其他方式表达所有观察到的事实。然而,我们可以确定的是,尽管精神素材理论受到了打击,但是并没有被摧毁。如果我们将意识归结于单细胞微生物的话,那么单个细胞就可以拥有意识,而且通过类推我们就可以将它归结于大脑中每一个被个别

于一种心灵状态——因为每一个心理状态必须完全是其所是,并且不是别的任何东西——而仅仅属于心理状态在不同程度上模糊地或者清晰地表象客体的方式之后;里普斯列举了那些据说注意力能使之更加清晰的感觉的例子。他说:"现在在晴朗的白天,此后在夜里,我知觉一个对象。将白天知觉的内容称作 a,并且将夜晚知觉的内容称作 a^1。在 a 和 a^1 之间可能存在相当大的差别。a 的颜色斑驳并且强烈,并且这些颜色之间有明显的界限;a^1 的颜色则不那么明亮,对比没有那么强烈,并且接近一种共同的灰色或褐色,并且颜色之间更多地混合起来。然而,像这样的两种知觉都完全是确定的,并且与所有其他的知觉截然不同。与 a 的颜色在我眼前看上去是明亮的和界限清晰的相比,a^1 的颜色看上去恰恰绝对是黯淡的和模糊的。但是现在我知道,或者我相信我知道,同一个实在的客体 A 与 a 和 a^1 都相符合。而且我相信,a 比 a^1 更好地再现了 A。然而,我没有用这种唯一正确的表述来表达我的信念,并且让我的意识内容与真实的客体 A、表象与它的意义,都彼此区分开来,相反,我用意识内容替代了实在的客体,并且在谈论经验时就好像它包含在同一个客体中(即被偷偷摸摸地引入进来的实在的客体),它创建了我们的意识内容两次,一次以清晰和明显的方式,另一次以朦胧和模糊的方式。现在我在谈论关于 A 的一种比较明显的意识和一种不那么明显的意识,然而我只能正当的谈论 a 和 a^1 这两种意识,它们自身同样的清楚,而且所假定的外部客体 A 以不同的清晰程度与它们相符合。(第 38 ~39 页)

And what a convenience would it not be for the psychologist if, by the adding together of various doses of this separate-cell-consciousness, he could treat thought as a kind of stuff or material, to be measured out in great or small amount, increased and subtracted from, and baled about at will! He feels an imperious craving to be allowed to *construct* synthetically the successive mental states which he describes. The mind-stuff theory so easily admits of the construction being made, that it seems certain that 'man's unconquerable mind' will devote much future pertinacity and ingenuity to setting it on its legs again and getting it into some sort of plausible working-order. I will therefore conclude the chapter with some consideration of the remaining difficulties which beset the matter as it at present stands.

Difficulty Of Stating The Connection Between Mind And Brain.

It will be remembered that in our criticism of the theory of the integration of successive conscious units into a feeling of musical pitch, we decided that whatever integration there was was that of the air-pulses into a simpler and simpler sort of physical effect, as the propagations of material change got higher and higher in the nervous system. At last, we said (p. 23), there results some simple and massive process in the auditory centres of the hemispherical cortex, to which, *as a whole*, the feeling of musical pitch directly corresponds. Already, in discussing the localization of functions in the brain, I had said (pp. 158–9) that consciousness accompanies the stream of innervation through that organ and varies in quality with the character of the currents, being mainly of things seen if the occipital lobes are much involved, of things heard if the action is focalized in the temporal lobes, etc., etc.; and I had added that a vague formula like this was as much as one could safely venture on in the actual state of physiology. The facts of mental deafness and blindness,

对待的单独的细胞。如果通过将不同剂量的这种单独细胞的意识加在一起,心理学家就能够将思想当作一种原料或者材料来对待,可以随意地用或大或小的量来对它进行测量,增加或者减少它,并且可以将它打包起来,那么这对于心理学家来说是多么方便啊！他感觉到一种迫切的渴望,渴望被允许对他所描述的连续的心理状态进行综合构建。精神素材理论这么容易地就认可了这种构建,因而似乎可以肯定的是,"人的不可征服的心灵"将会在未来更加顽强地和机智地致力于它的再次恢复,并使它进入某种看似合理的正常的运转状态。因此,我将对目前存在着的困扰这个问题的剩余难题做一些思考,并且以此来结束这一章。

陈述心脑间关系的困难

应当记得的是,在我们对连续意识单元聚合为乐音音高的感受的理论的批评中,我们断定,随着神经系统中的物质变化分布得越来越广泛,不管有什么样的聚合过程存在,这种聚合过程都是将空气振动聚合为一种越来越简单的物理结果。最后,我们说(第23页),在脑半球皮层的听觉中枢中导致了一些简单的和大规模的过程,对乐音音高的感受总体上直接与它相对应。在讨论大脑中的功能定位时,我已经说过(第158~159页),意识通过那个器官与神经支配流相伴随,并且在性质上随着神经流的特性而变化,如果大量地涉及到枕叶的话,它就主要是关于所见之物的,如果神经活动集中在颞叶,它就主要是关于所听之物的,等等,等等;而且我还补充说,像这样一种迷糊的方案就是人们在生理学发展的现状中至多可以安全提出的。心理失聪和失明的事实,以及听觉

of auditory and optical aphasia, show us that the whole brain must act together if certain thoughts are to occur. The consciousness, which is itself an integral thing not made of parts, 'corresponds' to the entire activity of the brain, whatever that may be, at the moment. This is a way of expressing the relation of mind and brain from which I shall not depart during the remainder of the book, because it expresses the bare phenomenal fact with no hypothesis, and is exposed to no such logical objections as we have found to cling to the theory of ideas in combination.

Nevertheless, this formula which is so unobjectionable if taken vaguely, positivistically, or scientifically, as a mere empirical law of concomitance between our thoughts and our brain, tumbles to pieces entirely if we assume to represent anything more intimate or ultimate by it. The ultimate of ultimate problems, of course, in the study of the relations of thought and brain, is to understand why and how such disparate things are connected at all. But before that problem is solved (if it ever is solved) there is a less ultimate problem which must first be settled. Before the connection of thought and brain can be explained, it must at least be *stated* in an elementary form; and there are great difficulties about so stating it. To state it in elementary form one must reduce it to its lowest terms and know which mental fact and which cerebral fact are, so to speak, in immediate juxtaposition. We must find the minimal mental fact whose being reposes directly on a brain-fact; and we must similarly find the minimal brain-event which will have a mental counterpart at all. Between the mental and the physical minima thus found there will be an immediate relation, the expression of which, if we had it, would be the elementary psycho-physic law.

Our own formula escapes the unintelligibility of psychic atoms by *taking the entire thought* (even of a complex object) *as the minimum*

和视觉失语症的事实向我们表明，如果某种思想要发生的话，整个大脑必须一起行动。意识自身是一个完整的、而不是由部分组成的东西，它同全部的大脑活动相对应，不管那在当时是什么。这是一种表达心脑关系的方法，在本书的剩余部分中我都不会抛弃这种方法，因为它无需提及假说就表达了赤裸裸的现象事实，而且不会暴露在如我们所发现的在坚持观念结合理论时所遭受到的那种逻辑责难之中。

不过，如果我们模糊地、实证地、或者科学地将这一方案当成一种单纯的关于我们的思想和我们的大脑相伴随的经验规律的话，它非常难以反驳，如果我们以为通过它可以表象任何更加本质或更加终极的东西的话，它就完全瓦解掉了。当然，在对思想和大脑的关系的研究中，最最终极的问题就是理解为什么这两种完全不同的东西竟会有联系，以及它们是如何联系起来的。但是在解决这个问题之前(如果它终究会得到解决的话)，这里有一个不那么终极的问题必须首先得到解决。在思想和大脑的关系能够被解释之前，它必须至少以一种基本的形式得到陈述；而要这样陈述它，还存在着极大的困难。要以一种基本的形式陈述它，人们就必须将它还原为其最低级的关系，并且知道哪个心理事实和哪个大脑事实可以说是直接并列着的。我们必须找到最小的心理事实，其存在直接依赖于大脑事实，并且我们必须同样找到最小的大脑事实，它无论如何都有一个心理对应物。在如此找到的精神的和物理的最小东西之间，将会存在一种直接的关系，对这种关系的表达，如果我们获有了它的话，就应当是基本的精神—物理规律。

我们自己的方案通过将整个思想(甚至是关于一个复杂对象

with which it deals on the mental side. But in taking the entire brain-process as its mini-mal fact on the material side it confronts other difficulties almost as bad.

In the first place, it ignores analogies on which certain critics will insist, those, namely, between the composition of the total brain-process and that of the *object* of the thought. The total brain-process is composed of parts, of simultaneous processes in the seeing, the hearing, the feeling, and other centres. The object thought of is also composed of parts, some of which are seen, others heard, others perceived by touch and muscular manipulation. "How then," these critics will say, "should the thought not itself be composed of parts, each the counterpart of a part of the object and of a part of the brain-process?" So natural is this way of looking at the matter that it has given rise to what is on the whole the most flourishing of all psychological systems-that of the Lock-ian school of associated ideas-of which school the mind-stuff theory is nothing but the last and subtlest offshoot.

The second difficulty is deeper still. *The 'entire brain-process ' is not a physical fact at all*. It is the appearance to an on looking mind of a multitude of physical facts. 'En-tire brain' is nothing but our name for the way in which a million of molecules arranged in certain positions may affect our sense. On the principles of the corpuscular or mechanical philosophy, the only realities are the separate molecules, or at most the cells. Their aggregation into a 'brain' is a fiction of popular speech. Such a fiction cannot serve as the objectively real counterpart to any psychic state whatever. Only a genuinely physical fact can so serve. But the molecular fact is the only genuine physical fact-whereupon we seem, if we are to have an elementary psycho-physic law at all, thrust right back upon something like the mind-stuff theory, for the molecular fact,

的思想)当作它用来处理精神方面问题的最小的东西从而避免了精神原子的不可理解性。但是在将整个大脑过程当作其物质方面的最小事实的时候,这个方案遇到了几乎同样糟糕的其他难题。

首先,它忽视了某些批评家所强调的类推,即整个大脑过程的组成与思想客体的组成之间的类推。整个大脑过程由部分所组成,由在视觉、听觉、触觉和其他中枢中同时进行的过程所组成。思想客体也由部分所组成,其中的一些是被看见的,另外一些是被听见的,还有一些是通过触摸和肌肉的运动而被知觉到的。这些批评家会说:“那么思想自身怎么不应当是由部分所组成,即客体的一个部分和大脑过程的一个部分的各个对应物呢?”看待问题的这种方式是如此的自然,以至于它产生了从整体上看是所有心理学体系中最为繁荣的一个体系——即主张联想观念的洛克学派体系——精神素材理论只不过是这一学派最后的和最精巧的一个分支。

第二个困难更加深刻。“整个大脑过程”根本不是一个物理事实。它对于一个旁观的心灵来说是许多物理事实的显现。“整个大脑”仅仅是我们用来称呼在特定位置上排列着的无数分子用来影响我们感觉的方式的名称。根据宇宙微粒论哲学或者机械论哲学的原理,唯一的实在是分离的分子,或者至多是细胞。它们聚合为大脑是大众言论的虚构。这样的一种虚构无论怎样也不能充当任何精神状态的客观的真实的对应物。只有真正的物理事实能够充当这种东西。而分子事实就是唯一真实的物理事实——如果我们无论如何要有一条基本的精神—物理规律,我们似乎又完全回到了某种像是精神素材理论的东西那里,因为作

being an element of the 'brain,' would seem naturally to correspond, not to the total thoughts, but to elements in the thought.

What shall we do? Many would find relief at this point in celebrating the mystery of the Unknowable and the 'awe' which we should feel at having such a principle to take final charge of our 'perplexities'. Others would rejoice that the finite and separatist view of things with which we started had at last developed its contradictions, and was about to lead us dialectically upwards to some 'higher synthesis' in which inconsistencies cease from troubling and logic is at rest. It may be a constitutional infirmity, but I can take no comfort in such devices for making a luxury of intellectual defeat. They are but spiritual chloroform. Better live on the ragged edge, better gnaw the file forever!

The Material-Monad Theory.

The most rational thing to do is to suspect that there may be a third possibility, an alternative supposition which we have not considered. Now there is an alternative supposition—a supposition moreover which has been frequently made in the history of philosophy, and which is freer from logical objections than either of the views we have ourselves discussed. It may be called the *theory of polyzoism or multiple monadism*; and it conceives the matter thus:

Every brain-cell has its own individual consciousness, which no other cell knows anything about, all individual consciousnesses being 'ejective' to each other. There is, however, among the cells one central or pontifical one to which *our* consciousness is attached. But the events of all the other cells physically influence this arch-cell; and through producing their joint effects on it, these other cells may be said to

为“大脑”元素的分子事实,似乎很自然地应当与思想中的元素相对应,而不是与整个思想相对应。

我们应该怎么办?此刻,很多人会在赞美那不可知事物的神秘中,会在这样一条原理最终掌管我们的混乱时我们所应该感受到的“敬畏”中得到慰藉。其他人会很高兴,我们所由以开始的对事物的有限的和分离主义式的看法最终揭露出了它的矛盾,并且将要引领我们辩证地向上达到某种“更高级的综合”,在这种综合中,矛盾不再令人烦恼,而且逻辑也停止了。这可能是一种生来就有的弱点,但是在这种使智性的失败变得很华贵的策略中我不能获得安慰。它们只是精神上的氯仿麻醉剂。最好是路途坎坷,最好是永远不懈地努力!

物质单子理论

可以做的最合理的事情就是猜想可能存在着第三种可能性,一种我们还没有考虑过的可供选择的推测。现在有一种可供选择的推测——而且是一种在哲学史上被经常做出的推测,它比我们自己已经讨论过的那两种观点都更有利于免除逻辑的反驳。它可以被称作多元物活论或者复合单子论;它是这样思考这个问题的:

每一个大脑细胞都有它自己的单独意识,所有其他的细胞对此都一无所知,所有单独的意识彼此都是“放逐的”。然而,在这些细胞中间,有一个我们的意识附着于其上的中心或者主宰细胞。但是所有其他的细胞事件都物理地影响着这个主宰细胞;并且通过对他产生共同的影响,这些其他细胞可以被称作是在“结

'combine.' The arch-cell is, in fact, one of those 'external media' without which we saw that no fusion or integration of a number of things can occur. The physical modifications of the arch-cell thus form a sequence of results in the production whereof every other cell has a share, so that, as one might say, every other cell is represented therein. And similarly, the conscious correlates to these physical modifications form a sequence of thoughts or feelings, each one of which is, as to its substantive being, an integral and uncompounded psychic thing, but each one of which may (in the exercise of its *cognitive* function) be *aware* of *THINGS* many and complicated in proportion to the number of other cells that have helped to modify the central cell.

By a conception of this sort, one incurs neither of the internal contradictions which we found to beset the other two theories. One has no unintelligible self-combining of psychic units to account for on the one hand; and on the other hand, one need not treat as the physical counterpart of the stream of consciousness under observation, a 'total brain-activity' which is non-existent as a genuinely physical fact. But, to offset these advantages, one has physiological difficulties and improbabilities. There is no cell or group of cells in the brain of such anatomical or functional pre-eminence as to appear to be the keystone or centre of gravity of the whole system. And even if there were such a cell, the theory of multiple monadism would, in strictness of thought, have no right to stop at it and treat it as a unit. The cell is no more a unit, materially considered, than the total brain is a unit. It is a compound of molecules, just as the brain is a compound of cells and fibres. And the molecules, according to the prevalent physical theories, are in turn compounds of atoms. The theory in question, therefore, if radically carried out, must set up for its elementary and irreducible psycho-physic couple, not the cell and its consciousness, but the primordial and eternal atom and its consciousness. We are back at Leibnitzian monadism, and therewith leave physiology behind us and dive into regions inaccessible to experience and verification;

合”。事实上,这主宰细胞是那些“外部媒介物”之一,我们知道,许多事物的融合或者聚合没有它们就不能发生。因此主宰细胞的物理更改形成了在其产生中每一个细胞都参与的一系列结果,因此正如人们可能会说的那样,每一个别的细胞在那里都得到了表象。同样,这些物理更改的意识相关物形成了一系列思想和感受,其中每一个思想和感受就其实体性存在而言都是一个完整的和非复合的精神事物,但是这每一个思想和感受(在其认知功能的行使中)都可能会意识到事物,这些事物在数量和复杂程度上与帮助了更改中心细胞的其他细胞的数量成正比。

通过这种概念,人们就不会招致我们已经发现的困扰着那其他两种理论的内部矛盾了。一方面,人们不用解释那种精神单元的不可理解的自我结合了;而另一方面,人们不用将作为一种真实的物理事实而不存在的“整个大脑活动”当作所考察的意识流的物理对应物来加以对待了。但是,人们有生理学方面的困难和不可能性,这抵消了这些优势。大脑中没有在解剖学方面或者在功能方面优秀得似乎是整个系统的拱心石或者是引力中心这样的细胞或者细胞群。并且即使存在这样一个细胞,从思维的严密性来说,复合单子论没有权利停留在它这里,并且把它作为一个单元来对待。从物质的方面来考虑,和整个大脑不是一个单元一样,细胞也不是一个单元。它是分子的复合物,就和大脑是细胞和纤维的复合物一样。根据盛行的物理学理论,分子依次又是原子的复合物。因此,如果要彻底贯彻相关理论的话,这种理论必须要确立其基本的并且不可还原的精神—物理对应物,不是细胞及其意识,而是原始的和永恒的原子及其意识。我们回到了莱布尼兹的单子论,并且随之将生理学留在了我们的身后,进入了经

and our doctrine, although not self-contradictory, becomes so remote and unreal as to be almost as bad as if it were. Speculative minds alone will take an interest in it; and. metaphysics, not psychology, will be responsible for its career. That the career may be a successful one must be admitted as a possibility—a theory which Leibnitz, Herbart, and Lotze have taken under their protection must have some sort of a destiny.

The Soul-Theory.

But is this my last word? By no means. Many readers have certainly been saying to themselves for the last few pages: "Why on earth doesn't the poor man say *the Soul* and have done with it?" Other readers, of anti-spiritualistic training and prepossessions, advanced thinkers, or popular evolutionists, will perhaps be a little surprised to find this much-despised word now sprung upon them at the end of so physiological a train of thought. But the plain fact is that all the arguments for a 'pontifical cell' or an 'arch-monad' are also arguments for that well-known spiritual agent in which scholastic psychology and com-mon-sense have always believed. And my only reason for beating the bushes so, and not bringing it in earlier as a possible solution of our difficulties, has been that by this procedure I might perhaps force some of these materialistic minds to feel the more strongly the logical respectability of the spiritualistic position. The fact is that one cannot afford to despise any of these great traditional objects of belief. Whether we realize it or not, there is always a great drift of reasons, positive and negative, towing us in their direction. If there be such entities as Souls in the universe, they may possibly be affected by the manifold occurrences that go on in the nervous centres.

验和实证无法达到的地方;而我们的学说,尽管没有自相矛盾,但却变得如此的遥远和不真实,以至于几乎和自相矛盾一样糟。只有思辨的心灵才会对它感兴趣;是形而上学,而不是心理学,将会对其进程负起责任。这种事业可能是成功的,这必须作为一种可能性而得到承认——在莱布尼兹、赫尔巴特和洛采的保护之下的理论一定有某种定数。

灵魂理论

但这就是我最后所说的话么?绝不是。很多读者在读前几页的时候一定对自己说过:"那个可怜的人究竟为什么不谈论灵魂,并且用它来解决问题呢?"其他接受过反唯灵论训练并且对其偏爱的读者、高深的思想家或者是流行的进化论者可能将会有些意外地发现,在带有如此浓厚的生理学意味的一连串思想的末尾,这个如今倍受轻视的词汇会突然出现在他们面前。但是明显的事实是,所有支持"主宰细胞"或者"主宰单子"的论证,也是支持那个为经院哲学心理学和常识理论所始终相信的广为人知的精神行动者的论证。我之所以这样到处搜索,并且没有在早些时候将它作为一种解决我们难题的可能方案提出来,就是因为通过这种程序,我可能会迫使一些这样的唯物主义者更加强烈地感觉到唯灵论立场在逻辑上值得尊敬之处。事实上,我们不能轻视任何一个传统的信仰对象。不论我们能否认识到它,这里总是有大量的理由,积极的和消极的,将我们拖入它们的方向。如果在宇宙中存在着像灵魂这样的本体,它们可能会受到在神经中枢中以各种形式发生的事件的影响。在某个既定的时刻,它

To the state of the entire brain at a given moment they may respond by inward modifications of their own. These changes of state may be pulses of consciousness, cognitive of objects few or many, simple or complex. The soul would be thus a medium upon which (to use our earlier phraseology) the manifold brain-processes *combine their effects.* Not needing to consider it as the 'inner aspect' of any arch-molecule or brain-cell, we escape that physiological improbability; and as its pulses of consciousness are unitary and integral affairs from the outset, we escape the absurdity of supposing feelings which exist separately and then 'fuse together' by them-selves. The separateness is in the brain-world, on this theory, and the unity in the soul-world; and the only trouble that remains to haunt us is the metaphysical one of understanding how one sort of world or existent thing can affect or influence another at all. This trouble, however, since it also exists inside of both worlds, and involves neither physical improbability nor logical contradiction, is relatively small.

I confess, therefore, that to posit a soul influenced in some mysterious way by the brain-states and responding to them by conscious affections of its own, seems to me the line of least logical resistance, so far as we yet have attained.

If it does not strictly *explain* anything, it is at any rate less positively objectionable than either mind-stuff or a material-monad creed. *The bare* PHENOMENON, *however, the* IMMEDIATELY KNOWN *thing which on the mental side is in apposition with the entire brain-process is the state of consciousness and not the soul itself.* Many of the stanchest believers in the soul admit that we know it only as an inference from experiencing its *states.* In Chapter X, accordingly, we must return to its consideration again, and *ask ourselves whether, after all, the ascertainment of a blank unmediated correspondence, term for term, of the succession of states of consciousness with the succession of total brain-processes, be not the simplest psycho-physic formula,*

们可以通过自己内在的改变来对整个大脑的状态做出反应。这些状态的改变可能是意识的瞬间波动，是对或多或少、或简单或复杂的对象的认识。因而，灵魂就是一种媒介物，通过它（使用我们早些时候的措辞），多种形式的大脑过程将它们的结果结合了起来。无需将它看作任何主宰分子或大脑分子的“内在方面”，我们避开了那种生理学方面的不可能性；并且由于其意识的瞬间波动从一开始就是单一的和完整的事件，我们避开了假设感受是单独存在的并且然后通过它们自己“融合在一起”这种谬论。按照这种理论，单独性存在于大脑世界，而统一性存在于灵魂世界；而且那唯一仍旧困扰着我们的麻烦是这样一种形而上学的麻烦，即理解某种类型的世界或存在物如何竟会影响或者作用于另一个世界或者存在物。然而，由于这种麻烦也存在于两个世界内部，并且它既不涉及物理方面的不可能性，也不涉及逻辑矛盾，它相对来说是个小麻烦。

因此，断定有一个灵魂，大脑状态以某种神秘的方式影响着它，并且它通过自己有意识的作用对它们做出反应，就我们已经达到的程度而言，这似乎对我来说是有最小逻辑阻力的一条思路。

如果它没有确实地解释任何东西，那么它无论如何不会像精神素材理论或物质单子理论那样肯定受到反驳。然而，那个赤裸裸的现象，那个在精神方面和整个大脑过程相并列的被直接得知的东西，是意识状态，而不是灵魂自身。很多最忠实的灵魂信仰者都承认，我们仅仅是将其作为一个从对其状态的体验而来的推论来了解的。相应地，在第 10 章中，我们必须再次回到这种思考上来，并且问我们自己，究竟对意识状态序列和整个大脑过程序列之间完全无媒介的一一对应的确定，是否不是最简单的精神一物

and the last word of a psychology which contents itself with verifiaive laws, and seeks only to be clear, and to avoid unsafe hypotheses. Such a mere admission of the empirical parallelism will there appear the wisest course. By keeping to it, our psychology will remain positivistic and non-metaphysical; and although this' is certainly only a provisional halting-place, and things must some day be more thoroughly thought out, we shall abide there in this book, and just as we have rejected mind-dust, we shall take no account of the soul. The spiritualistic reader may nevertheless believe in the soul if he will; whilst the positivistic one who wishes to give a tinge of mystery to the expression of his positivism can continue to say that nature in her unfathomable designs has mixed us of clay and flame, of brain and mind, that the two things hang indubitably together and determine each other's being, but how or why, no mortal may ever know.

理公式，并且不是那种满足于实证法则、只追求清晰、追求避免危险假说的心理学所要说的最后的话。像这样仅仅承认经验并行论，在那里看起来将是最明智的做法。通过对它的坚持，我们的心理学将依旧是实证的和非形而上学的；虽然这确实只是临时的停留地，并且事情必须在某一天得到更彻底的解决，但是在本书中，我们将停留在那里，而且正如我们已经拒绝了精神素材一样，我们也将不考虑灵魂。唯灵论读者如果愿意的话仍然可以相信灵魂；而想要在他的实证主义表述中增加一点神秘气息的实证主义者，可以继续说自然在它那深不可测的设计中已经用火焰和泥土、大脑和心灵混合成了我们，这两种东西不容置疑地结合在一起，并且决定着彼此的存在，但是它们是如何这样的和为什么这样的，凡人永远也不可能知道。

CHAPTER VII.

The Methods And Snares Of Psychology

We have now finished the physiological preliminaries of our subject and must in the remaining chapters study the mental states themselves whose cerebral conditions and concomitants we have been considering hitherto. Beyond the brain, however, there is an outer world to which the brain-states themselves ' correspond. ' And it will be well, ere we advance farther, to say a word about the relation of the mind to this larger sphere of physical fact.

Psychology Is A Natural Science.

That is, the mind which the psychologist studies is the mind of distinct individuals inhabiting definite portions of a real space and of a real time. With any other sort of mind, absolute Intelligence, Mind unattached to a particular body, or Mind not subject to the course of time, the psychologist as such has nothing to do. ' Mind, ' in his mouth, is only a class name for *minds*. Fortunate will it be if his more modest inquiry result in any generalizations which the philosopher devoted to absolute Intelligence as such can use.

To the psychologist, then, the minds he studies are *objects*, in a world of other objects. Even when he intro-spectively analyzes his

第七章　心理学的方法与陷阱

我们现在已经完成了为我们的学科而做的生理学准备工作,至今,我们一直在思考心理状态的大脑条件和伴随物,在其余的章节我们必须对心理状态自身进行研究。然而,在大脑之外还存在一个外部世界,大脑状态自身与之相对应。在我们进一步前进之前,对心灵和这一更大范围的物理事实之间的关系加以探讨是合理的。

心理学是一门自然科学

这就是说,心理学家所研究的心灵是存在于真实空间和真实时间的确定部分之中的独特个体的心灵。而其他类型的心灵,例如绝对理智、独立于独特肉体的心灵,或者不受时间进程影响的心灵,心理学家与它们没有任何关系。他嘴上所说的“心灵”,只是众多心灵的类名称。如果他那极为适度的探询所产生出的任何概括性的结果能够被致力于绝对理智本身的研究的哲学家所利用,这就是幸运的了。

那么,对心理学家来说,他所研究的心灵就是客体,存在于其他客体的世界之中。甚至当他内省地分析他自己的心灵,并且说

own mind, and tells what he finds there, he talks about it in an objective way. He says, for instance, that under certain circumstances the color gray appears to him green, and calls the appearance an illusion. This implies that he compares two objects, a real color seen under certain conditions, and a mental perception which he believes to represent it, and that he declares the relation between them to be of a certain kind. In making this critical judgment, the psychologist stands as much out-side of the perception which he criticises as he does of the color. Both are his objects. And if this is true of him when he reflects on his own conscious states, how much truer is it when he treats of those of others! In German philosophy since Kant the word *Erkenntnisstheorie*, criticism of the faculty of knowledge, plays a great part. Now the psychologist necessarily becomes such an *Erkenntnisstheoretiker*, But the knowledge he theorizes about is not the bare function of knowledge which Kant criticises-he does not inquire into the possibility of knowledge *überhaupt*. He assumes it to be possible, he does not doubt its presence in himself at the moment he speaks. The knowledge he criticises is the knowledge of particular men about the particular things that surround them. This he may, upon occasion, in the light of his *own* unquestioned knowledge, pronounce true or false, and trace the reasons by which it has become one or the other.

It is highly important that this natural-science point of view should be understood at the outset. Otherwise more may be demanded of the psychologist than he ought to be expected to perform.

A diagram will exhibit more emphatically what the assumptions of Psychology must be:

1The Psychologist	2TheThought Studied	3The Thought's Object	4The Psychologist's Reality

出他在那里发现了什么的时候，他也是以一种客观的方式来探讨它的。例如，他说在特定的情况下灰色在他看来是绿色，并且称这种显现是假象。这意味着，他对两种客体进行了比较，一种是在特定条件下看到的真实颜色，一种是他认为表象了它的心理知觉，并且他断言这两种客体之间有着某种特定的关系。在做出这样一种批判性的判断时，这位心理学家如他对待颜色时所做的一样，同样站在他所批判的知觉之外。两者都是他的客体。并且如果当他对自己的意识状态反省时情况对他来说是这样的，那么当他讨论其他人的意识状态时情况就更是如此了！在自康德以来的德国哲学中，知识理论这个词，即对认识能力的批判，起着非常重要的作用。现在，心理学家必然成为了这样一种知识理论家，但是他所理论化的认识不是康德所批判的那种纯粹的认识功能——他所探讨的不是认识究竟是如何可能的。他假设它是可能的，在他讲话的时候，他不怀疑它在他身上存在。他所批判的认识是独特的人对他们周围的独特事物的认识。有时，鉴于他自己未加怀疑的认识，他可以宣告认识是真还是假，并且追溯认识变成真的或者假的之理由。

极为重要的是，在开始的时候就应该理解这种自然科学的观点。否则的话，对心理学家的要求就会太多，从而超出了期望他应当完成的任务。

下面的图表将更有力地表明心理学的假设必须是什么：

1. 心理学家	2. 被研究的思想	3. 思想的对象	4. 心理学家的实在

These four squares contain the irreducible data of psychology. No. 1, the psychologist, believes No. 2, 3, and 4, which together form *his* total object, to be realities, and reports them and their mutual relations as truly as he can without troubling himself with the puzzle of how he can report them at all. About such *ultimate* puzzles he in the main need trouble himself no more than the geometer, the chemist, or the botanist do, who make precisely the same assumptions as he. ①

Of certain fallacies to which the psychologist is exposed by reason of his peculiar point of view—that of being a reporter of subjective as well as of objective facts, we must presently speak. But not until we have considered the methods he uses for ascertaining what the facts in question are.

The Methods Of Investigation.

Introspective Observation is what we have to rely on first and foremost and always. The word introspection need hardly be defined—it means, of course, the looking into our own minds and reporting what we there discover. *Every one agrees that we there discover states of consciousness.* So far as I know, the existence of such states has never been doubted by any critic, however sceptical in other respects he may have been. That we have *cogitations* of some sort is the *inconcussum* in a world most of whose other facts have at some time tottered in the breath of philosophic doubt. All people unhesitatingly believe that they feel themselves thinking, and that they distinguish the mental state as an inward activity or passion, from all the objects with which it

---

① On the relation between Pyschology and General Philosophy, see G. C. Robertson, 'Mind,' vol. VII. p. 1, and J. Ward, *ibid.* p. 153; J. Dewey, *ibid.* vol. IX. p. 1.

这四个方块包含了心理学不可还原的资料。第一个方块中的心理学家相信一起构成了他的全部对象的第二、三、四方块中的内容是实在,并且尽可能真实地报告它们及其相互间的关系,而且没有让他究竟如何能够报告它们这样的难题所困扰。关于这样的终极难题,他与跟他一样做出相同假定的几何学家、化学家或者植物学家一样,大体上不需要为此而使自己费心。①

我们现在必须谈谈心理学家容易犯的错误,它们的产生是因为心理学家的独特观点——作为主观事实和客观事实的报告者的观点。但是,在此之前,我将首先考虑一下他用来确定相关事实是什么的方法。

研究方法

内省观察是我们所不得不最先依赖、首要依赖和始终依赖的。内省这个词几乎不需要定义——它当然是指审视我们自己的心灵并且报告我们在那里发现了什么。每个人都承认我们在那里发现了意识状态。据我所知,不论批评家在其他方面是多么地喜欢怀疑,这种状态的存在从来没有被任何批评家怀疑过。在哲学的怀疑风气中,世界上的大部分其他事物都摇摇欲坠,而我们能够进行某种思考这一点在这个世界中是不动摇的。所有的人都毫不犹豫地相信,他们感受到自己在思考,并且他们将心理状态作为一种内部活动或者激情与心理状态可以在认识方面

① 关于心理学和一般哲学的关系,参见 G. C. 罗伯逊,《心灵》,第 7 卷,第 1 页,以及 J. 沃德,同上,第 153 页;J. 杜威,同上,第 9 卷,第 1 页。

may cognitively deal. *I regard this belief as the most fundamental of all the postulates of Psychology*, and shall discard all curious inquiries about its certainty as too metaphysical for the scope of this book.

A Question of Nomenclature. We ought to have some general term by which to designate all states of consciousness merely as such, and apart from their particular quality or cognitive function. Unfortunately most of the terms in use have grave objections. 'Mental state,' 'state of consciousness,' 'conscious modification,' are cumbrous and have no kindred verbs. The same is true of 'subjective condition.' 'Feeling' has the verb 'to feel,' both active and neuter, and such derivatives as 'feelingly,' felt, 'feltness,' etc., which make it extremely convenient. But on the other hand it has specific meanings as well as its generic one, sometimes standing for pleasure and pain, and being sometimes a synonym of '*sensation*' as opposed to *thought*; whereas we wish a term to cover sensation and thought indifferently. Moreover, 'feeling' has acquired in the hearts of platonizing thinkers a very opprobrious set of implications; and since one of the great obstacles to mutual understanding in philosophy is the use of words eulogistically and disparagingly, impartial terms ought always, if possible, to be preferred. The word *psychosis* has been proposed by Mr. Huxley. It has the advantage of being correlative to neurosis (the name applied by the same author to the corresponding nerve-process), and is moreover technical and devoid of partial implications. But it has no verb or other grammatical form allied to it. The expressions 'affection of the soul,' 'modification of the ego,' are clumsy, like 'state of consciousness,' and they implicitly assert theories which it is not well to embody in terminol-ogy before they have been openly discussed and approved. 'Idea' is a good vague neutral word, and was by Locke employed in the broadest generic way; but notwithstanding his authority it has not domesticated itself in the language so as to cover bodily sensations, and it moreover has no verb.

加以处理的所有客体区分开来。我把这种信念当作是所有心理学假定中最为基本的一个，并且将抛弃所有关于其确定性的好奇的质询，因为就本书的范围来看，它们太过于形而上了。

术语问题。我们应该有某个一般的术语，通过它来指出只是其自身的所有意识状态，并且脱离开它们特殊的性质和认识功能。不幸的是，所使用的大部分术语都具有严重的缺陷。“心理状态”、“意识状态”、“意识更改”用起来都很笨拙，并且没有相似的动词。“主观条件”也是如此。“感受”的动词是“感受”，它既是主动的，又是不及物的，并且还有诸如“感动地”、“被感受到”、“被感受到这一事实”等等派生词，这使得它极其方便。但是在另一方面，它既有具体的意义，又有一般的意义，有时候它代表快乐和痛苦，有时候它又是与思想相对立的“感觉”的同义词，而我们却想要一个术语来不加区别地包含感觉和思想。此外，感受在信奉柏拉图哲学的思想家们心中具有一系列臭名昭著的含义；并且，由于在哲学中相互理解的最大障碍之一就是褒扬地或者贬抑地使用词语，因此如果可能的话，不偏不倚的术语应该始终是首选的。赫胥黎先生提倡精神这个词，它有利于和神经（同样的作者将这个名称应用于神经过程）相关联，而且它是专业术语，没有偏袒性的含义。但是它没有动词或者与它有关联的其他语法形式。“灵魂的倾向”、“自我的变更”这些表达像“意识状态”一样是笨拙的表达，并且它们暗中维护了一些理论，在这些理论没有被公开讨论和证明之前就将它们体现在术语中是不好的。“观念”是一个很好的模糊的中性词，并且被洛克在最广泛的一般意义上使用过；但是尽管有洛克的权威，它还是没有在语言中使自己通俗得可以将身体的感觉包含进来，而且它也没有动词。如

'Thought' would be by far the best word to use if it could be made to cover sensations. It has no opprobrious connotation such as 'feeling' has, and it immediately suggests the omnipresence of cognition (or reference to an object other than the mental state itself), which we shall soon see to be of the mental life's essence. But can the expression 'thought of a toothache' ever suggest to the reader the actual present pain itself? It is hardly possible; and we thus seem about to be forced back on some *pair* of terms like Hume's 'impression and idea,' or Hamilton's 'presentation and representation,' or the ordinary 'feeling and thought,' if we wish to cover the whole ground.

In this quandary we can make no definitive choice, but must, according to the convenience of the context, use sometimes one, sometimes another of the synonyms that have been mentioned. *My own partiality is for either FEELING or THOUGHT.* I shall probably often use both words in a wider sense than usual, and alternately startle two classes of readers by their unusual sound; but if the connection makes it clear that mental states at large, irrespective of their kind, are meant, this will do no harm, and may even do some good. ①

The inaccuracy of introspective observation has been made a subject of debate. It is important to gain some fixed ideas on this point before we proceed.

The commonest spiritualistic opinion is that the Soul or *subject* of the mental life is a metaphysical entity, inaccessible to direct knowledge, and that the various mental states and operations of which we reflectively become aware are objects of an inner sense which does not lay hold of the real agent in itself, any more than sight or hearing gives us direct knowledge of matter in itself.

---

① Compare some remarks in Mill's Logic, bk. I. chap. III. § § 2, 3.

果能够让"思想"包含感觉的话,它就是目前可以使用的最好的词。它不具有像"感受"所具有的那种臭名昭著的内涵,而且它直接暗示了认知(或者是对一个对象的指称,而不是对心理状态自身的指称)的遍在,我们很快将会看到,认知就是精神生活的本质。但是,"关于牙疼的思想"这种表达能够向读者暗示出真实存在的疼痛自身吗?这几乎是不可能的;因此如果我们想要包括所有的范围,我们似乎又回到了像休谟的"印象和观念"、或者汉密尔顿的"呈现和再现"、或者普通的"感受和思想"这样的一些成对的术语上去了。

在这种进退两难的困境中,我们不能做出任何确定的选择,而是必须依从上下文的方便,有时使用已经提及的同义词中的某个术语,而有时使用另一个术语。我自己所偏爱的术语是感受或者思想。我可能会在一种比平常更广泛的意义上经常地使用这两个词,并且通过它们那不寻常的发音,轮流地让两类读者感到吃惊;但是,如果上下文的联系使得它清楚地指的是笼统的心理状态,并且与它们的种类无关,那么,这就不会带来坏处,甚至可以带来一些好处。①

内省观察的非精确性已经成为了争论的主题。在我们继续下去之前,就这一问题获得一些确定的想法是重要的。

最普通的唯灵论观点是,灵魂或者精神生活的主体是一个形而上的本体,对直接的认识而言是达不到的,并且我们通过反思而意识到的各种心理状态和操作,是内感的对象,这种内感不能够把握真实的动作者自身,就如同视觉和听觉不能给予我们关于

① 比较密尔的《逻辑学》中的评论,第1卷,第3章,第2、3节。

From this point of view introspection is, of course, incompetent to lay hold of anything more than the Soul's *phenomena*. But even then the question remains. How well can it know the phenomena themselves?

Some authors take high ground here and claim for it a sort of infallibility. Thus Ueberweg:

"When a mental image, as such, is the object of my apprehension, there is no meaning in seeking to distinguish its existence in my consciousness (in me) from its existence out of my consciousness (in itself); for the object apprehended is, in this case, one which does not even exist, as the objects of external perception do, in itself outside of my consciousness. It exists only within me."①

And Brentano:

"The phenomena inwardly apprehended are true in themselves. As they appear—of this the evidence with which they are apprehended is a warrant—so they are in reality. Who, then, can deny that in this a great superiority of Psychology over the physical sciences comes to light?"

And again:

"NO one can doubt whether the psychic condition he apprehends in himself *be*, and be *so*, as he apprehends it. Whoever should doubt this would have reached that *finished* doubt which destroys itself in destroying every fixed point from which to make an attack upon knowledge."②

Others have gone to the opposite extreme, and maintained that we

---

① Logic, § 40.

② Psychologie, bk. II. chap. III. §§ 1, 2.

物质本身的直接知识。出于这种观点，反省除了灵魂的现象以外不能把握任何东西。但尽管那样，问题依然存在。它在何种程度上能够认识现象自身呢?

一些作者提出了重要的理由并且声称它具有一种绝对的可靠性。尤伯维格如此说：

“当一个心理意象同样地是我理解的对象时，试图将它在我的意识中(在我之内)的存在与它在我的意识之外(在它自身之内)的存在区别开来是没有任何意义的；因为在这种情况下，被理解的对象，如同外部知觉的对象一样，是在它自身之内、在我的意识之外甚至根本不存在的。它只存在于我之内。”①

还有布兰塔诺也说：

“在内部被理解的现象在它们自身之内是真实的。由于它们显现了——它们能够得以理解这一证据就是它们显现了的根据——所以它们是实在的。那么，谁能否认在这一点上心理学相对于物理科学的一种极大的优越性显露出来了呢?”

还有：

“当人们理解精神条件的时候，没有人能够怀疑他所理解的在他自身之内的精神条件是否存在，以及是否如此存在。无论谁要怀疑这一点，他就到达了那种完结了的怀疑，这种怀疑在毁坏了由以向知识发起进攻的每一个固定的立足点的同时，也毁坏了它自己。②

其他一些人走到了相反的一个极端，主张我们根本不能拥有

---

① 《逻辑学》，第40节。

② 《心理学》，第2卷，第3章，第1、2节。

can have no introspective cognition of our own minds at all. A deliverance of Auguste Comte to this effect has been so often quoted as to be almost classical; and some reference to it seems therefore indispensable here.

Philosophers, says Comte,[1] have

"in these latter days imagined themselves able to distinguish, by a very singular subtlety, two sorts of observation of equal importance, one external, the other internal, the latter being solely destined for the study of intellectual phenomena.... I limit myself to pointing out the principal consideration which proves clearly that this pretended direct contemplation of the mind by itself is a pure illusion. ··· It is in fact evident that, by an invincible necessity, the human mind can observe directly all phenomena except its own proper states. For by whom shall the observation of these be made? It is conceivable that a man might observe himself with respect to the *passions* that animate him, for the anatomical organs of passion are distinct from those whose function is observation. Though we have all made such observations on ourselves, they can never have much scientific value, and the best mode of knowing the passions will always be that of observing them from without; for every strong state of passion... is necessarily incompatible with the state of observation. But, as for observing in the same way *intellectual* phenomena at the time of their actual presence, that is a manifest impossibility. The thinker cannot divide himself into two, of whom one reasons whilst the other observes him reason. The organ observed and the organ observing being, in this ease, identical, how could observation take place? This pretended psychological method is then radically null and void. on the one hand, they advise you to isolate yourself, as far as possible, from every external sensation, especially every intellectual work, —for if you were to busy yourself even with the simplest calculation,

---

① Cours de Philosophie Positive, I 34-8.

对我们自己的心灵的内省认识。奥古斯特·孔德对这一结果的意见被人们如此频繁的引用,以至于它几乎成为了经典;因此在这里对它有所提及似乎是绝对必要的。

孔德说,①哲学家们

“在近来这些日子里,想像他们自己能够通过一种非常特别的细微差别来区分开两种具有同等重要性的观察,一种观察是外部的,另一种是内部的,后者独自地以智性现象的研究为目的。……我将自己局限于指出这种重要的想法,它清楚地证明了这种伪称的心灵通过自身对自己直接沉思是一种纯粹的假象。……事实上很显然的是,通过一种不可征服的必然性,人类的心灵能够直接观察除了它自己的特有状态以外的所有现象。因为这些观察将由谁来完成呢?可以想像的是,一个人可以就激励它的激情来观察他自己,因为激情的解剖学器官与功能是观察的器官截然不同。尽管我们都对我们自己做过这样的观察,它们永远也不会有太多的科学价值,并且认识激情的最好方式始终是从外边观察它们的那种方式;因为每一种强烈的激情状态……都必然与观察状态不相容。但是,至于以同样的方式在智性现象真实出现的时候观察它们,那显然是不可能的。思维的人不能把他自己一分为二,一个在推理,同时另一个在观察他推理。在这种情况下,被观察的器官和观察的器官是同一的,观察如何能够发生呢?这种伪称的心理学方法因而根本就是无效的和没有用的。一方面,他们建议你尽量使你自己和所有的外部感觉、尤其是理智工作隔离开来——因为假如你使自己忙于甚至是最简单的计算,内部的观

① 《实证哲学教程》,1,第34~38页。

what would become of *internal* observation ? —on the other hand, after having with the utmost care attained this state of intellectual slumber, you must begin to contemplate the operations going on in your mind, when nothing there takes place! Our descendants will doubtless see such pretensions some day ridiculed upon the stage. The results of so strange a procedure harmonize entirely with its principle. For all the two thousand years during which metaphysicians have thus cultivated psychology, they are not agreed about one intelligible and established proposition. '*Internal observation*' gives almost as many divergent results as there are individuals who think they practise it,"

Comte hardly could have known anything of the English, and nothing of the German, empirical psychology. The 'results' which he had in mind when writing were probably scholastic ones, such as principles of internal activity, the faculties, the ego, the *liberum arbitrium indifferentice*, etc. John Mill, in replying to him, ①says:

"It might have occurred to M. Comte that a fact may be studied through the medium of memory, not at the very moment of our perceiving it, but the moment after: and this is really the mode in which our best knowledge of our intellectual acts is generally acquired. We reflect on what we have been doing when the act is past, but when its impression in the memory is still fresh. Unless in one of these ways, we could not have acquired the knowledge which nobody denies us to have, of what passes in our minds. M. Comte would scarcely have affirmed that we are not aware of our own intellectual operations. We know of our observings and our reasonings, either at the very time, or by memory the moment after; in either case, by direct knowledge, and not (like things done by us in a state of somnambulism) merely by their results.

① Auguste Comte and Positivism, 3d edition(I882), p. 64.

察会变成什么样子呢？——另一方面，在极为小心地获得了这种智性睡眠的状态之后，你必须在你的心中没有任何事情发生时才能开始沉思你心灵中进行的操作！我们的后代无疑会在某一天看到这样的主张在舞台上受到奚落。这种如此奇怪的过程结果完全和它的原则相一致。因为在形而上学家如此耕耘心理学的整整两千年之中，他们没有对一个可理解的和确定的命题达成一致。"内部观察"给出的存在分歧的结果差不多和认为自己在实践"内部观察"的个体一样多。"

孔德对英国的经验主义心理学几乎没有任何了解，并且对德国的经验主义心理学一无所知。当他写作的时候心里所想的"结果"可能是经院哲学家的结果，例如内部活动原理、机能原理、自我原则、无差别的行动自由原则等。约翰·密尔在对他的答复中说：①

"孔德先生可能想到过，一个事实可以通过记忆这种媒介，不是在我们感知它的那一刻，而是在其后的时刻得以研究：而这确实是我们通常获得关于我们智性活动的最好知识的方式。当行动结束了，但它在记忆中的印象依然鲜活的时候，我们反省我们做了些什么。除非以其中的一种方法，否则我们将不可能获得任何人都不能否认我们所拥有的、关于在我们心中所经过的事情的知识。孔德先生断言，我们对我们自己的智性活动没有意识。或者在我们进行观察和推理的时刻，或者在其后凭借着记忆，我们知道有观察和推理；在这两种情况下，我们是通过直接的知识，而不是（像在梦游症状态下我们所做的事情那样）仅仅通过它们的结果

---

① 《奥古斯特·孔德与实证主义》，第3版（1882年），第64页。

This simple fact destroys the whole of M. Comte's argument. Whatever we are directly aware of, we can directly observe."

Where now does the truth lie? Our quotation from Mill is obviously the one which expresses the most of *practical* truth a bout the matter. Even the writers who insist upon the absolute veracity of our immediate inner apprehension of a conscious state have to contrast with this the fallibility of our *memory* or *observation* of it, a moment later. No one has emphasized more sharply than Brentano himself the difference between the immediate *feltness* of a feeling, and its perception by a subsequent reflective act. But which mode of consciousness of it is that which the psychologist must depend on? If to *have* feelings or thoughts in their immediacy were enough, babies in the cradle would be psychologists, and infallible ones. But the psychologist must not only *have* his mental states in their absolute veritableness, he must report them and write about them, name them, classify and compare them and trace their relations to other things. Whilst alive they are their own property; it is only post-mortem that they become his prey. ① And as in the naming, classing, and knowing of things in general we are notoriously fallible, why not also here? Comte is quite right in laying stress on the fact that a feeling, to be named, judged, or perceived, must be already past. No subjective state, whilst present, is its own object;

① Wundt says: "The first rule for utilizing inward observation, consists in taking, as far as possible, experiences that are accidental, unexpected, and not intentionally brought about. . . *First* it is best as far as possible to rely on *Memory* and not on immediate Apprehension…. *second*, internal observation is better fitted to grasp clearly conscious states, especially voluntary mental acts: such inner processes as are obscurely conscious and involuntary will almost entirely elude it, because the effort to observe interferes with them, and because they seldom abide in memory." (Logik, II. 432.)

来知道它们的。这个简单的事实摧毁了孔德先生的全部论证。凡是我们直接意识到的东西,我们都能直接观察。"

真理现在存在于哪里呢?我们来自密尔的引文显然表达了关于这一问题的最实际的真理。甚至那些坚持认为我们对于一个意识状态直接的内部理解具有绝对准确性的作者,也不得不将我们较近的那一瞬间关于它的记忆和观察的易错性与此相对照。没有人比布兰塔诺自己更加犀利地强调了一个感受被直接感受到与通过其后的反省活动对这个感受的知觉之间的区别。但是在对它的意识方式中哪一种意识方式是心理学家必须要依赖的呢?如果拥有直接的感受和思想就足够了的话,摇篮中的婴儿也能成为心理学家了,而且是没有错误的心理学家。但是,心理学家不仅必须获得他们绝对真实的心理状态,他还必须报告和描写它们,命名它们,对它们进行分类并且比较它们,以及探索它们和其他事物的关系。当它们在运转的时候,它们是它们自己的所有物;只有在此之后它们才成为心理学家的猎物。[①] 而且,既然我们在命名、分类和知晓事物的时候一般而言是容易犯错误的(这是一个声名狼藉的事实),为什么在这里不也是如此呢?一个被命名、被判断、被知觉的感受必须是已经过去了的感受,孔德强调这一事实是非常正确的。没有主观状态在呈现的时候同时也是它自己

① 冯特说:"使用内部观察的第一条规则就是在于尽可能多得获得那些偶然的、意外的和不是有意地产生的经验。……首先,最好是尽可能地依赖于记忆,而不是即刻的理解。……第二,内部的观察更适合于把握明显的意识状态,尤其是主动的心理活动:那些像隐约有意识的并且是非主动的内部过程这样的内部过程,几乎会完全避开这种内部观察,因为观察的努力妨碍了它们,还因为它们很少在记忆中逗留。(《逻辑学》,2,第432页。)

its object is always something else. There are, it is true, cases in which we appear to be naming our present feeling, and so to be experiencing and observing the same inner fact at a single stroke. as when we say 'I feel tired,' 'I am angry,' etc. But these are illusory, and a little attention unmasks the illusion. The present conscious state, when I say 'I feel tired,' is not the direct state of tire; when I say. 'I feel angry,' it is not the direct state of anger. It is the state of *saying-I-feel-tired*, of saying-*I-feel-angry*,—entirely different matters, so different that the fatigue and anger apparently included in them are considerable modifications of the fatigue and anger directly felt the previous instant. The act of naming them has momentarily detracted from their force. ①

The only sound grounds on which the infallible veracity of the introspective judgment might be maintained are empirical. If we had reason to think it has never yet deceived us. we might continue to trust it. This is the ground actually maintained by Herr Mohr.

"The illusions of our senses." says this author, "have undermined our belief in the reality of the outer world; but in the sphere of inner observation our confidence is intact, for we have never found ourselves to be in error about the reality of an act of thought or feeling. We have never been misled into thinking we were *not* in doubt or

---

① In cases like this, where the state outlasts the act of naming it, exists before it, and recurs when it is past. we probably run little practical risk of error when we talk as if the state knew itself. The state of feeling and the state of naming the feeling are continuous. and the infallibility of such prompt introspective judgments is probably great. But even here the certainty of our knowledge ought not to be argued on the a *priorir* ground that *percipi* and *esse* are in psychology the same. The states are really two: the naming state and the named state are apart; '*percipi is esse*' is not the principle that applies.

的客体;它的客体永远是某些别的东西。确实有这样的情况存在,即当我们说"我感到累了","我生气了"等等时,我们似乎正在命名我们当前的感受,因此就是同时体验着并且观察着同一个内部事实。但是这些都是错觉,而且稍微注意一下就可以将这种错觉暴露出来。当我说"我感到累了"的时候,当前的意识状态不是疲劳的直接意识状态;当我说"我感到气愤"时,它不是气愤的直接意识状态。当前的意识状态是说我感到累了和说我感到气愤的意识状态——这是完全不同的内容,它们是如此的不同,以至于显然包含于其中的疲劳和气愤,与先前那个时刻所直接感受到的疲劳与气愤相比,已经有了相当大的改变。命名它们的活动即刻减损了它们的强度。①

主张内省判断具有确实可靠的准确性,其唯一可靠的根据是经验的。如果我们有理由认为它还从来没有欺骗过我们,我们就可以继续相信它。这是莫尔先生所实际维护的依据。

"我们感官的错觉,"这位作者说,"已经破坏了我们对外部世界的实在之信仰;但是在内部观察的范围内,我们的信心尚未动摇,因为我们从来没有发现自己对思想或者感受活动的实在之认识是错误的。我们还从来没有被误导去认为我们没有在怀疑或

---

① 在像这样的情况中,即这种状态比为它命名的活动持续得时间长,存在于它之前,并且当它过去了的时候又重新出现了,那么,当我们就好像状态知道它自己似的那样谈论的时候,我们实际上就可能很少有犯错误的风险。感受状态和命名感受的状态是连续的,并且这种即刻的内省判断可能具有很强的绝对可靠性。但是,即使是在这里,在心理学中,我们知识的确定性也不应该在下述这一先天的根据之上而得到论证,即被感知的和存在是相同的。这里的状态确实是两个:命名状态和被命名状态是分开的;"被感知的就是存在"这种原则在此是不适用的。

in anger when these conditions were really states of our consciousness。"①

But sound as the reasoning here would be, were the premises correct, I fear the latter cannot pass. However it may be with such strong feelings as doubt or anger, about weaker feelings, and about the *relations to each other* of all feelings, we find ourselves in continual error and uncertainty so Soon as we are called on to name and class, and not merely to feel. Who can be sure of the exact *order* of his feelings when they are excessively rapid? Who can be sure, in his sensible perception of a chair, how much comes from the eye and how much is supplied out of the previous knowledge of the mind? Who can compare with precision the *quantities* of disparate feelings even where the feelings are very much alike? For instance, where an object is felt now against the back and now against the cheek, which feeling is most extensive? Who can be sure that two given feelings are or are not exactly the same? Who can tell which is briefer or longer than the other when both occupy but an instant of time? Who knows, of many actions, for what motive they were done, or if for any motive at all? Who can enumerate all the distinct ingredients of such a complicated feeling as *anger*? and who can tell offhand whether or no a perception of *distance* be a compound or a simple state of mind? The whole mind-stuff controversy would stop if we could decide conclusively by introspection that what seem to us elementary feelings are really elementary and not compound.

Mr. Sully, in his work on Illusions, has a chapter on those of Introspection from which we might now quote. But, since the rest of this volume will be little more than a collection of illustrations of the difficulty of discovering by direct introspection exactly what our feelings

① J. Mohr: Grundlage der Empirischen Psychologie (Leipzig, 1882). p 47.

者在生气,当这些情况确实是我们的意识状态的时候。”①

假如前提正确,这里的推理就是合理的,但我恐怕前提不能通过。不管在诸如怀疑或者气愤这类强烈感受中情况会如何,对于比较弱的感受,以及所有感受彼此间的关系来说,一旦我们要对其进行命名和分类,而不仅仅是感受它们,我们就发现自己处于不断的犯错与不确定之中了。当感受非常快的时候,谁能够确定出他的感受的准确顺序呢?在对椅子的感性知觉中,谁能够确定出有多少东西来自于眼睛,又有多少东西是从先前心灵中的知识中补充进去的?甚至在感受非常相似的情况下,谁能够在量上对全异的感受进行精确地比较呢?例如,在一个感受时而被感受到贴着背部,时而被感受到贴着面颊的情况下,哪一个感受的范围最广泛呢?谁能够确定出两个被给定的感受是完全一样的,或者是完全不一样的呢?当两个感受都只占有很短的时间时,谁能够分辨出其中的哪一个比另一个更短或者更长呢?谁能够知道很多行为的完成是出于什么样的动机,或者是否完全出于任何动机呢?谁能够列举出像气愤这样的复杂感受的所有独特成分呢?又有谁能够当下说出对距离的一次知觉不管怎样都是一种复合的心理状态,或者是一个简单的心理状态呢?假如通过内省我们能够最后断定,似乎对我们来说是基本的感受的东西真的是基本的,而不是复合的,那么关于精神素材理论的整个论战就会停止了。

在萨利先生论错觉的著作中,有一章是关于内省错觉的,我们现在可以从中引用其内容。但是,由于这一卷的其余部分差不多全部是对通过直接内省发现我们的感受和它们的关系到底

① J. 莫尔:《经验心理学基础》(莱比锡,1882 年),第 47 页。

and their relations are, we need not anticipate our own future details, but just state our general conclusion that introspection is difficult and fallible; *and that the difficulty is simply that of all observation of whatever kind.* Something is before us; We do our best to tell what it is, but in spite of our good will we may go astray, and give a description more applicable to some other sort of thing. The only safeguard is in the final *consensus* of our farther knowledge about the thing in question, later views correcting earlier ones, until at last the harmony of a consistent system is reached. Such a system, gradually worked out, is the best guarantee the psychologist can give for the soundness of any particular psychologic observation which he may report. Such a system we ourselves must strive, as far as may be, to attain.

The English writers on psychology, and the school of Herbart in Germany, have in the main contented themselves with such results as the immediate introspection of single individuals gave, and shown what a body of doctrine they may make. The works of Locke, Hume, Reid, Hartley, Stewart, Brown, the Mills, will always be classics in this line; and in Professor Bain's Treatises We have probably the last word of what this method taken mainly by itself can do—the last monument of the youth of our science, still untechnical and generally intelligible, like the Chemistry of Lavoisier, or Anatomy before the microscope was used.

The *Experimental Method*. But psychology is passing into a less simple phase. Within a few years what one may call a microscopic psychology has arisen in Germany, carried on by experimental methods, asking of course every moment for introspective data, but eliminating their uncertainty by operating on a large scale and taking statistical means. This method taxes patience to the utmost, and could hardly have arisen in a country. whose natives could be *bored*. Such Germans as Weber, Fechner, Vierordt, and Wundt

是什么的困难之说明，我们无需过早使用我们自己后来将要使用的详细资料，而只需陈述一下我们的一般性结论：内省是困难的和易错的；而且这种困难只不过是所有的、不论任何一种的观察的困难。某些东西在我们前面；我们尽力地说出它是什么，但是尽管我们有好的意愿，我们还是会误入歧途，并且给出一种更适合于某种其他类型的东西的描述。唯一的防护措施在于我们关于相关事物的进一步的知识最终达成了一致，后面的观点纠正前面的观点，直到最后达到了一个连贯一致的和谐体系。这样一种逐渐建立起来的体系，是心理学家能够给出的可以报告的任何特殊的心理观察的合理性的最好保证。我们自己必须尽量地努力完成这样一种体系。

英国的心理学作者和德国的赫尔巴特学派，大体上使他们自己满足于像单独个体的直接内省所给出的这类结果，并且表明了他们可以提出一些什么样的学说。洛克、休谟、里德、哈特利、斯图尔德、布朗和密尔父子的著作是这方面的经典；而在《贝恩教授的论文》中，我们可能对这种方法主要被单独使用时它能做什么做出了最终的结论——我们年轻科学的最后纪念碑，依然是非专业性的和通常可以理解的，就像拉瓦锡的化学和在显微镜被使用之前的解剖学。

实验的方法。但是，心理学进入了一个不那么简单的阶段。在几年之内，人们可以称之为微观心理学的东西已经在德国出现了，它通过实验的方法而得以展开，当然在每时每刻都需要内省资料，但是通过大规模的操作和采用统计学的方法从而消除了它们的不确定性。这种方法需要极大的耐性，在国民对其厌倦的国家里，它是不可能出现的。像韦伯、费克纳、维尔罗特和冯特这样

obviously cannot; and their success has brought into the field an array Of younger experimental psychologists, bent on studying the *elements* of the mental life, dissecting them out from the gross results in which they are embedded, and as far as possible reducing them to quantitative scales. The simple and open method of attack having done what it Call, the method of patience, starving out, and harassing to death is tried; the Mind must submit to a regular *siege*, in which minute advantages gained night and day by the forces that hem her in must sum themselves up at last into her overthrow. There is little of the grand style about these new prism, pendulum, and chronograph-philosophers. They mean business, not chivalry. What generous divination, and that superiority in virtue which Was thought by Cicero to sire a man the best. insight into nature, have failed to do, their spying and scraping, their deadly tenacity and almost diabolic cunning, will doubtless some day bring about.

No general description of the methods of experimental psychology would be instructive to one unfamiliar with the instances of their application, so we will waste no words upon the attempt. *The principal fields of experimentation* so far haver been: 1) the connection of conscious states with their physical conditions, including the whole of brain-physiology, and the recent minutely cultivated physiology of the sense-organs, together with what is technically known as 'psychophysics,' or the laws of correlation between sensations and the outward stimuli by which they are aroused; 2) the analysis of space-perception into its sensational elements; 3) the measurement of the *duration* of the simplest mental processes; 4) that of the *accuracy of reproduction* in the memory of sensible experiences and of intervals of space and time; 5) that of the manner in which simple mental states *influence each other*, call each other up, or inhibit each other's reproduction; 6) that of the *number of facts* which consciousness can simultaneously discern; finally, 7) that of the elementary laws of obliviscence and retention. It must be said that in some of these fields

的德国人显然不可能对其感到厌烦；而且他们的成功已经为这一领域带来了一大批更年轻的实验心理学家，他们爱好研究精神生活的元素，将它们从它们所嵌入的大量结果中分离出来，并且尽可能地把它们还原成为数量等级。简单而开放的进攻方法已经完成了它的使命，忍耐、绝食以及折磨至死的方法也尝试过了；心灵一定会屈从于经常性的围攻，在其中，通过将它包围起来的力量而夜以继日地获得的那微小的优势，最后必定会汇总起来将它颠覆。对于这些使用多棱镜、钟摆、计时器的哲学家来说，几乎没有什么令人钦佩的风格。他们想要的是生意，而不是骑士精神。高尚的预言和借助于西赛罗所认为的赋予人对自然的最佳洞察力的优越性都无法做到的事情，在他们的窥探和挖掘中，在他们那极度的韧性与几乎是魔鬼般的狡猾中，无疑将会在某一天被完成的。

对于不熟悉实验心理学应用实例的人来说，对其方法的一般性描述没有什么教育性，因此我们将不会浪费笔墨来做这种尝试。迄今为止，主要的实验领域有：(1)意识状态与其物理条件的联系，包括整个大脑生理学，以及近来得到详细研究的感官生理学，还有被专业地称作“精神－物理学”的东西，或说关于感觉与激起它们的刺激之间的相互关系的法则；(2)关于将空间知觉分解为其感觉元素的分析；(3)对最简单的心理过程的持续时间的测量；(4)对感性经验在记忆中再现的准确性的测量，以及对空间和时间的间隔在记忆中再现的准确性的测量；(5)对简单的心理状态用以彼此影响、相互唤起、或者抑制彼此再现的方式的测量；(6)对意识能够同时辨别的事实数量的测量；最后，(7)对遗忘与记忆力的基本规律的测量。必须说的是，到目前为止，在一些这样

the results have as yet borne little theoretic fruit commensurate with the great labor expended in their acquisition. But facts are facts, and if we only get enough of them they are sure to combine. New ground will from year to year be broken, and theoretic results will grow. Meanwhile the experimental method has quite changed the face of the science so far as the latter is a record of mere work done.

The *comparative method*, finally, supplements the introspective and experimental methods. This method presupposes a normal psychology of introspection to be established in its main features. But where the origin of these features, or their dependence upon one another; is in question, it is of the utmost importance to trace the phenomenon considered through all its possible variations of type and combination. So it has come to pass that instincts of animals are ransacked to throw light on our own; and that the reasoning faculties of bees and ants, the minds of savages, infants, madmen, idiots, the deaf and blind, criminals, and eccentrics, are all invoked in support of this or that special theory about some part of our own mental life. The history of sciences, moral and political institutions, and languages, as types of mental product, are pressed into the same service. Messrs. Darwin and Galton have set the example of circulars of questions sent out by the hundred to those supposed able to reply. The custom has spread, and it will be well for us in the next generation if such circulars be not ranked among the common pests of life. Meanwhile information grows, and results emerge. There are great sources of error in the comparative method. The interpretation of the 'psychoses' of animals, savages, and infants is necessarily wild work, in which the personal equation of the investigator has things very much its own way. A savage will be reported to have no moral or religious feeling if his actions shock the observer unduly. A child

的领域里，这些结果与花费在获得结果的巨大劳动相比，它们几乎没有结出任何理论的硕果。但是，事实就是事实，而且只要我们获得了足够的事实，它们一定会结合起来。新的领域将会被年复一年地开垦出来，而且理论的结果将会增长。同时，就这门科学仅仅是对已经完成的工作的记录而言，实验的方法已经彻底改变了这门科学的面貌。

最后要说的是比较的方法，它是对内省方法和实验方法的补充。这种方法预先假定一种正规的内省心理学应该在其主要特征中得以确立。但是，这些特征或者这些特征之间的相互依赖关系起源于哪里还在争论之中，从所考虑现象的类型与结合的所有可能的变化中来对这种现象进行探索是极为重要的。因此就出现了这样的情况，为了将一缕光亮投向我们自己的本能，动物的本能得到了彻底地检查；而且蚂蚁和蜜蜂的推理能力，原始人、婴儿、疯子、白痴、聋哑人、罪犯、行为古怪的人的心灵，都被调用过来以支持关于我们自己的精神生活的某些部分的这种或那种特殊的理论。科学史、道德与政治制度以及语言，作为不同类型的精神产品，也同样被征用了过来。达尔文和高尔顿先生是这样一种榜样，他们将问题用数以百计的信函发送给了那些他们认为能够做出回答的人。这种习惯已经传播开来，而且如果这种信函不被列入生活的公害之列，对我们下一代人来说这就是适当的。与此同时，信息增长了，而且结果也出现了。大量的错误来源于比较的方法。对动物、原始人以及婴儿的“精神活动”的解释必然是一种任性的工作，在其中，研究者的个人因素在很大程度上左右着一切。如果一个原始人的行为使观察者过于震惊的话，这个原始人就会被报告说没有道德和宗教感。一个孩子因为以第三人

Will be assumed without self-consciousness because he talks of himself in the third person, etc., etc. No rules can be laid down in advance. Comparative observations, to be definite, must usually be made to test some pre-existing hypothesis; and the only thing then is to use as much sagacity as you possess, and to be as candid as you can.

The Sources Of Error In Psycholocy.

The first of them arises from the Misleading Influence of Speech. Language Was originally made by men who were not psychologists, and most men to-day employ almost exclusively the vocabulary of outward things. The cardinal passions of our life, anger, love, fear, hate, hope. and the most comprehensive divisions of our intellectual activity, to remember, expect, think, know, dream, with the broadest genera of aesthetic feeling, joy, sorrow, pleasure, pain, are the only facts of a subjective order which this vocabulary deigns to note by special words. The elementary qualities of sensation, blight, loud, red, blue, hot, cold, are, it is true, susceptible of being used in both an objective and a subjective sense. They stand for outer qualities and for the feelings which these arouse. But the objective sense is the original sense; and still to-day we have to describe a large number of sensations by the name of the object from which they have most frequently been got. An orange color, an odor of violets, a cheesy taste, a thunderous sound, a fiery smart, etc., will recall what I mean. This absence of a special vocabulary for subjective facts hinders the study of all but the very coarsest of them. Empiricist writers are very fond of emphasizing one great set of delusions which language inflicts on the mind. Whenever we have made a word, they say, to denote a certain group of phenomena, we are prone to suppose a substantive entity existing beyond the phenomena, of which the word shall be the name. But the *lack* of a word quite as often leads to the directly opposite error. We are then prone to suppose that no entity can be there;

称来谈论他自己，所以就被假定为没有自我意识，等等。任何原则都不能事先被放弃。需要明确的是，比较的方法通常必须被用来检验一些先前存在的假说；而且那时唯一可做的事情就是尽可能多地使用你获得的睿智，并且尽可能地公正。

心理学中的错误之源

第一个错误之源来自令人误解的言语的影响。语言最初不是由心理学家创造的，而且现今大多数人使用的词汇几乎全部是关于外部事物的词汇。我们生活中的主要情感——气愤、爱、恐惧、憎恨、希望，以及我们的智性活动中最具理解力的部分——记忆、预期、思维、认识、做梦，还有最宽泛的美感类别——喜悦、悲哀、快乐、痛苦，只有这些主观状态的事实被这种特殊的词汇指出来了。确实，感觉的基本性质——明亮、响亮、红、蓝、热、冷——是容许在主观和客观的意义上来使用的。它们表示外部的性质，也表示这些性质所引起的感受。但是，客观意义是最初的意义；而且现在我们仍然不得不通过使用能最频繁地引起感觉的客体的名称来描述大量的感觉。橙色、紫罗兰味、奶酪味、雷鸣般的声音、灼痛，等等，都表明了我说的意思。这种指称主观事实的特殊词汇的缺乏，妨碍了除对主观事实的最粗糙研究以外的所有对主观事实的研究。经验主义作家非常喜欢强调由语言在心灵中造成的大量的错觉。他们说，无论何时我们用一个词来指示某一现象群，我们都倾向于假定一个实体性的本体存在于现象之外，而这个词就是这个本体的名称。但是词汇的缺乏也同样会导致直接相反的错误。我们于是倾向于假定那里没有本体存在；

and so we come to overlook phenomena whose existence would be patent to us all, had we only grown up to hear it familiarly recognized in speech. ①It is hard to focus our attention on the nameless, and so there results a certain vacuousness in the descriptive parts of most psychologies.

But a worse defect than vacuousness comes from the dependence of psychology on common speech. Naming our thought by its own objects, we almost all of us assume that as the objects. are so the thought must be. The thought of several distinct things can only consist of several distinct bits of thought, or 'ideas;' that of an abstract or universal object can only be an abstract or universal idea. As each object may come and go, be forgotten and then though of again, it is held that the thought of it has a precisely similar independence, self-identity, and mobility. The thought of the object's recurrent identity is regarded as the identity of its recurrent thought; and the perceptions of multiplicity, of coexistence, of succession, are severally conceived to be brought about only through a multiplicity, a coexistence, a succession, of perceptions. The continuous flow of the mental stream is sacrificed, and in its place an atomism, a brickbat plan of construction, is preached, for the existence of which no good introspective grounds can be brought forward, and out of which presently grow all sorts of paradoxes and contradictions, the heritage of woe of students of the mind.

These words are meant to impeach the entire English psychology derived from Locke and Hume, and the entire German psychology derived

---

① In English we have not even the generic distinction between the thing-thought-of and the-thought-thinking-it, which in German is expressed by the opposition between *Gedachtes* and *Gedunke*, in Latin by that between *cogitatum* and *cogitatio*.

因此我们便忽视了这样的现象,即如果我们在成长的过程中经常很熟悉地听见它在谈话中被提及,那它的存在对我们所有人来说就是很明显的现象。[①] 将我们的注意力集中到没有名称的事物上是很难的,因此这就导致了在大部分心理学的描述部分中都存在一定程度上的空洞。

而且,一种比空洞更加糟糕的缺陷来自心理学对公共言语的依赖。在用思维自身的对象来命名我们的思维的时候,几乎我们所有人都认为,对象是什么,思想就必须同样是什么。对几个不同事物的思维只能由几个独特的思想或者观念所组成;对抽象的或者普遍的对象的思维只能是一个抽象的或者普遍的观念。由于每一个对象都可以来来去去,可以被忘记然后被想起来,人们坚持认为,对它的思维具有一种完全类似的独立性、自我同一性和灵活性。关于对象反复发生的统一性的思想,被看作是其反复发生的思维的同一性;关于多样性、共存性和连续性的知觉,分别被认为是仅仅由知觉的多样性、共存性和连续性所产生的。精神之流的连续流动被牺牲掉了,并且在其位置之上,一种原子论,一种碎砖式的构建计划得以宣扬,因为没有任何好的内省证据能够提示出它的存在,而且目前从这里头产生出来各种各样的悖论和矛盾,这是心灵研究者们的不幸的遗产。

这些话就是有意要对来自于洛克和休谟的整个英国心理学、以及来自于赫尔巴特的整个德国心理学表示怀疑的,这是就他们

---

① 在英语中,我们甚至没有在被思考的事物与思考着它的思维之间做出一般性的区分,在德语中,这种区分由被思维者和思维这两个词之间的对立而得以表达,在拉丁文中由被思维者和思维而得以表达。

from Herbart, So far as they both treat 'ideas' as separate subjective entities that come and go. Examples will soon make the matter clearer. Meanwhile our psychologic insight is vitiated by still other snares.

'*The psychologist's Fallacy.*' The *great* snare of the psychologist is the *confusion of his own standpoint with that of the mental fact* about which he is making his report. I shall hereafter call this the 'psychologist's fallacy' *par excellence.* For some of the mischief, here too, language is to blame. The psychologist, as we remarked above (p. 183), stands outside of the mental state he speaks of. Both itself and its object are objects for him. Now when it is a *cognitive* state (percept, thought, concept, etc.). he ordinarily has no other way of naming it than as the thought, percept, etc., *of that object.* He himself, meanwhile, knowing the self-same object in *his* way, gets easily led to suppose that the thought, which is *of* it, knows it in the same way in which he knows it, although this is often very far from being the case.① The most fictitious puzzles have been introduced into our science by this means. The so-called question or presentative or representative perception, of whether an object is present to the thought that thinks it by a counterfeit image of itself, or directly and without any intervening image at all; the question of nominalism and conceptualism, of the shape in which things are present when only a general notion of them is before the mind; are comparatively easy questions when once the psychologist's fallacy is eliminated from their treatment,—as we shall ere long see (in Chapter XII).

Another variety of the psychologist's fallacy is the assumption

---

① Compare B. P. Bowne's Metaphysics (1882), P. 408.

都将“观念”当作分离的、来来去去的主观本体而言的。一些例子将很快使这个问题更加清楚。与此同时，我们在心理方面的洞察力还受到了其他陷阱的损害。

“心理学家的谬误。”心理学家的一个巨大的陷阱，就是将他自己的立场与他正在报告的心理事实的立场相混淆。此后我将把这种情况称作典型的“心理学家的谬误”。对于一些这样的错误，语言在这里也应该受到责备。正如我们在上面所提到的那样（第183页），心理学家处于他所谈论的心理状态之外。心理状态自身和心理状态的对象都是他的对象。现在当它是一种认知状态（知觉、思维、概念，等等）时，他通常除了以对那个对象的思维、知觉等等的方式对它进行命名以外，他没有任何命名他的其他方式了。同时，他自己以他的方式认识了自我同一的对象，并且他很容易地致使自己假定对对象的思维以他知道对象的相同方式知道了对象，尽管情况通常远非如此。[1] 那最为虚伪的迷惑就是通过这样的方式被引入到我们的科学中来的。所谓的关于呈现的知觉或者再现的知觉的问题，关于一个对象是通过它自己的假冒的意象呈现在思考它的思维面前，还是直接地、在完全没有任何意象介入的情况下呈现在思维面前的问题；关于唯名论和概念论的问题，关于当事物只有一种一般概念出现在心灵面前时，事物所呈现出来的外形的问题；在对待这些问题的时候一旦消除掉了心理学家的谬误，这些问题就比较容易了，——正如我们不久将会看到的那样（在第12章）。

心理学家的谬误的另一种变化是这样一种假设，即被研究的

① 比较B. P. 鲍恩的《形而上学》（1882年），第408页。

that the mental state studied must be conscious of itself as the psychologist is conscious of it. The mental state is aware of itself only from within; it grasps what we call its own content, and nothing more. The psychologist, on the contrary, is aware of it from without, and knows its relations with all sorts of other things. What the thought sees is only its own object; what the psychologist sees is the thought's object, plus the thought itself, plus possibly all the rest of the world. We must be very careful therefore, in discussing a state of mind from the psychologist's point of view, to avoid foisting into its own ken matters that are only there for ours. we must avoid substituting what we know the consciousness is, for what it *is* a consciousness *of*, and counting its outward, and so to speak physical, relations with other facts of the world, in among the objects of which we set it down as aware. Crude as such a confusion of standpoints seems to be when abstractly stated, it is nevertheless a snare into which no psychologist has kept himself at all times from falling, and which forms almost the entire stock-in—trade of certain schools. We cannot be too watchful against its subtly corrupting influence.

Summary. To sum up the chapter, Psychology assumes that thoughts successively occur, and that they know objects in a world which the psychologist also knows. *These thoughts are the subjective data of which he treats, and their relations to their objects, to the brain, and to the rest of the world constitute the subject—matter of psychologic science.* Its methods are introspection, experimentation, and comparison. But introspection is no sure guide to truths *about* our mental states; and in particular the poverty of the psychological vocabu-lary leads us to drop out certain states from our consideration, and to treat others as if they knew themselves and their object as the psychologist knows both, which is a disastrous fallacy in the science.

心理状态必须意识到自身，如同心理学家意识到它那样。心理状态只能从内部意识到它自己；它把握的是我们称之为它自己的内容的东西，而且仅此而已。相反，心理学家是从外部意识到它，并且知道它与所有其他事物的关系。思维所看到的只是它自己的对象；心理学家所看到的是思维的客体，加上思维自身，还可能再加上世界上所有其余的东西。因此，从心理学家的观点讨论一种心理状态时，我们必须非常小心地避免在这种心理状态下自己的知识范围中私自添加进来仅仅是因为我们而存在的东西。我们必须避免用"一个意识是关于什么的"来替代"我们知道这意识是什么"，并且我们必须避免将它与世界上其他事实的外部的、而且因此可以说是物理的关系算在我们认为它所意识到的对象之内。当被抽象地表述出来的时候，这种立场的混淆似乎很拙劣，然而它却是一个所有心理学家都不能使他自己始终都不陷落进去的陷阱，而且它几乎构成了某些学派的所有存货。我们无论怎样警惕它那微妙的腐蚀作用也不为过。

概要。总结这一章，心理学假设思想的相继产生，并且假设它们知道心理学家也知道的世界中的对象。这些思想是他所处理的主观材料，并且这些思想与它们的对象的关系、与大脑的关系、与世界其余部分的关系构成了心理科学的主题。它的方法是内省、实验和比较。但是，内省不是通向关于我们心理状态的真理的可靠的向导；心理学词汇的贫乏尤其使得我们将某些状态排除在我们的思考之外，而将其他状态看作好像是它们知道它们自己和它们的对象，就如同心理学家也知道这两者一样，而这在这门科学中就是一种灾难性的谬误。

CHAPTER VIII.

The Relations Of Minds To Other Things.

Since, for psychology, a mind is an object in a world of other objects, its relation to those other objects must next be surveyed. First of all, to its

Time-Relations.

Minds, as we know them, are temporary existences. Whether my mind had a being prior to the birth of my body, whether it shall have one after the latter's decease, are questions to be decided by my general philosophy or theology rather than by what we call 'scientific facts'—I leave out the facts of so-called spiritualism, as being still in dispure. Psychology, as a natural science, confines itself to the present life, in which every mind appears yoked to a body through which its manifestations appear. In the present world, then, minds precede, succeed, and coexist with each other in the common receptacle of time, and of their collective relations to the latter nothing more can be said. The life of the *individual* consciousness in time seems, however, to be an interrupted one, so that the question:

Are we ever wholly unconscious?

becomes one which must be discussed. Sleep, fainting, coma, epilepsy, and other 'unconscious' conditions are apt to break in upon and occupy large durations of what we nevertheless consider the

第八章 心灵与其他事物的关系

既然对于心理学来说，心灵是客体，存在于包含其他客体的世界中，那么，接下来必须考察的是它与那些其他客体的关系。

时间关系

首先，它的时间关系如我们所知道的那样，心灵是暂时的存在。是否我的心灵在我的身体出生之前就存在，是否它在我死亡之后将依然存在，这些问题应当由我的一般哲学或者神学来加以决断，而不是我们称之为“科学事实”的东西——我省去了所谓唯灵论的事实，因为它们还在争论之中。作为一门自然科学，心理学将自身限制在当前的生活之中，在其中，每一个心灵似乎都被束缚在身体上，通过身体其表现才得以显现。因而，在现在的世界中，心灵在共同的时间容器中彼此之间有先、有后、有共存，并且就它们与后者的集合关系而言，没有更多的东西可说了。然而，个体意识的生命在时间中似乎是中断的，因此，

我们时常完全无意识吗？

这个问题就成了我们必须要讨论的问题。睡眠、昏厥、昏迷、癫痫以及其他“无意识”状态易于闯入我们依然称之为个人的精神历史的中，并且会持续很长的时间。如果承认了这种中断的事

mental history of a single man. And, the fact of interruption being admitted, is it not possible that it may exist where we do not suspect it, and even perhaps in an incessant and fine-grained form?

This might happen, and yet the subject himself never know it. We often take ether and have operations performed without a suspicion that our consciousness has suffered a breach. The two ends join each other smoothly over the gap; and only the sight of our wound assures us that we must have been living through a time which for our immediate consciousness was non-existent. Even in sleep this sometimes happens: We think we have had no nap, and it takes the clock to assure us that we are wrong. ① We thus may live through a real outward time, a time known by the psychologist who studies us, and yet not *feel* the time, or infer it from any inward sign. The question is, how often does this happen? Is consciousness really discontinuous. incessantly interrupted and recommencing (from the psychologist's point of view)? and does it only seem continuous to itself by an illusion analogous to that of the zoetrope? Or is it at most times as continuous outwardly as it inwardly seems?

It must be confessed that we can give no rigorous answer to this question. Cartesians, who hold that the essence of the soul is to think, can of course solve it a *priori*, and explain the appearance of thoughtless, intervals either by lapses in our ordinary memory, or by the sinking of consciousness to a minimal state, in which perhaps all that it feels is a bare existence which leaves no particulars behind to be

---

① Messrs. Payton spence (Journal of spec. Phil., X. 338, XIV. 286) and M. M. Garver (Amer. Jour. of Science, 3d series. XX. 189) argue, the one from speculative, the other from experimental grounds, that, the physical condition of consciousness being neural vtbration, the consciousness must itself be incessantly interrupted by unconsciousness—about fifty times a second, according to Garver.

实,那么它难道不可能存在于我们没有觉察到它的地方,而且甚至以一种不间断的和精细的形式存在吗?

这种情况可能发生,但是主体自己永远也不知道它。我们经常使用乙醚,然后进行手术,却从来没有怀疑过我们的意识已经产生了裂痕。两端越过裂缝平稳地连接了起来;而且只有看到了伤口我们才确信,我们一定是经历了一段对于我们当前的意识来说是不存在的时间。甚至在睡觉的时候,这种情况有时候也发生了:我们认为我们没有打盹,而钟表使我们确信我们错了。[①] 我们因此可以度过一段真实的外部时间,一段由研究我们的心理学家所知晓的时间,但是却感觉不到那段时间,或者不能从内部的迹象将它推断出它来。问题是,这种情况发生的周期是多少?意识真的是不连续的、不断地被中断并且又重新开始的吗(从心理学家的观点来看)?还有它只是通过一种与西洋镜假象相类似的假象才使得它对它自己来说似乎是连续的吗?或者在大部分时间里,它在外部是连续的和它似乎在内部是连续的是一样的吗?

必须承认的是,对这种问题我们不能给出严格的回答。笛卡儿主义者坚持认为灵魂的本质就是思维,他们当然能够先天地解决这个问题,或者通过我们日常记忆中的失误来解释无思维的时间间隔现象,或者通过意识降低到最小状态来解释它们,在这种状态中,它所能感受到的可能只是一种赤裸的存在,这种存在没有留下任何可以用来回忆的特殊的东西。然而,如果一个人没有

① 佩顿·思朋斯(《思辨哲学杂志》,10,338,14,286)和 M. 加弗(《美国科学杂志》,第 3 集,20,189)先生,一个从思辨的角度,另一个从实验的基础论证说,意识的物理条件是神经振动,意识自身一定会不断地被无意识所中断——根据加弗的观点,每秒 50 次。

recalled. If, however, one have no doctrine about the soul or its essence, one is free to take the appearances for what they seem to be, and to admit that the mind, as well as the body, may go to sleep.

Locke was the first prominent champion of this latter view, and the pages in which he attacks the Cartesian belief are as spirited as any in his Essay. "Every drowsy nod shakes their doctrine who teach that their soul is always thinking." He will not believe that men so easily forget. M. Jouffroy and Sir W. Hamilton, attacking the question in the same empirical way, are led to an opposite conclusion. Their reasons, briefly stated, are these:

In somnambulism, natural or induced, there is often a great display of intellectual activity, followed by complete oblivion of all that has passed. ①

On being suddenly a wakened from a sleep, however profound, we always catch ourselves in the middle of a dream. Common dreams are often remembered for a few minutes after waking, and then irretrievably lost.

Frequently, when awake and absent-minded, we are visited by thoughts and images which the next instant we cannot recall.

Our insensibility to habitual noises, etc., whilst awake, proves that we can neglect to attend to that which we nevertheless feel. similarly in sleep, we grow inured, and sleep soundly in presence of sensations of sound, cold, contact, etc., which at first prevented our complete repose. We have learned to neglect them whilst asleep as we should whilst awake. The mere *sense-impressions* are the same when the sleep is deep as when it is light; the difference must lie in a *judgment* on the part of the apparently slumbering mind that they are not worth noticing.

---

① That the appearance of mental activity here is real can be proved by suggesting to the 'hypnotized' somnambulist that he shall remember when he awakes He will then often do so.

关于灵魂及其本质的理论,他就可以自由地将这种显现看作是它们看上去所是的样子,而且承认心灵和身体都可以睡觉。

洛克是这后一种观点的第一个杰出的拥护者,他抨击笛卡儿信仰的那几页文字与他论文中的其他篇幅一样都充满了活力。"每一次昏昏欲睡的打盹都动摇了主张他们的灵魂始终在思维的人的理论。"他不会相信人会如此容易遗忘。朱弗罗伊先生和W.汉密尔顿爵士以同样经验的方式处理这个问题的时候,得出了相反的结论。简单地说,他们的理由如下:

在自然的或者是诱导的梦游症中,通常会有智性活动的大量展现,随之而来的就是对所有经过的事情的完全遗忘。①

突然从睡眠中被唤醒的时候,不管睡得有多么深,我们总是发现自己在做梦。普通的梦总是在醒来后的几分钟之内被记着,然后就不可挽回地消失了。

通常,在醒着并且心不在焉的时候,一些思想和意象会涌入我们的心头,而在下一个时刻我们却不能回忆起这些思想和意象。

当醒着的时候,我们对习惯了的噪音等的无感受性,证明了我们对不专注的事物依然有所感受。在睡眠中也同样如此,在最初阻碍我们入睡的对声音、寒冷、触碰等等的感觉在场的情况下,我们逐渐地习惯了,并且鼾声如雷。我们学会了在睡眠中忽略它们,如同在醒着时忽略它们一样。单纯的感官印象在深度睡眠和轻度睡眠中是一样的;差别一定在于显然正在睡眠的心灵部分做出了它们不值得注意这样的判断。

---

① 心理活动的显现在这里是真实的,这能够通过向"受到催眠"的梦游者暗示他在醒来的时候将会记得而得以证明。然后他通常就会记得。

This discrimination is equally shown by nurses of the sick and mothers of infants, who will sleep through much noise of an irrelevant sort, but waken at the slightest stirring of the patient or the babe. This last fact shows the *sense-organ* to be pervious for sounds.

Many people have a remarkable faculty of registering when asleep the flight of time. They will habitually wake up at the same minute day after day, or will wake punctually at an unusual hour determined upon overnight. How can this knowledge of the hour (more accurate often than anything the waking consciousness shows) be possible without mental activity during the interval?

Such are what we may call the classical reasons for admitting that the mind is active even when the person afterwards ignores the fact. ① Of late years, or rather, one may say, of late months, they have been reinforced by a lot of curious observations made on hysterical and hypnotic subjects, which prove the existence of a highly developed consciousness in places where it has hitherto not been suspected at all. These observations throw such a novel light upon human nature that I must give them in some detail. That at least four different and in a certain sense rival observers should agree in the same conclusion justifies us in accepting the conclusion as true.

---

① For more details, cf. Malebranche, Rech. de la Verité. bk. III. chap. I; J. Locke, Essay eonc. H. U., book II. ch. I; C. Wolf, Psychol. rationalis, § 59; Sir W. Hamilton, Lectures on Metaph., lecture XVLL; J. Bascom. Science of Mind, § 12; Th. Jouffroy, Melanges Philos., ‘du Sommeil’; H. Holland, Chapters on Mental Physiol., p. 80; B. Brodie, Psychol. Researches, p. 147; E. M. Chesley, Journ. of Spec. Phil., vol. XI. p. 72; Th. Ribot, Maladies de la Personnalite, pp. 8-10; H. Lotze, Meta. physics, § 533.

照顾病人的护士和照顾婴儿的母亲同样能够表现出这种辨别力，她们能够在大量不相关种类的噪音中睡觉，但是她们会在病人或者婴儿的最轻微的响动中醒来。这最后的事实表明感觉器官是可以接受声音的。

很多人在睡觉的时候拥有记录流逝的时间的非凡能力。他们日复一日地习惯性地在同一时刻醒来，或者准时在头天晚上决定的不寻常的时间里醒来。如果在那段时间间隔里没有心理活动的话，对时间的了解（常常比醒着的意识表现得更加准确）如何可能呢？

这些就是我们所说的承认下述观点的经典理由，即甚至当人们后来忽视了那个事实的时候，心灵也是活跃的。① 最近这些年来，或者毋宁说，最近几个月来，这些理由通过对患有歇斯底里症的被试和受到催眠的被试所做的许多奇特的观察而得以强化，这些观察证明了高度发展的意识存在于迄今完全没有被觉察到的地方。这些观察使我们对人类的本性有了如此新颖的了解，以至于我必须详细的讨论它们。如果至少有四个不同的并且在某种意义上说是相互竞争的观察者赞同相同的结论，那么这就证明我们将这种结论当作是真的来接受是正当的。

---

① 更多的细节可参见马尔布兰奇，《关于真理的研究》，第 3 卷，第 1 章；J. 洛克《人类理解论》，第 2 卷，第 1 章；C. 沃尔夫，《理性心理学》，第 59 节；W. 汉密尔顿爵士，《行而上学演讲》，第 17 讲；J. 巴斯科姆，《心的科学》，第 12 节；Th. 朱弗罗伊，《哲学杂谈》，“论睡眠”；H. 霍兰，《心理生理学章节》，第 80 页；B. 布罗迪，《心理学研究》，第 147 页；E. M. 切斯利，《思辨哲学杂志》，第 11 章，第 72 页；Th. 里伯特，《人格疾病》，第 8 ~ 10 页；H. 洛采，《行而上学》，第533 节。

'Unconsciousness' in Hysterics.

One of the most constant symptoms in persons suffering from hysteric disease in its extreme forms consists in alterations of the natural sensibility of various parts and organs of the body. Usually the alteration is in the direction of defect, or anaesthesia. One or both eyes are blind, or color-blind, or there is hemianopsia (blindness to one half the field of view), or the field is contracted. Hearing, taste, smell may similarly disappear, in part or in totality. Still more striking are the cutaneous anaesthesias. The old witch-finders looking for the 'devil's seals. learned well the existence of those insensible patches on the skin of their victims, to which the minute physical examinations of recent medicine have but recently attracted attention again. They may be scattered anywhere, but are very apt to affect one side of the body. Not infrequently they affect an entire lateral half, from head to foot; and the insensible skin of, say, the left side will then be found separated from the naturally sensitive skin of the right by a perfectly sharp line of demarcation down the middle of the front and back. Sometimes, most remarkable of all, the entire skin, hands, feet, face, everything, and the mucous membranes, muscles and joints so far as they can be explored, become *completely* insensible without the other vital functions becoming gravely disturbed.

These hysterical anaesthesias can be made to disappear more or less completely by various odd processes. It has been recently found that magnets, plates of metal, or the electrodes of a battery, placed against the skin, have this peculiar power. And when one side is relieved in this way, the anaesthesia is often found to have transferred itself to the opposite side, which until then was well. Whether these strange effects of magnets and metals be due to their direct physiological action, or to a prior effect on the patient's mind (expectant attention' or 'suggestion') is still a mooted question.

歇斯底里症发作中的“无意识”

在患有最严重的歇斯底里症的人中最恒定的症状之一，在于身体的不同部分和器官的自然感受性的变化。通常变化趋向于产生缺陷或者感觉缺乏。一只眼睛或者两只眼睛盲了，或者色盲了，或者出现了偏盲（视野的一半是盲的），或者视野收缩了。听力、味觉、嗅觉可以同样地部分或者全部消失。更引人注意的是皮肤的感觉缺乏。寻找“魔鬼标记”的年老的女巫发现者很清楚其受害人皮肤上的那些无感觉部分的存在，新近医学上的精确的物理检查只是在最近才将人们的注意力吸引到了这些部分上来。它们可以分散在任何地方，但是非常倾向于影响身体的一侧。它们从头到脚影响整整半边身体，这种情况也并非少见；并且无感觉的皮肤，比如说左侧的皮肤被发现通过一条非常明显的沿着身体前后的中间部分的分界线，与右侧自然有感觉的皮肤分离开来。有时最令人吃惊的是，整个皮肤——手、脚、脸、所有的一切，以及粘膜、肌肉和关节在它们能够被探测的范围之内变得完全没有感觉了，而其他重要的功能却没有受到严重的扰乱。

通过各种奇怪的方法可以使这些歇斯底里症中感觉缺乏差不多完全消失掉。最近发现，放置在皮肤上的磁铁、金属板、或者电池的电极就具有这种奇特的力量。而且，当一侧的感觉缺乏通过这种方法被解除之后，经常发现感觉缺乏独自转移到了直到那时还一直良好的相反的一边。无论这些磁铁和金属的奇怪效果是由于它们的直接的生理学作用所致，还是由于先前在病人的心中施加的影响所致（“预期注意”或者“暗示”），依然是一个有争

A still better awakener of sensibility is the hypnotic trance, into which many of these patients can be very easily placed, and in which their lost sensibility not infrequently becomes entirely restored. Such returns of sensibility succeed the times of insensibility and alternate with them. But Messrs. Pierre Janet ①and A. Binet ②have shown that during the times of anaesthesia, and coexisting with it, *sensibility* to *the ancesthetic parts is also there, in the form of a secondary consciousness* entirely cut off from the primary or normal one, but susceptible of being *tapped* and made to testify to its existence in various odd ways.

Chief amongst these is what M. Janet calls ' the method of *distraction*' These hysterics are apt to possess a very narrow field of attention, and to be unable to think of more than one thing at a time. When talking with any person they forget everything else. "When Lucie talked directly with any one," says M. Janet, "she ceased to be able to hear any other person. You may stand behind her, call her by name, shout abuse into her ears, without making her turn round; or place yourself before her, show her objects, touch her, etc., without attracting her notice. When finally she becomes aware of you, she thinks you have just come into the room again, and greets you accordingly. This singular forgetfulness makes her liable to tell all her secrets aloud, unrestrained by the presence of unsuitable auditors."

Now M. Janet found in several subjects like this that if he came up behind them whilst they Were plunged in conversation with a third party, and addressed them in a whisper, telling them to raise

---

① L' Automatisme Psychologique, Paris, 1889, *passim*.

② See his articles in the Chicago Open Court, for July, August and November. 1889. Also in the Revue Philosophique for 1889 and '90.

议的问题。一种更好的唤醒感受性的方法是催眠迷睡，在这种恍惚状态中，他们丧失了的感受性完全恢复了，这种情况并不少见。这种感受性的恢复发生在没有感受性的时期之后，并且与它们交替出现。但是，皮埃尔·詹尼特①和A. 彼耐特②先生已经表明，在感觉缺乏期间，对感觉缺乏部位的感受性也存在于那里，并且和感觉缺乏共存，它以次级意识的形式存在着，这次级意识完全与主要或者正常的意识相隔绝，但是容易受到敲击的影响，并且通过各种不寻常的方式可以证明它的存在。

这些方法中最主要的方法是詹尼特先生所说的"分心法"。这些歇斯底里症患者倾向于拥有非常狭小的注意域，并且一次只能思考一件事情。当和不管什么人谈话的时候，他们忘记了其他一切事情。"当露西直接和某人谈话的时候，"詹尼特先生说，"她不再能够听见其他任何人的讲话。你可以站在她身后，叫她的名字，朝着她的耳朵喊叫着说出辱骂的语言，这都不会使她转过身来；或者你可以站在她的面前，给她看一些东西，摸摸她，等等，这都不会引起她的注意。当最后她开始注意到你的时候，她认为你刚刚又来到了屋子里，并且因此向你打招呼。这种异常的健忘，使得她易于大声地讲出她的所有秘密，并且不合适的听众的出现也不会限制她这样做。"

现在，詹尼特在几个像这样的被试者中发现，如果他在他们正在和第三者谈话的时候走到他们的身后，并且低声地与他们说

---

① 《心理自动作用》，巴黎，1889年，书中各处。

② 参见他在《芝加哥公开法庭》中的文章，7月、8月和11月，1889年。也可参见他在1889年和1890年的《哲学评论》中的文章。

their hand or perform other simple acts, they would obey the order given, although their *talking* intelligence was quite unconscious of receiving it Leading them from one thing to another, he made them reply by signs to his whispered questions, and finally made them answer in writing, if a pencil were placed in their hand. The primary consciousness meanwhile went on with the conversation, entirely unaware of these performances on the hand' s part The consciousness which presided over these latter appeared in its turn to be quite as little disturbed by the upper consciousness' s concerns. This *proof by automatic' writing*, of a secondary consciousness' s existence, is the most cogent and striking one ; but a crowd of other facts prove the same thing. If I run through them rapidly, the reader will probably be convinced.

The apparently anaesthetic hand of these subjects, for one thing, *will often adapt itself discriminatingly* to whatever object may be put into it With a pencil it will make writing movements ; into a pair of scissors it will put its fingers and will open and shut them, etc. , etc. The primary consciousness, so to call it, is meanwhile unable to say whether or no *anything* is in the hand, if the latter be hidden from sight. "I put a pair of eyeglasses into Leonie' s anaesthetic hand, this hand opens it and raises-it towards the nose, but half way thither it enters the field of vision of Leonie, who sees it and stops stupefied : 'Why,' says she, 'I have an eyeglass in my left hand !'" M. Binet found a very curious sort of connection between the apparently anaesthetic skin and the mind in some Salpetriere-subjects. Things placed in the hand were not felt, but *thought* of (apparently in visual terms) and in no wise referred by the subject to their starting point in the hand' s sensation. A key, a knife, placed in the hand occasioned *ideas* of a key or a knife, but the hand felt nothing. Similarly the subject *thought of* the number 3, 6, etc. ,

话，告诉他们举起他们的手来，或者做出其他简单的动作，他们就会服从所下达的命令，尽管他们的谈话理智对于接受这个命令完全是无意识的。通过一件事情接着一件事情地引导他们，他使得他们通过手势来回答他低声说出的问题，并且最后使得他们用书写来回答问题，如果将一只笔放在他们手中的话。与此同时，主要的意识继续着谈话，对手所执行的这些操作完全没有意识。负责手的活动的意识似乎也同样没有由于上级意识的关注而受到打扰。“自动”书写证明了次级意识的存在，这种证明是最具说服力的，也是最显著的；而且许多其他的事实也证明了同样的问题。如果我们迅速地浏览一下这些事实，读者可能就会被说服了。

首先，这些被试的明显感觉缺乏的手，常常会使自己有区别地适应任何可以放在他手里的东西。放一只笔，它就会做出书写的动作；放上一把剪刀，它就会把它的手指伸进去，并且把剪刀张开又闭合，等等，等等。与此同时，如果手中的任何东西远离被试的视线的话，所谓主要的意识，是不能说出是否手中有任何东西的。“我把一副眼镜放进了里奥尼的感觉缺乏的手中，这只手将眼镜打开，并且把它向鼻子那边送去，但是在送过去的途中它进入了里奥尼的视野，她看见了它，并且停止了无感觉状态：‘为什么，’她说‘我有一副眼镜在我的左手里！’在一些感觉缺乏的被试者那里，彼耐特先生发现在明显感觉缺乏的皮肤和心灵之间有一种非常奇特的联系。放在手里的东西没有被感觉到，但是却被想起来了（明显是用视觉术语），并且被试决不会提及它们最初在手里的感觉。放在手里的一把钥匙、一把刀子会引起关于钥匙和刀子的观念，但是手却什么也感受不到。同样，如果操作者让被试的手或者是手指弯曲三次或者六次，或者如果他敲击被试的手或者手

if the hand or finger was bent three or six times by the operator, or if he stroked it three, six, etc. , times.

In certain individuals there was found a still odder phenomenon, which reminds one of that curious idiosyncrasy of ‘colored hearing’ of which a few cases have been lately described with great care by foreign writers. These individuals, namely, *saw* the impression received by the hand, but could not feel it ; and the thing seen appeared by no means associated with the hand, but more like an independent vision, which usually interested and surprised the patient. Her hand being hidden by a screen, she was ordered to look at another screen and to tell of any visual image which might project itself thereon. Numbers would then come, corresponding to the number of times the insensible member was raised, touched, etc. Colored lines and figures would come, corresponding to similar ones traced on the palm; the hand itself or its fingers would come when manipulated ; and finally objects placed in it would come ; but on the hand itself nothing would ever be felt. Of course simulation would not be hard here; but M. Binet disbelieves this (usually very shallow) explanation to be a probable one in cases in question. ①

The usual way in which doctors measure the delicacy of our touch is by the compass-points Two points are normally felt as one whenever they are too close together for discrimination ; but what is ‘too close’ on one part of the skin may seem very far apart on another. In the middle of the back or on the thigh, less than 3 inches may be too close; on the fingertip a tenth of an inch is far enough apart. Now, as tested in this way,

---

① This whole phenomenon shows how an idea which remains itself below the threshold of a certain conscious self may occasion associative effects therein. The skin-sensations unfelt by the patient’s primary consciousness awaken nevertheless their usual visual associates therein.

指三次或者六次，被试就会想到三或六这样的数字。

在某些个体那里发现了一种更加奇怪的现象，这使人们想起了令人好奇的“色听”特性，最近一些外国的作者十分认真地描述了关于“色听”的例子。即这些个体看见了由手接收到的印象，但是却不能感受它；而且被看见的东西似乎与手没有任何联系，但是更像是一种独立的视觉，这通常会引起患者的兴趣并且使他们感到惊讶。她的手藏在屏风后面，她被要求去看另一块屏风，并且说出可能投射于其上的任何视觉意象。于是数字将会出现在那里，与无感觉部位被抬起、触碰等等的次数相应。彩色线条和图形将会出现在那里，与在手掌上被画出的相似的线条和图形相应；当对她的手或者手指进行操作的时候，手或者手指将会出现在那里；最后，那里会出现放在手里的东西的意象；但是手本身却从来没有感受到任何东西。当然，在这里进行冒充并不困难；但是，彼耐特先生不相信对所讨论例子的这种解释（通常非常肤浅）是一种可能的解释。①

医生测量我们触觉敏感度的常用方法是使用罗经点。只要两个点彼此太靠近了以至于无法分辨出来，这两个点通常被感觉为一个点；但是在皮肤的某个部位上“太靠近”的两个点，在皮肤的另一个部位上就可能显得距离非常远。在后背的中部或者在大腿上，小于三英寸就可能是太靠近了；在手指尖上，十分之一英寸已经是足够远了。现在，以这种方式进行测试，如果诉诸主要

① 这整个现象表明，使自己处于某种有意识自我阈限之下的观念，是如何可以在那里引起联想效果的。患者的主要意识所感受不到的皮肤感觉，在那里还是唤醒了它们通常的视觉联想物。

with the appeal made to the primary consciousness, which talks through the month and seems to hold the field alone, a certain person's skin may be entirely anaesthetic and not feel the compass-points at all; and yet this same skin will prove to have a perfectly normal sensibility if the appeal be made to that other secondary or sub-consciousness, which expresses itself automatically by writing or by movements of the hand. M. Binet, M. Pierre Janet, and M. Jules Janet have all found this. The subject, whenever touched, would signify 'one point' or 'two points,' as accurately as if she were a normal person. She would signify it only by these movements; and of the movements themselves her primary self would be as unconscious as of the facts they signified, for what the submerged consciousness makes the hand do automatically is unknown to the consciousness which uses the mouth.

Messrs. Bernheim and Pitres have also proved, by observations too complicated to be given in this spot, that the hysterical blindness is no real blindness at all. The eye of an hysteric which is totally blind when the other or seeing eye is shut, will do its share of vision perfectly well when *both* eyes are open together. But even where both eyes are semi-blind from hysterical disease, the method of automatic writing proves that their perceptions exist, only cut off from communication with the upper consciousness. M. Binet has found the hand of his patients unconsciously writing down words which their eyes were vainly endeavoring to 'see,' i. e., to bring to the upper consciousness. Their submerged consciousness was of course seeing them, or the hand could not have written as it did. Colors are similarly perceived by the sub-conscious self, which the hysterically color-blind eyes cannot bring to the normal consciousness. Pricks, burns, and pinches on the anaesthetic skin, all unnoticed by the upper self, are recollected to have been suffered, and complained of, as soon as the under self gets a chance to express itself by the passage of the subject into hypnotic trance.

意识的话,主要意识用嘴说话并且似乎只是局限于这一活动领域之内,那么,某个人的皮肤可以完全是感觉缺乏的,并且根本感觉不到罗经点;然而,如果诉诸那另一个次级意识或说下意识,它通过书写或者手的动作自动地表达自己,那么,这同一块皮肤将证明具有完全正常的感受性。彼耐特先生、皮埃尔·詹尼特先生和朱尔斯·詹尼特先生都发现了这一点。被试无论什么时候被触碰,都会指出是“一点”或者是“两点”,就好像她是一个正常人一样准确。她只能通过这些动作来指出它;而她的主要的自我对这些动作自身是无意识的,对它们所指示的事实也同样是无意识的,因为使用嘴说话的意识不知道下意识让手自动去做的事情。

伯恩海姆先生和皮特里斯先生通过因过于复杂而不能在此加以陈述的观察也已经证明,歇斯底里症失明根本不是真正的失明。患有歇斯底里症的全盲的一支眼睛在另一只眼睛或者说能够看见的眼睛闭上的时候,可以很好地完成在两只眼睛都睁开时它自己的任务。而且,甚至在由于歇斯底里症而导致的两只眼睛都半盲的情况下,自动书写的方法证明了它们的知觉是存在着的,只是和上级意识的交流被切断了。彼耐特先生发现,他的病人的手无意识地写下了字,他们的眼睛再努力也看不到这些字,也就是说不能够将它们带入上级意识。他们的下意识当然看见了它们,否则手就不可能那样地书写。颜色也同样地被下意识自我所知觉,患有歇斯底里症色盲的眼睛不能将这些颜色带入正常的意识中。一旦下级自我由于被试进入了催眠的恍惚状态中而有机会得以表达自我,这些完全没有得到上级自我注意的在感觉缺乏皮肤上的刺痛、烧灼和夹痛都会被回忆起来,被试会记得他遭受了这样的痛苦,并且会对此抱怨。

It must be admitted, therefore, that *in certain persons*, at least, *the total possible consciousness may be split into parts which coexist but mutually ignore each other*, and share the objects of knowledge between them. More remarkable still, they are *complementary*. Give an object to one of the consciousnesses, and by that fact you remove it from the other or others. Barring a certain common fund of information, like the command of language, etc,, what the upper self knows the under self is ignorant of, and *vice versa*. M. Janet has proved this beautifully in his subject Lucie. The following experiment will serve as the type of the rest: In her trance he covered her lap with cards, each bearing a number. He then told her that on waking she should *not see* any card whose number was a multiple of three. This is the ordinary so-called 'posthypnotic suggestion,' now well known, and for which Lucie was a well-adapted subject. Accordingly, when she was awakened and asked about the papers on her lap, she counted and said she saw those only whose number was not a multiple of 3. To the 12, 18, 9, etc., she was blind. But the *hand*, when the sub-conscious self was interrogated by the usual method of engrossing the upper self in another conversation, wrote that the only cards in Lucie's lap were those numbered 12, 18, 9, etc., and on being asked to pick up all the cards which were there, picked up these and let the others lie. Similarly when the sight of certain things was suggested to the sub-conscious Lucie, the normal Lucie suddenly became partially or totally blind. "What is the matter? I can't see !" the normal personage suddenly cried out in the midst of her conversation, when M. Janet whispered to the secondary personage to make use of her eyes. The anaesthesias, paralyses, contractions and other irregularities from which hysterics suffer seem then to be due to the fact that their secondary personage has enriched itself by robbing the primary one of a function which the latter ought to have retained The curative indication is evident:

因此,必须承认的是,至少在有些人那里,全部可能的意识可以被分裂成不同的部分,这些部分共同存在,但是相互之间却忽视了对方,并且分享着它们之间知识的对象。更令人惊奇的是,它们是互补的。将一个对象给予其中的一个意识,由此你就将这个对象从另一个或者另一些对象那里移开了。关闭某种共同的信息储备,例如语言运用等等,上级自我所知道的东西,下级自我就不知道,反之亦然。詹尼特先生在他的被试露西身上漂亮地证明了这一点。下面的实验可以作为其他实验的典范:在她被催眠的恍惚状态中,他在她的腿上放了一些卡片,每张卡片上面都有一个数字。然后他告诉她,她在醒来的时候将看不见任何卡片上的数字是三的倍数的卡片。这就是平常所说的"催眠后暗示",现在它已广为人知了,而露西是一个对此适应得非常好的被试。相应地,当她被唤醒并被问及她腿上的卡片时,她数了一下,然后说她只看到那些数字不是三的倍数的卡片。对于12、18、9等等来说,她是盲的。但是,当下意识通过让上级自我全神贯注于另一场谈话这种寻常的方法而受到询问时,手就会写出在露西的腿上只有数字是12、18、9等等的卡片,而且当被要求拾起那里的所有卡片时,她只会拾起这些卡片,而将其他的卡片留在那里。同样,当将某些东西的视觉形象暗示给下意识的露西时,正常的露西会突然变得部分或者全部失明。当詹尼特先生悄悄地告诉次级人格使用她的眼睛的时候,正常的人格突然在她的谈话中间喊出声来,"怎么回事?我看不见了!"。歇斯底里症患者所遭受的感觉缺乏、瘫痪、收缩以及其他不正常现象因而似乎是由于这样的一个事实所致,即他们的次级人格通过剥夺主要人格应当保持的一种功能来充实自己。治疗暗示是明显的:通过诱导催眠或者无论

get at the secondary personage, by hypnotization or in whatever other way, and make her *give up* the eye, the skin, the arm, or whatever the affected part may be. The normal self thereupon regains possession, sees, feels, or is able to move again. In this way M. Jules Janet easily cured the well-known subject of the Salpetriere, Wit, of all sorts of afflictions which, until he discovered the secret of her deeper trance, it had been difficult to subdue. "Cessez cette mauvaise plaisanterie," he said to the secondary self—and the latter obeyed. The way in which the various personages share the stock of possible sensations between them seems to be amusingly illustrated in this young woman. When awake, her skin is insensible everywhere except on a zone about the arm where she habitually wears a gold bracelet This zone has feeling; but in the deepest trance, when all the rest of her body feels, this particular zone becomes absolutely anaesthetic.

Sometimes the mutual ignorance of the selves leads to incidents which are strange enough. The acts and movements performed by the sub-conscious self are withdrawn from the conscious one, and the subject will do all sorts of incongruous things of which he remains quite unaware. "I order Lucie [by the method of *distraction*] to make a *pied de nez*, and her hands go forthwith to the end of her nose. Asked what she is doing, she replies that she is doing nothing, and continues for a long time talking, with no apparent suspicion that her fingers are moving in front of her nose. I make her walk about the room; she continues to speak and believes herself sitting down."

M. Janet observed similar acts in a man in alcoholic delirium. Whilst the doctor was questioning him, M. J. made him by whispered suggestion walk, sit, kneel, and even lie down on his face on the floor, he all the while believing himself to be standing beside his bed. Such *bizarreries* sound incredible, until one has seen their like. Long ago, without understanding it, I myself saw a small example of the way in which a person's knowledge may be shared by the two selves.

其他什么方式到达次级人格,并且让她放弃眼睛、皮肤、胳膊或者无论哪一个可能受到影响的部位。于是,正常的自我收回了其所有物,看见了、能感受了或者能够再次移动了。用这种方法,朱尔思·詹尼特先生很容易地治愈了那个广为人知的感觉缺乏的被试——威特的各种痛苦,在发现她深层恍惚状态的秘密之前,这些痛苦一直是难以征服的。"停止这种低劣的玩笑,"他对次级自我说——并且后者服从了。各种人格分享可能的感觉材料的方式似乎在这位年轻妇女这里得到了有趣的说明。当醒着的时候,她的皮肤除了胳膊上习惯性地佩戴金手镯的区域以外,任何地方都没有感觉。这个区域有感觉;但是,在最深层的恍惚状态中,当身体的所有其余部分都有感觉的时候,这一特定区域就彻底地变得没有感觉了。

有时候自我彼此间的无知会导致相当奇怪的事情。由下意识自我执行的动作和运动从有意识自我那里消失了,并且被试会做出他仍然没有意识到的各种不合适的事情。"我让露西(通过分心法)做一个拇指顶鼻尖摇动其余四指的动作,她的手立刻会去到鼻尖处。问她在做什么,她说她什么也没有做,并且继续长时间的谈话,她对自己的手指在她的鼻子前边的摇动明显没有觉察。我让她在房间里走动;她继续谈话并且认为自己是坐着的。"

詹尼特先生在一个处于酗酒精神狂乱状态的人身上观察到了类似的动作。当医生正在问他问题的时候,詹尼特先生通过低声的暗示使得他行走、坐下、跪下、甚至脸朝下趴在地上,他却一直都相信自己正站在床边上。这么怪异的事情听起来是难以置信的,除非我们见到过类似的事情。很久以前,在还没有理解这种情况的时候,我自己看到过关于两个自我分享一个人的知识的

A young woman who had been writing automatically was sitting with a pencil in her hand, trying to recall at my request the name of a gentleman whom she had once seen. She could only recollect the first syllable. Her hand meanwhile, without her knowledge, wrote down the last two syllables. In a perfectly healthy young man who can write with the planchette, I lately found the hand to be entirely anesthetic during the writing act; I could prick it severely without the Subject knowing the fact. The *writing on the planchette*, however, accused me in strong terms of hurting the hand. Pricks on the *other* (non-writing) hand, meanwhile, which awakened strong protest from the young man's vocal organs, were denied to exist by the self which made the planchette go. ①

We get exactly similar results in the so-called post-hypnotic suggestion. It is a familiar fact that certain subjects, when told during a trance to perform an act or to experience an hallucination after waking, will when the time comes, obey the command. How is the command registered? How is its performance so accurately timed? These problems were long a mystery, for the primary personality remembers nothing of the trance or the suggestion, and will often trump up an improvised pretext for yielding to the unaccountable impulse which possesses the man so suddenly and which he cannot resist. Edmund Gurney was the first to discover, by means of automatic writing, that the secondary self is awake, keeping its attention constantly fixed on the command and watching for the signal of its execution. Certain trance-subjects who were also automatic writers, when roused from trance and put to the planchette,—not knowing then what they wrote, and having their upper attention fully engrossed by reading aloud, talking, or solving problems in mental arithmetic,—would inscribe

---

① See Proceedings of American Soc. for Psych. Research, vol. 1. p. 548.

方式的一个小例子。一个年轻的女子坐在那里,手中拿着一支铅笔,并且正在自动地书写着,在我的提问之下她正在努力地回忆一个她曾经见过的绅士的名字。她只能回忆起第一个音节。与此同时,在她不知道的情况下,她的手写下了后两个音节。在一个可以在占卜写板上书写的完全健康的年轻男子身上,我近来发现手在书写时是完全缺乏感觉的;我可以极其残暴地刺它,而被试却并不知道这件事。然而,在占卜写板上的字迹却用强硬的措辞谴责我刺痛了他的手。同时,刺他的另一只手(不写字的手),这就会激起来自年轻人的发声器官的强烈抗议,而负责在占卜写板上书写的那个自我却否认了这件事实的存在。①

我们在所谓的催眠后暗示中也得到了完全类似的结果。这是一个常见的事实,即当某个被试在催眠的恍惚状态中被告知在醒来之后要执行一个动作或者体验一种幻象时,他将在时间到来时服从那个命令。这个命令是如何被记录下来的呢?它的执行如何会这么准时呢?这些问题长期以来一直是个谜,因为主要人格对催眠恍惚状态和暗示都毫无记忆,并且经常会即兴编造一个借口,作为他屈从于如此突如其来地支配他、并让他无法抗拒的无法解释的冲动的托词。埃德蒙·格尼通过自动书写的方法第一个发现,次级自我是醒着的,不变地将其注意力固定在那个命令之上,并且守候着执行命令的信号。某些也是自动书写者的催眠被试,当从催眠恍惚状态中醒来并且开始使用占卜写板的时候——当时他们不知道写下了什么,并且他们的上级注意力完全贯注于大声朗读、谈话或者解决心算问题中了——就会记下

① 参见《美国心理研究协会会刊》,第1卷,第548页。

the orders which they had received, together with notes relative to the time elapsed and the time yet to run before the execution. ① It is therefore to no 'automatism' in the mechanical sense that such acts are due: a self presides over them, a split-off, limited and buried, but yet a fully conscious, self. More than this, the buried self often comes to the surface and drives out the other self whilst the acts are performing. In other words, the subject lapses into trance again when the moment arrives for execution, and has no subsequent recollection of the act which he has done. Gurney and Beaunis established this fact, which has since been verified on a large scale ; and Gurney also showed that the patient became *suggestible*; again during the brief time of the performance. M. Janet's observations, in their turn, well illustrate the phenomenon.

"I tell Lucie to keep her arms raised after she shall have awakened. Hardly is she in the normal state, when up go her arms above her head, but she pays no attention to them. She goes, comes, converses, holding her arms high in the air. If asked what her arms are doing, she is surprised at such a question, and says very sincerely: 'My hands are doing nothing; they are just like yours.'... I command her to weep, and when awake she really sobs, but continues in the midst of her tears to talk of very gay matters. The sobbing over, there remained no trace of this grief, which seemed to have been quite sub-conscious."

The primary self often has to invent an hallucination by which to mask and hide from its own view the deeds which the other self is enacting. Leonie 3 ②writes real letters, whilst Leonie 1 believes that she is

---

① Proceedings of the (London) See. for Psych. Remind, May 1887, p268 ff.

② M. Janet designates by numbers the different personalities which the subject may display.

他们已经接收到的命令，并且用符号记录下了已经过去的时间和在命令执行前还要经历的时间。[①] 因此，这些动作的产生不是由于机械意义上的"自动作用"：一个自我管理着它们，一个分裂出来的、有限的和隐藏的，但还是完全有意识的自我。此外，当动作正在进行的时候，隐藏的自我经常浮出水面并且赶走另一个自我。换句话说，当执行命令的时刻来临的时候，被试又一次进入了催眠恍惚状态，并且后来对他所做过的动作没有任何记忆。格尼和博尼斯确立了这一事实，此后这个事实在更大的范围上得到了证实；而且格尼还表明，在执行命令的短时间内患者又变得可暗示了。接下来，詹尼特先生的观察对这种现象做了很好的说明。

"我告诉露西在醒来之后把胳膊举着。当她的胳膊举过头顶的时候，她几乎还没有进入正常的状态，但是她并没有注意它们。她将胳膊高高地举在空中的同时，走过来，走过去，说着话。如果问她的胳膊正在做什么，她对这样的问题很是惊讶，并且非常真诚地说：'我的胳膊什么也没有做，它们就和你的一样。'……我命令她哭泣，当她醒来的时候她真的哭了，在哭的时候还继续谈论着非常愉快的事情。哭完了，也没有留下任何悲伤的痕迹，这悲伤似乎完全是下意识的。"

主要自我经常不得不虚构一种幻觉，通过它来掩饰或隐瞒它自己关于另一个自我正在做出的行为的观点。里奥尼 3[②] 真的在写信，而里奥尼 1 认为她自己在编织；或者露西 3 真的来到了医

① 《（伦敦）心理研究协会会刊》，1887 年 5 月，第 268 页以后。

② 詹尼特先生用数字来指明被试可以展示出来的不同的人格。

knitting; or Lucia 3 really comes to the doctor's office, whilst Lucia 1 believes herself to be at home. This is a sort of delirium. The alphabet, or the series of numbers, when handed over to the attention of the secondary personage may for the time be lost to the normal self. Whilst the hand writes the alphabet, obediently to command, the 'subject,' to her great stupefaction, finds herself unable to recall it, etc. Few things are more curious than these relations of mutual exclusion, of which all gradations exist between the several partial consciousnesses.

How far this splitting up of the mind into separate consciousnesses may exist in each one of us is a problem. M. Janet holds that it is only possible where there is abnormal weakness, and consequently a defect of unifying or co-ordinating power. An hysterical woman abandons part of her consciousness because she is too weak nervously to hold it together. The abandoned part meanwhile may solidify into a secondary or sub-conscious self. In a perfectly sound subject, on the other hand, what is dropped out of mind at one moment keeps coming back at the next. The whole fund of experiences and knowledges remains integrated, and no split-off portions of it can get organized stably enough to form subordinate selves. The stability, monotony, and stupidity of these latter is often very striking. The posthypnotic sub-consciousness seems to think of nothing but the order which it last received ; the cataleptic sub-consciousness, of nothing but the last position imprinted on the limb. M. Janet could cause definitely circumscribed reddening and tumefaction of the skin on two of his subjects, by suggesting to them in hypnotism the hallucination of a mustard-poultice of any special shape. "*J'ai tout le temps pense a votre sinapisme*," says the subject, when put back into trance after the suggestion has taken effect. A man N,... whom M. Janet operated on at long intervals, was betweenwhiles tampered with by another operator, and when put to sleep again by M. Janet, said he was 'too far away to receive orders, being in Algiers.' The other operator, having suggested that hallucination, had forgotten to remove it before waking the subject from his trance,

生的办公室，而露西1认为她自己在家里。这是一种暂时的精神错乱。当字母表或者数字序列被移交给次级人格去注意的时候，它们可能对正常的自我来说会消失一段时间。当手服从命令写字母表的时候，"被试"很是茫然地发现他自己不能回忆起它了，等等。很少有东西比这相互排斥的关系更加奇特的了，在这些关系当中，几个局部意识之间存在着各种等级。

存在于我们每个人之中的这种心灵分裂为单独的意识的情况可以达到什么样的程度，这是一个问题。詹尼特先生坚持认为只在当反常的弱点、以及由此产生的统一或者协调能力的无效出现的情况下它才是可能的。一位患有歇斯底里症的女子抛弃了她的一部分意识，是因为她的神经系统太脆弱了以至于不能将意识统一在一起。与此同时，被遗弃的部分可以固结成次级自我或下意识自我。另一方面，在一个完全健康的被试身上，在某一时刻退出心灵的东西不断地在下一个时刻回来。经验和知识的整个储备仍然是完整的，而且没有一个分裂出去的部分能够足够稳定地组织起来形成次级自我。这些次级自我的稳定性、单一性和鲁钝性通常十分惊人。催眠后的下意识似乎除了它最后接收到的命令以外什么都不想；全身僵硬症的下意识只思考被铭刻于肢体上的最后姿势。詹尼特先生通过向他的两个处于催眠状态中的被试暗示出关于任何特殊形状的芥末膏药的幻觉，能够在他们身上引起界限分明的皮肤红肿。在暗示起作用之后让被试回到催眠恍惚状态中的时候，被试说，"用全部时间想你们的芥子泥治疗法。"一个人N，……詹尼特先生以很长的时间间隔对他进行治疗，他偶尔受到了另一个手术人员的干预，当詹尼特先生再次催眠他的时候，他说他"在阿尔及尔，太远了不能接收命令。"是另一个手术人员暗示了这种幻觉，他在将被试从催眠状态中唤醒之

and the poor passive trance-personality had stuck for weeks in the stagnant dream. Leonie's sub-conscious performances having been illustrated to a caller, by a '*pied de nez*' executed with her left hand in the course of conversation, when, a year later, she meets him again, up goes the same hand to her nose again, without Leonie's normal self suspecting the fact.

All these facts, taken together, form unquestionably the beginning of an inquiry which is destined to throw a new light into the very abysses of our nature, It is for that reason that I have cited them at such length in this early chapter of the book. They prove one thing conclusively, namely, that *we must never take a person's testimony, however sincere, that he has felt nothing, as proof positive that no feeling has been there.* It may have been there as part of the consciousness of a 'secondary personage,' of whose experiences the primary one whom we are consulting can naturally give no account. In hypnotic subjects (as we shall see in a later chapter) just as it is the easiest thing in the world to paralyze a movement or member by simple suggestion, so it is easy to produce what is called a systematized anaesthesia by word of command. A systematized anaesthesia means an insensibility, not to any one element of things, but to some one concrete thing or class of things. The subject is made blind or deaf to a certain person in the room and to no one else, and thereupon denies that that person is present, or has spoken, etc. M. p. Janet's Lucie, blind to some of the numbered cards in her lap (p. 207 above), is a case in point. Now when the object is simple, like a red wafer or a black cross, the subject, although he denies that he sees it when he looks straight at it, nevertheless gets a 'negative after-image' *of it when he looks away again*, *showing that the optical impression* of it has been received. Moreover reflection shows

前忘记移除它了，而那个可怜的、被动的、处于恍惚状态的人格恪守在这个停滞的梦中达几个星期之久。里奥尼的下意识活动在一个访客面前得到了说明：她曾经在和他的谈话中用左手做过一个“拇指顶鼻尖摇动其余四指”的动作，当一年后她再次遇到他的时候，那同一只手再次伸到了鼻子那里，而里奥尼的正常的自我没有觉察到这个事实。

将所有这些事实放在一起，它们无疑形成了一项调查研究的开始，这项研究一定会将一缕新的光亮投向我们本性的最深处。正是出于这个原因，我才在这本书的前边章节中这么详细地引证了它们。它们结论性地证明了一件事情，即我们一定永远不要将一个人所说的他什么也没有感受到的证词当作那里没有感受存在的绝对证据，不论这证词多么真诚。它可以作为次级人格的意识而存在于那里，对于它的经验，我们所请教的主要人格自然不能给出任何说明。在易被催眠的被试那里（如我们将在后面的章节里看到的那样），正如通过简单的暗示使一个动作或者身体的一部分瘫痪是世界上最容易的事情一样，通过命令的语言来产生所谓的系统化感觉缺乏也很容易。系统化感觉缺乏不是指对事物的任意一种要素没有感受性，而是指对某一具体事物或者某一类事物没有感觉。被试可以变得对房间里的某一个人失明或失聪，但对其他人却不会，并且因此否认那个人在场或者说过话，等等。P. 詹尼特先生的露西对其腿上的一些标有数字的卡片而言是盲的（第 207 页以前），这就是佐证。现在当物体是简单的时候，像一个红色的圆片或者一个黑色十字架，尽管在被试直接看着它时否认他看见了它，但是当他再次移开视线的时候，他仍然得到了一个“负余象”，这表明它的视觉印象还是被接收了。而且

that such a subject must *distinguish the object from others like it in order to be blind to it*. Make him blind to one person in the room, set all the persons in a row, and cell him to count them. He will count all but that one. But how can he tell *which* one not to count without recognizing who he is? In like manner, make a stroke on paper or blackboard, and tell him it is not there, and he will see nothing but the clean paper or board. Next (he not looking) surround the original stroke with other strokes exactly like it, and ask him what he sees. He will point out one by one all the new strokes, and omit the original one every time, no matter how numerous the new strokes may be, or in what order they are arranged. Similarly, if the original single stroke to which he is blind be *doubled* by a prism of some sixteen degrees placed before one of his eyes (both being kept open), he will say that he now sees *one* stroke, and point in the direction in which the image seen through the prism lies, ignoring still the original stroke.

Obviously, then, he is not blind to the *kind* of stroke in the least. He is blind only to one individual stroke of that kind in a particular position on the board or paper—that is to a particular complex object; and, paradoxical as it may seem to say so, he must distinguish it with great accuracy from others like it, in order to remain blind to it when the others are brought near. He discriminates it, as a preliminary to not seeing it at all.

Again, when by a prism before one eye a previously invisible line has been made visible to that eye, and the other eye is thereupon closed or screened, *its* closure makes no difference ; the line still remains visible. But if then the prism be removed, the line will disappear even to the eye which a moment ago saw it, and both eyes will revert to

反省表明,这样的被试为了对一个对象来说是盲的,他必须将这一对象和其他对象区别开来。让他对房间里的一个人来说是盲的,让所有的人都站成一排,并且让他去数数这些人。除了那个人以外,他会把所有的人都数进去。但是他如何能够在没有认出那个人是谁的情况下辨别出哪个人不应该被数进去呢?同样,在纸上或者黑板上画上一笔,并且告诉他它不在那里,他就会除了干净的纸或黑板以外什么都看不见。然后(在他没有看见的情况下)将原来的笔画用和它完全相似的笔画包围起来,并且问他看见了什么。他将一个个地指出所有新的笔画,并且每次都将原来的笔画遗漏掉,而不管新的笔画有多么多,或者它们是以什么顺序排列的。同样地,如果原来他看不见的那一笔通过将一个大约16度的棱镜放在他的一只眼睛前面(两只眼睛是睁开的)而变成了两笔,他将说他现在看见了一笔,并且指出从棱镜中被看到的形象所在的方向,并且仍然忽视了最初的那一笔。

显然,他对这种笔画丝毫没有失明。他只对那种笔画中位于黑板或者纸上的一个特殊位置的一个单独笔画来说是失明的——这就是对一个特殊复杂的物体来说是失明的;而且,说起来似乎自相矛盾的是,他必须非常准确地将它与其他与之相似的笔画区别开来,以便当其他的笔画在它的附近的时候,他依然看不见它。作为完全看不见它的第一步,他辨别出了它。

此外,通过放在一只眼睛前面的棱镜,先前看不见的线条对那只眼睛来说变得可见了,并且另一只眼睛立即闭合起来或者被遮挡起来,此时另一个眼睛的闭合没有造成任何影响;线条依然是可见的。但是,如果当时把棱镜移走,那么,线条甚至对于刚刚还看见它的那只眼睛来说也消失掉了,并且两只眼睛都会回复到

their original blind state.

We have, then, to deal in these cases neither with a blindness of the eye itself, nor with a mere failure to notice, but with something much more complex; namely, an active counting out and positive exclusion of certain objects. It is as when one 'cuts' an acquaintance, 'ignores' a claim, or 'refuses to be influenced' by a consideration. But the perceptive activity which works to this result is disconnected from the consciousness which is personal, so to speak, to the subject, and makes of the object concerning which the suggestion is made, its own private possession and prey. ①

The mother who is asleep to every sound but the stirrings of her babe, evidently has the babe-portion of her auditory sensibility systematically awake. Relatively to that, the rest of her mind is in a state of systematized anaesthesia. That department, split off and disconnected from the sleeping part, can none the less wake the latter up in case of need. So that on the whole the quarrel between Descartes and Locke as to whether the mind ever sleeps is less near to solution than ever. *Onapriori* speculative grounds Locke's view that thought and feeling may at times wholly disappear seems the more plausible. As glands cease to secrete and muscles to contract, so the brain should sometimes cease to carry currents, and with this minimum of its activity might well

---

① How to conceive of this state of mind is not easy. It would be much simpler to understand the process, if adding new strokes made the first one visible. There would then be two different objects apperceived as totals,—paper with one stroke, paper with many strokes; and, blind to the former, he would see all that was in the latter, because he would have apperceived it as a different total in the first instance.

A process of this sort occurs sometimes (not always) when the new strokes, instead of being mere repetitions of the original one, are lines which combine with it into a total object, say a human face. The subject of the trance then may regain his sight of the line to which he had previously been blind, by seeing it as part of the face.

它们原来的失明状态。

因而，我们在这些例子中不得不处理的既不是眼睛本身的失明，也不是单纯的注意缺乏，而是更加复杂的东西；即主动地将某些对象计算在外，并且明确地将某些对象排除在外。当某人“冷落了”一个熟人、“忽视”了一个要求或者“拒绝”被某种思考所“影响”时，情况就是这样。但是，产生这种结果的知觉活动与对被试来说是个人(可以如此说)的意识是相分离的，并且这种知觉活动将暗示所针对的对象变成了它自己的私有财产和战利品。①

那位除了她孩子的响动以外可以在任何声音中睡着的母亲，显然系统让她的听觉感受性中对孩子的听觉部分醒着。与此相对，她心灵的剩余部分处于一种系统性感觉缺乏状态。那个从睡眠部分分离出来并与之断开联系的部门，依然能够在需要的情况下将睡眠部分唤醒。因此总体来说，笛卡儿和洛克之间就心灵是否睡觉的争论比以往更远离了问题的解决。在先天思辨的基础上，洛克关于思维和感受有时可以完全消失的观点似乎更有理一些。如同腺体会停止分泌，肌肉会停止收缩一样，因此大脑应该在某些时候会停止运送神经流，并且大脑的最小强度的活动可能

---

① 如何构想这种心理状态是不容易的。如果加进去新的笔画使得第一笔是可见的话，理解这种过程就会容易很多了。那么这里就会有都被感知为整体的两个不同的对象，——上面有一笔的纸，上面有许多笔画的纸；而且，虽然对前者而言他是盲的，但是他会在后者中看到所有东西，因为他首先将它感知为一个不同的整体。

当新的笔画不是原来笔画的单纯重复，而是与原来那一笔结合在一起构成一个完整对象(比如说一张人脸)的线条的时候，有时(但并非总是)会发生这种过程。那时处于催眠恍惚状态的被试，通过将先前看不见的线条看作是脸的一个部分，可以重新获得对那个他先前看不见的线条的视觉。

coexist a minimum of consciousness. On the other hand, we see how deceptive are appearances, and are forced to admit that a part of consciousness may sever its connections with other parts and yet continue to be. On the whole it is best to abstain from a conclusion. The science of the near future will doubtless answer this question more Wisely than we can now.

Let us turn now to consider the

Relations Of Consciousness To Space.

This is the problem known in the history of philosophy as the *question of the seat of the soul*. It has given rise to much literature, but we must ourselves treat it very briefly. Everything depends on what we conceive the soul to be, an extended or an inextended entity. If the former, it may occupy a seat. If the latter, it may not; though it has been thought that even then it might still have a *position*. Much hair-splitting has arisen about the possibility of an inextended thing nevertheless being *present* throughout a certain amount of extension. We must distinguish the kinds of presence. In some manner our consciousness is 'present' to everything with which it is in relation. I am *cognitively* present to Orion whenever I perceive that constellation, but I am not dynamically present there, I work no effects. To my brain, however, I am *dynamically* present, inasmuch as my thoughts and feelings seem to react upon the processes thereof. If, then, by the seat of the mind is meant nothing more than the locality With which it stands in immediate dynamic relations, we are certain to be right in saying that its seat is somewhere in the cortex of the brain. Descartes, as is well known, thought that the inextended soul was immediately present to the pineal gland. Others, as Lotze in his earlier days, and W. Volkmann, think its position must be at some point of the structureless matrix of the anatomical brain-elements, at which point they suppose that all nerve-currents may cross and combine.

适当地与最少的意识相共存。在另一方面,我们看到现象是多么地具有欺骗性,并且被迫承认一部分意识可以切断它与其他部分的联系而继续存在。总之,最好是放弃结论。在不远的将来科学无疑会比我们现在更精明地回答这个问题。

现在,让我们开始讨论

意识与空间的关系

这个问题就是哲学史上所说的灵魂的处所问题。关于这一问题已经出现了大量的文献,但是我们自己必须非常简洁地处理它。所有的事情都取决于我们认为灵魂是什么,一个广延的本体还是一个非广延的本体。如果是前者,它就可能占据一个处所。如果是后者,它就不可能如此;尽管人们曾经构想过即使是那样它依然可能有一个位置。关于无广延的事物通过一定量的外延而呈现的可能性问题,引起了大量的过于精细的区分。我们必须区别出呈现的种类。我们的意识以某种方式"呈现"给所有与之有关系的事物。每当我感知星座的时候,在认知上我呈现在猎户星座面前,但是我没有动力地呈现在那里,我产生不了任何影响。然而,我是动力地呈现在我的大脑面前的,因为我的思维和感受似乎对其中的过程起着作用。那么,如果心灵的处所不是指别的,仅仅是指与心灵有着直接动力关系的地点,我们说它的处所位于大脑皮层的某个地方就肯定是正确的。众所周知,笛卡儿认为,非广延的灵魂直接呈现给松果腺。其他人,如早期的洛采和W.沃尔克曼,认为它的位置一定位于解剖学意义上的大脑元素的无结构矩阵的某一点,他们假定在这一点上所有的神经流可以

The scholastic doctrine is that the soul is totally present, both in the whole and in each and every part of the body. This mode of presence is said to be due to the soul's inextended nature and to its simplicity. Two extended entities could only correspond in space with one another, part to part,—but not so does the soul, which has no parts, correspond with the body. Sir Win. Hamilton and Professor Bowen defend something like this view. I. H. Fichte, Ulrici, and, among American philosophers, Mr. J. E. Walter,① maintain the soul to be a space-filling principle. Fichte calls it the inner body, Ulrici likens it to a fluid of non-molecular composition. These theories remind us of the 'theosophic' doctrines of the present day, and carry us back to times when the soul as vehicle of consciousness was not discriminated, as it now is, from the vital principle presiding over the formation of the body. Plato gave head, breast, and abdomen to the immortal reason, the courage, and the appetites, as their seats respectively. Aristotle argues that the heart is the sole seat. Elsewhere we find the blood, the brain, the lungs, the liver the kidneys even, in turn assigned as seat of the whole or part of the soul. ②

The truth is that if the thinking principle is extended we neither know its form nor its seat ; whilst if unextended, it is absurd to speak of its having any space-relations at all. Space-relations we shall see hereafter to be *sensible* things. The only objects that can have mutual relations of position are objects that are perceived coexisting in the same felt space. A thing not perceived at all, such as the inextended soul must be, cannot coexist with any perceived objects in this way. No lines can be felt stretching from it to the other objects.

---

① Perception of Space and Matter, 1879, part II. chap. 3

② For a very good condensed history of the various opinions, see W. Volkmann yon Volkmar, Lehrbuch d. Psychologie, § 16, Anm. Complete references to Sir W. Hamilton are given in J. E. Walter, Perception of Space and Matter, pp. 65-6.

相交和结合。经院哲学的学说认为灵魂全部呈现于整个身体和身体的每个部分之中。呈现的方式据说是归因于灵魂的非广延本性和简单性。两个广延的本体只能在空间中彼此之间以及部分之间相互对应,——但是没有部分的灵魂却不是与身体如此对应的。Win. 汉密尔顿爵士和鲍温教授所辩护的观点与这种观点相似。I. H. 费希特、乌尔里希以及美国哲学家中的 J. E. 沃尔特[1]先生坚持认为灵魂是一种占有空间的本原。费希特称之为内部身体,乌尔里希把它比作一种非分子合成的流体。这些理论使我们想起了当今的"接神论"学说,并且把我们带回到了灵魂作为意识的媒介物还没有像现在这样与负责身体形成的生命本原区别开来的时代。柏拉图将头部、胸部和腹部分别看作是不朽的理性、勇气和欲望的处所。亚里士多德论证说心脏是唯一的处所。在别处我们发现大脑、血液、肺、肝脏依次被认作是整个灵魂或者部分灵魂的处所。[2]

真相是,如果思维的本原是广延的,我们既不知道它的形式也不知道它的处所;而如果它是非广延的,那么说它具有任何空间关系就完全是荒谬的。后面我们将会看到,空间关系是可感觉的事物。唯一能够具有相互位置关系的客体是在同一个被感受到的空间中被知觉到共同存在的客体。一个完全没有被知觉到的事物,例如无广延的灵魂就一定是这样,不能以这种方式和任何被知觉到的客体共存。我们感受不到任何路线从它这里伸展到

① 《空间和物质知觉》,1879 年,第 2 部分,第 3 章。

② 就一种非常好的浓缩了的各种观点的历史而言,可参见 W. 沃尔克曼·冯·沃尔克玛,《心理学教科书》,第 16 节,Anm。关于 W. 汉密尔顿的全部参考书目,参见 J. E. 沃尔特,《空间和物质知觉》,第 65 ~66 页。

It can form no terminus to any space-interval. It can therefore in no intelligible sense enjoy position. Its relations cannot be spatial, but must be exclusively cognitive or dynamic, as we have seen. So far as they are dynamic, to talk of the soul being ' present' is only a figure of speech. Hamilton's doctrine that the soul is present to the whole body is at any rate false : for cognitively its presence extends far beyond the body, and dynamically it does not extend beyond the brain. ①

The Relations Of Minds To Other Objects

are either relations to *other minds*, or to *material things*. The material things are either the mind's *own brain*, on the one hand, or *anything else*, on the other. The relations of a mind to its own brain are of a unique and utterly mysterious sort ; we discussed them in the last two chapters, and can add nothing to that account.

The mind's relations to other objects than the brain are *cognitive and emotional* relations exclusively, so far as we know. It *knows* them, and it inwardly *welcomes or rejects* them, but it has no other dealings with them. When it seems to *act* upon them, it only does so through the intermediary of its own body, so that not it but the body is what acts on them, and the brain must first act upon the body. The same is true when other things seem to act on it—they only act on the body,

① Most contemporary writers ignore the question of the soul's seat Lotze is the only one who seems to have been much concerned about it, and his views have varied. Cf. Medicinische Psychol., § 10. Microcosmus, bk. III. ch. 2. Metaphysic, bk. III. ch. 5. Outlines of Psychol., part II. ch. 3 See also G. T. Fechner, Psychophysik, chap, XXXVII.

了其他对象那里。它不能构成任何空间间隔的终点。因此它只能在不可理解的意义上享有位置。它的关系不能是空间的，而必须如我们已经看到的那样只是认知的和动力的。就它们是动力的而言，说灵魂是“呈现”的只是一种讲话的描绘。汉密尔顿关于灵魂呈现在整个身体面前的理论无论如何也是错的；因为它在认知上的呈现远远超出了身体，而在动力上的呈现它没有超出大脑。①

心灵与其他客体的关系

或者是与其他心灵的关系，或者是与其他物质事物的关系。物质事物一方面或者是心灵自身的大脑，另一方面或者是任何别的事物。心灵和大脑的关系是某种独特而且绝对神秘的关系；我们在最近的两章中讨论了它们，对那一论述我们不能再添加什么上去了。

据我们所知，心灵与大脑以外其他客体的关系就只是认知和情感的关系。它知道它们，并且它内部欢迎或者拒绝它们，但它与它们没有任何其他关系。当它似乎作用于它们的时候，它只是通过自己的身体这种媒介物来这样做的，因此不是它而是身体作用于它们，而且大脑必须首先作用于身体。当其他事物作用于他的时候，情况也同样如此——它们只作用于身体，并且通过身体

① 当代大部分作者都忽视了灵魂处所的问题。洛采是唯一似乎非常关注这一问题的人，而且他的观点发生过变化。参见《医学心理学》，第10节。《微观宇宙》，第3卷，第2章。《形而上学》，第3卷，第5章。《心理学概要》，第2部分，第3章。也可参见G.T.费克纳，《心理物理学》，第37章。

and through that on its brain.[①] All that it *can* do *directly* is to know other things, misknow or ignore them, and to find that they interest it, in this fashion or in that.

Now the *relation of knowing* is the most mysterious thing in the world. If we ask how one thing *can* know another we are led into the heart of *Erkenntnisstheorie* and metaphysics. The psychologist, for his part, does not consider the matter so curiously as this. Finding a world before him which he cannot but believe that *he* knows, and setting himself to study his own past thoughts, or someone else's thoughts, of what he believes to be that same world; he cannot but conclude that those other thoughts know it after their fashion even as he knows it after his. Knowledge becomes for him an ultimate relation that must be admitted, whether it be explained or not, just like difference or resemblance, which no one seeks to explain.

Were our topic Absolute Mind instead of being the concrete minds of individuals dwelling in the natural world, we could not tell whether that Mind had the function of knowing or not, as knowing is commonly understood. We might learn the complexion of its thoughts; but, as we should have no realities outside of it to compare them with,—for if we had, the Mind would not be Absolute, —we could not criticise them, and find them either right or wrong; and we should have to call them simply the thoughts, and not the *knowledge*, of the Absolute Mind. Finite minds, however, can be judged in a different way, because the psychologist himself can go bail for the independent reality of the objects of which they think. He knows these to exist outside as well as inside the minds in question; he thus knows whether the minds think and *know*, or only think;

---

① I purposely ignore 'clairvoyance and action upon distant things by mediums,' as not yet matter of common consent.

作用于它的大脑。[1] 所有它直接能够做的是知道其他事物,误解或者忽略它们,并且以这样或者那样的方式发现它们有利于它。

现在,认识关系是世界上最神秘的事情。如果我们问一个事物如何能够知道另一个事物,我们就被带入了知识论和形而上学的中心。就心理学家的任务来看,他不会这么好奇地考虑这一问题。他发现在他面前的世界只能是他相信他会知道的世界,并且使自己开始研究他自己过去的思想,或者其他某个人的思想,他认为这些思想都是同一个世界的思想;他只能得出结论说,那些其他思想按照它们的方式知道了世界,如同他以他的方式知道世界一样。知识对他来说变成了一种必须被承认的终极关系,不管它是否得到了解释,就像差异和相似一样,没有人想要解释它们。

假如我们的话题是绝对的心灵,而不是生活在自然世界中的个体的具体心灵,那么像认识被普遍理解的那样,我们也不能说出是否绝对心灵具有认识的功能。我们可以了解其思想的情况;但是,由于我们在它之外没有任何实在可以与它的思想相比较——因为如果我们有的话,绝对心灵就不是绝对的了——我们不能批评这些思想,并且不能发现它们正确与否;并且我们将不得不称它们为绝对心灵的思想,而不是知识。然而,有限的心灵能够以一种不同的方式被断定,因为心理学家能够为他们所思考的对象的独立实在性做担保。他知道这些对象既存在于所探讨心灵的内部,也存在于心灵的外部;因此他知道心灵是思考和认识,还是仅仅是思考;而且尽管他的知识理

---

① 我故意忽略掉了“通过媒介洞察并且作用于远处的事物”,因为这仍然是个未被普遍认可的问题。

and though his knowledge is of course that of a fallible mortal, there is nothing in the conditions that should make it more likely to be wrong in this case than in any other.

Now by what tests does the psychologist decide whether the state of mind he is studying is a bit of knowledge, or only a subjective fact not referring to anything outside itself ?

He uses the tests we all practically use. If the state of mind *resembles* his own idea of a certain reality ; or if without resembling his idea of it, it seems to imply that reality and refer to it by operating upon it through the bodily organs ; or even if it resembles and operates on some other reality that implies, and leads up to, and terminates in, the first one,—in either or all of these cases the psychologist admits that the state of mind takes cognizance, directly or remotely, distinctly or vaguely, truly or falsely, of the reality's nature and position in the world. If, on the other hand, the mental state under examination neither resembles nor operates on any of the realities known to the psychologist, he calls it a subjective state pure and simple, possessed of no cognitive worth. If, again, it resemble a reality or a set of realities as he knows them, but altogether fail to operate on them or modify their course by producing bodily motions which the psychologist sees, then the psychologist, like all of us, may be in doubt. Let the mental state, for example, occur during the sleep of its subject. Let the latter dream of the death of a certain man, and let the man simultaneously die. Is the dream a mere coincidence or a veritable cognition of the death ? Such puzzling cases are what the Societies for 'Psychical Research' are collecting and trying to interpret in the most reasonable way.

If the dream were the only one of the kind the subject ever had in his life, if the context of the death in the dream differed in many particulars from the real death's context, and if the dream led to no

所当然是易犯错误的凡人的知识,但是这里并不存在任何条件之下的事物,它们会使它在这种情况下比在其他任何情况下更容易出错。

现在,心理学家通过什么样的测试来判断他正在研究的心理状态是一点知识,或者仅仅是一种不指称它自身之外的任何事物的一种主观事实呢?

他使用的是我们实际上都在使用的测试。如果心理状态与他自己关于某个实在的观念相类似;或者如果与他关于实在的观念不相似,它似乎暗示出了那个实在,并且通过身体器官作用于它而指称它;或者即使它类似于并且作用于某个其他的实在,而这个实在暗示了、导向于并且中止于第一个实在——那么,在其中任何一种或者所有这些情况中,心理学家都承认心理状态直接地或者远距离地、清楚地或者模糊地、真实地或者错误地认识到了那个实在的本性以及在世界中的位置。在另一方面,如果被检查的心理状态既没有类似于也没有作用于心理学家所知道的任何实在,他称它为纯粹而简单的主观状态,不具有认识的价值。再则,如果它与他所知道的一个实在或者一组实在相类似,但是却完全不能通过心理学家所看到的产生身体运动而作用于它们或者改变它们的进程,那么心理学家就可能像我们所有人一样处于疑惑之中。例如,让心理状态出现在其主体的睡眠之中。让后者梦到某个人死了,并且让那个人与此同时死掉。梦仅仅是一个巧合,还是关于死亡的真正认识呢?“心理研究”协会正在收集这种令人迷惑的案例,并且尽量以最合理的方式对其做出解释。

如果那个主体在其一生中只做过一次这种类型的梦,如果梦中死亡的背景和真实死亡的背景在很多细节上都不同,并且如果

action about the death, unquestionably we should all call it a strange coincidence, and naught besides. But if the death in the dream had a long context, agreeing point for point with every feature that attended the real death; if the subject were constantly having such dreams, all equally perfect, and if on awaking he had a habit of acting immediately as if they were true and so getting 'the start' of his more tardily informed neighbors, ro we should probably all have to admit that he had some mysterious kind of clairvoyant power, that his dreams in an inscrutable way knew just those realities which they figured, and that the word 'coincidence' failed to touch the root of the matter. And whatever doubts any one preserved would completely vanish if it should appear that from the midst of his dream he had the power of *interfering* with the course of the reality, and making the events in it turn this way or that, according as he dreamed they should. Then at least it would be certain that he and the psychologist were dealing with the *same*. It is by such tests as these that we are convinced that the waking minds of our fellows and our own minds know the same external world.

The psychologist's attitude towards cognitions will be so important in the sequel that we must not leave it until it is made perfectly clear. *It is a thoroughgoing dualism.* It supposes two elements, mind knowing and thing known, and treats them as irreducible. Neither gets out of itself or into the other, neither in any way is the other, neither *makes* the other. They just stand face to face in a common world, and one simply knows, or is known unto, its counterpart. This singular relation is not to be expressed in any lower terms, or translated into any more intelligible name. Some sort of signal must be given by the thing to the mind's brain, or the knowing will not occur—we find as a matter of fact that the mere *existence* of a thing outside the brain is not a sufficient cause for our knowing it: it must strike the brain in some way, as well as be there, to be known.

那个梦没有导致关于死亡的任何行动，我们将毫无疑问地完全称其为一种奇怪的巧合。但是，如果梦中的死亡有着很长的来龙去脉，并且其细节和真实死亡的每一个特征都一一符合；如果主体不断地做这样的梦，所有的梦都同样精确，并且如果他醒来的时候有一种立即行动的习惯，就好像它们是真的一样，因此比那些消息迟缓的邻居们"占优势"，我们大家可能不得不承认，他拥有某种神秘的洞察力，他的那些梦以某种难以了解的方式恰恰知道它们所描绘的那些实在，而"巧合"这个词没能触及到问题的本质。而且如果下述情况出现的话，即在梦中他有能力干预现实的进程，并且使得事件按照他所梦见的它们所应该的那样朝这条路线或者那条路线发展，那么，任何人所持有的无论什么疑问就都消失了。那么，至少可以确定的是，他和心理学家在处理同样的事情。正是通过像这样的测试，我们确信我们同伴们的心灵和我们自己的心灵知道同一个外部世界。

心理学家对待认知的态度在产生结果方面是如此的重要，以至于我们必须把它弄得十分清楚，否则我们不会离开这一话题。它是一种彻底的二元论。它假设有两种要素，认识的心灵和被认识的事物，并且将它们看作是不可还原的。两者都不能从自身中出来，或者进入到另一个之中，二者都不能以任何方式是另一个，也都不能产生另一个。他们只是在共同的世界中面对面地存在着，并且一个仅仅是知道其对应物，或者为其对应物所知道。这种单一关系不能用任何低级的术语来表达，或者被翻译为更加容易理解的名称。事物必须将某种信号给予心灵的大脑，否则认识将不会发生——我们发现外在于大脑的某个事物的单纯存在并不是我们认识它的充足理由：为了被认识，它不仅必须存在于那

But the brain being struck, the knowledge is constituted by a new construction that occurs altogether in the mind. The thing remains the same whether known or not. ① And when once there, the knowledge may remain there, whatever becomes of the thing.

By the ancients, and by unreflecting people perhaps today, knowledge is explained as the *passage* of something from without into the mind-the latter, so far, at least, as its sensible affections go, being passive and receptive. But even in mere sense-impression the duplication of the object by an inner construction must take place. Consider, with Professor Bowne, what happens when two people converse together and know each other's mind.

"No thoughts leave the mind of one and cross into the mind of the other. When we speak of an exchange of thought, even the crudest mind knows that this is a mere figure of speech. . . . To perceive another's thought, we must construct his thought within ourselves;. . . this thought is our own and is strictly original with us. At the same time we owe it to the other; and if it had not originated with him, it would probably not have originated with us. But what has the other done?. . . This: by an entirely mysterious world-order, the speaker is enabled to produce a series of signs which are totally unlike [the] thought, but which, by virtue of the same mysterious order, act as a series of incitements upon the hearer, so that he constructs within himself the corresponding mental state. The act of the speaker consists in availing himself of the proper incitements. The act of the hearer is immediately only the reaction of the soul against the incitement. . . . All communion between finite minds is

① I disregard *consequences* which may later come to the thing from the fact that it is known. The knowing *per se* in no wise affects the thing.

里，还必须以某种方式冲击大脑。但是在大脑受到冲击的情况下，知识却由完全发生在心中的一种新的结构所组成。不管那个事物是否被认识，它依然是同样的事物。① 并且一旦知识存在于那里的时候，不论事物发生了何种变化，它依然可以保持在那里。

古代的人以及当今可能不反省的人，将知识解释为某物从外部进入到心灵中的通道——后者，至少就其可感觉的倾向而言，是被动的和接收的。但是，甚至在单纯的感官印象中，对客体的复制必须通过一种内部的建构才能发生。让我们和鲍恩教授一起考虑一下，当两个人在一起交谈，并且彼此了解对方的心灵的时候，会发生什么情况。

"没有思想会离开一个人的心灵然后穿越并进入另一个心灵。当我们说思想的交流的时候，甚至最拙劣的心灵也知道这仅仅是一种讲话的描绘。……要知觉另一个人的思想，我们必须在我们自己内部构建他的思想；……这种思想是我们自己的，并且确实是我们的原创。同时，我们应该将它归功于另一个人；假如它最初不是从他那里产生的，它可能也不会从我们这里产生。但是另一个人做了什么？……做了这些：通过一种完全神秘的世界秩序，谈话者能够产生一系列的符号，这些符号和（那个）思想完全不同，而且这些符号依靠同样神秘的秩序作为一系列的刺激物作用于听者，结果他就在自己的内部建构起了相应的心理状态。谈话者的行动在于利用适当的刺激物。听者的行动只是灵魂立刻对刺激做出反应。……有限个体间的所有交流都是这种类型

① 我没有理会事物被认识了这一事实后来可能会给这个事物带来的后果。认识本身决不影响那个事物。

of this sort. . . . Probably no reflecting person would deny this conclusion, but when we say that what is thus true of perception of another's thought is equally true of the perception of the outer world in general, many minds will be disposed to question, and not a few will deny it outright. Yet there is no alternative but to affirm that to perceive the universe we must construct it in thought, and that our knowledge of the universe is but the unfolding of the mind's inner nature. . . . By describing the mind as a waxen tablet, and things as impressing themselves upon it, we seem to get great insight until we think to ask where this extended tablet is, and how things stamp themselves on it, and how the perceptive act would be explained even if they did. . . . The immediate antecedents of sensation and perception are a series of nervous changes in the brain. Whatever we know of the outer world is revealed only in and through these nervous changes. But these are totally unlike the objects assumed to exist as their causes. If we might conceive the mind as in the light, and in direct contact with its objects, the imagination at least would be comforted; but when we conceive the mind as coming in contact with the outer world only in the dark chamber of the skull, and then not in contact with the objects perceived, but only with a series of nerve-changes of which, moreover, it knows nothing, it is plain that the object is a long way off. All talk of pictures, impressions, etc., ceases because of the lack of all the conditions to give such figures any meaning. It is not even clear that we shall ever find our way out of the darkness into the world of light and reality again. We begin with complete trust in physics and the senses, and are forthwith led away from the object into a nervous labyrinth, where the object is entirely displaced by a set of nervous changes which are totally unlike anything but themselves. Finally, we land in the dark chamber of the skull. The object has gone completely, and knowledge has not yet appeared.

的。……可能所有会反思的人都不会否认这一结论，但是当我们说对另一个人对思想的知觉的这种情况总体来说同样适用于对外部世界的知觉时，很多人倾向于对它提出质疑，而且还有不少人会立刻否定它。然而，这里没有别的选择，只能肯定的是，为了感知宇宙，我们必须在思想中构建它，并且我们关于宇宙的知识也是心灵内部本性的伸展。……通过将心灵描述为一块蜡板，并且事物使自己在上面留下印象，我们似乎获得了伟大的洞察力，直到我们想到要询问这个有广延的蜡板存在于哪里，事物是如何将它们自身印记其上的，以及即使它们这样做了，知觉活动又应该如何解释。……感觉和知觉的直接先行者是大脑中一系列神经变化。不论我们知道的外部世界是什么，它们只是在这些神经变化之中并且通过这些神经变化被显示出来。但是这些变化与被假设作为它们的原因而存在的客体完全不同。如果我们构想心灵在阳光之中，并且和其对象有着直接的联系，这种想像至少可以带来一些安慰；但是，当我们设想心灵只是在头盖骨这个黑暗的屋子里和外部世界发生联系，因而并不与所知觉的对象发生联系，而只是和一系列的神经变化相联系，此外，它对这些神经变化一无所知，显然对象还在远处。所有关于图像、印象等等的谈论都停止了，因为缺少赋予这种描述以任何意义的所有条件。甚至不清楚的是，我们是否还能找到一条离开黑暗、再次进入光明与实在的世界中的道路。我们从对物理和感官的完全信任开始，并且被引导着毫不犹豫地离开了客体，从而进入了神经的迷宫，在这里对象完全被一系列的神经变化所取代，这些变化除了自身之外和任何事物都不相象。最后，我们来到了头盖骨这个黑暗的屋子里。对象完全消失了，而知识还没有出现。按照最坚决的实

Nervous signs are the raw material of all knowledge of the outer world according to the most decided realism: But in order to pass beyond these signs into a knowledge of the outer world, we must posit an interpreter who shall read back these signs into their objective meaning. But that inter-preter, again, must implicitly contain the meaning of the universe within itself; and these signs are really but excitations which cause the soul to unfold what is within itself. Inasmuch as by common consent the soul communicates with the outer world only through these signs, and never comes nearer to the object than such signs can bring it, it follows that the principles of interpretation must be in the mind itself, and that the resulting construction is primarily only an expression of the mind' s own nature. All reaction is of this sort; it expresses the nature of the reacting agent, and knowledge comes under the same head, this fact makes it necessary for us either to admit a pre-established harmony between the laws and nature of thought and the laws and nature of things, or else to allow that the objects of perception, the universe as it appears, are purely phenomenal, being but the way in which the mind reacts against the ground of its sensations." ①

The dualism of Object and Subject and their pre-established harmony are what the psychologist as such must assume, whatever ulterior monistic philosophy he may, as an individual who has the right also to be a metaphysician, have in reserve. I hope that this general point is now made clear, so that we may leave it, and descend to some distinctions of detail.

There are two kinds of knowledge broadly and practically distinguishable: we may call them respectively *knowledge of acquaintance and knowledge-about*. Most languages express the distinction; thus, γνώναι, εἰδέναι; *noscere*, *scire*; *kennen*, *wissen*;

① B. P. Bowne: Metaphysics, pp. 407-10. Cf. also Lotze: Logik, §§308,326-7.

在论,神经迹象是所有关于外部世界的知识的原材料:但是为了越过这些迹象而进入关于外部世界的知识,我们必须安置一个解释者,它可以重复这些迹象并且把它们关于对象的意义诠释出来。而且,那个解释者又必须暗中将宇宙的意义包含在它自身之中;而且这些迹象真的只是引起灵魂将它自身之内的东西展开的刺激物。因为,由于人们一致同意灵魂只是通过这些迹象和外部世界交流的,而且灵魂到达客体的地方永远也不会超过这些迹象将它带到的地方,它所遵循的解释原则一定在心灵自身之中,而作为结果而发生的构建主要只是一种心灵自身本性的表达。所有的反应都属于这种类型;它表达了反应执行者的本性,知识也来自那同一个头脑,这一事实使我们必须承认,在思维的规律和本性与事物的规律和本质之间存在着一种预先设定的和谐,或者我们必须承认,对客体的知觉,和宇宙所显现出来的一样,纯粹是现象的,它只不过是心灵对其感觉基础做出反应的方式。"①

作为一个也有权利成为形而上学者的个体,无论这样的心理学家可以将什么样的一元论哲学作为其储备,客体和主体的二元论及其预先设定的和谐,是他们必须要假定的东西。我希望这个一般观点现在已经弄清楚了,因此我们可以离开它了,而详述一些细节方面的差异了。

有两种类型的知识是可以广泛地和真正地加以区分的:我们可以分别称它们为相识的知识和相知的知识。大多数语言表达了这种区别;因而就有,γνωναι,εἰδέναι; noscere,scire; kennen,

① B. P. 鲍恩:《形而上学》,第 407 ~ 410 页。也可参见洛采:《逻辑学》,第 308、326、327 节。

connaître, *savoir*.[①] I am acquainted with many people and things, which I know very little about, except their presence in the places where I have met them. I know the color blue when I see it, and the flavor of a pear when I taste it; I know an inch when I move my finger through it; a second of time, when I feel it pass; an effort of attention when I make it; a difference between two things when I notice it; but *about* the inner nature of these facts or what makes them what they are, I can say nothing at all. I cannot impart acquaintance with them to any one who has not already made it himself. I cannot *describe* them, make a blind man guess what blue is like, define to a child a syllogism, or tell a philosopher in just what respect distance is just what it is, and differs from other forms of relation. At most, I can say to my friends, Go to certain places and act in certain ways, and these objects will probably come. All the elementary natures of the world, its highest genera, the simple qualities of matter and mind, together with the kinds of relation that subsist between them, must either not be known at all, or known in this dumb way of acquaintance without *knowledge-about*. In minds able to speak at all there is, it is true, *some* knowledge about everything. Things can at least be classed, and the times of their appearance told. But in general, the less we analyze a thing, and the fewer of its relations we perceive, the less we know about it and the more our familiarity with it is of the acquaintance-type. The two kinds of knowledge are, therefore,

---

① Cf. John Grote: Exploratio Philosophica, p. 60; H. Helmholtz. Popular Scientific Lectures, London, p. 308-9.

woissen; connaître, savoir[1][2] 我同很多人和事相识，但除了它们在我遇见过它们的地方出现以外，我对它们知之甚少。当我看见蓝色时，我知道了蓝颜色，当我尝了一口梨时，我知道了梨的味道；当我的手指跨过了一英尺的距离时，我知道了一英尺；当我感受到一秒钟过去时，我知道了一秒钟的时间；当我努力去注意时，我知道了这次活动；当我注意到了两个事物间的区别时，我知道了它们之间的区别；但是关于这些事实的内部本性或者是什么使它们成其所是，我根本不能说些什么。我不能将我与它们的相识告诉任何没有亲自认识它们的人。我不能描述它们，不能让一个盲人猜测蓝色像什么，不能向一个孩子详细说明三段论法，或者告诉一个哲学家正是在什么方面，距离才恰恰是其所是，并且与其他的关系形式区别开来。至多，我能够对我的朋友们说，去到某个地方并且以某种方式行动，这些客体可能将会出现。世界的所有基本本性，其最高的类，物质和心灵的简单性质，以及存在于它们之间的关系的种类，必须或者完全不被知道，或者以这种不能说话的相识的方式被知道，而不带有相知的知识。在完全能够说话的心灵中，确实存在有关于任何事物的知识。事物至少能够被分类，并且它们显现的时间也能够被指出来。但是总体来说，我们对一个事物分析得越少，并且我们对其关系知觉得越少，我们就对其知道得越少，并且我们对它的熟悉程度就越是相识类型的。因此，这两类知识，正如人类的

① 参见约翰·格罗特：《哲学探索》，第60页；H. 赫姆霍尔茨，《通俗科学演讲》，伦敦，第308~309页。

〔2〕 它们分别是希腊语、拉丁语、德语和法语的“知道”的意思，但在熟悉程度上有所不同。

as the human mind practically exerts them, relative terms. That is, the same thought of a thing may be called knowledge-about it in comparison with a simpler thought, or acquaintance with it in comparison with a thought of it that is more articulate and explicit still.

The grammatical sentence expresses this. Its 'subject' stands for an object of acquaintance which, by the addition of the predicate, is to get something known about it We may already know a good deal, when we hear the subject named—its name may have rich connotations. But, know we much or little then, we know more still when, the sentence is done. We can relapse at will into a mere condition of acquaintance with an object by scattering our attention and staring at it in a vacuous trance-like way. We can ascend to knowledge *about* it by rallying our wits and proceeding to notice and analyze and think. What we are only acquainted with is only *present* to our minds; we have it, or the idea of it But when we know about it, we do more than merely have it; we seem, as we think over its relations, to subject it to a sort of *treatment* and to *operate* upon it with our thought The words *feeling* and *thought* give voice to the antithesis. Through feelings we become acquainted with things, but only by our thoughts do we know about them. Feelings are the germ and starting point of cognition, thoughts the developed tree. The minimum of grammatical subject, of objective presence, of reality known about, the mere beginning of knowledge, must be named by the word that says the least. Such a word is the interjection, as *lo*! *there*! *ecco*! *voilà*! or the article or demonstrative pronoun introducing the sentence, as *the*, it, *that*. In Chapter XII we

心灵实际对它们所操作的那样，是相对的术语。那就是说，关于一个事物的同一个思想在与一个相对简单一些的思想做比较时，可以被称作是关于这个事物的相知的知识，而在与一个表达更加清楚明晰的关于这个事物的思想做比较时，它可以被称作是关于这个事物的相识的知识。

语法正确的句子表达了这个意思。句子的"主语"代表了相识的对象，通过加上谓词，使得关于它的一些事情被了解了。当我们听到被指定的主语时，我们可能已经知道了许多——它的名称可能有丰富的内涵。但是，不论我们那时知道得有多少，当句子完成的时候，我们还是知道得更多了。通过分散我们的注意力，并且以一种散漫的、类似恍惚状态的方式看着客体，我们能够任意地回复到对那个客体的单纯的相识状态。通过集结我们的智慧，并且依次进行注意、分析和思考，我们能够上升到关于它的相知的知识。我们只是相识的东西仅仅是呈现给了我们的大脑的东西；我们拥有它或者它的观念。但是，当我们对它相知的时候，我们就不仅仅是拥有它了；由于我们思考着它的关系，我们似乎使之经历了某种处理，并且用我们的思维对其进行了操作。感受和思维这两个词表达了这种对立。通过感受，我们变得与事物相识了，但是只有通过我们的思维，我们才能与它们相知。感受是认知的萌芽与起点，思想是成长起来的大树。语法上的主语、客体的到场、被认识的实在，它们的最小值知识的纯粹起点必须通过说得最少的词语来加以命名。这样的词是像 lo! there! ecco! voilà 这样的插入语，[1] 或者是冠词，或者是像 the、it、that 这样的引入句子的指示代词。在第 12 章，我们将会更

[1] 它们分别是意大利语、英语、拉丁语和法语的"这儿"或者是"那儿"的意思。

shall see a little deeper into what this distinction, between the mere mental having or feeling of an object and the thinking of it, portends.

The mental states usually distinguished as feelings are the *emotions*, and the sensations we get from skin, muscle, viscus, eye, ear, nose, and palate. The 'thoughts,' as recognized in popular parlance, are the *conceptions* and *judgments*. When we treat of these mental states in particular we shall have to say a word about the cognitive function and value of each. It may perhaps be well to notice now that our senses only give us acquaintance with facts of body, and that of the mental states of other persons we only have conceptual knowledge. Of our own past states of mind we take cognizance in a peculiar way. They are 'objects of memory,' and appear to us endowed with a sort of warmth and intimacy that makes the perception of them seem more like a process of sensation than like a thought.

深入地了解到，在对一个客体纯粹的心理拥有或说感受与思考之间的区别预示着什么。

通常被区分为感受的心理状态是情绪和我们从皮肤、肌肉、内脏、眼睛、耳朵、鼻子和上颚得到的感觉。和在通俗说法中得到认可的一样，“思想”是概念与判断。当我们对这些心理状态特别加以讨论的时候，我们将不得不对它们各自的认知功能和价值加以论述。现在也许充分注意到的是，我们的感官只是使得我们对身体的事实有所了解，而对于其他人的心理状态的事实我们只有概念上的知识。我们以一种特别的方式认识我们自己过去的心理状态。它们是“记忆的对象”，并且它们被赋予了某种温暖与亲密的性质而显现在我们面前，而这使得对它们的知觉似乎更像是一种感觉过程，而不像是一种思维了。

CHAPTER IX.

The Stream Of Thought.[①]

We now begin our study of the mind from within. Most books start with sensations, as the simplest mental facts, and proceed synthetically, constructing each higher stage from those below it. But this is abandoning the empirical method of investigation. No one ever had a simple sensation by itself. Consciousness, from our natal day, is of a teeming multiplicity of objects and relations, and what we call simple sensations are results of discriminative attention, pushed often to a very high degree. It is astonishing what havoc is wrought in psychology by admitting at the outset apparently innocent suppositions that nevertheless contain a flaw. The bad consequences develop themselves later on, and are irremediable, being woven through the whole texture of the work. The notion that sensations, being the simplest things, are the first things to take up in psychology is one of these suppositions. The only thing which psychology has a right to postulate at the outset is the fact of thinking itself, and that must first be taken up and analyzed. If sensations then prove to be amongst the elements of the thinking, we shall be no worse off as respects them than if we had taken them for granted at the start.

---

① A good deal of this chapter is reprinted from. an article 'On some Omissions of Introspective Psychology' which appeared in 'Mind' for January 1884.

第九章 思想之流①

现在我们从内部开始我们对心灵的研究。多数书籍从感觉开始，将其作为最简单的心理事实，然后综合地继续下去，从下面的阶段构建起每一个更高级的阶段。但这是在弃绝经验的研究方法。还没有人获有过简单的感觉自身。从我们出生的那一天起，意识就具有关于对象和关系的丰富的多样性，并且我们所说的简单的感觉是辨别注意的结果，而且它常常被推到了一个非常高的高度。令人吃惊的是，通过在一开始就承认显然是天真的、然而却包含错误的假设已经在心理学中造成非常大的破坏。坏的结果后来自己发展了起来，并且是不可挽回的，因为它们渗透进了这项工作的整个结构中。感觉作为最简单的事物在心理学中是要最先加以对待的东西，这种观点就是其中的一个假定。心理学在一开始有权假定的唯一东西，就是思维这一事实本身，并且它必须最先得以处理和分析。如果感觉因而证明存在于思维的要素之中，就对它们的考虑而言，我们的情况不会比假如我们从一开始就对它们信以为真时的情况更糟。

---

① 这一章的很多内容都是从"论内省心理学的一些遗漏之处"这篇文章中再版过来的，这篇文章刊登在1884年1月的《心灵》杂志上。

The first fact for us, then, as psychologists, is that thinking of some sort goes on. I use the word thinking, in accordance with what was said on p. 186, for every form of consciousness indiscriminately. If we could say in English 'it thinks,' as we say 'it rains' or 'it blows,' we should be stating the fact most simply and with the minimum of assumption. As we cannot, we must simply say that *thought goes on.*

Five Characters In Thought.

How does it go on? We notice immediately five important characters in the process, of which it shall be the duty of the present chapter to treat in a general way:

1) Every thought tends to be part of a personal consciousness.

2) Within each personal consciousness thought is always changing.

3) Within each personal consciousness thought is sensibly continuous.

4) It always appears to deal with objects independent of itself.

5) It is interested in some parts of these objects to the exclusion of others, and welcomes or rejects—*chooses* from among them, in a word all the while.

In considering these five points successively, we shall have to plunge *in medias res as* regards our vocabulary, and use psychological terms which can only be adequately defined in later chapters of the book. But every one knows what the terms mean in a rough way; and it is only in a rough way that we are now to take them. This chapter is like a painter's first charcoal sketch upon his canvas, in which no niceties appear.

1) Thought tends to Personal Form.

作为心理学家,对我们来说,第一个事实就是,某种思想在进行着。我使用思想这个词是按照我在第186页所说的那个意思,它不加区分地表示每一种意识形式。如果我们能够用英语说"(它)思想了",如同我们说"(它)下雨了"或者"(它)刮风了"一样,我们就可以最简单地、并且以最少的假定来陈述这个事实。由于我们不能,我们必须简单地说,思想在进行着。

思想的五个特征

它是如何进行的呢?我们在这个过程中立即注意到五个重要的特征,当前这一章的职责就是以一种概括的方式对其加以论述:

(1)每一个思想都倾向于是个人意识的一部分。

(2)在每一个个人意识中,思想总是在变化着。

(3)在每一个个人意识中,思想很容易被觉察到是连续的。

(4)它显现为始终在处理独立于它自身的客体。

(5)它对这些客体的某些部分感兴趣,而排除了其他一些部分,并且欢迎和拒绝它们——一句话,从它们中间进行选择——它始终如此。

在相继地考虑这五点的时候,我们将不得不在词汇方面陷入进去,并且使用只能在本书后面的章节才能够被充分定义的术语。但是每一个人都粗略地知道这些术语的意思是什么;而且现在我们也只是粗略地使用这些术语。这一章就像是一个画家在其画布上最初用炭笔画下的草图,细节尚未在其中显现。

1.思想倾向于个人的形式

When I say *every thought is part of a personal con-sciousness*, 'personal consciousness' is one of the terms in question. Its meaning we know so long as no one asks us to define it, but to give an accurate account of it is the most difficult of philosophic tasks. This task we must confront in the next chapter; here a preliminary word will suffice.

In this room—this lecture-room, say—there are a multitude of thoughts, yours and mine, some of which cohere mutually, and some not. They are as little each-for-itself and reciprocally independent as they are all-belonging-together. They are neither: no one of them is separate, but each belongs with certain others and with none beside. My thought belongs with my other thoughts, and your thought with your other thoughts. Whether anywhere in the room there be a mere thought, which is nobody's thought, we have no means of ascertaining, for we have no experience of its like. The only states of consciousness that we naturally deal with are found in personal consciousnesses, minds, selves, concrete particular I's and you's.

Each of these minds keeps its own thoughts to itself. There is no giving or bartering between them. No thought even comes into direct *sight* of a thought in another personal consciousness than its own. Absolute insulation, irreducible pluralism, is the law. It seems as if the elementary psychic fact were not *thought or this thought or that thought*, but *my thought*, every thought being *owned*. Neither contemporaneity, nor proximity in space, nor similarity of quality and content are able to fuse thoughts together which are sundered by this barrier of belonging to different personal minds. The breaches between such thoughts are the most absolute breaches in nature. Everyone will recognize this to be true, so long as the existence of *something* corresponding to the term 'personal mind' is all that is insisted on, without any particular view of its nature being implied.

当我们说每一个思想都是个人意识的一部分时,“个人意识”就是相关的术语之一。只要没有人要求我们对它进行定义,我们就知道它的意思,但是,要对它做出一个精确的论述,这就是一项最困难的哲学任务了。我们必须在下一章面对这项任务。在这里,有一个初步的词汇就足够了。

在这间房间里——比如,在这间教室里——存在有众多的思想,你们的和我的,其中的一些相互凝聚,而另一些却不是这样。正如它们并非全部归属一处一样,它们也同样不是自足的和相互独立的。它们两者都不是:它们中没有任何一个是单独的,而且它们每一个都隶属于某些其他的思想,并且只隶属于它们。我的思想隶属于我的其他的思想,而你们的思想隶属于你们的其他的思想。是否在房间的任何地方存在一种纯粹的思想,它不是任何人的思想,我们无法确定,因为我们没有任何像它这样的经验。我们自然地加以处理的唯一的意识状态,被发现存在于个人的意识、心灵、自我、具体而特殊的你的意识和我的意识之中。

这每一个心灵将它自己的思想保留给自己。心灵之间不存在给予或者是交换。甚至没有任何思想能够直接进入在另一个个人意识中而并非是它自己的意识中的某个思想的视野。绝对的隔离和不可还原的多元是这里的法则。情况看起来就好像是基本的精神事实不是思想,或者不是这个思想或那个思想,而是我的思想,每一个被拥有的思想。共时性、空间上的接近、以及性质和内容的相似性都不能将思想融合在一起,这些思想被属于不同的个人心灵这一屏障给分离开了。在这些思想间的裂缝是自然中最绝对的裂缝。只要与术语“个人心灵”相对应的某种东西是存在的这一点被坚定地认可了,并且它没有暗示出任何关于其

On these terms the personal self rather than the thought might be treated as the immediate datum in psychology. The universal conscious fact is not 'feelings and thoughts exist,' but 'I think' and 'I feel.' ① No psychology, at any rate, can question the *existence* of personal selves. The worst a psychology can do is so to interpret the nature of these selves as to rob them of their worth. A French writer, speaking of our ideas, says somewhere in a fit of anti-spiritualistic excitement that, misled by certain peculiaritities which they display, we 'end by personifying' the procession which they make,—such personification being regarded by him as a great philosophic blunder on our part. It could only be a blunder if the notion of personality meant something essentially different from anything to be found in the mental procession. But if that procession be itself the very 'original' of the notion of personality, to personify it cannot possibly be wrong. It is already personified. There are no marks of personality to be gathered *aliunde*, and then found lacking in the train of thought. It has them all already; so that to whatever farther analysis we may subject that form of personal selfhood under which thoughts appear, it is, and must remain, true that the thoughts which psychology studies do continually tend to appear as parts of personal selves.

I say 'tend to appear' rather than 'appear', on account of those facts of sub-conscious personality, automatic writing, etc., of which we studied a few in the last chapter. The buried feelings and thoughts proved now to exist in hysterical anæsthetics, in recipients of post-hypnotic suggestion, etc; themselves are parts of *secondary personal selves*. These selves are for the most part very stupid and contracted,

① B. P. Bowne: Metaphysics, p. 363.

本质的特殊观点，那么每个人都会承认这是真的。基于这些观点，个人的自我而不是思想就可能作为心理学的直接资料而加以对待。普遍的意识事实不是“感受和思想存在着”，而是“我思维”，和“我感受”。[①] 无论如何，任何心理学都不能怀疑个人自我的存在。心理学能做的最坏的事情，就是对这些自我的本性加以解释，并且剥夺了它们自身的价值。一位法国的作家，在反唯灵论的时候，一时激动在某处说到了我们的观点，他说，由于我们被他们所表现出来某些特性所误导了，我们“通过人格化而中止了”他们制造出来的进程——他将这种人格化看作是我们这边犯下的一个极大的错误。如果人格化的概念意味着与在心理进程中所发现的任何东西有着本质区别的某些东西，那么它才可能是错误的。但是，如果那个进程自身恰恰是人格观点的原型，那么将它人格化就不可能是错的。它已经被人格化了。这里不存在从其他地方被聚集起来，然后被发现在思想的序列中是缺失了的人格的任何迹象，它已经完全拥有它们了；因此无论我们对在其中思想得以出现的个人自我的那种形式做怎样的进一步分析，心理学所研究的思想确实不断地趋向于显现为个人自我的某些部分这一点是真的，而且也必须一直是真的。

我说“趋向于显现”而不是“显现”，是由于我们在上一章做了一些研究的下意识人格、自动书写等等那些事实。这些被隐藏起来的思想现在被证明存在于患有歇斯底里感觉缺乏症的人那里，存在于催眠后暗示的接收者那里，等等；它们自身是次级个人自我的组成部分。这些次级自我的绝大部分都是非常愚蠢和缩小了的，并

① B. P. 鲍恩：《形而上学》，第 363 页。

and are cut off at ordinary times from communication with the regular and normal self of the individual; but still they form conscious unities, have continuous memories, speak, write, invent distinct names for themselves, or adopt names that are suggested; and, in short, are entirely worthy of that title of secondary personalities which is now commonly given them. According to M. Janet these secondary personalities are always abnormal, and result from the splitting of what ought to be a single complete self into two parts, of which one lurks in the background whilst the other appears on the surface as the only self the man or woman has. For our present purpose it is unimportant whether this account of the origin of secondary selves is applicable to all possible cases of them or not, for it certainly is true of a large number of them. Now although the *size* of a secondary self thus formed will depend on the number of thoughts that are thus split-off from the main consciousness, the *form* of it tends to personality, and the later thoughts pertaining to it remember the earlier ones and adopt them as their own. M. Janet caught the actual moment of inspissation (so to speak) of one of these secondary personalities in his anaesthetic somnambulist Lucie. He found that when this young woman's attention was absorbed in conversation with a third party, her anæsthetic hand would write simple answers to questions whispered to her by himself. "Do you hear?" he asked. "*No*," was the unconsciously written reply. "But to answer you must hear." "*Yes, quite so*." Then how do you manage?" "*I don't know*." "There must be some one who hears me." "*Yes*." "Who?" "*Someone other than Lucie*." "Ah! another person. Shall we give her a name?" "*No*." "Yes, it will be more convenient." "*Well, Adrienne, then*." "Once baptized, the subconscious personage," M. Janet continues, "grows more definitely outlined and displays better her psychological characters. In particular she shows us that she is conscious of the feelings excluded from the consciousness of the primary or normal personage.

且与正常的人体自我之间的交流通常是中断的；但是，它们依然形成了意识的统一体，有意识的记忆、谈话、书写，可以为它们自己发明独特的名称，或者采纳被暗示出来的名称；而且，简言之，它们完全配得上现在普遍赋予它们的次级人格这个头衔。按照詹尼特先生的观点，这些次级人格总是不正常的，由于本来应该是一个完整的自我分裂成两个部分而产生，这两个部分中的一个潜伏在不引人注目的地方，而另一个作为男人或者女人所唯一拥有的自我浮出了水面。就我们当前的目的来说，是否这种论述也适用于它们的所有可能的情况，这是无关紧要的，因为情况对于它们中的大多数来说的确是这样的。现在，尽管如此形成的次级自我的大小将取决于从主要的意识中分离出来的思想的数量，但是它的形式往往是倾向于人格化的，而且后来的隶属于它的思想记得前面的思想，并且把它们当成是自己的而加以采纳。詹尼特先生在其感觉缺乏的梦游者——露西那里，抓住了这样一种真实瞬间，在此刻，这些次级人格中的一种次级人格浓缩了（可以这么说）。他发现当这个年轻女性的注意力完全被吸引到了与第三方的谈话中时，她的感觉缺乏的手可以写下他小声向她提出的问题的答案。“你听见了吗？”他问道。“没有”这是无意识写出的回答。“但是要回答你必须听见呀。”“是的，确实如此。”“那么你是如何做到的呢？”“我不知道。”“一定有人听见我了。”“是的。”“谁？”“一个不是露西的人。”“哈！另一个人。我们给她起个名字行吗？”“不行。”“行，这会更方便些的。”“好吧，那么就叫阿德里尼吧。”“一旦被命名了，”詹尼特先生继续说，“下意识人格就变得更加轮廓清晰了，并且能更好地展现她的心理特征了。尤其是，她向我们表明了她能够意识到从主要的或说正常的人格的意

She it is who tells us that I am pinching the arm or touching the little linger in which Lucie for so long has had no tactile sensations." ①

In other cases the adoption of the name by the secondary self is more spontaneous. I have seen a number of incipient automatic writers and mediums as yet imperfectly 'developed,' who immediately and of their own accord write and speak in the name of departed spirits. These may be public characters, as Mozart, Faraday, or real persons formerly known to the subject, or altogether imaginary beings. Without prejudicing the question of real ' spirit- control' in the more developed sorts of tranceutterance, I incline to think that these (often deplorably unintelligent) rudimentary utterances are the work of an inferior fraction of the subject's own natural mind, set free from control by the rest, and working after a set pattern fixed by the prejudices of the social environment. In a spiritualistic community we get optimistic messages, whilst in an ignorant Catholic village the secondary personage calls itself by the name of a demon, and proffers blasphemies and obscenities, instead of telling us how happy it is in the summer-land. ②

Beneath these tracts of thought, which, however rudimentary, are still organized selves with a memory, habits, and sense of their own identity, M. Janet thinks that the facts of catalepsy in hysteric patients drive us to suppose that there are thoughts quite unorganized and

---

① L' Automatisme Psychologique, p. 818.

② Cf. A. Constans: Relation sur une Epidémie d' bystéro-démonopathie en 1861. 2me ed. Paris, 1863.—Chiap e Franzolini: L' Epidemia d' istero-demonopatie in Verzegnis. Reggio, 1879.—See also J. Kerner's little work : Nachricht von dem Vorkommen des Besessenseina. 1836,

识中被排除了的感受。是她告诉我们，我正在捏她的胳膊或者我正在触摸她的小拇指，而在这些部位中，露西已经好久没有触觉了。”①

在其他情况中，次级自我对名字的采用更具有自发性。我见过许多尚未“发展”完善的早期的自动书写者和灵魂，他们直接地并且主动地以逝去的灵魂的名义书写和讲话。这些灵魂可以是像莫扎特、法拉第这样的公众人物，或者是被试以前认识的真实的人，还可以是完全虚构的存在。在没有损害关于在进一步发展了的恍惚说话种类中真实的“精神控制”这一问题的情况下，我倾向于认为，这些（常常是可悲地蠢钝的）尚未发展的说话方式，是被试自己天生的心灵的次级部分的作品，这次级部分从心灵的剩余部分的控制中解放了出来，并且按照对社会环境的偏见所确定的固定模式而工作。在唯灵论的社会中，我们得到了令人乐观的信息，而在一个无知的天主教的村庄里，次级人格以魔鬼的名义称呼它自己，并且说着亵渎和淫秽的话语，而没有告诉我们它在这放牧之地上是多么的幸福。②

詹尼特先生认为在患有歇斯底里症病人中出现的全身僵硬的事实驱使我们假设，在这些无论发展得多么不完善、却仍然通过记忆、习惯和它们自己的身份感而组织起来的思想系统之下，存在着彻底无组织的和非个人的思想。一个处于全身僵硬症恍

① 《心理自动作用》，第 818 页。

② 参见 A. 康斯坦斯：《论 1861 年的魔鬼附身和歇斯底里流行病的关系》，第 2 版，巴黎，1863 年。Chiap e 弗兰佐里尼：《魔鬼附身癔病在韦尔兹格尼斯地方的流行》，Reggio，1879 年。也可参见 J. 克纳的短篇著作：《关于意识现象的报告》，1836 年。

impersonal. A patient in cataleptic trance (which can be produced artificially in certain hypnotized subjects) is without memory on waking, and seems insensible and unconscious as long as the cataleptic condition lasts. If, however, one raises the arm of such a subject it stays in that position, and the whole body can thus be moulded like wax under the hands of the operator, retaining for a considerable time whatever attitude he communicates to it. In hysterics whose arm, for example, is anaesthetic, the same thing may happen. The anæsthetic arm may remain passively in positions which it is made to assume; or if the hand be taken and made to hold a pencil and trace a certain letter, it will continue tracing that letter indefinitely on the paper. These acts, until recently, were supposed to be accompanied by no consciousness at all: they were physiological reflexes. M. Janet considers with much more plausibility that feeling escorts them. The feeling is probably merely that of the position or movement of the limb, and it produces no more than its natural effects when it discharges into the motor centres which keep the position maintained, or the movement incessantly renewed. ①Such thoughts as these, says M. Janet, "are known by *no one*, for disaggregated sensations reduced to a state of mental dust are not synthetized in any personality." ②He admits, however, that these very same unutterably stupid thoughts tend to develop memory,—the cataleptic ere long moves her arm at a bare hint; so that they form no important exception to the law that all thought tends to assume the form of personal consciousness.

2) Thought is in Constant Change.

I do not mean necessarily that no one state of mind has any

---

① For the Physiology of this compare the chapter on the Will

② *Loc. cit.* p. 316.

惚状态(在某些受到催眠的被试那里也能够人工地产生这种状态)的患者醒来的时候没有记忆,并且只要全身僵硬的状态持续着,他似乎是无感觉和无意识的。然而,如果有人抬起这样的被试的胳膊,它就会停留在那个位置上,而且整个身体因此在手术人员手里就像是蜡块一样能够被造型,能够很长时间地保持着他传达给它的无论何种姿势。在例如其胳膊是感觉缺乏的歇斯底里症患者那里,同样的事情也可以发生。感觉缺乏的胳膊会被动地保持在它被摆放的位置上;或者如果那只手被拿了起来,并且让它拿起一支笔描画某个字母,它将不确定地连续在纸上描画那个字母。直到最近,这些行动还是被认为完全没有任何意识相伴随:它们是生理反射。詹尼特先生似乎更有理地认为,感受陪同着它们。感受可能仅仅是对肢体的那个位置或者运动的感受,并且当它释放到了使这个位置得以保持或者使运动不断重复的运动中枢里的时候,它仅仅引起了其自然的效果。① 詹尼特先生说,像这样的思想,"没有人知道,因为分解了的感觉还原为一种精神微粒了,它们没有在任何人格中被综合起来。" ②然而,他承认这些完全同样有着非语言所能表达的愚钝的思想趋向于发展出记忆,——患有全身僵硬症的病人不久就能在单纯的暗示下移动他的胳膊,因此对所有的思想趋向于采取个人意识形式这一规律来说,它们没有构成任何重大的例外。

2. 思想在不断地变化

我没有必要表达出所有的心理状态都没有任何持续时间

① 关于这方面的生理学,可比较《意志》这一章。

② 在上述引文中,第316页。

duration—even if true, that would be hard to establish. The change which I have more particularly in view is that which takes place in sensible intervals of time; and the result on which I wish to lay stress is this, that *no state once gone can recur and be identical with what it was before.* Let us begin with Mr. Shadworth Hodgson's description:

"I go straight to the facts, without saying I go to perception, or sensation, or thought, or any special mode at all. What I find when I look at my consciousness at all is that what I cannot divest myself of, or not have in consciousness, if I have any consciousness at all, is a sequence of different feelings. I may shut my eyes and keep perfectly still, and try not to contribute anything of my own will; but whether I think or do not think, whether I perceive external things or not, I always have a succession of different feelings. Anything else that I may have also, of a more special character, comes in as parts of this succession. Not to have the succession of different feelings is not to be conscious at all. . . . The chain of consciousness is a sequence of *differents*." ①

Such a description as this can awaken no possible protest from any one. We all recognize as different great classes of our conscious states. Now we are seeing, now hearing; now reasoning, now willing; now recollecting, now expecting; now loving, now hating; and in a hundred other ways we know our minds to be alternately engaged. But all these are complex states. The aim of science is always to reduce complexity to simplicity; and in psychological science we have the celebrated 'theory of *ideas*' which, admitting the great difference among each other of what may be called concrete conditions of mind, seeks to show how this is all the resultant effect of variations in the *combination* of certain simple elements of consciousness that always remain the same.

① The Philosophy of Reflection, I. 248, 290.

——即使是真的，这也难以确立。我尤为关注的那种变化是在可感知的时间间隔中所发生的变化；而我想要强调的结果就是，状态一旦消失就不能够重现，并且不能与它以前所是的东西是同一的。让我们从沙德沃斯·霍奇森先生的描述开始：

“我径直来到了事实那里，而根本没有说我来到了知觉、感觉、思想或者任何特殊的模式之中。当我观察我的意识的时候，我所有的发现就是，我自己不能摆脱的东西，或者如果我确实有任何意识的话，我在意识中不能不拥有的东西，是一系列不同的感受。我可以闭上眼睛，完全保持静止，并且尽量不让我自己的意志中的任何东西起作用；但是，不论我是否思考，不论我是否在知觉外部的事物，我总是拥有一连串不同的感受。我也可以拥有一些其他东西，其具有更特殊的性质，它们作为这一序列的组成部分也来到这里。要是没有一连串不同的感受就根本不会有意识。……一系列意识就是一系列不同之物。”①

像这样的一种描述不可能引起任何人的反对。我们所有人都承认，我们的意识状态具有一些不同的大的类别。我们时而在看，时而在听；时而在推理，时而在意欲；时而在回忆，时而在期待；时而在爱，时而在恨；而且我们知道我们的心灵以数以百计的其他方式交替地忙碌着。但是所有这些都是复杂的状态。科学的目标总是将复杂还原为简单；并且在心理科学中，我们有著名的“观念理论”，它承认在每个我们可以称之为心灵的具体状态的东西之间存在着巨大的差异，它试图表明，这种情况如何完全是某些始终同一的简单的意识要素在结合上的变化所造成的结果。

① 《反映哲学》，1，第248、290页。

These mental atoms or molecules are what Locke called 'simple ideas.' Some of Locke's successors made out that the only simple ideas were the sensations strictly so called. Which ideas the simple ones may be does not, however, now concern us. It is enough that certain philosophers have thought they could see under the dissolving-view-appearance of the mind elementary facts of *any* sort that remained unchanged amid the flow.

And the view of these philosophers has been called little into question, for our common experience seems at first sight to corroborate it entirely. Are not the sensations we get from the same object, for example, always the same? Does not the same piano-key, struck with the same force, make us hear in the same way? Does not the same grass give us the same feeling of green, the same sky the same feeling of blue, and do we not get the same olfactory sensation no matter how many times we put our nose to the same flask of cologne? It seems a piece of metaphysical sophistry to suggest that we do not; and yet a close attention to the matter shows that *there is no proof that the same bodily sensation is ever got by us twice.*

What *is got twice is the same* OBJECT. We hear the same *note* over and over again; we see the same *quality* of green, or smell the same objective perfume, or experience the same *speries* of pain. The realities, concrete and abstract, physical and ideal, whose permanent existence we believe in, seem to be constantly coming up again before our thought, and lead us, in our carelessness, to suppose that our 'ideas' of them are the same ideas. When we come, some time later, to the chapter on Perception, we shall see how inveterate is our habit of not attending to sensations as subjective facts, but of simply using them as stepping-stones to pass over to the recognition of the realities whose presence they reveal. The grass out of the window now looks to me of the same green

这些精神原子或者分子就是洛克所说的“简单观念”。洛克的一些后继者进一步认为,唯一的简单观念严格说来就是感觉。然而,简单观念可以是那些观念,这现在与我们无关。了解到下述这一点就足够了,即某些哲学家认为,他们能够在心灵那消融的风景显现之下,看到在流动中保持不变的任何种类的基本事实。

并且这些哲学家的观点很少受到质疑,因为我们的共同经验乍一看似乎完全确证了它。例如,我们从同一个对象那里获得的感觉难道不是始终一样的吗?以相同的力度敲击同一个钢琴的琴键,这难道不是以相同的方式使我们听见了吗?难道同样的草儿没有给予我们同样的绿色的感受,难道同样的天空没有给予我们同样的蓝色的感受,又难道不论我们多少次将鼻子伸向同一个科隆香水瓶,我们没有得到相同的气味的感觉吗?似乎是一种形而上学的诡辩在暗示说我们没有;然而,如果紧密地关注这一问题,它就会向我们表明,这里没有任何关于我们曾经两次获有过同一个感觉的证据。

两次被得到的是那同一个对象。我们一次又一次地听到了同一个音符;我们看到了相同的绿色的性质,或者闻到了相同的真实的香水,或者体验到了相同种类的疼痛。那些具体的和抽象的、物理的和观念的、我们相信其永久存在的实在,似乎不断地再一次地出现在我们的思想面前,并且在我们漫不经心的情况下使我们推想,我们关于它们的“观念”是相同的观念。当我们今后进入到知觉这一章时,我们将会看到,下述的这种习惯是多么地根深蒂固,即我们在不经意间将一些感觉作为了主观事实,但我们却简单地将它们作为踏脚石来使用,通过它们来识别实在,当然这些实在的呈现是由它们揭示出来的。现在窗外的草在阳光下

in the sun as in the shade, and yet a painter would have to paint one part of it dark brown, another part bright yellow, to give its real sensational effect. We take no heed, as a rule, of the different way in which the same things look and sound and smell at different distances and under different circumstances. The sameness of the *things* is what we are concerned to ascertain; and any sensations that assure us of that will probably be considered in a rough way to be the same with each other. This is what makes off-hand testimony about the subjective identity of different sensations well-nigh worthless as a proof of the fact. The entire history of Sensation is a commentary on our inability to tell whether two sensations received apart are exactly alike. What appeals to our attention far more than the absolute quality or quantify of a given sensation is its *ratio* to whatever other sensations we may have at the same time. When everything is dark a somewhat less dark sensation makes us see an object white. Helmholtz calculates that the white marble painted in a picture representing an architectural view by moonlight is, when seen by daylight, from ten to twenty thousand times brighter than the real moonlit marble would be. ①

Such a difference as this could never have been *sensibly* learned; it had to be inferred from a series of indirect considerations. There are facts which make us believe that our sensibility is altering all the time, so that the same object cannot easily give us the same sensation over again. The eye's sensibility to light is at its maximum when the eye is first exposed, and blunts itself with surprising rapidity. A long night's sleep will make it see things twice as brightly on wakening, as simple rest by closure will make it see them later in the day. ②We feel things

① Populäre Wissenschaftliche Vorträge, Drittes Heft (1876), p. 72.

② Fick, in L. Hermann's Handb. d. Physiol., Bd. III. Th. I. p. 225.

和在阴暗处对我来说看起来都一样绿,但是画家却不得不将它的一部分画成暗褐色,另一部分画成亮黄色,以便使它获有真实的感觉效果。通常,我们并不留意同样的事物在不同的距离和不同的情形下看起来、听起来和闻起来的不同方法。事物的一致性是我们所想要确定的;并且任何使我们确保那种一致性的感觉可能将粗略地被认为是彼此间相同的感觉。正是这一点使得关于不同感觉的同一性的当下证词作为那种事实的证据几乎没有了任何价值。感觉的整个历史都是关于下述内容的注释,即我们没有能力辨别出我们分别接受到的两个感觉是否完全相同。吸引我们注意力的东西远不是一个给定感觉的绝对的质与量,而是我们在那一时刻可能获有的无论何种别的感觉与它的比率。当一切都是暗色的时候,稍微亮一点点的感觉就会使我们看见一个对象是白色的。赫姆霍尔茨计算过,为了再现月光下建筑物的风景而在一幅画上画下的白色大理石,在日光下看上去比真正月光下的大理石要明亮一到两万倍。①

像这样一种差异永远不能被感性地认识到,它不得不从一些间接的思考中被推论出来。这里有一些事实可以使我们相信我们的感受性始终是在变化的,因此同一个对象不能很容易地再次给予我们相同的感觉。当眼睛最初暴露在阳光之下,它对光的感受性达到了其最大值,并且以令人吃惊的速度又变得迟钝了。一夜长时间的睡眠,使得醒来时眼睛看东西的明亮度是白天简单的闭眼休息之后眼睛看东西的明亮度的两倍。② 相应地当我们睏了

① 《通俗科学报告集》,第3册(1876年),第72页。

② 菲克,在L.赫尔曼的《生理学手册》中,第3卷,第1册,第225页。

differently according as we are sleepy or awake, hungry or full, fresh or tired; differently at night and in the morning, differently in summer and in winter, and above all things differently in childhood, manhood, and old age. Yet we never doubt that our feelings reveal the same world, with the same sensible qualities and the same sensible things occupying it. The difference of the sensibility is shown best by the difference of our emotion about the things from one age to another, or when we are in different organic moods. What was bright and exciting becomes weary, flat, and unprofitable. The bird's song is tedious, the breeze is mournful, the sky is sad.

To these indirect presumptions that our sensations, following the mutations of our capacity for feeling, are always undergoing an essential change, must be added another presumption, based on what must happen in the brain. Every sensation corresponds to some cerebral action. For an identical sensation to recur it would have to occur the second time *in an unmodified brain.* But as this, strictly speaking, is a physiological impossibility, so is an unmodified feeling an impossibility; for to every brain-modification, however small, must correspond a change of equal amount in the feeling which the brain subserves.

All this would be true if even sensations came to us pure and single and not combined into 'things.' Even then we should have to confess that, however we might in ordinary conversation speak of getting the same sensation again, we never in strict theoretic accuracy could do so; and that whatever was true of the river of life, of the river of elementary feeling, it would certainly be true to say, like Heraclitus, that we never descend twice into the same stream.

But if the assumption of 'simple ideas of sensation' recurring in

或者清醒了、饿了或者饱了、精力充沛或者疲劳的时候，我们感受事物是不同的；在晚上和白天不同，在夏天和冬天不同，尤其在童年、成年和老年的时候，我们感受事物是不同的。然而，我们从来也没有怀疑过这一点，即我们的感受揭示了同一个世界，这个世界有着相同的可感觉的性质，并且有相同的可感觉的事物占据着它。当我们处于不同的年龄时，或者当我们处于不同的机体情绪状态时，我们对事物的不同情绪的体验，最明显地表现出了感受性的差异。原本是令人欢快和兴奋的东西变得令人厌烦、无聊和无利可图了。小鸟的歌声是沉闷的，微风令人忧郁，天空令人悲伤。

随着我们感受能力的变化，我们的感觉也始终在经历着本质的变化，在这样一些间接的假定之上，基于在大脑中所必须发生的事情，必须加上另一个假定。每一个感觉都与某种大脑活动相对应。要使同一个感觉重现，它将不得不在没有变化的大脑中再次出现。但是，由于严格说来这在生理学上是不可能的，因此一个未更改的感受也是不可能的；因为每一次大脑的改变，不论有多么小，必须和大脑所促生的感受中的等量变化相对应。

即使我们所获得的感受是纯粹而单一的，并且还没有结合为“事物”，所有这一切也都是真的。甚至在那时，我们也不得不承认，无论我们可以在平常的谈话中如何说我们又一次获得了相同的感觉，就严格的理论准确性而言，我们永远也不能做到这一点；并且无论对生命之河而言何种东西是真实的，无论对基本感受之河而言何种东西是真实的，如赫拉克利特所说，我们永远也不能两次踏入同一条河流，这样说当然是真实的。

而且，如果“简单感觉观念”以不变的形式再现这一假定这么

immutable shape is so easily shown to be baseless, how much more baseless is the assumption of immutability in the larger masses of our thought!

For there it is obvious and palpable that our state of mind is never precisely the same. Every thought we have of a given fact is, strictly speaking, unique, and only bears a resemblance of kind with our other thoughts of the same fact. When the identical fact recurs, we *must* think of it in a fresh manner, see it under a somewhat different angle, apprehend it in different relations from those in which it last appeared. And the thought by which we cognize it is the thought of it-in-those-relations, a thought suffused with the consciousness of all that dim context. Often we are ourselves struck at the strange differences in our successive views of the same thing. We wonder how we ever could have opined as we did last month about a certain matter. We have outgrown the possibility of that state of mind, we know not how. From one year to another we see things in new lights. What was unreal has grown real, and what was exciting is insipid. The friends we used to care the world for are shrunken to shadows; the women, once so divine, the stars, the woods, and the waters, how now so dull and common! the young girls that brought an aura of infinity, at present hardly distinguishable existences ; the pictures so empty; and as for the books, what *was* there to find so mysteriously significant in Goethe, or in John Mill so full of weight? Instead of all this, more zestful than ever is the work, the work; and fuller and deeper the import of common duties and of common goods.

But what here strikes us so forcibly on the flagrant scale exists on every scale, down to the imperceptible transition from one hour's outlook to that of the next. Experience is remoulding us every moment,

容易就表明是没有根据的，那么，关于我们更加大量的思想中的不变性的假设，又会是多么地更加没有根据啊！

因为在那里我们的心理状态永远都不是完全一样的，这是显而易见和明显的。严格说来，我们所获有的关于一个既定事实的每一个思想都是独一无二的，并且只是和我们关于同一事实的其他的思想在种类上有相似之处。当同一个事实重现的时候，我们必须以一种全新的方式来思考它，以一种略微不同的角度来观察它，在与上次它显现于其中的关系有所不同的关系中来理解它。而且我们所由以认知它的思想是关于它在那些关系中的思想，一个充满着关于那整个模糊的关系背景的意识的思想。我们自己也为我们对同一个事物的相继看法中的奇怪的差异而常常感到惊奇。我们想知道，我们上个月对某一个事件如何竟会有那样的想法。我们的成长使得那种心理状态的出现变得不大可能了，我们也不知道怎么会这样。年复一年，我们以新的视角看待问题。以前不真实的东西变得真实了，以前令人兴奋的东西变得没有味道了。我们过去最最在乎的朋友，皱缩成了影子；曾经如此神圣的女人、星星、森林还有流水，现在是如此的无趣与普通！那些给人带来永恒的感受的年轻女孩，现在成了几乎难以辨别的人；照片变得如此空洞；而至于书籍，在歌德那里曾经发现具有如此神秘意义的东西是什么呢？或者在约翰·密尔那里如此沉重的东西又是什么呢？尽管如此，比所有这一切更有滋味的是工作，就是工作；公共职责和公共利益的意义也变得更加充实和深刻了。

而且，存在于众所周知的等级之上并且在这里强有力地令我们感到惊奇的东西，也存在于每一个等级之上，向下一直到此时观点到彼时观点的不可觉察的转变之上。经验每时每刻都在改

and our mental reaction on every given thing is really a resultant of our experience of the whole world up to that date. The analogies of brain-physiology must again be appealed to corroborate our view.

Our earlier chapters have taught us to believe that, whilst we think, our brain changes, and that, like the aurora borealis, its whole internal equilibrium shifts with every pulse of change. The precise nature of the shifting at a given moment is a product of many factors. The accidental state of local nutrition or blood-supply may be among them. But just as one of them certainly is the influence of outward objects on the sense-organs during the moment, so is another certainly the very special susceptibility in which the organ has been left at that moment by all it has gone through in the past. Every brain-state is partly determined by the nature of this entire past succession. Alter the latter in any part, and the brain-state must be somewhat different. Each present brain-state is a record in which the eye of Omniscience might read all the foregone history of its owner. It is out of the question, then, that any total brain-state should identically recur. Something like it may recur ; but to suppose it to recur would be equivalent to the absurd admission that all the states that had intervened between its two appearances had been pure nonentities, and. that the organ after their passage was exactly as it was before. And (to consider shorter periods) just as, in the senses, an impression feels very differently according to what has preceded it; as one color succeeding another is modified by the contrast, silence sounds delicious after noise, and a note, when the scale is sung up, sounds unlike itself when the scale is sung down ; as the presence of certain lines in a figure changes the apparent form of the other lines, and as in music the whole æsthetic effect comes from the manner in which one set of sounds alters our feeling of another; so, in thought, we must admit that those portions of the brain that have just been maximally excited

造着我们,而且我们对每一个既定事物的心理反应,真的是到那时为止我们关于整个世界的经验的结果。为了确证我们的观点,我们必须再次诉诸于大脑生理学的类推。

我们前面的章节已经使我们相信,当我们思考的时候,我们的大脑也变化着,并且就像北极光一样,它的整个内部的平衡随着每一次变化的波动而改变。在一个既定时刻,改变的确切本质是由许多因素造成的。局部营养和供血的偶然状态可能就是其中的因素。其中因素之一肯定还包括在那个时刻外部的对象对感觉器官所造成的影响,这样看来还有一个因素是在那一时刻感官通过其过去的全部经历而形成的那种十分特殊的感受性。每一个大脑状态都部分地由这些过去相继发生的所有事情所决定。改变后者的任何一个部分,那么大脑状态必定会有所不同。每一个当前的大脑状态都是一份记录,全知者可以从中读出其拥有者的过去的全部历史。那么,任何完整的大脑状态将会完全相同地重现,这是绝对不可能的。某种与它相似的东西可能会出现;但是假设它会重现的话,就等于荒谬地承认,介于它的两种显现之间的所有状态都是不存在的了,并且器官在它们通过了以后,和它以前是完全一样的。而且(考虑一下较短的时间)正如在感官那里,一个印象依照在它之前所发生的事情感受起来是非常不同的;比如在一种颜色之后出现的另一种颜色会由于对比而发生变化,在噪音过后,安静是宜人的,一个音符,当音阶在上行时听起来和当音阶在下行时是完全不一样的;比如在一个图形上出现了某些线条会改变其他线条的外观形式,又比如在音乐中,整个审美效果取决于一组声音改变我们对另一组声音的感受的方式;所以,在思想中,我们必须承认,已经极度兴奋过的大脑的那

retain a kind of soreness which is a condition of our present consciousness, a codeterminant of how and what we now shall feel.[①]

Ever some tracts are waning in tension, some waxing, whilst others actively discharge. The states of tension have as positive an influence as any in determining the total condition, and in deciding what the *psychosis* shall be. All we know of submaximal nerve-irritations, and of the summation of apparently ineffective stimuli, tends to show that *no* changes in the brain are physiologically ineffective, and that presumably none are bare of psychological result. But as the brain-tension shifts from one relative state of equilibrium to another, like the gyrations of a kaleidoscope, now rapid and now slow, is it likely that its faithful psychic concomitant is heavier-footed than itself, and that it cannot match each one of the organ's irradiations by a shifting inward iridescence of its own? But if it can do this, its inward iridescences must be infinite, for the brain-redistributions are in infinite variety. If so coarse a thing as a telephone-plate can be made to thrill for years and never reduplicate its inward condition, how much more must this be the case with the infinitely delicate brain?

I am sure that this concrete and total manner of regarding the mind's changes is the only true manner, difficult as it may be to carry it out in detail. If anything seems obscure about it, it will grow clearer as we advance. Meanwhile, if it be true, it is certainly

---

① It need of course not follow, because a total brain-state does not recur, that no *point* of the brain can ever be twice in the same condition. That would be as improbable a consequence as that in the sea a wave-crest should never come twice at the same point of space. What can hardly come twice is an identical *combination* of wave-forms all with their crests and hollows reoccupying identical places. For such a total combination as this is the analogue of the brain-state to which our actual consciousness at any moment is due.

些部分保留着某种痛苦,它是我们当前意识的一个条件,是我们现在该如何感觉和感觉什么的一个共同决定因素。①

在任何时候,一些神经通道在紧张状态中正在逐渐变小,一些在逐渐增大,而另一些则活跃地释放。紧张状态对确定整个条件,以及决定精神将会是什么都同样地起着积极的作用。我们所知道有关亚极大神经刺激、显然无效的刺激的聚合的全部内容都趋向于表明,大脑中的所有变化在生理学的意义上都不是无效的,并且都会引起心理结果。而且由于大脑张力从一种相对平衡的状态转到另一种状态,就像一个万花筒的旋转,时而快时而慢,那么有没有可能它的忠实的精神伴随物比它自己行动得更迟缓些呢,并且有没有可能它不能通过改变它自己内部的彩虹来和器官的每一次照射相匹配呢?但是,如果它能够这样做,那么它内部的彩虹就必须是无限的,因为大脑的重新分布状态是无限多样的。如果像电话盘这样粗糙的东西都能够震颤多年而从不重复其内部条件,那么这种情况对于无限精致的大脑而言不是必定更加如此了吗?

我确信这种看待心灵变化的具体而完整的方式是唯一真实的方式,虽然将它详细地完成是困难的。如果关于它的某些事情似乎是模糊的,随着我们的进展它就会变得清楚了。同时,如果

---

① 当然不需要由此推论的是,因为整个大脑状态不会重现,所以大脑的任何一个点不能两次处于同一个状态。这是一种不可能的推论,如同大海中的波峰永远不能到达空间中的同一个点两次这种推论一样。很难发生两次的是,波形与其再次占据相同空间的所有波峰和波谷的完全相同的结合。因为像这样的一种完全结合,类似于导致我们在任何时刻形成真实的意识的大脑状态的活动。

also true that no two 'ideas' are ever exactly the same, which is the proposition we started to prove. The proposition is more important theoretically than it at first sight seems. For it makes it already impossible for us to follow obediently in the footprints of either the Lockian or the Herbartian school, schools which have had almost unlimited influence in Germany and among ourselves. No doubt it is often *convenient* to formulate the mental facts in an atomistic sort of way, and to treat the higher states of consciousness as if they were all built out of unchanging simple ideas. It is convenient often to treat curves as if they were composed of small straight lines, and electricity and nerve-force as if they were fluids. But in the one case as in the other we must never forget that we are talking symbolically, and that there is nothing in nature to answer to our words. A *permanently existing 'idea' or 'Vorstellung' which makes its appearance before the footlights of consciousness at periodical intervals, is as mythological an entity as the Jack of Spades.*

What makes it convenient to use the mythological formulas is the whole organization of speech, which, as was remarked a while ago, was not made by psychologists, but by men who were as a rule only interested in the facts their mental states revealed. They only spoke of their states as *ideas of this or of that thing*. What wonder, then, that the thought is most easily conceived under the law of the thing whose name it bears! If the thing is composed of parts, then we suppose that the thought of the thing must be composed of the thoughts of the parts. If one part of the thing have appeared in the same thing or in other things on former occasions, why then we must be having even now the very same 'idea' of that part which was there on those occasions. If the thing is simple, its thought is simple. If it is multitudinous, it must require a multitude of thoughts to think it. If a succession, only a succession of thoughts can know it.

它是真实的，那么，没有两个“观念”曾完全相同，这也当然是真的，而这正是我们开始时要证明的命题。这个命题在理论上比它初次看上去要更加重要。因为它已经使得我们不再顺从地追随洛克学派或者是赫尔巴特学派的足迹了，这些学派在德国和我们自己中间几乎产生了无限的影响。毫无疑问，以一种原子论的方式来阐明心理事实，并且将高级的意识状态看作好像完全是由不变的简单观念而构建起来的，这常常是很方便的。将曲线看作好像是由小的直线组成的，将电和神经力看作是流体，这常常是很方便的。但是在这样或那样的情况下，我们必须永远牢记我们是以象征的方式进行讨论的，并且自然界中不存在与我们的话语相对应的任何东西。以一定周期的时间间隔使自身显现在意识的舞台前的永久存在的“观念”或者“联想”，如黑桃杰克一样是虚构的本体。

言语的整个结构使得使用虚构的话语变得方便起来，正如不久前所提到的那样，它不是由心理学家制造出来的，而是由那些通常只是对他们的心理状态所揭示的事实感兴趣的人们制造出来的。他们只是把他们的状态称之为关于这个事物或者那个事物的观念。那么，思想最容易在它所包含其名称的事物的规律下而被构想，这又有什么可奇怪的呢！如果事物是由部分所组成的，那么我们就假设关于事物的思想一定是由思想的不同部分所组成的。如果事物的一个部分在以前的场合里出现在同一个事物或者其他事物中了，那么甚至现在我们也拥有在那些场合显现的部分的完全相同的“观念”。如果事物是简单的，它的思想也是简单的。如果它是多种多样的，要思考它就必须需要众多的思想。如果它是连续的，只有一组连续的思想才能认识它。如果它

If permanent, its thought is permanent. And so on *ad libitum*. What after all is so natural as to assume that one object, called by one name, should be known by one affection of the mind ? But, if language must thus influence us, the agglutinative languages, and even Greek and Latin with their declensions, would be the better guides. Names did not appear in them inalterable, but changed their shape to suit the context in which they lay. It must have been easier then than now to conceive of the same object as being thought of at different times in non-identical conscious states.

This, too, will grow clearer as we proceed. Meanwhile a necessary consequence of the belief in permanent selfidentical psychic facts that absent themselves and recur periodically is the Humian doctrine that our thought is composed of separate independent parts and is not a sensibly continuous stream. That this doctrine entirely misrepresents the natural appearances is what I next shall try to show.

3) *Within each personal consciousness, thought is sensibly continuous.*

I can only define ' continuous' as that which is without breach, crack, or division. I have already said that the breach from one mind to another is perhaps the greatest breach in nature. The only breaches that can well be conceived to occur within the limits of a single mind would either be *interruptions*, time-gaps during which the con-sciousness went out altogether to come into existence again at a later moment; or they would be breaks in the *quality*, or content, of the thought, so abrupt that the segment that followed had no connection whatever with the one that went before. The proposition that within each personal consciousness thought feels continuous, means two things:

1. That even where there is a time-gap the consciousness after it feels as if it belonged together with the consciousness before it, as

是永久的,关于它的思想也是永久的。并且可以像这样随意地说下去。究竟是什么使人们如此自然的假设,通过一个名称而被称呼的一个对象,应当通过心灵的某个倾向来认识呢?但是,如果语言必须如此地影响我们,那么粘着性的语言,甚至带有词尾变化的希腊语和拉丁语都将是更好的指南了。名称在这些语言中并非不变的显现,而是改变它们的外形以适合它们所处的语境。那时一定比现在更容易设想,同一个对象在不同的时刻是在不同的意识状态中被思考的。

随着我们的进展,这一点也会变得更加清楚起来。与此同时,永久的自我同一的精神事实周期性地使自己消失和重现,这种信念产生了一个必然的结果,它就是休谟的学说,这种学说认为,我们的思想由各自独立的部分所组成,并且不是一种可感知的连续的流。我接下来将要表明的是,这种学说完全错误地再现了那种自然显现。

3. 在每一个个人意识中,思想明显是连续的

我只能将“连续的”定义为它是没有破裂、裂缝或者分界线的。我已经说过,一个心灵到另一个心灵之间的裂缝可能是自然界中最大的裂缝。能够被适当地构想的在有限的单个心灵中出现的裂痕,或者是中断、时间裂缝,在其间意识完全消失,而在后来的时刻又再次出现了;或者它们就是思想的性质或者内容的断裂,这断裂是如此的突然,以至于随后的部分和前面过去的部分没有任何联系。在每一个个人意识中,思想感受起来是连续的,这一命题有两个意思:

1. 甚至在存在时间断裂的地方,在这之后的意识感受起来就好像它作为同一个自我的另一个部分,完全和在这之前的意识同

another part of the same self;

2. That the changes from one moment to another in the quality of the consciousness are never absolutely abrupt.

The case of the time-gaps, as the simplest, shall be taken first. And first of all, a word about time-gaps of which the consciousness may not be itself aware.

On page 200 we saw that such time-gaps existed, and that they might be more numerous than is usually supposed. If the consciousness is not aware of them, it cannot feel them as interruptions. In the unconsciousness produced by nitrous oxide and other anaesthetics, in that of epilepsy and fainting, the broken edges of the sentient life may meet and merge over the gap, much as the feelings of space of the opposite margins of the 'blind spot' meet and merge over that objective interruption to the sensitiveness of the eye. Such consciousness as this, whatever it be for the onlooking psychologist, is for itself unbroken. It *feels* unbroken; a waking day of it is sensibly a unit as long as that day lasts, in the sense in which the hours themselves are units, as having all their parts next each other, with no intrusive alien substance between. To expect the consciousness to feel the interruptions of its objective continuity as gaps, would be like expecting the eye to feel a gap of silence because it does not hear, or the ear to feel a gap of darkness because it does not see. So much for the gaps that are unfelt.

With the felt gaps the case is different. On waking from sleep, we usually know that we have been unconscious, and we often have an accurate judgment of how long. The judgment here is certainly an inference from sensible signs, and its ease is due to long practice in the particular field.① The result of it, however, is that the consciousness

① The accurate registration of the 'how long' is still a little mysterious.

处一处。

2. 意识的性质从一个时刻到另一个时刻所发生的变化，从来都不是绝对突然的。

由于时间断裂的情况最为简单，它将首先被拿来加以讨论。首先讨论的是，意识自身可能没有觉察到的时间断裂。

在第200页我们看到，这样的时间断裂是存在的，而且它们可能比通常所假设的还要多。如果意识没有觉察到它们，它就不能把它们感受为中断。在由一氧化二氮和其他麻醉药物引起的无意识中，在癫痫和昏厥所造成的无意识中，有感觉力的生命的断裂边缘，可以越过那个裂口，相遇并且融合起来，很像对“盲点”的相对边缘的空间感受，可以越过眼睛感受性的客观中断，相遇并且融合起来，不管像这样的意识对于旁观的心理学家来说是什么样的，在其自身看来它是没有断裂的。它感受起来是没有断裂的；在醒着的一天里，只要这一天还在继续，就可以感觉到它是一个单元，在每段时间自身都是单元的意义上，它们的所有部分都是彼此紧挨着的，没有任何相异的物质侵入其间。期望意识将它的客观连续性的中断感受为裂缝，就好像期望眼睛感受到安静的断裂，因为它听不见，或者又好像期望耳朵感受到黑暗的断裂，因为它看不见。关于未被感受到的裂缝就谈到这里吧。

就被感受到的裂缝而言，情况是不同的。从睡眠中醒来的时候，我们通常知道我们曾是无意识的，并且我们常常对无意识的持续时间有着精确的判断。这里的判断当然是一种从可感觉的迹象中的推论，并且它之所以容易是由于在特殊领域中的长期训练而造成的。①

① “多长时间”的精确记录依然有一点神秘。

is, for *itself*, not what it was in the former case, but interrupted and discontinuous, in the mere sense of the words. But in the other sense of continuity, the sense of the parts being inwardly connected and belonging together because they are parts of a common whole, the consciousness remains sensibly continuous and one. What now is the common whole? The natural name for it is *myself*, *I*, or *me*.

When Paul and Peter wake up in the same bed, and recognize that they have been asleep, each one of them mentally reaches back and makes connection with but *one* of the two streams of thought which were broken by the sleeping hours. As the current of an electrode buried in the ground unerringly finds its way to its own similarly buried mate, across no matter how much intervening earth; so Peter's present instantly finds out Peter's past, and never by mistake knits itself on to that of Paul. Paul's thought in turn is as little liable to go astray. The past thought of Peter is appropriated by the present Peter alone. He may have *aknowledge*, and a correct one too, of what Paul's last drowsy states of mind were as he sank into sleep, but it is an entirely different sort of knowledge from that which he has of his own last states. He *remembers* his own states, whilst he only *conceives* Paul's. Remembrance is like direct feeling; its object is suffused with a warmth and intimacy to which no object of mere conception ever attains. This quality of warmth and intimacy and immediacy is what Peter's *present* thought also possesses for itself. So sure as this present is me, is mine, it says, so sure is anything else that comes with the same warmth and intimacy and immediacy, me and mine. What the qualities called warmth and intimacy may in themselves be will have to be matter for future consideration. But whatever past feelings appear with those qualities must be admitted to

然而，其结果是，意识就其自身而言已经不是在前面的情况中它所是的东西了，而且它是中断的和不连续的，这是在词语的纯粹意义上来说的。但是在连续性的其他意义上，在下述这种意义上，即关于部分的感觉内在地联系在一起，并且同处一处，因为它们是共同整体的组成部分，意识依然是显然连续的和完整的。现在，那个共同的整体是什么呢？它自然的名称是我自己、主格的我或者宾格的我。

当保罗和彼得在同一张床上醒来，并且承认他们刚才睡着了的时候，他们各自在精神上进行回顾，并且只与由睡眠时间所中断的两个思想流中的一个进行联系。就像埋在地下的电极的电流，不管要穿越多少介于其间的土地，也会准确无误地找到同样埋在地下的它自己的配偶；因此彼得的现在立即找到彼得的过去，并且从来不会错误地和保罗的过去连在一起。相应地，保罗的思想也不大可能误入歧途。彼得的过去的思想被现在的彼得所单独占有。他知道当保罗进入睡眠的时候，他最后那昏昏欲睡的心灵状态是什么，他可以拥有这种知识，并且这也是一种正确的知识，但是这是一种与他对他自己过去的状态所拥有的知识完全不同的一种知识。他记得他自己的状态，而他只能构想保罗的状态。记忆就像是直接的感受；它的对象充满了对任何纯粹概念的对象来说从来不曾获有的温暖与亲密。这种温暖、亲密和直接的性质也是彼得现在的思想自身所拥有的东西。如此确定的是，这个现在就是我，是我的。同样确定的是，任何带有这同样的温暖、亲密和直接的性质的其他东西，就是我，是我的。被称作温暖和亲密的性质，其自身究竟是什么，这个问题将不得不留给未来去思考。但是，必须要承认的是，凡是带着这些性质显现的过去

receive the greeting of the present mental state, to be owned by it, and accepted as belonging together with it in a common self. This community of self is what the time-gap cannot break in twain, and is why a present thought, although not ignorant of the time-gap, can still regard itself as continuous with certain chosen portions of the past.

Consciousness, then, does not appear to itself chopped up in bits. Such words as 'chain' or 'train' do not describe it fitly as it presents itself in the first instance. It is nothing jointed; it flows. A 'river' or a 'stream' are the metaphors by which it is most naturally described. *In talking of it hereafter, let us call it the stream of thought, of consciousness, or of subjective life.*

But now there appears, even within the limits of the same self, and between thoughts all of which alike have this same sense of belonging together, a kind of jointing and separateness among the parts, of which this statement seems to take no account. I refer to the breaks that are produced by sudden *contrasts in the quality* of the successive segments of the stream of thought. If the words 'chain' and 'train' had no natural fitness in them, how came such words to be used at all? Does not a loud explosion rend the consciousness upon which it abruptly breaks, in twain? Does not every sudden shock, appearance of a new object, or change in a sensation, create a real interruption, sensibly felt as such, which cuts the conscious stream across at the moment at which it appears? Do not such interruptions smite us every hour of our lives, and have we the right, in their presence, still to call our consciousness a continuous stream?

This objection is based partly on confusion and partly on a superficial introspective view.

The confusion is between the thoughts themselves, taken as

的感受，都必须要得到当前心理状态的迎接，被它所拥有，并且与它共处在一个共同的自我之中。这个自我共同体就是时间断裂不能将其一分为二的东西，也是现在的思想，尽管没有忽视时间断裂，依然能够将自己看作是与过去某些选定部分相连续的原因。

因而，意识并没有向自身显现为被砍碎了的碎块。像“链条”或者“序列”这样的词语，并没有恰当地将它最初呈现给它自己时的样子给描述出来。它不是连接起来的东西，它流动着。通过“河”或者“流”这样的比喻，它被最自然地描述了出来。在后面谈到它的地方，让我们称呼它为思想之流、意识之流或者主观的生活之流吧。

但是现在，甚至在同一个自我界限之内，以及在同样地拥有共处一处这种相同意义的所有思想之间，似乎出现了一种部分间的连接与分离，上述这种论述似乎对此没有加以考虑。我指的断裂是由思想之流的相继部分在性质上出现了突然的差异而产生的断裂。如果“链条”和“序列”这些词语天生就不适合它们，那么，这样的词语如何竟会被投入使用？难道一声巨大的爆炸没有把它所中断的意识一分为二吗？难道每一次突然的震惊、一个新对象的显现或者感觉的变化不会产生出一种真实的、可以被那样明显感受到的、在其显现的那一刻将穿过的意识之流切断的中断吗？难道这样的中断没有在我们生活的每时每刻折磨着我们，并且在它们出现的时候，难道我们还有权利称我们的意识是连续的流吗？

这种异议，部分基于混淆，部分基于一种肤浅的内省观点。

混淆存在于作为主观事实的思想自身和思想所意识到的事

subjective facts, and the things of which they are aware. It is natural to make this confusion, but easy to avoid it when once put on one's guard. The things are discrete and discontinuous; they do pass before us in a train or chain, making often explosive appearances and rending each other in twain. But their comings and goings and contrasts no more break the flow of the thought that thinks them than they break the time and the space in which they lie. A silence may be broken by a thunder-clap, and we may be so stunned and confused for a moment by the shock as to give no instant account to ourselves of what has happened. But that very confusion is a mental state, and a state that passes us straight over from the silence to the sound. The transition between the thought of one object and the thought of another is no more a break in the *thought* than a joint in a bamboo is a break in the wood. It is a part of the *consciousness* as much as the joint is a part of the *bamboo*.

The superficial introspective view is the overlooking, even when the things are contrasted with each other most violently, of the large amount of affinity that may still remain between the thoughts by whose means they are cognized. Into the awareness of the thunder itself the awareness of the previous silence creeps and continues; for what we hear when the thunder crashes is not thunder *pure*, but thunder-breaking-upon-silence-and-contrasting-with-it[①] Our feeling of the same objective thunder, coming in this way, is quite different from what it would be were the thunder a continuation of previous thunder. The thunder itself we believe to abolish and exclude the silence; but the *felling* of the thunder is also a feeling of the silence as just gone; and it would be difficult to find in the actual concrete consciousness of man a feeling so limited to the present as not to have an inkling of anything that went before. Here,

① Cf. Brentano; Psychologie, vol. I. pp. 219-20. Altogether this chapter of Brentano's on the Unity of Consciousness is as good as anything with which I am acquainted.

物之间。出现这种混淆是很自然的，但是一旦人们对此有所提防，它是很容易避免的。事物是离散的和不连续的；它们确实以序列或者链条的形式从我们面前经过，常常会爆发性地显现出来，并且使彼此分离开来。但是它们的到来、离去和差异并没有中断思考着它们的思想之流，就如同它们没有使它们位于其中的时间和空间中断一样。安静可以被雷鸣所打断，并且我们会由于这种震颤而在一段时间里感到非常震惊和困惑，以至于我们自己竟不能立刻了解到发生了什么事情。但是那种混乱是一种心理状态，一种直接使我们从安静过渡到声响的状态。关于一个对象的思想和关于另一个对象的思想之间的转换，在思想中不是一种中断，就像竹子上的竹节并没有在竹子上产生中断一样。和竹节是竹子的一部分一样，它也是意识的一部分。

肤浅的内省观点忽略了这一点，即甚至在事物彼此间的对比最为强烈的时候，在这些事物由以得到认知的思想之间依然可以存在着大量的相似之处。对先前的安静的知觉悄悄地溜进了对雷声的知觉之中，并且继续着；因为当打雷的时候，我们所听到的并不是纯粹的雷声，而是破坏了安静并且与安静相对照的雷声。①以这种方式到来的我们对同一个客观雷声的感受，和在它是前一个雷声的继续时我们对它的感受是不同的。我们相信雷声自身打破并消除了安静；但是对雷声的感受也是对刚刚离去的安静的感受；在人的真实而具体的意识中，很难发现一个感受是如此地局限于现在，以至于对以前发生的任何事情都一无所知。这里，

① 参见布兰塔诺：《心理学》，第1卷，第219～220页。总而言之，布兰塔诺关于意识的统一性这一章是我所熟悉的好的论述之一。

again, language works against our perception of the truth. We name our thoughts simply, each after its thing, as if each knew its own thing and nothing else. What each really knows is clearly the thing it is named for, with dimly perhaps a thousand other things. It ought to be named after all of them, but it never is. Some of them are always things known a moment ago more clearly; others are things to be known more clearly a moment hence.① Our own bodily position, attitude, condition, is one of the things of which *some* awareness, however inattentive, invariably accompanies the knowledge of whatever else we know.

---

① Honor to whom honor is due! The most explicit acknowledgment I have anywhere found of all this is in a buried and forgotten paper by the Rev. Jas Wills, on 'Accidental Association,' in the Transactions of the Royal Irish Academy, vol XXI. part I (1846). Mr. Wills writes:

" At every instant of conscious thought there is a certain sum of perceptions, or reflections, or both together, present, and together constituting one whole state of apprehension. Of this some definite portion may be far more distinct than all the rest; and the rest be in consequence proportionally vague, even to the limit of obliteration. But still, within this limit, the most dim shade of perception enters into, and in some infinitesimal degree modifies, the whole existing state. This state will thus be in some way modified by any sensation or emotion, or act of distinct attention, that may give prominence to any part of it; so that the actual result is capable of the utmost variation, according to the person or the occasion. . . To any portion of the entire scope here described there may be a special direction of the attention, and this special direction is recognized as strictly what is *recognized* as the idea present to the mind. This idea is evidently not commensurate with the entire state of apprehension, and much perplexity has arisen from not observing this fact. However deeply we may suppose the attention to be engaged by any thought, any considerable alteration of the surrounding phenomena would still be perceived; the most abstruse demonstration in this room would not prevent a listener, however absorbed, from noticing the sudden extinction of the lights. Our mental states have always an *essential unity*, such that each state of apprehension, however variously compounded, is a single whole, of which every component is, therefore, strictly apprehended (so far as it is apprehended) as a part. Such is the elementary basis from which all our intellectual operations commence. "

语言又一次同我们对真相的知觉作起对来。我们简单地依照每一个思想所指的事物命名我们的思想，就好像每一个思想只知道它自己所指的事物，而不知道其他任何东西。实际上为每一个思想所知道的不仅无疑有它所命名的那个事物，而且模模糊糊地还可能有许许多多其他的事物。它应当依照所有这些事物来命名，但是它从来没有这样过。其中一些总是在片刻之前被认识得更加清楚的事物；而另一些是在片刻之后被认识得更加清楚的事物。[1] 我们自己的身体位置、姿势和状态就是这些事物之一，我们对其有所知觉，不管这知觉有多么无意，它们总是不变地和我们

---

① 向应当受到尊敬的人致敬！我向尊敬的 J. 威尔斯所写的一篇关于“偶然联想”文章献上我最最明确的谢意，这篇被埋葬、被遗忘了的文章发表在《爱尔兰皇家科学院学报》，第 21 卷，第 1 部分(1846)。威尔斯先生写到：

“在每一个有意识思维的瞬间，都有一定数量的知觉或者反应出现，或者两者一起出现，并且一起构成了整个理解状态。就这些而言，某些确定的部分可能比所有剩余的部分要清楚得多；结果，那些剩余的部分就相应地模糊一些，甚至达到了消除的界限边缘。但是，在这个界限之内，最模糊的知觉依然进入到了整个现存的状态，并且在极小的程度上改变着这个状态。这个状态因此将会以某种方式被任何感觉、情绪或者明显的注意作用所改变，这些感觉、情绪或者注意作用可以使它的任何一部分突出出来；因此，根据人或者场合的不同，实际的结果能够发生最大限度的变化。……这里可能有一种特殊的注意方向指向这里所描述的整个范围的任何部分，并且对这种特殊方向的辨认完全和对呈现给心灵的观念的辨认一样。这个观念显然和整个理解状态不相称，而且很多困惑与混乱就出自没有观察到这一事实。不论我们可以设想任何思想如何深入地吸引着注意力，周围现象的任何明显的变化还是可以被知觉到；不论一个听者如何地聚精会神，这个房间里的最深奥的论证还是不能阻止这个听者注意到灯光的突然熄灭。我们的心理状态始终具有这样一种基本的统一性，即每一种理解状态，不论它是多么不同地被复合起来的，都是一个单一的整体，因此它的每一个成分都被严格地理解(只要它被理解了)为它的一个部分。这就是我们的知性的活动所由以开始的初步基础。”

We think; and as we think we feel our bodily selves as the seat of the thinking. If the thinking be *our* thinking, it must be suffused through all its parts with that peculiar warmth and intimacy that make it come as ours. Whether the warmth and intimacy be anything more than the feeling of the same old body always there, is a matter for the next chapter to decide. *Whatever* the content of the ego may be, it is habitually felt *with* everything else by us humans, and must form a *liaison* between all the things of which we become successively aware. ①

On this gradualness in the changes of our mental content the principles of nerve-action can throw some more light . When studying, in Chapter III, the summation of nervous activities, we saw that no state of the brain can be supposed instantly to die away. If a new state comes, the inertia of the old state will still be there and modify the result accordingly. Of course we cannot tell, in our ignorance, what in each instance the modifications ought to be. The commonest modifications in sense-perception are known as the phenomena of contrast. In æsthetics they are the feelings of delight or displeasure which certain particular orders in a series of impressions give. In thought, strictly and narrowly so called, they are unquestionably that consciousness of the *whence* and the *whither* that always accompanies its flows. If recently the braintract a was vividly excited, and then *b*, and now vividly c, the total present consciousness is not produced simply by *c*'s excitement, but also by the dying vibrations of a and *b* as well. If we want to represent the brain-process we must write it thus: ${}_{a}{}^{b}c$—three different processes coexisting, and correlated with them a thought which is no one of the three thoughts which they would have produced had each of them occurred alone. But whatever this fourth thought may exactly be,

① Compare the charming passage in Taine on Intelligence (N. Y. ed.), I. 83-4.

所知道的无论其他什么样事物的知识相伴随。我们思考,并且当我们思考时,我们感受到我们身体的自我就是思考的处所。如果思考是我们的思考,那么它就一定使它的所有部分都充满了使它成为我们的思考的那种温暖和亲密。一直存在于那里的那种温暖和亲密是否不仅仅是对同一个原来的身体的感受,是我们在下一章将要决断的问题。不论自我的内容会是什么,我们人类都习惯性地将它和所有其他的事物一起感受出来,而且它一定在我们相继知觉到的所有事物之间形成了一种联系。①

神经活动的原理能够使我们更进一步地理解在我们心理内容变化中的这种渐次性。当在第三章中研究神经活动的聚合时,我们看到,我们不能设想任何大脑状态会立刻消失。如果一个新的状态来了,旧的状态的惯性将依然存在,并且会相应地改变结果。当然以我们的无知我们不能说出在每一时刻的改变应当是什么。在感知觉中,最普通的改变被认为是对比现象。在审美中,它们是一系列印象的某些特殊秩序所引起的快乐或不快乐的感受。在所说的严格意义上的和狭义的思想中,它们无疑是始终伴随其流动的关于从何处来和到何处去的意识。如果在最近大脑神经纤维束 a 明显被刺激了,然后是 b,现在又是 c 明显被刺激了,那么当前的整个意识并不完全是由对 c 的刺激所引起的,而且也是由 a 和 b 的振动所引起的。如果我们想要再现大脑过程,我们必须这样写:$_{a}{}^{b}c$——三个不同的过程共同存在,而且有一个思想和它们相关联,这个思想并不是这三个过程单独发生时所产生的那三个思想中的任意一个思想。但是不管这第四个思想究

① 比较泰恩《智能》(纽约版)第1卷第83~84页中那迷人的段落。

it seems impossible that it should not be something *like* each of the three other thoughts whose tracts are concerned in its production, though in a fast-waning phase.

It all goes back to what we said in another connection only a few pages ago (p. 233). As the total neurosis changes, so does the total psychosis change. But as the changes of neurosis are never absolutely discontinuous, so must the successive psychoses shade gradually into each other, although their *rate* of change may be much faster at one moment than at the next.

This difference in the rate of change lies at the basis of a difference of subjective states of which we ought immediately to speak. When the rate is slow we are aware of the object of our thought in a comparatively restful and stable way. When rapid, we are aware of a passage, a relation, a transition *from* it, or *between* it and something else. As we take, in fact, a general view of the wonderful stream of our consciousness, what strikes us first is this different pace of its parts. Like a bird's life, it seems to be made of an alternation of flights and perchings. The rhythm of language expresses this, where every thought is expressed in a sentence, and every sentence closed by a period. The resting-places are usually occupied by sensorial imaginations of some sort, whose peculiarity is that they can be held before the mind for an indefinite time, and contemplated without changing; the places of flight are filled with thoughts of relations, static or dynamic, that for the most part obtain between the matters contemplated in the periods of comparative rest.

Let us call the resting-places the 'substantive parts,' and the places of flight the 'transitive parts,' of the stream of thought. It then appears that the main end of our thinking is at all times the attainment of some other substantive part than the one from which we have just been dislodged. And we may say that the main use of the transitive parts is

竟是什么,似乎不可能的是,它不和另外三个思想中的每一个思想有些相似,尽管以一种衰落的方式,但这三个思想的神经通道还是和它的产生有关。

所有这一切又回到了我们在几页前(第223页)所说的另一个联系上来,由于整个神经变化了,因此全部精神也变化了。而且,由于神经的变化从来都不是绝对不连续的,因此连续的精神也逐渐地相互变化,尽管它们的变化速度可能在一个时刻比在下一个时刻要快得多。

这种变化速度的不同是主观状态不同的基础,我们应当对后者立即展开讨论。当速度慢的时候,我们以一种比较平静和稳定的方式意识到我们思维的对象。当速度快的时候,我们意识到一种从它而来、或者在它与某些其他事物之间的转变、关系和过渡。事实上,当我们采纳了关于奇妙的意识之流的一种一般观点的时候,最先打动我们的就是其各部分的不同速度。就像一只小鸟的生命,它似乎是由飞行和栖息的交替所构成的。语言的节奏表达了这一点,其中每一个思想在一个句子中被表达了出来,并且每一个句子以一个句号结尾。栖息之地通常被某种感觉想像所占据,它的特殊性在于,它们能够无限长时间地保持在心灵面前,并且被思忖时也没有发生变化;飞行之地充满着关于静态关系或者动态关系的思想,这些关系大部分是从在比较平静的期间得到沉思的事物之间获得的。

让我们将栖息之地称作思想之流的"实体性部分",将飞行之地称作思想之流的"过渡部分"。因而似乎我们思考的主要目的始终都是去获得某种与我们刚刚离开的实体性部分不同的其他实体性部分。并且我们可以说过渡部分的主要用途就是将我们

to lead us from one substantive conclusion to another.

Now it is very difficult, introspectively, to see the transitive parts for what they really are. If they are but flights to a conclusion, stopping them to look at them before the conclusion is reached is really annihilating them. Whilst if we wait till the conclusion *be* reached, it so exceeds them in vigor and stability that it quite eclipses and swallows them up in its glare. Let anyone try to cut a thought across in the middle and get a look at its section, and he will see how difficult the introspective observation of the transitive tracts is. The rush of the thought is so headlong that it almost always brings us up at the conclusion before we can arrest it. Or if our purpose is nimble enough and we do arrest it, it ceases forthwith to be itself. As a snowflake crystal caught in the warm hand is no longer a crystal but a drop, so, instead of catching the feeling of relation moving to its term, we find we have caught some substantive thing, usually the last Word we were pronouncing, statically taken, and with its function, tendency, and particular meaning in the sentence quite evaporated. The attempt at introspective analysis in these cases is in fact like seizing a spinning top to catch its motion, or trying to turn up the gas quickly enough to see how the darkness looks. And the challenge to *produce* these psychoses, which is sure to be thrown by doubting psychologists at anyone who contends for their existence, is as unfair as Zeno's treatment of the advocates of motion, when, asking them to point out in what place an arrow *is* when it moves, he argues the falsity of their thesis from their inability to make to so preposterous a question an immediate reply.

The results of this introspective difficulty are baleful. If to hold fast and observe the transitive parts of thought's stream be so hard, then the great blunder to which all schools are liable must be

从一个实体性的结论引领到另一个实体性的结论中。

要内省地了解过渡的部分真正是些什么，现在是很困难的。如果它们只是向结论飞行，在它们到达结论之前让它们停下来并去观察它们，这其实就是在消灭它们。而如果我们一直等着它到达了结论，这结论在强度和稳定性方面都远远地超过了它们，以至于它的光芒就完全将它们遮蔽和吞没了。让任何人设法在中途切断一个思想，并且来观察一下思想的片断，那么他就会发现对这个过渡阶段的内省观测有多么困难了。思想的急流以如此快的速度前进，以至于它几乎总是在我们能够捕捉到它之前就把我们带到了结论那里。或者如果我们的意图足够机敏，并且我们确实抓住了它，它就立刻不再是它自己了。就像被一只温暖的手捉住的一片雪花晶体不再是一片雪花而是一滴水一样，我们发现我们没有捕捉到对发展的关系的感受，而是捕捉到了一些实体性事物，通常是我们所说出的最后一个词，它是被静态地把握的，与它一起被把握的还有在那个已经完全消失掉了的句子中的功能、趋向和特殊意义。在这些情况下对内省分析的尝试，事实上就像是抓住一个旋转着的陀螺去把握它的运动，或者就像试图以足够快的速度打开燃气灯来看看黑暗是什么样子的。有疑问的心理学家无疑会对任何提倡这种精神存在的人进行挑战，但是对展示这种精神的公然对抗就如同芝诺对待运动提倡者一样是不公平的，当时，他要求他们指出当箭在运动的时候它处于什么位置，由于他们不能对如此荒谬的问题立即作以回答，他就论证说他们的论题是错误的。

这种内省困难的结果是有害的。如果要牢牢捉住并且观察思想之流的过渡部分是如此的困难，那么，所有学派都容易犯的

the failure to register them, and the undue emphasizing of the more substantive parts of the stream. Were we not ourselves a moment since in danger of ignoring any feeling transitive between the silence and the thunder, and of treating their boundary as a sort of break in the mind? Now such ignoring as this has historically worked in two ways. One set of thinkers have been led by it to *Sensationalism*. Unable to lay their hands on any coarse feelings corresponding to the innumerable relations and forms of connection between the facts of the world, finding no *named* subjective modifications mirroring such relations, they have for the most part denied that feelings of relation exist, and many of them, like Hume, have gone so far as to deny the reality of most relations *out* of the mind as well as in it. Substantive psychoses, sensations and their copies and derivatives, juxtaposed like dominoes in a game, but really separate, everything else verbal illusion,—such is the upshot of this view.① The *Intellectualists*, on the other hand, unable to give up the reality of relations *extra mentem*, but equally unable to point to any distinct substantive feelings in which they were known, have made the same admission that the feelings do not exist. But they have drawn an opposite conclusion. The relations must be known, they say, in something that is no feeling, no mental modification continuous and consubstantial with the subjective tissue out of which sensations and other substantive states are made. They are known, these relations, by something that lies on an entirely different plane, by an *actus purus* of Thought, Intellect, or Reason, all written with capitals and considered to mean something unutterably superior to any fact of sensibility whatever.

---

① E. g.: "The stream of thought is not a continuous current, but a series of distinct ideas, more or less rapid in their succession; the rapidity being measurable by the number that pass through the mind in a given time." (Bain: E. and W., p. 29.)

但是从我们的观点来看,理性主义者和感觉主义者都错了。如果确实存在着像感受这样的东西,那么,对象间的关系也肯定存在于物理世界之中,而且更加肯定的是,认识这些关系的感受也存在着。在人类的言语中,没有一个连词或者前置词、并且几乎没有一个副词短语、句法形式或者声音的变形,没有表达了关系中的这样或那样的细微差别,这些关系是我们有时确实感受到的存在于我们思想的众多对象之间的关系。如果我们客观地说,是真实的关系似乎被揭示出来了;如果我们主观地说,是思想之流通过它自己的内在特色与它们中的每一个相匹配。在这两种中任何一种情况下,关系是无数的,并且现存的语言不能公平对待它们所有的细微区别。

与我们乐意说蓝色的感受或者寒冷的感受一样,我们也应当乐意说"并且"的感受、"如果"的感受、"但是"的感受以及"通过"的感受。然而我们没有:我们只承认实体性部分的存在这种习惯是如此地根深蒂固,以至于语言几乎拒绝了使自己用于别的用途。经验主义者经常详述其使我们产生下述假设的影响,即只要我们有一个单独的名称,那么一个单独的事物就必须存在并与它相对应;而且在没有任何证据的提出比这更有利于他们的情况下,他们还正确地否定了众多抽象本体、原理和力的存在。但是,他们对我们在第7章(见195页)所说的那个与之相对的错误却什么也没说,这个错误就是假定在没有名称的地方也就没有本体存在。由于这个错误,所有无声的或者无名的精神状态都被沉着自若地压制了;或者,如果它们最终还是得到了认可,它们也是依照它们所导致的实体性的知觉而被命名的,例如"关于"这个或者那个对象的思想,那个呆板的词语"关于",就将它所有的精细的

idiosyncrasies in its monotonous sound. Thus the greater and greater accentuation and isolation of the substantive parts have continually gone on.

Once more take a look at the brain. We believe the brain to be an organ whose internal equilibrium is always in a state of change,—the change affecting every part. The pulses of change are doubtless more violent in one place than in another, their rhythm more rapid at this time than at that. As in a kaleidoscope revolving at a uniform rate, although the figures are always rearranging themselves, there are instants during which the transformation seems minute and interstitial and almost absent, followed by others when it shoots with magical rapidity, relatively stable forms thus alternating with forms we should not distinguish if seen again; so in the brain the perpetual rearrangement must result in some forms of tension lingering relatively long, whilst others simply come and pass. But if consciousness corresponds to the fact of rearrangement itself, why, if the rearrangement stop not, should the consciousness ever cease? And if a lingering rearrangement brings with it one kind of consciousness, why should not a swift rearrangement bring another kind of consciousness as peculiar as the rearrangement itself? The lingering consciousnesses, if of simple objects, we call 'sensations' or 'images,' ac-cording as they are vivid or faint; if of complex objects, we call them 'percepts' when vivid, 'concepts' or 'thoughts' when faint. For the swift consciousnesses we have only those names of 'transitive states,' or 'feelings of relation,' which we have used. ①

---

① Few writers have admitted that we cognize relations through feeling. The intellectualists have explicitly denied the possibility of such a thing—e. g. , Prof. T. H. Green ('Mind,' vol. VII. p. 28): "No feeling, as such or as felt, is [of?] a relation. . . Even a relation between feelings is not itself a feeling or

特性吞没在了其单调的声音中了。因此对实体性部分越来越显著的强调和孤立就一直在继续着。

让我们再一次观察一下大脑。我们认为大脑是内部平衡始终处于变化状态的器官,——这种变化影响着每一个部分。变化的波动无疑在一个地方比在另一个地方更激烈,它们的节奏在这一时刻比在那一时刻更快。就像在一只以始终如一的速度旋转着的万花筒中,尽管图形总是重新排列它们自己,这里还是有一些瞬间,在其间变化似乎很微小,并且是有间隙的,甚至几乎是不存在的。这些变化的后面跟随着以神奇的速度射出的其他变化,因此相对稳定的形式和如果我们再次看到也不会分辨出来的形式交替进行着;因此在大脑中永久的重新排列一定会导致一些拖延时间相对长一些的张力形式,而其他的形式只不过是来了又去。但是,如果意识和重新排列自身这一事实相应,那么,为什么如果重新排列停止了而意识还没有停止呢?并且如果一个延迟了的重新排列随之带来了一种意识,那么,为什么一个快速的重新排列不能带来另一种和这种重新排列自身一样独特的意识呢?延迟了的意识,如果是关于简单对象的,我们就依照它们的清晰与模糊称之为"感觉"或者"意象";如果是关于复杂对象的,那么,当它们是清楚的,我们就称之为"知觉",当它们是模糊的,就称之为"概念"或者"思想"。对于快速的意识,我们只有"过渡状态"或者"对关系的感受"这样一些我们已经使用过的名称。①

① 很少有作者承认,我们通过感受来认知关系。理性主义者已经明确地否认了这种情况的可能性——例如T. H. 格林教授(《心灵》,第7卷,第28页)说:"没有像这样的或者被感受到了的感受是(关于?)一种关系的。……甚至在感受之间的关系自身也不是一种感受,或者被感受到了。"在另一方

As the brain-changes are continuous, so do all these consciousnesses

---

felt." On the other hand, the sensationists have either smuggled in the cognition without giving any account of it, or have denied the relations to be cognized, or even to exist, at all. A few honorable exceptions, however, deserve to be named among the sensationists. Destutt de Tracy, Laromiguière, Cardaillac, Brown, and finally Spencer, have explicitly contended for feelings of relation, consubstantial with our feelings or thoughts of the terms 'between' which they obtain. Thus Destutt de Tracy says. (Eléments d'Idéologie, T. Ier, chap, IV): "The faculty of judgment is itself a sort of sensibility, for it is the faculty of feeling the relations among our ideas; and to feel relations is to feel." Laromiguière writes (Lecons de Philosophie, IIme Partie, 3me Lecon):

"There is no one whose intelligence does not embrace simultaneously many ideas, more or less distinct, more or less confused. Now, when we have many ideas at once, a peculiar feeling arises in us; we feel, among these ideas, resemblances, differences, relations. Let us call this mode of feeling, common to us all, the feeling of relation, or relation-feeling (*sentimemt-rapport*). One sees immediately that these relation-feelings, resulting from the propinquity of ideas, must be infinitely more numerous than the sensation-feelings (*sentiments-sensationts*) or the feelings we have of the action of our faculties, The slightest knowledge of the mathematical theory of combinations will prove tills. . . . *Ideas* of relation originate in feelings of relation. They are the effect of our comparing them and reasoning about them."

Similarly, de Cardaillac (Études Éémentaires de Philosophie, Section I. chap, VII):

"By a natural consequence, we are led to suppose that at the same time that we have several sensations or several ideas in the mind, we feel the relations which exist between these sensations, and the relations which exist between these ideas.... If the feeling of relations exists in us, ... it is necessarily the most varied and the most fertile of all human feelings: 1° the most varied, because, relations being more numerous than beings, the feelings of relation must be in the same proportion more numerous than the sensations whose presence gives rise to their formation; 2°, the most fertile, for the relative ideas of which the feeling-of-relation is the source... are more important than absolute ideas, if such exist.... If we interrogate common speech, we find the feeling of relation expressed there in a thousand different ways. If it is easy to seize a relation, we say that it is *sensible*, to distinguish it from one which, because its terms are too remote, cannot be as quickly perceived. A sensible difference, or resemblance.... What is taste in the arts, in intellectual productions? What but the feeling of those relations among the parts which constitutes their merit? ... Did we not feel relations we should never attain to true knowledge, ... for almost all our knowledge is of relations.... We never have an isolated sensation; ... we are therefore never without the feeling of relation.... An *object* strikes our senses; we see in it only a sensation.... The relative is so near the absolute, the relation-feeling so near the sensation-feeling, the two are so intimately fused in the composition of the object, that the relation appears to us as part of the sensation itself.

由于大脑变化是连续的，因此所有这些意识也相互融合，就

面，感觉主义者要么将认识偷运进来而没有给予任何说明，要么完全否认关系能够被认识，或者甚至否认了其存在。然而，在这些感觉主义者中有几个例外值得一提。德斯杜特·德特拉西、拉罗米吉埃、卡代拉克、布朗，最后还有斯宾塞，都明确地主张有关系感受，它们与他们所获有的我们对术语“在……之间”的感受或思想同质。因此德斯杜特·德特拉西说（《意识形态原理》，第1册，第4章）：“判断能力自身是一种感受性，因为它是感受我们观念间的关系的能力；并且感受关系就是感受。”拉罗米吉埃写到（《哲学教程》，第2部分，第3讲）：

“没有一个人的理智中不同时包含着许多在不同程度上清晰或混乱的观念。现在当我们同时拥有很多观念的时候，一种奇特的感受在我们心里出现了：在这些观念之中，我们感受到了类同、差异和关系。让我们称这种我们所有人都共有的感受模式为对关系的感受，或者关系感受（关系感觉）。人们立刻看到，这些产生于观念接近的关系感受，在数量上必须无限地多于感觉-感受（情绪-感觉）或者对我们的功能运行的感受。极少数学结合理论能够证明这一点。……关系观念起源于关系感受。它们是我们对它们进行比较和推论的结果。”

同样地，卡代拉克（《哲学基础研究》，第1部分，第7章）说：

“一种自然的推论使得我们假设，当我们在心中同时拥有几个感觉和几个观念的时候，我们感受到了存在于这些感觉之间的关系，以及存在于这些观念间的关系。……如果对关系的感受确实存在于我们心里，……它肯定是人类所有感受中最多样和最丰富的感受：（1）最多样的，因为关系比存在在数量上更多，对关系的感受一定以相同的比例在数量上比感觉要多，这些感觉的出现造成了关系感受的形成；（2）最丰富的，因为以关系感受为来源的关系概念比绝对观念更重要，如果这种绝对观念存在的话。……如果我们考察公共言语，我们发现对关系的感受以数千种不同方式在那里被表达了出来。如果捕捉住一个关系很容易，我们说它是可感觉的，从而将它同另一种关系区别开来，这另一种关系因其太细微，不能同样快地被知觉出来。一种可感觉的差异或者类同。……在艺术中和在智性产品中的鉴赏力是什么？除了对构成其价值的部分间的那些关系的感受以外还有什么？……如果我们没有感受到关系，我们就永远也不能获得真正的知识，因为几乎我们所有的知识都是关于关系的。……我们从来也没有一种单独的感官；……我们因此一直都有对关系的感受。……一个对象激起了我们的感觉；我们在它那里只看到了一个感觉。……关系是如此接近于绝对之物，关系-感受是如此接近于感觉-感受，这两者如此亲密地融合在对象的构成之中，以至于关系在我们看了是感觉自身的一部分。毫无疑问的是，形而上学者对

each other like dissolving views. Properly they are but one

It is doubtless to this sort of fusion between sensations and feelings of relation that the silence of metaphysicians as to the latter is due; and it is for the same reason that they have obstinately persisted in asking from sensation alone those ideas of relation which it was powerless to give."

Dr. Thomas Brown writes (Lectures, XLV. *init.*): "There is an extensive order of our feelings which involve this notion of relation, and which consist indeed in the mere perception of a relation of some sort. . . . Whether the relation be of two or of many external objects, or of two or many affections of the mind, the feeling of this relation . . . is what I term a relative suggestion; that phrase being the simplest which it is possible to employ, for expressing, without any theory, the mere fact of the rise of certain feelings of relation, after certain other feelings which precede them; and therefore, as involving no particular theory, and simply expressive of an undoubted fact. . . . That the feelings of relation are states of the mind essentially different from our simple perceptions, or conceptions of the objects, . . . that they are not what Condillac terms *transformed sensations*, I proved in a former lecture, when I combated the excessive simplification of that ingenious but not very accurate philosopher. There is an original tendency or susceptibility of the mind, by which, on perceiving together different objects, we are instantly, without the intervention of any other mental process, sensible of their relation in certain respects, as truly as there is an original tendency or susceptibility by which, when external objects are present and have produced a certain affection of our sensorial organ, we are instantly affected with the primary elementary feelings of perception; and, I may add, that as our sensations or perceptions are of various species, so are there various species of relations;—the number of relations, indeed, even of external things, being almost infinite, while the number of perceptions is, necessarily, limited by that of the objects which have the power of producing some, affection of our organs of sensation. . . . Without that susceptibility of the mind by which it has the feeling of relation, our consciousness would be as truly limited to a single point, as our body would become, were it possible to fetter it to a single atom."

Mr. Spencer is even more explicit. His philosophy is crude in that he seems to suppose that it is only in transitive states that outward relations are known; whereas in truth space-relations, relations of contrast, etc., are felt along with their terms, in substantive states as well as in transitive states, as we shall abundantly see. Nevertheless Mr. Spencer's passage is so clear that it also deserves to be quoted in full (Principles of Psychology, § 65):

"The proximate components of Mind are of two broadly-contrasted kinds—Feelings and the relations between feelings. Among the members of each group there exist multitudinous unlikenesses, many of which are extremely strong; but such unlikenesses are small compared with those which distinguish members of the one group from members of the other. Let us, in the first place, consider what are the characters which all Feelings have in common, and what are the characters which all Relations between feelings have in common."

"Each feeling, as we here define it, is any portion of consciousness which occupies a place sufficiently large to give it a perceivable individuality; which has its individuality marked off from adjacent portions of consciousness by qualitative contrasts; and which, when introspectively contemplated, appears to be homogeneous.

像消融的风景一样。它们可能就是一个在时间上延伸的意

关系感受的沉默是由于这种在感觉和关系感受间的融合所致;并且也是出于同样的原因,他们顽固地坚持单独向感觉索求感觉无力给予的那些关系观念。"

托马斯·布朗博士写到(《演讲》,45,init.):"我们有一大类感受涉及了这种关系概念,并且它们确实是在于对某种关系的纯粹知觉。……不管这关系是关于两个还是多个外部对象间的关系,也不管这关系是关于两种还是多种心灵的倾向间的关系,这种关系感受……就是我称之为关系暗示的东西;这个术语是最简单的,它有可能在没有任何理论的情况下,用来表达某种关系感受在先于它们的某种其他感受之后而出现了这一单纯事实;并且由于它不涉及任何特殊的理论,因此它只不过表达了某种毫无疑问的事实。……关系感受是本质上区别于我们对客体的简单的知觉或概念的心理状态,……它们不是孔狄拉克所命名的转化了的感觉的东西,我在前面的章节已经证明了这一点,当时,我驳斥了这个具有创造性,但却不是十分正确的哲学家的观点,因为他将问题过于简化了。心灵有一种原初的倾向或感受性,通过它们对不同的客体一块进行知觉的时候,我们在没有任何其他心理过程干涉的情况下立刻感觉到了它们在某方面的关系,同样真实的是,还存在一种原初的倾向和感受性,当外部对象出现并且引起了我们感觉器官的某种倾向的时候,通过它们我们立即受到了主要的基本知觉感受的影响;并且,我可以补充的是,由于我们的感觉或知觉有不同种类,因此也存在有不同种类的关系;——确实,关系的数量,甚至是外部关系的数量都几乎是无限的,而知觉的数量必然受限于有能力引起我们感觉器官某些倾向的客体数量的限制。……如果没有那种心灵由以获有关系感受的感受性,我们的意识将真的会局限于一个单一的点上,就如同如果有可能将我们的身体束缚到一个单一的原子上,我们的身体也将真的局限于一个单一的点上。"

斯宾塞先生说得更加清楚。他的哲学是粗糙的,因为他似乎假定只有在过渡状态中外部的关系才被认识了;然而,正如我们将会大量看到的那样,真相是,空间关系、对比关系等等是在实体性状态中以及在过渡状态中和它们的条件一起被感受到的。不过斯宾塞先生的行文是如此的清晰,它也值得被全部引述出来(《心理学原理》,第65节):

"心灵大致有两种对比鲜明的成分——感受和感受间的关系。在每一组的成员之间存在着大量的差别,很多差别的对比是非常强烈的;但是这种差别和组与组之间的成员间的差别比起来就小很多。首先,让我们考虑一下所有感受所共同具有的特征是什么,以及感受间的所有关系共同具有的特征是什么。"

"每一个感受,如我们这里对它定义的那样,是意识的任何部分,它占据着一个可以给它一个可知觉的个性的足够大的位置;这个意识部分的个性通过性质上的对比和其邻近部分的意识相区别;并且当内省地沉思它时,它显现出来

protracted consciousness, one unbroken stream.

These are the essentials. Obviously if, under introspection, a state of consciousness is decomposable into unlike parts that exist either simultaneously or successively, it is not one feeling but two or more? Obviously if it is indistinguishable from an adjacent portion of consciousness, it forms one with that portion—is not an individual feeling, but part of one. And obviously if it does not occupy in consciousness an appreciable area, or an appreciable duration, it cannot be known as a feeling."

"A Relation between feelings is, on the contrary, characterized by occupying no appreciable part of consciousness. Take away the terms it unites, and it disappears along with them; having no independent place, no individuality of its own. It is true that, under an ultimate analysis, what we call a relation proves to be itself a kind of feeling—the momentary feeling accompanying the transition from one conspicuous feeling to an adjacent, conspicuous feeling. And it is true that, notwithstanding its extreme brevity, its qualitative character is appreciable; for relations are (as we shall hereafter see) distinguishable from one another only by the unlikenesses of the feelings which accompany the momentary transitions. Each relational feeling may, in fact, be regarded as one of those nervous shocks which we suspect to be the units of composition of feelings; and, though instantaneous, it is known as of greater or less strength, and as taking place with greater or less facility. But the contrast between these relational feelings and what we ordinarily call feelings is so strong that we must class them apart. Their extreme brevity, their small variety, and their dependence on the terms they unite, differentiate them in an unmistakable way."

"Perhaps it will be well to recognize more fully the tenth that this distinction cannot be absolute. Besides admitting that, as an element of consciousness, a relation is a momentary feeling, we must also admit that just as a relation can have no existence apart from the feelings which form its terms, so a feeling can exist only by relations to other feelings which limit it in space or time or both. Strictly speaking, neither a feeling nor a relation is an independent element of consciousness: there is throughout a dependence such that the appreciable areas of consciousness occupied by feelings can no more possess individualities apart from the relations which link them, than these relations can possess individualities apart from the feelings they link. The essential distinction between the two, then, appears to be that whereas a relational feeling is a portion of consciousness inseparable into parts, a feeling, ordinarily so called, is a portion of consciousness that admits imaginary division into like parts which are related to one another in sequence or coexistence. A feeling proper is either made up of like parts that occupy time, or it is made up of like parts that occupy space, or both. In any case, a feeling proper is an aggregate of related like parts, while a relational feeling is undecomposable. And this is exactly the contrast between the two which must result if, as we have inferred, feelings are composed of units of feelings, or shocks."

识,一个不间断的流。

是相似的。这些就是基本要素。明显地,如果在反省之下一个意识状态可以被分解为或者同时存在或者相继存在的不同部分,难道它不是一个或者两个感受吗?明显地,如果它和意识的邻近部分是无法区别的,那么它与那个部分就形成了一个感受——它不是一个单独的感受,而是一个感受的一部分。还很明显地是,如果它没有在意识中占据了一个可感知的区域,或者一个可感知的期限,那么它就不能作为一个感受而被认识。"

"相反,感受间的关系以不占据可感知的意识部分为特征。拿走由它所联合起来的条件,那么它就和它们一起消失了;它没有独立的位置,自身也没有个性。确实,在最终的分析之下,我们所称之为关系的东西证明它自身是一种感受——一种伴随着从一个显著的感受到一个邻近的显著的感受间的过渡的瞬间感受。确实,虽然它极其短暂,但是它的性质特征是可以感知的;因为关系(如我们今后将要看到的那样)之间只有通过伴随着瞬间过渡的感受的不同才能被区分开来。事实上,每一个关系感受都可以被看作是我们怀疑是感受组成单元的那些神经震荡中的一次震荡;而且,尽管是瞬间的,它可以被认作是具有或大或小的强度,并且是以不同的难易程度而发生的。但是这些关系感受和我们平常称之为感受的东西之间的对比是如此强烈,以至于我们必须将它们区分开来。它们的极度短暂性、较少的多样性以及它们对自己所联合起来的条件的依赖性,以准确无误的方式将它们区分了出来。"

"可能,更全面地认识下述真理将是很好的,即这种区分不可能是绝对的。除了承认关系作为意识的一种元素是一种瞬间的感受,我们还必须承认,正如一种关系离开了构成其条件的感受就不存在了一样,一个感受也只能通过在空间、时间或者这两方面给它以限制的其他感受的关系才能够存在。严格说来,一个感受或者一种关系都不是一种意识的独立元素:到处存在一种这样的依赖性,即由感受所占据的可感知的意识区域离开了连接它们的关系就不能获有任何个性,同样关系离开了它们所连接的感受也不能获有任何个性。因而,这两者之间的本质区别似乎是,鉴于关系感受是不能再进行分割的意识部分,通常所说的一个感受是这样一种意识部分,它容许在想像中将意识分割为以相继或者共存的方式彼此关联的相同部分。严格意义上的感受或者由占据时间的相同部分所组成,或者由占据空间的相同部分所组成,或者由占据空间和时间的相同部分所组成。无论如何,严格意义上的感受是有关系的相同部分的集合,而一个关系感受是不可分解的。而且如果如我们所推断的那样,感受是由感受单元或者震荡所组成的,那么这正是必定会导致的二者间的对比。"

Feelings of Tendency.

So much for the transitive states. But there are other unnamed states or qualities of states that are just as important and just as cognitive as they, and just as much unrecognized by the traditional sensationalist and intellect-ualist philosophies of mind. The first fails to find them at all, the second finds their *cognitive function*, but denies that anything in the way of *feeling* has a share in bringing it about. Examples will make clear what these inarticulate psychoses, due to waxing and waning excitements of the brain, are like. ①

Suppose three successive persons say to us: ‘Wait!’ ‘Hark!’ ‘Look!’ Our consciousness is thrown into three quite different attitudes of expectancy, although no definite object is before it in any one of the three cases. Leaving out different actual bodily attitudes,

① M. Paulhan (Revue Philosophique, XX. 455-6), after speaking of the faint mental images of objects and emotions, says: “We find other vaguer states still, upon which attention seldom rests, except in persons who by nature or profession are addicted to internal observation. It is even difficult to name them precisely, for they are little known and not classed; but we may cite as an example of them that peculiar impression which we feel when, strongly preoccupied by a certain subject, we nevertheless are engaged with, and have our attention almost completely absorbed by, matters quite disconnected therewithal. We do not then exactly think of the object of our preoccupation; we do not represent it in a clear manner; and yet our mind is not as it would be without this preoccupation. Its object, absent from consciousness, is nevertheless represented there by a peculiar unmistakable impression, which often persists long and is a strong feeling, although so obscure for our intelligence.” “A mental sign of the kind is the unfavorable disposition left in our mind towards an individual by painful incidents erewhile experienced and now perhaps forgotten. The sign remains, but is not understood; its definite meaning is lost.” (P. 458.)

对倾向的感受

关于过渡状态就谈这么多吧。但是还存在一些其他未命名的状态或者状态的性质，它们也同样重要，同样是认知的，而且同样没有太多地得到传统的感觉主义和理性主义心灵哲学的承认。前者完全没有发现它们，后者只发现了它们的认知功能，却否认了感受方面的任何东西在认识功能的实现中起作用。一些例子将会澄清由对大脑的逐渐增强和减弱的刺激所导致的这些没能得到清楚表达的精神是什么样子的。①

假设三个人依次对我们说："等等!""听!""看!"我们的意识就陷入了三种完全不同的期望态度，尽管在这三种情况中都没有确定的对象出现在意识面前。不考虑身体的不同的真实姿势，也

① 波尔汉先生(《哲学评论》,20,第455~456页)在谈论完了对象和情绪的模糊的心理意象之后说："我们还发现了其他的模糊状态，注意力很少停留其上，只有在一些由于天性或者职业的缘故有着内部观察嗜好的人那里情况才不是这样。要精确地命名它们甚至都是困难的，因为它们很少被认识，而且也没有被分类；但是我们可以引用那奇特的印象作为它们的例子，当我们强有力地全神贯注于一个特定的主题，我们仍然从事着与之完全无关的事情，并且我们的注意力也几乎完全被这样的事情所吸引了，此时我们就感受到了这种奇特的印象。在那时我们并没有完全思考我们所全神贯注的对象；我们没有以一种清晰的方式再现它；然而，如果没有这种全神贯注，我们的心灵就不会是其将是的那样了。它的对象不在意识之中，却仍然被一种奇特的、准确无误的印象在那里被再现了出来，这种印象常常持续很长时间，并且是一种强烈的感受，尽管对我们的理智来说是如此的模糊。""这种心理迹象是一种在我们心里留下的朝向一个个体的倾向，它是由不久前经历过、而且现在可能被忘记了的令人痛苦的事件所引起的。迹象保留着，但是没有被理解；它的确切意义不为人知。"(第458页)

and leaving out the reverberating images of the three words, which are of course diverse, probably no one will deny the existence of a residual conscious affection, a sense of the direction from which an impression is about to come, although no positive impression is yet there. Meanwhile we have no names for the psychoses in question but the names hark, look, and wait.

Suppose we try to recall a forgotten name. The state of our consciousness is peculiar. There is a gap therein; but no mere gap. It is a gap that is intensely active. A sort of wraith of the name is in it, beckoning us in a given direction, making us at moments tingle with the sense of our closeness, and then letting us sink back without the longed-for term. If wrong names are proposed to us, this singularly definite gap acts immediately so as to negate them. They do not fit into its mould. And the gap of one word does not feel like the gap of another, all empty of content as both might seem necessarily to be when described as gaps. When I vainly try to recall the name of Spalding, my consciousness is far removed from what it is when I vainly try to recall the name of Bowles. Here some ingenious persons will say: "How *can* the two consciousnesses be different when the terms which might make them different are not there? All that is there, so long as the effort to recall is vain, is the bare effort itself. How should that differ in the two cases? You are making it seem to differ by prematurely filling it out with the different names, although these, by the hypothesis, have not yet come. Stick to the two efforts as they are, without naming them after facts not yet existent, and you'll be quite unable to designate any point in which they differ." Designate, truly enough. We can only designate the difference by borrowing the names of objects not yet in the mind. Which is to say that our psychological vocabulary is wholly inadequate to name the differences that exist, even such strong differences as these. But namelessness is compatible with existence. There are innumerable consciousnesses of emptiness, no one of which

不考虑这三个词反射出来的意象，这些意象当然是多样的，可能没有人会否认残留的意识倾向的存在，这是对一个印象将要到来的方向的感觉，尽管实际的印象还没有出现在那里。同时，我们没有这种相关精神的名称，而只有听、看和等这些名称。

假设我们设法回忆一个忘记了的名称。我们的意识状态是奇特的。这里存在着一道裂缝，但不仅仅是裂缝。它是一个极为活跃的裂缝。名称的某种灵魂存在于其中，在一个既定的方向上召唤着我们，使我们不时地由于感到接近目标而兴奋起来，然后又使我们由于没有得到渴望得到的词语而消沉起来。如果错误的名称被提示给了我们，这个异乎寻常地明确的裂缝就会立刻行动起来以否定它们。它们不适合它的模子。并且一个词语的裂缝感觉起来不像另一个词语的裂缝，虽然当把它们描述为裂缝的时候，它们的内容似乎应该必然是空的。当我徒劳地设法回忆斯波尔丁这个名字时，我的意识与当我徒劳地设法回忆鲍尔斯这个名字时的意识相去甚远。在这里，一些聪明的人会说："当可以使得意识不同的两个术语不存在的时候，这两个意识如何可能不同呢？只要回忆的努力是徒劳的，所有存在于那里的只是努力自身。在这两种情况中怎么会有区别呢？尽管根据假设，这些名称还没有出现，但是你是通过过早地将不同的名称填充进去而使得它似乎是不同的。坚守那两种努力的本来的样子，并且不要以还没有出现的事实来命名它们，那么你将完全不能指出它们在哪一点上不同。"指出，确实不假。我们只能通过借用还没有在心中出现的对象的名称来指出那种区别。这就是说，我们的心理学词汇完全不足以命名存在着的差异，甚至像这样如此强烈的差异。但是没有名称的东西和存在是相容的。这里有数不清的空虚的意

taken in itself has a name, but all different from each other. The ordinary way is to assume that they are all emptinesses of consciousness, and so the same state. But the feeling of an absence is *toto coelo* other than the absence of a feeling. It is an intense feeling. The rhythm of a lost word may be there without a sound to clothe it; or the evanescent sense of something which is the initial vowel or consonant may mock us fitfully, without growing more distinct. Every one must know the tantalizing effect of the blank rhythm of some forgotten verse, restlessly dancing in one's mind, striving to be filled out with words.

Again, what is the strange difference between an experience tasted for the first time and the same experience recognized as familiar, as having been enjoyed before, though we cannot name it or say where or when? A tune, an odor, a flavor sometimes carry this inarticulate feeling of their familiarity so deep into our consciousness that we are fairly shaken by its mysterious emotional power. But strong and characteristic as this psychosis is—it probably is due to the submaximal excitement of wide-spreading associational brain-tracts—the only name we have for all its shadings is ' sense of familiarity. '

When we read such phrases as 'naught but,' 'either one or the other,' 'a is b, but,' 'although it is, nevertheless,' ' it is an excluded middle, there is no *tertium quid*,' and a host of other verbal skeletons of logical relation, is it true that there is nothing more in our minds than the words themselves as they pass? What then is the meaning of the words which we think we understand as we read? What makes that meaning different in one phrase from what it is in the other? 'Who?' 'When?'

识，其中没有一个本身就有名称，但是它们彼此之间都是不同的。通常的方法就是假设它们都是意识的空虚，并且因此是相同的状态。但是对不在的感受与感受的不在是截然相反的。它是一种强烈的感受。一个遗忘了的词语的节奏可能还存在，只是没有给它穿上声音的外衣罢了；或者对最初是元音或辅音的某种东西的逐渐消失的感觉会断断续续地嘲弄我们，只是没有变得更加清晰罢了。每个人一定知道某些被遗忘的诗句的空白韵律所产生的那令人着急的效果吧，它不安地在人的心中舞动，努力用词语使自己得以填充。

还有，一个是首次尝试过的体验，另一个是因为过去感受过，尽管我们不能命名它或者说出在哪里或什么时候经历过它，但是被我们辨认出是熟悉的相同的体验，这二者之间奇怪的差异是什么呢？一首曲调、一袭气味、一种味道有时就将这种未经表达的熟悉的感受深深地带入到了我们的意识之中，我们完全为它的神秘的情感力量所震撼了。可是，虽然这种精神是强烈而显著的——这种情况可能是由于普遍联系着的大脑神经束的亚极大兴奋所致——但是我们就其所有细微差别所拥有的唯一名称是“熟悉感”。

当我们阅读像这样的短语，例如“没有，但是”，“或者是这个，或者是那个”，“a 是 b，但是”，“尽管它是，然而”，“它是被排除的中部，不存在中部”，以及其他许多表述逻辑关系的骨架词语时，真的除了这些经过的词语自身之外，在我们的心中不存在任何更多的东西了吗？当我们阅读这些词语的时候，我们认为自己所理解了的这些词语的意义那么又是什么呢？什么使得这些意义在一个短语中与在另一个短语中有所不同呢？“谁？”“何时？”“何

'Where?' Is the difference of felt meaning in these interrogatives nothing more than their difference of sound? And is it not (just like the difference of sound itself) known and understood in an affection of consciousness correlative to it, though so impalpable to direct examination? Is not the same true of such negatives as 'no,' 'never,' 'not yet'?

The truth is that large tracts of human speech are nothing but *signs of direction* in thought, of which direction we nevertheless have an acutely discriminative sense, though no definite sensorial image plays any part in it whatsoever. Sensorial images are stable psychic facts; we can hold them still and look at them as long as we like. These bare images of logical movement, on the contrary, are psychic transitions, always on the wing, so to speak, and not to be glimpsed except in flight. Their function is to lead from one set of images to another. As they pass, we feel both the waxing and the waning images in a way altogether peculiar and a way quite different from the way of their full presence. If we try to hold fast the feeling of direction, the full presence comes and the feeling of direction is lost. The blank verbal scheme of the logical movement gives us the fleeting sense of the movement as we read it, quite as well as does a rational sentence awakening definite imaginations by its words.

What is that first instantaneous glimpse of some one's meaning which we have, when in vulgar phrase we say we 'twig' it? Surely an altogether specific affection of our mind. And has the reader never asked himself what kind of a mental fact is his *intention of saying a thing* before he has said it? It is an entirely definite intention, distinct from all other intentions, an absolutely distinct state of consciousness, therefore; and yet how much of it consists of definite sensorial images, either of words or of things? Hardly anything! Longer, and the words and things come into the mind; the anticipatory intention, the divination

地?”在这些疑问词中被感受到的意义的差别仅仅是其声音的差别吗?而且,尽管用直接的检查完全感触不到它,但是,难道它没有(就如同声音差别自身一样)在与之相关的意识倾向中被认识和理解吗?难道对像“不”、“从不”、“还没有”这样的否定词而言情况不也是同样如此吗?

真相是,大量的人类言语只是思想中的方向符号,对其我们还是有一种敏锐的辨别感,尽管没有任何确定的感觉意象在其中起任何作用。感觉意象是稳定的精神事实;我们能够一直获有它们并且想观察它们多久就观察它们多久。相反,这些逻辑运动的空洞意象是精神的过渡,可谓总是在飞行,并且只有在飞行中才能被瞥见。它们的功能就是从一组意象导向另一组意象。当它们通过的时候,我们以一种总之是奇特的并且与意象的完全呈现相当不同的方式,感受到了逐渐增强和减弱的意象。如果我们试图牢牢把握住对方向的感受,那么完全的呈现就会到来,而对方向的感受就丧失掉了。当我们阅读逻辑运动结构的空白词语时,这种空白的词语结构给了我们一种飞逝的运动感,就如同一个合理的句子通过它的词语唤起了明确的想像。

当我们用通俗的短语说我“了解”了它的时候,我们所获有的对某人的意思的最初的瞬间一瞥是什么呢?当然是我们心灵的一种完全明确的倾向。当读者在说某件事情之前,难道他从来没有问过自己他说这件事情的意图是何种心理事实吗?它是一种完全明确的意图,和所有其他的意图截然不同,因此是一种绝对独特的意识状态;然而,它在多大程度上是由关于词语的或者关于事物的明确的感觉意象所构成的呢?几乎没有!在时间长一些之后,并且在词语和事物进入到心灵中之后,预期的意向,预言

is there no more. But as the words that replace it arrive, it welcomes them successively and calls them right if they agree with it, it rejects them and calls them wrong if they do not. It has therefore a nature of its own of the most positive sort, and yet what can we say about it without using words that belong to the later mental facts that replace it? The intention *to-say-so-and-so* is the only name it can receive. One may admit that a good third of our psychic life consists in these rapid premonitory perspective views of schemes of thought not yet articulate. How comes it about that a man reading something aloud for the first time is able immediately to emphasize all his words aright, unless from the very first he have a sense of at least the form of the sentence yet to come, which sense is fused with his consciousness of the present word, and modifies its emphasis in his mind so as to make him give it the proper accent as he utters it? Emphasis of this kind is almost altogether a matter of grammatical construction. If we read 'no more' we expect presently to come upon a 'than'; if we read 'however' at the outset of a sentence it is a 'yet,' a 'still,' or a 'nevertheless,' that we expect. A noun in a certain position demands a verb in a certain mood and number, in another position it expects a relative pronoun. Adjectives call for nouns, verbs for adverbs, etc., etc. And this foreboding of the coming grammatical scheme combined with each successive uttered word is so practically accurate that a reader incapable of understanding four ideas of the book he is reading aloud, can nevertheless read it with the most delicately modulated expression of intelligence.

Some will interpret these facts by calling them all cases in which certain images, by laws of association, awaken others so very rapidly that we think afterwards we felt the very *tendencies* of the nascentimages to arise, before they were actually there. For this school

就不再存在了。而且当替代它的词语到来的时候，如果它们和它是一致的，它就继续欢迎它们并且称它们是正确的，如果它们和它不一致，它就拒绝它们并且称它们是错误的。因此它自己拥有一种最明确的本性，然而如若没有使用后来取代了它的属于随后的心理事实的词语，我们又能对它说些什么呢？“如此说的意图”是它唯一能够获得的名称。人们可能会承认，我们足有三分之一的精神生活在于对这些尚未表达出来的思维系统进行快速的预料。当一个人首次大声地朗读某些东西的时候，他直接能够正确地强调他所朗读的所有词语，除非在一开始的时候他至少对就要到来的句子形式有一种感觉，这感觉与他对当前词语的意识融合在了一起，并且在他的心灵中修正词语的着重点，以便在他发出它的时候使他能够给它以适当的强调，不然这种情况如何会发生呢？这种类型的强调几乎完全是一个语法构建的问题。如果我们读到“不多”的时候，我们目前期望读到“于”字；如果我们读到“然而”，我们就期望在句子的开头有“还”、“还是”、或者“不过”这些词。处于某个位置上的一个名词需要某种产生语态和数的变化的动词，当它处于另一个位置上时，它需要一个关联代词。形容词需要动词，动词需要副词，等等。而且，这种对即将到来的与每一个相继读出的词语相结合的语法系统的预感实际上是如此的精确，以至于一个不能完全理解他正在大声朗读的书中观点的读者，仍然能够用经过最精细地调整的理智表达来朗读它。

一些人将通过下述内容来解释这些事实，他们认为它们的情况是这样的，即在其中某些意象通过联想规律，以非常快的速度唤醒了其他意象，以至于我们后来认为，我们在初生的意象实际出现之前，感受到了将要出现的意象的真实倾向。对这一学派而

the only possible materials of consciousness are images of a perfectly definite nature. Tendencies exist, but they are facts for the outside psychologist rather than for the subject of the observation. The tendency is thus a *psychical* zero; only its *results* are felt.

Now what I contend for, and accumulate examples to show, is that 'tendencies' are not only descriptions from without, but that they are among the *objects* of the stream, which is thus aware of them from within, and must be described as in very large measure constituted of *feelings* of *tendency*, often so vague that we are unable to name them at all. It is, in short, the re-instatement of the vague to its proper place in our mental life which I am so anxious to press on the attention. Mr. Galton and Prof. Huxley have, as we shall see in Chapter XVIII, made one step in advance in exploding the ridiculous theory of Hume and Berkeley that we can have no images but of perfectly definite things. Another is made in the overthrow of the equally ridiculous notion that, whilst simple objective qualities are revealed to our knowledge in subjective feelings, relations are not. But these reforms are not half sweeping and radical enough. What must be admitted is that the definite images of traditional psychology form but the very smallest part of our minds as they actually live. The traditional psychology talks like one who should say a river consists of nothing but pailsful, spoonsful, quartpotsful, barrelsful, and other moulded forms of water. Even were the pails and the pots all actually standing in the stream, still between them the free water would continue to flow. It is just this free water of consciousness that psychologists resolutely overlook. Every definite image in the mind is steeped and dyed in the free water that flows round it. With it goes the sense of its relations, near and remote, the dying echo of whence it came to us, the dawning sense of whither it is to lead.

言，唯一可能的意识材料就是有非常确定的本质的意象。倾向是存在着的，但是它们只是对外在的心理学家而言才是事实，而对观察的被试而言就不是事实。因而，倾向是精神上的无；只是其结果被感受到了。

现在我所主张的，以及我所收集的例子将要表明的是，“倾向”不仅仅是从外部的描述，而且它们也是思想之流的对象，因而思想之流是从内部感知到它们的，而且，思想之流必须被描述为在很大范围内是由对倾向的感受而构成的，这些倾向感受常常非常模糊，以至于我们完全不能命名它们。简言之，我如此急于要引起人们注意，就是在于将这些模糊的东西复原到其在我们精神生活中的固有位置上来。正如我们将在第 18 章中看到的那样，高尔顿先生和赫胥黎教授在推翻休谟和贝克莱关于我们只能拥有完全确定事物的意象的理论中，已经预先迈出了第一步。在推翻同样荒唐的观点中，即简单的客观性质在主观感受中得以揭示给了我们的知识，而关系却没有，他们又迈出了一步。但是这些改革不够彻底和全面。必须承认的是，传统心理学中的确定意象，如它们所实际存在的那样，只构成了我们心灵中极小的一部分。传统心理学说起话来很像这样一个人，他说一条河流只是由提桶形状的水、勺状的水、夸脱罐状的水、大木桶状的水以及其他模具形状的水所组成的。即使那些提桶和罐子实际上就竖立在河流之中，在它们之间依然有空闲的水继续流动。心理学家所坚决忽视掉的正是意识中这空闲的水。心灵中每一个确定意象都浸染在流动在它周围的这些空闲的水中。与它在一起的还有其近处的和远处的关系感觉，还有正在消逝的它从哪里来到我们这里的回响，以及开始出现的对它将要到哪里去的感觉。这意象的

The significance, the value, of the image is all in this halo or penumbra that surrounds and escorts it,—or rather that is fused into one with it and has become bone of its bone and flesh of its flesh; leaving it, it is true, an image of the same *thing* it was before, but making it an image of that thing newly taken and freshly understood.

What is that shadowy scheme of the 'form' of an opera, play, or book, which remains in our mind and on which we pass judgment when the actual thing is done? What is our notion of a scientific or philosophical system? Great thinkers have vast premonitory glimpses of schemes of relation between terms, which hardly even as verbal images enter the mind, so rapid is the whole process. [①]We all of us have this permanent consciousness of whither our thought is going. It is a feeling like any other, a feeling of what thoughts are next to arise, before they have arisen. This field of view of consciousness varies very much in extent, depending largely on the degree of mental freshness or fatigue. When very fresh, our minds carry an immense horizon with them. The present image shoots its perspective far before it, irradiating in advance the regions in which lie the thoughts as yet unborn.

---

① Mozart describes thus his manner of composing: First bits and crumbs of the piece come and gradually join together in his mind; then the soul getting warmed to the work, the thing grows more and more, "and I spread it out broader and clearer, and at last it gets almost finished in my head, even when it is a long piece, so that I can see the whole of it at a single glance in my mind, as if it were a beautiful painting or a handsome human being; in which way I do not hear it in my imagination at all as a succession—the way it must come later—but all at once, as it were. It is a rare feast! All the inventing and making goes on in me as in a beautiful strong dream. But the best of all is the *hearing of it all at once.*"

意义和价值全部在于环绕着它和陪同着它的这种晕轮和半影之中,——或者毋宁说,其意义和价值全部在于和它融为一体并且与它骨肉相连的晕轮和半影之中;如果离开它,它确实还是以前那同一个事物的意象,但这却使得它成为了一个以新的方式被采纳和理解的那同一事物的意象了。

一部歌剧、一部戏剧或者一本书之"形式"的那种模糊的安排,一直保留在我们的心中,并且当真实的事情完成的时候,我们在其之上进行判断,那么这"形式"安排是什么呢?我们对科学和哲学系统的观点是什么?伟大的思想家对术语间的安排有大量的预见性的"一瞥",整个过程是如此迅速,以至于它们甚至几乎没有作为词语意象就进入了心灵中。[①] 我们所有人都拥有这种永久的关于我们的思想将要去哪里的意识。它像任何其他感受一样,它是在思想还没有出现之前,一种对接下来将要出现什么思想的感受。意识的这种视野在范围上变化很大,这在很大程度上取决于心灵的精神饱满或疲劳的程度。当精神非常饱满的时候,我们的心灵就获得极为广阔的视野。当前的意象将其远景远远地投射到它的前面,预先照射到了尚未出现的思想所位于的区

① 莫扎特这样描述他的作曲方法:在他的心灵中,最初作品的零星碎片出现了,并且逐渐地连接在了一起;然后灵魂激昂地工作起来,东西变得越来越多,"并且我更宽泛地、更清楚地将它展开,最后它几乎在我的头脑里完成了,甚至当它的篇幅很长时也是如此,所以我在我心灵中只要瞥上一眼就能够看到整个作品,就仿佛它是一幅美丽的图画或者是一个英俊的人;以这种方式,我在我的想像之中没有把它听成是一个连续的作品——这种方法必须随后出现——而是同时听到它,就好像它是同时出现的一样。这是一种少有的享受!所有的发明和制造都在我的心中进行着,就像在一个美丽而强烈的梦中似的。但是,其中最美妙的事情还是同时听到了它。"

Under ordinary conditions the halo of felt relations is much more circumscribed. And in states of extreme brain-fag the horizon is narrowed almost to the passing word,—the associative machinery, however, providing for the next word turning up in orderly sequence, until at last the tired thinker is led to some kind of a conclusion. At certain moments he may find himself doubting whether his thoughts have not come to a full stop; but the vague sense of a *plus ultra* makes him ever struggle on towards a more definite expression of what it may be; whilst the slowness of his utterance shows how difficult, under such conditions, the labor of thinking must be.

The awareness that our *definite* thought has come to a stop is an entirely different thing from the awareness that our thought is definitively completed. The expression of the latter state of mind is the falling inflection which betokens that the sentence is ended, and silence. The expression of the former state is 'hemming and hawing,' or else such phrases as 'et cetera,' or 'and so forth.' But notice that every part of the sentence to be left incomplete feels differently as it passes, by reason of the premonition we have that we shall be unable to end ii The 'and so forth' casts its shadow back, and is as integral a part of the object of the thought as the distinctest of images would be.

Again, when we use a common noun, such as *man*, in a universal sense, as signifying all possible men, we are fully aware of this intention on our part, and distinguish it carefully from our intention when we mean a certain group of men, or a solitary individual before as. In the chapter on Conception we shall see how important this difference of intention is. It casts its influence over the whole of the sentence, both before and after the spot in which the word *man* is used.

Nothing is easier than to symbolize all these facts in terms of brain-action. Just as the echo of the *whence*, the sense of the starting point of our thought, is probably due to the dying excitement of processes but a moment since vividly aroused; so the sense

域。在通常的情况下，被感受到的晕轮是非常有限的。并且在大脑极度疲劳的状态中，视野几乎缩小到了经过的词语之上，——然而，联想机制为下一个词语以有序的顺序出现而做着准备，直到最后疲劳的思想者被引领到了某种结论之上。在某些时候，他可能发现自己在怀疑他的思想是否还没有完全结束；但是对最远点的东西的模糊感觉，使他不断地挣扎下去，以获得一种更明确的对它可能是什么的表达；同时，他缓慢的言语表明，在这样的情况下，思维的劳作肯定是多么艰苦啊。

对我们明确的思想已经停止了的感知与对我们的思想已经明确地完成了的感知相比，它是一个完全不同的东西。对后一种心理状态的表达是预示语句结束和寂静的降调。对前一种状态的表达是“支支吾吾”，或者像“及其他”以及“等等”这样的其他短语。但是要注意的是，尚未完成的句子的每一个部分在经过时感受起来都不一样，原因在于我们所获有的我们将无法完成它的预感。这“等等”将它的阴影投射回来，并且像最清楚的意象一样，是思维对象的一个应有部分。

还有，当我们在一种普遍的意义上使用像男人这样的普通名词来表示所有可能的男人时，我们在我们这方面完全意识到了这种意图，并且将它同我们意指某个特定的男人群体或者我们面前一个单独个体时的意图小心地区别开来。在关于概念的一章中我们将会看到这种对意图的区分是多么地重要。在男人这个词被使用的那个位置的前后，它对整个句子施加着影响。

没有什么比依照大脑活动将所有的这些事实用符号表示出来更简单的了。正像来自所来之处的回声，对我们思想起点的感觉，可能是由于正在消逝的只是片刻之前才出现的过程的兴奋所

of the whither, the foretaste of the terminus, must be due to the waxing excitement of tracts or processes which, a moment hence, will be the cerebral correlatives of some thing which a moment hence will be vividly present to the thought. Represented by a curve, the neurosis underlying consciousness must at any moment be like this:

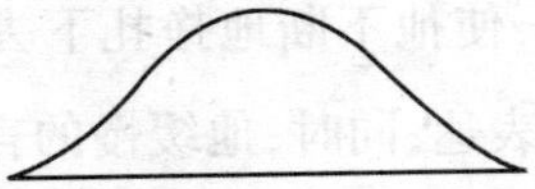

FIG. 27

Each point of the horizontal line stands for some brain-tract or process. The height of the curve above the line stands for the intensity of the process. All the processes are *present*, in the intensities shown by the curve. But those before the latter's apex *were* more intense a moment ago; those after it *will* be more intense a moment hence. If I recite *a*, *b*, *c*, *d*, *e*, *f*, *g*, at the moment of uttering *d*, neither *a*, *b*, *c*, nor *e*, *f*, *g*, are out of my consciousness altogether, but both, after their respective fashions, 'mix their dim lights' with the stronger one of the d, because their neuroses are both awake in some degree.

There is a common class of mistakes which shows how brain-processes begin to be excited before the thoughts attached to them are *due*—due, that is, in substantive and vivid form. I mean those mistakes of speech or writing by which, in Dr. Carpenter's words, "we mispronounce or misspell a word, by introducing into it a letter or syllable of some other, whose turn is shortly to come; or, it may be, the whole of the anticipated word is substituted for the one which ought to

致;因此,对目的地的感觉,对终点的预示,一定是由于一些逐渐增强的神经束或过程的兴奋所致,它们在片刻之后将成为在稍后将会生动地呈现给思想的某些事物的大脑相关物。用一条曲线来再现潜在于意识之下的神经活动,它在任何时候都一定像这样:

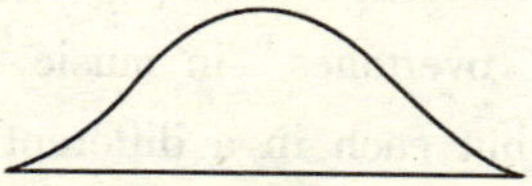

图 27

水平线上的每一个点都代表某种大脑神经束或者过程。水平线上方的曲线高度代表过程的强度。所有的过程都以曲线所表明的强度呈现了出来。但是,在曲线顶点之前的那些过程在片刻之前要更强一些;在曲线顶点之后的那些过程在片刻之后要更强一些。如果我背诵 a、b、c、d、e、f、g,在说出 d 的那一刻,a、b、c 和 e、f、g 都完全没有离开我的意识,而且这两者都依照它们各自的方式,将“它们的黯淡的光芒”和 d 的更强烈的光芒“混合在了一起”,因为它们的神经活动都在某种程度上进行着。

这里有一种普通类型的错误,它们展示了大脑过程如何在隶属于它们的思想应该到来——即以实体性和生动的形式到来——之前就开始兴奋了。我指的是那些言语和书写的错误,用卡彭特博士的话说,由于这些错误,“我们错读或者错拼了一个词,我们是通过将某些其他词语的一个字母和一个发音引入到这个词中而出错的,而这些其他的词是即刻就要出现的词;或者情况也可能是,被预料到随后将要出现的整个词代替了,本来应该表达

have been expressed."① In these cases one of two things must have happened: either some local accident of nutrition *blocks* the process that is *due*, so that other processes discharge that ought as yet to be but nascently aroused; or some opposite local accident *furthers* the *later processes* and makes them explode before their time. In the chapter on Association of Ideas, numerous instances will come before us of the actual effect on consciousness of neuroses not yet maximally aroused.

It is just like the 'overtones' in music. Different instruments give the 'same note,' but each in a different voice, because each gives more than that note, namely, various upper harmonics of it which differ from one instrument to another. They are not separately heard by the ear; they blend with the fundamental note, and suffuse it, and alter it; and even so do the waxing and waning brain-processes at every moment blend with and suffuse and alter the psychic effect of the processes which are at their culminating point.

Let us use the words *psychic overtone*, *suffusion*, or *fringe*, to designate the influence of a faint brain-process upon our thought, as it makes it aware of relations and objects but dimly perceived. ②

---

① Mental Physiology, § 236. Dr. Carpenter's explanation differs materially from that given in the text.

② Cf. also S. Stricker: Vorlesungen über allg. u. exp. Pathologie (1879), pp. 462-3, 501, 547; Romanes: Origin of Human Faculty, p. 82. It is so hard to make one's self clear that I may advert to a misunderstanding of my views by the late Prof. Thos. Maguire of Dublin (Lectures on Philosophy 1885). This author considers that by the 'fringe' I mean some sort of psychic material by which sensations in themselves separate are made to cohere together, and wittily says that I ought to "see that uniting sensations by their 'fringes' is more vague than to construct the universe out of oysters by platting their beards" (p. 211). But the fringe, as I use the word, means nothing like this; it is part of the *object cognized*, —substantive *qualities* and *things* appearing to the mind in a *fringe of relations*. Some parts—the transitive parts—of our stream of thought cognize

出来的词。"[1]在这些情况中,两个事件中的任何一件必定发生过:或者在营养方面的某个突发事件妨碍了应该出现的过程,结果其他至今才应该被唤起的过程释放了;或者某种相反的局部突发事件促进了后来的过程,并且使它们提前爆发了。在关于观念联想的章节里,我们将会涉及大量关于在最大程度上尚未被激起的神经活动对意识产生真正影响的例子。

这正像音乐中的"泛音"。不同的乐器奏出"相同的音",但是每种乐器都是以一种不同的声音来奏出它的,因为每种乐器奏出的不仅仅是那个音,即它们奏出的还有这个音的上部泛音列,而这泛音列在不同的乐器那里是不同的。耳朵没有单独地听到它们;它们和基音混合在了一起,并且弥漫于它的周围,改变了它;而逐渐增强和减弱的大脑过程甚至也是如此,它们每时每刻都和达到顶点的过程的精神效果相混合,弥漫于它,并且改变它。

让我们使用精神泛音、弥漫或者边缘这些词来指明一个微弱的大脑过程对我们的思想所造成的影响,因为这使得我们的思想意识到了被模糊知觉到的关系和对象。[2]

---

① 《心理生理学》,第236节。卡彭特博士的解释和文中给出的解释有实质性的区别。

② 也可参见S.斯特里克:《普通和实验病理学讲座》(1879年),第462、463、501、547页;里奇特:《人类官能的起源》,第82页。让别人明白自己的观点是如此的困难,以至于我应当注意到已故的都柏林托马斯·马奎尔教授对我们观点的误解(《哲学演讲》,1885年)。这位作者认为,我用"边缘"是指某种精神材料,通过它,分离的感觉自身得以结合起来,并且他还机智地说,我应该"看到,用感觉的'边缘'来结合感觉,比通过给牡蛎的须毛编辫子的方法用牡蛎来构建宇宙还要更加含糊"(第211页)。但是我所使用的边缘这个词完全不是这个意思;它是被认知的对象的一部分,——实体性的性质和事物在关系的边缘中呈现给心灵。我们思想之流的一些部分——过渡部分认知的

If we then consider the *cognitive function* of different states of mind, we may feel assured that the difference between those that are mere 'acquaintance,' and those that are 'knowledges-*about*' (see p. 221) is reducible almost entirely to the absence or presence of psychic fringes or overtones. Knowledge *about* a thing is knowledge of its relations. Acquaintance with it is limitation to the bare impression which it makes. Of most of its relations we are only aware in the penumbral nascent way of a 'fringe' of unarticulated affinities about it. And, before passing to the next topic in order, I must say a little of this sense of affinity, as itself one of the most interesting features of the subjective stream.

In all our voluntary thinking there is some topic or subject about which all the members of the thought revolve. Half the time this topic is a problem, a gap we cannot yet fill with a definite picture, word, or phrase, but which, in the manner described some time back, influences us in an intensely active and determinate psychic way. Whatever may be the images and phrases that pass before us, we feel their relation to this aching gap. To fill it up is our thoughts' destiny. Some bring us nearer to that consummation. Some the gap. negates as quite irrelevant. Each swims in a felt fringe of relations of which the aforesaid gap is the term. Or instead of a definite gap we may merely carry a mood of interest about with us. Then, however vague the mood, it will still act in the same way, throwing a mantle of felt affinity over such representations, entering the mind, as suit it, and tingeing with the feeling of tediousness or discord all those with which it has no concern.

---

the relations rather than the things; but both the transitive and the substantive parts form one continuous stream, with no discrete 'sensations' in it such as Prof. Maguire supposes, and supposes me to suppose, to be there.

然后，如果我们考虑不同心理状态的认知功能，我们可能会感到确定的是，那些“相识”和“相知”的知识之间的区别，几乎可以完全被还原为精神边缘或精神泛音的存在与不存在（见第221页）。对一个事物的相知的知识是对其关系的知识。对它的相识的知识则局限于它所造成的单纯印象。就其大多数关系而言，我们只能通过那没有得到明确表达的关于它的亲和性的“边缘”在半影中初步意识到它。而且，在依次转到下一个话题之前，我必须对这种亲和感稍加讨论，因为它是主观之流最有趣的特征之一。

在我们所有的主动思考中，存在着某种主题或题目，思维的所有成分都卷入其中。这个主体常常是一个问题，一个我们尚不能用明确的图画、词语或者短语填满的裂缝，但是，它依照我们前面所描述的那样，以一种极为活跃和确定的精神方式影响着我们。不论在我们面前经过的意象和短语是什么，我们感受到了它们与这令人痛心的裂缝的关系。将它填满是我们思维的宿命。有些意象和短语把我们带到了离其完成更近的地方，有些由于完全不相关而被裂缝否定掉了。每一个意象或短语都在被感受到了的关系边缘中漂浮着，上述裂缝就是表达关系边缘的术语。或者我们可能没有一个明确的裂缝，我们仅仅是带着一种感兴趣的心情。那么，不论这种心情有多么模糊，它将依然以相同的方式起作用，即将感受到了的亲和性的覆盖物投掷到这些表象之上，如果这些表象适合这覆盖物，这些表象就进入到了心灵中，而对于所有它不关注的表象，它则觉得厌烦与不和。

是关系而不是事物；但是过渡的和实体性的部分共同形成了一条连续的流，没有像马奎尔教授所设想的那种“感觉”存在于其中，而且他还假设说我也如此设想。

Relation, then, to our topic or interest is constantly felt in the fringe, and particularly the relation of harmony and discord, of furtherance or hindrance of the topic. When the sense of furtherance is there, we are 'all right;' with the sense of hindrance we are dissatisfied and perplexed, and cast about us for other thoughts. Now *any* thought the quality of whose fringe lets us feel ourselves 'all right,' is an acceptable member of our thinking, whatever, kind of thought it may otherwise be. Provided we only feel it to have a place in the scheme of relations in which the interesting topic also lies, that is quite sufficient to make of it a relevant and appropriate portion of ouar train of ideas.

For the important thing about a train of thought is its conclusion. That is the *meaning*, or, as we say, the topic of the thought. That is What abides when all its other members have faded from memory. Usually this conclusion is a word or phrase or particular image, or practical attitude or resolve, whether rising to answer a problem or fill a pre-existing gap that worried us, or whether accidentally stumbled on in revery. In either case it stands out from the other segments of the stream by reason of the peculiar interest attaching to it. This interest *arrests* it, makes a sort of crisis of it when it comes, induces attention upon it and makes us treat it in a substantive way.

The parts of the stream that precede these substantive conclusions are but the means of the latter's attainment. And, provided the same conclusion be reached, the means may be as mutable as we like, for the 'meaning' of the stream of thought will be the same. What difference does it make what the means are? "*Qu'importe le flacon, pourvu qu'on ait l'ivresse?*" The relative unimportance of the means appears from the fact that when the conclusion is there, we have always forgotten most of the steps preceding its attainment. When we have uttered a proposition,

因而，与我们主题或兴趣的关系不断地在边缘中被感受到，尤其是同主题和谐与不和谐的关系，以及促进和妨碍主题的关系在边缘中被感受到了。如果有促进的感觉，我们就“没事”；如果有妨碍的感觉，我们就感到不满和困惑，并且在我们的周围寻找其他的思想。现在任何其边缘的性质使我们感到自己“没事”的思想，无论它在其他方面是何种思想，都是我们的思维可以接受的成员。只要我们感受到它在有趣的主题也存在其中的关系系统中获有一席之地，这就足以使它成为我们观念序列中一个相关且适当的部分。

因为思想序列的重要之处在于其结论。那就是意义，或者如我们所说，是思想的主题。那就是当思想的所有其他成分都从记忆中消逝了，却依然保留下来的东西。通常这种结论是一个词或者短语，或者是精确的意象，又或者是一种实际的态度和决心，无论它们的出现或者是为了回答一个问题，要么是为了填满一个先前就存在着并且困扰着我们的裂缝，又或者是否它们是在沉思中被无意撞上的。在任何一种情况下，它因为从属于它的奇特兴趣而从思想之流的其他部分中突显出来。这种兴趣捉住了它，当它到来的时候，给它制造了某种危机，将注意力引导到了它这里来，并且使我们以一种实体性的方式来对待它。

思想之流中先于这些实体性结论的部分只是获得结论的手段。而且，只要达到了相同的结论，手段可以随着我们的意愿而变化，因为思想之流的“意义”是相同的。手段是什么难道会使它产生什么区别吗？“喝一小瓶酒有什么关系，但愿一醉方休？”下述事实表明了手段相对来说是不重要的，当结论出现了的时候，我们总是忘记了在结论获得之前的大部分步骤。当我们说出一

we are rarely able a moment afterwards to recall our exact words, though we can express it in different words easily enough. The practical upshot of a book we read remains with us, though we may not recall one of its sentences.

The only paradox would seem to lie in supposing that the fringe of felt affinity and discord can be the same in two heterogeneous sets of images. Take a train of words passing through the mind and leading to a certain conclusion on the one hand, and on the other hand an almost wordless set of tactile, visual and other fancies leading to the same conclusion. Can the halo, fringe, or scheme in which we feel the words to lie be the same as that in which we feel the images to lie ? Does not the discrepancy of terms involve a discrepancy of felt relations among them ?

If the terms be taken *quâ* mere sensations, it assuredly does. For instance, the words may rhyme with each other, —the visual images can have no such affinity as *that*. But *quâ* thoughts, *quâ* sensations *understood*, the words have contracted by long association fringes of mutual repugnance or affinity with each other and with the conclusion, which run exactly parallel with like fringes in the visual, tactile and other ideas. The most important element of these fringes is, I repeat, the mere feeling of harmony or discord, of a right or wrong direction in the thought. Dr. Campbell has, so far as I know, made the best analysis of this fact, and his words, often quoted, deserve to be quoted again. The chapter is entitled "What is the cause that nonsense so often escapes being detected, both by the writer and by the reader ?" The author, in answering this question, makes (*inter alia*) the following remarks: ①

① George Campbell: Philosophy of Rhetoric, book Ⅱ. chap. Ⅶ.

个命题的时候，我们很少能够在片刻之后回忆起我们确切的用词，尽管我们可以用不同的词语非常容易地表达它。我们依然记得自己阅读过的书籍中的实际结果，尽管我们可能已经回忆不出书中的任何一个句子了。

唯一的矛盾似乎在于假设感受到的亲和性和不和谐的边缘，在两组完全不同的意象中会是相同的。一方面是经过心灵并且导致某个结论的词语序列，而另一方面是几乎没有词语的触觉、视觉或其他意象，而它们也导致了相同的结论。我们所感受到的词语存在于其中的晕轮、边缘或者系统，与我们所感受到的意象存在于其中的晕轮、边缘或者系统会是一样的吗？难道所用词语的差异不涉及它们之间感受到了的关系的差异吗？

如果所用词语被看作是纯粹的感觉，它确实如此。例如，词语间可以互相押韵——而视觉意象却不可能具有这种亲和性。而且如果表达项被看作是思想，被看作是理解了的感觉，那么词语相互之间以及词语和结论之间的不一致和亲和性的长长的联系边缘就会约定这些词语，这些边缘与在视觉观念、触觉观念以及其他观念中的相似的边缘是完全平行的。我要重申的是，这些边缘的最重要的元素是对和谐与不和谐的单纯感受，以及思想中正确方向和错误方向的单纯感受。据我所知，坎贝尔博士对这一事实做了最好的分析，而且他的论述经常被引用，他的论述在这里值得再次引用。那一章的题目是“是什么原因使得废话如此经常地不为作者和读者所察觉？”作者在回答这一问题的时候，（专门）做出了下述评论：①

---

① 乔治·坎贝尔：《修辞学哲学》，第2卷，第7章。

"That connection [he says] or relation which comes gradually to subsist among the different words of a language, in the minds of those who speak it, . . . is merely consequent on this, that those words are employed as signs of connected or related things. It is an axiom in geometry that things equal to the same thing are equal to one another. It may, in like manner, be admitted as an axiom in psychology that ideas associated by the same idea will associate one another. Hence it will happen that if, from experiencing the connection of two things, there results, as infallibly there will result, an association between the ideas or notions annexed to them, as each idea will moreover be associated by its sign, there will likewise be an association between the ideas of the signs. Hence the sounds considered as signs will be conceived to have a connection analogous to that which subsisteth among the things signified; I say, the sounds considered as signs; for this way of considering them constantly attends us in speaking, writing, hearing, and reading. When we purposely abstract from it, and regard them merely as sounds, we are instantly sensible that they are quite unconnected, and have no other relation than what ariseth from similitude of tone or accent. But to consider them in this manner commonly results from previous design, and requires a kind of effort which is not exerted in the ordinary use of speech. In ordinary use they are regarded solely as signs, or, rather, they are confounded with the things they signify; the consequence of which is that, in the manner just now explained, we come insensibly to conceive a connection among them of a very different sort from that of which sounds are naturally susceptible."

"Now this conception, habit, or tendency of the mind, call it which you please, is considerably strengthened by the frequent use of language and by the structure of it. Language is the sole channel through which we communicate our knowledge and discoveries to others,

“(他说)在说某种语言的人们的心中,逐渐出现于这种语言中的不同词语间的联系或者关系,……只是在下述情况之中作为结果而出现的,即那些词语是作为相关联的和相联系的事物的符号来使用的。在几何学中这是一条公理,即那些与同一个事物相等的事物彼此间也相等。以同样的方式,它也可以被看作是心理学中的一条公理,即那些和同一个观念相联系的观念彼此间也联系着。因此,这样的情况就会发生,即如果由于经验到了两个事物之间的联系,从而导致了附加于这两个事物之上的观点或概念间的联系,因为它会绝对无误地导致这种情况出现,那么,由于每一个观念都会通过其符号而进一步联系起来,这里就同样会有关于符号的观念间的联系。因此,被看作是符号的声音就被认为具有一种和存在于所指事物间的联系相类似的联系;我说声音被看作是符号;因为我们在说、写、听和读中经常以这种方式来考虑它们。当我们故意将这种联系分离出来,并且只把它们看作是声音,我们就立刻感觉到它们是没有联系的,并且除了由语调和重音的相似而产生的关系之外,它们之间没有任何关系。但是,以这种方式考虑它们一般是由于先前的计划所致,并且需要一种在日常的言语使用中无需做出的努力。在日常的使用中,它们被单独地看作符号,或者毋宁说,它们和它们所指的事物是混淆在一起的;其结果就是,以刚刚解释过的方式,我们不知不觉地就开始构想它们之间有一种和声音自然就有的那种联系非常不同的联系。”

“现在心灵的这种概念、习惯或者倾向——你想怎么称呼它都可以——通过语言的频繁使用和语言的结构而被极大地巩固了。语言是这样一种唯一的渠道,通过它我们将我们的知识和发

and through which the knowledge and discoveries of others are communicated to us. By reiterated recourse to this medium, it necessarily happens that when things are related to each other, the words signifying those things are more commonly brought together in discourse. Hence the words and names by themselves, by customary vicinity, contract in the fancy a relation additional to that which they derive purely from being the symbols of related things. Farther, this tendency is strengthened by the structure of language. All languages whatever, even the most barbarous, as far as hath yet appeared, are of a regular and analogical make. The consequence is that similar relations in things will be expressed similarly; that is, by similar inflections, derivations, compositions, arrangement of words, or juxtaposition of particles, according to the genius or grammatical form of the particular tongue. Now as, by the habitual use of a language (even though it were quite irregular), the signs would insensibly become connected in the imagination wherever the things signified are connected in nature, so, by the regular structure of a language, this connection among the signs is conceived as analogous to that which subsisteth among their archetypes."

If we know English and French and begin a sentence in French, all the later words that come are French; we hardly ever drop into English. And this affinity of the French words for each other is not something merely operating mechanically as a brain-law, it is something we feel at the time. Our understanding of a French sentence heard never falls to so low an ebb that we are not aware that the words linguistically belong together. Our attention can hardly so wander that if an English word be suddenly introduced we shall not start at the change. Such a vague sense as this of the words belonging together is the very minimum of fringe that can accompany them, if 'thought' at all. Usually the vague perception that all the words we hear belong to the same language

现传达给别人，而别人的知识和发现也通过它来传达给我们。通过反复地求助于这一媒介，下述情况必然会发生，即当事物彼此之间有联系的时候，指称那些事物的词语在谈话中就更加经常地被结合到一起。因此，语言和名称通过它们自身，通过习惯上的连接，在完全由于它们是相关事物的符号而造成的关系之上，在想像中又约定出了一种关系。此外，这种倾向还被语言的结构所强化了。所有的语言，不论它是哪一种，甚至是最原始的语言，只要它已经出现了，就都具有规则的和相似的构造。结果是，在事物中的相似的关系会被相似地表达出来；即依照特殊语言的特色和语法形式，通过相似的词语变形、派生、复合、排列，或者词缀的并列而被表达出来。现在，因为，通过语言的习惯性使用（尽管它是很不规则的），只要符号所指称的事物在自然界是有联系的，符号在想像中就会不知不觉地变得有联系，所以，通过语言有规则的结构，这种符号间的联系就被构想为是与存在于它们原型间的联系相类似的联系。”

如果我们懂英语和法语，并且用法语开始一个句子，随后而来的词语都是法语词；我们几乎从来不曾不知不觉地用上英语。法语单词彼此间的这种亲和性并不仅仅是某种作为一条大脑规则而机械地起作用的东西，它是某种我们在当时感受到的东西。我们对所听到的一个法语句子的理解，从来也不曾如此地衰微，以至于我们没有意识到词语属于一种语言。我们的注意力几乎从来也不可能如此的涣散，以至于假如一个英语单词突然被引入进来了，我们居然不会对这种改变而感到吃惊。像这样一种词语属于一个整体的模糊感觉，如果被“思维”到了的话，是能够伴随词语的最小边缘。我们所听到的所有词语属于同一种语言，并且

and to the same special vocabulary in that language, and that the grammatical sequence is familiar, is practically equivalent to an admission that what we hear is sense. But if an unusual foreign word be introduced, if the grammar trip, or if a term from an incongruous vocabulary suddenly appear, such as 'rattrap' or 'plumber's bill' in a philosophical discourse, the sentence detonates, as it were, we receive a shock from the incongruity, and the drowsy assent is gone. The feeling of rationality in these cases seems rather a negative than a positive tiling, being the mere absence of shock, or sense of discord, between the terms of thought.

So delicate and incessant is this recognition by the mind of the mere fitness of words to be mentioned together that the slightest misreading, such as 'casualty' for 'causality,' or 'perpetual' for 'perceptual,' will be corrected by a listener whose attention is so relaxed that he gets no idea of the *meaning* of the sentence at all.

Conversely, if words do belong to the same vocabulary, and if the grammatical structure is correct, sentences with absolutely no meaning may be uttered in good faith and pass unchallenged. Discourses at prayer-meetings, reshuffling the same collection of cant phrases, and the whole genus of penny-a-line-isms and newspaper-reporter's flourishes give illustrations of this. "The birds filled the tree-tops with their morning song, making the air moist, cool, and pleasant," is a sentence I remember reading once in a report of some athletic exercises in Jerome Park. It was probably written unconsciously by the hurried reporter, and read uncritically by many readers. An entire volume of 784 pages lately published in Boston①

① Substantialism or Philosophy of Knowledge, by 'Jean Story' (1879).

属于这种语言中相同的特殊词汇，并且语法顺序也是熟悉的，这种对它们的模糊知觉通常实际上等于承认我们所听到的是意义。而且，如果一个不寻常的外语单词被引入了进来，如果语法出错了，又如果一个来自于不适宜的词汇中的术语突然出现了，例如在一次哲学演讲中出现了诸如“捕鼠夹”或者“水管工的账单”这样的词语，句子便爆炸了，宛如我们受到了这种不协调的冲击，而且那昏昏欲睡的赞同也随之消失了。在这些情况中，对合理性的感受似乎是一种消极的东西，而不是一种积极的东西，它是纯粹的冲击的缺失，或者是纯粹的思维所用术语间的不和谐感觉的缺失。

心灵的这种对一起提及的词语的纯粹的适切性的认知是如此精细并且是不间断的，以至于最细小的误读，例如将“因果性”误读为“伤亡”，将“知觉的”误读为“永久的”，都将被一个注意力是如此涣散以至于根本没有理解句子意思的读者所更正。

相反，如果词语确实属于相同的词汇，并且如果语法结构也是正确的，绝对没有意义的句子就可以欺诈性地被说出来，并且也不会受到质疑。在祈祷会上的演讲，只是重组了相同集合中的说教性的短语，不值钱的文章和报纸记者的所有华丽辞藻，都可以作为这种情况的例证。“清晨，鸟儿的歌声萦绕在枝头，让空气变得湿润、凉爽和愉快起来”，这个句子我记得我曾在一篇关于杰罗姆公园中某些体育锻炼的报道中读到过。它可能是被一个匆匆忙忙的记者在无意识中写下的，而又被许多读者不加批评的阅读了。波士顿最近出版的一本 784 页的书[①]，完全都是由随意

① 《实体论或知识哲学》“琼·斯托里”著(1879 年)。

is composed of stuff like this passage picked out at random.

" The flow of the efferent fluids of all these vessels from their outlets at the terminal loop of each culminate link on the surface of the nuclear organism is continuous as their respective atmospheric fruitage up to the altitudinal limit of their expansibility, whence, when atmosphered by like but coalescing essences from higher altitudes,—those sensibly expressed as the essential qualities of external forms,—they descend, and become assimilated by the afferents of the nuclear organism."①

There are every year works published whose contents show them to be by real lunatics. To the reader, the book quoted from seems pure nonsense from beginning to end. It is impossible to divine, in such a case, just what sort of feeling of rational relation between the words may have appeared to the author's mind. The border line between objective sense and nonsense is hard to draw; that between subjective sense and nonsense, impossible. Subjectively, any collocation of words may make sense—even the wildest words in a dream—if one only does not doubt their belonging together. Take the obscurer passages in Hegel: it is a fair question whether the rationality included in them be anything more than the fact that the words all belong to a common vocabulary, and are strung together on a scheme of predication and relation,—immediacy,

---

① M. G. Tarde, quoting (in Delboeuf, Le Sommeil et les Reves (1885), p. 226) some nonsense-verses from a dream, says they show how prosodic forms may subsist in a mind from which logical rules are effaced . . . . I was able, in dreaming, to preserve the faculty of finding two words which rhymed, to appreciate the rhyme, to fill up the verse as it first presented itself with other words which, added, gave the right number of syllables, and yet I was ignorant of the sense of the words. . . . Thus we have the extraordinary fact that the words called each other up, without calling up their sense. . . . Even when awake, it is more difficult to ascend to the meaning of a word than to pass from one word to another; or to put it Otherwise, *it is harder to be a thinker than to be a rhetorician*, and on the whole nothing is commoner than trains of words not understood.

选出的同下述段落一样的素材所组成的。

"所有这些导管里传出的液体在核生物体表面的每一个顶点链环的终端回路上从它们的端口流出，随着它们各自的大气结果达到了它们扩展性高度的极限，它一直都是连续的，据此，当被来自更高的高度的相似而且结合着的本质所气化时——那些被明显地表达为外部形式的本质性质的东西——它们下降了，并且由于核生物的传入物而变得可以被吸收了。"①

每年都有一些著作出版，其内容表明它们出自疯子之手。对于读者而言，上面引用过的那本书从头至尾都纯粹是废话。在这样一种情况下，很难猜想是一种什么样的词语间的理性关系感受出现在了作者的心中。客观意义和无意义之间的界限是很难划分的；主观意义和无意义之间的界限是不可能划分的。在主观方面，词语的任何排列都可以获有意义——甚至梦中最混乱词语也可以如此——只要人们不怀疑它们彼此有关联。就拿黑格尔的比较晦涩的段落来说：提出下述这个问题是公平的，即是否包含在段落中的合理性不仅仅是下述事实，即所有的词语都属于同一类词汇，并且是在论断和关系的系统之上被拼凑起来的——这

---

① G. 塔德先生(《睡觉和梦》，德博甫，1885年，第226页)引用了一些来自梦中的无意义的诗句，他说，"它们表明了在逻辑规则被抹消掉了的心灵中韵律的形式如何可以存在。……在梦中，我能够找到两个成韵的字，我还能赏韵，我甚至还能用其他附加进来的并且能给出正确音韵的词语填充最先呈现其自身的诗句，然而，我对这些词语的意义却是无知的。……因此，我们就获得了一件异乎寻常的事实，即词和词之间能够彼此唤起对方，而没有召唤出它们的意义。……甚至当醒着的时候，理解一个词的意义要比从一个词过到另一个词更困难；或者用别的方式表达，做个思想家比做个修辞学家更困难，并且一般来说，没有什么东西比一系列不能被理解的词语更常见的了。

self-relation, and what not,—which has habitually recurred. Yet there seems no reason to doubt that the subjective feeling of the rationality of these sentences was strong in the writer as he penned, them, or even that some readers by straining may have reproduced it in themselves.

To sum up, certain kinds of verbal associate, certain grammatical expectations fulfilled, stand for a good part of our impression that a sentence has a meaning and is dominated by the Unity of one Thought. Nonsense in grammatical form sounds half rational; sense with grammatical sequence upset sounds nonsensical; e. g., " Elba the Napoleon English faith had banished broken to he Saint because Helena at. " Finally, there is about each word the psychic ' overtone ' of feeling that it brings us nearer to a forefelt conclusion. Suffuse all the words of a sentence, as they pass, with these three fringes or haloes of relation, let the conclusion seem worth arriving at, and all will admit the sentence to be an expression of thoroughly continuous, unified, and rational thought. ①

Each word, in such a sentence, is felt, not only as a word, but as having a meaning. The ' meaning ' of a word taken thus dynamically in a

① We think it odd that young children should listen with such rapt attention to the reading of stories expressed in words half of which they do not understand, and of none of which they ask the meaning. But their thinking is in form just what ours is when it is rapid. Both of us make flying leaps over large portions of the sentences uttered and we give attention only to substantive starting points, turning points, and conclusions here and there. All the rest, ' substantive ' and separately intelligible as it may *potentially* be, actually serves only as so much transitive material. It is *internodal* consciousness, giving us the sense of continuity, but having no significance apart from its mere gap-filling function. The children probably feel no gap when through a lot of unintelligible words they are swiftly carried to a familiar and intelligible terminus.

些关系有直接性、自我相关性，等等——它们是习惯性地重复发生的。然而，这里似乎没有理由怀疑，当作者书写这些句子的时候，对这些句子的合理性的主观感受在作者那里是强烈的，或者甚至一些读者在费力阅读之后也可以在他们自己身上重现这种感受。

总之，某些种类的词语伴随物，某些实现了的语法预期，在很大程度上支持了我们的印象，即一个句子有一个意思，并且被一个思想的统一体所支配。符合语法形式的无意义的话听起来有部分合理性；语法顺序混乱的意义听起来是无意义的；例如"埃尔巴拿破仑英国的信念曾经流放打破他圣人因为海伦娜在。"最后，在每一个词语周围都有感受的精神"泛音"，它将我们带到离预感到的结论更近的地方。当一个句子中的所有词语经过时，让这三种关系边缘或者晕轮都弥散在它们之中，让结论看起来是值得到达的，那么，所有人将会承认，句子是完全连续的、统一的和合理的思想表达。①

在这样的一个句子中，每一个词语，不仅作为一个词语，而且还具有一种意义，都被感受到了。在一个句子中如此动态地获得

---

① 我们认为奇怪的是，小孩子们能够如此全神贯注地听人们讲故事，而故事所由以表达的词语他们有一半都不理解，而且他们也不问所不理解词的意义是什么。而且当思维在快速运作时他们的思维和我们的都处于相同的状态。我们都在所说语句的庞大部分上进行着飞一般的跳跃，而且我们只注意各处的实体性的起点、转折点和结论。所有其余的部分，尽管它们可能潜在地是"实体性的"并且是可以单独理解的，实际上只不过是充当了那些大量的过渡性材料。是节间意识给我们以连续的感觉，但是它除了单纯的填补裂缝的功能以外，没有任何意义。当孩子们通过大量无法理解的词语被带到了一个熟悉的和可以理解的终点时，他们可能没有感受到裂缝。

sentence may be quite different from its meaning when taken statically or without context. The dynamic meaning is usually reduced to the bare fringe we have described, of felt suitability or unfitness to the context and conclusion. The static meaning, when the word is concrete, as ' table, ' ' Boston, ' consists of sensory images awakened; when it is abstract, as ' criminal legislation, ' ' fallacy, ' the meaning consists of other words aroused, forming the so-called ' definition. '

Hegel's celebrated dictum that pure being is identical with pure nothing results from his taking the words statically, or without the fringe they wear in a context. Taken in isolation, they agree in the single point of awakening no sensorial images. But taken dynamically, or as significant,—as *thought*,—their fringes of relation, their affinities and repugnances, their function and meaning, are felt and understood to be absolutely opposed.

Such considerations as these remove all appearance of paradox from those cases of extremely deficient visual imagery of whose existence Mr. Galton has made us aware (see below). An exceptionally intelligent friend informs me that he can frame no image whatever of the appearance of his breakfast-table. When asked how he then remembers it at all, he says he simple ' *knows* ' that it seated four people, and was covered with a white cloth on which were a butterfish, a coffee-pot, radishes, and so forth. The mind-stuff of which this ' knowing ' is made seems to be verbal images exclusively. But if the words ' coffee, ' ' bacon, ' ' muffins, ' and ' eggs ' lead a man to speak to his cook, to pay his bills, and to take measures for the morrow's meal exactly as visual and gustatory memories would, why are they not, for all practical intents and purposes, as good a kind of material in which to think ? In fact, we may suspect them to be for most purposes better than terms with a richer imaginative coloring. The scheme of relationship and the conclusion being the essential things in thinking,

的一个词的意义,可能同静态地或者没有语境的情况下获得的这个词的意义完全不同。动态意义通常被还原为我们已经描述过的所感受到的与语境和结论适合或不适合的纯粹边缘。静态的意义,当这个词是具体的,例如“桌子”、“波士顿”,由被唤醒的感觉意象所组成;当这个词是抽象的,例如“刑法”、“谬误”,意义由被引起的形成所谓“定义”的其他词语所组成。

黑格尔的著名格言,即纯粹的存在和纯粹的无是同一的,这是由于他静态地或者在离开语境中词语所携带的边缘来对待词语而造成的。孤立地看,它们只是在没有唤起感觉意象这一点上是一致的。但是动态地看,或者将它们看作是有意义的——看作思想——它们的关系边缘、它们的亲和性和不一致性,它们的功能和意义,就会被感受到或理解为是绝对相反的。

像这样的一些考虑将所有自相矛盾的现象,从高尔顿先生使我们意识到其存在的那些极不完善的视觉意象的例子中,排除了出去(见下文)。一个异常聪明伶俐的朋友告诉我,他对其早餐桌的显观无论怎样也不能形成任何意象。当问他如何竟能记得它时,他说他只是“知道”它是供四人坐的桌子,上面铺着白布,白布上面有一个黄油盘子、一个咖啡壶和一些萝卜等等。这种“知道”所由以构成的精神素材似乎完全是词语意象。但是,如果“咖啡”、“熏肉”、“松饼”和“鸡蛋”这些词致使一个人和他的厨师说话,付账单,并且着手准备次日的饭菜,那么,对于所有实际目的和意图来说,它们为什么不能同视觉和味觉记忆一样,同样是一种很好的用以思维的材料呢?事实上,我们可以猜想,就大多数目的而言,它们比具有更丰富的想像色彩的表达项要更好一些。关系系统和结论是思维中最为本质的东西,就此目的而言,那种

that, kind of mind-stuff which is handiest will be the best for the purpose. Now words, uttered or unexpressed, are the handiest mental elements we have. Not only are they very *rapidly* revivable, but they are revivable as actual sensations more easily than any other items of our experience. Did they not possess some such advantage as this, it would hardly be the case that the older men are and the more effective as thinkers, the more, as a rule, they have lost their visualizing power and depend on words. This was ascertained by Mr. Galton to be the case with members of the Royal Society. The present writer observes it in his own person most distinctly.

On the other hand, a deaf and dumb man can weave his tactile and visual images into a system of thought quite as effective and rational as that of a word-user. *The question whether thought is possible without language* has been a favorite topic of discussion among philosophers. Some interesting reminiscences of his childhood by Mr. Ballard, a deaf-mute instructor in the National College at Washington, show it to be perfectly possible. A few paragraphs may be quoted here.

"In consequence of the loss of my hearing in infancy, I was debarred from enjoying the advantages which children in the full possession of their senses derive from the exercises of the common primary school, from the every-day talk of their school-fellows and playmates, and from the conversation of their parents and other grown-up persons."

"I could convey my thoughts and feelings to my parents and brothers by natural signs or pantomime, and I could understand what they said to me by the same medium; our intercourse being, however, confined to the daily routine of home affairs and hardly going beyond the circle of my own observation. . . ."

"My father adopted a course which he thought would, in some measure, compensate me for the loss of my hearing. It was that of taking me with him when business required him to ride abroad;

最容易到手的精神素材就是最好的。现在,说出的和未经表达的词语是我们所拥有的最容易到手的心理元素。它们不仅可以非常迅速地活跃起来,而且它们作为真实的感觉比我们经验中的任何其他东西都容易活跃起来。如果它们不拥有像这样的一些优势,就很难出现下述情况了,即通常年纪较大的人越是丧失其形象化能力,并且越是依赖于词语,那么,他们作为思想家就越是给人留下了深刻的印象。这一点已经被高尔顿先生所确认,皇家学会的成员的情况确实如此。当前的笔者也在自己身上清楚地观察到了这一点。

另一方面,一个聋哑人能够同词语使用者一样,同样有效与合理地将其触觉和视觉意象编织进思想体系中。没有语言,思想是否可能这一问题一直是哲学家们喜欢讨论的一个话题。坐落于华盛顿的国家大学中的聋哑人教师巴拉德先生,有一些关于童年的有趣回忆,这些回忆表明它完全是有可能的。在这里应当引用几个段落来表明。

“由于幼年丧失了听力的缘故,我不能享有拥有全部感官的儿童从普通小学的各种练习中、从和他们的学校伙伴和玩伴的日常谈话中、以及从他们的父母和其他成年人中的谈话中得来的那些好处。”

“我能够通过自然的符号或者手势向我的父母和兄弟传递我的思想和感受;通过同样的媒介,我能够理解他们对我说了些什么;然而,我们的交流局限于日常家庭事物,并且几乎没有超越我自己的观察范围……”

“我父亲采取了一种做法,他认为这多少可以为我的听力丧失做一些补偿。这种做法就是,当有生意需要他出国的时候,他

and he took me more frequently than he did my brothers; giving, as the reason for his apparent partiality, that they could acquire information through the ear, while I depended solely upon my eye for acquaintance with affairs of the outside world. . . . "

"I have a vivid recollection of the delight I felt in watching the different scenes we passed through, observing the various phases of nature, both animate and inanimate; though we did not, owing to my infirmity, engage in conversation. It was during those delightful rides, some two or three years before my initiation into the rudiments of written language, that I began to ask myself the question : *How came the world into being* ? When this question occurred to my mind, I set myself to thinking it over a long time. My curiosity was awakened as to what was the origin of human life in its first appearance upon the earth, and of vegetable life as well, and also the cause of the existence of the earth, sun, moon, and stars."

"I remember at one time when my eye fell upon a very large old stump which we happened to pass in one of our rides, I asked myself, 'Is it possible that the first man that ever came into the world rose out of that stump ? But that stump is only a remnant of a once noble magnificent tree, and how came that tree ? Why, it came only by beginning to grow out of the ground just like those little trees now coming up.' And I dismissed from my mind, as an absurd idea, the connection between the origin of man and a decaying old stump. . . . "

"I have no recollection of what it was that first suggested to me the question as to the origin of things. I had before this time gained ideas of the descent from parent to child, of the propagation of animals, and of the production of plants from seeds. The question that occurred to my mind was: whence came the first man, the first animal, and the first plant, at the remotest distance of time,

就带着我和他一起走，并且他带我出去要比带我的兄弟们出去得更频繁一些；他为这种明显偏爱所给出的理由是，他们能够通过耳朵来获得信息，而我只能依靠我的眼睛来熟悉外部世界所发生的事情。……”

“我还清楚地记得当我们观赏我们所经过的不同景色时，当我们观察各种有生命的或者无生命的自然状态时，我所感受到的那种喜悦；尽管由于我的缺陷，我们并没有交谈。正是在这些愉快的旅行期间，大约是我开始学习书面语言基础知识的两三年前，我开始问自己这样一个问题：世界是如何产生的？当这个问题出现在我的心中时，我让自己思考这个问题思考了很久。最初显现在地球上的人类生命以及植物生命的起源是什么，还有地球、太阳、月亮和星星的存在原因是什么，对于这些问题，我的好奇心被唤醒了。”

“我记得有一次，当我的目光落在了在我们的一次旅行中偶然遇到的一棵非常大的古老树桩上时，我问自己，‘第一个来到世界上的人有可能来源于那个树桩吗？但是那个树桩只是一棵曾经高贵宏伟的大树的残留物，而且那棵大树是怎么来的呢？哎呀呀，它的出现只是由于开始从土地上生长出来而实现的，就像现在正在生长着的小树那样。’于是我将人的起源与一棵腐朽的老树桩之间的联系，当作一种荒谬的观点，从心中排除了出去。……”

“我不记得是什么最初向我提示了事物的起源这一问题。我在这之前已经获得了从父母到孩子的家系观念、动物繁殖的观念以及种子生成植物的观念。出现在我心中的问题是，在最早的时候，并且在此之前没有人、动物、植物存在的时候，那第一个人、第

before which there was no man, no animal, no plant; since I knew they all had a beginning and an end."

"It is impossible to state the exact order in which these different questions arose, i. e., about men, animals, plants, the earth, son, moon, etc. The lower animals did not receive so much thought as was bestowed upon man and the earth; perhaps because I put man and beast in the same class, since I believed that man would be annihilated and there was no resurrection beyond the grave,—though I am told by my mother that, in answer to my question, in the case of a deceased uncle who looked to me like a person in sleep, she had tried to make me understand that he would awake in the far future. It was my belief that man and beast derived their being from the same source, and were to be laid down in the dust in a state of annihilation. Considering the brute animal as of secondary importance, and allied to man on a lower level, man and the earth were the two things on which my mind dwelled most."

"I think I was five years old, when I began to understand the descent from parent to child and the propagation of animals. I was nearly eleven years old, when I entered the Institution where I was educated; and I remember distinctly that it was at least two years before this time that I began to ask myself the question as to the origin of the universe. My age was then about eight, not over nine years."

"Of the form of the earth, I had no idea in my childhood, except that, from a look at a map of the hemispheres, I inferred there were two immense disks of matter lying near each other. I also believed the sun and moon to be round, flat plates of illuminating matter; and for those luminaries I entertained a sort of reverence on account of their power of lighting and heating the earth. I thought from their coming up and going down, travelling across the sky in so regular a manner that there must be a certain something having power to govern their course. I believed the sun went into a hole at the west and came out of another at the east, travelling through a great tube in the earth,

一个动物和第一个植物是从哪里来的;因为我知道它们都有一个开端和结尾。"

"说出这些不同问题出现的确切顺序是不可能的,这些问题是关于人、动物、植物、地球、太阳、月亮等等的问题。对低等动物的思考不像对人和地球的思考那样多;可能是因为我把人和兽类放入了同一类中了,因为我相信人是会死的,并且不会从坟墓中复活——尽管我母亲在回答我的问题的时候,她以我的一个已故叔叔为例,这位叔叔在我看来就好像是睡着了,她试图使我理解,他是会在遥远的未来醒来的。我相信,人和兽类的存在得自于相同的来源,并且会在一种死亡的状态中被放入泥土中。考虑到野兽是次等重要的,并且在较低的层次上和人相关联,人和地球就成为我的心灵沉思最多的两种事物了。"

"我想我是在五岁的时候开始理解从父母到孩子的家系和动物的繁殖的。大约在十一岁的时候,我进入了一家教育机构,在那里我受到了教育;而且我还清楚地记得,至少是在这个时间的两年前我就开始问自己宇宙的起源这种问题了。当时我大概八岁,没有超过九岁。"

"关于地球的形状,除了在地图上看到的那两个半球,并且从中推断出存在有两个彼此离得很近的巨大的物质圆盘,此外,我在童年时代对其一无所知。我还相信太阳和月亮是由发光物质构成的圆的、扁平的盘子;由于它们具有照亮和温暖地球的力量,我对那些发光体怀有一种尊敬之情。我想,由于它们升起来又降下去,以一种非常规律的方式在天空中穿行,一定存在有某种东西,它有能力控制它们的行程。我相信太阳落入了西边的一个洞中,而且从东边的另一个洞中出来,其间穿过了地球中的一个大

describing the same curve as it seemed to describe in the sky. The stars seemed to me to be tiny lights studded in the sky."

"The source from which the universe came was the question about which my mind revolved in a vain struggle to grasp it, or rather to fight the way up to attain to a satisfactory answer. When I had occupied myself with this subject a considerable time, I perceived that it was a matter much greater than my mind could comprehend; and I remember well that I became so appalled at its mystery and so bewildered at my inability to grapple with it that I laid the subject aside and out of my mind, glad to escape being, as it were, drawn into a vortex of inextricable confusion. Though I felt relieved at this escape, yet I could not resist the desire to know the truth; and I returned to the subject; but as before, I left it, after thinking it over for some time. In this state of perplexity, I hoped all the time to get at the truth, still believing that the more I gave thought to the subject, the more my mind would penetrate the mystery. Thus I was tossed like a shuttlecock, returning to the subject and recoiling from it, till I came to school."

"I remember that my mother once told me about a being up above, pointing her finger towards the sky and with a solemn look on her countenance. I do not recall the circumstance which led to this communication. When she mentioned the mysterious being up in the sky, I was eager to take hold of the subject, and plied her with questions concerning the form and appearance of this unknown being, asking if it was the sun, moon, or one of the stars. I knew she meant that there was a living one somewhere up in the sky; but when I realized that she could not answer my questions, I gave it up in despair, feeling sorrowful that I could not obtain a definite idea of the mysterious living one up in the sky."

管子，并且其行进的路线和在天空中描画出的曲线似乎相同。星星似乎在我看来是镶嵌在天空中的微弱的发光体。”

“宇宙的起源问题一直萦绕在我心中，为了把握它，或者毋宁说为了尽力地获得一个满意的答案，我付出了徒劳的努力。当我在相当长的时间里使自己专注于这个问题的时候，我认识到这个问题太大了，我的心灵不能理解；而且我还清楚地记得，我对这个问题的神秘性感到非常地惊骇，并且对我没有能力战胜它而感到非常地困惑，因而我把这个问题放到了一边，并且让它离开了我的心中，好像为避免了卷入无法解脱的混乱漩涡中而感到高兴。虽然这种逃避使我感到解脱了，但是我还是无法抗拒认识真理的欲望；而且我再一次回到了这一问题上来；但是，和以前一样，在对它仔细地思考了一段时间之后，我还是遗弃了它。在这种困惑混乱的状态中，我始终希望到达真理，而且我仍然相信，我越是思考这一问题，我的心灵就越是能看穿这种神秘性。从而，我就像一个被投掷的羽毛球，返回到这一问题上来，然后又反弹了回去，直到我进入了学校。”

“我记得我母亲有一次给我讲天上的一个存在，她用手指指着天空，脸上带着严肃的表情。我不记得导致这次交流的详细情况了。当她提到天空中那神秘的存在时，我渴望把握这一问题，并且不断地向她提出关于这个未知的存在的形式和显现的问题，询问它是否是太阳、月亮或者是其中的一颗星星。我知道她的意思是说，在天空中某个地方有一个有生命的存在；但是当我意识到她不能回答我的问题的时候，我在绝望中放弃了它，我感到遗憾的是我不能对天空中神秘的有生命的存在获得一个明确的观念。”

"One day, while we were haying in a field, there was a series of heavy thunder-claps. I asked one of my brothers where they came from. He pointed to the sky and made a zigzag motion with his finger, signifying lightning. I imagined there was a great man somewhere in the blue vault, who made a loud noise with his voice out of it; and each time I heard[①] a thunder-clap I was frightened, and looked up at the sky, fearing he was speaking a threatening word."[②]

Here we may pause. The reader sees by this time that it makes little or no difference in what sort of mind-stuff, in what quality of imagery, his thinking goes on. The only images *intrinsically* important are the halting-places, the substantive conclusions, provisional or final, of the thought. Throughout all the rest of the stream, the feelings of relation are everything, and the terms related almost naught. These feelings of relation, these psychic overtones, halos, suffusions, or fringes about the terms, may be the same in very different systems of imagery. A diagram may help to accentuate this indifference of the mental means where the end is the same. Let *A* be some experience from which a number of thinkers start. Let *Z* be the practical conclusion rationally inferrible from it.

---

① Not literally *heard*, of course. Deaf mutes are quick to perceive shocks and jars that can be felt, even when so slight as to be unnoticed by those who can hear.

② Quoted by Samuel Porter: 'Is Thought possible without Language?' in Princetou Review, 57th year, pp 108-12 (Jau. 1881?). Cf. also W. W. Ireland : The Blot upon the Brain (1886), Paper X, part Ⅱ; G. J. Romanes : Mental Evolution in Man, pp. 81-83, and references therein made. Prof. Max Muller gives a very complete history of this controversy in pp. 30-64 of his ' Science of Thought' (1887). His own view is that Thought and Speech are inseparable; but under speech he includes any conceivable sort of symbolism or even mental imagery, and he makes no allowance for the wordless summary glimpses which we have of systems of relation and direction.

“一天，当我们正在田间割草的时候，响起了一阵巨大的雷鸣声。我问我的一个兄弟说，它们从哪里来。他指着天空并且用他的手指做了一个Z字形动作，表示闪电。我设想，在蓝色拱顶中的某个地方有一个巨人，他用自己的嗓子发出了喧闹的噪音；而且我每次听见①雷声时都感到害怕，我抬头看着天空，害怕他正在说着一个吓人的词。”②

在这里我们可以停下来了。读者这次看到了，他的思维的进行是凭借着一种什么精神素材，是凭借着什么样性质的意象，这都没有太大的不同，或者说这都一样。具有本质重要性的唯一意象就是思想的犹豫之处、思想的暂时的实体性结论和最终的实体性结论。在思想之流的所有剩余部分中，关系感受就是一切，而相关的表达项几乎是无。这些关系感受，这些围绕着那些表达项的精神泛音、晕轮、弥漫或者边缘，在非常不同的意象系统中可能都是一样的。下面的图示可能有助于强调，在目的是一样的情况下，心理手段是无关紧要的。让*A*代表一些思想者所由以开始的一些经验。让*Z*代表从*A*合理地推断出来的实际结论。一个人

---

① 当然不是字面意义上的听见。聋哑人能够很快地知觉到能够被感受到的冲击和震动，甚至当冲击和震动是如此地微小以至于没有引起那些能听到的人的注意的时候，他们也能够如此。

② 塞缪尔·波特的引文：“没有语言思想是可能的吗？”《普林斯顿研究》，第57年，第108~112页（1881年？1月）。也可参见W. W. 爱尔兰：《大脑的瑕疵》（1886年），第10篇，第2部分；G. J. 里奇特：《人的心理进化》，第81~83页，以及那里指出的参考书目。马克思·弥勒在其《思想科学》（1887年，第30~64页）中，对这一争论的历史做了一个完整的记录。他自己的观点是，思想和言语是不可分的；但是他将能够想得到的所有符号或者甚至是心理意象都包括在了言语之下，但是他没有将我们所说的对关系和方向系统的无言的即刻一瞥也包括进去。

One gets to the conclusion by one line, another by another; one follows a course of English, another of German, verbal imagery. With one, visual images predominate; with another, tactile. Some trains are tinged with emotions, others not; some are very abridged, synthetic and rapid, others, hesitating and broken into many steps. But when the penultimate terms of all the trains, however differing *inter se*, finally shoot into the same conclusion, we say and rightly say, that all the thinkers have had substantially the same thought. It would probably astound each of them beyond measure to be let into his neighbor's mind and to find how different the scenery there was from that in his own.

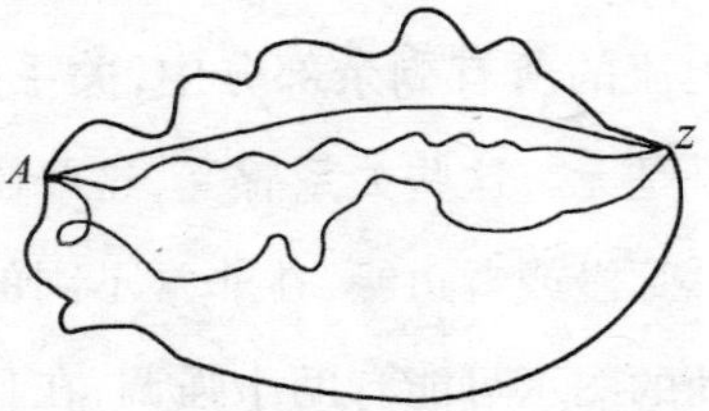

FIG. 28

Thought is in fact a kind of Algebra, as Berkeley long ago said, "in which, though a particular quantity be marked by each letter, yet to proceed right, it is not requisite that in every step each letter suggest to your thoughts that particular quantity it was appointed to stand for." Mr. Lewes has developed this algebra-analogy so well that I must quote his words:

" The leading characteristic of algebra is that of operation on relations. This also is the leading characteristic of Thought. Algebra cannot exist without values, nor Thought without Feelings. The

由一条线到达结论，另一个人由另一条线到达结论；一个人遵循的是使用英语词语意象的线路，另一个人遵循的是使用德语词语意象的线路。在一个人那里，视觉意象占优势；在另一个人那里，触觉意象占优势。一些序列里夹杂着情绪，而其他的则没有；有些序列非常精简、综合和迅速，而其他的则是犹豫的，并且分解为许多步骤。但是，当所有序列的倒数第二个表达项，不论它们之间如何不同，最终进入了同一个结论的时候，我们就说，而且是正确地说，所有的思想者实质上获有了相同的思想。如果将这些思想者领入其同伴的心中，他将会发现那里的风景和他自己的比起来有多么地不同，这种情况可能会使他们中的每一个人都极为吃惊。

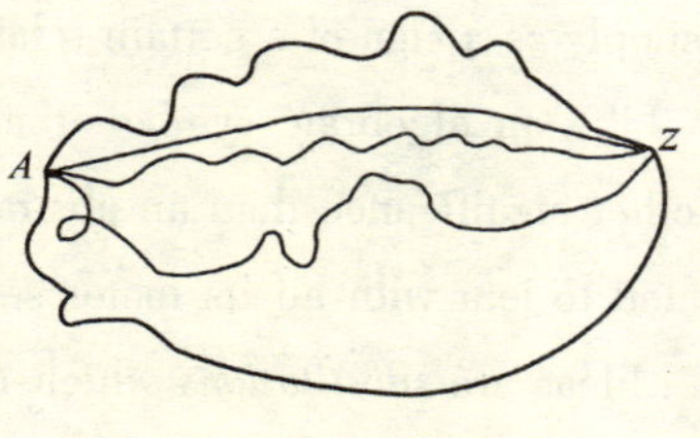

图 28

事实上思想是一种代数，如贝克莱在很久以前所说的那样，"在其中，尽管每一个特殊的量都由一个字母所表示，然而要正确地进行下去，每一个字母不需要在每一步中都向你的思想提示它被指定用来代表的那个特殊的量。"路易斯先生非常好地发展了这种代数类比的说法，因而我必须引用他的话：

"代数的首要特征是对关系的运算。这也是思维的首要特征。代数不能离开值而存在，思维也不能离开感受而存在。在赋值之

operations are so many blank forms till the values are assigned. Words are vacant sounds, ideas are blank forms, unless they symbolize images and sensations which are their values. Nevertheless it is rigorously true, and of the greatest importance, that analysts carry on very extensive operations with blank forms, never pausing to supply the symbols with values until the calculation is completed; and ordinary men, no less than philosophers, carry on long trains of thought without pausing to translate their ideas (words) into images. . . . Suppose some one from a distance shouts 'a lion!' At once the man starts in alarm. . . . To the man the word is not only an . . . expression of all that he has seen and heard of lions, capable of recalling various experiences, but is also capable of taking its place in a connected series of thoughts without recalling any of those experiences, without reviving an image, however faint, of the lion—simply as a sign of a certain relation included in the complex so named. Like an algebraic symbol it may be operated on without conveying other significance than an abstract relation: it is a sign of Danger, related to fear with all its motor sequences. Its logical position suffices. . . . Ideas are *substitutions* which require a secondary process when what is symbolized by them is translated into the images and experiences it replaces; and this secondary process is frequently not performed at all, generally only performed to a very small extent. Let anyone closely examine what has passed in his mind when he has constructed a chain of reasoning, and he will be surprised at the fewness and faintness of the images which have accompanied the ideas. Suppose you inform me that 'the blood rushed violently from the man's heart, quickening his pulse at the sight of his enemy.' Of the many latent images in this phrase, how many were salient in your mind and in mine? Probably two—the man and his enemy—and these images were faint. Images of blood, heart,

前，运算一直都是很多空白的形式。除非词语和观念象征了作为它们的值的意象和感觉，否则词语是空白的声音，观念是空白的形式。然而，确切无疑和至关重要的是，分析者用空白的形式进行非常广泛的运算，在计算完成之前，从来不会停下来给符号赋值；而且普通人和哲学家一样，在进行很多步骤的思维时，也不会停下来将他们的观念（词语）转化成意象。……设想某人在远处喊，'一只狮子！'那个人立刻开始惊慌了。……对那个人来说，这个词不仅仅表达了他对狮子的所见所闻，能够使他回忆起各种各样的经历，而且这个词在没有使他回忆起任何那些经历的情况下，在没有唤醒任何关于狮子的无论多么微弱的意象的情况下，它也能在一系列有联系的思想中占有一席之地——仅仅作为了某个包含在被如此命名的联合体中的关系的符号。像代数符号一样，对它进行运算的时候，它除了传递抽象关系以外可以不传达其他意义：它是一个关于危险的符号，以其所有运动序列与恐惧相关。它的逻辑地位是充分的。……观念将是需要一个次级过程的替代物，当通过次级过程的作用它所象征的东西被转化成了它所替换了的意象和经验的时候，观念就成为了替代物；并且这种次级过程常常完全得不到执行，通常只是在很小的范围里才得以执行。让任何一个人仔细地检查一下，当他构建一个推理链条的时候，有什么东西从他的心灵中经过了，那么，他将会惊奇的是，与观念相伴随的意象是多么地少、多么地微弱。假设你告诉我，'看到敌人，血液猛烈地从那个人的心脏中喷涌了出来，加速了他的脉搏跳动。'就这个句子中的许多潜在的意象而言，在你的心中以及在我的心中有多少是显而易见的呢？可能有两个——那个人和他的敌人——并且这些意象是微弱的。关于血液、心

violent rushing, pulse, quickening, and sight, were either not revived at all, or were passing shadows. Had any such images arisen, they would have hampered thought, retarding the logical process of judgment by irrelevant connections. The symbols had substituted *relations* for these *values*. . . . There are no images of two things and three things, when I say 'two and three equal five;' there are simply familiar symbols having precise relations. . . . The verbal symbol' horse,' which stands for all our experiences of horses, serves all the purposes of Thought, without recalling one of the images clustered in the perception of horses, just as the sight of a horse's form serves all the purposes of *recognition* without recalling the sound of its neighing or its tramp, its qualities as an animal of draught, and so forth. "①

It need only be added that as the Algebrist, though the sequence of his terms is fixed by their relations rather than by their several values, must give a real value to the *final* one he reaches; so the thinker in words must let his concluding word or phrase be translated into its full sensible-image-value, under penalty of the thought being left unrealized and pale.

This is all I have to say about the sensible continuity and unity of our thought as contrasted with the apparent discreteness of the words, images, and other means by which it seems to be carried on. Between all their substantives elements there is 'transitive' consciousness, and the words and images are 'fringed,' and not as discrete as to a careless view they seem. Let us advance now to the next head in our description of

① Problems of Life and Mind, 3d Series, Problem IV, chapter 5. Compare also Victor Egger: La Parole Intérieure (Paris, 1881), chap. VI.

脏、猛烈的喷涌、脉搏、加速以及看见这些意象，或者完全没有被唤醒，或者成了经过的影子。如果这些意象出现的话，他们会妨碍思维，通过不相关的连接来延迟判断的逻辑过程。符号用关系替代了这些值。……当我说‘二加三等于五’的时候，这里没有关于两个事物和三个事物的意象；这里有的仅仅是获有精确关系的熟悉的符号。……代表我们关于马的所有经验的词语符号，适用于思维的所有意图，而无需回忆起簇生于对马的知觉之中的任何一个意象，正如关于马的形状的视觉适用于所有识别的意图，而无需回忆起它的嘶叫声或脚步声，以及它作为一个拉运东西的动物所具有的品质，等等。”①

唯一需要补充的是，作为一个代数学家，尽管他所用术语的序列是通过它们的关系而不是通过它们各自的值而得以固定的，但是他必须将一个真实的值赋予他最后到达的那个术语；因此使用词语的思考者必须将他的结论性的词语或者句子转化为完全的感觉意象值，否则就会受到思想没能实现并且变得苍白的惩罚。

作为与思维似乎由以进行的词语、意象以及其他手段的明显不连续性相对照的、我们思维的可感觉的连续性和统一性，对它我必须要说的就这么多了。在它们的所有实体性要素之间，存在有“过渡性”意识，并且词语和意象都是有“边缘”的，并且不像对一种疏忽的观点而言它们似乎是不连续的，它们不是不连续的。现在，让我们进入到对思想之流的下一个描述中，并开始这

① 《生命与心灵的问题》，第 3 卷，问题 4，第 5 章。也可以比较维克多·埃格：《内部话语》（巴黎，1881 年），第 6 章。

Thought's stream.

4) *Human thought appears to deal with objects independent of itself; that is, it is cognitive, or possesses the function of knowing.*

For Absolute Idealism, the infinite Thought and its objects are one. The Objects are, through being thought; the eternal Mind is, through thinking them. Were a human thought alone in the world there would be no reason for any other assumption regarding it. Whatever it might have before it would be its vision, would be there, in *its* 'there,' or then, in *its* 'then'; and the question would never arise whether an extra-mental duplicate of it existed or not. The reason why we all believe that the objects of our thoughts have a duplicate existence outside, is that there are *many* human thoughts, each with the *same* objects, as we cannot help supposing. The judgment that *my* thought has the same object as *his* thought is what makes the psychologist call my thought cognitive of an outer reality. The judgment that my own past thought and my own present thought are of the same object is what makes *me* take the object out of either and project it by a sort of triangulation into an independent position, from which it may *appear* to both. *Sameness* in a multiplicity of objective appearances is thus the basis of our belief in realities outside of thought.① In Chapter XII we shall have to take up the judgment of sameness again.

To show that the question of reality being extra-mental or not is not likely to arise in the absence of repeated experiences of the *same*, take the example of an altogether unprecedented experience, such as a

---

① If but one person sees an apparition we consider it is private hallucination. If more than one, we begin to think it may be a real external presence.

一描述吧。

4. 人类的思想显现为处理独立于它自身的对象；更确切地说，它是认知的，或者拥有认识的功能。

对于绝对的唯心主义而言，无限的思想和其对象是一个东西。对象是通过被思考而存在；永恒的心灵是通过思考它们而存在。如果世界上只有一个人的思想，那就没有任何理由对它做出任何其他的假定。无论它面前有什么，那都是它的幻象，将会在那里，在它的"那里"，或者将会在那时，在它的"那时"；并且它的精神以外的副本是否存在这一问题将永远也不会出现。我们所有人之所以相信我们的思想对象有一个副本存在于外界，是因为存在有许多人类的思想，每一个都是关于相同对象的，所以我们禁不住要如此假设。我的思维和他的思维拥有相同的对象，这一判断使得心理学家称我的思维对外部实在是认知的。我自己的过去的思想和现在的思想是关于相同对象的思想，这一判断使得我将对象从二者中拿了出来，并且通过形成某种三角形的方法将它投射到一个独立的位置上来，从那里它可以向两者显现出来。对象显现的多样性中的同一性因此是我们相信在思想之外有实在的基础。① 在第 12 章，我们将再次讨论同一性判断。

为了表明实在是否存在于精神之外这一问题在没有出现重复的相同经验的情况下是不可能出现的，让我们列举一个完全是史无前例的经验的例子，比如喉咙里的一种新味道。它是一个主

---

① 如果只有一个人看见了离奇的东西，我们就认为它是私人的幻觉。如果有不止一个人看见了，我们就会开始认为，它可能是一个真实的外部存在。

new taste in the throat. Is it a subjective quality of feeling, or an objective quality felt? You do not even ask the question at this point. It is simply *that taste*. But if a doctor hears you describe it, and says: "Ha! Now you know what *heartburn* is," then it becomes a quality already existent *extra mentem tuam*, which you in turn have come upon and learned. The first spaces, times, things, qualities, experienced by the child probably appear, like the first heartburn, in this absolute way, as simple *beings*, neither in nor out of thought. But later, by having other thoughts than this present one, and making repeated judgments of sameness among their objects, he corroborates in himself the notion of realities, past and distant as well as present, which realities no one single thought either possesses or engenders, but which all may contemplate and know. This, as was stated in the last chapter, is the *psychological* point of view, the relatively uncritical non-idealistic point of view of all natural science, beyond which this book cannot go. A mind which has become conscious of its own cognitive function, plays what we have called 'the psychologist' upon itself. It not only knows the things that appear before it; it knows that it knows them. This stage of reflective condition is, more or less explicitly, our habitual adult state of mind.

It cannot, however, be regarded as primitive. The consciousness of objects must come first. We seem to lapse into this primordial condition when consciousness is reduced to a minimum by the inhalation of anæsthetics or during a faint. Many persons testify that at a certain stage of the anæsthetic process objects are still cognized whilst the thought of self is lost. Professor Herzen says:①

---

① Revue Philosophique, vol. XXI. p. 671.

观性质的感受，还是一个被感受到了的客观性质？在这种情况下你甚至都不会问这样的问题。它仅仅是那种味道。但是，如果一个医生听到你描述了它，并且说："哈！现在你知道什么是胃灼热了吧。"从而，它就变成了一种已经超出思想事物之外而存在的性质了，反过来说，你遇上了它，并且了解了它。被孩子所体验到的最初的空间、时间、事物、性质，可能和最初的胃灼热一样，作为简单的存在，以这种绝对的方式，既不在思想中也不在思想之外显现了出来。但是后来，由于除了这个当前的思想之外又有了别的思想，并且通过在这些对象之间反复地做出同一性判断，他就在自己心中确证了实在的观点，这些过去的、遥远的以及目前的实在，任何一个单独的思想都不能拥有它们或者产生它们，但是所有的思想都可以对它们进行沉思和认识。如上一章所陈述的那样，这就是心理学的观点，是相对而言可以不加批判的所有自然科学的非唯心主义观点，本书的讨论不能超越这一观点。一个已经变得能够意识到自己的认知功能的心灵，对其自身扮演的是我们所说的"心理学家"的角色。它不仅知道显现在它面前的事物，而且它还知道它知道它们。这一或多或少明确的反省状态，就是我们惯常的成年人的心理状态。

然而，它不能被认作是原始的。关于对象的意识必须首先出来。当意识由于麻醉剂的吸入或者在昏厥期间减小到最小值的时候，我们似乎就堕入了这种原始状态。许多人都证明了，在麻醉过程的某一特定阶段，对象依然能够被认知，而对自我的思维却丧失了。赫茨恩教授说：①

① 《哲学评论》，第 21 卷，第 671 页。

" During the syncope there is absolute psychic annihilation, the absence of all consciousness; then at the beginning of coming to, one has at a certain moment a vague, limitless, infinite feeling—a sense of *existence in general* without the least trace of distinction between the me and the not-me."

Dr. Shoemaker of Philadelphia describes during the deepest conscious stage of ether-intoxication a vision of

" two endless parallel lines in. swift longitudinal motion... on a uniform misty background ... together with a constant sound or whirr, not loud but distinct... which seemed to be connected with the parallel lines.... These phenomena occupied the whole field. There were present no dreams or visions in any way connected with human affairs, no ideas or impressions akin to anything in past experience, no emotions, of course no idea of personality. There was no conception as to what being it was that was regarding the two lines, or that there existed any such thing as such a being; the lines and waves were all." ①

Similarly a friend of Mr. Herbert Spencer, quoted by him in 'Mind' (vol Ⅲ. p. 556), speaks of " an undisturbed empty quiet everywhere except that a stupid presence lay like a heavy intrusion *somewhere*—a blotch on the calm." This sense of objectivity and lapse of subjectivity, even when the object is almost indefinable, is, it seems to me, a somewhat familiar phase in chloroformization, though in my own case it is too deep a phase for any articulate aftermemory to remain. I only know that as it

---

① Quoted from the Therapeutic Gazette; by the N. Y. Semi-weekly Evening Post for Nov. 2, 1886.

"在昏厥期间会出现绝对的精神覆没,所有意识都消失了;然后在开始苏醒的时候,在某一时刻人们会有一种模糊的、无限的、极大的感受——一种关于一般存在的感觉,这种感觉在我和非我之间没有任何区分的迹象。"

费城的舒梅克博士描述了在乙醚致醉最深的意识阶段期间出现的一种幻象:

"两条没有尽头的、在快速的纵向运动中的平行线……处于相同的薄雾背景之下……与它们一起的还有一种持续的声音或说呼呼声,声音不大但却清楚……这声音似乎是与平行线有联系的。……这些现象占据了整个视野。这里没有出现以任何方式与人类事物相联系的梦或幻象,没有任何与过去经验中的任何事物相类似的观念或印象,没有情绪,当然也没有任何人格观念。对于关注着这两条线的是一个什么样的存在而言,或者对于这里存在着作为这样一种存在的任何这样的东西而言,则完全没有任何概念;线条与波动就是一切。"①

同样,赫伯特·斯宾塞先生的一个朋友说:"到处都是安静的没有受到打扰的空虚,除了在某处有一种令人乏味的存在以外,它放置在那里就像是一种严重的侵扰——平静中的一个大斑点(这些话被斯宾塞先生在其《心理》中引用了,第 3 卷,第 556 页)。"这种客观性的感觉和主观性的丧失,甚至当对象几乎是无法定义的时候,似乎对我而言也是氯仿麻醉中一个有些熟悉的阶段,尽管在我自己这里,它是一个十分深层的阶段,不能为任何表达清晰的随后记忆所保留。我只是知道,当它消失了的时候,我

---

① 引自《治疗学报》;转引自《纽约半周邮报》,1886 年 11 月 2 日。

vanishes I seem to wake to a sense of my own existence as something additional to what had previously been there. ①

Many philosophers, however, hold that the reflective consciousness of the self is essential to the cognitive function of thought. They hold that a thought, in order to know a thing at all, must expressly distinguish between the thing and its own self. ②This is a perfectly wanton assumption, and not the faintest shadow of reason exists for supposing it true. As well might I contend that I cannot dream without dreaming that I dream, swear without swearing that I swear, deny without denying that I deny, as maintain that I cannot know without knowing that I know. I may have either acquaintance-with, or knowledge-about, an object O without think about myself at all It suffices for this that I think O, and

① In half-stunned states self-consciousness may lapse. A friend writes me: "We were driving back from—in a wagonette. The door flew open and X., alias 'Baldy,' fell out on the road. We pulled up at once, and then he said, 'Did anybody fall out?' or 'Who fell out?'—I don't exactly remember the words. When told that Baldy fell out, he said, 'Did Baldy fall out? Poor Baldy!'"

② Kant originated this view. I subjoin a few English statements of it. J. Ferrier, Institutes of Metaphysic, Proposition I: "Along with whatever any intelligence knows it must, as the ground or condition of its knowledge, have some knowledge of itself." Sir Wm. Hamilton, Discussions, p. 47: "We know, and we know that we know,—these propositions, logically distinct, are really identical; each implies the other.... So true is the scholastic brocard: *non sentimus nisi sentiamus nos sentire.*" H. L. Mansel, Metaphysics, p. 58: "Whatever variety of materials may exist within reach of my mind, I can become conscious of them only by recognizing them as mine.... Relation to the conscious self is thus the permanent and universal feature which every state of consciousness as such must exhibit." T. H. Green, Introduction to Hume, p. 12: "A consciousness by the man ... of himself, in negative relation to the thing that is his object, and this consciousness must be taken to go along with the perceptive act itself. Not less than this indeed can be involved in any act that is to be the beginning of knowledge at all. It is the minimum of possible thought or intelligence."

似乎认识到一种自我存在的感觉，它作为了先前已经存在于那里的东西的附加物。①

然而，很多哲学家坚持认为，反省式的自我意识是思维认知功能的本质。它们主张，为了完全认识一个事物，思维必须清楚地区分开那个事物和它的自我。② 这是一个很荒唐的假定，连假设它为真的最微弱的理由的影子都不存在。假如我主张我不能在没有知道我知道的情况下知道，我倒不如主张我不能在没有梦见我做梦的情况下做梦，我不能在没有发誓说我发誓了的情况下发誓，不能在没有否认说我否认了的情况下否认。我可以在完全没有考虑我自己的情况下，拥有关于对象 O 的相识的知识以及相知的知识。我思考着 O，并且它存在着，这就足够了。如果除了

---

① 在半昏迷状态，自我意识可能会丧失。一个朋友写信告诉我："我们正在往回行驶——乘坐的是四轮游览轻便马车。车门突然打开了，化名为'鲍迪'的 X 摔倒在路上。我们立刻停下来，这时他说，'有人摔出来了吗？'或者'谁摔出来了？'——我不能准确地记起他说了什么。当告诉他说是鲍迪摔出来了，他说，'鲍迪摔出来啦？可怜的鲍迪！'

② 康德首创了这种观点。我补充几个关于它的英文陈述。J. 费里尔，《形而上学原理》，命题 1："与任何理智所知道的不论什么东西相伴随的，必须是一些关于理智自身的知识，它是其知识的基础和条件。"Wm. 汉密尔顿先生，《讨论》，第 47 页："我们知道，并且我们知道了我们知道，——这两个命题在逻辑上截然不同，实际上却是同一的；每个命题都蕴含着另一个命题。……那句经院哲学的格言是如此真实：假如我们不觉得我们觉得，我们就不觉得。"L. 曼塞尔先生，《形而上学》，第 58 页："不论在我的心灵所及之处存在着什么样的多样性材料，我只有通过将它们认作是我的这种方法才能变得对它们有意识。……因此，与自我意识的关系就是每一个像这样的意识状态必须展示出来的永久的和普遍的特征。"T. H. 格林，《休谟导论》，第 12 页："人……对他自己的意识，与作为其对象的事物处于消极的关系之中，并且这种意识必须被看作是与知觉活动自身相伴随的。至少这确实是作为知识开端的任何活动完全要涉及的东西。它是可能的思维和理智的最小值。"

that it exist. If, in addition to thinking O, I also think that I exist and that I know O, well and good; I then know one more thing, a fact about O, of which I previously was unmindful. That, however, does not prevent me from having already known O a good deal. O *per se*, or O *plus* P, are as good objects of knowledge as O *plus me is*. The philosophers in question simply substitute one particular object for all others, and call it *the* object *par excellence*. It is a case of the 'psychologist's fallacy' (see p. 197). *They* know the object to be one thing and the thought another; and they forthwith foist their own knowledge into that of the thought of which they pretend to give a true account. To conclude, then, *thought may, but need not, in knowing, discriminate between its object and itself.*

We have been using the word Object. *Something must now be said about the proper use of the term Object in Psychology.*

In popular parlance the word object is commonly taken without reference to the act of knowledge, and treated as synonymous with individual subject of existence. Thus if anyone ask what is the mind's object when you say 'Columbus discovered America in 1492,' most people will reply 'Columbus,' or 'America,' or, at most, 'the discovery of America.' They will name a substantive kernel or nucleus of the consciousness, and say the thought is 'about' that, —as indeed it is, —and they will call that your thought's 'object.' Really that is usually only the grammatical object, or more likely the grammatical subject, of your sentence. It is at most your 'fractional object;' or you may call it the 'topic' of your thought, or the 'subject of your discourse.' But the *Object* of your thought is really its entire content or deliverance, neither more nor less. It is a vicious use of speech to take out a substantive kernel from its content and call that its object;

思考 O 之外,我还想,我存在着并且我知道 O,这很合适并且很好;那么我就又知道了一件事情,一个关于 O 的事实,我以前对它是不留心的。然而,这并不妨碍我对 O 已经有了很多了解。O 本身,或者 O 加上 P,与 O 加上我一样,都是很不错的知识的对象。相关的哲学家只是用一个特殊的对象代替了所有其他的对象,并且称其为那个与众不同的对象。这种情况是关于“心理学家的谬误”的一个例子(见第 197 页)。他们知道对象是一种东西,而思维是另一种东西;并且它们立刻将他们自己的知识私自添加到他们伪称要给予真实论述的关于思维的知识之中了。因而,一句话,思维在进行认识的时候,可以但却不是必须在它的对象和它自身之间做出区分。

我们一直在使用对象这个词。现在必须讨论一下“对象”这一术语在心理学中的特有用法。

在一般人的谈话中,对象这个词的使用通常与认识活动无关,并且它被看作是与单独存在的主题同义的。因此,如果有人问,当你说“哥伦布在 1492 年发现了美洲”时,心灵的对象是什么,大多数人将会回答说是“哥伦布”、“美洲”或者至多是“美洲的发现”。他们将会指出意识的一个实体性的内核或说核子,并且说思维就是“关于”这些东西的思维,——好像它确实如此,——然后他们将会把这些东西称作你的思维的“对象”。事实上,那通常只是你所说句子的语法上的宾语,或者更可能是语法上的主语。它至多是你的“部分对象”;或者你可以把它称作你的思想的“主题”,或者“你谈话的题目”。但是,你的思维的对象事实上是它的全部内容或说意见,不多也不少。将一个实体性的内核从它的内容中提取出来并且称那是它的对象,这是对言语的一

and it is an equally vicious use of speech to add a substantive kernel not articulately included in its content, and to call that its object. Yet either one of these two sins we commit, whenever we content ourselves with saying that a given thought is simply 'about' a certain topic, or that that topic is its 'object.' The object of my thought in the previous sentence, for example, is strictly speaking neither Columbus, nor America, nor its discovery. It is nothing short of the entire sentence, 'Columbus-discovered-America-in-1492.' And if we wish to speak of it substantively, we must make a substantive of it by writing it out thus with hyphens between all its words. Nothing but this can possibly name its delicate idiosyncrasy. And if we wish to *feel* that idiosyncrasy we must reproduce the thought as it was uttered, with every word fringed and the whole sentence bathed in that original halo of obscure relations, which, like an horizon, then spread about its meaning.

Our psychological duty is to cling as closely as possible to the actual constitution of the thought we are studying. We may err as much by excess as by defect. If the kernel or 'topic,' Columbus, is in one way less than the thought's object, so in another way it may be more. That is, when named by the psychologist, it may mean much more than actually is present to the thought of which he is reporter. Thus, for example, suppose you should go on to think: 'He was a daring genius!' An ordinary psychologist would not hesitate to say that the object of your thought was still 'Columbus.' True, your thought is *about* Columbus. It 'terminates' in Columbus, leads from and to the direct idea of Columbus. But for the moment it is not fully and immediately Columbus, it is only 'he,' or rather 'he-was-a-daring-genius;' which, though it may be an unimportant difference for conversational purposes,

种恶意使用;而且,将一个没有被清楚地看到包含在它的内容中的实体性的内核添加进它的内容里,并且称那是它的对象,这同样是对语言的一种恶意使用。然而,只要我们使自己满足于说一个给定的思想仅仅是“关于”某个特定的主题的,或者说那个主题是它的“对象”,那么我们就会犯下这两种错误中的任何一种错误。例如,在前面的那句话中,我的思维的对象严格说来既不是哥伦布,也不是美洲,更不是发现。它完全是整个句子,“哥伦布在1492年发现了美洲”。而且如果我们想要实体性地讨论它,我们必须通过在写出它的时候将所有的词语用连字号连起来的方式使它成为一个独立存在的实体。只有这样才有可能指出其精致的特性。而且如果我们希望感受到那特性,我们就必须像它被说出来的那样再现这种思想,让每一个词语都被缘饰在那种模糊关系的原初晕轮之中,让整个句子都沐浴在那种模糊关系的原初晕轮之中,这晕轮就像是一道地平线,在它的意义周围分散开来。

我们心理学的任务就是尽可能地贴近我们所研究的思想的真实构造。过度与不足都会使我们犯错误。如果哥伦布这个内核或主题在一种情形下少于思维的对象,那么在另一种情形下它就会多于思维的对象。也就是说,当心理学家命名它的时候,它的含义可能比心理学家所报告的那个思想所实际呈现出来的意义要更多一些。因而,例如,假设你会继续想:“他是一个有胆量的天才!”一位普通的心理学家会毫不犹豫地说,你的思维的对象依然是“哥伦布”。确实,你的思想是关于哥伦布的。它“终止于”哥伦布,引起并且导致哥伦布的直接观念。但是,此时它并非完全并且直接地就是哥伦布,它只是“他”,或者毋宁说它是“他是一个有胆量的天才”;尽管这对于谈话意图而言是一种不重要的区

is, for introspective psychology, as great a difference as there can be.

The object of every thought, then, is neither more nor less than all that the thought thinks, exactly as the thought thinks it, however complicated the matter, and however symbolic the manner of the thinking may be. It is needless to say that memory can seldom accurately reproduce such an object, when once it has passed from before the mind. It either makes too little or too much of it. Its best plan is to repeat the verbal sentence, if there was one, in which the object was expressed. But for inarticulate thoughts there is not even this resource, and introspection mast confess that the task exceeds her powers. The mass of our thinking vanishes for ever, beyond hope of recovery, and psychology only gathers up a few of the crumbs that fall from the feast.

The next point to make clear is that, *however complex the object may be, the thought of it is one undivided state of consciousness.* As Thomas Brown says:①

"I have already spoken too often to require again to caution you against the mistake into which, I confess, that the terms which the poverty of our language obliges us to use might of themselves very naturally lead you; the mistake of supposing that the most complex states of mind are not truly, in their very essence, as much one and indivisible as those which we term simple—the complexity and seeming coexistence which they involve being relative to our feeling② only, not to their own absolute nature. I trust I need not repeat to you that, in itself, every notion, however seemingly complex, is, and must be, truly

① Lectures on the Philosophy of the Human Mind, Lecture 45.

② Instead of saying *to our feeling only*, he should have said, to the *object* only.

别,但是对于内省心理学来说,这是一个这里能够存在着的大得不能再大的区别了。

因而,每一个思维的对象就恰好是思维所思考的一切,不论事件有多么复杂,也不管思考它的方式多么具有象征性,都正如思维思考它那样。无需说的是,一旦对象从心灵面前经过了,记忆很少能够准确地再现这样一个对象。它要么再现得太少,要么再现得太多。最好的方法就是重复对象所由以表达的语句,如果这里有的话。但是对于未被清楚表达的思想来说,甚至连这种资源也没有,于是反省必须承认,这种任务超出了它的能力。我们的大部分思想都永远地消失了,没有恢复的希望,而心理学只是收集了一些从盛宴上散落下来的面包屑。

下一个要弄清楚的要点是,无论对象可能多么复杂,关于它的思想是一个未被分开的意识状态。如托马斯·布朗所说:①

“我已经说得太频繁了,以至于不需要再次警告你们不要犯这种错误,我承认,我们语言的贫乏迫使我们使用这些术语,而这些术语自身就可以很自然地把你们引向这种错误;这个错误就是假设最复杂的心理状态,事实上,其真正本质并不像我们称之为简单事物的东西那样是完整的和不可分割的——它们所涉及的复杂性和表面上的共存只是相对于我们的感受②而言的,而不是相对于它们自己的绝对本性。我相信我无需向你们重复,在它自身之内,每一个观念,无论多么复杂,都是而且必须是真正简单

① 《人类心灵哲学演讲》,第45讲。

② 不应该说只是相对于我们的感受,而应该说只是相对于我们的对象。

simple—being one state or affection, of one simple substance, mind. Our conception of a whole army, for example, is as truly this one mind existing in this one state, as our conception of any of the individuals that compose an army. Our notion of the abstract numbers, eight, four, two, is as truly one feeling of the mind as our notion of simple unity."

The ordinary associationist-psychology supposes, in contrast with this, that whenever an object of thought contains many elements, the thought itself must be made up of just as many ideas, one idea for each element, and all fused together in appearance, but really separate, ①The enemies of this psychology find (as we have already seen) little trouble in showing that such a bundle of separate ideas would never form one thought at all, and they contend that an Ego must be added to the bundle to give it unity, and bring the various ideas into relation with each other. ②We will not discuss the ego just yet, but it is obvious that if things are to be thought in relation, they must be thought together, and in one *something*, be that something ego, psychosis, state of consciousness, or whatever you please. If not thought with each other, things are not thought in relation at all. Now most believers in the ego make the same mistake as the associationists and sensationists whom they oppose. Both agree that the elements of the subjective stream are discrete and separate and constitute what Kant calls a 'manifold.' But while the associationists think that a 'manifold' can form a

---

① "There can be no difficulty in admitting that association does form the ideas of an indefinite number of individuals into one complex idea; because it is an acknowledged fact. Have we not the idea of an army? And is not that precisely the ideas of an indefinite number of men formed into one idea?" (Jas. Mill's Analysis of the Human Mind (J. S. Mill's Edition), vol. I. p. 264.)

② For their arguments, see above.

的——是一个简单实体心灵的一种状态或者一种倾向。例如，我们关于一整支军队的概念真正是指这一个心灵存在于这一个状态之中，正如我们关于构成一支军队的个体的概念所指的那样。我们关于抽象数字8、4、2的概念和我们关于简单的个体的概念一样，都真的是我们心灵的一种感受。”

与此相对照，普通的联想主义心理学假设，只要思想的某个对象包含众多要素，思想自身必须同样是由众多的观念所组成的，一个观念对应一个要素，并且所有的观念在显现中都融合在一起，但实际上是分离的。① 这种心理学的敌人没有费多少力气(如我们已经看到的那样)就表明，这样一捆分离的观念根本永远也不能形成一个思想，而且他们主张必须将自我加到那捆分离的观念之上，以便使它统一起来，并且使得各种不同的观念彼此有了联系。② 现在我还不想对自我加以讨论，但是显而易见的是，如果事物要在关系中被思考，它们必须被共同思考，并且必须在某个东西中被思考，这个东西可以是自我、精神、意识状态，或者随你怎么称呼它都行。如果不是在彼此之间进行思考，事物就完全不能在关系中被思考。现在，大多数相信自我的人，和他们所反对的联想主义者和感觉主义者一样，犯下了相同的错误。双方都同意，主观之流的元素是非连续的和分离的，并且构成了康德所说的“杂多”。而且，联想主义者认为“杂多”可以形成单一的知

---

① “承认联想确实将数量不确定的个体的观念构成为一个复杂的观念，这不会有任何困难；因为这是一个公认的事实。难道我们没有关于一支军队的观念吗？而且难道这不正是由数量不确定的人的观念所构成的一个观念吗?”(Jas. 密尔，《人类心灵分析》，J. S. 密尔版，第1卷，第264页。)

② 关于它们的论证，见前面的论述。

single knowledge, the egoists deny this, and say that the knowledge comes only when the manifold is subjected to the synthetizing activity of an ego. Both make an identical initial hypothesis; but the egoist, finding it won't express the facts, adds another hypothesis to correct it. Now I do not wish just yet to 'commit myself' about the existence or nonexistence of the ego, but I do contend that we need not invoke it for this particular reason—namely, because the manifold of ideas has to be reduced to unity. *There is no manifold of coexisting ideas*; the notion of such a thing is a chimera. *Whatever things are thought in relation are thought from the outset in a unity, in a single pulse of subjectivity, a single psychosis, feeling, or state of mind.*

The reason why this fact is so strangely garbled in the books seems to be what on an earlier page (see p. 196 ff.) I called the psychologist's fallacy. We have the inveterate habit, whenever we try introspectively to describe one of our thoughts, of dropping the thought as it is in itself and talking of something else. We describe the things that appear to the thought, and we describe other thoughts *about* those things—as if these and the original thought were the same. If, for example, the thought be 'the pack of cards is on the table,' we say, "Well, isn't it a thought of the pack of cards? Isn't it of the cards as included in the pack? Isn't it of the table? And of the legs of the table as well? The table has legs—how can you think the table without virtually thinking its legs? Hasn't our thought then, all these parts—one part for the pack and another for the table? And within the pack-part a part for each card, as within the table-part a part for each leg? And isn't each of these parts an idea? And can our thought, then, be anything but an assemblage or pack of ideas,

识，而自我主义者却否认了这一点，并且说只有当杂多受到自我的综合作用的支配时知识才会到来。双方都做出了同样的最初假说；但是自我主义者发现它不能表达事实，就加上了另一个假说来纠正它。现在我还不希望对自我的存在与不存在“表态”，但是我的确主张，我们不需要为这个特殊的理由而调用它——这个理由是，因为观念的杂多性必须被还原为一致性。不存在共存观念的杂多性；关于这种东西的观念是一种狂想。凡是在关系中被思考的东西，它们从一开始就是在一致性中，在主观性的单一律动中，在单一的精神、感受或者心理状态中被思考的。

这一事实之所以在那些书中被如此奇怪地歪曲，似乎就是因为我在前面几页（见 196 页以后）所说的心理学家的谬误所致。我们都有一种根深蒂固的习惯，无论何时我们设法反省地描述我们的一个思想，我们就会丢掉在其自身之内的那个思想，并且谈论一些其他的事情。我们描述显现给那个思想的事物，我们还描述关于那些事物的其他一些思想——就好像这些思想和原初的那个思想是相同的。例如，如果思想是“那副牌在桌子上”，我们说，“噢，它难道不是关于那幅牌的思想吗？它难道不是关于那副牌里的纸牌的思想吗？它难道不是关于桌子的思想吗？它难道不也是关于桌子腿的思想吗？桌子是有腿的——你如何能够在思考桌子的时候事实上没有思考到它的腿呢？那么，我们的思想难道不全都是这些部分吗——一部分是关于那副牌的，另一部分是关于那张桌子的？并且在关于那副牌的部分思想中难道没有一个部分是关于每一张纸牌的思想，在关于那张桌子的部分思想中难道没有一个部分是关于桌子的每一条腿的思想？这每一部分难道不是一个观念吗？那么，我们的思想除了是观念的集合或者集

each answering to some element of what it knows ?"

Now not one of these assumptions is true. The thought taken as an example is, in the first place, not of ' a pack of cards. ' It is of 'the-pack-of-cards-is-on-the-table,' an entirely different subjective phenomenon, whose Object implies the pack, and every one of the cards in it, but whose conscious constitution bears very little resemblance to that of the thought of the pack *per se*. What a thought *is*, and what it may be developed into, or explained to stand for, and be equivalent to, are two things, not one. ①

An analysis of what passes through the mind as we utter the phrase *the pack of cards is on the table* will, I hope, make this clear, and may at the same time condense into a concrete example a good deal of what has gone before.

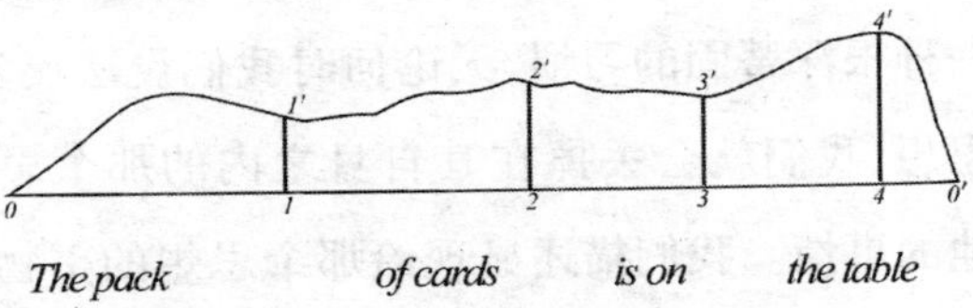

FIG. 29. —The Stream of Consciousness.

① I know there are readers whom nothing can convince that the thought of a complex object has not as many parts as are discriminated in the object itself. Well, then, let the word parts pass. Only observe that these parts are not the separate ' ideas ' of traditional psychology. No one of them can live out of that particular thought, any more than my head can live off of my particular shoulders. In a sense a soap-bubble has parts; it is a sum of juxtaposed spherical triangles. But these triangles are not separate realities; neither are the ' parts ' of the thought separate realities. Touch the bubble and the triangles are no more. Dismiss the thought and out go its parts. You can no more make a new thought out of ' ideas ' that have once served than you can make a new bubble out of old triangles. Bach bubble, each thought, is a fresh organic unity, *sui generis*.

群以外，其中每一个观念和它所知道的东西的某种要素相对应，除此之外，它还能是什么呢？"

此刻，这些假设中没有一个是正确的。被用来作为例子的那个思想，首先就不是关于"一副牌"的思想。它是关于"那副牌在桌子上"的思想，这是一个完全不同的主观现象，其对象包含有那副牌，以及那副牌中的每一张纸牌，但是每一张纸牌的意识构造和关于那副牌的思想本身的意识构造几乎没有相同之处。一个思想是什么，以及它可以发展为什么，或者被解释为代表什么，还有，它等同于什么，这是两类东西，不是一种东西。①

当我们说出句子"那副牌在桌子上"时，什么经过了我们的心灵，我希望，对这一问题的分析会使得这一点清楚起来，并且还可以使以前所讨论过的大量内容浓缩到一个具体的例子中来。

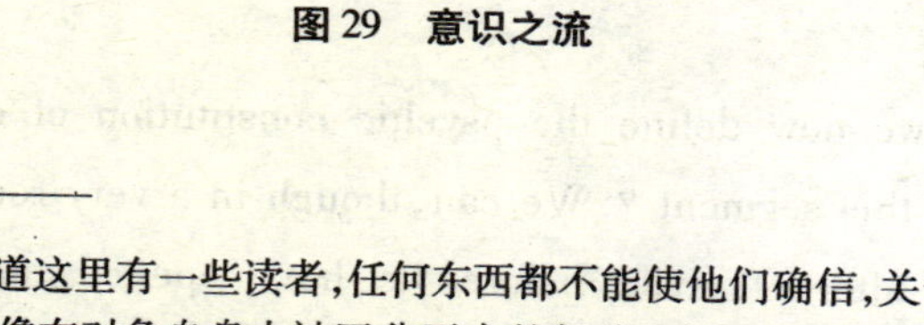

图 29　意识之流

---

① 我知道这里有一些读者，任何东西都不能使他们确信，关于一个复杂对象的思想不像在对象自身中被区分开来的部分那样，是由和对象一样多的部分所组成的。那么很好，让词语部分过去。只说这些部分不是传统心理学的分离的"观念"。它们中的任何一个部分离开这一特殊的思想都不能存在，就像我的头离开了我所特有的肩膀就不能存活了。在某种意义上，肥皂泡有部分，它是并列在一起的球面三角形的聚合物。但是这些三角形不是分离的实在；思想的"部分"也不是独立的实在。碰一下那个肥皂泡，三角形就不再存在了。消除那个思想，它的部分也就离去了。正如你不能用过去的三角形造出一个新的肥皂泡来，你也不能从曾经被使用的"观念"中造出一个新的思想来。每一个肥皂泡，每一个思想，都是一个新的、独特的有机体。

It takes time to utter the phrase. Let the horizontal line in Fig. 29 represent time. Every part of it will then stand for a fraction, every point for an instant, of the time. Of course the thought has *time-parts*. The part 2-3 of it, though continuous with 1-2, is yet a different part from 1-2. Now I say of these time-parts that we cannot take any one of them so short that it will not after some fashion or other be a thought of the whole object' the pack of cards is on the table.' They melt into each other like dissolving views, and no two of them feel the object just alike, but each feels the total object in a unitary undivided way. This is what I mean by denying that in the thought any parts can be found corresponding to the object's parts. Time-parts are not such parts.

Now let the vertical dimensions of the figure stand for the objects or contents of the thoughts. A line vertical to any point of the horizontal, as 1-1′, will then symbolize the object in the mind at the instant 1; a space above the horizontal, as 1-1′-2′-2, will symbolize all that passes through the mind during the time 1-2 whose line it covers. The entire diagram from O to O′ represents a finite length of thought's stream.

Can we now define the psychic constitution of each vertical section of this segment? We can, though in a very rough way. Immediately after O, even before we have opened our mouths to speak, the entire thought is present to our mind in the form of an intention to utter that sentence. This intention, though it has no simple name, and though it is a transitive state immediately displaced by the first word, is yet a perfectly determinate phase of thought, unlike anything else (see p. 253). Again, immediately before O′, after the last word of the sentence is spoken, all will admit that we again think its entire content as we inwardly realize its completed deliverance.

说出这句话需要时间。让图 29 中的水平线代表时间。那么，水平线上的每一个部分将代表一段时间，每一个点代表时刻。当然思想也有时间部分。思想的部分 2 ~ 3，尽管和部分 1 ~ 2 是相连续的，但是却和部分 1 ~ 2 不同。现在，关于这些时间部分我要说的是，我们不能将它们中的任何一个部分看得太短，以至于它怎么也不会是关于“那副牌在桌子上”这整个对象的思想。它们彼此溶入对方，就像消融的风景，每两个部分都不会感受到对象是正好一样的，但是每个部分都以一种统一和完整的方式感受到了整个对象。这就是我要说的意思，我用它否认了思想中的任何部分被发现能够和对象的部分相对应。时间部分不是这样的部分。

现在，让垂直纬度的图形代表思想的对象或内容。那么，和水平线上任何一点相垂直的线，如 1 ~ 1′，将代表在时刻 1 时心灵中的对象；水平线上的空间如 1 ~ 1′ ~ 2′ ~ 2′，将代表在线段 1 ~ 2 所覆盖的时间间隔 1 ~ 2 期间经过心灵的一切。从 O 到 O′的整个图示代表思想之流的有限长度。

我们现在能够详细说明这个片断的每一个垂直部分的精神构造吗？我们能够如此，尽管是以一种非常粗略的方式。紧接着 O 之后，甚至在我们已经开口说话之前，整个思想就以一种要说出那个句子的意向的形式呈现给了我们的心灵。这个意向，尽管没有简单的名称，尽管它是一个立刻就会被第一个词所取代的过渡状态，但是它仍然是思想的一个完全确定的状态，和任何其他的事物都不一样(见第 253 页)。还有，紧接着 O′之前，在句子的最后一个词被说出以后，所有人都会承认，当我们在内部意识到它已经全部完成了的时候，我们又一次思考了它的全部内容。用

All vertical sections made through any other parts of the diagram will be respectively filled with other ways of feeling the sentence's meaning. Through 2, for example, the cards will be the part of the object most emphatically present to the mind; through 4, the table. The stream is made higher in the drawing at its end than at its beginning, because the final way of feeling the content is fuller and richer than the initial way. As Joubert says, "we only know just what we meant to say, after we have said it." And as M. V. Egger remarks, "before speaking, one barely knows what one intends to say, but afterwards one is filled with admiration and surprise at having said and thought it so well."

This latter author seems to me to have kept at much closer quarters with the facts than any other analyst of consciousness. ①But even he does not quite hit the mark, for, as I understand him, he thinks that each word as it occupies the mind *displaces* the rest of the thought's content. He distinguishes the 'idea' (what I have called the total *object* or meaning) from the consciousness of the words, calling the former a very feeble state, and contrasting it with the liveliness of the words, even when these are only silently rehearsed. "The feeling," he says, "of the words makes ten or twenty times more noise in our consciousness than the sense of the phrase, which for consciousness is a very slight matter." ②And having distinguished these two things, he goes on to separate them in time, saying that the idea may either precede or follow the words, but that it is a 'pure illusion' to suppose them

① In his work, La Parole Intérleure (Paris, 1881), especially chapters VI and VII.

② Page 301.

图示中的任何其他部分所组成的所有垂直部分将分别由感受句子意义的其他方式所充满。例如,通过 2 的时候,纸牌就是最有力地呈现于心灵中的那部分对象;经过 4 的时候,是桌子。思想之流在结尾之处比在开始之处要高一些,因为感受内容的最后方式比最初方式要更充分、更丰富。如朱伯特所说,“在我们已经说完之后,我们才知道刚刚我们想说什么。”如 V. 埃格先生所说,“在讲话之前,人们几乎不知道自己想要说什么,但是在说完之后,他就会为他如此得当地想出和说出了它而感到自豪和惊讶。”

这后一位作者似乎在我看来比任何其他意识分析者都更接近事实。① 但是,即使是他也没有完全击中目标,因为,以我对他的理解,他认为,当每一个词语占据心灵的时候,它取代了思想的剩余内容。他将“观念”(这是我所称之为全部对象或者意义的东西)和词语的意识区分了开来,称前者为一种非常微弱的状态,并且将它与词语的活泼性相对照,甚至当这些词语只是被默默地背诵出来的时候。他说,“对词语的感受在我们的意识中产生的喧闹比对句子的感觉所产生的喧闹要大十到二十倍,对句子的感觉对于意识来说是一个非常微小的事件。”②并且在区分完这两种事物之后,他继续在时间上将它们分离开来,说观念或者可以先于词语,或者可以跟随在词语之后,而且说如果假设它们是同时

① 见他的著作,《内部话语》(巴黎,1881 年),尤其是第 6 章和第 7 章。
② 第 301 页。

simultaneous. ①Now I believe that in all cases where the words are *understood*, the total idea may be and usually is present not only before and after the phrase has been spoken, but also whilst each separate word is uttered. ② It is the overtone, halo, or fringe of the word, *as spoken in that sentence*. It is never absent; no word in an understood sentence comes to consciousness as a mere noise. We feel its meaning as it passes; and although our object differs from one moment to another as to its verbal kernel or nucleus, yet it is *similar* throughout the entire segment of the stream. The same object is known everywhere, now from the point of view, if we may so call it, of this word, now from the point of view of that. And in our feeling of each word there chimes an echo or foretaste of every other. The consciousness of the 'Idea' and that of the words are thus consubstantial. They are made of the same 'mind-stuff,' and form an unbroken stream.

---

① Page 218. To prove this point, M. Egger appeals to the fact that we often hear some one speak whilst our mind is preoccupied, but do not understand him until some moments afterwards, when we suddenly 'realize' what he meant. Also to our digging out the meaning of a sentence in an unfamiliar tongue, where the words are present to us long before the idea is taken in. In these special cases the word does indeed precede the idea. The idea, on the contrary, precedes the word whenever we try to express ourselves with effort, as in a foreign tongue, or in an unusual field of intellectual invention. Both sets of cases, however, are exceptional, and M. Egger would probably himself admit, on reflection, that in the former class there is some sort of a verbal suffusion, however evanescent, of the idea, when it is grasped—we hear the echo of the words as we catch their meaning. And he would probably admit that in the second class of cases the idea persists after the words that came with so much effort are found. In normal cases the simultaneity, as he admits, is obviously there.

② A good way to get the words and the sense separately is to inwardly articulate word for word the discourse of another. One then finds that the meaning will often come to the mind in pulses, after clauses or sentences are finished.

的,那是一种“纯粹的错觉”。[1] 现在我认为,在所有词语得到理解的情况下,整个观念可以并且通常不仅在句子被说出之前或者说出之后就出现了,而且在每一个单独的词语被说出的时候它也出现了。[2] 这就是在那个句子中被说出的词语的泛音、晕轮、或者边缘。它从来没有缺席过;一个得到理解的句子中的所有词语不会作为一个纯粹的声音来到意识之中。当它经过的时候,我们感受到了它的意义;并且尽管对其词语内核或者核子来说,我们的对象每时每刻都在变化着,但是在思想之流的整个片断中,它是相同的。这同一个对象在各处都得到了认识,时而从这个词的观点(如果我们可以如此称呼它的话)来认识它,时而从那个词的观点来认识它。并且在我们对每一个词的感受中,都回响着所有其他词语的回声及其预示。因而,“观念”的意识和词语的意识是同质的。它们都是由相同的“精神素材”所组成的,并且形成了一条不间断

---

① 第218页,为了证明这一点,埃格先生求助于下述事实,我们常常全神贯注地听某人讲话,但是我们却不能理解他,直到后来的某一时刻,我们突然“认识到”他所说的意思是什么。当我们从不熟悉的语言中挖掘出了一个句子的意思,情形也是如此,在这种情况下,在观念被采纳以前,词语已经呈现给我们好久了。在这些特殊的情况下,词语确实真的先于观念。相反,只要我们设法尽力地表达我们自己,例如用一种外语来表达自己,或者在一个不同寻常的知识创新领域中表达自己,观念就先于词语。然而,两种情况都有例外,而且,埃格先生自己可能在深思熟虑之后会承认,在前一种情况下,存在有某种观念的词语弥漫,无论它多么容易消散,当观念得到把握的时候——我们在捕获它们的意义的时候我们听到了词语的回声。而且在第二种情况下,他也可能会承认,在如此费力地找到那些词语之后,观念仍然继续着。在通常的情况下,如他所承认的那样,同时性显然是存在的。

② 一种单独理解词语及其意义的好的方式是,小声地逐字读出另一个人的讲话。然后,人们就会发现,意义常常是在从句或句子完成之后脉冲式地来到心灵之中的。

Annihilate a mind at any instant, cut its thought through whilst yet uncompleted, and examine the object present to the cross-section thus suddenly made; you will find, not the bald word in process of utterance, but that word suffused with the whole idea. The word may be so loud, as M. Egger would say, that we cannot *tell* just how its suffusion, as such, feels, or how it differs from the suffusion of the next word. But it does differ; and we may be sure that, could we see into the brain, we should find the same processes active through the entire sentence in different degrees, each one in turn becoming maximally excited and then yielding the momentary verbal 'kernel,' to the thought's content, at other times being only sub-excited, and then combining with the other sub-excited processes to give the overtone or fringe. ①

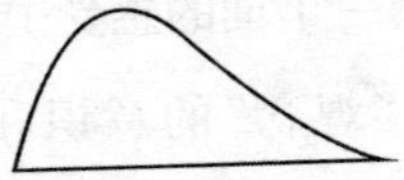

The pack of cards is on the table

FIG. 30.

"We may illustrate this by a farther development of the diagram on p. 279. Let the objective content of any vertical section through the stream be represented no longer by a line, but by a plane figure, highest opposite whatever part of the object is most prominent in consciousness at the moment when the section is made. This part, in verbal thought, will usually be some word. A series of sections 1-1′, taken at the moments 1, 2, 3, would then look like this: The horizontal breadth

① The nearest approach (with which I am acquainted) to the doctrine set forth here is in O. Liebmann's Zur Analysis der Wirklichkeit, pp. 427-438.

的流。在任何一个时刻让心灵消失，在思想尚未完成的时候切断它，并且检验呈现给由此突然造成的横截面的对象；你所发现的将不是那个处于说话过程中的光秃秃词，而是弥散着整个观点的那个词。如埃格先生所说，那个词可以如此地响亮，以至于我们不能辨别像这样的一种弥漫感受起来是什么样的，我们也不能辨别它同下一个词的弥漫有何种区别。但是，它确实不同；而且我们可以确定的是，假如我们能够看穿大脑的话，我们将会看到同样的一些过程在不同的程度上活跃于整个句子被说出的期间，每一个过程依次变得最为兴奋，然后产生出思想内容的瞬间词语"内核"，在其他时间里只是处于亚兴奋状态，然后和其他亚兴奋过程结合在一起形成泛音或边缘。①

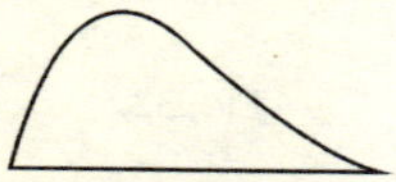

那副牌在桌子上

图 30

"我们可以通过进一步发展在第 279 页上的那个图示来说明这一点。让思想之流的任意垂直部分的客观内容不再由一条线所表示，而是由一个平面图形来表示，与对象的无论哪一个部分相对应的最高点，代表此刻在那一截面做出的时候意识中最显著的东西。在语言思想中，这一部分通常就是一些词语。在时刻 1，2，3 所截取的截面 1 ~ 1′序列因而看上去就是这样的：水平宽度

① 与这里提出的学说最为接近的观点（对其我很熟悉）可以在 O. 李普曼的《论现实的分析》中找到，第 427 ~ 438 页。

stands for the entire object in each of the figures; the height of the curve above each part of that object marks the relative prominence of that part in the thought. At the moment symbolized by the first figure *pack* is the prominent part; in the third figure it is *table*, etc."

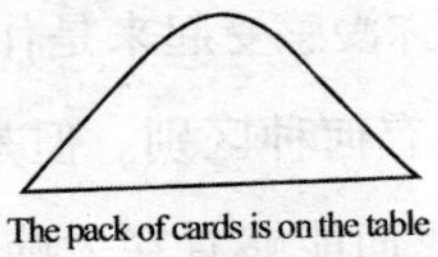

FIG. 31.

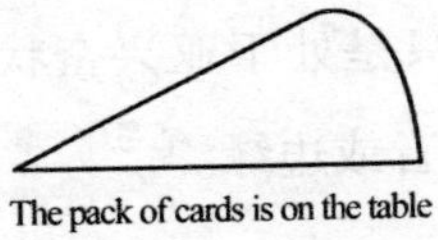

FIG. 32.

We can easily add all these plane sections together to make a solid, one of whose solid dimensions will represent time, whilst a cut across this at right angles will give the thought's content at the moment when the cut is made.

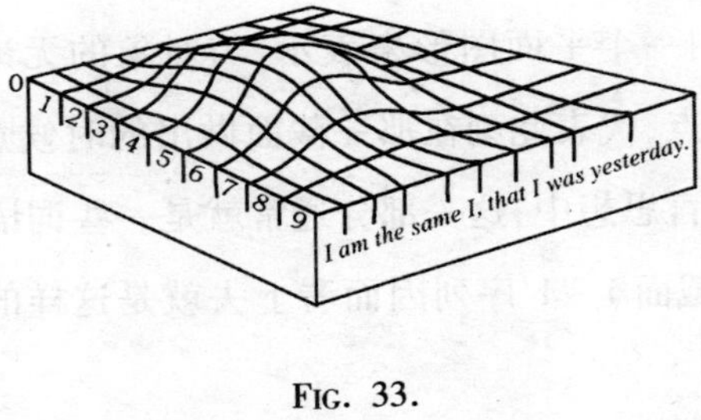

FIG. 33.

代表在每一个图形中的整个对象;对象的每一个部分上方的曲线的高度代表在思想中那个部分的相对显著程度。在第一个图形所代表的那一时刻,‘副’是最显著的部分;在第三个图形中,‘桌子’是最显著的部分,等等。”

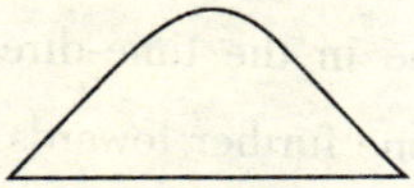

图 31

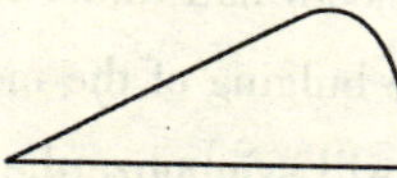

图 32

我们能够很容易地将这些平面部分加在一起,从而形成一个立体图形,它的一个立体纬度将代表时间,同时对这一纬度进行垂直切割,得出切割的那一时刻的思想内容。

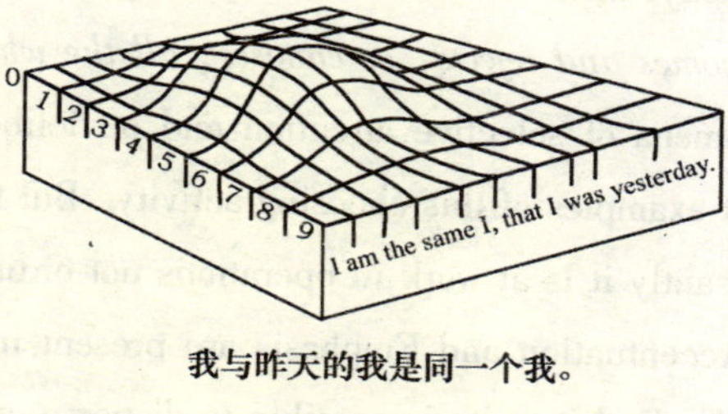

我与昨天的我是同一个我。

图 33

Let it be the thought, 'I am the same I that I was yesterday.' If at the fourth moment of time we annihilate the thinker and examine how the last pulsation of his consciousness was made, we find that it was an awareness of the whole content with *same* most prominent, and the other parts of the thing known relatively less distinct. With each prolongation of the scheme in the time-direction, the summit of the curve of section would come further towards the end of the sentence. If we make a solid wooden frame with the sentence written on its front, and the time-scale on one of its sides, if we spread flatly a sheet of India rubber over its top, on which rectangular co-ordinates are painted, and slide a smooth ball under the rubber in the direction from 0 to 'yesterday,' the bulging of the membrane along this diagonal at successive moments will symbolize the changing of the thought's content in a way plain enough, after what has been said, to call for no more explanation. Or to express it in cerebral terms, it will show the relative intensities, at successive moments, of the several nerve-processes to which the various parts of the thought-object correspond.

The last peculiarity of consciousness to which attention is to be drawn in this first rough description of its stream is that

5) *It is always interested more in one part of its object than in another, and welcomes and rejects, or chooses, all the while it thinks.*

The phenomena of selective attention and of deliberative will are of course patent examples of this choosing activity. But few of us are aware how incessantly it is at work in operations not ordinarily called by these names. Accentuation and Emphasis are present in every perception we have. We find it quite impossible to disperse our attention impartially over a number of impressions. A monotonous succession of sonorous strokes is broken up into rhythms, now of one sort, now of another, by the different accent which we place on different strokes. The

让这个图代表思想“我与昨天的我是同一个我。”如果在第4个时刻,我们让思想者停下来,并且检查一下他的意识的最后跳动是如何完成的,我们发现,它是一个对整个内容的意识,并且“同一的”是最显著的,而所知事物的其他部分则相对不是那么明显。随着图示在时间方向上的每一次延伸,截面曲线的顶点就会逐渐地朝着句子的结尾部分靠近。如果我们将这个句子写在一个立体的木制结构前面,并且将时间刻度写在它的另一个边上,如果我们在它的顶部平铺上一块印度橡胶,并且在其上画上矩形坐标,在从0到“昨天”的方向上在橡胶下面滚动一个光滑的圆球,在相继的时刻里,沿着这条对角线而出现的隔膜的凸起,就以一种足够简单的方式象征出了思想内容的变化,由于前面已经做过论述,对此就不做进一步的解释了。或者用大脑方面的术语来表达它就是,它表明了在相继的时刻几个神经过程的相对强度,这几个神经过程和思想—对象的各个部分相对应。

在这最初的对意识之流的粗糙描述中,需要引起注意的意识的最后一个特性是:

5. 在思考时,它总是对其对象的一个部分比对另一个部分更感兴趣,它始终在欢迎和拒绝,或说它总是在选择。

选择性注意和有意意志的现象当然是这种选择活动的明显例子。但是我们很少人能意识到,它是如何不断地在通常不是以这种名称来称呼的操作中起作用的。在我们所拥有的所有知觉中,着重与强调都是存在着的。我们发现将我们的注意力公平地分配给众多的印象是完全不可能的。一系列响亮而单调的敲击声,通过我们所放置在不同的敲击声上的不同的重音,被分解成了不同的节奏,时而是这一种,时而是那一种。这些节奏中最简

simplest of these rhythms is the double one, tick-tóck, tick-tóck, tick-tóck. Dots dispersed on a surface are perceived in rows and groups. Lines separate into diverse figures. The ubiquity of the distinctions, *this* and *that*, *here* and *there*, *now* and *then*, in our minds is the result of our laying the same selective emphasis on parts of place and time.

But we do far more than emphasize things, and unite some, and keep others apart. We actually *ignore* most of the things before us. Let me briefly show how this goes on.

To begin at the bottom, what are our very senses themselves but organs of selection? Out of the infinite chaos of movements, of which physics teaches us that the outer world consists, each sense-organ picks out those which fall within certain limits of velocity. To these it responds, but ignores the rest as completely as if they did not exist. It thus accentuates particular movements in a manner for which objectively there seems no valid ground; for, as Lange says, there is no reason whatever to think that the gap in Nature between the highest sound-waves and the lowest heat-waves is an abrupt break like that of our sensations; or that the difference between violet and ultra-violet rays has anything like the objective importance subjectively representted by that between light and darkness. Out of what is in itself an undistinguishable, swarming *continuum*, devoid of distinction or emphasis, our senses make for us, by attending to this motion and ignoring that, a world full of contrasts, of sharp accents, of abrupt changes, of picturesque light and shade.

If the sensations we receive from a given organ have their causes thus picked out for us by the conformation of the organ's termination, Attention, on the other hand, out of all the sensations yielded, picks out certain ones as worthy of its notice and suppresses all the rest. Helm-holtz's work on Optics is little more than a study of those visual sensations

单的一种就是滴答、滴答、滴答的二拍子节奏。[1] 在水平面上散布开的圆点，是以行列和组来感知的。线条被分解成不同的图形。在我们的心灵中到处存在的那些区分，这个和那个、这里和那里、这时和那时，是我们对地点和时间部分进行同样的选择性强调的结果。

但是我们所做的远远不止于强调事物，将一些联合起来，并且将其他一些分离开来。我们实际上忽略了在我们面前的大部分事物。让我简要地表明这是如何发生的。

让我们从最基本的地方开始，我们的感官自身不是选择的器官又会是什么呢？在运动的无限混乱之中，物理学告诉我们外部世界就是由此组成的，每一种感觉器官都挑选出处于某种速度范围之内的运动。它对这些运动做出反应，但是会完全忽略其余的部分，就好像它们不存在一样。它因而就以一种客观上似乎没有正当根据的方式强调了某些特殊的运动；因为，如兰格所说，这里没有任何理由认为，自然界中最高声波和最低声波之间的裂缝是一个突然的中断，就像在我们感觉中的裂缝一样；也没有理由认为紫色光线和紫外线之间的区别具有任何像由光明与黑暗之间的区别而主观地再现出来的那种客观重要性。从其自身之中那难以区分的、密集的、缺乏差别和强调的连续统一体中，我们的感官通过注意这种运动并且忽略那种运动为我们构造了一个世界，这个世界充满着差异、着重的强调、突然的变化以及独特的光亮与阴暗。

如果我们之所以从一个既定器官接收到感觉，是因为这个器官的终端构造为我们挑选了这些感觉，那么，在另一方面，注意力从所有产生的感觉中挑选出它值得注意的某些感觉，并且抑制了所有剩余的感觉。赫姆霍尔茨的光学著作几乎完全就是对普通

〔1〕“强弱”节奏。

of which common men never become aware—blind spots, *muscce volitantes*, after-images, irradiation, chromatic fringes, marginal changes of color, double images, astigmatism, movements of accommodation and convergence, retinal rivalry, and more besides. We do not even know without special training on which of our eyes an image falls. So habitually ignorant are most men of this that one may be blind for years of a single eye and never know the fact.

Helmholtz says that we notice only those sensations which are signs to us of *things*. But what are things? Nothing, as we shall abundantly see, but special groups of sensible qualities, which happen practically or aesthetically to interest us, to which we therefore give substantive names, and which we exalt to this exclusive status of independence and dignity. But in itself, apart from my interest, a particular dust-wreath on a windy day is just as much of an individual thing, and just as much or as little deserves an individual name, as my own body does.

And then, among the sensations we get from each separate thing, what happens? The mind selects again. It chooses certain of the sensations to represent the thing most *truly*, and considers the rest as its appearances, modified by the conditions of the moment. Thus my table-top is named *square*, after but one of an infinite number of retinal sensations which it yields, the rest of them being sensations of two acute and two obtuse angles; but I call the latter *perspective* views, and the four right angles the *true* form of the table, and erect the attribute squareness into the table's essence, for aesthetic reasons of my own. In like manner, the real form of the circle is deemed to be the sensation it gives when the line of vision is perpendicular to its centre—all its other sensations are signs of this sensation. The real sound of the cannon is the sensation it makes when the ear is close by. The real color of the brick is the sensation it gives when the eye looks squarely at it from a near point,

人从来不会意识到的那些视觉感觉的研究——这些视觉感觉包括盲点、飞蝇幻视、后象、放射、色彩边缘、颜色的边缘变化、双像、散光、调节和集中运动、视网膜的对抗，等等。没有特殊的训练我们甚至都不知道图像会落到哪只眼睛上。大部分人都将此习惯性地忽略掉了，这种习惯是如此的根深蒂固，以至于有人在自己的一只眼睛瞎了好多年之后，可能依然不知道这一事实。

赫姆霍尔茨说，我们只注意到那些对我们来说是事物的符号的感觉。但是事物是什么呢？如我们将要大量看到的那样，它们只是特殊的可感知的性质群，它们碰巧实践地或者审美地使我们感兴趣，我们因此给它们以实体性的名称，并且我们将它们提升到这种独一无二的独立与高贵的地位上来。但是在它自身之内，抛开我的兴趣，大风天里的特殊的一圈尘埃，就像我自己的身体一样，同样是一个单独的事物，多少也应该得到一个单独的名称。

那么，在我们从每一个单独的事物那里获得的感觉之间，又有什么发生了呢？心灵再次选择。它选择那些特定的能够最真地再现事物的感觉，并且把剩余的感觉当作是它的现象，这些现象为当时的条件所改变。因此，我的桌面被称为是正方形的，其根据是桌面所产生出来的无限多的视网膜感觉中的一个感觉，其余的感觉都是两个锐角和两个钝角的感觉；但是，出于我自己的审美方面的理由，我将后者称作透视法式的观察，并且称四个直角是桌子的真实形状，将正方形这种属性植入在桌子的本质中。同样，圆形的真实形状被认为是当视线垂直于它的中心时，它所给予的感觉——它的所有其他感觉都是这种感觉的符号。大炮的真实声音是当耳朵靠近它的时候，它所造成的感觉。砖头的真实颜色是当眼睛避开阳光却又不是在阴暗处、并且从近处正

out of the sunshine and yet not in the gloom; under other circumstances it gives us other color-sensations which are but signs of this—we then see it looks pinker or blacker than it really is. The reader knows no object which he does not represent to himself by preference as in some typical attitude, of some normal size, at some characteristic distance, of some standard tint, etc., etc. But all these essential characteristics, which together form for us the genuine objectivity of the thing and are contrasted with what we call the subjective sensations it may yield us at a given moment, are mere sensations like the latter. The mind chooses to suit itself, and decides what particular sensation shall be held more real and valid than all the rest.

Thus perception involves a twofold choice. Out of all present sensations, we notice mainly such as are significant of absent ones; and out of all the absent associates which these suggest, we again pick out a very few to stand for the objective reality *par excellence.* We could have no more exquisite example of selective industry.

That industry goes on to deal with the things thus given in perception. A man's empirical thought depends on the things he has experienced, but what these shall be is to a large extent determined by his habits of attention. A thing may be present to him a thousand times, but if he persistently fails to notice it, it cannot be said to enter into his experience. We are all seeing flies, moths, and beetles by the thousand, but to whom, save an entomologist, do they say anything distinct? On the other hand, a thing met only once in a lifetime may leave an indelible experience in the memory. Let four men make a tour in Europe. One will bring home only picturesque impressions—costumes and colors, parks and views and works of architecture, pictures and statues. To another all this will be non-existent; and distances and prices, populations and drainage-arrangements, door and window-fastenings, and other useful statistics

对着它看时，它所给予我的感觉；在其他情形下，它给予我们的其他颜色感觉只是这种感觉的符号——那时我们看见它似乎比实际的样子要更粉红一些，或者更黑一些。读者所知道的对象，无不是他通过优先选择某种典型姿势、某种正常尺寸、某个特定距离、某种标准色彩等等而将对象再现给他自己的。但是所有这些本质的特征一起为我们构成了事物的真实客观性，并且与在某个时刻它产生给我们的被称作是主观感觉的东西相对照，而它们只不过是和后者一样的感觉。心灵选择了按照自己的意愿做事，并且确定了什么样的特殊感觉应该被认为比所有其他的感觉更真实、更有效。

因此，知觉涉及双重选择。从所有出现的感觉中，我们主要注意像这样对不在的感觉有意义的感觉；从这些感觉所提示的所有不在的联系中，我们又选出很少的一些来代表典型的客观实在。我们不能获有更精致的选择活动的例子了。

这种活动继续处理由此在知觉中被给出的事物。一个人的经验思想依赖于他所经历过的事物，但是这些思想将会是什么则在很大程度上是由他的注意习惯所决定的。一个事物可能会上千次地呈现给他，但是如果他总是没有注意到它，那么就不能说它进入了他的经验之中。我们都上千次地看见过苍蝇、蛾子和甲虫，但是，除了昆虫学家以外，有谁能够说出它们的区别之处呢？另一方面，在一生中只遇到过一次的东西，可能会在记忆中留下去除不掉的经验。假设四个人去欧洲旅行。其中的一个人带回家的只有栩栩如生的印象——服装和色彩，公园、风景和建筑作品，绘画和雕像。对另一个人来说，所有这一切都将是不存在的；而距离和价格、人口和污水系统的布置，门窗插销以及其他有

will take their place. A third will give a rich account of the theatres, restaurants, and public balls, and naught beside; whilst the fourth will perhaps have been so wrapped in his own subjective broodings as to tell little more than a few names of places through which he passed. Each has selected, out of the same mass of presented objects, those which suited his private interest and has made his experience thereby.

If, now, leaving the empirical combination of objects, we ask how the mind proceeds *rationally* to connect them, we find selection again to be omnipotent. In a future chapter we shall, see that all Reasoning depends on the ability of the mind to break up the totality of the phenomenon reasoned about, into parts, and to pick out from among these the particular one which, in our given emergency, may lead to the proper conclusion. Another predicament will need another conclusion, and require another element to be picked out. The man of genius is he who will always stick in his bill at the right point, and bring it out with the right element—'reason' if the emergency be theoretical, 'means' if it be practical—transfixed upon it. I here confine myself to this brief statement, but it may suffice to show that Reasoning is but another form of the selective activity of the mind.

If now we pass to its aesthetic department, our law is still more obvious. The artist notoriously selects his items, rejecting all tones, colors, shapes, which do not harmonize with each other and with the main purpose of his work. That unity, harmony, 'convergence of characters,' as M. Taine calls it, which gives to works of art their superiority over works of nature, is wholly due to *elimination*. Any natural subject will do, if the artist has wit enough to pounce upon some one

用的统计数据将取代它们的位置。第三个人却能对剧院、饭馆和公共舞会做出非常充分的解说，而除此以外就没什么了；而第四个人可能一直沉浸在他自己的主观沉思之中，结果他只能说出一些他所经过的地方的名称。他们每一个人都从呈现给他们的那些大量的相同对象中进行了选择，并且选择出了适合自己私人兴趣的那些对象，从而获得了各自的经验。

现在，如果离开对象的经验结合，我们问心灵是如何理性地依次把它们连接起来的，那么，我们就会又一次发现选择是无所不能的。在未来的章节我们将会看到，所有的推理都取决于心灵的这种能力，即将所推理的现象的整体性打破，并将其分解成各个部分，然后从这些部分中选出特殊的一个，它在我们给定的紧急情况中可以导向适当的结论。另一个困境需要另一个结论，因而需要选出另一个要素。天才是这样的人物，他总是在正确的地方扔下他的钩子，并且在取出钩子的时候，正确的要素已经扎在钩子上了——如果紧急情况是理论方面的，这要素就是“理由”，如果紧急情况是实践方面的，这要素就是“手段”。在这里我只将自己局限在这种简要的论述中，但是这种论述足以表明，推理只不过是心灵选择活动的另一种形式。

现在如果我们过渡到心灵的审美部门，我们的规律就更加显而易见了。众所周知，艺术家选择其项目，拒绝所有彼此间不和谐以及同作品的主要意图不和谐的音调、色调和形状。这种统一、和谐、“特征趋同”（泰恩先生如此称呼它），使得艺术作品比自然之作优越，这种统一、和谐、“特征趋同”完全是由于“排除”所致。如果艺术家有足够的才智可以抓住自然的某一个特征作为它的典型特征，并且将所有和这一典型特征不和谐的、仅仅是

feature of it as characteristic, and suppress all merely accidental items which do not harmonize with this.

Ascending still higher, we reach the plane of Ethics, where choice reigns notoriously supreme. An act has no ethical quality whatever unless it be chosen out of several all equally possible. To sustain the arguments for the good course and keep them ever before us, to stifle our longing for more flowery ways, to keep the foot unflinchingly on the arduous path, these are characteristic ethical energies. But more than these; for these but deal with the means of compassing interests already felt by the man to be supreme. The ethical energy *par excellence* has to go farther and choose which *interest* out of several, equally coercive, shall become supreme. The issue here is of the utmost pregnancy, for it decides a man's entire career. When he debates, Shall I commit this crime? choose that profession? accept that office, or marry this fortune? —his choice really lies between one of several equally possible future Characters. What he shall *become* is fixed by the conduct of this moment. Schopenhauer, who enforces his determinism by the argument that with a given fixed character only one reaction is possible under given circumstances, forgets that, in these critical ethical moments, what consciously *seems* to be in question is the complexion of the character itself. The problem with the man is less what act he shall now choose to do, than what being he shall now resolve to become.

Looking back, then, over this review, we see that the mind is at every stage a theatre of simultaneous possibilities. Consciousness consists in the comparison of these with each other, the selection of some, and the suppression of the rest by the reinforcing and inhibiting agency of attention. The highest and most elaborated mental products are filtered from the data chosen by the faculty next beneath,

偶然的东西抑制住，那么任何自然的主题都将比自然之作优越。

如果提升得再高一些，我们就到达了伦理学的高度，众所周知，在这里选择是最高的统治。只有当一个行为是从几个都同样具有可能性的行为中选择出来的时候，这个行为才具有与伦理有关的性质。确定好的行为的理由，并且让这些理由永远保留在我们心里，抑制我们对更加奢华的生活方式的渴望，让脚步在艰辛的道路上永不畏缩，这些是典型的伦理力量。但伦理力量比这些还要多；因为这些只是涉及了实现利益的手段，这些利益是已经为人们所感受到是至高的利益。典型的伦理力量必须走得更远，并且必须在几个具有同等强制性的利益中，选择出哪一个应该成为至高的利益。这里的问题具有极为深远的意义，因为它决定着人的整个生涯。当他思考着，我应该犯这种罪吗？选择那个职业吗？接受那个职位，或者嫁给这大量的财产吗？——他的选择实际上是对几个同等可能的未来品格的选择。此刻的行为决定了他将来会变成什么。叔本华通过下述论点来强调他的决定论，对于一个既定的固定品格而言，在既定的情形之下，只有一种反应是可能的，他忘记了，在这些与伦理有关的关键时刻，所意识到似乎正在被讨论的东西是品格自身的情况。那个人所面临的问题与其说是他现在应当选择做出什么行为，不如说他现在应当决定他要变成什么样的人。

回顾这些评论，那么我们就会看到，心灵在每个阶段都是一个同时存在多种可能性事物的剧场。意识就在于将这些可能性事物相互加以比较，通过注意力的强调和抑制作用，从中选出一些可能性事物，并且抑制剩余的可能性事物。最高级和最精致的精神产品是从下一级机能所选择的资料中过滤出来的，这些资料

out of the mass offered by the faculty below that, which mass in turn was sifted from a still larger amount of yet simpler material, and so on. The mind, in short, works on the data it receives very much as a sculptor works on his block of stone. In a sense the statue stood there from eternity. But there were a thousand different ones beside it, and the, sculptor alone is to thank for having extricated this one from the rest. Just so the world of each of us, howsoever different our several views of it may be, all lay embedded in the primordial chaos of sensations, which gave the mere *matter* to the thought of all of us indifferently. We may, if we like, by our reasonings unwind things back to that black and jointless continuity of space and moving clouds of swarming atoms which science calls the only real world. But all the while the world *we* feel and live in will be that which our ancestors and we, by slowly cumulative strokes of choice, have extricated out of this, like sculptors, by simply rejecting certain portions of the given stuff. Other sculptors, other statues from the same stone! Other minds, other worlds from the same monotonous and inexpressive chaos! My world is but one in a million alike embedded, alike real to those who may abstract them. How different must be the worlds in the consciousness of ant, cuttle-fish, or crab!

But in my mind and your mind the rejected portions and the selected portions of the original world-stuff are to a great extent the same. The human race as a whole largely agrees as to what it shall notice and name, and what not. And among the noticed parts we select in much the same way for accentuation and preference or subordination and dislike. There is, however, one entirely extraordinary case

是从再下一级机能所提供的众多资料中选出来的,而这众多资料又是从更大量、却更简单的材料中筛选出来的,等等。简而言之,心灵处理它所接收到的资料,很像雕塑家处理他的石块。从某种意义上说,雕像永久以来就矗立在那里了。但是,除了这尊雕像以外还存在有上千尊不同的雕像,而且这尊雕像能从剩余的雕像中摆脱出来只能归功于那位雕塑家。我们每一个人的世界也正是如此,无论我们各自对它的看法可能有多么地不同,所有观点都根植于感觉的原始混乱之中,它们毫无差别地将纯粹的物质给予了我们所有人的思想。如果我们愿意的话,我们可以通过自己的推理将事物放回到黑暗的和无接缝的空间连续性中,放回到挤满原子的移云中,科学称它们是唯一真实的世界。但是,我们所感受与居住的世界,一直是这样一个世界,我们的祖先和我们自己,通过慢慢地积累起一次次的选择,使它从混乱中摆脱出来,就像雕塑家那样,通过简单地拒绝既定材料的某些部分,使雕像脱颖而出。其他的雕塑家,从相同的石头中解脱出其他的雕像!其他的心灵,从同样单调和无表现力的混乱中解脱出其他的世界!我的世界只是对那些可以抽象出它们的人来说,同样根植于混乱之中、同样真实的百万个世界中的一个世界。蚂蚁、墨鱼和螃蟹的意识中的世界必定有多么地不同啊!

但是,在你的心灵中和在我的心灵中,原初世界材料的被拒绝部分和被选择部分在很大程度上是相同的。就应该注意和命名什么、不应该注意和命名什么而言,总体上来说人类在很大程度上意见是一致的。并且在被注意到的部分中,人类以大致相同的方式因为重要和偏爱、次要和不喜欢的原因而进行选择。然而,存在有一种完全非同寻常的情况,这就是从来没有两个人被

in which no two men ever are known to choose alike. One great splitting of the whole universe into two halves is made by each of us; and for each of us almost all of the interest attaches to one of the halves; but we all draw the line of division between them in a different place. When I say that we all call the two halves by the same names, and that those names are '*me*' and '*not-me*' respectively, it will at once be seen what I mean. The altogether unique kind of interest which each human mind feels in those parts of creation which it can call me or *mine* may be a moral riddle, but it is a fundamental psychological fact. No mind can take the same interest in his neighbor's *me* as in his own. The neighbor's me falls together with all the rest of things in one foreign mass, against which his own *me* stands out in startling relief. Even the trodden worm, as Lotze somewhere says, contrasts his own suffering self with the whole remaining universe, though he have no clear conception either of himself or of what the universe may be. He is for me a mere part of the world; for him it is I who am the mere part. Each of us dichotomizes the Kosmos in a different place.

Descending now to finer work than this first general sketch, let us in the next chapter try to trace the psychology of this fact of self-consciousness to which we have thus once more been led.

认为是以同样的方式进行选择的。将整个宇宙分为二等分是由我们每一个人来完成的；并且对我们每一个人来说，几乎所有的兴趣都隶属于其中的一半；但是我们都在不同的地方划分出了这两半之间的界限。当我说我们都用相同的名称来称呼这两半，并且说它们的名称分别是“我”和“非我”，我所说的意思立刻就可以得以理解了。每一个人类的心灵在那些可以称作“我”或者“我的”的创造部分中所感受到的那种完全独特的兴趣，可能是一个道德之谜，但是它却是一个基本的心理学事实。没有任何一个心灵能够从他的邻居的“我”中获得和他自己的“我”中一样的兴趣。邻居的“我”和所有剩余的事物一起被归为一个异质集团，以此为背景，他自己的“我”又极为鲜明地突出了出来。如洛采在某个地方所说，甚至连脚下的蠕虫也将它自己那苦难的自我和整个剩余宇宙相对照，尽管它没有任何关于它自己或者关于宇宙是什么的清晰概念。它对我而言仅仅是世界的一部分；我对它而言也仅仅是世界的一部分。我们每一个人都在不同的地方将宇宙对分为二。

现在，让我们往下进入到比这最初的一般性概述更为精细的工作中，让我们在下一章中试图探索关于自我意识这一事实的心理学，因而我们又一次地被引到自我意识这一事实上来了。

译者后记

威廉·詹姆斯(William James)的《心理学原理》共28章,根据笔者现有的资料来看,国内有两个译本,一本是唐钺先生翻译的,由商务印书馆出版,另一本是田平先生翻译的,由中国城市出版社出版。这两个译本都是选译本,笔者重新翻译了其中的第1~9章。

《心理学原理》的第1~9章是全书中非常重要的部分。首先,这几章的内容使我们认识到了心理学是如何从哲学中分离出来的,哲学和心理学各自的研究对象有什么不同,心理学的研究方法如何必须是经验科学式的而不是形而上学式的,以及心理学家的任务和哲学家的任务有什么不同,哪些问题心理学家不需要涉及。其次,在第2、3章中,我们尤其看到了心理学作为一门自然科学是如何用实验和比较的方法来进行研究的,就研究心理现象的条件而言,实验心理学为什么有权利成为心理学中重要的内容之一;而在第5、6章中,我们又看到了詹姆斯先生作为一名心理学家,是如何对形而上学提出质疑的,而又作为一名哲学家,又是如何告诫心理学家应该如何避免"心理学家的谬误"的,尤其当心理学家使用实验和比较的方法的时候。这四章的论证风格截然不同:一种是综合归纳式的、从而是自下而上的,它将一个最为简单的命题用丰富的资料层层展开，最后得出一个经过修正的合理的结论；另一种是分析演绎式的，它将错误的命题推到逻辑的尽头，使之漏洞百出，最后提出相反的结论。最后，在第九章，詹姆斯先生最为重要的、也是为后人所津津乐道的观点出现了。詹姆斯将认识活动中那通过内省很难了解的、只有通过观察才能引起注意的、被大多数人所忽视的内容表述了出来，这就是"思想之流"的观点。

为了方便读者阅读，笔者必须简要地说明一些专业术语的翻译情况。1. senses 翻译为"感官"；sensation 翻译为"感觉"，既可指感觉活动，又可指感觉内容；sensibility 翻译为"感受性"或"感性"；sensational、sensory、sensorial 统一翻译为"感觉的"，其中 sensory 是相对于物理的、生理的感觉过程而言的，sensorial 是相对于精神的、心理的感觉过程而言的，而 sensational 是相对于两种感觉过程之和而言的，是总体的、抽象的表述；sensitive 翻译为有"感觉的"，sensible 翻译为"可感觉的"。2. feel 和 feeling 翻译为"感受"，和感觉相区别，feeling 也有情感的意思，关于 sensation 和 feeling 的区别，詹姆斯做了详细的说明，读者可以在本书中找到，这里就不重复了。3. thought 翻译为"思想"和"思维"，thought 不仅指思维的内容，而且也指思维本身，是在综合的意义上来使用的，笔者根据上下文的语境将思维和思想与之对应，如果只是讲思维活动，就翻译成"思维"，如果讲的是思维的内容便翻译成"思想"，如果二者兼而有之，则统一翻译成"思想"。4. unconscious 翻译为"无意识"，并没有翻译成弗洛伊德的"潜意识"，其原因是詹姆斯承认存在下意识（subconscious），即次级人格所拥有的、对主要人格而言是离散的和无意识的意识，它可以和弗洛伊德的潜意识相对应，而且詹姆斯之所以驳斥精神分析论中的无意识(unconscious)，主要是为了驳斥精神微粒说，并没有提及弗洛伊德的潜意识(unconscious)，通过詹姆斯对无意识与下意识的论述，反而会使我们对潜意识的界定更加明确。5. presentation 翻译为“呈现”，强调主体与对象的在场；appearance 翻译为“显现”，强调主体的智性活动，但显现出来的东西可能是假象；representation 翻译为“表象”，它有再现的意思，所以表象是经验知识，具有客观实在性。它们与现象(phenomenon)相对应。6. intellect 翻译为“智性”，intelligence 翻译为“理智”(见邓晓芒的译著《纯粹理性批判》中的德汉术语索引)，前者强调人的认知活动，后者还包括人的实践活动。7. a priori 和 a posteriori 翻译为“先天”和“后天”，同康德所说的先验(transcendental)和超验(transcendent)相对照。8. knowledge of acquaintance 和 knowledge－about 这两个词分别翻译为“相识的知识”和“相知的知识”，这两个词是针对认识事物的程度而言的，前者指的是刚刚认识，对对象还不了解，甚至只是给对象起了个名字，后者是指对事物已经很熟悉，对它的认识已经很深刻了。虽然相知和相识本意是指人与人之间的熟悉程度和认识深度，但是如果我们从中可以引申出它们不仅指人与人之间的认识，而且也指人与物之间的认识，并且正是通过对物的认识、对人的创造物的认识，人才更加深刻地认识到了自己这层含义的话，这两个词的翻译还是较为妥当的。9. reflection 翻译为“反省”，introspection 翻译为“内省”，前者是对人类的文化符号进行反思，尤其是对人类的科学知识、制度与习惯进行反思，通过这种反思，最终是为了回答人是如何的，或者更确切地说人是应该如何的，因此反省是哲学的主要研究方法；后者是指个体的人在完成了某次心理活动或行为活动之后,对自己刚刚完成的心理活动或行为活动进行反思,为的是找到个体的人进行心理活动和行为活动的原因、方法与规律,因此内省是心理学的主要研究方法,并且也正是因为心理学的研究方法是以内省为主的,心理学才是一门形而下的自然科学。

笔者在翻译的过程中,参阅了田平先生翻译的《心理学原理》(威廉·詹姆斯著)、唐钺先生翻译的《心理学原理》(威廉·詹姆斯著)、高觉敷先生翻译的《精神分析引论新编》(弗洛伊德著)、邓晓芒先生翻译的《纯粹理性批判》(康德著)和《实践理性批判》(康德著)、庞景仁先生翻译的《未来形而上学导论》(康德著)、林方先生和王景先生翻译的《近代心理学历史引导》(墨菲、柯瓦奇著)以及张春兴先生的著作《现代心理学》等书。在此,对上述各位学者前辈表示衷心的感谢!

需要指出的是,威廉·詹姆斯的《心理学原理》还对研究西方的实用主义哲学有着极为重要的价值,所以笔者期待有兴趣的学者可以将詹姆斯的《心理学原理》全部翻译出来,从而填补国内这一学术空白。

郭　宾

2006 年 8 月

《西方学术经典文库》(第一辑)

功利主义	[英]约翰·斯图亚特·穆勒
诗学·诗艺	[古希腊]亚里士多德 [古罗马]贺拉斯
经济发展理论	[美]约瑟夫·阿洛伊斯·熊彼特
经济学原理	[英]阿尔弗雷德·马歇尔
国民财富的性质与原理	[英]亚当·斯密
联邦党人文集	[美]亚历山大·汉密尔顿
就业、利息和货币通论	[英]约翰·梅纳德·凯恩斯
尼各马可伦理学	[古希腊]亚里士多德
道德情操论	[英]亚当·斯密
君主论	[意]尼科洛·马基雅弗利
新教伦理与资本主义精神	[德]马克斯·韦伯
古代法	[英]亨利·萨姆奈·梅因
第一哲学沉思集	[法]勒内·笛卡儿
查拉图斯特拉如是说	[德]弗里德里希·威廉·尼采
哲学研究	[英]路德维希·维特根斯坦
实践理性批判	[德]伊曼努尔·康德
社会契约论	[法]让·雅克·卢梭
理想国	[古希腊]柏拉图
心理学原理	[美]威廉·詹姆斯
精神现象学	[德]威廉·弗里德里希·黑格尔
神圣者的观念	[德]鲁道夫·奥托
小逻辑	[德]威廉·弗里德里希·黑格尔

论人类不平等的起源	[法]让·雅克·卢梭
道德形而上学基础	[德]伊曼努尔·康德
人性论	[英]戴维·休谟
政府论	[英]约翰·洛克
论法的精神	[法]查尔斯·路易斯·孟德斯鸠
代议制政府	[英]约翰·斯图亚特·穆勒
英国法与文艺复兴	[英]弗雷德里克·威廉·梅特兰
法律社会学基本原理	[奥]尤根·埃利希
论美国民主	[法]夏尔·阿列克西·德·托克维尔
原始社会结构与功能	[英]A. R. 拉德克利夫-布朗
政治学	[古希腊]亚里士多德
罗马帝国编年史	[古罗马]科尔涅里乌斯·塔西佗
普通语言学教程	[瑞士]费尔迪南·德·索绪尔
货币哲学	[德]格奥尔格·西梅尔
法理学讲演录	[英]约翰·奥斯丁
思想录	[法]布莱兹·帕斯卡
利维坦	[英]托马斯·霍布斯
意识形态与乌托邦	[德]卡尔·曼海姆
忏悔录	[古罗马]圣·奥古斯丁
西太平洋上的航海者	[英]布罗尼斯拉夫·马林诺夫斯基
历史学:理论和实际	[意]贝内德托·克罗齐
逻辑哲学论	[英]路得维希·维特根斯坦